archaeology
AEGEAN ISLANDS

PUBLICATION CO-ORDINATOR   Athina Ragia

ENGLISH TRANSLATION   Alexandra Doumas

EDITING OF GREEK TEXTS   Kiki Birtacha

CARTOGRAPHY   Kelly Kalogirou

PAGINATION   Theoni Soupiona

IMAGE REPRODUCTION   TOXO S.A.

PRINTING   EPIKOINONIA Co. Ltd

BINDING   Moutsis Bros & Co.

ISBN   960 204 2729

1st edition: December 2006

© 2006 MELISSA Publishing House
58 Skoufa St, Athens 106 80
Tel. 210 3611692, Fax 210 3600865
www.melissabooks.com

All rights reserved. No part of this publication may be reproduced or republished, wholly or in part, or in summary, paraphrase or adaptation, by mechanical or electronic means, by photocopying or recording, or by any other method, without the prior written permission of the editor. Law 2121/1993 and the regulations of International Law applicable in Greece.

archaeology
AEGEAN ISLANDS

Scientific editor
Andreas G. Vlachopoulos

MELISSA PUBLISHING HOUSE

CONTENTS

FOREWORD
ARCHAEOLOGY IN THE AEGEAN ISLANDS — 8
    Christos Doumas — 14

PART I
AEGEAN ISLANDS: HISTORICAL AND ARCHAEOLOGICAL BACKGROUND

Stone Age   Adamantios Sampson — 32

Bronze Age   Christos Boulotis — 38

Geometric and Archaic periods
    Alexandros Mazarakis Ainian — 50

Classical period   Lydia Palaiokrassa-Kopitsa — 60

Hellenistic and Roman periods
    Sophia Aneziri – Georgia Kokkorou-Alevra — 70

PART II
NORTH AND EAST AEGEAN

Thasos   Chaido Koukouli-Chrysanthaki — 80

Samothrace   Dimitris Matsas — 92

Imbros   Dimitris Matsas — 100

Tenedos   Dimitris Matsas — 104

Lemnos   Luigi Beschi — 106

Aghios Efstratios   Aglaia Archontidou-Argyri — 115

Lesbos   Aglaia Archontidou-Argyri — 116

Chios   Aglaia Archontidou-Argyri — 126

Oinouses   Aglaia Archontidou-Argyri — 134

Psara   Aglaia Archontidou-Argyri — 136

Samos   Constantinos Tsakos — 140

Ikaria   Maria Viglaki-Sophianou — 150

Phournoi   Maria Viglaki-Sophianou — 155

SPORADES

North Sporades — 158
    Skiathos   Argyroula Doulgeri-Intzesiloglou — 159
    Skopelos   Argyroula Doulgeri-Intzesiloglou — 161
    Alonnisos   Argyroula Doulgeri-Intzesiloglou — 165
    Deserted islands of the Sporades
        Argyroula Doulgeri-Intzesiloglou — 167

Skyros   Amalia A. Karapaschalidou — 168

ARGOSARONIC ISLANDS

Salamis   Yannos G. Lolos — 176

Psyttaleia   Yannos G. Lolos — 181

Aegina   Eva Simantoni-Bournia — 182

Poros   Eva Simantoni-Bournia — 190

Hydra   Yannos G. Lolos — 192

Dokos   Yannos G. Lolos — 195

Islets and rocky islets   Yannos G. Lolos — 196

Spetses   Yannos G. Lolos — 197

KYTHERA, ANTIKYTHERA

Kythera   Aris Tsaravopoulos — 198

Antikythera   Aris Tsaravopoulos — 202

CYCLADES

Kea   Yanna Venieri — 206

Makronisos   Evangelos Ch. Kakavoyannis — 212

Andros   Christina A. Televantou — 214

Gyaros   Alexandros P. Gounaris — 220

Tenos   Olga Philaniotou — 222

Syros   Marisa Marthari — 226

Mykonos   Photeini N. Zapheiropoulou — 230

Delos   Photeini N. Zapheiropoulou — 232

Rheneia   Photeini N. Zapheiropoulou — 244

Kythnos Alexandros Mazarakis Ainian	246
Seriphos Alexandros Mazarakis Ainian	250
Siphnos Alexandros Mazarakis Ainian	252
Islets of the Western Cyclades	256
Seriphopoula Peggy Pantou – Zozi Papadopoulou	256
Kitriani Peggy Pantou – Zozi Papadopoulou	257
Polyaigos Peggy Pantou – Zozi Papadopoulou	258
Paros Photeini N. Zapheiropoulou	260
Antiparos Photeini N. Zapheiropoulou	269
Saliagos Photeini N. Zapheiropoulou	269
Despotiko Yannos Kourayos	269
Naxos Olga Philaniotou – Vassilis Lambrinoudakis	272
Lesser Cyclades	286
Donousa Olga Philaniotou	286
Kouphonisia Olga Philaniotou	287
Keros Olga Philaniotou	288
Schinousa Olga Philaniotou	289
Herakleia Olga Philaniotou	289
Amorgos Lila Marangou	290
Ios Marisa Marthari	298
Sikinos Marisa Marthari	302
Pholegandros Marisa Marthari	302
Kimolos Ismini Trianti	304
Melos Ismini Trianti	306
Thera Christos Doumas – Maya Efstathiou	312
Anaphe Christina A. Televantou	326

DODECANESE

Milesian islands	330
Agathonisi Anastasia Dreliossi-Herakleidou	330
Arkioi Maria Michalaki-Kollia	330
Marathi Maria Michalaki-Kollia	330
Patmos Anastasia Dreliossi-Herakleidou	332
Leipsoi Anastasia Dreliossi-Herakleidou	333
Pharmakonisi Anastasia Dreliossi-Herakleidou	333
Leros Anastasia Dreliossi-Herakleidou	334
Kalymnos Anastasia Dreliossi-Herakleidou	336
Telendos Anastasia Dreliossi-Herakleidou	339
Pserimos Anastasia Dreliossi-Herakleidou	339
Kos Dimitrios Bosnakis	340
Astypalaia Maria Michalaki-Kollia	352
Syrna Maria Michalaki-Kollia	353
Nisyros Melina Filimonos-Tsopotou	354
Yali Melina Filimonos-Tsopotou	355
Telos Melina Filimonos-Tsopotou	356
Syme Eleni Farmakidou	358
Rhodes Toula Marketou – Ioannis Ch. Papachristodoulou	360
Chalke Kalliopi Bairami	372
Alimnia Kalliopi Bairami	373
Castellorizo Kalliopi Bairami	373
Rho Kalliopi Bairami	375
Karpathos Fotini Zervaki	376
Kasos Fotini Zervaki	378

CRETE

Prehistoric times Maria Andreadaki-Vlazaki – Lefteris Platon	384
Historical times Thomas Brogan – Natalia Vogeikoff	410

AEGEAN: AN UNDERWATER MUSEUM

Katerina P. Dellaporta	434

SELECTED BIBLIOGRAPHY   446
BIOGRAPHICAL NOTES   457
SOURCES OF ILLUSTRATIONS   462

FOREWORD

"Aegean Islands", the first book in the series "Archaeology", produced by the MELISSA Publishing House, is a review of archaeological activity in the islands of the Archipelago from the nineteenth century to the present day, with emphasis on the most important field research, findings and finds of the last twenty years.

The book aims at a comprehensive and collective assessment of the Aegean island world and its culture. This was the basic idea and it is this that we consider is the value and the contribution of the work to the contemporary bibliography, as archaeological approaches to the Aegean have until now been fragmentary and focused on single islands or island groups.

The introduction outlines briefly the history of archaeological activity in the Aegean, the factors that stimulated it and the persons who conducted it.

Part I comprises five chapters offering an illuminating synthesis by chronological period of the Aegean's course in history, art and society, from the earliest settlement of the islands until the end of the ancient world, which is marked by the prevailing of Christianity.

The main body of the book presents all the islands – from the largest and best known to the tiny uninhabited islets – with concise texts and ample illustrations, which give an overview of the particular physiognomy of each place, as this is documented by the archaeological remains and their interpretation.

Despite the strictures of space and the condensing of the texts and illustrations into just a few pages per island, the forty-six authors provide a full, informative and comprehensible account, placing particular emphasis on archaeological activity over the past few years and frequently presenting for the first time finds from recent excavations. So, "Aegean Islands" is essentially a compendium, by the most authoritative researchers today, of the archaeology of the Aegean Islands. Euboea, the second largest island in the Archipelago, is not included in this volume because its geographical and, in part, cultural "fidelity" to the Greek Mainland were considered more appropriate to its examination along with Central Greece, in the next volume of the series "Archaeology".

Archaeological research, by its very nature multi-dimensional and demanding in personnel and funding, is not exempted from the social and scientific dictates, as well as the political conjunctures, of each era. After the large-scale excavations of the nineteenth and the early twentieth century, at major sites in the ancient world, which were the field of extensive investigations by the Foreign Archaeological Schools and the Archaeological Society at Athens, the front of research turned from the 1960s onwards to the systematic study and publication of these important ensembles. Taking as axiomatic that excavation is an irreversible intervention in the material remains, and as such destructive, the scale of investigations was reduced. Moreover, these began to become inter-disciplinary in character and to employ modern methodological tools for the sounder approach to the societies of the past.

In this same period there was an upsurge in the research activity of the Archaeological Service of the Hellenic Ministry of Culture, which was called on to carry out thousands of excavations, under the pressure of the rapid pace of building "development" in the islands, often with limited means and extremely few personnel.

For many years, and perhaps still today, archaeology was perceived by the general public as an introverted and agoraphobic discipline. Archaeologists were seen as a special category of scholars, often quaint, who had another conception of space, time and – primarily – modern society. This image, frequently reinforced by the fact that very important finds were never exhibited in the state museums, but lay mouldering in dusty storerooms, and that remains of historical significance, humiliated and undocumented, ended up as "old stones" in citizens' eyes, was very slow in altering.

Over the past twenty years, militant archaeology has for the first time become aware of its responsibility for the management of this enormous volume of antiquities. Today, even though pressures are still as asphyxiating, archaeology in Greece appears to be establishing its social and educational role. The arrangement of archaeological sites in the islands, some of which are models or exemplars of the enhancement of antiquities, and the considerable museological and publishing activity noted in parallel, have radically changed the archaeological and the environmental landscape.

Aim and hope of this book, which endeavours to present so many and so diverse islands in just 460 pages, is to help promote this direction, by offering a modern look at Antiquity. Through a voyage calling at many harbours, starting from Macedonian Thasos and ending at Gavdos in the Libyan Sea, and passing from Attic Psyttaleia to Karian Megiste, it enriches our knowledge of the past, provides a conspectus of historical time and publicizes some of the most important achievements of a great civilization, the Aegean.

And something more: it shows that archaeological finds – from the "wondrous" that capture the public imagination, to the "humble" – emerge from correctly investigated excavation assemblages and that they are not exclusively works of art, like those which – products of antiquities looting and illegal export – are exhibited in private collections and museums, violently wrenched from the womb of their original environment.

The authors of this volume, most of them archaeologists with a long career in the Archaeological Service, the universities and the wider academic-research domain, collaborated closely with one another to enrich each unit in information and photographs, facilitating their colleagues who have written texts about other islands. Consequently, their contribution is to be found in many more pages than those they sign. The MELISSA Publishing

House and the editor of the volume express their sincerest thanks to all, for their participation and collaboration in all stages of preparing the book, over the last three years.

For photographs from the excavations and from their personal or service archives – many of them hitherto unpublished – we address our warm thanks to professors N. Arslan (Tenedos) and H. Huryilmaz (Imbros); Dr L. Parlama and the Scientific Committee for the Conservation and Enhancement of Palamari, Skyros, Dr E. Sapouna-Sakellaraki (Skyros), Professor J.J. Kienast and Dr V. Yannouli (Samos), Professor F. Felten and Dr W. Gauss (Aegina), Dr B. Wells (sanctuary of Poseidon, Poros), Dr Y. Sakellarakis and Professor I. Petrocheilos (Aghios Georgios and Palaiokastro, Kythera), M. Caskey (Aghia Irini, Kea), The Scientific Committee for the Conservation and Enhancement of Ancient Karthaia, Kea, I. Demolin-Osipenco and the archive of P. Spitaels (Makronisos), professors G. Despinis and N. Kourou (Aghia Thekla and Xobourgo, Tenos), Professor C. Renfrew (Saliagos), Dr V. Vasilopoulou (Chrysospilia, Pholegandros), Dr C. Zachos (Zas, Naxos), the Union of Melians (Phylakopi, Melos), E. Skerlou (sanctuary of Herakles, Kos) and Dr P. Triantaphyllidis (Rhodes).

For enriching the demanding chapter on Crete, we are most grateful to V. Niniou-Kindeli (Tsiskiana, Aptera), Dr A. Kanta (Monastiraki), professors N. Stampolidis and P. Themelis (Eleutherna), E. Tegou (Pantanassa, Amari), the excavators of Archanes Y. and E. Sakellarakis, Dr G. Rethemiotakis (Galatas) and N. Dimopoulou (Poros), Dr A. Vasilakis (Trypiti), professors J. and M. Shaw (Kommos), Dr J.-A. MacGillivray (Palaikastro), V. Apostolakou (Trypitos), as well as the directors of the excavations at Azoria (professors D. Haggis and M. Mook), Mochlos (professors J. Soles and C. Davaras), and Kavousi (professors G. Gesell and L. P. Day).

Many thanks for permission to use photographs are due to the Archaeological Receipts Fund (TAPA) and especially to its director K. Romiopoulou and to T. Chrysochoidou, to the National Archaeological Museum and E. Morati, as well as to the Directorate of Culture of the Ministry of the Aegean and Island Policy. Also to the Museum of Cycladic Art – N.P. Goulandris Foundation and its director Professor N. Stampolidis for providing photographs from the catalogues of the exhibitions Neolithic Culture in Greece, Sea Routes *and* Eleutherna. *Last, to him and to A. Karetsou for kindly providing photographs from the catalogue of the exhibition* Dodecanese – Crete – Cyprus, 16th-6th c. BC. *We express our thanks to Emlen, Arthur and David Myers for allowing us to use photographs from the outstanding album of their parents, Wilson and Ellie Myers,* Aerial Atlas of Crete. *Also to the photographic archives of the Archaeological Society at Athens (I. Ninou), the French Archaeological School (K. Christophi), the Italian Archaeological School (I. Symiakaki), the British School at Athens (A. Kakisi), the German Archaeological Institute (Dr M. Krumme), the American School of Classical Studies, the Numismatic Museum, Athens, the Glyptothek Munich, the Louvre Museum and the Vatican Museums. The chapter on under-water antiquities in the Aegean was enriched with photographs from the archive of the Hellenic Institute of Marine Archaeology.*

Elias Eliadis processed especially for this book a large number of photographs, including that on the front cover. The collaboration with photographers A. Voliotis, S. Efstathopoulos, K. Xenikakis, N. Kaseris. G. Koukas, Ch. Papanikolopoulos and D. Sakatzis significantly enriched the volume with new shots. We thank them all warmly. Substantial too was the assistance of the publishing companies "Adam", "Ekdotike Athenon", "Esperos" and "Toubis", which permitted us to use photographs from their archives. The source of each photograph (archive and photographer) is recorded at the end of the book, as this was declared to the editor by the authors.

The marking of the archaeological toponyms on the maps and the literary editing of the Greek texts were undertaken by the archaeologist and editor Kiki Birtacha, to whose experience and comments significant improvements in the form of the book are due.

The book was conscientiously translated into English by Alexandra Doumas at an intensive pace, to ensure it was ready on time.

The idea of Aegean Islands, *first volume in the series "Archaeology", was conceived by Annie Ragia in 2002 and given the form of a book thanks to Athina Ragia, with the invaluable collaboration of Theoni Soupiona on the pagination and Kelly Kalogirou on the cartography. The dummy of the Greek edition was scrutinized on Andros, in 2005, by Professor Dimitris Philippidis, whom I thank for his critical comments on the final result.*

Fully aware of the honour and the responsibility of the project entrusted to me, I wish to dedicate this book to Yorgos Ragias, for over fifty years now father of MELISSA.

Andreas G. Vlachopoulos PhD
Archaeologist

Archaeology in the Aegean Islands

CHRISTOS DOUMAS

The discipline of Archaeology was dilatory in realizing the leading role played by the small remnants of land in the Aegean Sea, in shaping the Aegean Culture. And this despite the fact that in very many cases archaeological research started from small remnants such as these. The ancient Greeks called the islands *Nesoi*, presumably because in men's first contact with them – perhaps from the Upper Palaeolithic period – they imagined them as floating, moving pieces of land, since in the absence of instruments of orientation it was difficult if not impossible to revisit them.[1] It seems that the birth of myths that islands were stabilized after divine intervention is due to this conception. Myth has it that Zeus anchored Delos, Apollo Anaphe, Poseidon Nisyros, Herakles Mykonos, and so on. Virgil's remark that "you'd think that the Cyclades, broken off, are swimming"[2] appears to preserve the echo of this conception. Consequently, the etymology of the word island in Greek (νήσος, νησί) has nothing to do with solitariness; quite the opposite it means mobility. Even so, foreign researchers lacking in Classical education and led astray by the meaning of terms of Latin derivation, such as insularity and isolation, have tried to interpret the cultural processes in the Aegean islands from the viewpoint of seclusion. In this approach their guide was anthropologists' studies of peoples in the islands and archipelagos in the great oceans, islands that are hundreds or even thousands of miles away from major landmasses. Is it valid, however, to compare the islands of the Aegean with those of the Pacific? Especially when it is well known that in whatever direction you cross the Aegean, you never lose sight of at least a tiny piece of land?

The Aegean, this swathe of sea between two continents, scattered with thousands of islands and rocky islets, is a unique geographical phenomenon. And it is to this, I believe, that it owes the uniqueness of its culture. Two major sea currents, the Eastern Mediterranean current and the Bosporos current, move respectively northwards and southwards in the Aegean. In their flow between the island groups they are split into a host of local cyclonic and anticyclonic currents, making this sea a bridge between East and West, North and South, betwixt three continents. As recent specialist studies have shown,[3] the tremendous variety in marine circulation enhanced each of the islands as a port of call for the circulation not only of material goods but also of ideas. The great twentieth-century historian Fernand Braudel had already pointed out this role of the islands in 1949, when he wrote: "when the islands are included in the sea lanes and for one reason or another become a link in a chain" they cease to be cut off, but "on the contrary are involved actively in the affairs of the outside world, less cut off from these than some inaccessible mountainous regions".[4]

The variety of archaeological institutions conducting research in the Aegean means that their findings are published in a variety of languages. For this reason, those studying the archaeology of the Aegean must be conversant in several languages, in order to have access to as much data as possible. Otherwise their approach is in danger of being incomplete and their conclusions unrelated to reality. Unfortunately, this has happened with some researchers studying the Aegean islands, mainly English-speaking (with the brilliant exception of Colin Renfrew), who instead of confessing this weakness have preferred to ignore research itself and to impose a kind of embargo on non-English publications. So, for example, the Italian publications of research on Lemnos have been ignored consistently, even in very recent British publications, which restrict the Bronze Age Aegean between... Thebes and Crete.[5] Of course, the Cyclades, represented adequately in the Anglo-Saxon bibliography, were admitted in the cultural process of the Bronze Age Aegean. The linguistic imperialism enhanced by the conception *aliena sunt, non leguntur* nurtured a kind of arrogance which was expressed in the form of expert authority on issues of island archaeology. Such "expert authorities" on the island archaeology of the Aegean also ignored the existence of Braudel for at least twenty-three years, that is until the French historian's work was published in English translation (1972), when his ideas were suddenly espoused and promoted by would-be pioneers of archaeological thought with the fanaticism typical of every provincial new convert. However, the islands of the Aegean, all the islands, always existed and the mechanisms of their participation in the cultural events did not wait from the archaeologists to set them in motion.[6]

Consequence of the diachronic interaction among the islands, both between each other and between them and the large landmasses nearby, was that each island formed its own cultural identity. The limitations characteristic of the islands in terms of natural resources on the one hand formed the frugal character of their inhabitants and on the other hand stimulated quests for ways and means of improving living conditions. From the synergy of these two factors the island societies in the Aegean emerged, which from early on were in the vanguard of the cultural process. The invention of ever safer and faster seagoing vessels, observation of the currents, meteorological phenomena and the star-spangled sky facilitated the islander's voyages, which brought them into contact with other peoples and other cultures. These contacts made them pioneers not only in early technology but also in liberal thought. The need for survival impelled them to develop ties with the nearby landmasses, which came to function as their *Lebensraum*, their *peraia*.

The Aegean islands, the majority clustered in small archipelagos, formed individual societies with common characteristics. These characteristics may differ from archipelago to archipelago, or even from island to island, depending on the possibilities of communication with the landmass opposite.

North Aegean

The islands of the North Aegean include Thasos, Samothrace, Aghios Efstratios, Tenedos, Imbros and Lemnos. Common trait of them all is their location on the sea current that flows down from the Hellespont, in a northwestern course, constituting an essential factor of communication.

Thasos An island rich in minerals and marble, Thasos was exploited from early times. Although sporadic researches into its past began in the mid-nineteenth century, the first systematic excavation commenced in 1911, by the French School at Athens, at modern Limenas, ancient Thasos. This excavation, which still continues, and rescue excavations of the Greek Archaeological Service, have revealed unique works of ancient Greek art, as well as important monuments dedicated to cult. Together with the rich epigraphic material, these creations reveal the significant role the island played after Parian colonists settled there in the seventh century BC.

The island's prehistoric past remained essentially unknown until the 1970s, when investigations were begun – at first rescue operations and later more systematic – by the XIII Ephorate of Prehistoric and Classical Antiquities. These have brought to light prehistoric ochre mines and settlements at Skala Sotiros, Limenaria and Aghios Ioannis, which date the early habitation of the island back to at least the Neolithic Age.

Samothrace The archaeologist's pick has uncovered remains of the ancient city at Palaiopoli on the northwest coast of the island, a little to the west of the sanctuary of the Great Gods, and a prehistoric settlement on the hillock of Mikro Vouni, on the southwest coast.

The sanctuary was identified by the discovery of the statue of the Nike (Victory) in 1863, by the French Consul in Adrianople. M. Champoiseau. The removal of the statue to Paris made Samothrace famous and attracted the interest of the archaeological community. In 1866 a French mission under Deville and Coquart assumed the task of mapping the ruins of the sanctuary of the Great Gods and opening excavation trenches. There followed the investigations by the Austrian Alexander Conze (1873 and 1875), which have been dubbed the "beginning of modern excavations in Greece".[7] After an interruption of half a century, research at the site was resumed as a collaboration between the French School at Athens and the Institute of Prague (1823-1927). Activities ceased until just before the Second World War, when research was begun anew in 1938 by the Institute of Fine Arts, New York University. The series of volumes under the general title *Samothrace: Excavations Conducted by the Institute of Fine Arts, New York University* hosts studies and articles relating to the monuments and to the cult of the Kabeiroi. Their sanctuary on Samothrace was of panhellenic character and vied in fame with the other great centre of mystery cult, the sanctuary of Demeter in Eleusis.

Investigations at Mikro Vouni are being carried out by the XIV Ephorate of Prehistoric and Classical Antiquities. This settlement was founded in the Final Neolithic period and continued in existence until the end of the Middle Bronze Age. Although research is still in progress, the preliminary reports present evidence that documents relations with Middle Minoan Crete.

Aghios Efstratios, Tenedos, Imbros The history of these three small islands is known more from the literary sources than from archaeological research. Only Imbros can boast intensive excavation activity in recent years, and indeed with the collaboration of Greek and Turkish archaeologists. These investigations confirm yet again the rule that cultural boundaries almost never coincide with administrative ones.

Lemnos Lying at the entrance to the Hellespont and on the point of convergence of two currents, the East Mediterranean current flowing towards the Euxine Pontus (Black Sea) and the Bosporos current flowing towards the Aegean, Lemnos enjoyed the most privileged position for relations with the world of Pontos. Nevertheless, this was not the reason why archaeological researches on the island began. Aim of the

1. Aim of the old excavations was to reveal impressive monuments, which required large teams: from the excavation at Poliochni in the 1930s.

2. The dynamic excavator of Thermi on Lesbos, Winifred Lamb.

Etruscan specialist Alessandro Della Seta (fig. 17) was to determine whether the Etruscans of Italy and the Tyrrhenians of Lemnos had a common origin. He commenced excavations in the city of historical times, Hephaistia, in 1923.[8] However, his interest quickly shifted to the east coast of the island, where at the village of Kaminia the famous stele with the inscription in the Etruscan alphabet had been found. From 1930 until the entrenchment of Fascism in Italy and the introduction of racist laws, when Della Seta's work was violently interrupted (1938), he had uncovered a considerable part of the prehistoric settlement at nearby Poliochni (fig. 1). With seven Neolithic phases and as many again in the Bronze Age, Poliochni offered a rich stratigraphy for studying the early history of the Northeast Aegean and became a reference point for the development of culture in the region. The continuation of research after the Second World War and the monumental two-volume publication of the results by Luigi Bernabò Brea[9] brought Lemnian archaeology to the forestage once more. Urban planning, public utilities (paved streets, sewerage network, community wells for water supply, fortification wall), division of labour and advanced pyrotechnology (metallurgy, pottery production) established Poliochni not only as the earliest urban centre in the Aegean, not excepting nearby Troy, but also the earliest city on European soil.

Recent investigations at other prehistoric sites confirm the important role that Lemnos played in cultural processes in the Early Bronze Age Aegean. Evidence brought to light in excavations conducted by the XX Ephorate of Prehistoric and Classical Antiquities in the island's capital, Myrina, attests to the existence of an urban centre there at least equal in importance to that at Poliochni. A third centre is being revealed on the islet of Koukkonisi in Moudros Bay, in excavations conducted by the Academy of Athens. The geographical location and the orientation of these three prehistoric settlements document the radiation of activities on Lemnos to the outside world. Thanks to its strategic position in relation to the Hellespont, and with its three coastal settlements, Poliochni on the east, Myrina on the west and Koukkonisi on the south, Lemnos functioned as a centre for trafficking goods and ideas, linking the entire Aegean with the world of the East, the world of the Euxine Pontus.[10]

Lemnos kept its strategic significance in historical times, as the ancient literary sources and the monuments attest. In the interwar years the Italian Archaeological School at Athens had already uncovered part of the eponymous city of the smith-god Hephaistos, Hephaistia, on the northeast peninsula of the island, as well as the ruins of the neighbouring sanctuary of the Great Gods, the Kabeirion.

East Aegean

The East Mediterranean current flows up between the islands of the East Aegean and the Asia Minor coast, making this strip of water a true sea-lane. The east coasts of the islands were ideal for establishing ports of call for seagoing vessels in all periods, while at the same time they were in direct contact with their *peraia* opposite. This explains why throughout their history the basic centres of settlement on these islands faced eastward.

Lesbos Lesbos is not only the largest island in the East Aegean but also has a rich soil that favours many and varied crops. This fact, in conjunction with the island's proximity to Asia Minor, contributed to its development from prehistoric times, as archaeological investigations have confirmed. More or less contemporary with the Italian research

on Lemnos, a British mission led by Winifred Lamb (fig. 2) excavated the prehistoric settlement at Thermi, a short distance to the north of Mytilene. All five successive phases of this small city date to the third millennium BC and display an admirable urban organization. Because Lamb's immediate and exemplary publication of the results of the excavation (1936) preceded the publication of Poliochni, it was for many years the sole source of information on the Northeast Aegean in the Early Bronze Age.

Archaeological research on the monuments of historical times on Lesbos has been conducted exclusively by the XX Ephorate of Prehistoric and Classical Antiquities. Of the five cities (*pentapolis*) of ancient Lesbos, two were dominant: Mytilene and Methymna, monuments from which were revealed by D. Evangelidis in the interwar years (1922-1928). After the Second World War, excavations at these sites were continued by the successive Ephors of Antiquities for the region. The impressive aqueduct, the ancient theatre of Mytilene, the so-called House of Menander – thus named after the mosaic depictions of scenes from comedies by the poet –, the ancient sanctuary at Mesa, as well as a host of works of art bear witness to Lesbos's contribution to Aegean Civilization. These material testimonies also make it easier to comprehend the development of the literary arts and the emergence of such personalities as Pittakos and Alkaios from Mytilene, Sappho from Eressos, Arion from Methymna. I. D. Kontis's book entitled "*Lesbian Polyptych*" (1973, in Greek) was at the time the best-documented synopsis of the island's archaeological wealth.

Chios The island of Chios, with its abundance of monuments spanning prehistory to Late Antiquity, was rather late in attracting the attention of the archaeological community. The British School at Athens showed a lively interest in the island's antiquities and members were particularly active during the 1930s. At Kato Phana the sanctuary of Apollo Phanaios was investigated (1934-1935), at the site of Delphini on the northeast coast parts of the fortification of the ancient acropolis were brought to light, while at the northwest tip of Chios, in the Aghio Galas Cave, remains of habitation dating back to the Early Neolithic period were found (1938). In the same year the large-scale excavation at Emporio, on the souheast coast, began. Work there continued in the 1950s, revealing phases extending from the Early Bronze Age into historical times, from which were presented in a model publication the related find.

Research in the city of Chios itself, one of the renowned ancient cities of Ionia, were begun quite recently by the XX Ephorate of Prehistoric and Classical Antiquities, mainly as rescue excavations in building plots, as the ancient city lies buried beneath the modern capital of the island. Despite their sporadic character, these excavations have helped to determine the boundaries of the city in Archaic and Classical times and have uncovered notable building remains, pottery workshops and important artworks.

Psara Though small, this islet, the Psyrie of Homer, evidently played a significant role in Antiquity, as remains of its past attest. It was unknown archaeologically until 1961, when the then Ephor of Antiquities, Serapheim Charitonidis, located a Mycenaean cemetery at the northwest tip, in Archontiki Bay, and an ancient settlement at the site of Paliokastro, the Mavri Rachi immortalized for all Greeks by the national poet Dionysios Solomos. Systematic excavations at these sites have been conducted since the 1980s by personnel of the XX Ephorate of Prehistoric and Classical Antiquities.

Samos Samos was one of the most important centres of the ancient Hellenic world and museums in many countries proudly host great works of art from here. That is why archaeological interest in Samos began early. After all, Herodotus' descriptions of the famed panhellenic sanctuary of Hera and the still standing column of the goddess's temple were an enduring challenge. As early as 1702, at the behest of King Louis XIV, the French naturalist J. Pitton de Tournefort conducted a small excavation around the aforesaid column. In the early twentieth century (1902-1903) a new excavation was made by P. Kavvadias and Th. Sofoulis, on behalf of the Archaeological Society at Athens. However, the extensive investigations that are continued to this day by the German Archaeological Institute at Athens started in 1910 under the direction of Th. Wiegand. Since then whole contingents of German scholars have been trained through studying the finds from the sanctuary of Hera (fig. 3), which are published regularly in a series of volumes under the general title *Samos*. Apart from the information on the history of the Heraion, the excavations there have also brought to light evidence of prehistoric habitation, which place Samos in the same cultural ambit as the other East Aegean islands.

Remains of prehistoric habitation also came to light in the excavations conducted by W. Wrede (1928) and U. Jantzen (1963-1968) on Kastrou tou Lykourgou Hill in the area of former Tigani, now known as Pythagoreio. Pythagoreio occupies only a small part of the ancient city of Samos, the monuments of which are preserved in quite good condition. Excavations in the city, occasional at first, by the German Archaeological Institute (1894) and the Greek Archaeological Service (1924), have been continued since 1966 as systematic rescue interventions by the XXI Ephorate of Prehistoric and Classical Antiquities. Famed among the city's monuments is the Eupalineion Aqueduct, work of the engineer Eupalinos from Megara, who dared to open a tunnel 1,036 metres long under the mountain in order to bring water from the spring to the city. Another monumental project of the time of the tyrant Polykrates is the mole, 360 metres long and with foundations to a depth of 30 metres, which protected the city's cosmopolitan harbour and survives to this day.

Ikaria Lying in the midst of the open sea and orientated northwest-southeast, the long narrow island of Ikaria constitutes as it were a protective wall for those sailing in this invariably tempestuous area of the Aegean. That is why even today it has two harbours, Evdilos in the north and Aghios Kirykos in the south, which are used depending on the prevailing weather. Lacking in large tracts of arable land and with limited natural resources, Ikaria evidently owed its significance in Antiquity to its strategic position. This is attested by the imposing Hellenistic tower at Drakano, at the northeast tip of the island.

After the excavation by L. Politis in the sanctuary of Artemis Tauropolos (1939) in the coastal village of Kampos, ancient Oinoe, the Ephor of Antiquities N. Zapheiropoulos expressed archaeological interest in Ikaria, as part of his effort to organize the Ephorate in the 1960s. Rescue excavations here and there indicated the stock-raising character of the island's ancient settlements, which were small clusters of farmsteads.

North Sporades

The North Sporades constitute to an archipelago of small islands and rocky islets, rarely more than 6 kilometres apart, while Skiathos is only 4 kilometres away from the coast of Thessaly. Another distructive feature of this island group is its location in an area that is the junction of sea routes in the Aegean. The currents, one cyclonic and the other anticyclonic, moving between east and west, linked the area of the Hellespont with mainland Greece, offering the possibility of maritime travel in all seasons of the year. Bearing these geographical parameters in mind, it is easy to realize why the North Sporades were a challenge for the prehistoric inhabitants of Thessaly. Thus the early evidence of human habitation, such as the Mesolithic level in the Cyclops' Cave on Youra and the Early Neolithic level at Aghios Petros on Kyra Panaya can be understood. There is no doubt that such early steps towards the islands led gradually to the development of sea communications and the transformation of the Aegean economy into one of middlemen. The discovery of a Late Minoan II grave on Skopelos (ancient Peparethos) prompted N. Platon (1949) to link the island with the myth of Staphylos, fruit of the union of Dionysos and Ariadne, since tradition has it that Peparethos was colonized by Cretans.

After lying in the archaeological doldrums for decades, investigations in the North Sporades started some twenty years ago and are being continued by the XIII Ephorate of Prehistoric and Classical Antiquities.

Skyros Excavations on Skyros were always small-scale rescue operations by members of the Archaeological Service. D. Evangelidis (1918), I. Papadimitriou (1935), Ph. Stavropoulos (1939), P. Themelis (1967-1968), A. Choremis (1970-1971) brought to light evidence of the island's continuous involvement in the cultural affairs of the Aegean during historical times. For earlier periods the survey by D. Theocharis (1974) identified Neolithic remains at the site of Papa to Chouma. Of longer duration and more systematic is the excavation of the Early Bronze Age settlement on the most windswept tip of northern Skyros, Palamari. These investigations, which began in 1981 and are still in progress, confirm the significance of the sea currents for communications in the prehistoric Aegean. For it is surely not fortuitous that Palamari is situated on the very point where the cyclonic and the anticyclonic current towards the Hellespont meet, making communication possible in both summer and winter.

Argosaronic Islands - Kythera

The small archipelagos formed within the Argolic and Saronic gulfs are, in a way, miniatures of the larger island complexes in the Aegean. And their role is similar to these too, although on a smaller scale, mainly for relations between the eastern Peloponnese and western Attica. It is well known that the sea current from the Hellespont flows southwards, skirting the east shoreline of mainland Greece. In this privileged position, the islands of the Argosaronic Gulf undoubtedly played a role in the early circulation of goods and raw materials to and from the Cyclades and Attica, and vice versa. Indeed, the circulation of obsidian and kaolin from Melos, and of andesite millstones from the Methana region is confirmed from at least the Neolithic Age. The shipwrecks located or explored in this region also testify to these islands' contribution to early trade.

Aegina Thanks to the visible monuments as well as to the references in the ancient sources, Aegina was a focus of archaeological interest from early on. In 1814, C. R. Cockerel had carried out an excavation next to the harbour, at Kolona, where part of the column of the opisthodomos of the temple of Apollo – initially attributed to Aphrodite – was visible. Eighty years later, in 1894, Valerios Stais returned to the site, excavating on behalf of the Archaeological Society at Athens. Since then, work at Kolona has been continued by the Austrian Archaeological Institute, through whose publications in the series *Alt-Ägina* the island's rich cultural history is enhanced. In the Neolithic Age a settlement was founded at this site, which was destined to play a leading role in Aegean affairs not only in prehistoric but also in historical times.

Situated on the northern sea current, which flows along the east coasts of the Greek Mainland, Aegina was in a strategic position for communications between the North and South Aegean. The settlement at Kolona was therefore enhanced as a communications node of seminal importance, a role it kept in early historical times too. For it is not fortuitous that in this settlement the most tangible evidence of advanced metallurgy, after Poliochni on Lemnos, is encountered. Just as it is not insignificant that Aegina was the first city in Greece to mint its own coinage.

Thanks to its economic autonomy in historical times, Aegina was in the artistic vanguard among the Greek cities. The architectural monuments in the sanctuary of Aphaia and their sculpted decoration were acknowledged as representing a landmark in the history of ancient art, which is why King Ludwig of Bavaria purchased the sculptures in 1813. Systematic investigations in the Aphaia sanctuary were conducted in the early twentieth century by the German archaeologist A. Furtwangler.

Salamis Although the island was inhabited from the Neolithic Age it does not seem to have played a role in any way comparable to that of Aegina, perhaps because of its propinquity to Attica. Nonetheless, excavations carried out by the Archaeological Society at Athens from the nineteenth century by P. Kavvadias (1893) and A. Keramopoullos (early 20th century), as well as more recently by members of the Archaeological Service, have revealed notable Mycenaean, Submycenaean and Classical cemeteries, as well as parts of the Classical city. Signifi-

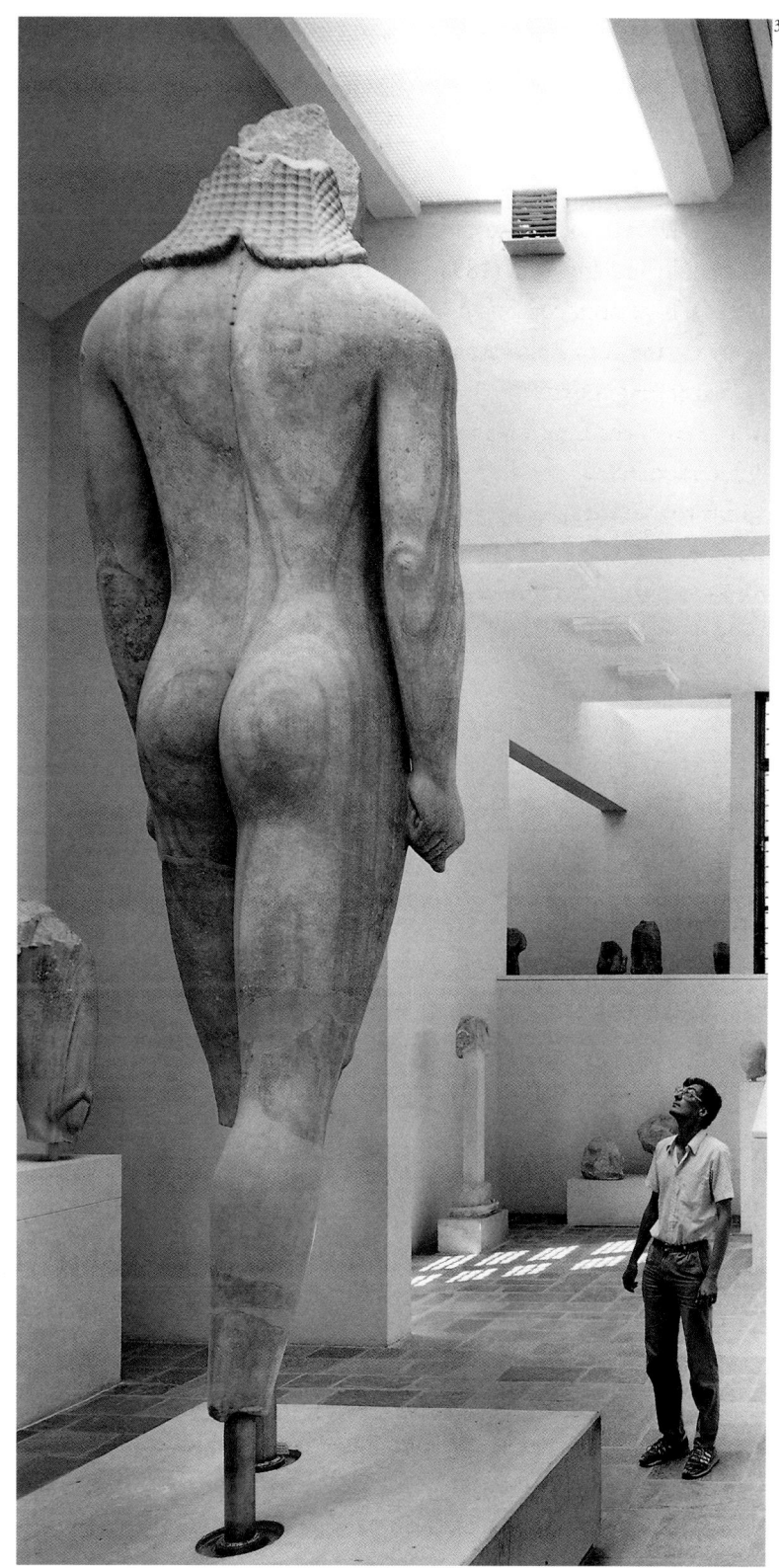

3. A new wing of the Samos Museum had to be built to house the colossal kouros, triple life-size, from the Heraion.

cant remains from Neolithic into historical times have been brought to light in the ongoing investigations in the "Cave of Euripides", and of late work is in progress on the Mycenaean citadel at Kanakia.

Poros The sanctuary of Poseidon in Kalaureia was explored by the Swedish Archaeological Institute, which has resumed excavations there. Surface surveys and small-scale excavations on the rest of the island have confirmed the existence of remains from all periods of Antiquity.

Kythera, Antikythera Although these islands are geographically outside the Aegean Sea, it was considered apposite to include them in this volume because they have an insular culture and because they constitute the western gateway to the Aegean. Kythera, which lies on this maritime crossroad, was often visited by travellers, many of whom described its monuments. In the years of British Rule (1808-1864) the few excavations carried out there were of amateur character, if not by antiquities looters, bearing in mind that the first publication (1862) of archaeological finds from Kythera was by the Professor of Archaeology at the University of Athens, Athanasios Rousopoulos, who operated as a supplier of antiquities to foreigners! Immediately after the island's unification with Greece, the Archaeological Society at Athens expressed interest in its antiquities, but it was not until 1915 that a Mycenaean tomb was excavated by the Kytherian Valerios Stais. In 1963 the British School at Athens, in collaboration with the University of Pennsylvania Museum, conducted excavations at Kastri. In recent years the systematic excavation at Aghios Georgios sto Vouno has uncovered one of the very few peak sanctuaries known outside Crete.

Cyclades

The Cyclades, scattered in the Central Aegean, contribute more than any other island group to breaking up the major sea currents in this area into numerous local ones, so creating much variety in sea circulation. As far as archaeological research is concerned, we could say that the first excavations in these islands were carried out in 426/5 BC, when the Athenians, on the pretext of absolving Delos of the pollution of death, proceeded to the purification (*catharsis*) of the island, disinterring all those who had been buried there until that time and transferring their remains to Rheneia opposite. Thucydides at least analyses this act as an excavation of the past. In later times too, the archaeological community expressed interest in the Cyclades from early on, with the appointment of Ludwig Ross as first Ephor of Antiquities. His work *Reisen auf den griechischen Inseln des ägäischen Meeres* (1840) gives some of the first reliable information on their archaeological wealth. Since then scholars and amateurs, clandestine diggers and antiquities looters have applied themselves zealously to uncovering and enhancing – each from his own standpoint – the monuments of these islands' past. Given that, as in the case of all the islands, the nearest large landmass to them exerted both economic and cultural influence, and given too that the Cyclades extend for a long way along the mainland coastlines, it is to be expected that the culture of the individual islands differs slightly, depending on the mainland region with which they had close relations.

Kea Famed in Classical Antiquity for its laws and its sons (such as the two lyric poets Simonides and Bacchylides), as well as for its monuments, which are mentioned in the literary sources, Kea naturally attracted the attention of archaeological research.[11] After all, ancient inscriptions and works of art have never ceased turning up by chance, while monuments of the four ancient cities, Ioulis (mod. Chora), Poiessa (Poises), Karthaia (Poles) and Korrhesia, the imposing tower at Aghia Marina, were always visible. Travellers in the seventeenth and eighteenth centuries frequently refer to these remains and sometimes looted them. Before the founding of the Greek State, in 1811, the first excavations were carried out at Karthaia by the Danes P. O. Brøndsted and M. J. Kinch. The former published the findings of this project in 1826, in his work *Reisen und Untersuchungen in Griechenland*. Ninety years later, in 1902, the Belgian epigraphist P. Graindor, as member of the French School of Archaeology at Athens, embarked on a second major excavation at Karthaia. Although the Greek State showed an early interest in the antiquities of Kea, not until after the Second World War was it possible to conduct systematic research. In the 1960s interest in the archaeology of Kea was rekindled. On the one hand the Ephorate of Antiquities for the Cyclades, under the direction of N. Zapheiropoulos, started new investigations at Karthaia, and on the other the University of Cincinnati, with Professor John L. Caskey (fig. 5), commenced excavations on the small peninsula of Aghia Irini, in Aghios Nikolaos Bay (1960-1967). Later systematic surveys by Greek universities and other research foundations have brought Kea into the forefront of archaeological scholarship.

Makronisos, Gyaros These inhospitable islands were used from early times by different regimes as places of exile for undesirable opponents to their authority and were neglected by archaeological research. In the 1970s and 1980s a Belgian archaeological mission conducted small-scale excavations at the Neolithic site at Provatsa on Makronisos.

Andros Despite the fact that there are visible monuments on Andros, such as the impressive Hellenistic tower at Aghios Petros, archaeologists were rather late in showing interest in the island. Important monuments of the ancient capital, present Palaiopoli, were brought to light in the 1950s (N. Kontoleon), and in the 1960s trial trenches were opened on Cape Zagora (N. Zapheiropoulos). Systematic research was subsequently conducted (1967-1977) by the Archaeological Society at Athens in collaboration with the University of Sydney, which uncovered a settlement of the Geometric period (900-700 BC), unique in terms of its layout and the evidence yielded on the religious practices, everyday activities and artistic inquiries of its inhabitants.

The excavations at Palaiopoli are being continued by a team from the University of Athens, while significant sites have been located and investigated by the XXI Ephorate of Prehistoric and Classical Antiquities. These include the Geometric settlement at Ypsili and the Neolithic settlement at Strophilas. The concentration of sites on the west coast of the island, if not fortuitous and due to the coincidence of research, is perhaps indicative of the island's importance for maritime communications. Sheltered from the stormy northeast winds, this coast offered protection for vessels sailing from and to the Gulf of Euboea, an even safer route for communication with the North Aegean.

4. The founder of prehistoric archaeology in Greece and the first excavator in the Cyclades, Christos Tsountas.

5. The excavator of Aghia Irini on Kea, John L. Caskey, inside the prehistoric shrine, looking for a way of dealing with the seawater flooding it.

Tenos Lying at the east edge of the northern Cyclades, Tenos has been explored archaeologically since the early twentieth century. The sanctuary identified by L. Ross in 1837, at the site of Kionia near the present capital, was excavated systematically by the Belgians H. Demoulin and P. Graindor, on behalf of the French School of Archaeology at Athens. In the years before the Second World War research was confined to studying the monuments in the sanctuary and small-scale excavations in the countryside. Even after the war, investigations were limited. In the 1950s the Archaeological Society (N. Kontoleon) excavated the sanctuary of Demeter at Xobourgo. Recently archaeological activity on the island has intensified, with projects of the XXI Ephorate of Prehistoric and Classical Antiquities, the University of Athens and the French School of Archaeology.

Syros Because Hermoupolis was founded on the site of the ancient city of Syros, the monuments of the latter remain virtually unknown. For example, remnants of the ancient theatre, with three rows of seats, are to be found in the basement of a house in the Aniphoraki neighbourhood. However, the situation regarding the material remains of the island's prehistoric past is very different from that for its Classical antiquities. Investigations began in the middle years of the nineteenth century, with the first excavations by G. Papadopoulos (1861-1862, 1865). His work was followed by the Syran anthropologist Klon Stephanos (1872-1875) and at the end of the century by the systematic researches of Christos Tsountas (1898, fig. 4). From the 1960s onwards the XXI Ephorate of Antiquities has shown continuous interest in the cemetery at Chalandriani and the adjacent Early Cycladic fortified settlement at Kastri.

Mykonos In the shadow of the panhellenic sanctuary of Delos, Mykonos was until recently dismissed as of little archaeological interest even though some sporadic prehistoric antiquities had been noted on the surface. It was simply used to house the finds from the excavations on Rheneia; the Mykonos Archaeological Museum was founded to avoid the sacrilege of returning the yields of the ancient purification *Bothros* to the sacred isle of Delos. The chance discovery in Chora

(1961) of the famous Archaic pithos with relief scenes of the Trojan War changed the archaeological image of Mykonos. The rapid development of tourism and the consequent building boom all over the island prompted systematic excavations by the Ephorate of Antiquities. As a result, important antiquities of the Neolithic Age (Ftelia) and the Mycenaean period (Angelika) have come to light.

Delos – Rheneia The ruin of Delos, a pirates' lair during the Ottoman period, was literally plundered after the Liberation of Greece, in order to build the Neoclassical town of Hermoupolis on Syros; the island's monuments were the "quarry" from which abundant, cheap and finely-worked marble was readily obtained. Systematic excavations were begun in 1873, by the French School of Archaeology at Athens (C. Picard, R. Vallois, A. Plassart. Ph. Bruneau) and continue to this day. The uncovering of part of the city, its harbours, sanctuaries and public buildings, brought to light monuments, inscriptions and works of art (fig. 6) through which the history and glorious past of this small but cosmopolitan centre of the ancient world can be reconstructed. The enormous wealth of finds from these excavations has been studied by hundreds of scholars, many of whom were bright stars in the firmament of Classical archaeology.

Excavations on neighbouring Rheneia were conducted by the Archaeological Service (D. Stavropoulos) in the late nineteenth century, revealing the famous *Bothros*, the pit in which the Athenians had deposited the objects from the purification of Delos, to rid the birthplace of the god of light, Apollo, from the miasma of death.

Kythnos, Seriphos Apart from references in the works of travellers, these two islands were until very recently *terra incognita* for archaeological research. Some work was carried out sporadically on Seriphos in the 1960s, while in the last few years systematic surface surveys and excavations have commenced on Kythnos, with significant finds from the site of the ancient city and Maroulas.

Siphnos Of the 200 or so ancient towers identified in the Aegean islands, 54 are on Siphnos. This is not surprising, considering the island's mineral wealth. The extraction of metal ores and the production of lead and silver go back to at least the third millennium BC, as demonstrated by recent research in ancient mines. During the Archaic period Siphnos also produced gold, which ensured it sufficient economic affluence to participate in the cultural affairs of the Hellenic world, erecting imposing monuments such as the renowned Siphnian Treasury in the sanctuary of Apollo at Delphi.

As was the case with many Aegean islands, the first scientific approach to the antiquities of Siphnos – after the descriptions of the travellers – was made by L. Ross (1835-1837). However, systematic investigations were undertaken by the Archaeological Society, with excavations conducted initially by Ch. Tsountas (1898) and subsequently by Iakovos Dragatsis (1915, 1922-1924). Before the Second World War (1935-1937) J. K. Brock and G. M. Young carried out research on the ancient acropolis, on behalf of the British School at Athens. After the war and throughout the 1970s, the Siphnian archaeologist Varvara Philippaki explored the Mycenaean citadel at Aghios Andreas, continuing the excavation started by

6. Mykonians still wore traditional baggy trousers (*vrakes*) when the French Archaeological School began excavations on Delos, as can be seen in this snapshot of a worker amidst the ancient statues.

7. Part of the euthynteria of the "one-hundred-foot" (*hekatompedon*) temple on the acropolis of ancient Paros (Paroikia), which was excavated by O. Rubensohn.

8. The systematic search for material cultural remains of ancient societies transformed the "treasure-hunting" character of the old excavations: view of the British excavation at Saliagos near Antiparos.

9. Only by continuous pumping of the sea, under the level of which the prehistoric settlement at Grotta on Naxos lies, was it possible to glean valuable information on the island's history.

10. The Mycenaean cemetery at Kamini on Naxos, in the course of its excavation: Ephor of Antiquities Nikolaos Zapheiropoulos with his team.

11. Part of the German excavations at ancient Thera, with the so-called "Palazzo".

12. The excavator of Akrotiri, Spyridon Marinatos, examining finds from Akrotiri.

Tsountas. Last, noteworthy is the investigation of the island's ancient mines by the scientific team of the Max-Plank Institut für Kernphysik, of Mainz/Heidelberg, in the 1980s, which proved the huge contribution of Siphnos to Aegean culture and civilization.

Paros, Antiparos, Despotiko Paros and the smaller islands to the southwest of it attracted archaeological interest quite early on. The British traveller Theodore Bent was the first to excavate on Antiparos and Despotiko, uncovering 40 Early Cycladic graves (1883). Investigations by Ch. Tsountas followed (1897), with excavations of mainly Early Cycladic cemeteries on Paros, Antiparos and Despotiko. In the early twentieth century research by the German Archaeological Institute, under O. Rubensohn, brought to light part of the ancient acropolis of Paros in the modern town of Paroikia (fig. 7) and evidence that the island's harbour today was in use since at least the end of the third millennium BC. The Asklepieion and the sanctuary of Apollo Pythios, as well as the sanctuary of Apollo and Artemis (Delion), on Kynthos (Vigla) Hill, overlooking Paroikia from the north, were also uncovered in the early 1900s.

Archaeological interest in the islands of the group revived after the Second World War, with rescue excavations carried out by the Ephorate of Antiquities. A systematic British excavation on the islet of Saliagos, between Paros and Antiparos (1964-1965), revealed for the first time a Neolithic settlement in the Cyclades (fig. 8). Recent excavations by the XXI Ephorate of Prehistoric and Classical Antiquities for the Cyclades have brought to light important parts of the ancient city at Paroikia on Paros, while a notable Mycenaean settlement has been found at Koukounaries, above the Bay of Naousa. Ongoing systematic excavations on Despotiko are uncovering an impressive sanctuary of the Archaic period, with masterpieces of ancient sculpture.

Naxos The largest and most fertile island in the Cyclades, Naxos was home to human communities from earliest times, material evidence of which is dispersed all over its area. Characteristic visible monuments are the Archaic temple in Chora (Palatia) and the colossal kouroi still in the marble quarries. However, the first excavations were directed at prehistoric sites. Dozens of Early Cycladic cemeteries were discovered by Klon Stephanos on behalf of the Archaeological Society, in the opening decade of the twentieth century, while a small investigation by Gabriel Welter in the settlement at Grotta and below the temple of Apollo at Palatia (1930) unearthed remains from the Neolithic Age. Before the Second World War (1937), the Archaeological Society (Ch. Karouzos and N. Kontoleon) excavated the south cemetery of Naxos. The Archaeological Society resumed activity after the war, with the large-scale excavation at Grotta (fig. 9), directed initially by N. Kontoleon (1949-1972) and continued after his death. The project was completed with the organization of the model *in-situ* museum (1999). Among the numerous rescue excavations was that of the Mycenaean cemetery at Kamini, carried out by N. Zapheiropoulos (fig. 10) on behalf of the Archaeological Society (1959-1960).

In the 1960s the Greek State reacted to the scourge of illicit digging by intensifying rescue excavations, primarily of Early Cycladic sites in the

countryside. In recent years the University of Athens has placed considerable emphasis on the enhancement of archaeological sites. The ancient sanctuaries at Yria and at Gyroulas near Sangri have brought Naxos into the front line of archaeological heritage management.

Lesser Cyclades The little archipelago in the triangle of sea between Naxos, Ios and Amorgos, comprising the islands of Keros, Ano and Kato Kouphonisi, Schinousa, Herakleia and Donousa, at the northernmost tip, lying on what is known to the domestic ferryboat service as the "barren line", have attracted archaeological attention relatively recently. Only Keros was known, on account of the Early Cycladic marble figurines that flooded the antiquities market mainly from the mid-1950s onwards. Both the activity of looters and the rapid development of tourism on these islands of late pressurized the authorities to undertake systematic investigations. Noteworthy are the Early Cycladic cemeteries on the Kouphonisia and the settlement of the Geometric period on Donousa.

Ios Although the monuments on Ios had attracted the attention of L. Ross, the first excavations were not undertaken until 1904, when the Belgian archaeologist P. Graindor, member of the French School of Archaeology, began work in Chora, which stands on the site of the ancient city. After half a century of inertia, interest in the archaeology of Ios was revived from the 1960s onwards, with the scheduling of archaeological sites and surface surveys. The first programmed systematic excavation on the island is underway in the Early Cycladic settlement at Skarkos.

Amorgos Located on the crossroad of routes between the Cyclades and the Dodecanese, Amorgos has always been a pole of attraction with important cultural development in prehistoric and historical times. Its past, known from the ancient sources, caught the interest of researchers from early on and in the course of the nineteenth century scores of scholars, following the fashion of the time, applied themselves to studying inscriptions, scattered and accessible in the environs of the island's three ancient cities, Aigiale, Minoa and Arkesine. Only over the last twenty years or so have studies of the ancient art of Amorgos appeared and excavations been undertaken. The British traveller T. Bent excavated an Early Cycladic grave in 1883 and the German F. Duemmler a similar grave in 1886, while monuments of the three ancient cities were exposed two years later (1888) by G. Deschamps, member of the French School of Archaeology. Last, Ch. Tsountas, in the framework of his researches in the Cyclades in 1894, 1897 and 1898, investigated Early Cycladic sites at various points on the island. In the first quarter of the twentieth century epigraphic studies were predominant in the archaeological bibliography on Amorgos, with occasional articles on its art. Not until 1981 was the first large-scale systematic excavation begun by the Archaeological Society at Minoa. This tardiness of archaeological interest in an island with such a wealth of monuments is only explicable in terms of the checkered history of Modern Greece. After the Second World War the islands were marginalized with respect to development programmes for the country, and Amorgos was no exception, given its remoteness. Since no development projects were implemented, no need for rescue excavations arose.

Sikinos, Pholegandros These islands, known in later history as places of exile for political dissenters under various regimes, only attracted the attention of archaeological research quite recently. The first significant publication is the article by A. Frantz, H. Thompson and J. Travlos on the ancient temple of Sikinos (1969).

Melos A landmark in the history of Greek archaeology was the British excavation at Phylakopi, under the direction of C. Harcourt Smith (1894-1895). This was the second stratigraphic excavation after Troy in the whole of the Eastern Mediterranean, and with it order began to be put in the chronological sequence of the individual phases of the Cycladic Culture. Synchronisms were identified with the second city of Troy (Phylakopi I), as well as with the early shaft graves at Mycenae (Phylakopi II). Mycenaean architecture and a palace were uncovered in the third city at the site (Phylakopi III). The stratigraphic sequence at Phylakopi helped Sir Arthur Evans, excavator of Knossos, to distinguish the phases of what he dubbed the Minoan Civilization on Crete and to propose a single chronological scheme for the entire Aegean. The results of research at Phylakopi were published in the collective volume *Excavations at Phylakopi in Melos* (1904), which provided a valuable tool for researchers into the prehistoric Aegean.

Kimolos Only since the 1960s has archaeological interest been expressed in this satellite island of Melos.

Thera – Therasia The quarrying of Theran pozzuolana to be used as insulating material in the construction of the Suez Canal, by the French engineer Ferdinand de Lesseps (1866), led to the discovery of prehistoric antiquities on Therasia. This was the beginning of archaeological research in the islands of the Cyclades. A small excavation was carried out three years later (1870) by the French School of Archaeology, at the site of Favatas, south of the present village of Akrotiri on Thera. At the turn of the century (1895-1902), a mission of the German Archaeological Institute, led by Hiller von Gaertringen, carried out large-scale excavations in ancient Thera (fig. 11), while a small team dug trenches again in the vicinity of Akrotiri, at the site of Potamos. A milestone in archaeological research on Thera was the visit to the island in 1961 by the first post-war Chancellor of West Germany (as it was then), Konrad Adenauer, grandson of Hiller von Gaertringen. In order to facilitate access to the excavations, the then Minister of Co-ordination, Spyridon Markezinis, a native of Thera, decided to widen the road leading up from Kamari to ancient Thera. In the course of this operation the impressive Archaic cemetery at Sellada was discovered, which was subsequently excavated systematically by N. Zapheiropoulos, under the auspices of the Archaeological Society. A few years later, in 1967, Spyridon Marinatos, also under the auspices of the Archaeological Society, began excavating the Bronze Age city at Akrotiri, opening up new horizons in our understanding of Aegean prehistory (fig. 12).

Anaphe Yet another island for political exiles in Modern Greece, Anaphe remained on the margins of archaeological interest and only since the 1970s has the XXI Ephorate of Prehistoric and Classical Antiquities undertaken works on its monuments.

Dodecanese (South Sporades)

With the exception of Karpathos and Kasos, which lie in the open sea, all the other islands in this group are strung out along the Asia Minor coast, on the northward-flowing East Mediterranean current. In particular, the bevy of islets interposed between the larger islands and the opposite littoral zone of Asia Minor with its indented shoreline, were from time immemorial incentives as well as havens for seafarers in this region, however primitive their craft. This explains the presence of archaeological finds on even the smallest islands.

Milesian islands The archipelago south of Samos, chief islands in which are Patmos, Leros, Agathonisi, Arkioi, Leipsoi and Pharmakonisi, undoubtedly played a seminal role in early seafaring in the Aegean, since their density turns them into "stepping stones", to "leap" from one to the other across the intervening sea. Although there are visible archaeological remains, systematic investigation of these islands is essentially still awaited. However, the XXII Ephorate of Prehistoric and Classical Antiquities for the Dodecanese has made commendable progress in recording the monuments.

Kalymnos The island is of considerable archaeological interest and the earliest systematic excavations there date from the period of Italian Rule (1912-1948). After the unification of the Dodecanese with Greece, mainly rescue excavations have been carried out.

Kos Thanks to its proximity to Asia Minor and its fertile land, Kos developed into one of the most important centres in Graeco-Roman Antiquity. The island's enormous archaeological wealth quickly attracted the interest of the Italian Archaeological Service of the Dodecanese, which conducted extensive excavations in the town of Kos and in the countryside. Large parts of the ancient city were revealed under the present capital and there was wide-scale expropriation of land in order to create a protective zone, while in the countryside the great sanctuary of Asklepios was uncovered. Important remains of Neolithic habitation have been explored in the Aspri Petra Cave (fig. 17), and large cemeteries of the Late Bronze Age and the Early Iron Age have come to light at the sites of Elaionas and Lagada.

After the unification with Greece (1948) and mainly from the 1960s onwards, a period of rapid development of tourism, the XXII Ephorate of Prehistoric and Classical Antiquities has carried out excavations in many places, with remarkable results. Last, the University of Athens excavation in the sanctuary of Apollo at ancient Alasarna (mod. Kardamaina) has revealed another significant cult centre in the Dodecanese.

Astypalaia More is known about the island in Antiquity from the literary sources and inscriptions than from its monuments. Nevertheless, surface surveys and rescue excavations by the XXII Ephorate of Antiquities for the Dodecanese have identified and uncovered notable monuments spanning almost the entire Bronze Age. Very interesting is the cemetery exclusively for infant burials, being investigated on the outskirts of the present settlement of Chora.

13

Nisyros, Telos, Chalke, Syme, Megiste Although these islands have visible ancient remains, archaeological research on them is limited. Small-scale excavations were undertaken on Nisyros and Chalke in the period of Italian Rule. In 1915 the Italian Archaeological Service excavated some graves on Megiste (Castellorizo). After the unification with Greece, archaeological investigations were limited to surface surveys, conservation of monuments and rescue excavations. In the 1970s the University of Athens in collaboration with the Natural History Museum of Vienna explored the Charkadio Cave on Telos, where fossils of dwarf elephants were found under Early Bronze Age remains. The only systematic excavation, on the islet of Yali, has uncovered evidence of habitation in the Neolithic Age.

Rhodes The excavating activity on Rhodes, which began in the mid-nineteenth century, was little more than the looting of ancient cemeteries, since its sole aim was to find antiquities for sale. The vice-consul of Great Britain on the island, Sir Alfred Billiotti, joined forces with Auguste Saltzmann to carry out extensive excavations in the ancient cemeteries in the area of Kamiros, from 1859 to 1865. Between October 1863 and June 1864 they dug at the behest of the British Museum. In 1866 their collaboration ceased, Saltzmann continued his activity in the Kamiros area, on behalf of a French collector, while Billiotti turned his sights on Ialysos, where he excavated 42 Mycenaean chamber tombs between 1868 and 1871. After Saltzmann's death (1874), Billiotti returned to Kamiros, resuming excavations in 1880. The finds from these operations were sold to various museums, such as the British Museum and the Berlin Museum, as well as to private collections.

The first systematic excavations on Rhodes were conducted between 1902 and 1914 by the Danish scholars Christian Blinkenberg and Karl Frederik

Kinch, on the acropolis of Lindos, at Vroulia and at Exochi, near Lardos. The results of their researches were presented in a series of volumes under the title *Lindos*, published by the National Museum of Copenhagen. The Italian Occupation (1912) marked the beginning of an illustrious period of archaeological exploration in the Dodecanese (fig. 14). A permanent Archaeological Service was set up, based on Rhodes, and Amedeo Maiuri was appointed as the first Ephor (1914), while in parallel the Archaeological Institute (FERT) was founded and endowed with a notable scientific library. Ambitious programmes of conservation and restoration of the monuments were combined with large-scale excavation projects. One of the most important Late Bronze Age centres in the Dodecanese, perhaps on a par with Akrotiri on Thera, was brought to light in the Italian excavations at Trianda (ancient Ialysos), confirming the role played by Rhodes in cultural processes in the Eastern Mediterranean. This city was apparently of long duration, judging from the extensive cemeteries of the Mycenaean period. Excavations carried out by the Italian Archaeological Service of the Dodecanese brought to light ancient Kamiros, the monuments on the acropolis of ancient Ialysos at Philerimos, the acropolis of ancient Rhodes. The special scientific periodical published by the Archaeological Institute FERT, *Clara Rhodos*, in its ten volumes (1928-1941) hosted important articles relating to the island's monuments.

In addition to excavations, restorations and publications, the Italian Archaeological Service of the Dodecanese made extensive expropriations of land, in order to create a protective zone around the monuments and archaeological sites.

After the Second World War and the unification of the Dodecanese with Greece (1948), the Ephorate of Antiquities for the Dodecanese was founded, first Ephor of which was Ioannis Kontis (fig. 13), who was suc-

ceeded by Grigoris Constantinopoulos. Kontis's study of the street plan of the ancient city of Rhodes proved to be the most effective tool for the rescue excavations in later years, when tourism developed apace in the modern town. Thanks to the pre-existing infrastructure of the Italian Administration, the XXII Ephorate of Prehistoric and Classical Antiquities evolved into a model archaeological institute by Greek standards. The extensive research, although in the form of rescue interventions, all over the island has filled in considerable gaps in our knowledge, giving us a fairly full picture of the history of Rhodes in all phases of Antiquity.

Karpathos, Kasos These largely rocky islands were important mainly as natural ports of call on the communications route between the southeast Aegean and Crete. Their relations with Crete are confirmed by sporadic finds in different parts of the island. The most important of the few archaeological investigations is the rescue excavation conducted by the Archaeological Service at Pigadia on Karpathos, where there was a notable Late Bronze Age installation.

Crete

Crete is an island in geographical terms only. It has the cultural characteristics of a rich mainland. Thanks to its economic self-sufficiency it was the "promised land" for the inhabitants of the smaller islands in the Aegean. From early times Crete evidently needed to exchange its agricultural surplus for navigational services and technical know-how in sectors such as shipbuilding and metallurgy, in which the Aegean islanders were pioneers. That is why it never needed to develop shipping activities itself,

as corroborated by the ancient adage: "the Cretan is ignorant of the sea". The radiation of Cretan Civilization to the islands, particularly those closest to it, is indisputable. Nonetheless, this radiation should be seen as an influence it exerted on the islands that saw it as a kind of *peraia* for them. Consequently Crete cannot be encompassed in the island culture of the Aegean and is included in this volume as the southernmost physical boundary of the Archipelago. Its high culture and its monuments, both of prehistoric and historical times, were the focus of archaeological research from early on and the history of this would require several volumes, with contributors far better qualified than I am to present it. Suffice it to say that among the many scholars involved with the excavation of the palatial centres and the monuments of Crete were personalities such as Minos Kalokairinos, Iossif Chatzidakis, Stephanos Xanthoudidis (fig. 16), Arthur Evans (Knossos, fig. 15), Doro Levi (Phaistos), Henri van Effenterre (Malia), Nikolaos Platon (Zakros, fig. 18) and Spyridon Marinatos (Amnisos, Vathypetro, etc.). Moreover, the archaeology of Crete was *par excellence* the research domain of foreign archaeological schools, such as the British, the French, the Italian, the American, the Swedish Institute and other more recent foundations. Over the past two decades the three Ephorates of Prehistoric and Classical Antiquities of the Ministry of Culture (XXIII, XXIV, XXV) have been particularly active in research, as well as other institutions such as the University of Crete and the Archaeological Institute of Crete.

Hundreds of surface surveys and excavations have been carried out on Crete since the nineteenth century, as apparent from the references in the texts in the relevant chapter of this volume.

---

1. The ancient Greek verbs νέω and νήχομαι mean to float, to swim (cf. νήσσα = duck).
2. Pelago credas innare revulsas Cycladas (Aen. XIII, 691).
3. Papageorgiou D., Θαλάσσιοι δρόμοι στο προϊστορικό Αιγαίο κατά τη Νεολιθική και την Πρώιμη Εποχή του Χαλκού (doctoral dissertation, University of Athens, Athens 2002).
4. Braudel, F., *La Méditerranée et le monde méditerranéen à l'époque de Philippe II*, Arman Colin, Paris 1949.
5. E.g. Dickinson, O., *The Aegean Bronze Age*, Cambridge University Press 1994.
6. Doumas, C., Aegean Islands and Islanders, in J. Cherry, C. Scarr and S. Shennan (eds), *Explaining Social Change: Studies in honour of Colin Renfrew*, McDonald Institute Monographs, Cambridge 2004, 215-226.
7. Gran-Aymerich, E., L'archéologie française en Grèce: politique archéologique et politique méditerranéenne, 179-1945, in Roland Étienne (ed.), *Les politiques d' archéologie du milieu du XIXe siècle à l'orée du XXIe*, École française d' Athène 2000, 72.
8. Αρχαιολογική Εφημερίς 1937, 609ff.
9. *Poliochni* I (1964), II (1976), L'Erma di Bretschneider, Roma.
10. See Doumas, Ch. and La Rosa, V. (eds), *Poliochni and the Early Bronze Age in the North Aegean*, Italian Archaeological School at Athens – University of Athens, Athens 1997.
11. For more detailed information on the history of archaeological research on Kea see L. G. Mendoni, Αρχαία Κέα: Ιστοριογραφία και αρχαιολογικές έρευνες, in L. G. Mendoni και A. I. Mazarakis Ainian (eds), *Κέα-Κύθνος: Ιστορία και Αρχαιολογία*, KERA Athens 1998, 17-48.

13. Ioannis Kontis, the inspired first Greek Ephor of Antiquities in the Dodecanese.

14. View of the Italian excavations in the area of the ancient harbour of Rhodes.

15. The large team of labourers employed by Sir Arthur Evans to uncover the imposing parts of the palace of Knossos.

16. The Minoan villa at Nirou Chani, brought to light by Stephanos Xanthoudidis.

17. Scene from the Italian excavation in the Aspri Petra Cave on Kos. Visible are the first excavator of Poliochni on Lemnos, Alessandro Della Seta (right, behind) and the then young Doro Levi (right, front).

18. Systematic collection and documentation of the archaeological evidence in the excavation of the Minoan palace at Zakros (1960s). Visible is the kind-hearted excavator Nikolaos Platon (centre, right).

AEGEAN ISLANDS: HISTORICAL AND ARCHAEOLOGICAL BACKGROUND

Stone Age

ADAMANTIOS SAMPSON

19

19. Mesolithic fishhooks from the Cyclops' Cave on the islet of Youra. The 45 hooks of animal bone are unique finds, without parallel in Greece to date. They vary in size from 6 mm. to 7 cm. It is characteristic that the form of the fishhook has not changed essentially to this day, indicating that long experience had preceded its invention and specialization had been created in the sector of fishing. Volos Archaeological Museum.

20. The islet of Youra is harbourless, while its precipitous coasts are badly eroded. In the interior, however, there are still remnants of woodland, which has been destroyed by intensive grazing, fires and tree felling in recent centuries. On the successive habitation floors in the Cyclops' Cave, hearths and food residues have been found, consisting of hundreds of thousands of bones of animals, birds and mainly fish. In all the Mesolithic levels there are also huge quantities of marine molluscs and land snails. The presence of the last points to humid conditions, which palaeo-climatic studies have confirmed for this era.

21. Mesolithic burial on Kythnos. The skeleton was found in supine position but in highly contracted pose, with the knees bent up to the height of the shoulders. The arms were folded on the chest. The state of the skeleton is good, even though there is a hard incrustation of stone on the bones. Small stones all around delimit the burial.

Palaeolithic and Mesolithic Age
(*circa* 700,000-6500 BC)

Over the past forty years particular emphasis has been placed on research into the early prehistory of Greece and as a result our knowledge has been extended back several millennia prior to the Bronze Age, which was already well known. Excavations mainly in Thessaly, but also further south in Greece, have brought to light considerable evidence of the Neolithic Age, which commenced around 6500 BC, while in recent years investigations in caves and at open-air sites have produced new data on the economy, the climate and the palaeo-environment. In the past two decades, several Greek researchers have been exploring earlier eras, such as the Palaeolithic. Whereas this was considered almost non-existent in Greece, we now know that it was present almost everywhere at least 100,000-10,000 BP, while stone tools and human fossils dating from 400,000-200,000 BP or even earlier have been identified.

Research in the Aegean region has been limited so far, while some foreign archaeologists were convinced that the islands were inhabited after the fifth millennium BC. However, the case of Crete was already known, which was inhabited from at least the seventh millennium BC. Excavations in the North Sporades (island of Youra), the Cyclades and the Dodecanese have overturned many of the hitherto prevailing views and it has become clear that the Aegean conceals very ancient remains of habitation, which only intensive surface surveys and excavations will locate. Some pre-Neolithic finds have been identified on Naxos, but they are not from stratified context. There is also the problem that the earlier Palaeolithic and Mesolithic sites must now be on the seabed, since sea level was much lower in that period. In the North Sporades finds have been identified from the Middle Palaeolithic period, when these islands were no longer joined to Thessaly.

In Upper Palaeolithic times (18,000-16,000 BC) most of the islands of the Cyclades, excepting, Kythnos, Melos and a few others, formed one huge island about two-thirds the size of Cyprus, capable of sustaining rich fauna and flora for Palaeolithic hunters-gatherers.

From the Mesolithic Age the islands of the central and southern Aegean constituted natural stepping stones for the transition from mainland Greece to Asia Minor and vice versa. Astypalaia linked the Cyclades with the Dodecanese, while Mykonos was an important stopping place on the route eastwards via Ikaria and Samos. It is natural, therefore, that there were contacts with Asia Minor (Antalya), Cyprus and perhaps with the Near East, with which there seem to have been similarities and analogies.

Excavations in the Cyclops' Cave on Youra (1992-1996) opened up new horizons in the study of Aegean prehistory (figs 20, 225). Of particular interest are the deepest strata, belonging to the Mesolithic Age and dating from the ninth to the seventh millennium BC. Outstanding among the finds are a few dozen fishhooks made of animal bones, unique in Greece to date, which belie a previous long experience of specialization in the fishing sector (fig. 19). The discovery of skeletons of very big fish, mainly of the tuna species, as well as the presence of tools of Melian obsidian in the Mesolithic levels, are indirect testimonies that the fishermen in this period had mastered advanced techniques of seafaring. Some types of tools are similar to those recovered from Mesolithic caves at Antalya in Asia Minor and possibly reveal movements and contacts between the two regions. Another highly significant ascertainment from the study of the archaeological material in the cave is that already from the Lower Mesolithic (8600-7600 BC) pig, sheep and goats had been domesticated in the Aegean region. This finding prompts the reconsideration of views of scholars who place these achievements in the East.

Early domestication of caprines and of cereals is encountered at Knossos, from 7000 BC. Although many scholars have sought the provenance of the Aceramic/Pre-pottery Neolithic period in Crete in the Middle East or Asia Minor, if we accept that the Mesolithic inhabitants of the Aegean were capable of covering long distances by sea, it is very possible that they could proceed towards the Neolithic way of life, by bringing ideas from the East and domesticating the local ancestors of plants and animals. Consequently, Crete was probably inhabited by Aegean populations and it is futile to seek for migrations from abroad.

Excavations at the site of Maroulas, Loutra on the island of Kythnos began in 1996 and are continuing as a collaboration between the University of the Aegean and the XXI Ephorate of Prehistoric and Classical Antiquities for the Cyclades. From the first season, excavation at different points in the site revealed ten skeletons in the contracted pose characteristic of the period (fig. 21). The dead were placed in a rock-cut hollow or a pit, lined with slabs or stones and covered by large slabs. In addition to the burials, circular constructions with flagstones, that were the paved floors of huts, were noted over the entire area.

The occupants of the site made tools of Melian obsidian and primarily quartz, a material that abounds on the island. The stone industry includes types of the Mesolithic Age, while characteristic microlithic tools are also present. There are copious land molluscs (snails) over the entire settlement, as well as seashells and fish bones. Animal bones are much rarer. All these elements belong to the Mesolithic model and display analogies with finds from the Cyclops' Cave on Youra. The date of the settlement has been determined by three samples, which gave dates of 8600 to 7800 BC. Consequently, Maroulas on Kythnos is a site contemporary with the Cyclops' Cave on Youra and the Franchthi Cave at Hermionida in the Argolid, the Mesolithic phase (Lower and Upper) of which lasted for two thousand years (8500-6500 BC).

Neolithic Age
(6500-3300/3000 BC)

Research over the last twenty years has enriched our knowledge of the Neolithic Age in the Aegean. The Early (6500-5800 BC) and the Middle Neolithic period (5800-5300 BC) are present in the Cyclops' Cave, at Aghios Petros of Kyra-Panaya, on Skyros, at Aghio Galas on Chios, on Euboea and on Crete (Knossos), while recently they have been identified also on the island of Imbros. The Late Neolithic (5300-3200 BC) is the best-known period and in addition to the North Aegean (North Sporades, Thasos [fig. 27], Lemnos, Samothrace), it is encountered in the Cyclades, on Chios, Lesbos, Samos, in the Dodecanese and on Crete (fig. 31).

A large part of the deposits in the Cyclops' Cave on Youra dates to the Neolithic Age (6300-4000 BC) and spans the Early, the Middle and the early phase of the Late Neolithic period. The painted pottery of the early sixth millennium BC, similar to that found at Aghios Petros of Kyra-Panaya, attains perfection, with decorative motifs influenced by the contemporary arts of weaving or embroidery (fig. 22).

Neolithic sites in the Cyclades were until recently little known, the most important being on the islet of Saliagos, off Antiparos (figs 28, 30), where in the 1960s the British School at Athens conducted a pioneering interdisciplinary investigation of a walled settlement that flourished in the Late Neolithic period (first half of 5th millennium BC). In 1995 excavations commenced at the significant Neolithic site of Ftelia on Mykonos, which are still in progress (figs 23, 29). The settlement here, covering an area of 0.8-0.9 hectares, was thriving in the Late Neolithic I period (5100-4600 BC, according to carbon 14 dates) and was contemporary with the settlement

22. The earliest Neolithic levels yielded painted pottery, which in the next phase (Middle Neolithic period, early 6th millennium BC) attains perfection, with motifs influenced by the weaving or embroidery of the time. These are sherds from about 20 globular vases found all together in a particular place in the cave. Vases with similar decoration had been found earlier in the Neolithic settlement at Aghios Petros of Kyra-Panaya, but are totally absent from other regions outside the North Sporades. It seems that they are the products of a local pottery workshop with singular decoration, which is one of the distinctive traits of the "Youra – Kyra-Panaya Culture". Volos Archaeological Museum.

23. Mykonos. The settlement at Ftelia faces north and is exposed to the strong north winds. In Neolithic times the sea was 300 m. further away and the settlement was surrounded by a fertile plain. Noteworthy is the pair of peculiar little buildings. These are careful constructions of elliptical plan with walls standing to a height of 1.70 m., unusual by the standards of the Neolithic Age. The manner of construction of the two buildings, their shape, small size and the lack of finds on their floor suggest that they were not used as a house. Possibly they served as granaries in which the agricultural surplus of the settlement was stored.

34 | AEGEAN ISLANDS: HISTORICAL AND ARCHAEOLOGICAL BACKGROUND

on Saliagos. The thick deposits, of 1.60-2.30 metres, have preserved four building phases, the earliest of which is the best preserved. Similar buildings are unusual in the Neolithic Age and their survival to a height of 1.50-1.70 metres is without precedent in the Aegean.

The similarity between the finds from Ftelia and those from Tharrounia on Euboea reveals the provenance of the inhabitants from the Greek Mainland, despite the views of scholars who believe that the islands were colonized by populations from Asia Minor. Excavations in the Skoteini Cave at Tharrounia on Euboea (1986-1991) uncovered an undisturbed stratigraphy from the end of the Middle to the end of the Late Neolithic period (5700-5300 BC), permitting the establishment of a new chronological scheme for the Neolithic Age, beginning basically from central and southern Greece. This scheme led to the division of the long last period of the Neolithic Age into two periods, Late Neolithic I (5300/5200-4300/4200 BC) and Late Neolithic II (4300/4200-3300/3200 BC), replacing the terms Late (5300-4500 BC) and Final Neolithic (4500-3200 BC), which had been used earlier when research was in its initial stages and there were very few absolute dates. Nonetheless, many archaeologists continue to use the traditional chronological system.

Strophilas on Andros, a Late Neolithic site belonging to the final phase of the Neolithic Age, is particularly important because of its fortification and its rock-carvings (figs 291, 292). The Neolithic Age in the Cyclades ends with the smooth transition to the Early Bronze Age, as indicated by the settlement and the cemetery excavated at Kephala on Kea (late 4th millennium BC). At the same period there was human presence in the Zas Cave on Naxos, where investigations (1985-1986) brought to light significant finds for early metallurgy in the Aegean (fig. 24).

24. Gold strip with holes in its four corners, from the Zas Cave on Naxos. Dated to the final period of the Neolithic Age (4500-3200 BC). Naxos Archaeological Museum.

25. Yali. The excavation site with the northeast part of the island in the background, where there are deposits of obsidian. Ethno-archaeological research at the same site has revealed hundreds of buildings of the Ottoman period, pointing to intensive exploitation by inhabitants of Nisyros.

26. Excavations and surface surveys on Yali started in 1986 and are still in progress. Of particular interest are the island's geological formations, which are the result of volcanic eruptions.

STONE AGE | 35

Until twenty years ago the Neolithic Age in the Dodecanese was virtually unknown and its chronology vague. Only after surface surveys and excavations in caves (1977 1980) was its significance realized. Excavations in two caves on the island of Rhodes, on Leros and on the islet of Alimia brought to light building remains and abundant Neolithic deposits in which four phases of the Late Neolithic period (*circa* 5300-3300 BC) were distinguished. Indeed, in the lowest level of the deposits in the Kalythies Cave on Rhodes painted pottery reminiscent of that from Haçilar in Asia Minor was recovered, which is dated 5700-5600 BC. Even so, the Neolithic Age in the Dodecanese charted a course of its own.

Important Neolithic activity has been confirmed by excavations and surface surveys on Yali, the little island with obsidian deposits that lies between Kos and Nisyros (figs 25, 26). Pottery dispersed all over the island and building remains mainly in the mountainous parts are dated to the last two phases of the Late Neolithic period (Late Aegean Neolithic period 3 and 4). The most notable find was a building in the southwest part of the island, almost on the summit of the mountain, in the woods. A notable cemetery was located at another point on the island, pointing to the exploitation of the land by scattered population groups. The choice of sites on Yali, particularly in mountainous areas, shows that the inhabitants were involved in the familiar economic activities of agriculture and stock raising. Ethno-archaeological study of Yali (1990-1996) revealed the intensive exploitation of the island by poor inhabitants of Emporio on Nisyros during the closing centuries of Ottoman rule, which could provide a model for understanding the seasonal exploitation of small islands by transhumant cultivators and herdsmen.

27. Prehistoric settlement at Limenaria on Thasos. A tripod vessel of the earliest phase of the Late Neolithic period (mid-6th millennium BC). Thasos Archaeological Museum.

28. General view of the settlement on Saliagos, during the excavation. Because of the intense erosion, the building remains were badly destroyed. The site presents the same habitation model as Ftelia on Mykonos, with which it is contemporary. Study of the geomorphology at Ftelia has shown that sea level was 10-12 m. below the present level, which means that Saliagos was not an islet but a hillock in a plain, since the depth of the sea between Paros and Antiparos is no more than 5 m.

29. The excavation at Ftelia yielded numerous figurines, some of which are large enough to be called statuettes. The "Lady of Ftelia" is a female figurine, the greater part of which is preserved and is 33 cm. high. Of a type characteristic of figurines in this period, it displays similarities with figurines from the Skoteini Cave at Tharrounia on Euboea. Late Neolithic I period (5100-4600 BC). Mykonos Archaeological Museum.

30. The "Fat Lady of Saliagos", a small marble figurine (h. 5.9 cm.), the head and right shoulder of which are missing, renders a steatopygous female figure sitting cross-legged. Late Neolithic period (5300-4500 BC). Paros Archaeological Museum.

31. Clay figurine of a sitting female, from Hierapetra. The modelling of the breasts, the abdomen, the buttocks and the legs is emphasized by incisions filled with white paste. Middle-Late Neolithic period (5800-4800 BC). Herakleion Archaeological Museum.

STONE AGE | 37

Bronze Age (3000-1050 BC)

Christos Boulotis

To the degree that culture is man's response to the challenges of the natural environment, the Aegean – a sea littered with numerous islands and closed on three sides by land, and with the elongated island of Crete as horizontal boundary to the south – was an ideal setting for the development of flourishing cultures. With the preparatory dynamic of the Neolithic Age and the transitional Chalcolithic Age, these cultures gradually acquired during the Bronze Age (3rd-2nd millennium BC) an identity and an ambit that went far beyond their narrow geographical limits. Thanks to the intensification of seafaring, this blessed sea that is home to myths, legends and beliefs, united more than it divided, making its acculturating effects felt far into the hinterland of the surrounding landmasses.

Among the chief characteristics and the culminating achievements that triggered a chain of mechanisms and processes in man's material and intellectual life, beginning from the Early Bronze Age (3rd millennium BC), outstanding is the phenomenon of early urbanization. With this came the apparent social stratification, the rapid developments in metalworking, already evident in the Late Neolithic period, with bronze first and foremost, which in contradistinction to the working of stone led to the conventional name of the new age, and even the progressive craft specialization, the now co-ordinated practice of seafaring and trade; elements that became more widespread in the ensuing centuries, particularly in the Minoan and the Mycenaean world. The Middle and the Late Bronze Age (2nd millennium BC) definitively set their seal on the emergence of the palatial societies of Minoan Crete initially (2000/1900 BC) and of Mycenaean Greece subsequently (late 15th century BC), which had a beneficial effect in one way or another on the rest of the island world. The take off in the quantity and quality of production and of all aspects of material culture – often to the point of extravagance –, the emergence and establishment of religious and social institutions, the consolidation of intra-Aegean contacts and the development of "international" relations now enhanced the Aegean as a western counterweight to the high civilizations of the Eastern Mediterranean, and at the same time as a cultural forestage of Europe and incubator of the Hellenic Civilization of historical times. Climactic achievement of the Aegean in the second millennium BC was without doubt the invention and diffusion of the supreme cultural good of writing, specifically in its syllabic form, the so-called Linear A and Linear B scripts. Indeed, Linear B marked the passage from prehistory to protohistory, bequeathing us from the fourteenth and thirteenth centuries BC the most ancient texts in the Greek language.

At this time too, the inhabitants of the Aegean region appear eponymous for the first time in the written sources of their great

32. Part of a stone slab with pecked representation of a ship and its crew, from Korfi t'Aroniou on Naxos. It was found together with other slabs bearing similar rock-carvings, perhaps marking an open-air shrine. Late 3rd millennium BC. Apeiranthos Archaeological Collection.

33. Marble figurine of a harpist, from Keros. A superb example of Early Cycladic art and one of the rare male figures in marble sculpting of the period. Together with a figurine of a flute-player (fig. 425), also from Keros, these are the earliest representations of musicians in the Aegean. H. 22.5 cm. Second half of 3rd millennium BC. Athens, National Archaeological Museum.

contemporary palatial worlds: the Cretans first, in Egyptian texts and inscribed representations of them of the 18th Dynasty (mid-2nd millennium BC), as gift-bearers with the name Keftiu or, more generally together with other Aegean peoples (primarily Cycladic islanders?), as inhabitants of "the islands in the midst of the sea", or of the "land of the Keftiu and of the islands in the midst of the Great Green (sea)", which sea is the Aegean. The Mycenaean Achaeans later (14th-13th century BC), in the archives of Hatusha, capital of the Hittites, who are named indirectly through various references to the mighty kingdom of Ahhiyawa. Indeed, various sites in Crete and the Mycenaean Peloponnese are incised on a statue base from the mortuary temple of Pharaoh Amenophis III (1392-1355/4 BC), bearing witness to the journey of an official Egyptian embassy in the Aegean during the fourteenth century BC – a sea voyage, presumably of diplomatic-mercantile character, comparable to those made by the Keftiu and the other inhabitants of the Aegean to the land of the Nile. Included among the most important cities of Crete (Kaftu) enumerated in this itinerary are Knossos (Kunuscha), Amnissos (Amnischa) and Kydonia (Kutunaja), and among those in the Peloponnese (Tanaja/u, from Danaos), Mycenae (Mukanu), while mentioned too are Kythera (Kutir/la) as the mission's intermediate island port of call.

By adopting an absolutely symmetrical, although conventional, tripartite system of dating, those who study Aegean archaeology have divided the entire Bronze Age into the Early (3000/2800-1900 BC), Middle (1900-1700/1650 BC) and Late (1700/1650-1100/1050 BC), each of which is subdivided into three periods and these into sub-periods. However, in order to stress the particular physiognomy of the geographically distinct cultural cycles, they have used in parallel for the Greek Mainland the terms Early Helladic, Middle Helladic and Late Helladic, for the Cyclades respectively Early Cycladic, Middle Cycladic and Late Cycladic, while for Crete, Early Minoan, Middle Minoan and Late Minoan, or, on the criterion of the constructional history of the palaces, Prepalatial, Protopalatial, Neopalatial and Post-palatial (fig. 587). Within this conventional timeframe, the absolute dates, which are a constant desideratum of research, are achieved through correspondences on the one hand, primarily, with the Egyptian chronological system (see especially Minoan and Mycenaean Civilization) and on the other, in recent decades, with the help of the physical sciences (mainly the methods of carbon 14 and dendrochronology). Nonetheless, the picture of the Aegean chronological system is far from calm: the momentous eruption of the Thera volcano, which certainly had multiple repercussions on the Aegean scene in the second millennium BC, evidently dealing a severe blow to the flourishing Minoan Civilization, has of late caused turbulence in the familiar timeframe too, since the physical sciences date it to 1640/30 BC, in contrast to the traditional date of around 1500 BC.

In an overview of the settlement pattern mainly in the Early Bronze Age, from the vantage point of the sea, the reasons underlying the choice of sites become immediately clear. For many of these – from Lemnos (Poliochni [fig. 127], Koukonisi, Myrina) and Lesbos (Thermi), to Aegina (Kolona [figs 35, 246]), the Cyclades (Aghia

33

BRONZE AGE | 39

Irini on Kea [fig. 280], Phylakopi on Melos [fig. 465], Skarkos on Ios [figs 447, 448], Akrotiri on Thera) and Crete (Pseira, Mochlos), as well as the surrounding coasts (Troy, Pefkakia near Volos, Askitario and Aghios Kosmas in Attica) – the shore with safe haven was the basic criterion for founding a settlement and a favourable precondition of prosperity, particularly when there was fertile arable land and pasturage nearby, to ensure sufficiency of products of primary production and the essential surplus for barter trade. The cultural cycles of the period, the identity of which was determined largely by the islands' geographical position in the Aegean and their geomorphology, are distinguished principally into the robust Prepalatial culture of Crete, which was a self-sufficient island in many ways, into the extremely singular Early Cycladic, with the dense cluster of islands in the South Aegean, literally a maritime crossroad, and lastly into the culture of the North and Northeast Aegean, the most important centres of which were Lemnos, Thasos, Samothrace, Lesbos, Chios and Samos, which were apparently gateways of entry for the advanced technical know-how introduced via Asia Minor. Nonetheless, significant settlements developed on other islands too, such as Euboea (Manika, Lefkandi), Skyros (Palamari [fig. 229]) and Rhodes (Asomatos [fig. 555]). In all cases the vital contacts of the island settlements with one another as well as with their neighbouring *peraia*, first and foremost, maintained a continuous flow of fertile interactions and reciprocal influences, at least at the level of material culture. In such a dense network of Aegean settlements the affluence aspired to and, above all, the sustaining of this, were anything but self-evident. The fortification walls observed in many island and/or coastal settlements of the period, indeed some peculiarly mighty or wisely designed (Poliochni, Troy, Thermi, Palamari [fig. 229], Kolona, Kastri on Syros [figs 316, 317], Markiani on Amorgos, Panormos on Naxos [fig. 397]), vividly annotate the dangers of incursions mainly from the sea.

If Poliochni on Lemnos stands out as the most important proto-urban island centre of the Early Bronze Age, with an organized layout, strong fortifications, notable community amenities (fig. 129) and obvious economic prosperity (see also its treasure of gold jewellery), at the other end of the Aegean, in Crete, a precursor form of "palace" at Vasiliki, Hierapetra and at Phournou Koryphi, Myrtos, as well as the Prepalatial beehive tombs with their rich grave goods of the Mesara (fig. 595) and Archanes (fig. 598), in which members of a clan were buried, advocated in common with other indications a different social structure, different orientations and a different dynamic, as well as an ever-increasing opening of trade to the Eastern Mediterranean. Between these two geographical extremes, with the divergent cultural physiognomies, the Cy-

34. "*Depas amphikypellon*", from the prehistoric settlement at Koukonisi on Lemnos. This peculiar type of clay vase, invented in Asia Minor, is known in numerous varieties and was widely distributed in the Aegean region. Examples proliferate during the second half of the 3rd millennium BC. Myrina Archaeological Museum.

35. Maquette of an indicative sector of the fifth settlement at Kolona on Aegina (2200-2050 BC), with housing complexes developed lengthwise, alongside the fortification wall, which is reinforced with horseshoe-shaped bastions. Aegina Archaeological Museum.

40 | AEGEAN ISLANDS: HISTORICAL AND ARCHAEOLOGICAL BACKGROUND

clades shaped their own cultural persona, presenting striking singularities in diverse aspects of material culture, such as settlement and funerary architecture, pottery, marble-carving, as well as in the mortuary habits and the religious beliefs that are documented mainly through the typical marble figurines, supreme creations of Aegean art in general in the third millennium BC (fig. 33). The dissemination of the marble figurines and peculiar vessels outside the Cyclades, for example to Crete, the Attic coast, Euboea, Lemnos, Miletos, bears irrefutable witness to the mobility of the Cycladic islanders and their artworks (fig. 596). Indeed, when the "export" of typically Cycladic elements included mortuary habits and burial practices (see cemetery at Tsepi near Marathon and at Aghios Kosmas in Attica), then migratory routes are also indicated. Obsidian from Melos, for making tools, lost nothing of its earlier capital importance as a raw material that was traded (fig. 463). Concurrently, the mines of silver and lead on Siphnos, of copper on Kythnos and most probably Seriphos – together with the mines of argentiferous lead and copper (?) at Laurion – added, by the standards of the new age, extra mercantile prestige to the Cyclades. However, apart from raw materials and precious artworks, the ships of the day traded pottery too, as confirmed *inter alia* by the cargo of a ship that sunk in the late third millennium BC whilst skirting the coast of the islet of Dokos (figs 667-669) near Hydra. A valuable tool for the relative chronology, pottery, thanks to the wide geographical distribution of distinctive shapes (e.g. "*depas amphikypellon*" [figs 34, 132], "*kymbe*" or "sauceboat" [figs 264, 597], one-handled cup with funnel mouth), becomes primarily from this period, also a pilot for the better understanding of maritime trade and the nature of intra-Aegean contacts. Direct and indirect,

36. Drawing of one of the four manned ships in the frieze on the shoulder of the matt-painted pithos from Kolona on Aegina (fig. 243). Middle Cycladic period (18th c. BC). Aegina Archaeological Museum.

37. Part of the miniature "wall-painting of the fleet" or "flottila fresco", which adorned the West House at Akrotiri on Thera. The ships illustrated in the frieze reveal much information on the craft of shipbuilding of the period, as well as on nautical symbolism. The frolicking dolphins, the "escorting genii", here indicate fair sailing. Late Cycladic IA period (1550-1500 BC, according to the traditional dating). Museum of Prehistoric Thera.

BRONZE AGE | 41

38. Stone rhyton in the form of bull's head with gilded horns, from the Little Palace at Knossos. Reflecting the importance of the paramount sacred animal of the Minoans, the bull, rhyta of this kind, in a variety of materials, held a special place in cult practice. Late Minoan I period (1550-1450 BC). Herakleion Archaeological Museum.

38

39. The gold signet "ring of Minos", from Gypsades, south of the palace of Knossos. A wonderful example of Minoan minor art and condensed narrative sacred iconography, in which the marine world is combined in cult with the vegetation cycle. Late Minoan IB-Late Minoan II period (15th c. BC). Herakleion Archaeological Museum.

these contacts resulted in the creation of a first common Aegean cultural expression, which did not however overshadow the local identities.

In such a context, the seafaring skills of the Aegean peoples, detectable in the archaeological record from at least the seventh millennium BC (e.g. Melian obsidian in the Franchthi Cave in the Argolid), now acquired a more explicit character. The insular and nautical direction that the Early Bronze Age culture necessarily took surely also influenced its ideological content. The ship, as the oldest complex "machine" in the Aegean region and as essential medium for movements by sea, was henceforth enhanced as definitive agent of culture, since together with all manner of material goods and raw materials fertilizing ideas were circulated as well, bringing about cultural osmoses. Precisely this importance of the ships is reflected in the representations of them by the mariners *par excellence* of the third millennium BC, the Cycladic islanders; representations of long rowboats, mainly incised on clay "frying-pan" vessels (fig. 318) or pecked on stone slabs, like those from Korfi t'Aroniou on Naxos (figs 32, 396). Indeed, on the "frying-pan" vessels the representations of ships amidst a superb mesh of spirals, constitute the earliest seascapes, with the restive spiral successfully rendering the turbulent waters of the Aegean Sea. However, Cycladic marine iconography dates back even further, to the Chalcolithic Age (4th millennium BC), as borne out by the numerous carvings of ships on the fortification wall of the settlement being excavated at Strophilas on Andros (figs 291, 292).

In a cyclical dynamic, the development of metalworking, and particularly bronze-working, in the proto-urban island centres to which Lemnos belonged, led to the production of more effective tools. These in their turn contributed to the building of bigger and technically better ships, and therefore to the undertaking of longer and safer voyages for trading and other reasons. These voyages brought by association greater wealth to the island and coastal communities, surely having a catalytic effect on their social structures. However, beyond the contribution of shipping to the internal development of the settlements and to the diverse cultural osmoses, its continuous development brought, as was to be expected, improved knowledge of the sea currents, the winds and of course the constellations, of great assistance on the voyage at sea, the study of which gradually laid the foundations of the science of astronomy.

The end of the third millennium BC and the transition from the Early to the Middle Bronze Age does not seem to have taken place smoothly everywhere and in the same way. Alongside settlements that suffered severe disasters, decline, temporary or long-term abandonment – events correlated on the Greek Mainland mainly with the advent of Hellenic tribes –, other settlements, many of them on the islands, such as Koukonisi (Lemnos [fig. 133]), Emporio (Chios [fig. 163]), Kolona (Aegina), Phylalopi (Melos) or Akrotiri (Thera), continued to be inhabited, and were to enjoy a great heyday in the Middle Bronze Age. In fact Kolona, which has yielded, on pottery, notable depictions of ships with crews of warriors (figs 36, 243, 244), appears to have distinguished itself in maritime trade, while the Cyclades continued to be an active nucleus of exchanges, with inter-Cycladic ones now becoming evident mainly through the dissemination of Melian pottery. Like Aegina, the islands of Kythera and Kea functioned as bridgeheads for influences from Crete, on account of their proximity to the Greek Mainland.

42 | AEGEAN ISLANDS: HISTORICAL AND ARCHAEOLOGICAL BACKGROUND

39

40

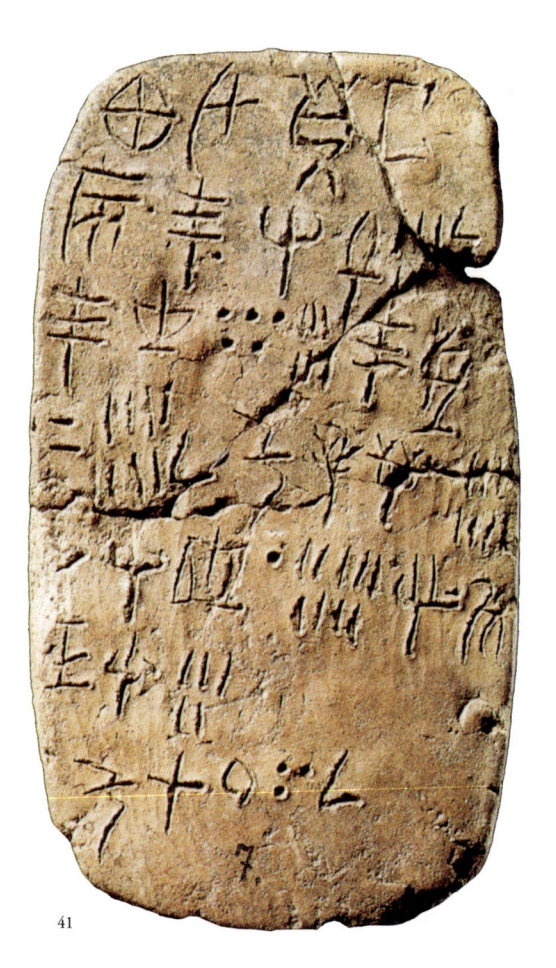

41

However, the smooth transition from the third to the second millennium BC and the continual cultural evolution are evidenced in exemplary manner in Minoan Crete, whose self-sufficiency in primary-sector products and extra-Aegean contacts, in conjunction with internal developmental processes, led at the dawn of the second millennium BC to the appearance of palatial structures modelled *mutatis mutandis* on Egyptian and Eastern prototypes. The palaces of Crete (Knossos [figs 589, 608], Phaistos [fig. 609], Malia [figs 606. 607], as well as the smaller ones such as Zakros [figs 604, 605], Petras, Galatas [fig. 611], Kydonia) were multi-dynamic centres of political and religious authority, economic activities, co-ordinated practice of various arts – frequently to the point of extreme refinement – and in general regulators of virtually all aspects of material culture and intellectual life. This character and role is better known to us from their Neopalatial phase, that is the phase of their zenith and greatest radiance (fig. 38). For the more effective function of the complex palatial machine, the invention and use of script, combined with the use of seals, was an absolute necessity, once again imposed by palatial models from outside the Aegean region. Although the Minoan script in its two main forms – Hieroglyphic and Linear A (figs 40, 41) – served first and foremost the economy and administration, it soon opened up into other sectors, such as religion. Indeed, with the flow of multiple cultural influences from Crete to the Aegean region – particularly the south – during the sixteenth century BC the wonderful journey of script, specifically Linear A, began to places of obvious Minoan character, such as Kythera (fig. 267), Akrotiri (Thera), Aghia Irini (Kea), Phylakopi (Melos), as well as Miletos, which according to later tradition was founded by Cretans. Minoan hieroglyphic script had travelled even earlier (18th century BC) and indeed as far as the North Aegean, as attested by examples of it from the settlement at Mikro Vouni on Samothrace (figs 104, 106). The legendary Thalassocracy of Minos, which is recorded mainly by Thucydides (I 1-8) and Diodorus (E 84,1), and is echoed in many ancient traditions according to which the lineage of the mythical king of Knossos conquered or colonized various islands and coastal areas, now finds additional support in the archaeological reality. The expansion of the Minoans into the Aegean, in parallel with the turn of their trading interests towards Cyprus, the world of the Near East and of Egypt, becomes tangible through the dissemination of peculiar shrines, such as the so-called "peak sanctuaries" (Aghios Georgios sto Vouno on Kythera [figs 268, 269], Troulos on Kea, Philerimos (?) on Rhodes), cult vessels and figurines (see mainly the "temple" at Aghia Irini on Kea [figs 279, 281]). It is also evidenced by their script and their metrical and ponderal systems, the art of narrative wall-painting and the iconography – especially the religious and symbolist –, as well as by diverse other facets of material culture, from precious prestige objects to humble clay conical cups, which can be con- sidered in a way the "trademark" of Minoan influence or presence.

In interpreting the various Minoan or Minoanizing cultural elements outside Crete, archaeologists often find themselves in a dilemma or support contending views: are these colonies, emporia or merely influences in the context of tendencies towards cultural simulation of the splendid Minoan model? All these versions, as well as gradations of them, are tenable by case. Whereas Kythera, neighbour of Crete, was indeed a Minoan colony, the few Cretan elements at Mikro Vouni on Samothrace, for example, or at Koukonisi on Lemnos, that is at the northernmost reaches of the Aegean, present the picture of short-lived or *ad hoc* emporia, possibly associated with the quest for and the trafficking of metals. More problematical are the Cycladic settlements (Akrotiri, Aghia Irini, Phylakopi) or the settlement at Trianda on Rhodes (figs 557, 558), where the Minoan element, particularly overt and manifold, is interwoven in the local cultural tradition. In the same period, the sixteenth and fifteenth centuries BC, Minoan radiance also dazzled the élite of the Greek Mainland in many ways, as is reflected most clearly in the grave goods of Grave Circles A and B at Mycenae, as well as in the early tholos tombs of the Peloponnese (Vapheio in Lakonia, Peristeria and Kakovatos in Messenia). Henceforth, and under the beneficial influence of Minoan Crete, the Mycenaean world gradually shaped its own cultural identity, until the emergence of its palatial structures *circa* 1400 BC. Even more intensive in their case was the centralization and the complicated bureaucratic system, which Linear B script – that is the adaptation of Minoan Linear A to the needs of the Greek language – was summoned to serve effectively.

Contacts by sea, founding of emporia and colonies, infiltration of the economic spheres of influence, population movements and the like certainly entailed numerous hazards. These were exacerbated by piracy, which, again according to Thucydides, the fleet of Minos undertook to combat in the Aegean. Narrative representations of the late sixteenth century BC illustrate martial episodes, such as that on the silver "siege rhyton" from Grave Circle A at Mycenae, showing a walled city threatened by an approaching fleet. Such events, certainly with a kernel of historical truth, were not only imprinted in the visual arts but also nurtured for the first time epic poetry, which was later monumentalized in the nautical campaign against Troy. Because hidden behind Troy are surely numerous earlier sieges of coastal cities, which have remained anonymous. Maritime voyages brought wealth, and despite the inherent dangers they were in this respect a constant challenge for the societies of the age. It is not fortuitous that the two major maritime epic cycles, the Argonautic and later the Trojan, which date back to the Late Bronze Age Aegean, are ventures of mercantile-seafaring character. From the same temporal horizon as the "siege rhyton" is the "flotilla frieze" from the West House at Akrotiri on Thera (figs 37, 482, 488). This narrative polyptych has the sea as its warp and a proud fleet of sailing ships and rowboats – exceptional examples of the shipwright's craft – as its weft. After a voyage taking them to various coastal cities, these vessels now enter the harbour of their home city, presumably Akrotiri itself, where their return is greeted with celebrations and the sacrifice of a bull. In this rich narrative canvas, the artistic negotiation of which is literally a watershed in Aegean iconography of the period, martial incidents are present, as well as "accidents" at sea, that is wrecks or pirate attacks. The "flotilla frieze" is the high-spot of Aegean marine iconography, which had been initiated here in the Cyclades, many centuries earlier, with the ships in the rock-carvings at Strophilas on Andros and was continued by the Cycladic ships of the third millennium BC, all of them eloquent images of seafaring skills.

However, the panoramic opening up of the visual arts to the world of the sea during the second millennium BC is owed essentially to palatial Crete, from which there is an inexhaustible relat-

40-42. Characteristic examples of Aegean script on clay tablets. On the opposite page: above, Minoan Hieroglyphic from the palace of Knossos (18th c. BC), below, Linear A from the Minoan villa at Aghia Triada (*c.* 1450 BC). Here: Mycenaean Linear B from the palace of Pylos. The first two tablets are exhibited in the Herakleion Archaeological Museum, the third in the National Archaeological Museum, Athens.

43. Ritual vase of chlorite in the form of a triton shell, from the palace of Malia. Vessels of this kind were probably associated specifically with marine cults. This particular triton is decorated in relief with "Minoan genii" performing a libation. Late Minoan I period (1550-1450 BC). Aghios Nikolaos Archaeological Museum.

44. The "Lady of Phylakopi". A clay cult figurine (h. 45 cm.) from the West Shrine in the Mycenaean settlement at Phylakopi on Melos. Female figurines of comparable size were found in the shrines at Mycenae and Tiryns. Late Helladic IIIA2 period (second half 14th c. BC). Melos Archaeological Museum.

ed iconography of ship representations – particularly in seal engraving – as well as primarily of marine creatures. With the artists' bold, inquisitive eye, it dives below the surface to the seabed (fig. 43). In the great glorification of Nature that the Minoan world emits, the sea, as a living environment of multiple importance, was the womb from which diverse religious beliefs were born. Beliefs detectable mainly through contemporary representations, such as those in seal-engraving which depict the maritime voyage of a female deity, the most representative examples being the famous gold "ring of Minos" (fig. 39) and another ring from Mochlos – a symbolic voyage that was linked conceptually with the cycle of vegetation. It seems that postmortem beliefs too were associated with the watery element of the sea, judging from convergent clues and mainly from the painted representation on the Aghia Triada sarcophagus (mid-14th century BC), where first among the offerings to the eminent deceased depicted is a ship model (fig. 631). Perhaps beliefs concerning the Isles of the Blessed have their roots in this temporal horizon.

On the Aegean stage from the mid-fifteenth century BC onward the balance of power was tilting decisively in the Mycenaeans' favour. The installation of an Achaean dynasty in Crete (figs 626, 627), which certainly did not take place peacefully, set is seal on their sovereignty. Palpable proof of this are the "warriors' tombs" in the vicinity of Knossos, and, above all, the keeping of archives in the palace there, as well as that in Kydonia (Chania), in the Greek language of Linear B script (fig. 629). The Minoan influence on the Mycenaeans, which had commenced in the sixteenth century BC, was now strengthened, and indeed on Cretan soil, leading to a powerful cultural amalgam and syncretism apparent also in the religious domain. Culmination of this was the conflation of the Mycenaean god Zeus with the Minoan young dying god of vegetation, in the person of Zeus Diktaios, attested in Linear B tablets from Knossos (*dikatajo diwe*).

On the Greek Mainland, the great palatial centres of the age (Mycenae, Tiryns, Pylos, Thebes), together with other comparatively smaller ones (Athens, Menelaion in Sparta, Midea in the Argolid, Orchomenos and Glas in Boeotia, Iolkos) set up Mycenaean realms from Thessaly to the southern Peloponnese. Within these territories there developed a dense network of satellite settlements, Cyclopean fortifications, royal tholos tombs and richly-furnished burials in chamber tombs, highly productive palatial workshops and huge public benefit projects, such as the draining of Lake Kopais in Boeotia.

43

AEGEAN ISLANDS: HISTORICAL AND ARCHAEOLOGICAL BACKGROUND

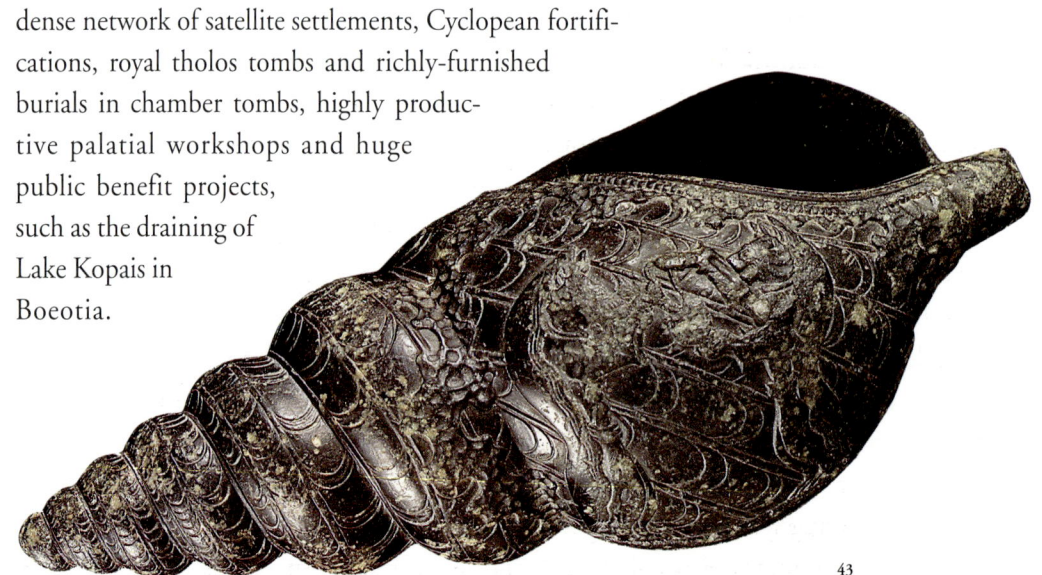

The narrative iconography together with a host of other archaeological evidence compose the picture of a prosperous stratified society of pyramidal structure, at the apex of which was the *wanaka*, the *anax* (ἄναξ), surrounded by a military aristocracy which, like the Homeric one later, promoted the ideal of male valour (ἀνδρεία) as ultimate value. Thanks to the decipherment of Linear B script, by the British architect Michael Ventris in 1952, the Mycenaean world is for us an articulate world. In a relationship of reciprocal complementarity, what is found archaeologically frequently finds its voice in the Linear B tablets (fig. 42), which notwithstanding their abbreviated accounting character offer us express testimonies of political, military and religious institutions, name craft specializations, artifacts, trading transactions, labour relations, and so on. Concurrently, however, the tablets reveal to us an early form of the Olympian Pantheon, as this was crystallized in the Homeric epics; among the Mycenaean deities recorded Poseidon (*posedao*), the mighty Homeric god of the sea, already holds a special place, and indeed with his female cult consort Posidaeia (*posideja*). The worship of the Winds, with the officiating *anemo ijereja* (= priestess of the winds), attested on a Linear B tablet from Knossos, should be understood in relation to the success of sea voyages, while in the menologion of Pylos a spring wind has the evocative name of *porowito*, a derivative of the verb to sail (πλέω), that is, it is the month in which the season of seafaring begins or reaches its peak.

For the vigorous Mycenaeans as an ascendant power, and consonant with the dictates of the age, opening to the sea and domination at sea were concomitants of power, as they were the essential preconditions for acquiring raw materials and conducting trade beyond the bounds of the Aegean, in the Euxine Pontus, the markets of Cyprus, Egypt and the East, in the Western Mediterranean, as far as Spain. In such a framework, the presence of Mycenaeans in the Aegean islands and the Asia Minor littoral zone, circumstantially, was even more pronounced than that of the Minoans previously, with greater density of settlements and many important centres, such as Ialysos on Rhodes, Seraglio on Kos, Grotta on Naxos, Phylakopi on Melos (fig. 44) and, of course, Miletos and Iasos in Asia Minor. Particularly indicative in this respect is the founding of a Mycenaean trading station even on the remote island of Psara (figs 177-180), while the ubiquitous Mycenaean traits (primarily the typical figurines) in the settlement excavated at Koukonisi on Lemnos, the strategic maritime-mercantile node at the entrance to the Hellespont, exactly opposite Troy, confirm a permanent installation of Mycenaeans.

If the hearths of the so-called "Mycenaean *Koine*", that is the obvious uniformity in almost all manifestations of material culture during the fourteenth and principally the thirteenth century BC, were the palaces, it nevertheless owed its consolidation and wide geographical ambit for the most part to the available mercantile-maritime force. Indeed, recorded expressly in the Linear B tablets of these years are the earliest shipbuilding and nautical terms in the Greek language, such as *nauodomo* (shipwright) and *ereta* (oarsman) – 600 (!) oarsmen are mentioned in the tablets from Pylos – while the formation of Mycenaean male names with the word *naus* (= ship) as first or second component (e.g. *nausikete*[*we*], *eunawo*, *okunawo*) is also in its way indicative of seafaring skill. Illuminating too are the indirect references in the tablets to maritime trade, to movements of people by sea, and to associated expeditions, not always of a

44

45. Ivory plaque of a Mycenaean warrior with figure-eight shield, boars'-tusk helmet and javelin, from the Artemision on Delos. Late Helladic IIIB period (13th c. BC). Delos Archaeological Museum.

46. Characteristic stirrup jar of the island "Close Style", with schematic representation of octopus, from the Mycenaean chamber-tomb cemetery at Kamini on Naxos. Late Helladic IIIC period (mid-12th c. BC). Naxos Archaeological Museum.

peaceful character. For example, by crossing the Aegean the Milesian man (*miratijo*) recorded in the tablets of Thebes would have reached Boeotia, while women from Knidos (*kinidija*), Miletos (*miratija*) and Lemnos (*raminija*) must have made a similar voyage to end up as weavers in the palace of Pylos – these, it seems, as captives in the turbulent demise of the thirteenth century BC, when the Mycenaeans were active in the East Aegean islands and the Asia Minor littoral zone, that is in the years of the legendary Trojan War. Alongside the word for copper (*kako*), there are copious references in the Linear B tablets to other precious materials imported from the East, (*kuwano* = *kyanos*/glass paste, *erepa* = *elephas*/ivory, *kuruso* = *chrysos*/gold), which were acquired by sea in order to supply mainly palatial workshops and manufactories. The importance of sea trade, in the Aegean and beyond, during the Mycenaean Age is thrown into relief by the combination of Linear B testimonies, actual artworks and raw materials, and the wrecks of merchant ships close to the shores of southwest Asia Minor – at Uluburun, opposite Castellorizo, and Cape Gelidonya (in the waters off Halikarnassos), dated to the late fourteenth and the thirteenth century BC respectively. These ships, transporting among other things cargoes of copper ingots (talents) and bars of glass paste (*kyanos*), were sailing from harbours of the Near East and Cyprus to the island markets of the Aegean (fig. 45) and thence to the palatial centres. "Trademark" of the ubiquitous Mycenaean presence from now on is the stirrup jar (in Linear B *karareu* = *chlareus*), a Minoan invention, sometimes inscribed, which because of its peculiar shape was ideally suitable for the storage, transport and trade of wine and, mainly, olive oil. Perfumed oil in particular seems to have been essentially the mainstay of the palatial Mycenaean economy and maritime trade.

The Mycenaean societies in both Mainland Greece and the islands at this time were of necessity and of their own volition turned towards the sea. The magnitude of their maritime might is echoed, albeit with a dose of poetic excess, in the "List of Ships" in Homer's *Iliad* (II 487-760), which is considered to be one of the earliest authentic passages in this epic. Of largely Mycenaean origin, it enumerates by geographical regions and kingdoms the 1,186 (!) ships that participated in the campaign against Troy. The contribution of Aegean islands to this combined fleet was substantial, with most important that of Crete (80 ships), followed by Salamis (12 ships) and the Dodecanese – Rhodes, Kos, Nisyros, Karpathos, Kasos, Syme, Kalydnai islands – with 42 ships in all. If the cited harbours of the Greek Mainland are also counted in, then the "List of Ships" could be considered as the earliest portolan of the Aegean.

With the collapse of the palatial systems around 1200 BC, apparently caused by external and internal factors, the Mycenaean world went into decline. The invasion by the "Sea Peoples" mentioned in the Egyptian texts, who at this very same period engulfed the kingdom of the Hittites and the entire coastal zone of the Eastern Mediterranean, even threatening Egypt, cut the Mycenaeans off from their vital markets there. The recession of sea trade outside the Aegean dealt a mortal blow to the palatial economy, resulting in the weakening of the central authority. Domestic conflicts, hostile incursions, assaults and pressures by the Hellenic tribes who had heretofore been on the margins of the Mycenaean world, were perhaps responsible for the destruction of the palaces. Hasty military mobilizations in the coastal zone of the kingdom of

Pylos, as can be seen through the Linear B tablets from the palace there, dating from the last days before the final catastrophe, are a sign of the troubled times (fig. 42).

The twelfth century BC was a century of drastic changes to the map and the internal structure of the Mycenaean world, as marked population migrations are now observed, to the coasts of eastern Attica, for example, and the Peloponnese (Perati, Asine, Monemvasia), and of course to the islands, primarily the Aegean islands, with the migratory wave reaching as far as Cyprus. The density of settlements in Crete, the Cyclades and the Dodecanese (mainly Rhodes) was particularly high, as well as in other islands where new settlements were founded too (e.g. Koukounaries on Paros [fig. 376], Emporio on Chios, Aghios Andreas on Siphnos [fig. 365], Kanakia on Salamis [fig. 239]), some of which flourished. The Aegean continued to be a route of communication and a source of enrichment for its inhabitants, whose efforts to revive led to a second, this time shorter-lived and less splendid, "*Koine*". The centres of this *Koine* kept only a few contacts with the harbours of the Near East and these, it seems, indirect, with the intervention of Cyprus, while trading relations with Egypt were evidently more direct. Olive oil and perfumed oil, as of old, were among the trade goods still in high demand, with the stirrup jars now decorated in accordance with the so-called "Close Style" (figs 46, 526), which is considered to be a creation of the Argolid, but enriched by island painting traits (especially on the Cycladic and Cretan examples).

The rekindling of the small "Aegean *Koine*" in the twelfth century BC was succeeded by instability, new realignments and an even greater recession in maritime trade, resulting in the fall in living standards. The Aegean in the eleventh century BC, with the new historical conditions that would ignite new developments already visible, was a troubled and dangerous sea.

The loss of the good of syllabic script was perhaps one of the most serious consequences of the dissolution of the Mycenaean palatial world, which made the so-called Dark Age seem even darker. When script reappeared in the eighth century BC, this time in alphabetic form, through other processes and in different historical-social circumstances, the Homeric epics were given their final form, essentially marking the starting point of historical times. And although much of the *Iliad* and the *Odyssey* echoes their age, they are nonetheless a poetic mirror – even through refraction – of the Mycenaean world, with the Aegean and the other seas claiming either vociferously or *sotto voce* a generous share.

46

Geometric (1050-700 BC) and Archaic periods (700-480 BC)

ALEXANDROS MAZARAKIS AINIAN

Scholars often examine the Aegean island region in connection with the surrounding mainland. Although the latter undoubtedly influenced to a considerable degree historical and cultural developments in the former, nonetheless the geographical integrity of each island in the Aegean resulted in each developing and preserving singular cultural characteristics. This singularity was apparently particularly pronounced at the beginning of historical times, and was gradually tempered when the city-states were consolidated and major powers, such as Athens, set out to dominate the Aegean. On the other hand, this "chain" of islands itself was the bridge of communication not only with the mainland shores surrounding it, but also, directly or indirectly, with far more distant lands and peoples, such as those in the Euxine Pontus (Black Sea) and the Eastern Mediterranean.

The review that follows does not include Euboea and most of the regions belonging to the so-called "Euboean *Koine*" (it does however include the islands of the "*koine*", i.e. some of the Cyclades, Skyros and Kos). Thus, the role of the Euboeans, who, as is well known, led the way in contacts between East, North and West, and had a decisive influence on the cultural development of many islands in the Aegean, is not discussed here.

The period between the end of the Late Bronze Age until Classical times, that is from the mid-eleventh to the early fifth century BC, is divided conventionally into sub-periods: the so-called Protogeometric (1050-900 BC), Geometric (900-700 BC) and Archaic (700-480 BC). The final phase of the Late Bronze Age, after the widespread destructions of the palatial centres on the Greek Mainland, that is the twelfth century BC, is known as the Late Helladic IIIC period and the Late Minoan IIIC period on Crete, while in some regions a brief phase is identified in pottery production between Late Helladic/Late Minoan IIIC and the Protogeometric period, which is known as the Submycenaean/Subminoan period.

The end of the thirteenth and the whole of the twelfth century BC (end of Late Helladic IIIB and Late Helladic IIIC period) in the Aegean region are marked by successive violent destructions. Some can be attributed confidently to human agency (e.g. at Koukounaries on Paros, fig. 51), while others were due to earthquakes, which shook the wider region at this period (e.g. Phylakopi on Melos and Grotta on Naxos). In the Dodecanese, in contrast to most Aegean regions, the number of excavated graves points to a demographic increase during the twelfth century BC. This is usually interpreted as due to the arrival of new population groups, perhaps from the Peloponnese. In most regions, however, the usual watershed between the Late Bronze Age and the Early Iron Age is observed.

On Crete, destructions are evident at many sites at the end of the Bronze Age, some of them perhaps caused by piratical raids. Certainly in most places the transition from Late Minoan IIIB

47. Bronze male figurine from Delos. Possibly dating to the early Geometric period (9th c. BC). Delos Archaeological Museum.

48. Crete. Aerial photograph of the "refuge-settlement" at Kastro, Kavousi (800 m. a.s.l.), which was founded in the 12th-11th c. BC. It was reorganized with houses of oblong plan during the 10th-9th c. BC and abandoned in the 7th c. BC.

49. Tenos, Xobourgo. The natural acropolis dominates the entire southern part of the island and is a considerable distance from the sea. The megalithic ("Cyclopean") wall of the settlement was built during the turbulent years between the end of the Bronze Age and the beginning of the Iron Age, probably in the 12th c. BC, and remained in use into at least Classical times.

50. Chios, Emporio. General view of the so-called "Megaron Hall" of the Early Archaic period (7th c. BC). This was the only building inside the fortified acropolis, close to the gateway and the sanctuary of Athena. It is considered to have been the residence of the ruler.

51. Paros, Koukounaries. Aerial photograph of the settlement of the Late Mycenaean into the Early Archaic period (12th-7th c. BC). The settlement was abandoned peacefully some time in the 7th c. BC, perhaps due to the phenomenon of synoecism: the inhabitants may have moved to the city of Paros, on the site of modern Paroikia.

48 49
50 51

GEOMETRIC AND ARCHAIC PERIODS | 51

to Late Minoan IIIC was smooth and without violence. However, it is now proven that the Achaeans settled on Crete in this period. In this same troubled period in the Aegean, several settlements appeared that can be described as "refuges", because they were founded at naturally fortified sites, difficult of access, such as Karphi, Vrokastro and Kavousi (fig. 48) in eastern Crete, Xobourgo on Tenos (fig. 49), the fortified acropolises of Salamis, and so on. The majority of these sites are not coastal, from which it is deduced that one of the dangers came from the sea. On Crete the inhabitants, indigenes and Achaeans together, apparently took refuge at these sites when the first Dorian tribes began to settle on the island.

The collapse of the mighty centres of authority and the movements of populations in the Greek Mainland, as well as to the islands and the Asia Minor littoral, led gradually to the formation of the geopolitical map of historical times. During the so-called "Dark Age" (11th-10th century BC) – a term used by research for the previously barely-known period from the eleventh to the ninth century BC – there was a realignment of social and political forces in the wider Aegean region, and a new ruling class was instituted in the framework of the new but weakened social structures. As a rule, a city-state was founded on each island (excepting the larger ones, such as Crete), sometimes upon the ruins of the most important Bronze Age settlement. Of interest is the fragmentation of the territory of some islands into several city-states. The reasons for this differentiation are not always easy to comprehend.

Although the turbulent and hazardous environment outlined above (incursions, piracy, natural disasters, etc.) led to a reduction in contacts, the sea-lanes of communication were not entirely forgotten. During the Subminoan period (second half of 11th century BC) Crete maintained contacts with Cyprus, to which Cretans had emigrated at the end of the Late Minoan IIIC period (early 11th century BC). In some regions communications were kept up throughout the eleventh and tenth centuries BC (e.g. relations between Crete and the Dodecanese and Cyprus, or between the flourishing settlement at Lefkandi on Euboea and the Eastern Mediterranean). These were expanded and intensified from the ninth century BC onwards, thanks to the general improvement in living conditions. All manner of transactions were surely supported also by the appearance of script, at least from the first half of the eighth century BC (see early graffiti from Euboea, Naxos and Andros). Archaeological finds document on the one hand movements of craftsmen, mainly metalworkers, from the East to the Aegean islands, and on the other contacts of islanders, especially in the East Aegean, with Asia Minor and the Eastern Mediterranean. This intercourse between artisans, merchants, even mercenaries, and the local population groups, led to an osmosis that was to be a significant parameter in the cultural transformation and the development of art in the islands at the dawn of the first millennium BC. The production of iron objects had a drastic effect on societies throughout the Mediterranean during the Early Iron Age. Some Aegean islands, including Crete, played an important role in the development of the new technology, thanks to their iron ore deposits, as well as in the transmission of the technical know-how, which research indicates passed from East to West.

Most of the islands flourished during the Geometric and especially the Archaic period, until the outbreak of the Persian Wars. As a norm, during this period each island still enjoyed its political

52. Detail of the scene of *prothesis* (lying in state) of the dead, on the neck of an amphora of the Geometric period (second half of the 8th c. BC) from the "*polyandrion*" of ancient Paros. The deceased is possibly a warrior who fell in the battle depicted on the belly of the same vase. The standing figure leaning over in front of him holds an arrow, perhaps a visual reminder of the way in which the warrior was killed. Paros Archaeological Museum.

53. Late 7th c. BC krater decorated in the "Wild Goat Style". The main centre of production of vases of this type was in Ionia, possibly Miletos. The vase illustrated was found in the cemetery of Kamiros on Rhodes. Paris, Musée du Louvre.

autonomy. Some islands founded colonies or trading stations (e.g. Naxos, Paros, Andros, Thera, Samos, Rhodes). Some played a seminal role in the major conflicts of the era of the birth of the city-states (such as the War for the Lelantine Plain, in which Paros sided with Eretria, whereas Naxos and Samos sided with Chalkis), while competition for control of trade and seafaring led to clashes between the islands (Naxos-Paros, Samos-Aegina, etc.). Archaeological investigations sometimes detect episodes in these hostilities (e.g. the *polyandria* of Paros [figs 52, 380, 382, 383], the battlefield identified at Choriza on Hydra).

In Crete and the Cyclades the buildings of early historical times were constructed entirely of stone and were as a rule of rectangular plan. The settlements consist of rectangular houses forming building complexes with tiered flat roofs (e.g. Karphi on Crete, Zagora on Andros). In contradistinction to most regions on the Greek Mainland at this period, where the norm is isolated rectangular or apsidal houses, on the islands a dense honeycomb urban tissue is encountered. At many sites (as in the aforementioned Cretan settlements, as well as at Smari, Prinias and Eleutherna) buildings have been uncovered – usually of megaron type – that could be identified as rulers' residences, but which also accommodated political, economic and religious activities.

On Crete the survival of the Minoan tradition is observed in many sectors, such as architecture or religious beliefs. In several *loci sancti* on the great island (e.g. in caves such as the Ida Cave and in rural sanctuaries such as that at Kato Symi) and to a lesser degree in the Cyclades (Aghia Irini on Kea, Yria on Naxos) an unbroken continuity of worship is confirmed, without this meaning that the cultic customs remained stagnant. On Crete specifically, continuity is observed also in iconographic subjects. At Aghia Irini on Kea parts of the prehistoric temple were used in Protogeometric and Geometric times, while the head of a clay statue from the Late Helladic II horizon (mid-15th century BC) was placed upon a cylindrical terracotta base, as if a cult effigy.

Examination of the archaeological data recovered so far from excavated settlements and sanctuaries in the Aegean islands of Protogeometric, Geometric and Early Archaic times, leads to some fundamental ascertainments. The first urban temples were built in the late eighth century BC. Until that time worship in the sanctuaries of settlements was in the open air, usually focused on an altar or a pit (*bothros*) for votive offerings (e.g. Emporio on Chios, Zagora on Andros, Koukounaries on Paros). In direct propinquity to these open-air sanctuaries there were often "aristocratic" residences (e.g. Emporio, Zagora and Crete). Some sectors of society, presumably the members of the aristocratic élite, partook of meals offered by the local ruler of the settlement (king with actual authority or simply *primus inter pares*, depending on the case), in his

53

GEOMETRIC AND ARCHAIC PERIODS | 53

residence. It should be noted here that from the eighth century BC onwards the division of inhabitants into at least two social classes can be observed through the burial customs and the grave goods, as well as in the organization of the settlements, as for example at Zagora on Andros and Emporio on Chios (fig. 50).

Concurrently, from early on peri-urban sanctuaries also operated, at varying distances from the settlements (e.g. Aghia Irini on Kea, Yria on Naxos, Samos and elsewhere). In time, some of these acquired a supra-local importance, such as the Heraion on Samos, but only the sanctuary of Delos (fig. 47) was to attain panhellenic radiance. There were also rural sanctuaries that served the inhabitants of a wider region and did not belong to a specific settlement. Noteworthy is the case of the extra-urban sanctuary at Kommos in southern Crete, where one of the earliest temples of historical times has been excavated, which appears to have been used also for ritual meals.

Another important temple with similar function is that in the extra-urban sanctuary at Yria on Naxos (fig. 56). Those settlements that did not establish urban temples early on seem to have failed to develop into cities (e.g. Zagora, Aghios Andreas on Siphnos, Emporio, and others). Conversely, wherever temples dedicated to the patron deity were built, the settlements evolved into cities (characteristic examples are Minoa on Amorgos and Dreros on Crete). Exceptions to this rule can be explained by individual local peculiarities and conditions, which are however difficult to detect (see e.g. the case of Koukounaries on Paros, where the settlement was abandoned even though it had acquired a temple).

Indeed, many settlements were abandoned peacefully in about the same period, around 700 BC or slightly later, which fact is perhaps due to the phenomenon of synoecism, that is when the inhabitants of two or more villages or towns gathered together at a new site and founded a city (e.g. Zagora and Ypsili on Andros when Palaiopoli was founded, Koukounaries when the inhabitants moved to Paroikia on Paros). This phenomenon of synoecism is observed already from the eighth century BC, but spread throughout Greece towards the end of the century and in the first half of the seventh century BC. Many small settlements of early historical times failed to evolve into cities and were therefore abandoned, while some others continued in existence but did not succeed in developing further (e.g. Aghios Andreas on Siphnos).

The construction of urban or peri-urban monumental and sometimes *hekatompedon* temples (Samos), and the construction of fortifications surrounding the settlements were the outcome of collective decisions and not of individual initiatives. Towards the end of the Geometric period, the temples, initially sacred *oikoi* of multiple purpose (e.g. for holding ritual meals, depositing votive offerings and safekeeping the cult statue of the deity), gradually changed function (*naos* = house of the deity) and architectural form (monumental or *hekatompedon* temples and/or temples with peristyle).

In parallel, separate edifices were founded, such as treasuries, hestiatoria and prytaneia, which were intended for other cult rituals and political functions that were previously accommodated under the same roof. The components that echo the institutions of the city-state can now be de-

54. Delos. Marble statue of a winged Nike, dated around the mid-6th c. BC. If the inscribed base found near the sculpture is related to it, then this is a work of Archermos, which was dedicated to Apollo in his sanctuary on Delos by the sculptor's father Mikkiades from Chios. H. 0.90 m. Athens, National Archaeological Museum.

55. Naxos. Reconstruction drawing of the Archaic temple of Dionysos at Yria (*c.* 580-570 BC). This three-aisled prostyle temple with a marble pitched roof was a characteristic contribution of Naxos to the development of Ionian monumental architecture. Drawing by the architect Manolis Korres.

56. Naxos. View of the Archaic temple of Dionysos at Yria, after restoration works. This is one of the most important sanctuaries on the island, as is deduced from the use of marble for constructing all the main architectural elements of the temple and from the decrees found at the site.

GEOMETRIC AND ARCHAIC PERIODS | 55

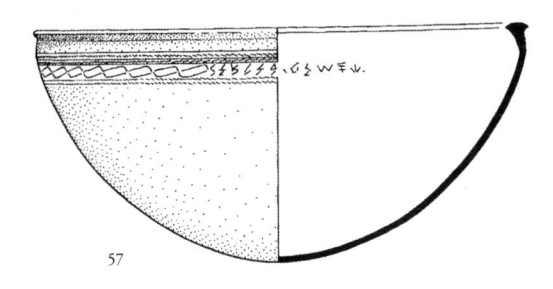

57. Drawing of a bronze inscribed Phoenician bowl found at Knossos, in a grave of two young girls, and dated *c.* 900 BC. This is the earliest alphabetic inscription in the Aegean (incised is the name and patronymic of the vessel's original owner). Herakleion Archaeological Museum.

58. Samos. Torso of an Archaic kouros (*c.* 560-550 BC) with Cycladic influences, found in the west sector of the ancient city. Inscribed on the left thigh is the name of the dedicator: ΛΕΥΚΙΟΣ ΑΝΕΘΗΚΕ ΤΩΙ ΑΠΟΛΩΝΙ (Leukios dedicated [it] to Apollo). Pres. h. 1 m. Samos Archaeological Museum.

tected thanks to excavations. At Dreros on Crete, for example, the nucleus of the early phase of the city has come to light, which includes an agora, a temple to the patron deity with cult statues, and a prytaneion. At other sites, open spaces have been interpreted as an early agora (Zagora on Andros, Emporio on Chios), while elsewhere the temple of the patron deity is in proximity to a building that could be identified as the prytaneion (Prinias on Crete, Koukounaries on Paros).

Last, the phenomenon of the cult of heroes, particularly the heroization of the dead, as on the Greek Mainland, appeared from the ninth century BC and was consolidated by the late eighth century BC (Naxos, Minoa on Amorgos, Paros, Psara, Thasos). This phenomenon is correlated directly with the birth of the *polis* and the spread of the Homeric epics. Specifically, the data from the excavation in Metropolis Square in Naxos reveal that at the beginning the cult was no different from the usual practice of the cult of the dead. Gradually the honours to the dead took the form of abstract worship of the ancestors (9th and early 8th centuries BC), which with the advent of the Late Geometric period evolved further into cult of heroes.

An important development in which the islands were evidently prime movers was the diffusion of the alphabet. Inscriptions dated to the second half of the eighth and the early seventh century BC come, among other places, from Aegina, Zagora on Andros, Grotta on Naxos, Thera, Amorgos, Anaphe, Syros, Rhodes, Kalymnos, Samos, Kommos and Phaistos on Crete. It is agreed that the Greeks borrowed the alphabet from the Phoenicians, in order to write the sounds of the Greek language. The harmonious coexistence of Greeks and Phoenicians in the Aegean and their common aims give credence to the view that the Phoenician alphabet was adopted in a place where the two peoples were living together. Phoenician presence is attested on several islands, either through finds or tradition (e.g. Crete, Rhodes, Antiparos, Despotiko, Kythnos, Kythera). Particularly illuminating is the case of the sanctuary at Kommos on Crete (fig. 636): at the centre of the Geometric temple an unusual three-pillar altar of Phoenician type (three colonnettes inserted in a stone base) was found, while a repository (*apothetes*) outside the temple contained also sherds of Phoenician vases of the ninth century BC. This evidence reveals that the sanctuary at Kommos served Phoenicians too, who were either visiting or living on the island. Additional evidence for the second hypothesis are Phoenician gravestones (*cippi*) found at Eleutherna and Knossos, and the numerous imported grave goods accompanying burials of the Geometric period. An inscribed bronze Phoenician bowl (fig. 57) was found in a grave of 900 BC at Knossos, while from Gavalomouri, Kisamos on Crete comes a funerary amphora with strong Dodecanesian influence, dated even earlier, incised with a Phoenician graffito *sin* (W) under the rim. According to one view, the alphabet was disseminated from the Dorian islands (Crete, Thera, Rhodes). Advocates of this view accept that the alphabet passed through many stages of development before acquiring its final form, which explains why initially the additional letters phi, chi, psi (φ, χ, ψ) are absent, as is the case in the inscriptions from Phaistos and Thera. However, the view that alphabetic script was disseminated by the Euboeans remains the most likely.

From the seventh century BC onwards contacts were intensified with the East, and this century is alternatively known as the "Orientalizing period". The promulgation of the Homeric epics from the second half of the eighth century BC and the tendency to redefine the identity of the new social formations in relation to the Mycenaean past, led to a series of innovations (e.g. the development of narrative scenes in vase- painting) or behaviours (e.g. the aforementioned phenomenon of hero worship, or the aristocratic burials of "Homeric" character). This was undoubtedly a period of ferment and social realignments, with the economic affluence acquired by the lower orders, such as merchants and mariners, which led to readjustment of the framework of political and social organization. In some cases this was also manifested in the writing down of the laws (e.g. Crete).

Concurrently, the sense of individualism was cultivated, as can be seen for example from lyric poetry, dedicatory inscriptions, the local variations of the Greek alphabet and the local workshops for artifacts. The island workshops of metalworking, jewellery-making, vase-making and sculpture each display different traits. By exploiting the excellent quality marble, the Naxians, the Parians and the Tenians were emboldened to carve colossal stone *ex-votos* and funerary monuments, contributing decisively to the development of great sculpture from as early as the seventh century BC (fig. 54). Among the earliest works of so-called "Daedalic" sculpture are creations of the Naxian (*ex-voto* of Nikandre [fig. 416], 660-650 BC, Delos kouroi) and the Cretan ("Dame d'Auxerre" [fig. 639]) workshop. Examples of monumental sculpture have come to light on Thera (fig. 498) and Samos (figs 58, 187, 190), although these are probably not products of local workshops. In vase-painting the workshops followed different directions, as a rule conservative, primarily those of the islands in the Central Aegean (the most important being the Naxian and Parian), which for an interval continued the tradition of Geometric times, and those of the East Aegean, which assimilated with a relative delay the models of the East (Samos, Rhodes, Chios ["Wild Goat Style"], fig. 53). A special place in narrative art is held by the relief pithoi from the Cyclades, the most important workshop being the Tenian (figs 310, 327).

59. Small glass vases of the Archaic period (6th c. BC), from the city of Mytilene. There were various centres of production and circulation of such vases, the most important of which was Rhodes. Mytilene Archaeological Museum.

60. Glass head-shaped pendant of the 6th-5th c. BC, from the temple of ancient Kythnos. The object was produced in a Mediterranean workshop (possibly in the Aegean), where glass-working rivalling that of Punic-Carthaginian workshops developed during this period. Archaeological Collection of Chora, Kythnos.

Important advances were made in architecture. One of the means used by the rising city-states, for reasons of rivalry, was monumental architecture. Many Aegean islands, the more affluent ones, were trailblazers in the development of monumental Greek architecture, starting from the late eighth century BC. On Delos the so-called "Oikos of the Naxians" (perhaps the temple of Apollo) was built in the early seventh century BC and divided into three aisles by two wooden colonnades. A second large temple was dedicated by the Naxians to Artemis (Artemision E). These two temples surely echo the monumental architecture on Naxos itself: the monumental temple in the peri-urban sanctuary at Yria is dated to the Late Geometric period (it replaced a smaller temple of the early eighth century BC). This temple was remodelled in the early seventh century BC, when a four-column prostasis was added. The first *hekatompedon* temple was constructed in the Heraion on Samos around 700 BC (the earlier view was that this temple dated to the early eighth century BC and was peripteral has been vigorously doubted in recent years). At the far end of the temple, now detached from the wall (e.g. the "bench" of the cult statue in the temple of Apollo at Dreros [fig. 640]), there was a stone base for the cult statue.

The islands played a decisive role in the development of the Ionic order (temple of Apollo at Palatia on Naxos [fig. 415], Yria [figs 55, 56] and Gyroulas on Naxos, Heraion on Samos [fig. 186]), as well as of the Aeolic (Lesbos [fig. 152]). In contrast to the Doric temples of the Greek Mainland, the architects emphasized the façade of the temples (prostasis of temple at Yria, dipteral temples of Samos). Marble tiling of the roof is considered to be a Naxian innovation (see signature of the Naxian marble-mason Byzes on the marble tiles from the Acropolis of Athens and the marble tiles of the fourth temple at Yria). The rivalry between the islands, and especially between Naxos and Paros, is recorded in the sculptural and architectural monuments in the pan-Ionian sanctuary of Delos (fig. 54). This rivalry sometimes went beyond the narrow limits of the island region, particularly as the major panhellenic sanctuaries were enhanced as the places for projecting prowess (e.g. Treasury of the Siphnians at Delphi [fig. 362]). Large-scale public works, such as the construction of imposing fortification walls, sometimes of marble (Siphnos), or the ambitious hydraulic projects (Eupalineion Aqueduct of Samos [figs

59

58 | AEGEAN ISLANDS: HISTORICAL AND ARCHAEOLOGICAL BACKGROUND

192, 193], aqueduct at Melanes on Naxos) are interpreted either as collective works of the powerful city-states, or as outcome of the policy of the tyrants (Polykrates of Samos, Kleoboulos of Lindos, Lygdamis of Naxos). In contrast, recent excavations on Kythnos confirm that even the seemingly poorer islands were able to avoid isolation through an extensive network of communications, and to attract affluent visitors from all over the Mediterranean basin, particularly the eastern part (fig. 60).

The Archaic temples on Crete differ from those in the rest of the island region, not only because they keep the *eschara* and the benches in their interior, but because some are adorned with unusual sculpted decoration (Prinias [figs 637, 638]) or have a peculiar architectural form (Gortyn), due on the one hand to a very long tradition and to Minoan survivals, and on the other to influences from the Orient. In the sixth century BC there was a marked decline in the number of visitors to most sanctuaries. This same "gap" is observed in the settlements too. Nevertheless, this seems to be due to a gap in archaeological (and primarily excavation) research, rather than to an actual decline of Crete during this period, even though it is quite widely believed that the phenomenon points to important social changes, perhaps due to a fall off in contacts with the Eastern Mediterranean. There is no drastic change in the architectural character of the settlements or the burial habits during the Archaic period, even though architectural types such as the megara appear, which share a common prostoon, such as those at Goulediana, which are reminiscent of corresponding houses at Vroulia on Rhodes, as well as on the Greek Mainland. In mortuary customs we note that the aristocratic class is appreciably differentiated from the other social strata.

The dual dimension of the islands, the watery element that surrounds them and isolates them, and the bridges of communication they create due to their medley, resulted on the one hand in conservatism and on the other in selective assimilation of cultural elements from places near and far. The geopolitical significance of the islands led in Classical and Hellenistic times to the more powerful ones laying claim to dominion in the Aegean, as did the great powers of the wider region.

Classical period (480-323 BC)

LYDIA PALAIOKRASSA-KOPITSA

Throughout Antiquity the Aegean islands were of prime importance in the historical development of the Hellenic world, due to their position on the sea routes linking Greece with Egypt, the Propontis and the Euxine Pontus, Cyprus and the East. The Aegean became an arena of mercantile transactions and circulation of cultural goods.

The development of each island differed, as this was dependent on its location and its natural resources. It was affected by the fertility of the ground, the wealth of the subsoil and, primarily, the position of each island – more or less strategic –, as well as by influences from the civilizations of the East, of Egypt and of the Greek Mainland. Consequently, the economy and the artistic progress of the islands display remarkable variety. Exploitation of the natural wealth of the coasts close to each island, the *peraia*, contributed to the even greater development of some, as is the case of Thasos, Lesbos, Chios, Rhodes. The commercial development of the three last, for example, was due to their strategic position, their direct contacts with eastern civilizations, the growth of trade, as well as to their fertile earth. The mobility of the island mariners and merchants, and the economic development of the islands with the extensive trafficking of goods, are reflected directly in certain artifacts, such as coins or transport amphorae.

Particularly notable was the development of Thasos in the second half of the sixth century BC, which was due not only to the location, the fertile soil and the natural resources of the island and of its *peraia* in neighbouring Thrace, but also to the impetus and input of the Parian colonists. Renowned in Antiquity, beyond the island's bounds, was the Thasian marble used in sculpture and in architecture.

The inhabitants of Chios applied themselves to trade and shipping, from which they prospered to such an extent that Thucydides (VIII 45,4) considered them the "wealthiest of the Hellenes". The possession of the *peraia* on the opposite coast, where there were gold mines, contributed to the island's development and to the Chians gathering in their hands the transit trade of the East. Chian merchants traded products mainly between the East and the Euxine Pontus, while also promoting their own commodities, foremost among them Chian wine (fig. 61). Chios also had the largest number of slaves in Greece, after Sparta (Thucydides VIII 40), and played a leading role in the slave trade, together with Corinth and Aegina. The superiority of the Chians and the Aeginetans in trade generally is also vouched for by Aristotle (*Politics* IV 4. 1291B 24).

Aegina was in fact a special case in historical times. The Aeginetans' old enmity with the Athenians and their sympathies for the Spartans decided their fate. The great naval and commercial power ended up at this time as a vassal of the Athenians (431 BC), who expelled the island's population and put an end to its prosperity.

61. Silver stater of Chios, with obverse type the figure of a Sphinx, emblem of the city, and a transport amphora in front of her, denoting the island's main product, wine. On the reverse of the coin is an incuse square. 478-431 BC (?). Athens, Numismatic Museum.

62. Although the First Athenian League was dissolved after the Athenians' defeat by the Spartans, its spirit lived on, as attested by decrees of the Athenian State, inscribed between 405 and 403/2 BC, honouring Samians and granting them additional special privileges. The stele with the text of the decrees is crowned by a relief representing the patron goddesses of the two cities, Athena and Hera, in a gesture of *dexiosis* (handshake). Athens, Acropolis Museum.

Lesbos, also in a strategic position controlling the sea route to the Euxine Pontus and Thrace, was densely populated in Classical times and highly developed, thanks to its fertile soil and the exploitation of its *peraia*.

Most of the islands in the Cyclades developed because of shipping and trade, in which their inhabitants were involved, as well as in some cases because of the rich soil or subsoil. Paros owed its economic and artistic development in particular to its excellent quality marble. Keos was famed for beekeeping and mainly for the export of red ochre or ruddle and of argentiferous lead.

On other islands, such as Thera or Karpathos, more introverted societies developed, due to under-exploitation – for different reasons – of the potential offered by the sea. Leros, Patmos and the lesser islands in the Dodecanese were directly dependent on Miletos. Other islands were at various times under the influence of their more powerful neighbours, such as Megiste (Castellorizo) and Chalke in the fourth century BC, which were subject to the Rhodians.

In Classical times most of the islands developed into economic-mercantile and naval powers, with harbours that were important ports of call for shipping and for trading goods, as well as because of their strategic position. For these reasons their contribution was significant to the hegemonic designs of the Athenians, who to a large degree controlled the development of the majority. Their fate was decided by the policy of the two great powers of the period, Athens and Sparta, which aimed at the hegemony of the Hellenes. Almost all the islands were members of the Delian-First Athenian League (487/77 BC) and of the Second Athenian League (378/7 BC), until the battle of Chaironeia (338 BC), when the Athenians' possessions were restricted to Samos, Lemnos, Skyros, Imbros and Delos.

In the first decade of the fifth century BC the Aegean islands were captured by or sided with the Persians, some with very severe consequences, such as Thasos, which having surrendered in 492 BC, suffered the demolition of its walls and the obligation to pay tribute. The islands did not have a uniform stance to Xerxes' campaign in 480 BC, but the majority aligned with the Persians.

After the successful outcome of the Persian Wars, the Aegean islands gained their freedom, and shortly after most of them joined – some under duress – the Delian-Athenian League, initial aim of which was the common confrontation of the Persian threat. Exceptions were Crete and Kythera, which because of their location were controlled by Sparta, apart from the period of the Peloponnesian War (424 BC onwards).

A special case is Delos, which was a vassal of Athens and did not gain its independent until 314 BC. The existence of the famous sanctuary of Apollo, centre of worship for the Ionian Greeks, distinguished it from the other islands and to this it owed its designation as hub of the Delian Amphictyony. The Athenians, who were in full control of the island, decided on its "*catharsis*" in 426/5 BC, reorganized the festival and built a new temple, between the Archaic one and that of the Delians. Also of decisive importance for the island was the existence of the harbour.

Most of the islands remained loyal to Athens, such as Lemnos and Chios, while some reacted to its domination at various times, such as Naxos (469 BC), Thasos (465 BC), Samos (440 BC), Aegina (431 BC) and Lesbos (Mytilene, 428 BC); these insurrections were suppressed, however, with serious consequences for some islands, such as the loss of autonomy, the surrender of their ships to the Athenians or the demolition of their fortifications. Athenian control was intensified with the installation of cleruchs (lot-holders) on many islands (447 BC onwards), in the framework of the League, which the Athenians gradually transformed into a hegemony. One of the first islands to receive Athenian citizens as lot-holders was Skyros (474/3 BC), because of its location on the sea route between Attica and Thrace. This was followed by the settling of cleruchs on Andros, Imbros, Lemnos, Naxos and Samos, and during the Peloponnesian War on Aegina, Lesbos and Melos. The amount of tax the islands paid to the League is indicative of their prosperity, which for some (Thasos, Aegina, Paros, Andros) was considerable. Other islands managed to keep their independence, such as Chios, and for shorter intervals Lesbos and Samos.

The cities of Amorgos, as *koinon*, and Dorian Thera appear with some delay in the League's lists, in 434/3 BC and 430/29 BC respectively. By 416/5 BC the rest of the Dorian Cyclades (Anaphe, Sikinos, Pholegandros, Kimolos) had joined the League, and only Melos hung on to its autonomy until that year, when it was captured by the Athenians, with tragic consequences for its populace.

The tremendous influence exerted by Athens on political developments in the islands is also ascertained from the instituting of oligarchic regimes on Thasos, Andros, Tenos and Paros, in 411 BC, as well as previously with the participation of several islands in the Sicilian Expedition. Within the unstable clime of these years Lesbos and Chios seceded from the League in 412 BC, but were captured by the Athenians before the year was out.

An important event was the founding of the new city of Rhodes, with the synoecism of 408/7 BC, which strengthened the island's political and economic role. The new city was built in accordance with the Hippodamean system of urban planning.

Athenian domination in the Aegean ended earlier for some islands, such as Lesbos, Rhodes and Kos, and finally and permanently after the Athenian defeat in the naval battle of Aigos Potamoi (404 BC). The islands entered the Spartan sphere of influence, with unfavourable repercussions for some cities, such as Chios. Nevertheless, there are indications that the Athenian presence in the islands continued (fig. 62), such as the Athenian cleruchs remaining on Lemnos in the early 380s BC.

Spartan domination ended with the removal of the Spartans after Konon's victory at Knidos (394 BC) and finally in the Aegean in 376 BC. The inclusion of the islands in the Second Athenian League (378/7 BC) was disturbed only temporarily in a few cases (Paros, Naxos, Kos, Rhodes). The Athenians' siege of Samos resulted in the expulsion of the Samians and the installation of Athenian cleruchs (lot-holders) on the island (365-322 BC). Cleruchs settled on other islands too, such as Imbros, Lemnos and Skyros. The three cities of Keos formed a federation, which was dissolved by Athenian intervention in the mid-fourth century BC.

After the Peace of Antalkides (386 BC), the Parians, supported by the Tyrant of Syracuse Dionysios I, founded their second colony, Pharos, in the Adriatic. In 366 BC Kos followed the example of Rhodes, founding a new city organized on the principles of the Hippodamean system of urban planning, which soon brought prosperity to the island. The new heyday of Thasos is

63. Part of a marble grave stele with the figure of a young man, from Amorgos, 440-430 BC. Ascribed to a Parian workshop, the relief displays the characteristics of the local island-Ionian tradition. Athens, National Archaeological Museum.

64. The marble grave stele set up on the tomb of Philis. The name of the deceased, who is represented seated on a stool and holding a jewellery casket (*pyxis*), is recorded in the inscription on the regula above the figure. The stele was crowned by a pediment. Attic influence can be discerned in the relief, but there are also clear traits of the Parian workshop. 450-440 BC. Paris, Musée du Louvre.

Classical Period | 63

65. Grave stele of Krito and Timarista, from Rhodes. Peculiar is the curved top of the stele, which is crowned by an akroterion. Attic influence is obvious in both figures. *Circa* 410 BC. Rhodes Archaeological Museum.

attested by the founding of a new colony in Pangaion, Krenides (subsequently Philippi), in 360 BC. During the Allied War (357-355 BC), the Athenians installed garrisons with an Athenian commander, on Amorgos and Andros. In the second quarter of the fourth century BC (362 BC?) other islands were attacked and sacked by the forces of Alexander, Tyrant of Pherrhai, who also took captive the population of Tenos.

An outstanding feature of many islands in the Classical period, particularly in the fourth century BC, is the presence of towers in the countryside, as can be seen on Ios, Keos (fig. 284), Kythnos, Seriphos (fig. 359), Siphnos (fig. 368), Tenos, Amorgos (fig. 439), Andros, Thasos, Lesbos, Peparethos (Skopelos) and Ikos (Alonnisos [fig. 223]). The increase of installations in the countryside, some of them fortified, was the outcome of the interest in utilizing the land, of the related expansion of the rural population and the intensification of agriculture. Some towers were associated with farmsteads, a few have been identified as lighthouses (fig. 370) and others as *phryktories* (for fire signals), while some on Seriphos and Siphnos were probably related to the exploitation of these islands' mineral resources.

Already from the mid-fourth century BC, with the appearance of the power of Macedonia, balances in the Aegean were upset, beginning from the north (see Thasos). Again, Athenian domination ended earlier in some islands, in 357 BC, albeit temporarily (Chios, Rhodes, Kos, Kalymnos), and finally with the break up of the League (338/7 BC). Even so, Athenian occupation continued after the battle of Chaironeia, on Samos, Lemnos, Skyros, Imbros and Delos. Athens had now ceased to be a maritime power in the Aegean, after the defeat of its fleet in the naval battle of Amorgos (332 BC).

Crete during Classical times was a special case. The political and social organization of its cities was characterized by introversion, conservatism and stagnation. Indicative of this are the laws of Gortyn. Some development is noted in social organization, but this was far behind that of the other islands.

The Cretans kept their distance from the important developments in the rest of Greece, during the Persian Wars, the hegemony of Athens and its conflict with Sparta, even though Cretan cities were a source of mercenaries.

The economy of the Cretan cities was basically agricultural, with limited trading transactions. Nonetheless, the various cities maintained relations with their metropolises, such as Argos, Sparta, Aegina, as well as with the major centres of the time, such as Athens, Rhodes and Cyprus. Contacts with Athens, attested by imported Attic vases, were due to the supply of mercenaries, but mainly to the island's location on the sea route to the grain markets of North Africa.

Conservatism and stagnation are apparent also in the art and architecture of Crete, which cleaved to the old tradition and influences mainly from the radiant art of Attica, to which it subscribed a leading personality, the sculptor Kresilas from Kydonia.

Athens' domination was not only political, as has been ascertained, but also economic, since during the fifth and fourth centuries BC the Athenians had succeeded in controlling the circulation of goods and securing the sufficiency of their imports, mainly of grain. In particular, after the outbreak of the Peloponnesian War one of the priorities of Athenian policy was to ensure the grain supply for the city and to prevent its distribution towards the Peloponnese. For this reason the Athenians showed special interest in Kythera, which was a port of call on the route from Egypt, Crete and Cyprus towards the Peloponnese. Of analogous importance for Athens was Thasos, as well as Lemnos – Imbros – Tenedos in that period, due to the location of the first island next to the Thracian littoral and of the other islands on the route to the Propontis and the Euxine Pontus, regions rich in grain, timber and metals. According to the textual sources, Lemnos, Thasos and Skiathos were grain-growing islands.

There is considerable evidence to document Athenian domination, such as the decision of the Keians (Koressia, first half of 4th century BC) to restore Athens' monopoly on the export of red ochre, or the decree of the Athenians (third quarter of 5th century BC) imposing the use of their own coins, weights and measures on the allies.

Athenian control even extended to the sector of worship, through the cleruchs who participated in the administration of local sanctuaries, such as of Hera on Samos, or of the Kabeiroi at Hephaistia on Lemnos.

In sculpture during the first half of the fifth century BC, the Archaic roots were still adhered to in the islands and the characteristics of the various workshops, such as the Naxian, the Thasian, the Samian and the East Greek or Ionian, are clearly discernible. Two general directions are observed in sculpture production, in which the island-Ionian and the East Greek-Ionian (fig. 200) traits held sway. The most active artistic centre however was Paros, which kept is pre-eminence until the time when its craftsmen were absorbed by the work team of the Parthenon. Sculptures ascribed to the Parian workshop are easily distinguished by their excellent marble and outstanding workmanship, as the Parian artists successfully amalgamated the aforementioned trends during Classical times. The examples that document these ascertainments are numerous and come mainly from the island region (fig. 467), especially Paros itself or its colony Thasos, in whose sculpture – as well as architecture and vase-painting – the Ionic influences of the metropolis (fig. 64), but also of northern Ionia, the Aeolis and Chios are apparent. Indicative too of the influence of Paros on its colony is the use of the Parian alphabet in inscriptions until the end of the fifth century BC, when it was replaced by the Attic Eukleidian alphabet after 404/3 BC.

Whilst the building programme of Pericles was in full swing in Athens and after its completion, the hitherto prevailing directions in sculpture changed. For the needs of this programme sculptors had flocked to Athens from the leading centres of the age, such as the Lemnian (of Athenian origin) Alkamenes and the Parian Agorakritos, the most notable pupils of Pheidias. Classical art at Athens, with the Parthenonian tradition, influenced production in the rest of the Hellenic world, even though this kept its own expression (figs 63, 198). These influences,

66. Incised stele with figures of four female dancers with *kalathiskos*, in which direct influence of the sculptor Kallimachos can be seen. Late 5th c. BC. Chios Archaeological Museum.

67. Red-figure hydria with representation of a horse race, from the cemetery of Kamiros. Product of an Attic pottery workshop, the vase is attributed to the early mannerist painters of 560-450 BC. Rhodes Archaeological Museum.

which are apparent even in the fourth century BC (fig. 102), were strong not only in the work of famed island sculptors, principally Parians, but also in secondary production, of grave and votive reliefs (figs 65, 66).

Significant sculptors originated from the islands, such as Skopas from Paros, also an architect, who was active throughout Greece and Asia Minor, and Thrasymedes, who too hailed from Paros, while others worked in the islands, such as Bryaxis on Rhodes.

Comparable was the development of architecture, in which the survival of the Ionian, on most islands, or the Aeolian tradition can be seen.

In pottery too the preservation of local traditions from Archaic times is noted at first, while the influence of Athens is obvious later. In the pottery of Thasos, for example, Parian influences are clear until the early fifth century BC, and subsequently Chian and Athenian.

Thasos itself was promoted by the work of the great painter Polygnotos, who had a decisive impact on the development of monumental painting. Another important painter in Antiquity, Parrhasios from Ephesos, worked on Rhodes, while Agathargos from Samos (third quarter of 5th century BC) is mentioned as the exponent of perspective. Another fifth-century BC painter was Timanthes from Kythnos.

The pottery of Lesbos was also influenced by Attic tradition, although the production of local grey ware continued from the Archaic period. The finds from almost all the islands, especially the smaller ones where there was no notable local pottery production, bear witness to relations with Athens and the import of products of the Athenian Kerameikos (figs 67, 69, 183, 320, 321, 573).

Of considerable importance for the study of pottery was the discovery on Rheneia of the "purification *bothros*", where the contents removed from the graves of Delos had been deposited.

Indicative of the robust economy of most islands is their coinage. Nonetheless, the policy of Athens in the fifth century BC led most cities to interrupt minting coins, with the exception of Chios. Some islands resumed activity in this sector in the fourth century BC, while others delayed until Hellenistic times. However, there were cases of islands with limited coin production, which mainly served local needs, such as Imbros, Samothrace, Lemnos, Amorgos, Syros, Tenos, the islands of the North Sporades and Crete.

Representations on coins frequently have religious, mythological or historical symbolism and in many cases draw on the principal cult of each island, as on Thasos (Herakles, Dionysos, fig. 71), Ikaria (Artemis Tauropolos), Tenos (Poseidon), Thera (Apollo), Andros, Naxos and Peparethos (Dionysos), Skiathos (Hermes), or local mythological traditions, such as Kea (Aristaios), Crete (e.g. Minotaur and Labyrinth on the coins of Knossos, fig. 70). Other representations refer to local products and flora and fauna, such as of Paros (she-goat) or Skyros (fig leaf between two antithetic she-goats).

Significant was the coinage of Thasos in the fifth and fourth centuries BC (fig. 71), and of Lesbos, with the mint of Mytilene (fig. 160), the leading city, and of Methymna, its second city. Tenedos issued silver tetradrachms from the early fourth century BC, with a Janus-like head on the obverse and a double axe on the reverse. Samos ceased minting coins in 439 BC, after its capture by the Athenians, while its mint resumed production in the early fourth century BC. The wealthy island of Chios also circulated silver and copper coins (fig. 61), but its mint stopped operating in the mid-fourth century BC.

Of the Argosaronic islands, Aegina, although it was the first Greek city to mint coins that circulated widely in Archaic times (fig. 251), was ousted from its prominent position by Athens in Classical times. Even so, an appreciable number of cities in this period adopted the Aeginetan weight standard for their coinage, such as the cities of Crete, Eretria, Chalkis and Abdera. The Aeginetans continued to apply themselves to trade, being mainly involved in the grain market, as is borne out by the discovery of hoards of the island's coins of Classical times from Egypt (Fayum) to Lemnos or the Peloponnese.

The particularly notable numismatic presence of some Cycladic islands in the Archaic period was also cut short by the Athenian domination, with sole exceptions the issues of Melos and Siphnos. The Melos mint stopped production only for the duration of the Athenian occupation of the island (416-405/4 BC). The coinage of many islands recommenced in the first half of the fourth century BC (Andros, Keos, Naxos). In the fourth century BC Tenos minted silver coins on the Attic and the Rhodian weight standard.

The Dodecanese also enjoyed a conspicuous numismatic presence, consequence of their vigorous commercial development. One of the loveliest examples of early Classical coins is the silver tridrachm of Kos (fig. 524). The representations on the island's issues in the fourth century BC relate to the worship of Herakles.

The three cities of the island of Rhodes (Lindos, Ialysos, Kamiros) minted coins prior to their synoecism in 408 BC. Noteworthy is the peculiarity of the coins of Ialysos

68. Bossed kalyx, h. 6.1 cm., from the west necropolis of Rhodes. Heat-formed by pressing glass into a mould and with a wheel, the vessel is decorated with incised continuous Doric petals in radiate arrangement, ending at the level of the curved shoulder in a horizontal zone of incised lozenge and mesh pattern. Rhodian glass vessels of the 4th c. BC were kalykes and mainly shallow bowls, of small dimensions. 375-379 BC. Rhodes Archaeological Museum.

69. Part of an Attic red-figure volute krater with Dionysiac scene, from the sanctuary of the Mother of the Gods, on Samothrace. *Circa* 400 BC. Samothrace Archaeological Museum.

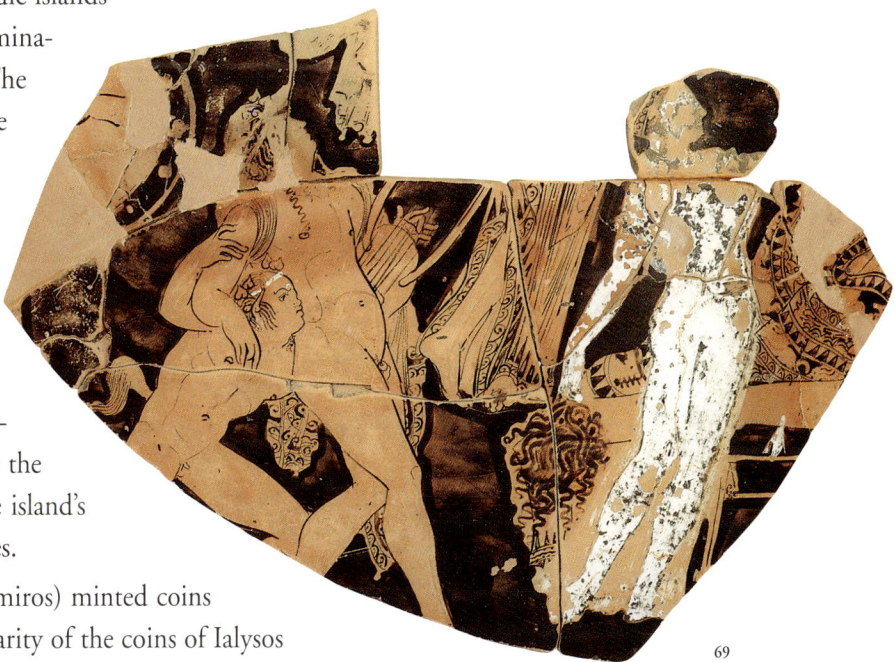

70. Silver stater of Knossos, with representation of the Minotaur on the obverse and of the Labyrinth on the reverse. Dated between 425 and 370 BC. Berlin, Staatliche Museen – Münzkabinett.

71. Represented on the new issues of Thasos are the city's two protecting gods: the head of bearded Dionysos on the obverse, and Herakles archer with the inscription ΘΑΣΙΟΝ on the reverse. Silver drachma, 290-335 BC. Berlin, Staatliche Museen – Münzkabinett.

in the fifth century BC, in terms of iconography, style and weight, which follows the Phoenician standard, attesting influences from the coinage of Lycia, Cyprus and Cyrene. The mint of the new city of Rhodes (fig. 566) emerged from the early fourth century BC as the most important in Karia and influenced the issues of other cities, such as Samos and Nisyros.

The issues of the cities of Crete were somewhat delayed, appearing in the mid-fifth century BC, initially of Gortyn, Phaistos and Lyttos, and subsequently of Knossos, while the island's coinage reached its peak in the fourth century BC, receiving influences mainly from the Peloponnese. This heyday is related to the recovery in trade and the general development of Crete in that period.

In addition to its coinage, Rhodes was famed in Antiquity for its coroplastic art and glass-making (fig. 68). The flourishing coroplastic production in the sixth century BC, mainly of plastic vases, continued into Classical times, especially during the fifth century BC. Likewise in glass-making, opaque vases were produced by the core technique from early historical times until the end of the fifth century BC, while transparent heat-formed glass vessels, influenced by Achaemenid tradition, appeared from the early fourth century BC.

As has been said already, some islands were famed for their wine. Excellent quality wine was one of the principal products of Thasos and the state passed legislation to control its production and trade. Thasian wine was exported in transport amphorae (fig. 72), mainly to the Thracian hinterland, Macedonia, Athens, the islands and the regions of the Euxine Pontus, particularly Istros, Kallatis and Tomoi, where from the second quarter of the fourth century BC Thasian imports were far in excess of all others.

Chios was also famed for its wine, which was of choice quality and distinguished as *austeros* (dry), *glykazon* (sweetish) and *autokraton* (full-bodied). The Chians' mercantile activities are attested by the discovery of Chian amphorae (fig. 73) in large quantities in Athens, as well as in Aegina, Corinth, Thasos, Akanthos, Cyprus and, last, in such far-flung places as Gordion in Phrygia, Olbia, Istros on the Danube and Tomoi further south. Characteristic of relations between Chios and Athens is that the number of Chian amphorae found in Athens more or less doubled in the period 425-410 BC, while after that a reduction is observed. Perhaps this increase was associated with the transportation of grain from the Euxine Pontus to feed the Athenian army and navy. In general, there was a fall off in Chian exports after 412 BC.

Lesbos too was renowned for its wine in Classical times and Lesbian transport amphorae are distinguished by their grey clay and the characteristic finial of the handles on the shoulder.

Rhodes during the fourth century BC developed into an important commercial centre that vied with Athens, and into one of the biggest grain markets. From this period too it exported its renowned wine, as did Kos, to the cities of the Euxine Pontus (Kallatis).

Another wine-producing city was Samothrace, whose amphorae travelled to the Thracian hinterland and the Euxine Pontus, which was also reached by wine from Peparethos (figs 218, 219) and Ikos (fig. 222). Last, Samian amphorae were used not only for transporting wine but also, primarily, olive oil, which was an important product of the island.

Many of the islands were the birthplace of leading figures in Letters and Sciences, only a few of whom were active in their native city, such as the poet Philoxenos from Kythera, composer of dithyrambs. The work of the poet Ion from Chios (485/80-421 BC) was diverse, while noteworthy is the significant *oeuvre* of the lyric poet Bacchylides from Keos (481-431 BC), the epic poet Choirilos from Samos (5th century BC), Hegemon from Thasos, first author of the parody of the epic (5th century BC) and the poetess Herinna from Telos (4th century BC).

Important was the work of the prose writer and historiographer Hellanikos from Mytilene (5th century BC) and of Theopompos from Chios (4th century BC), as well as of the mathematicians Oinopodes and Hippokrates from Chios (5th century BC). Outstanding personality in the domain of philosophy is Theophrastos from Eresos, pupil and successor of Aristotle in the peripatetic school, who lived on Lesbos for two years, as well as on Thasos for a time.

Another sector in which another Aegean island, Kos, was well known is Medicine. The most important medical schools in Antiquity were in Knidos and Kos, while there is no information about the school on Rhodes. The school on Kos was the most renowned, on account of the personality of Hippokrates (5th century BC), who charted new directions for the physicians' art in that period. He also offered his services on Thasos, for about four years. Therapeutic baths were also related to the curing of the human body and these operated from at least the late fifth century BC at Thermes, one of the two main cities on Ikaria.

All the deities of the Dodecatheon were worshipped in the Aegean islands, as well as local heroes (e.g. Perseus on Seriphos) or historical persons (Euripides on Salamis). However, some islands were famed for the cult of a specific god or goddess, such as Delos of Apollo, Samos of Hera, Lemnos of Hephaistos, the Kabeiroi and the Great Goddess, Kythera of Aphrodite, Samothrace of the Great Gods, where mysteries were celebrated (figs 107-109), Kalaureia (Poros [fig. 256]) and Tenos of Poseidon (fig. 312), Andros and Naxos of Dionysos.

72. Thasian transport amphorae are distinguished initially by their globular shape and their button-shaped embolon, while in the 4th c. BC they became more attenuated, with biconical body and long embolon. Systematic stamping of these vases began quite early on, with the same representations as appeared on the coins (Herakles archer). Early 4th c. BC. Thasos Archaeological Museum.

73. Chian transport amphorae are distinguished into two types, on the basis of the change in the form of the neck from swollen to straight-sided, in 425 BC. This change is considered to denote also a change in the capacity of the vases. The Chians were the first to stamp their amphorae on the base of one handle, after the change in the type. The representation on the stamp was the same as that on the city's coins. During the 4th c. BC amphorae – such as the one illustrated – acquired more slender forms and no longer have the button-shaped embolon. Chios, Volissos Archaeological Collection.

Hellenistic (323-31 BC) and Roman periods (31 BC-AD 324)

Historical outline

SOPHIA ANEZIRI

The geographical position of the Aegean islands, between the Greek Mainland and the Asia Minor coast, determined the important role these played in trade and shipping, as well as made them an apple of discord between the dominant powers in the Early Hellenistic period (late 4th-early 3rd century BC). The navies of the Antigonids and the Ptolemies, successors to Alexander the Great, tried persistently to control the islands and therefore the sea routes in the Aegean. From the late fourth and during the first half of the third century BC an important part of their claims concerned the Cyclades and control of the *Koinon* of Islanders. There were serious clashes between the kings of Macedonia and of Egypt even over the islands in the East Aegean and Crete, while from time to time the Attalids and the Seleucids too made their presence felt in the Aegean.

A special case was the island of Rhodes, which because of its great maritime and mercantile power, as well as its geographical location between the Aegean and the Eastern Mediterranean, not to mention the rich *peraia* under its control, succeeded in escaping the suffocating embrace of the Hellenistic rulers. Nonetheless, it was weakened by the Third Macedonian War, when its ambition for greater autonomy was punished by its hitherto allies, the Romans, who took away Karia and Lycia (167 BC), and declared Delos a free port (166 BC), which event dealt a direct blow to Rhodian commerce.

During Hellenistic times the Aegean islands experienced not only military but also political rivalries for control of their harbours and trade. This was a period of intensive migrations and installations of new populations, coming mainly from Eastern Mediterranean lands and Italy. The foreign merchants and mariners, alone or organized in associations, became bearers of new cultural and cultic practices, which were combined creatively with the rich religious and cultural substrate of the Aegean region. The most characteristic example of these processes is Delos. Sacred isle at the heart of the Cyclades, a panhellenic cult centre and very important harbour, it enjoyed a long period of relative autonomy (314-166 BC), under the hegemony-influence of the Antigonids, the Ptolemies and later of Rhodes, until in 166 BC, on the initiative of the Romans, it returned to the domination of Athens. From that time and until its desolation by the forces of King Mithridates of Pontos (99 and 69 BC), Delos experienced a cosmopolitan heyday.

Movements in the Aegean region were not linked exclusively with trade. Religious festivals and their accompanying games, which were held on all the islands, and mainly those hosting cults of panhellenic appeal, such as Samothrace with the Kabeiria, Samos with the Heraia, Kos with the Asklepieia and of course Delos with the festivals in honour of Apollo and Artemis, attracted official representatives, pilgrims, athletes, artists, as well as traders from all over the Hellenic world.

74. Colossal head of Helios, Sun-god of Rhodes. The god, in impetuous movement, as indicated by the turn of the head, the dishevelled hair and the half-open mouth, was perhaps represented driving his chariot. The holes around the hair were for inserting the metal rays of his wreath. A work of around the mid-2nd c. BC, possibly echoing the "Colossus of Rhodes". Rhodes Archaeological Museum.

75. Delos. General view of the archaeological site. Visible are the agora of the Delians or Square Agora in the foreground, the stoas lining the sacred way in the middle distance, part of the sanctuary of Apollo right and part of the theatre quarter left. In the background are the islets of Megalos and Mikros Rematiaris, and in the distance is Rheneia.

HELLENISTIC AND ROMAN PERIODS | 71

76. Warehouse of transport amphorae in Rhodes. The pointed-base amphora was the characteristic vessel for storing and trading wine and olive oil in Graeco-Roman Antiquity. Almost all the important commercial centres produced their own distinctive transport amphorae. The pointed end, used as a third handle, facilitated the carrying of the jars and the ovoid shape facilitated their storage.

77. Statue of Poseidon from Melos. Larger than life-size, it was sculpted in two pieces that were joined in the area where the swathing of the himation begins. In his right hand he held an upright trident, while next to his right leg is a dolphin, attribute of the god. The *contrapposto*, "centrifugal" movement of the figure's limbs is characteristic of Late Hellenistic sculptures, while the plasticity of the curls on the hair and beard echoes baroque creations of the mature Hellenistic period. Perhaps a work of the Rhodian School. Second half of 2nd c. BC. Athens, National Archaeological Museum.

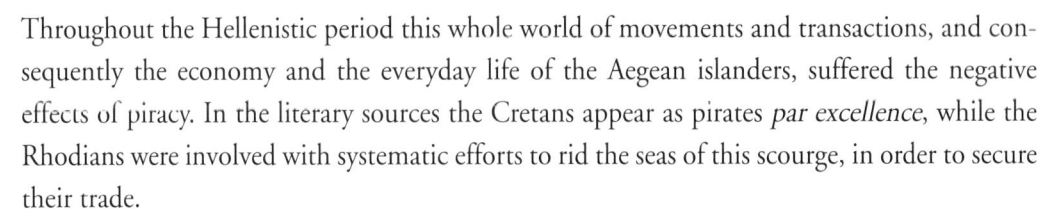

Throughout the Hellenistic period this whole world of movements and transactions, and consequently the economy and the everyday life of the Aegean islanders, suffered the negative effects of piracy. In the literary sources the Cretans appear as pirates *par excellence*, while the Rhodians were involved with systematic efforts to rid the seas of this scourge, in order to secure their trade.

In the first century BC the islands were affected by the attacks of Mithridates and the hostilities of the civil wars of the Roman Republic.

In Imperial times (1st century AD) stability was established in the Aegean region, with the incorporation of the islands in the Roman provinces (of Achaea, Macedonia, Asia, Crete-Cyrenaica) and the successful combating of piracy. However, the trade routes of the Roman Oecumene had now been extended throughout the Eastern and Western Mediterranean. Within the fold of the single *imperium*, the Aegean no longer had the nodal importance it enjoyed when the Hellenistic monarchies were at their peak.

Archaeological evidence

GEORGIA KOKKOROU-ALEVRA

On the basis of the historical outline given above, it is only natural that some Aegean islands, particularly those that were important commercial nodes with robust economies, were enhanced as major cultural centres, in which new concepts of urban planning, innovations and experiments in architecture, distinguished schools of sculpture with distinctive traits, thriving pottery workshops, coinage, the minor arts and jewellery flourished during the Hellenistic period.

A new element in the large sanctuaries was the "staging" of space as a single unity, usually with the temple as central axis, which is surrounded symmetrically by stoas and to which lead magnificent propyla and wide staircases with many steps. The most characteristic examples are the Asklepieion on Kos (figs 539, 540) and the sanctuary of Athena Lindia at Lindos on Rhodes (fig. 568). The basic pre-Hellenistic nucleus of both sanctuaries was expanded in Hellenistic times upon spacious terraces framed by long stoas in Π-shaped arrangement, with numerous columns set wide apart so as to create intense contrasts of light and shade. Monumental staircases and propyla led up to the terraces, so that as the *loci sancti* "welcomed" the faithful they created an aura of mystery and divine expectancy for the temple and the altar where cult was celebrated. The landscape, that is the natural setting, played an active role in these new conceptions of architecturally designed space and is included organically in them. The same trend is ascertained also in the very ancient and originally "haphazardly" organized sanctuary of Apollo on Delos, where the stoa of Antigonos (250 BC) delimits its enlarged space from the north, while shortly before 200 BC the double stoa of Philip V – a novelty of the period – framed with one branch the sacred way, on the west, while simultaneously "looking" towards the harbour with the other. Corresponding to the Stoa of Philip V is the South Stoa, which stands on the east of the main thoroughfare of the sanctuary, which thus acquires a majestic character.

More specifically on Delos, with its cosmopolitan ambience and multiethnic population, impressive is the number of sanctuaries of foreign deities, the worship of which had been introduced and established on the island. This is attested by the erection of splendid sanctuaries with temples of the Hellenized Syrian deities Atargatis and Haddad, the Serapeion III for the cult of Serapis, Isis and Anubis, the sanctuary of Agathe Tyche (Good Fortune) or Philadelpheion for the cult of Ptolemy II Philadelphos and his consort Arsinoe. It is further evidenced by the sanctuary of Zeus Hypsistos for the worship of Baal, the sanctuary of the gods of Ashkelon, *ex-voto* of the banker Philostratos from Ashkelon in Palestine, and last, by the three open-air sanctuaries of Semitic type on the summit of Kynthos, dedicated to the cult of Baal-Zebul. Even a Jewish synagogue, the oldest known synagogue outside Palestine, had been built on Delos by the first century BC. A Jewish community is also attested in Hellenistic Kos, where there was similarly a flourishing community of Italian merchants, as on Rhodes.

The initiative for these architectural arrangements and the edifices in the large sanctuaries were usually taken by powerful rulers, who in this way publicized their might, their wealth and their hegemonic ambition.

In front of the stoas in the sanctuaries, as well as at various other points in them, semicircular and rectangular exedras were set up, usually adorned with statues of their dedicators, offering places where pilgrims could relax and also adding to the resplendence of the site. The same role was played by the host of *ex-votos*, portrait statues of eminent men as well as distinguished women, set on high pedestals or simple bases, equestrian statues of rulers, martial statue groups with propagandist overtones, statues of animals, and so on, which concurrently project in the most emphatic manner both those represented and the sponsors. The place of the model figures of Archaic society, that is the kouroi and korai statues of the sixth century BC, which silently served the gods, as well as of the great outstanding personalities – statesmen, athletes, poets and orators of Classical times – who honoured, enhanced and "saved" their cities in critical periods –, was now taken by portrait statues of rulers, himation-clad politicians, mythological and heroic groups. The theatrical and frequently pompous tone is obvious also in the individual *ex-votos*, such as the statue of the Nike of Samothrace upon a ship's prow (fig. 114), which was set up in an artificial lake to give the impression of the open sea in which the victorious naval battle that occasioned the dedication of the sculpture had been fought.

Large altars were also founded in this period, in reality monumental edifices, sometimes decorated with colonnades and statues, like the altar in the Asklepieion on Kos in its second- century BC phase, which is reminiscent of the altar of Zeus and Athena at Pergamon, and sometimes simpler, as in the sanctuary of Poseidon and Amphitrite on Tenos, and in the sanctuary of the Kabeiroi on Samothrace. There the enormous tholos dedicated by Arsinoe of Egypt, a traditional circular building but in a Hellenistic version, constitutes one of the most impressive and

77

HELLENISTIC AND ROMAN PERIODS | 73

most famous sacred edifices of Hellenistic times (fig. 78). Last, the architectural forms of the buildings themselves acquired a more complex and extravagant character, as they often combined heteroclite elements from different orders – Ionic, Doric and Corinthian.

Spacious agoras were built or remodelled in virtually all the large cities in the Aegean islands, such as Kos (fig. 532) and Delos. On the latter island in particular (fig. 75), with the enormous growth in trade – and indeed in the slave trade – and the cosmopolitan ambience, as merchants of different ethnic groups flocked there in the period when it was a free port, four agoras were built in Hellenistic times – the agora of the Hermaists or Competaliasts (2nd century BC), the agora of the Delians or the Square Agora (mid-2nd century BC), the agora of Theophrastos (2nd century BC) and the two-storey agora of the Italians (late 2nd century BC). All these agoras were very large, usually rectangular open-air spaces, with peristyles inside and stoas outside. Inside there were alcoves with statues (fig. 79) and sculptural groups of gods and of mortals, as well as exedras, latrines and bathhouses. The Hypostyle Hall on Delos, an unusual building type with internal columns, was a centre of banking and trading transactions, and of intercourse in general, a kind of stock exchange. The *Koinon* of Poseidoniasts of Berytos (fig. 344), a building *ex-voto* "… of the Poseidoniast merchants and shipowners and agents" with residential apartments, religious spaces, niches with statues and so on, likewise documents the cosmopolitan commercial character of the once sacred isle of Apollo.

Two- and even three-storey houses with peristyles (fig. 337), luxurious symposium rooms with elaborate mosaic floors (figs 335, 341, 343) and marble dadoes, with many ancillary facilities, with statues, marble vases, underground water cisterns (fig. 80) existed on Delos, foreshadowing the opulent, often labyrinthine Roman residences of Kos, Rhodes and Lesbos. The funerary monuments became analogous, particularly the tomb complexes of Rhodes (fig. 82), the impressive formations of which are sometimes evocative of natural caves.

The flowering of sculpture was anything but fortuitous on those islands enjoying a commercial and economic heyday. One of the greatest centres of sculpture was Rhodes, representative both of Hellenistic baroque and of the light and airy rococo (fig. 74). Apart from Chares of Lindos, creator of the renowned colossal bronze statue of Helios, which stood in the harbour of Rhodes and was counted among the Seven Wonders of the Ancient World, Rhodes was also the birthplace of the sculptor Menekrates, the "Pheidias" of the famous altar of Zeus and Athena at Pergamon. Apollonios and Tauriskos, creators of the well-known Dirke group, hailed from Tralleis in Asia Minor but were the adopted sons of the Rhodian Menekrates and certainly his pupils. Furthermore, some of the most famous statues of the Late Hellenistic period, such as the Aphrodite (Venus) of Melos (fig. 474) and the Poseidon of Melos (fig. 77), which adorned sanctuaries and public places on that island, are possibly works of the Rhodian School of sculpture. The famous Laokoon group (fig. 572) was also, according to the textual sources, a creation of Rhodian sculptors; even if it should be dated in the first century AD, then it without doubt bears witness to the acme of Rhodian sculpture in Roman times too. The sculptures in the grotto of Tiberius at Sperlonga in Italy were also most probably works of the same Rhodian artists – since their signature was found in the cave. The sculpors were invited to Rome, like many

78. Samothrace, sanctuary of the Great Gods. Parapet decorated with rosette between bucrania, from the tholos of Arsinoe II. Decoration with garlands, bucrania and rosettes is typical of many monuments of the Hellenistic period, particularly grave altars. Source of inspiration was the festive bedecking of the sanctuaries and altars with actual garlands and ox heads.

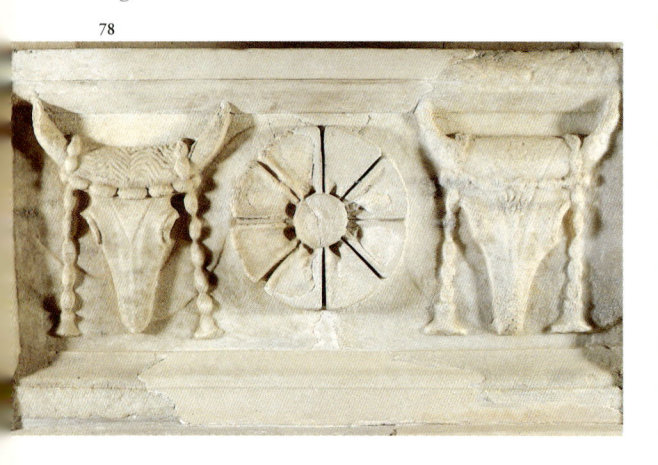

74 | AEGEAN ISLANDS: HISTORICAL AND ARCHAEOLOGICAL BACKGROUND

79. Statue of a wounded Gaul, from Delos. The ruffled hair, the mouth half-open from pain and effort, and the pronounced musculature convey the tension of the struggle and bring to mind baroque figures of the Pergamene School. An enemy arrow was lodged in the hole in the right thigh, while the warrior's Galatian helmet rests beside the same leg. Perhaps dedicated to commemorate the victory of Marios over the Cimbrians and Teutons in 101 BC. Possibly a work by Agasias son of Menophilos, from Ephesos. Athens, National Archaeological Museum.

HELLENISTIC AND ROMAN PERIODS

other Greek sculptors, to decorate temples as well as other civic and private buildings. After all, charming statues of Nymphs with bases imitating natural rock – possibly a Rhodian innovation – adorned sanctuaries, public and private places in Rhodes, creating the illusion of an idyllic natural landscape.

Kos too produced sculptural creations in a distinctive Koan style. In particular the Koan portrait statues, which combine Hellenistic types of himation-clad males, common in many centres, with a realism of Italian inspiration in representing the personal features and personality, bring to mind analogous portrait statues of Delos, in which the classicistic and the realistic style coexist.

Delos attracted the leading sculptors of the age, from Ephesos, Pergamon, Athens and elsewhere, as attested by the surviving inscriptions on the statue bases (the Ephesian Agasias son of Menophilos, the Parian Aristander son of Skopas, the Athenians Dionysios and Timarchides, sons of Timarchides, Sopatros son of Archias from Soloi, and many more). The large number of unfinished works reproducing the same types and with technical innovations bears witness to the operation of sculpture workshops on the island, especially in the Late Hellenistic period. Known types of Classical statues were adapted or remodelled in order to represent gods and mortals, in a rich variety of styles and subjects. Although it is not possible to speak of a school of sculpture on Delos, with a single style, the presence of so many great sculptors with different styles certainly contributed to the dissemination of the styles developing in the major centres of sculpture in those years.

Paros continued to be a major centre of sculpture, with eponymous artists – Aristander the second son of Skopas, Antiphanes son of Thrasonides, Protogenes son of Karpos, Timotheos son of Timotheos, and an anonymous son of Timotheos – recorded mainly in the texts. Indeed, it is possible to speak of a "Neoparian" sculpture workshop, by analogy to the "Neoattic". Relief grave stelai, small cylindrical or cuboid altars, as well as grave *trapezai* with garlands and bucrania, were carved in almost every city, to cover the needs of private and funerary cult (fig. 82).

Humbler arts flourished too on the Aegean islands in these times (fig. 81). Vases of Hadra ware were produced on Rhodes and Crete, pointed-base amphorae for transporting wine and olive oil (fig. 76), were made in almost all the islands, with distinctive traits in each, coins with the particular symbols of each city facilitated trading transactions (fig. 122). Concurrently, black-glaze skyphoi with relief decoration were imported from centres in Asia Minor and elsewhere in the Mediterranean, imitating the luxurious and expensive metal table vessels. Terra sigillata ware and relief lamps, often with interesting mythological and other representations, were imported too. Pottery imports increased during the period of Roman rule, when alongside the Greek vases Italian ones appeared throughout the Mediterranean, while the production and distribution of glass vases was flourishing as well. At this period there was a gradual fall off in sculpture, although the demand for portrait statues of the Roman emperors (fig. 419) and grave stelai invigorated output to a degree in the aforementioned centres. Nonetheless, Parian sculpture continued to thrive, creating a characteristic type of sarcophagus, while grave altars

80. Water cistern on Delos. Eight arches constructed of granite blocks supported the roof of the cistern, the interior dimensions of which are 22.50 x 6.50 m. It received the waters from the drain of the orchestra in the theatre. 3rd c. BC.

81. Gemstone of Early Roman times (1st c. BC-1st c. AD) with intaglio representation of an official, from Minoa on Amorgos. Amorgos Archaeological Collection.

82. Rhodes. Interior of a monumental rock-cut tomb from the tomb complex at Aghios Ioannis. Magnificent tomb complexes of this type, with impressive architectural and other decoration carved in the living rock, occur on Rhodes, bespeaking the prosperity of the city's inhabitants in Hellenistic times. The cinerary urns, the larnakes, the stelai, and the altars with garlands and bucrania, are the usual markers of the tombs.

appeared, as well as stelai with relief representations of gladiators, the new popular "athletes" in Roman times. Furthermore, temples built on high crepises – podia –, agoras, porticoed buildings and luxurious villas that continued the Hellenistic architectural tradition, were enriched with Roman elements. Vespasians (public latrines) and bathhouses (fig. 196) also added a Roman note to public spaces.

Particularly important was the art of mosaic, which created masterpieces depicting mainly subjects from Greek mythology, but also simpler abstract patterns and motifs. The mosaic floors of Mytilene (Menander House [fig. 155]), Kos (fig. 537) and Rhodes are the best known of the period. The economic crisis in the third century AD and the prevailing of the new religion, Christianity, brought to an end the artistic creation of Antiquity. However, this was to be the substrate for the development of Early Christian art, which predominated in the Aegean islands from the fifth century onwards.

HELLENISTIC AND ROMAN PERIODS | 77

THASOS
SAMOTHRACE
IMBROS
LEMNOS
TENEDOS
AGHIOS EFSTRATIOS
LESBOS
PSARA
CHIOS
ANTIPSARA
OINOUSES
SAMOS
IKARIA
PHOURNOI

NORTH AND EAST AEGEAN

Thasos

Chaido Koukouli-Chrysanthaki

The geographical position and the natural resources of Thasos were decisive factors in shaping its cultural identity during prehistoric and historical times. In the northern reaches of the Aegean world, a short distance from the coasts of Europe and Asia, Thasos creatively assimilated cultural influences from both continents. By exploiting the fertility of its soil and the wealth of its subsoil, its inhabitants secured economic self-sufficiency and autonomous development.

Given the rich metal ore deposits, which set their seal on the island's prosperity in historical times, it is no accident that the first human presence on Thasos is associated with mining activity. The Palaeolithic hunters on the island and the opposite mainland with which it was joined had located the ochre – iron oxide – in the abundant lodes of haematite in southern Thasos and had developed techniques of extracting and collecting this mineral (figs 83, 84). The earliest traces of ochre extraction at Tzines in the area of Limenaria date back to the Upper Palaeolithic (*circa* 18,000 BC). Recent research has identified other traces of Palaeolithic man's presence on the island.

No evidence of habitation in the Mesolithic and the Early Neolithic period has yet been found on Thasos. The earliest known traces of settlement date to the late Middle Neolithic period and exist in the south of the island. The Neolithic inhabitants were arable farmers and stock-raisers, who supplemented their diet by hunting and fishing. They lived on low hills close to the sea (settlement at Limenaria [fig. 27]), as well as at mountainous sites some distance inland (settlement at Kastri Theologos). Traces of Neolithic installations have been identified in northern Thasos (acropolis of ancient Thasos), while there are indications that Neolithic man dwelt also in the island's caves (Skala Marion, Drakotrypa Panayas).

The earliest Neolithic settlement known so far is at Limenaria, which was inhabited in the transitional phase between the Middle and Late Neolithic periods (5500-5200 BC, according to carbon 14 dates) and continued into the final phases of the Late Neolithic and the Early Bronze Age (3rd millennium BC). The highland Neolithic settlement at Kastri was particularly dynamic in the final phase of the Late Neolithic period.

Throughout its history Thasos remained bound to the opposite mainland, yet also displays particular cultural traits that refer to the Aegean world. Moreover, the island's early inclusion in the distribution network for obsidian from Melos also attests its direct or indirect contacts with the Aegean.

The prehistoric coastal settlement at Aghios Ioannis Theologos, which dates to the fourth millennium BC, is important for bridging the chronological and cultural gap between the Neolithic and the Early Bronze Age.

Early Bronze Age (3rd millennium BC) settlements exist at coastal sites which were either occupied then for the first time (Skala Sotiros, Aghios Antonios at Potos) or succeeded earlier Neolithic installations (Limenaria, Drakotrypa Cave). The Aegean features of the architecture of this period are enhanced clearly in the walled settlement at Skala Sotiros (fig. 85). A significant find from the excavations here are the fragments of stone anthropomorphic stelai, which were incorporated in the enceinte and the buildings of the settlement (fig. 87). These date to a cultural horizon that is earlier than the settlement but the chronological termini of which have not been determined. However, fortuitous finds from other sites on Thasos (fig. 86), as well as on the opposite coast of Macedonia, bear witness to the diffusion of the anthropomorphic stele in the North Aegean.

In the Late Bronze Age (1600-1050 BC) there was a new movement of the population from the coasts to the hinterland, which was completed in the Early Iron Age (1050-800 BC). The central settlement of this period was at the naturally-fortified site of Kastri, which was reoccupied in the latter years of the Late Bronze Age, after a long interval of desertion. Extensive cemeteries (figs 88, 89) and small satellite settlements around the Kastri settlement bespeak the demographic growth hereabouts during the Early Iron Age.

In the late second and the early first millennium BC Thasos was part of the cultural *koine* that existed in Macedonia east of the River Axios and in Aegean Thrace (fig. 90). Distant from the sea routes leading to the Hellespont, it is not mentioned in the Homeric epics. Nonetheless, the archaeological finds, such as Mycenaean pottery, indicate that the island was not cut off from the Aegean world in either the Late Bronze Age or the Early Iron Age.

Archaeometric analyses of metal objects and slag from smelting metal ores have shown that the inhabitants of the settlement at Kastri were involved in mining the local deposits of lead, copper and iron, and that they were familiar with the alluvial gold in the area of Koinyra, prior to the arrival of the Phoenicians.

Metalliferous Thasos, like the opposite mainland coasts, belongs to the cultural group of Southeast Europe, in which evidence of copper metallurgy exists already from the earliest phase of the Later Neolithic period (5th millennium BC). Lead isotope analyses have demonstrated the use of Thasian copper from the latest phase of the Late Neolithic period, and archaeometric research has confirmed the extraction of silver from the local lead deposits during the Early Bronze Age.

According to the textual sources, at the turn from prehistoric to historical times the island's inhabitants were Thracians. Indeed, one of the island's names preserved in the literary tradition, Odonis, refers to the Thracian tribe of Edonians of Pangaion.

Excavations have uncovered a late eighth-century BC settlement at the northeast edge of the island, on the site were the ancient *polis* of Thasos was founded later. Its destruction in the early seventh

83, 84. Thasos. "Tzines", Limenaria. Excavation in the ochre mine T1. The early miners proceeded from the natural crevices above ground to opening tunnels underground. They used as wedges long bones or horns/antlers of animals – mainly deer – and as percussion tools pebbles. The successive floors bear witness to periodic extractions. Upper Palaeolithic Age (*c.* 18,000 BC).

85. Thasos. Early Bronze Age settlement at Skala Sotiros (3rd millennium BC). The small area of the walled settlement and the form of the buildings designated it as a citadel. Fortified citadels of analogous type are known from the Cyclades, as well as from islands in the Northeast Aegean and the west coast of Asia Minor.

86. Thasos. Anthropomorphic stele. A fortuitous find from the area of Potos in southern Thasos.

87. Thasos. Fragments of marble anthropomorphic stelai with incised and painted decoration, from the Early Bronze Age settlement at Skala Sotiros (3rd millennium BC). The anthropomorphic stelai of Thasos, with their schematic bearded or beardless figures, are among the earliest examples of monumental sculpture in the Aegean world. Thasos Archaeological Museum.

88. Thasos, Kastri. An Early Iron Age tomb (1050-800 BC) from the cemetery of the settlement at Kastri. Characteristic of the stone-built tomb above ground are the corbelled walls that slope inwards, on top of which rests a large schist capstone.

89. Thasos, Kastri. The clusters of family tombs with multiple burials in the *loculi* reflect the clan-based social structure.

century BC is contemporary with the destruction and abandonment of the settlement at Kastri, and marks the end of the prehistoric period on the island.

The appearance in the late eighth and the early seventh century BC of wheel-made vases with Subgeometric decoration, which refer to the Greek colonies in the Macedonian littoral, the Northeast Aegean islands (Lemnos, Lesbos) and the coast of northwest Asia Minor (Troy), signifies for Thasos too the beginning of the movement of the great Greek colonization.

In the early seventh century BC, Parians led by the *oikistes* Telesikles founded at the northeast tip of the Thasos the colony that was to bring the island of Thracians into the Hellenic world. The colonists brought not only the worship of Apollo Pythios, Athena Polias and the mystery cult of Demeter from their homeland, but also the institutions and the culture of the Greek *polis*, which were to transform the prehistoric society of the island. This smooth passage to civilization is recorded by the first lyric poet in Europe, Archilochos. Son of the *oikistes* Telesikles and a first-generation colonist, Archilochos, "although a servant of Lord Enyalios [Ares, god of war]… also knows well the lovely gifts of the Muses" describes in his poems the colony's difficult early years: the battles between the Parians and the other wretched Greeks who followed them, the battles with the local Thracian tribes, the harsh life of the soldier colonist, the nostalgia of the emigrant.

Archaeological finds confirm that the Parians quickly conquered the land that the Delphic oracle had promised them. The colonists built their "conspicuous city" upon the ruined settlement of the Thracians they had expelled. At the summit of the acropolis was the sanctuary to the paternal gods, Apollo Pythios and Athena Poliouchos (fig. 92). At the foot of the acropolis, next to the sanctuaries of Artemis and of Herakles, were the first residential neighbourhoods of the colonists and the agora of the city (figs 93, 94).

The Parian colonists, who had marble-working skills from their homeland, immediately set about quarrying the local marble to build their city and to sculpt statues of their gods to adorn their sanctuaries (figs 96, 97). The numerous Cycladic vases (fig. 95) also reflect ties with the Cyclades and the metropolis Paros. Vases from other Greek cities, jewellery and artifacts, attest to the early opening of the Parian colony to the Hellenic world and the Eastern Mediterranean.

Recent excavations have shown that the colony was soon fortified with a wall. The Gate of the Theoroi, which the city enhanced two centuries later as a sacred symbolic passage between the agora and the sanctuary of Artemis, is a memory of the wall of Telesikles' and Archilochos' city. Outside this first enceinte was discovered the base of the cenotaph of Glaukos, an early colonist declared a hero after his death.

The Parian colonists, masters of the island from the mid-seventh century BC, as finds from the sanctuary of Halyke at the south end of Thasos confirm (fig. 100), expanded to the shores opposite, where they founded the first colonies before the seventh century BC was over: Neapolis (pres. Kavala), Oisyme and Galepsos. By the late sixth century BC the Thasians had completed their colonial state, which encompassed a series of walled *emporeia* between the estuaries of the rivers Strymon and Nestos, as well as two outposts east of the Nestos: Stryme and an *emporeion* of indefinable character to the east of it, known as "Thasion Kephalai". The recent

THASOS | **83**

identification of Berge and its correlation with Thasos extends the Thasians' early colonial penetration beyond the littoral zone into the hinterland of the Strymon Valley.

The city-state of Thasos, metropolis of this extensive colonial state, enjoyed a sustained heyday in the second half of the sixth century BC. The population in the *asty* increased, new neighbourhoods and sanctuaries were established (Thesmophorion, sanctuary of Dionysos), and new temples and cult buildings were constructed in the old sanctuaries (sanctuary of Athena Poliouchos, Herakleion, sanctuary of Halyke). In the late sixth century BC the city minted its first coinage (fig. 99). Around 500 BC it acquired a new defensive wall, 4.5 km. long (fig. 98), and fortified its naval harbour (figs 682, 683).

The mighty walls of Thasos withstood the siege by the Tyrant of Miletos Histiaios, in 494 BC, but did not protect the city in the Persian Wars. In 492 BC the city surrendered to the Persian general Mardonius, who demolished its walls, and was forced to pay tribute to Darius I. During Xerxes' campaign (480 BC), the Thasians spent the mythical sum of 400 talents on a banquet for the king, when he marched across the Thasian *peraia*, *en route* to southern Greece.

When the Persian Wars ended, Thasos attained its zenith, thanks to the incomes from the island and the *peraia*. Intensive cultivation of the arable land and exploitation of the marble and metal resources were achieved through a system of large private properties, which underpinned the aristocratic structure of society. Epigraphic testimonies document the city's legislative interventions to improve urban space and to control the production and trade of wine.

Arts and manufacturing on the island and in its *peraia* continued to reflect the Parian colony's Ionian roots. The temples and the cult buildings kept the small scale of Cycladic architecture, with the sculptural decoration drawing on the thematic repertoire and style of Archaic art in the Cyclades. The Parian tradition formed the character of Thasian sculpture too (figs 96, 97, 101) and survived in Thasian vase-making until the late sixth-early fifth century BC. The pottery also displays dynamic influences from other cities, such as Chios and Athens, while the motifs in the architectural terracottas that adorned the roofs of Late Archaic buildings refer to the Aeolian cities of northwestern Asia Minor.

In the first half of the fifth century BC the names of outstanding Thasian citizens were known throughout the Hellenic world, such as the athlete Theagenes, who was victor in two Olympiads (*disolympios*), in 480 and 476 BC, and the great painter Polygnotos, renowned for his works in Athens.

In 477 BC Thasos joined the First Athenian League, of which it was evidently a powerful member, judging by the high annual tax it contributed. However, it broke away in 465 BC, when it realized that its mines and colonies on the coast of Thrace were threatened by Athenian expansion into the Strymon estuary. The head-on clash with Athens ended in total submission. In 464 BC Thasos pulled down its walls, surrendered

90. Thasos, Kastri. Late Bronze Age handmade vases from the settlement. Thasos Archaeological Museum.

91. Thasos. Seal for stamping the handle of a Thracian amphora: ΘΑΣΙΩΝ ΑΣΤΥΚΡΕΩΝ. Thasian wine was stored and traded in transport amphorae made in special workshops all over the island and dependent on the vineyard owners. The city's control of the production and trade of wine is indicated also by the stamps on the amphora handles, already from the early 5th c. BC. At first only symbols were used, but from the early 4th c. BC inscriptions appear with the ethnic of the city (ΘΑΣΙΩΝ) and the names of the responsible annual archon, the maker or the owner of the vineyard-wine, accompanied by their symbols.

92. Thasos. View of the acropolis of ancient Thasos. Visible at the top of the acropolis, which to this day "is crowned by wild woodland", as Archilochos described it, is the monumental terrace of the sanctuary of Athena Poliouchos.

93, 94. Thasos. The agora of the ancient city, which lay at the foot of the acropolis.

THASOS | 85

95. Thasos. A Cycladic plate found in the sanctuary of Artemis, in which it was a votive offering. Work of a Parian potter, it echoes the polychrome monumental painting of its period. The mythical hero Bellerophon, riding on Pegasos, the winged horse presented to him by Athena, slays the Chimaera, a terrible monster with the head of a lion, the body of a goat and a snake as a tail. In the mid-7th c. BC Cycladic vase-painting, with its rich decoration and daemonic figures reflecting influences from Oriental art, presents the first depictions of Greek myths and promotes the human figure, which was to be the dominant subject in Greek art in the ensuing centuries.
Thasos Archaeological Museum.

its fleet, lost its colonies and adapted its institutions to conform to the Athenian democratic model. The economic recession after the defeat is recorded in the dramatic drop in its annual tax to the Athenian League, to three talents. Nonetheless, the re-appearance of Thasos in the fiscal lists of the Athenian League for the interval 446-443 BC, with tax of 30 talents, points to economic recovery and restoration of partial control of its colonies in Thrace.

During the Peloponnesian War (431-405 BC) Thasos vacillated between the opposing camps of the Athenians and the Spartans, remaining for long periods on the Athenian side.

The panhellenic conflict does not seem to have impeded the movement of people or the transport of goods. In the late fifth century BC Hippokrates arrived on the island and stayed there for two years. Thasos renewed its legislation regulating trade in Thasian wine, which circulated all over the Greek world. At Athens, as Aristophanes' comedy *Lysistrata* narrates, the women bound their oath with Thasian wine. Polygnotos decorated the Poikile Stoa in the Agora, and the Thasian poet Hegemon entertained the Athenians with his parodies and became a friend of Alcibiades.

In 411 BC Thasos, swept up in the tide of upheavals between oligarchs and democrats in Athens, with the support of Athenian oligarchs reinstated the city's old institutions and in 410 BC went over to the Spartan side. After its violent return to the Athenian camp (407 BC), it paid the heavy price of defeat at the end of the war. The Spartan general Lysander captured Thasos immediately after his victory at Aigos Potamoi (405 BC) and deceiving the democrats with Attic sympathies who had gone into hiding, gathered them all in the sanctuary of Herakles, where he slaughtered them in cold blood.

In the first half of the fourth century BC Thasos enjoyed a new period of prosperity. A member of the Second Athenian League from 375 BC, it rescued the colony of Stryme from the Maronians and strengthened its presence in the *peraia* by founding a new colony, Krenides, in the rich interior of the gold-bearing Pangaion Mountains, in 360 BC.

The archaeological finds confirm the island's economic and cultural floruit in the first half of the fourth century BC. The spectacular increase of population in the countryside was certainly related to the intensification of viticulture. Thasian wine, stored in transport amphorae stamped with the name of the city and of its archons, travelled all over the ancient world (figs 72, 91). It was particularly popular on the coasts of the Euxine Pontus and in the Thracian heartland, where Thasian merchants were accorded privileged treatment by the Thracian dynasts.

Thanks to the prosperity, it was possible to implement new large-scale construction programmes. The walls were repaired and the agora was laid out as the political and religious centre of the city. In the early fourth century BC the temple of Zeus Agoraios was erected in the main square and the buildings intended to house the civic authorities were put up on its northeast side.

However, in the mid-fourth century BC the political equilibrium in the North Aegean changed, with the appearance of the new rising power of Hellenism, the Kingdom of Macedon.

96, 97. Thasos. The ram-bearing (*kriophoros*) kouros in the Thasos Museum is one of the earliest works of Thasian sculpture. The Parian colonists brought to their new homeland not only the characteristic figure of Archaic art, the kouros, but also the monumental dimension of the colossal kouros that Naxian and Attic artists had represented in marble. The statue is dated *circa* 600 BC and was destined for the sanctuary of Apollo Pythios. It is not certain whether it represents the god or the dedicator bringing the animal for sacrifice to him. Because of the crack in the marble, the statue was abandoned unfinished and later used as building material in the city wall. Fig. 96 shows the upper part of the kouros in the entrance to the first Archaeological Museum on Thasos (1918).

THASOS | 87

98. Thasos, Silenus Gate. The carving of relief divine and daemonic figures on the marble jambs of the gateways is a particular feature of the defensive wall of Thasos, which reflects influences from the East. The earliest in the series of gateway reliefs is that of the ithyphallic Silenus, which is contemporary with the construction of the wall, around 500 BC. The small rock-cut niche in front of the figure was for placing offerings to the guardian of the gateway and protector of the city.

99. Silver stater of Thasos, 520-510 BC. Silenus lifting a Maenad in his arms. The first coinage of Thasos is dated to the closing decades of the 6th c. BC and is one of the earliest in the Hellenic world. The early coins are silver and feature daemonic figures from the Dionysiac cycle, Sileni and Maenads. Paris, Bibliothèque Nationale – Cabinet des Médailles.

Thasos first lost Krenides, which Philip II captured and renamed Philippi (356 BC). This was followed by the conquest of the other cities in the Thasian *peraia* and then by the annexation of the metropolis Thasos to the Macedonian realm.

The loss of its political integrity as a city-state had little effect on the thriving economic and cultural life of Thasos, which by preserving its domestic autonomy remained, despite the loss of its *peraia*, a flourishing city in the Kingdom of Macedon. The Thasian wine trade was dynamic until the mid-third century BC and the quarrying of Thasian marble was intensified to cover not only internal demand but also trading outside the island. With the input of wealthy citizens too, the construction programmes continued in the agora, on the wall and on other public buildings in the city. The theatre acquired a monumental proscenium and a huge building for public assemblies was put up next to the sanctuary of Herakles. The splendid choregic monuments in the sanctuary of Dionysos testify not only to the flourishing theatrical culture but also to the flowering of Thasian sculpture, which followed the evolution of the Classical tradition in Hellenistic times (fig. 102).

As part of the Hellenistic *oikoumene* formed after the death of Alexander the Great, Thasos survived the clashes between the Hellenistic kingdoms and creatively assimilated the diffuse religious and cultural currents circulating in the Eastern Mediterranean. Towards the end of the fourth century BC a new festival was introduced on Thasos, the Alexandreia. The small temple in the square between the agora and the sanctuary of Artemis was most probably dedicated to the cult of the deified Alexander.

Prior to Macedonia's subjugation to the Romans, Thasos formed a new framework of autonomy as a free city and an ally of Rome (192 BC). The minting of silver tetradrachms, jointly with Maroneia, also an ally of Rome, defined the new beginning. With the construction of the Via Egnatia, the role of the Thracian *peraia*, through which the road artery passed, was upgraded. A loyal ally of Rome in the Mithridatan War (88 BC), Thasos regained part of its *peraia* as a gift of the Roman Senate (80 BC). However, this was lost, along with other privileges, when the island found itself on the side of the defeated after the battle of Philippi (42 BC). With an intervention of Augustus, the Thasians later returned to this part of their *peraia*, where their rights were ratified by decrees of the emperors Vespasian and Trajan, in return for the upkeep of the section of the Via Egnatia there.

Although the political and economic role of Thasos in the region was downgraded after the founding of the Roman *colonia* at Philippi, Thasos never became the economic or the cultural *peraia* of this city. The flourishing trade in Thasian marble secured its economic self-sufficiency and its cultural infrastructure determined its quality as a Greek city in the Roman East.

Literary and epigraphic testimonies describe the social stratification and the ideological-cultural physiognomy of Roman Thasos, which is revealed also by the archaeological finds from the agora (figs 93, 94), the sanctuaries and the civic buildings, as well as from the private houses and the necropolises. The citizens of the ruling class, who were pro-Caesar and ardent patriots, were united around the cult of the emperor, who ensured them political authority. The first

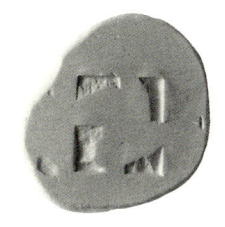

100. Thasos, sanctuary of Halyke. Sporadic finds and a cult cave have been revealed from the sanctuary of the 7th c. BC. The two oikoi with square *eschara*-altars at the centre date to the 6th c. BC. Inscriptions attest the worship of Apollo and other gods, such as the Dioskouroi, who were protectors of seafarers. At the centre of an area in which there was intensive marble quarrying, the sanctuary was enhanced as a revered *locus sanctus* for the city and the countryside, which continued in use well into Late Antiquity. The quarrying of marble on the peninsula continued at the same rate even in Early Christian times. The ancient temples were succeeded by two Early Christian basilicas on the nearby hill.

members of the imperial family to be worshipped in the central square of the agora were Augustus and his deified adopted sons, Gaius Caesar and Lucius Caesar. Statues and honorary pedestals of the emperors and of Roman patrons were also erected in the agora. The Thasians honoured Emperor Hadrian, beloved of the Greek cities, with a magnificent statue in a special building in the agora. New buildings were erected there in Roman times, the theatre was converted into an arena, the city acquired an odeum, its streets were paved and a system of drains-sewers was installed. A monumental arch was raised for Emperor Caracalla. Particularly prominent was the presence of affluent citizens, both men and women, who donated landholdings to the city, undertook the expenses of repairing public edifices and sanctuaries (fig. 103), and set up for their families honorific monuments, exedras, statues and monumental tombs. Women were distinguished as priestesses in the sanctuaries of the gods and in the imperial cult.

Disaster struck the city of Thasos when it was raided by the Heruls in the second half of the third century AD. It recovered, however, and prospered again in Early Christian times. The total destruction of the city came – as at Philippi – in the early seventh century AD, as a result of a catastrophic earthquake and barbarian incursions.

Thasos was known for its antiquities, thanks to European travellers who visited the island from the fifteenth to the nineteenth century. In the late nineteenth and the early twentieth century the first excavators came, whose aim was to enrich the museums of their homelands with their finds, which were dispatched to the Musée du Louvre in Paris and the Archaeological Museum in Istanbul.

The first systematic excavations on Thasos commenced in 1911, under the direction of the French School of Archaeology, which continues its archaeological investigations to this day.

Systematic research by the Greek Archaeological Service began after the Second World War. Since 1969 this has been extended to the prehistoric period.

101. Thasos. The head in the Wix Collection in the Copenhagen Glyptothek was considered to be from a kouros, until it was found to belong to a fragment of the torso of a sphinx found in the ancient city of Thasos. Work of 570-560 BC. Thasos Archaeological Museum.

102. Thasos. Head of a statue of Dionysos on a choregic monument in the sanctuary of Dionysos. The patron god of the theatre, flanked by the statues of Comedy, Tragedy and Nychterinos, was housed in a temple-shaped building. The Thasian sculptor remodelled an Attic creation of the School of Praxiteles or Leochares. Second half of 4th c. BC. Thasos Archaeological Museum.

103. Thasos. Aphrodite on a dolphin. An *ex-voto* from the sanctuary of Poseidon, where Aphrodite was also worshipped. The half-naked goddess rides the waves on the back of a dolphin, on whose tail sits her infant son Eros. Remodelling of a Praxitelean prototype. 2nd-1st c. BC. Thasos Archaeological Museum.

103

Samothrace

DIMITRIS MATSAS

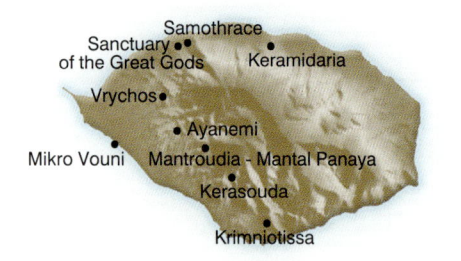

The small isolated island of Samothrace was on the frontiers of the ancient Greek world. Nonetheless, it was distinguished from neighbouring Imbros and more distant Tenedos because it was the locus of the mysteries whose fame radiated far and wide throughout Antiquity.

Samothrace dominates the Thracian Sea, by virtue of its imposing mountainous massif, 1664 metres a.s.l., and lies 22 miles from the coast of Thrace. The seafarer approaching this richly watered island – unusual by Aegean standards – had to confront the lack of a natural harbour. Samothrace, approximately 182 sq. km. in area, is situated at the north edge of the Aegean continental shelf. The sheer slopes on the southeast coast continue beneath the sea, to a depth of 1000 metres, in the North Aegean trough. Upon the earlier metamorphic sedimentary rocks are an ophiolitic geological sequence and neritic sediments. The granite massif in the central part of the island has intruded the ophiolites and post-sediments, while volcanic rocks extend on its periphery, on the lowest altitudes of which are Pliocene and more recent marine deposits.

Archaeological research to date has found no traces of habitation on Samothrace before the sixth millennium BC. The coastal settlement on the Mikro Vouni tell, in the southwest part of the island, has yielded remains of human occupation in the Late Neolithic (late 6th-first quarter of 4th millennium BC), the Middle and the Late Bronze Age, and was abandoned around 1700 BC (figs 104-106). The excavation at Mikro Vouni has included investigation of the cultural sequence at the site, as this is documented in the deposits some 9 metres deep on the highest central terrace of the tell, and horizontal exploration of the uppermost building levels in the same area. On present evidence it emerges that the houses of the final phase of the settlement, that is the end of the Middle Bronze Age, were single-storey and of rectangular plan, with two rooms, measuring about 4 x 9 metres. They stood side by side, with narrow passages between them. The walls had a stone socle of large beach pebbles and an upper structure most probably of mud brick reinforced with a timber frame. In the Early Bronze Age (mid-3rd millennium BC) there were also stone walls, in one case with herringbone masonry. The floors are of beaten earth, which in the Late Neolithic period was reinforced with sea shingle, while in the earliest phase of the settlement they had a bedding of pebbles. Stone-paved floors have only been located in parts of external spaces.

From its early phases, the settlement at Mikro Vouni seems to have been incorporated in the Aegean exchange network. Obsidian from Melos reached Samothrace already in the Late Neolithic period. However, the most important finds that confirm these exchanges come from the Middle Bronze Age levels (19th-18th century BC). Belonging in the developed framework of the palatial economy of Crete, perhaps of Knossos, and most probably related to the supply of metals from the Northeast Aegean region, these are Minoan documents in clay (fig. 104), which

104

92 | NORTH AND EAST AEGEAN

are the earliest to have been found so far away from Crete. They comprise two Linear A inscriptions and seal impressions with hieroglyphic signs-syllabograms, dominant among which are the double axe and the cuttlefish, symbols of religious character, which perhaps point to a religious mantle for the activities of the Minoan ruling class in the Aegean at that time.

For the Early Iron Age, the textual tradition refers to the successive settling of two Thracian tribes on the island, the Dardanians and the Saians. The Thracian settlements dating from the end of the Late Bronze Age (11th century BC) onwards are located in naturally or artificially fortified sites, at a short or longer distance from the sea and concentrated mainly in the south, southwest and west parts of the island, in a zone between the 300 and 600 metre contours. These were abandoned in the late fourth-early third century BC, when the Thracians were incorporated into the flourishing Greek society of Samothrace.

The most important site to have been investigated is the acropolis and the settlement on the summit and slopes respectively of Vrychos Hill, west of the present village of Chora. The construction of the enceinte is dated to the beginning of the Early Iron Age, while habitation on the hill slopes, where five megalithic tombs have been identified, is dated to both phases of the Early Iron Age (11th-6th century BC). Greek colonists reached Samothrace in two streams, first a small one from northwest Asia Minor or Lesbos, *circa* 700 BC, and second a larger one from Samos, in the early sixth century BC. As research in the sanctuary of the Great Gods and in two rural sanctuaries of Cybele, as Meter (Mother) or Meter Oreia, has shown, relations between the Greek colonists and the Thracian population were peaceful.

By the early fifth century BC Samothrace belonged to the satrapy of Thrace and in the naval battle of Salamis a Samothracian ship fought on the side of the Persians. The island's annual contribution to the treasury of the First Athenian League was initially six talents, which was re-

104. Samothrace, Mikro Vouni. Minoan clay nodulus. On one face a seal impression with the first part of a Minoan Libation Formula (hieroglyphic signs-syllabograms of the double axe and the cuttlefish), on the other an incised inscription in Linear A script (19th-18th c. BC). Samothrace Archaeological Museum.

105. Samothrace, Mikro Vouni. Early Bronze Age tripod vase of closed shape with incised and impressed decoration. Late 3rd millennium BC. Samothrace Archaeological Museum.

106. Samothrace, Mikro Vouni. Building remains of the late 3rd millennium BC.

107. Samothrace. Plan of the sanctuary of the Great Gods.

1-3. Unidentified Late Hellenistic buildings (1st c. BC)
4. Unfinished Early Hellenistic building (late 4th-early 3rd c. BC)
5. Medieval fortification (10th c.)
6. Milesian Dedication (2nd half 3rd c. BC)
7. Hestiatoria (late 4th c. BC-early 2nd c. AD)
8, 10. Spaces of unspecified purpose (3rd-2nd c. BC)
9. Archaistic niche (3rd-2nd c. BC)
11. Stoa (1st half 3rd c. BC)
12. Nike Monument (1st half 2nd c. BC)
13. Theatre (1st half 2nd c. BC)
14. Altar Court (340-330 BC)
15. "Hieron" (325-150 BC)
16. "Hall of Votive Gifts" (4th c. BC)
17. Hall of Choral Dancers (c. 340 BC)
19. Sacred rock (1st half 4th c. BC)
20. Rotunda of Arsinoe II (288-270 BC)
21. Structure Orthostate (1st half 4th c. BC)
22. Sacristy (1st c. AD)
23. Anaktoron (1st c. AD)
24. Dedication of Philip III and Alexander IV (323-317 BC)
25. Circular area (late 5th-early 4th c. BC)
26. Propylon of Ptolemy II (285-281 BC)
27. South Necropolis (mid-6th c. BC-early 2nd c. AD)
28. Doric Rotunda (2nd half 4th c. BC)
29. Neorion (275-250 BC)
30. Hestiatorion (mid-3rd c. BC)

108. Samothrace. Aerial photograph of the sanctuary of the Great Gods with the Eastern Hill and the circular area (fig. 107:25). c. 400 BC.

109. Samothrace, sanctuary of the Great Gods. View of the "Hieron" with the restored part of the colonnade on the façade (fig. 107:15). 150-125 BC.

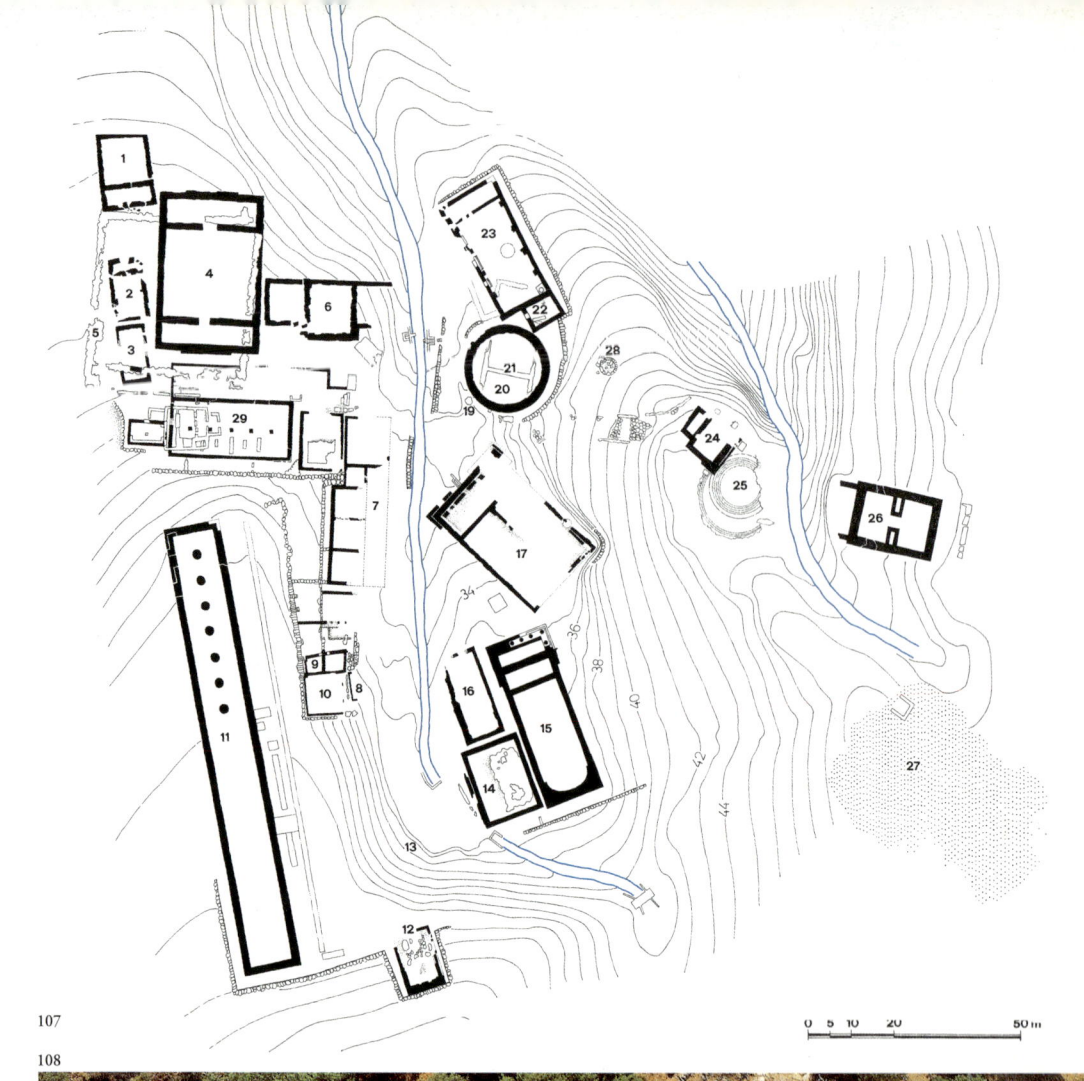

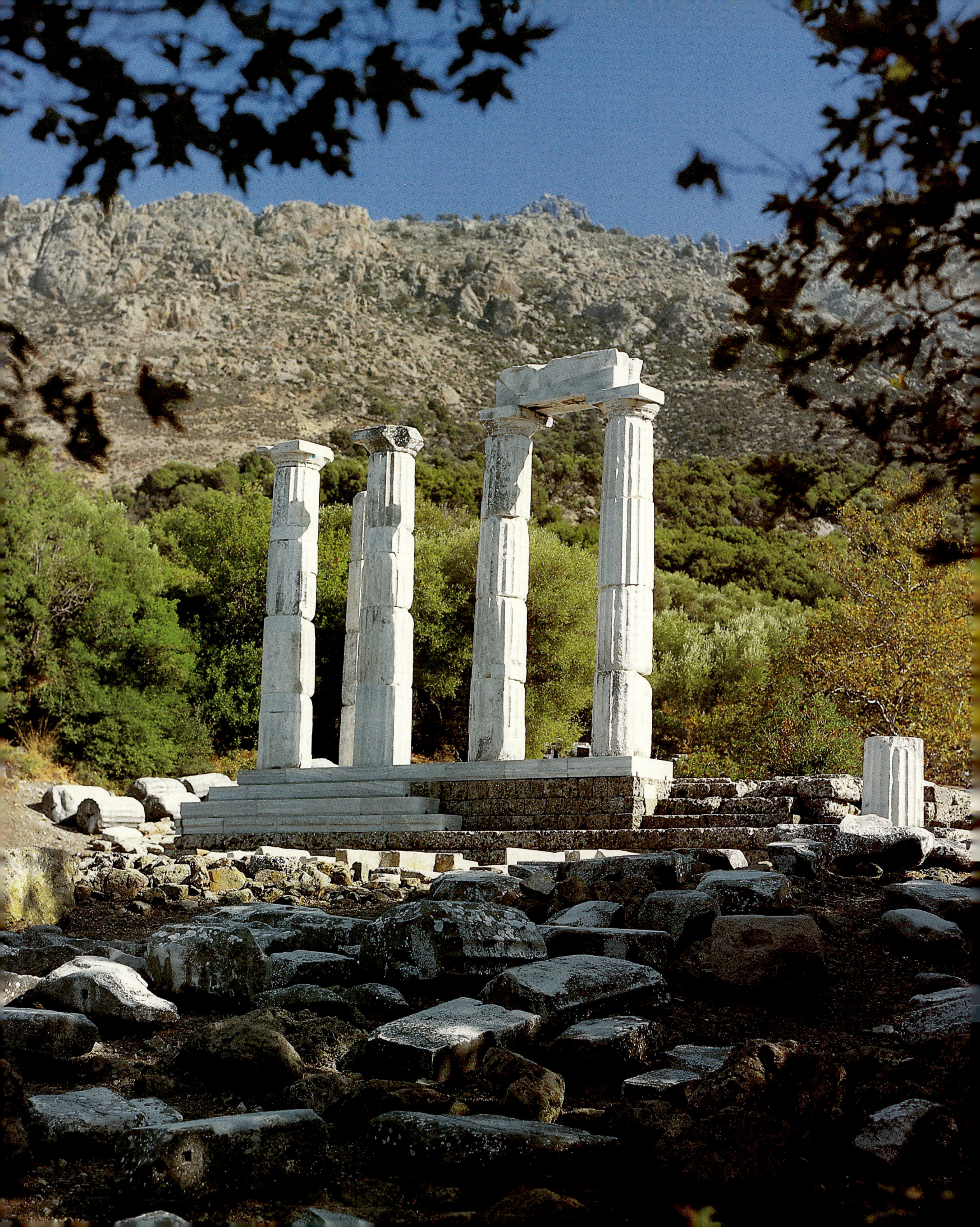

110. Samothrace. Part of the marble relief frieze of the Hall of Choral Dancers, which probably referred to the ritual – of the marriage of Kadmos and Harmonia – which was re-enacted inside the building (*c.* 340 BC). Samothrace Archaeological Museum.

111. Samothrace, Southern Necropolis. Terracotta figurines of seated, nude, armless females. Of religious significance, these objects were connected with the cult of a Great Goddess and fertility. Late 2nd or early 1st c. BC. Samothrace Archaeological Museum.

duced later to two. At the end of the Peloponnesian War (404 BC) Samothrace came under Spartan control. A brief interval of Athenian sovereignty followed, prior to the King's Peace (386 BC), after which Samothrace returned to the Spartans until 378/7 BC, when it became a member of the Second Athenian League. In 340 BC it belonged officially to the Kingdom of Macedon. The mint of Samothrace, which had closed *circa* 475 BC, resumed operation in the late fourth century BC.

The ancient city of Samothrace was located on the northwest coast, in the northern foothills of a counterscarp of the central mountainous massif. The most impressive feature today is the wall, which is 2.4 km. long and dates from the fourth (?) to the third century BC. Inside the ancient city an important section of the Medieval fortification survives, which was built when Emperor John VIII surrendered the island to the Genoese Gattilusi family (1431-1433).

On the north shore, five kilometres east of the ancient city, a complex of pottery workshops (4th century BC-3rd century AD) has been investigated. The excavation of one of the dump of wasters (second half 4th-3rd century BC) yielded a considerable number of stamped amphorae handles, which also indicate the dispersion (Thracian littoral, Troas, Euxine Pontus, Balkan heartland) of Samothracian amphorae in the regions to which the island's wine was most probably exported.

Just southwest of the ancient city, inside two gullies, is the sanctuary of the Great Gods, the most important religious buildings in which extend between the west and the east stream (figs 107-109). From the nineteenth century interest in the Great Gods and the mysteries caught the imagination of European archaeologists. The first excavation on Samothrace was made in the sanctuary in 1854, while the French diplomat Charles Champoiseau discovered the state of Nike (Victory) there in 1863 (fig. 114). Over a century and a half of archaeological investigations at the site have not been sufficient to cover the gap in the limited literary corpus of references and allusions, nor to reveal the essence and the content of the mysteries. And even though we know the names of the Great Gods (Axieros, Axiokersa, Axiokersos and Kasmilos), we do not understand the initiation, from the rite of which we know some details, such as the "*homologia*" (confession) that the initiate made about the most illicit act in his life, the purple girdle that participants in the mysteries fastened below their abdomen, and the iron finger rings they wore, representing their union with the gods. The myths associated with the mysteries

96 | NORTH AND EAST AEGEAN

were privilege, since they were central themes of the rites. However, it seems that the Samothracian myth of abduction concerned a divine couple, perpetrator and victim respectively, Kadmos, the traveller of foreign origin, and Harmonia, who was found at sea and brought home by her brothers Dardanos and Iasion/Aetion, who are frequently identified as the two basic Kabeiroi/Great Gods. This salvation is related to the purpose of the initiation, which was rescue from hazards at sea. The epiphany of the four on Samothrace was linked with the happy event of the couple's marriage, which was the climax of the initiation experience, in the Hall of Choral Dancers (figs 107:17, 110). Prior to this, the participants in the mysteries, after the preliminary initiation within the circular area, proceeded with eyes closed towards the centre of the sacred space, where they began to search for the lost goddess whose abduction was already a fact at the start of the rite in the Hall of Choral Dancers. The last was obviously the initiation building, the Anaktoron or Telesterion, which view necessitates a reconsideration of the earlier identification of the building (fig. 107:23), while the identification of the "Hieron" (fig. 107:15), as well as its relation to the initiation in to the second degree of the mysteries, "*epopteia*" (supervision), is doubted.

Excavations have given a picture of the sanctuary and its development (fig. 107). There are indications of religious activity from the seventh century BC, but construction of the monumental buildings began only in the fourth century BC and is associated with the generosity and the political interests of the royal house of Macedon, already from the reign of Philip II. Royal support continued in the time of the successors to Alexander the Great and the sanctuary enjoyed its heyday during the third and second centuries BC. The marriage of Arsinoe, the first of the great females in the family of Ptolemies, to the King of Thrace Lysimachos, and then to her brother Ptolemy II, was of special significance for Samothrace, on account of the royal couples' close religious relations with the island's sanctuary (fig. 78). Samothrace passed under Egyptian sovereignty in the second half of the third century BC, while towards the end of the century the first signs of Roman interest in the sanctuary appeared. The island passed into the hands of Philip V after 200/199 BC, to be inherited by his son and successor Perseus, who after the battle of Pydna (168 BC) sought refuge on Samothrace, where he surrendered finally to the Romans. Worship of the Great Gods and initiation into their mysteries ceased at the end of the fourth century AD. The

112. Samothrace, south necropolis. Cinerary black-figure pelike attributed to the "Eucharides Painter", with scene of the vintage in the presence of the gods (left Herakles, at the centre Dionysos). *C.* 500 BC. Samothrace Archaeological Museum.

SAMOTHRACE | 97

Early Christian finds from Samothrace show that it followed the fate of the sanctuary of the Great Gods only after the reign of Justinian, when the decline of settlement characteristic of the early Middle Byzantine period began.

Excavations in the necropolises have brought to light numerous burials, both cremations (6th-4th century BC, 1st century BC) and inhumations (4th century BC-2nd century AD). The latter include burials in amphorae and pithoi, composite sarcophagi of tailored slabs (*thekai*), stone sarcophagi and tile-shelter tombs, while there are also two marble monuments (1st century BC-1st century AD). Noteworthy among the finds from the necropolises is the Attic pottery (6th-4th centuries BC). The earliest Attic vases are almost all black-figure and date from the second half to the end of the sixth century BC. Imports of Attic vases – now red-figure – were repeated around 470 BC and continued throughout the fifth century BC. The Attic vases used in cremations during the sixth and fifth centuries BC were amphorae, pelikes (fig. 112) and sometimes hydrias, while those used in funerary rituals were kraters, cups and bowls. The frequent appearance of Dionysiac subjects is associated with Dionysos' quality as god of death and resurrection. From the mid-sixth century BC local vases as well as those from other regions, such as Lemnos and an as yet unidentified East Aegean workshop, were used as cinerary urns. Most of the pottery of the Hellenistic and Roman periods is mould-made (2nd-late 1st century BC), black-glaze kantharoi (3rd century BC), pyxides (*circa* 250-225 BC) and unguentaria (3rd-1st century BC). Lamps were used frequently in mortuary rites, in which terracotta figurines (figs 111, 113) also played an important role, since they were not intended as grave goods but were of religious and secular character. Terracotta figurines were not common in the necropolises of Samothrace before the Hellenistic period, whereas there is a remarkable proliferation of figurines in first half of the third and the second half of the first century BC. The majority represent enthroned female figures (fig. 111). The imported figurines must come from some unknown site on the Asia Minor coast with strong influences from Myrina on Lemnos.

At the beginning of the Hellenistic period (last quarter of 4th century BC) gold suddenly appeared, but the gold jewellery from the Hellenistic burials on Samothrace is inferior to that found at other sites in the Aegean. Mainly gold wreaths, earrings and finger rings are encountered, the best examples of which were imported from centres perhaps in Macedonia and possibly in Asia Minor.

Noteworthy among the other metal finds from the necropolises are the small bronze vases, mainly phialai and oinochoai (late 6th-5th century BC), and the bronze mirrors, the earliest of which date from the second half of the fourth century BC. Almost all the bone and ivory objects, the most elegant of which are the little pyxides, date from the Early Roman period. Last, an exceptionally important category of finds from the necropolises of Samothrace is the glassware. The earliest glass objects (second half of 6th century BC) are made in the core technique, which lived on into Early Roman times. A small number of "cast" glass bowls date to the second half of the first century BC, but the blown glass that reached Samothrace at the end of the century quickly ousted all other techniques, while blown-glass bottles superceded the clay unguentaria of corresponding shape.

113. Samothrace, Southern Necropolis. Terracotta figurine of winged Eros, 250-225 BC. Samothrace Archaeological Museum.

114. Samothrace, sanctuary of the Great Gods. The Nike (Victory) of Samothrace (190-180 BC). The Nike wears a flimsy chiton and a heavy himation, which, due to the strong wind and the violent movement, cling to the body, emphasizing its plasticity. Majestic, with wings still outspread, she has just alighted on the prow of a ship, an allusion to the dedication of the statue by the victor in a naval battle. It is very probable that the commander of the allied fleet, the Rhodian admiral Eudamos, dedicated the statue in the panhellenic sanctuary, after his victory over the forces of Antiochos III (190 BC). The work, created by the Rhodian Pythokritos, is one of the most famous original sculptures of the Hellenistic period and representative of the Rhodian "baroque" style then in vogue. Paris, Musée du Louvre.

NORTH AND EAST AEGEAN

114

Imbros

DIMITRIS MATSAS

Imbros (Turk. Gökçeada), in a particularly important location for navigation, lies just 9.5 miles northwest of the entrance to the Hellespont and even closer to the shore of the Thracian Chersonese (Gallipoli Peninsula), 11 miles from Lemnos – together with which it is frequently mentioned in history – and 13.5 miles from Samothrace. It is 285 sq. km. in area and has a hilly terrain with volcanic rocks (andesite, lava, tuff) and valleys on flysch, which together with limestone are the oldest sedimentary formations.

Homer describes Imbros as "*paipaloessa*" (precipitous), an epithet only befitting of its north coast, which is dominated by the highest peak, just over 450 metres a.s.l. Information on the island's prehistoric and historical past is based on recent archaeological surveys which, after many years of inactivity, aimed to record and to salvage a host of antiquities scattered all over Imbros. Important too are the data from the excavation of the Yenibademli/Aghios Floros tell in the Büyükdere Valley (Megalos Potamos of the Imbrians), about 1.7 km. southwest of the village of Kaleköy (Kastro) and 1.5 km. from the present beach in Kale Bay (Aghios Nikolaos). This river, the largest and most important on the island, is the Ilissos of the Athenian cleruchs who settled on Imbros in the early fifth century BC. Miltiades, son of Kypselos, was most probably the first eponymous Athenian to disembark (494 BC) on the island, which the Persians had captured in 509 BC. The Deme of "the Athenians in Imbros" was organized after the model of the Athenian body politic, followed the Attic calendar (*menologion*) and used Athenian types along with local symbols on the coinage.

The earliest traces of human presence date back to the time when Imbros was still joined to the Gallipoli Peninsula and have been found on the surface over a large area in the southeastern part of the island, with a stone industry reminiscent of corresponding Palaeolithic sites in the region of Marmara. One possibly Early Neolithic site is known from surface finds, on a low tell in the southwest part of Imbros, with pottery similar to that of the earliest phase at the site of Hoca Çeşme on the eastern delta of the Evros (anc. Hebros) in East Thrace. This tell also has surface sherding of the Late Neotlithic period (late 6th-early 4th millennium BC), as does the tell on Cape Pyrgos/Yuvalı (anc. Naulochos) on the southwest shore. According to surface finds, the last site, which owes its name to the Medieval fortification on the top of the tell, was inhabited also from the Early to the Late Bronze Age (3rd-2nd millennium BC) and in Hellenistic and Roman times (fig. 120). Surface finds of the Late Neolithic period are also reported from the sites of Vaniyeri/V'ni I and V'ni III on the northeast coast.

During the Early Bronze Age (3rd millennium BC) there was an increase in the number of sites on Imbros, from most of which surface pottery typical of the phases Troy I and II (*circa* 2920-2450 BC) has been collected, while characteristic is the absence of pottery typical of Troy III-IV (*circa* 2450-1700 BC). In addition to the aforementioned Pyrgos/Yuvalı and the Yenibademli/Aghios Floros tell, which will be referred to more thoroughly below, nine settlements that are coastal or very close to the present shoreline have been located, all on the southeast, east and northeast coasts, and ranging in area from 600 sq. m. to at least 2.2 hectares. At six sites fortifications have been noted, common characteristics of which are the horseshoe bastions and the ramps leading to the entrances to the enceintes. Their concentration in the east part of Imbros, opposite the Thracian Chersonese and the Hellespont, points to the island's significance in maritime communications and trade of the period (fig. 115).

The second millennium BC is represented most fully at Pyrgos/Yuvalı, where one Minoan sherd and three Mycenaean sherds with painted decoration of local production were collected. The Mycenaean presence on the island is also confirmed by pottery from Yenibademli/Aghios Floros, while on a Linear B tablet from Knossos there is mention of the ethnic *i-mi-ri-jo* (Imbrios).

The prehistoric settlement at the Yenibademli/Aghios Floros tell (approx. area 1.5 hectares, present altitude 18 m.) was situated on the coast of the southeast creek of a bay occupying the entire north (lower) part of the present valley with Quartenary alluvial deposits (fig. 116). The ongoing excavation, which commenced in 1996 and is part of a wider archaeological research project in the Troas, focused on Troy, has revealed remains of a fortified enceinte on the west terrace and in the south part of the tell, where the wall is about 5 metres thick a ramp securing access to the fortification from the southwest.

The settlement sequence has been investigated mainly in the central-east and north parts of the tell, where so far six "architectural levels" have been investigated, which yielded homogeneous pottery that follows the shapes and decoration of the tradition of Troy I and is dated to the first half of the third millennium BC. The deposit 2.00-3.35 metres thick that has been excavated here represents the upper part of the cultural sequence at the site, while a deposit 2-3 metres thick, which awaits excavation, most probably includes also the Pre-Troy phases (Late Neolithic), as at Mikro Vouni on Samothrace.

The architectural plan in general comprises groups of buildings of rectangular ground-plan and, in the later architectural levels, with partywalls on the long sides, a feature observed also at Mikro Vouni on Samothrace. The walls were built of mud bricks on stone socles (in one case there is a wall entirely of stone) and the flat roofs were supported by wooden posts.

In addition to the pottery, the Northeast Aegean Culture of the third millennium BC is represented by the clay and stone figurines, mainly of females, with schematic decoration (figs 117, 118), which are an aspect of the inhabitants' ideology, and in the enigmatic stone anchors. In the area of the ramp on the southwest slope of the tell, five architectural levels have been uncovered, the uppermost of which dates to the Late Bronze Age (second half of 2nd millennium BC) and has been linked with a small Mycenaean installation, whereas the four lower levels date to the Early Bronze Age. In the Late Bronze Age the

115. Imbros. Cylindrical cup, h. 11 cm., hammered from a sheet of electrum (natural alloy of gold and silver). The diameter of the ring base is 2.8 cm. and of the rim 6.6 cm. Below the rim, three horizontal and five vertical grooves form four rectangular panels, from the midpoint of the lower side of which five grooves run at right angle to the base. Found on Imbros (Yaniyeri/V'ni I?) on 1 March 1917, auctioned for the first time on 15 July 1918 at Sotheby's (£ 150), and for the second time on 28 April 2004, again at Sotheby's (estimate £ 400,000-£ 600,000). Dated *c.* 2600-2300 BC.

115

surface of the ramp was repaired using pebbles of different sizes, among which have been found over 200 sherds of Mycenaean vases, mainly of local manufacture, which are dated between the fourteenth and the twelfth century BC.

The ancient city of Imbros occupied the same site as the modern village of Kaleköy (Kastro), on the south slope of a low hill between two bays on the north coast. The greater part of the city wall has been restored recently and it has become clear that its extension thrust much further to the southwest than had been thought. At the east foot of the hill remnants of the seats of the theatre have been located, while the city's cemeteries lie *extra muros* to the southeast and the northeast.

The Late Byzantine castle (fig. 119), of rubble masonry without mortar and incorporating numerous *spolia* in its construction, stands in the north-central part of the ancient city. It is of much smaller dimensions and has an almost trapezoidal plan. The west, south and east sides were reinforced with towers, while two entrances have been identified on the east and northeast sides. At the west end of the Kale/Aghios Nikolaos Bay, in the area of Arida, surface remains point to habitation in Hellenistic and Roman times.

The sanctuary of the Great Gods, which is known only from inscriptions and ancient sources, is placed in the area of Roxado, a valley southwest of the ancient city, in a location analogous to that of the corresponding sanctuary on Samothrace (but at a higher altitude). The retaining walls that survive to this day (fig. 121) date to the Late Classical-Early Hellenistic period (4th century BC).

In the southwest of the island, close to the church of the Virgin Gerakia, an ancient farmhouse dating from the fourth century BC onwards, has been identified. However, it has been associated with the indigenous population of Imbros, bearer of an age-old cultural tradition. North of the Virgin Gerakia, a Late Byzantine hilltop fortress of dry-stone rubble masonry is known as Palaiokastro (Eski Kale) and should perhaps be identified with the second well-fortified city on the island, which is mentioned in the early fifteenth century. Two smaller fortresses of dry-stone rubble masonry, at Arasia (Kesıktaş) and Palaiokastraki (Eren), in the central part of the island, were obviously nodes in a network of lookout posts.

116. Imbros. View of the Yenibademli/Aghios Floros tell in 1991 (before excavation), from the south.

117, 118. Imbros, Yenibademli/Aghios Floros tell. Clay figurines. On the female figurine the arms are denoted as small stumps and the breasts are button-shaped. The incisions on the front are perhaps a schematic rendering of a garment. Early Bronze Age (1st half of 3rd millennium BC).

102 | NORTH AND EAST AEGEAN

119. Imbros, Kaleköy/Kastro. View of the Late Byzantine fortification with ancient architectural members (*spolia*) built into its fabric.

120. Imbros, Yuvalı/Pyrgos. Late Antique inscription. The site is on the southwest coast, opposite Lemnos, and has evidence of occupation in the Late Neolithic period, the Bronze Age, Hellenistic and Roman times.

121. Imbros, Roxado. The extant retaining walls of the sanctuary of the Great Gods, which date to the Late Classical-Early Hellenistic period (late 4th c. BC).

Tenedos

DIMITRIS MATSAS

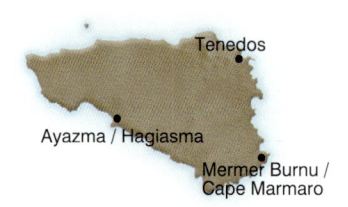

Tenedos (Turk. Bozcaada), 39 sq. km. in area, lies about 11 miles south-southwest of the mouth of the Hellespont, 16 miles south of Imbros, 27 miles east of Lemnos and approximately 2.5 miles from the coast of Asia Minor. Its terrain is distinguished by rolling hills in the north and a flat plain in the south, extending from east to west and occupying two-thirds of the island. The highest point on Tenedos is the summit of Göz Tepe/Prophitis Ilias (190 m. a.s.l.), a trachyte hill in the northeast. The southeast part consists of limestone and schist. On Mermer-Burnu/Cape Marmaro, on the east coast, are the ancient quarries. The west part of Tenedos is a low plate of later Tertiary sediments.

Although small, Tenedos never lost its importance in Antiquity and the Middle Ages, thanks to its strategic geographical position at the entrance to the Hellespont. It was a safe anchorage for ships sailing into the straits when northeast winds were blowing. It was also famed for its wine. The heyday it enjoyed in the Hellenistic period is evident from its significant coinage (fig. 122).

Apart from the coins, the most notable archaeological finds come from the graves of the ancient city, offering crucial information on the society and economy, the art and foreign relations of the island. The necropolis in the south part of today's main village, spreads east of Yeni Kale, west of the harbour of the ancient city, in a small cove in the north part of the east coast (fig. 124). Forty-nine graves have been uncovered, dating from the Early Bronze Age (first half of 3rd millennium BC) and the Early Iron Age (late 8th/early 7th century BC) into Roman times (2nd century BC). These are of different types: cist graves (first half of 3rd millennium BC, late 8th/early 7th-4th century BC), pithoi burials (6th-2nd century BC), cinerary amphorae (5th-4th century BC), clay sarcophagi and chamber tombs (6th-5th century BC).

About 1 km. west of the harbour, a building of rectangular plan and three cist graves dating from the Early Bronze Age (first half of 3rd millennium BC) have been excavated. The graves, which are later than the building, are formed of upright stone slabs (orthostats) in rectangular-trapezoidal arrangement. One of the graves accommodated a double burial, with the dead, as in another grave, placed in contracted pose. Although the grave goods recovered are closely related to the material culture of the Northeast Aegean and the Troas, inhumation was not common practice in this period. Moreover, unusual in Northeast Aegean architecture are the wooden posts impacted in the pisé wall of the rectangular building.

Among the grave goods of historical times are grey ware from western Asia Minor, which is associated with the Aeolians, Subgeometric painted pottery (late 8th/early 7th century BC), terracotta figurines

122. Silver tetradrachm of Tenedos, *c.* 150 BC. On the obverse Janiform heads, one male and one female (Zeus and Hera ?). On the reverse the double axe within a laurel wreath, the inscription ΤΕΝΕΔΙΩΝ (of Tenedians), a bunch of grapes with monogram bottom left and small winged figure holding a wreath. The double axe, which is usually a symbol of a female deity and was of special significance for Tenedos, could be considered a vestige of Cretan presence on the island in the Bronze Age. Athens, Numismatic Museum.

123. Tenedos. Fortification of Mohamed II, from the southeast. It stands at the north end of the harbour of the ancient city.

124. Tenedos. View of the excavation of the necropolis, from the east. Photograph taken in 1991.

125, 126. Tenedos. Semicircular gold sheet with repoussé decoration. The representation of the male and female figures in the chariot is associated with the Greek art of the eastern Aegean, where the ornament was probably made (Ephesos ?) in the early 6th c. BC. Çanakkale Archaeological Museum.

(6th and 5th centuries BC), Corinthian aryballoi (6th century BC), Attic black-figure kylikes (late 6th/early 5th century BC), black-glaze kylikes (4th century BC) and a rich assemblage of metal objects (figs 125, 126). The fibulae from the Geometric and Early Archaic graves display marked affinity with those from the Aegean islands and western Asia Minor, while the Corinthian and Attic pottery attests to close relations with Corinth and Athens during the sixth and fifth centuries BC.

The ruins of the ancient city of Tenedos, which was apparently designed on some kind of grid system, lie on the site occupied by the present main village. The theatre, on the east slope of Yeni Kale Hill, overlooks the shore of Alexandria Troas. Our knowledge of the ancient city is limited to a few architectural members as well as part of a street and a network of drains-sewers. On the hill at the north edge of the cove of the natural harbour stands the fortification built by Mohamed II (fig. 123). The ground plan of the present internal fortification should be largely identical with that of the Medieval one. A second ancient settlement has been located on the southwest coast, in Sulubahçe Bay, close to the Hagiasma, the spring and single-aisle basilica of the Ottoman period, dedicated to St Paraskevi.

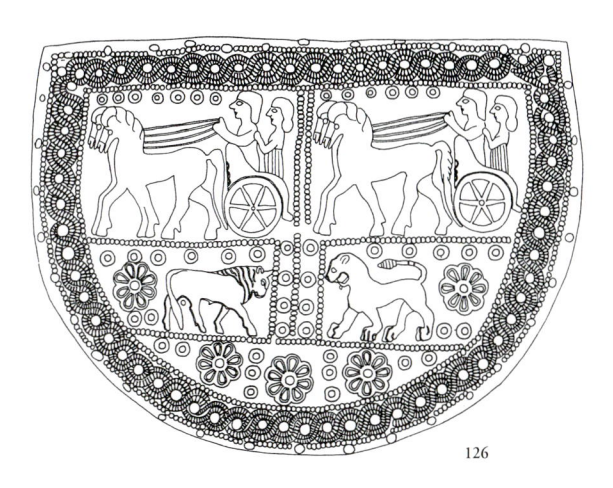

ΤΕΝΕΔΟΣ

Lemnos

Luigi Beschi

Lemnos lies opposite the Hellespont, on an important sea-lane linking the Aegean Sea with the Black Sea, a short distance from the coasts of Thrace and the Troas. Its location was nodal for communication and trading exchanges already from prehistoric times.

A narrow strip of land between the deep bays of Moudros and Pournias divides the island into the western mountainous region with the precipitous indented coastline, and the eastern plain with low hills projecting in the vast sandy bays. The igneous rocks (lava, trachyte, tuff), gneiss, poros and sandstone were the building materials used in all periods, creating polychromy in the island's architecture.

During prehistoric times two settlements were predominant on Lemnos, at Poliochni and Myrina, which stand out among the smaller unexplored or partly explored settlements, such as Koukonisi in the creek of Moudros Bay and Hephaistia in Pournias Bay. In historical times too Lemnos was *dipolis* – a rare case in the Aegean – with the two cities of Myrina and Hephaistia.

According to Homeric tradition, the smith-god Hephaistos fell from heaven onto Lemnos, where he was helped by the Sintians, a Thracian tribe that learnt the art of metallurgy from him. The hillock of Mosychlos near Hephaistia, on which the god landed, has always had the aspect of burnt and barren earth. The *terra lemnia* extracted from here in a ceremonial manner was an antidote to poisons and was sealed and sold everywhere as a medicament.

Hephaistos gave his name to Hephaistia, the largest city on "most friendly" Lemnos, which acquired the epithet "*amichthaloessa*" (smoke-shrouded) from the smoke of its workshops and its volcanic ground. The island was synonymous with its principal deity, the Great Goddess Lemnos, who is identified with the Greek Artemis, the Thracian Bendis and the Great Mother of the Phrygians. Although correspondence between myth and history is precarious, we surmise that the cult of the two deities Hephaistos and Lemnos was deeply rooted in the religious tradition of the island, which was inhabited by Thracians prior to its historical phases, the Mycenaean-Minyan (13th-8th century BC), the Pelasgian-Tyrrhenian (late 8th-6th century BC) and lastly the Attic, when Lemnos was a cleruchy of Athens.

The prehistoric phases at Poliochni and Myrina place the island on the route to the East, which led to the quest for and the working of metals. The introduction of the eastern cult of the Kabeiroi, descendants of the two traditional deities, who were considered daemons of fire, fertility, wine and seafaring, possibly coincides with the arrival of the Tyrrhenians, a non-Hellenic tribe whose origin and language are still contentious issues for research but whose culture undoubtedly belongs in the Northeast Aegean sphere.

Many other myths are projected against this backdrop, the best known being those of the "Lemnian Curse". The earliest myth is associated with the worship of Aphrodite, possibly a hypostasis of the Great Goddess: the women, through neglect

127

of their duties, were afflicted by a bad smell, which caused the unfaithfulness of the men, whom they then murdered. The island without men was colonized by Jason and the Argonauts, who stayed there briefly *en route* to Colchis. This is an allusion to the Mycenaean period, in exactly the same way as the abandonment of Philoktetes *en route* for Troy. The second curse is connected with the Tyrrhenian phase, namely the murder of the Athenian women whom the Tyrrhenians had abducted at Brauron. This was possibly the reason why Miltiades captured the island around 500 BC, after the Persian invasion in 511 BC.

Excavations conducted on Lemnos have shown that the foremost settlement in prehistoric times was that at Poliochni. Excavated by the Italian School of Archaeology, it is the most fully studied installation on the island. Continuous research and the wealth of data accrued have demonstrated that habitation at this very important site was continuous for over 1,500 years (fig. 128). Poliochni, one of the earliest examples of urbanization in the Aegean (the oldest city with assembly spaces and urban planning), is situated on a hill overlooking a large bay on the east coast opposite the Troas, with which it had, to a considerable degree, common building and cultural phases in its long history.

From the beginning of the excavation, the sequence of chronological phases at Poliochni was distinguished conventionally by colours. Habitation starts in the Late Chalcolithic period, that is, before the founding of Troy, in the form of a village of ellipsoidal huts belonging to the so-called "black" period (4th millennium BC). This is followed by the "blue" period (3000-2800 BC) at the beginning of the Early Bronze Age, which is a significant step in its development: the village passed to a first form of urban organization, with rectangular buildings, a fortification wall and access from the fertile plain to the west. This period coincides with the first phase of Troy (Troy I). At the entrance to the citadel are two important buildings: on the left a large storage space, the so-called "granary", and on the right a space with benches on the long sides, the so-called "bouleuterion", for political-administrative or religious assemblies (fig. 129).

In the "green" period at Poliochni (2800-2500 BC) houses were organized in building *insulae* and were of *megaron* type, of square plan with antechamber. The pottery starts to be differentiated from that of the East and received Aegean influences, mainly from the Cyclades and Crete. The ensuing "red" period (2500-2300 BC), which corresponds to Troy II, presents minor differences. By now close relations with the Aegean and in particular Crete are visible. The city was reinforced by two large semicircular bastions and the building *insulae* were arranged either side of winding streets.

The "yellow" period at Poliochni (2300-2000 BC) is the richest in architectural remains and variety of pottery, met-

127. Lemnos. Gold earrings from the Poliochni hoard, akin to "Priam's Treasure" from Troy, 2300-2000 BC. Athens, National Archaeological Museum.

128. Lemnos, Poliochni. The city extends on a low hill on the east coast of the island and is the best-excavated and best-studied centre of the Northeast Aegean Culture of the 3rd millennium BC.

129. Lemnos, Poliochni. The assembly hall with the benches (the so-called bouleuterion). Recent research has demonstrated that there were built benches along the two long sides, which could accommodate 90 persons (3000-2800 BC).

al tools and precious objects, such as gold jewellery comparable to that of the so-called "Priam's Treasure" from Troy III-IV (figs 127, 131, 132). A catastrophic earthquake sealed the buildings and their contents, facilitating the reconstruction of the city's urban plan, which had two main street axes, stone-paved squares and community wells. One of the buildings is considered to have been the residence of a pre-eminent person.

After a short interval of crisis and desertion come the "brown" (1950-1600 BC) and the "mauve" period (1600-1400 BC). The city was in decline in relation to the past and shrunk in area. Mycenaean pottery is rare, but this gap in the archaeological record has been filled by the recent finds from Hephaistia and Koukonisi, where an important settlement centre that continued to flourish during the Middle and the Late Bronze Age has been excavated over the past few years (figs 133, 134). The archaeological evidence thus verifies the information in the literary sources (Homeric epics and Classical drama) and the content of a Linear B tablet from the palace of Pylos, which refers to female weavers from Lemnos.

Notable finds of the prehistoric era have come to light in Myrina, which occupied one of the least accessible promontories on the island. Recent investigations by the Greek Archaeological Service have revealed buildings and artifacts (fig. 130) corresponding to the earliest phases at Poliochni (black to yellow period). The settlement appears to have covered a wide area in space and time, constituting a new urban centre of the third millennium BC.

Preserved on the margins of ancient Myrina is a Cyclopean wall, most probably Mycenaean, at the base of which is part of a wall of isodomic masonry from the time of the Attic cleruchy. The settlement was smaller than that at Hephaistia, but its mythological tradition is richer. Here reigned Thoas, who had arrived from Crete, and his daughter Hypsipyle; here the Argonauts dropped anchor and from here Euneos sent aid to the Achaeans below the walls of Troy.

In the second half of the nineteenth century, an assemblage of votive figurines of Sirens (fig. 141) and Sphinxes, similar to those in the rich sacral repository (*apothetes*) of the Archaic sanctuary of Hephaistia, was discovered to the north of the modern town of Myrina. The foundations of a temple were also uncovered, and some decrees of the city, inscribed on marble and set up in a conspicuous position, as noted also in an Athenian decree of the Classical period, which specifies the sanctuary of Artemis.

North of Myrina, at the site of Avlona, an interesting though puzzling ensemble of buildings has been excavated (fig. 138), which are dated from the Archaic (fig. 139) to the Roman period. A central core of two overlying imposing apsidal buildings of the Archaic period is complemented by rectangular spaces of the Classical and mainly the Hellenistic period. Rooms built on terraces supported by strong retaining walls on the seaward side face onto wide stone-paved spaces.

130. Lemnos. "Fruitstand" of the early 3rd millennium BC ("blue" period, 3000-2800 BC), from the excavation of the settlement north of Myrina. Myrina Archaeological Museum.

131. Lemnos. Tripod cooking pot from Poliochni, "yellow" period (2300-2000 BC). This is the commonest type of domestic vessel. Myrina Archaeological Museum.

132. Lemnos, Poliochni. "*Depas amphikypellon*" from the "yellow" period (2300-2000 BC), a peculiar vase type encountered in the mature phase of the Early Bronze Age, from Troy as far as the Central Aegean. Myrina Archaeological Museum.

108 | NORTH AND EAST AEGEAN

In the eastern sector of the modern town (site of Tsas) the pottery workshops of the Archaic and Hellenistic periods have been revealed, which extended over a wide area with rooms, courtyards, remains of kilns, materials (lumps of clay, moulds, stamps) and products (figurines, lamps, Megarian bowls corresponding to those of Hephaistia). In the same area a large necropolis of Hellenistic and Roman times has been excavated, as well as the foundations of a temple-shaped edifice. Unfortunately, the urban tissue of modern Myrina prevents fuller investigation of the ancient centre, over the agora of which – according to the texts – the shadow of Mount Athos loomed in the west.

When the church of St Alexander at Kaminia, in the vicinity of Poliochni, was demolished in 1884 a grave stele of the second half of the sixth century BC was recovered, with representation of a warrior armed with spear and shield, and bearing Tyrrhenian inscriptions of analogous content (fig. 135). After repeated attempts to interpret these inscriptions, they were for years the expression of the "Tyrrhenian Question" on Lemnos. Ultimate aim of the subsequent research at Hephaistia by the Italian School of Archaeology was to bring this important epigraphic monument out of isolation.

Hephaistia was the most extensive city on Lemnos, spreading on the edges of a large cape with a deep natural harbour, the greater part of which is now filled by sand. On the flat interior zone of the isthmus spread the necropolis. Here, on a Late Classical tomb pedestal, important pottery finds and remains of Mycenaean buildings were uncovered. Close by was the cemetery with cremations, of the Late Geometric period (late 8th-second half of 7th century BC), which made known the local pottery production, but which mainly gave a full picture of the Tyrrhenians' mortuary customs. A little further to the south was the cemetery of the next period, of the Athenian cleruchy, with inhumations and grave goods confirming relations primarily with Attica.

One of the most important complexes for our knowledge of the Tyrrhenians' architecture, art and religious beliefs are the remains of a sanctuary on the west slope of the Hephaistia Peninsula. The rectangular buildings are arranged on two levels: the lower with remnants of a row of spaces of the first half of the seventh century BC and the upper with a row of three rooms opening onto a square, in use from the mid-seventh to the late sixth century BC. The central building has a low pavement of poros blocks, upon which remains of offerings were found. To the south, around a baetyl-cippus, a rich sacral repository (*apothetes*) was discovered, with local objects and imports from Athens, Corinth, Chios and Rhodes, attesting to a widespread network of communications. Especially noteworthy are terracotta fountain models, a type of figurine with raised arms (fig. 140), a palladium, a winged Artemis and series of Sirens (fig. 142) and Sphinxes. A well in the same room yielded evidence of the vi-

133. Lemnos, Koukonisi. The settlement was thriving mainly in the Early and the Middle Bronze Age. However, the finds from the Late Bronze Age or Mycenaean period enhance the importance of Lemnos in the expansion of Mycenaean Civilization in the Northeast Aegean.

134. Lemnos, Koukonisi. Hydria of the final phases of the Middle Bronze Age (1700-1600 BC), with red-burnished surface and incised decoration of geometric motifs filled with white paste. Myrina Archaeological Museum.

135. Lemnos. The stele from Kaminia. Both inscriptions, on the front and the side face, are in a language akin to Etruscan, raising the problem of the provenance of the Tyrrhenians of Lemnos, second half of 6th c. BC. Athens, National Archaeological Museum.

136. Lemnos, Hephaistia. View of the Archaic sanctuary, a type of telesterion with a small adyton right and benches along the long walls. Built in the 7th c. BC, it was destroyed by the Persians in 512-511 BC and abandoned. In Hellenistic times it was arranged as a pottery workshop.

137. Lemnos, Hephaistia. The Hellenistic theatre (4th-3rd c. BC), with proscenium of the Roman phase, is only partly preserved. Recently, a very important level of Archaic buildings has been excavated in the area.

138. Lemnos. The so-called Artemision at Avlona, with various phases spanning the Archaic to the Roman period.

olent destruction of the sanctuary, possibly by the Persians (511 BC), since ash, charcoal and skeletal remains of a fifty-year-old man, together with a spearhead, were found in its depths. This find is very important because it is the unique skeletal material of the period, since the Tyrrhenians exclusively cremated their dead. The quality of the offerings, the majority from females, suggests worship of the Great Goddess of Lemnos, and certainly not of the Kabeiroi, who received offerings of another type. This was confirmed later by the author's investigations (1977-1982), which revealed a temple on the central axis of the sacred precinct (*temenos*) (fig. 136). Of rectangular plan with spacious hall and benches along the sides, it is delimited left by a kind of adyton with high bench for offerings, while the bench right ends in front of the adyton with a wide stone-paved space. Upon this and on the axis of the adyton, in front of a little apse, are two large cylindrical stands (one decorated with confronted serpents), probably for ritual use, as is deduced from the typology of the vases found *in situ*. The building should be associated with the cult of the Great Goddess, assimilated with Cybele, the Great Mother of the East. It was founded around the mid-seventh century BC and abandoned after a fire in the late sixth century BC. On the ruins of the Archaic sanctuary, which was not rebuilt, an extensive workshop quarter developed between the third and second centuries BC, producing mainly relief pottery analogous to that of Myrina.

Investigations have brought to light various buildings dispersed in the city, which did not yet have a clear urban plan. To the west, upon the ruins of the Archaic houses, a theatre was constructed in the Early Hellenistic period. Visible are remains of the marble seats of the proedria, the cavea with four cunei and a skene building with two phases, Hellenistic and Roman (fig. 137). To the south of the sanctuary, a building unit of the city has been excavated. The general picture seen today is of the Hellenistic phase, although remains from the Archaic and the Roman period are preserved. Between the theatre and the neighbourhood, exactly as on the walls of the isthmus, some particularly well-built Roman residences and a Mycenaean settlement have been explored. Close to the inner edge of the harbour are remains of a Hellenistic bathhouse. Systematic research begun recently has already produced notable data. Proof of the continuous habitation of the city are the Early Christian buildings, constructed and in use before their gradual abandonment, from the early fifth century AD.

The sanctuary of the Kabeiroi is located at the end of a sheltered bay in the north, not far from the entrance to the harbour of Hephaistia. The cult, which some literary sources is correlated with the presence of Tyrrhenians in Archaic times, is rooted in earlier religious traditions. The sanctuary was enclosed by a precinct wall (*peribolos*) and was developed on two terraces reinforced with retaining wall on the seaward side. On the north terrace there are the foundations of a large building comprising four elements: a portico with twelve Doric columns on the façade and two on the sides, a wide central space divided into three aisles by two rows of four Ionic columns, a corridor or bema and a suite of rooms at the far end (fig. 143). The central part of the upper structure was about 15 metres high. The ground plan of the building, which displays affinity with those of assembly halls (such as the telesterion at Eleusis and the bouleuteria at Athens and Dodona), characterizes it as a telesterion, bigger than that in the sanctuary

LEMNOS | 111

on Samothrace. Construction commenced in the first half of the second century BC but it was never completed, perhaps because of the conflict between Romans and Macedonians in the reign of Philip V. The telesterion was in use for some four hundred years, until its destruction around AD 200.

Preserved on the south terrace is a humbler construction, largely built of earlier architectural material (*spolia*) and dated to the third century AD. It copies on a smaller scale the plan of the large Hellenistic telesterion, with a three-aisled hall divided by two rows of four columns, here closed at the far end by an elevated corridor and two rooms at the back, on the central axis of which the base of an adyton survives. Access to the building was through a simple eight-columned portico founded on a strong retaining wall on the seaward side and with benches for the initiates in its lateral aisles. In 1990, remains of the first telesterion, dated to the seventh century BC and therefore erected by the Tyrrhenians, were revealed in its foundations (fig. 144). This was an almost rectangular space with mud-brick benches around its walls, to accommodate about 50 initiates. At the far end of the cella is a rectangular base, in front of which is a semicircular projection, upon which was found a tripod vase (lebes), supporting the view that the construction is an *eschara* (place for sacred fire). The plan is comparable not only to that of other primitive telesteria but also to that of the Archaic temple in neighbouring Hephaistia. Both are linked with examples of architecture in the Late Geometric and Early Archaic tradition, intended for rituals and provided with an internal sacrificial space. However, what is particularly important about the Lemnian telesterion is the discovery of clay vessels on the floor, which confirm the ritual character of worship at the moment of the Persian destruction. This is an assemblage of some forty vases, the majority of which (primarily the ritual "karchesia") bear incised dedicatory inscriptions; for example, scratched on the neck of one jug is the Tyrrhenian word *novaisna*, which is correlated with the Etruscan *aisna*, meaning divine, sacred, holy.

Of seminal importance for reconstructing the life of the sanctuary were two rich sacral repositories (*apothetai*) found at the bases of the terrace walls. The first yielded clay vessels of the seventh and sixth centuries BC, most for libations and bearing inscriptions, again with the word *novaisna*. A second big *apothetes* was in part on top of the Archaic one. This contained votive figurines and vases together with domestic pottery. Striking is the large number of lamps, confirming the nocturnal rites referred to by Cicero, and of drinking and libation vases, indicative of the type of ceremonial. The material dates from the mid-fifth to the early second century BC and is consequently no later than the construction of the Hellenistic telesterion. The last decades of life in the sanctuary must have been played out on the south terrace, before worship ceased in the fourth century AD, with the subsequent destruction and desertion but no sign of a Christian installation. Gathered here were the most important inscriptions and the most precious *ex-votos*, which had been vandalized by the early Christians.

The contribution of Lemnos to ancient poetry and thought was significant. The island sired the sophist Antilochos, the naturalist Apollodoros, the prolific family of the Philostratids, essayists and authors, and the sculptor Alkamenes. Nor should the beneficial effect of the island on Athens be overlooked; the bronze statue of Athena Lemnia, created by Pheidias, stood at the

139. Lemnos. Archaic vase from the excavations at Avlona. Late 7th-6th c. BC. Myrina Archaeological Museum.

140. Lemnos. Anthropomorphic figurine from the sanctuary of Hephaistia, which belongs in the great figural tradition of Creto-Mycenaean figurines with raised arms, late 7th c. BC. Athens, National Archaeological Museum.

141. Lemnos. Head of a Siren. Votive offering in the sanctuary of Myrina, second half of 6th c. BC. Myrina Archaeological Museum.

142. Lemnos. Siren, votive offering from the Archaic sanctuary of Hephaistia, mid-6th c. BC. Myrina Archaeological Museum.

LEMNOS | 113

143. Lemnos. The large Hellenistic telesterion, where initiation into the mysteries of the Kabeiroi took place.

144. Lemnos, Kabeirion. The Archaic telesterion (7th-6th c. BC), under the remains of the Late Roman telesterion. Preserved is the brick bench, visible between the foundations of the Roman columns.

entrance to the Acropolis. Lemnian myths were brought to life on the stage of the theatre of Dionysos, in the plays *Kabeiroi* by Aeschylus, *Lemnian Women* by Aristophanes, *Philoktetes* by Sophocles. In the last work, the hero on departing for Troy greets the island passionately, after the long and solitary abandonment (lines 1453-1468):

Hail Lemnos sea-girt plain

Aghios Efstratios

AGLAIA ARCHONTIDOU-ARGYRI

Aghios Efstratios lies between Lemnos and Lesbos. It is a rocky mountainous isle, just 43 sq. km. in area, which emerged from the depths of the sea during geological upheavals in the region. The modern village spreads on the west coast, around the harbour, where a settlement existed from the Hellenistic period (fig. 145). The earliest indications of human presence have been found on the east coast and date from Mycenaean times, while there are remains from the historical period over virtually its entire barren and almost impenetrable extent (fig. 146). Noteworthy are the Archaic retaining walls (fig. 147) near the cemetery and the Hellenistic tombs around the harbour.

In the ancient Greek literary texts the island is referred to by the Homeric name Chryse (Gold), later the name Nea (New), because it rose up from the sea, and Hiera (Holy), because of St Eustratios.

145. Aghios Efstratios. The harbour, around which the ancient settlement developed.

146. Aghios Efstratios. Millstone of ancient material.

147. Aghios Efstratios. Retaining wall of the Archaic period (7th-6th c. BC) with the characteristic polygonal Lesbian masonry.

Lesbos

AGLAIA ARCHONTIDOU-ARGYRI

Of all the names given to the island in Antiquity, Makaria, Pelasgia, Issa, Imerte, Lasia, Aigeira, Aithiope, Mytonis, Lesbos, the last prevailed, after the homonymous Thessalian hero, son of Lapethos and grandson of Aiolos.

The first mythical king of the island was Makar, son of Helios and Rhode, or according to another version, Makareus, son of Krinax and grandson of Zeus. His daughters, Mytilene, Methymna, Antissa, Arisbe, Issa and Pyrrha, and his son Eresos, gave their names to the subsequent cities.

The earliest remains of human activity on Lesbos date from the Final Neolithic period (late 4th millennium BC). During the Early and the Middle Bronze Age (*circa* 3000-1600 BC) the island belonged culturally and historically within the sphere of the so-called Trojan Culture. A settlement of this period has been excavated systematically on the coast of Thermi (fig. 148), where large narrow-fronted houses have been uncovered, in continuous alignment and of megaron type with closed prodomos, flat roof, entrance on the narrow side and pebbled floors. This important proto-urban centre, in which five settlement phases have been distinguished, was destroyed by fire at the time of the arrival of the first Aeolian tribes on the island.

Homer, giving the geographical bounds of Priam's realm in the *Iliad*, refers to Lesbos as "*Makaros edos*". However, the most significant archaeological evidence of the Mycenaean period on the island is confined to the entrance and the shores of the Gulf of Kalloni, where a settlement and cemetery have been found, and to the west coast of the Gulf of Gera, where a pottery workshop has been excavated, with successive destruction levels from the middle to the end of the second millennium BC (fig. 149).

In the period of the great colonization, Achaeans reached Lesbos from the Peloponnese and Aeolians from Thessaly and Boeotia. In the city of Mytilene, the government was in Achaean hands, but the mores, customs and traditions of the Aeolian tribes held sway.

In the eighth century BC, when the city-state came into being, six cities are mentioned on Lesbos: Mytilene, Pyrrha, Arisbe, Methymna and Eresos, of which Mytilene and Methymna emerged as the mightiest.

The main reasons for the development and power of Lesbos were its proximity to the Asia Minor coast, its robust economy due to the fertile soils and the rich fishing grounds in its bays, and its advantageous geographical position. The city of Mytilene was found on Nesi, a natural fortification separated from the land by the Euripos, ending in two natural harbours, the naval "triereme harbour" to the south and the commercial "*malloeis* harbour" to the north.

Control of the city of Sigeion at the entrance to the Hellespont was the pretext for the clash between Mytilene and Athens, which ended in 607 BC in Mytilene's favour, with the well-known episode of the duel fought between the commanders of the two warring camps. Pittakos slew the leader of the Athenian army, the Olympic victor Phrynon, and became a hero. Henceforth Mytilene controlled the straits and until the fifth century BC kept its domination in all the Asia Minor cities, from Sigeion to Smyrna. In the literary and historical sources the Asia Minor shores, from Sigeion and Pitane down to Smyrna, are called "coastal cities", "Mytilenians' shore (*Mytilenaion aigialos*)", "*peraia*" or "*colonia*". Mytilene kept its influence on the coastal cities even after the Persian Wars, losing it at the end of the Peloponnesian War, when the Lacedaemonian Kallikratis besieged the city in 406 BC. Henceforth it was limited to the "*Mytilenaion aigialos*".

From the seventh to the fifth century BC the cities of Lesbos played a dynamic role in creating the so-called Hellenic spirit and civilization, and were associated primarily – betwixt myth and reality – with the shaping of Greek music and poetry. Lyric poetry was born on Lesbos, with principal representatives Alkaios and Sappho, dubbed the tenth Muse. The role of Lesbos in forming music and poetry is echoed in the myth of Orpheus. After his death in the mountains of Pieria, the waves carried his lyre to Mytilene, where it was kept in the sanctuary of "Apollo Malloes", and his severed head to Antissa, where it was kept in the sanctuary of Dionysos, which was also an oracle shrine.

Lesbos contributed to the architectural evolution of the Greek temple and to the elaboration of the so-called Aeolic or Proto-Ionic order. The superb Aeolic column capitals of the seventh and sixth centuries BC, in the Mytilene Archaeological Museum (fig. 152), are the most characteristic features of buildings of this category.

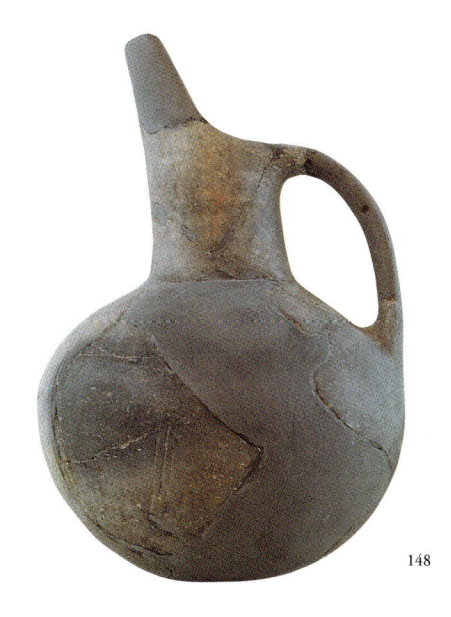

148. Lesbos. Beak-spouted jug from the Early Bronze Age settlement at Thermi (3rd millennium BC). Mytilene Archaeological Museum.

149. Lesbos. Excavations on the west coast of the Gulf of Gera have brought to light remains of a Mycenaean settlement and pottery workshops of Mycenaean, Hellenistic and Roman times.

The absence of monumental sculpture, with few exceptions, is due to the fact that no systematic excavations have been conducted in the sanctuaries and cities. The pottery workshops of Archaic Lesbos produced not only vases in reddish brown clay but also a grey ware known as "*bucchero*". The island's excellent olive oil and wine were transported in large *bucchero* amphorae to harbours in the Euxine Pontus and Egypt, in return for grain, copper, precious metals and perfumes, the last brought to the island in expensive glass vials (fig. 59).

From the eighth to the late seventh century BC, period of the creation of the city-state and of the change of regime from timocratic to democratic, the life of the Lesbian cities was bedevilled by political strife. Among the personalities who played a significant part in the return to normality and the consolidation of democracy were the *aisymnetes* Pittakos and the lyric poets Alkaios and Sappho, sometimes working together in the same political faction and sometimes as rivals in different factions.

After the dissolution of the Lydian State in 546 BC, the cities of Lesbos, along with the other East Aegean islands and the cities in the Asia Minor littoral, had to contend with the expansionist designs of the Persians. The successive uprisings against the conquerors culminated in the Ionian Revolt in 499 BC, in which the cities played an active part and were punished with extremely harsh economic and military reprisals.

In the period of the Persian Wars the Lesbian cities joined the Athenian League. In the events of the Peloponnesian War the island's wealthiest and most important city, Mytilene, was epicentre of marginal episodes in the struggle between the two rivals, Sparta and Athens, for influence on the Greek cities. Climactic event for Lesbos, which is mentioned by Thucydides, was the apostasy of the Mytilenians. In the efforts of the Aeolian cities of Lesbos and Asia Minor to break away from the influence of the Athenian State, they planned a coalition with Mytilene as political, commercial and administrative centre. This necessitated the city's expansion onto the land beyond the Euripos, in order to cope with the new order. The attempt to do so in 428 BC failed. The removal of parts of the fortifications and the quays, the execution of one thousand ephebes and the humiliating terms of the treaty forced upon the deme adversely affected life and development in the city for the next two hundred years.

After 428 BC, Athenian cleruchs settled on the richest farms in the Lesbian countryside, with olive groves, vineyards, vegetable gardens and grain fields. The Athenian cleruchy on Lesbos was abolished after Kallikratis' successful siege of Mytilene, the prevailing of the Lacedaemonians and the return of the exiled supporters of oligarchy in 406 BC. Only in 377 BC did the Lesbian cities become members of the Second Athenian League and in 338 BC they took part in the panhellenic anti Persian alliance of Corinth, under the leadership of King Philip II of Macedon.

Archaeological research has shown that Lesbos was densely populated in the Classical period. On the rich estates already existing from Archaic

150. Lesbos. Female acrobat figurine from Pyrrha, of the 5th c. BC. Mytilene Archaeological Museum.

151. Lesbos. Gold wreath, found with jewellery and exquisite figurines in a grave on a farm of Mytilene. *c.* late 3rd c. BC. Mytilene Archaeological Museum.

152. Lesbos, sanctuary at Klopedi. The Aeolic column capital is the main architectural element of the homonymous order. Late 6th c. BC. Mytilene Archaeological Museum.

153, 154. Lesbos. The octastyle prostyle Ionic temple of the 4th c. BC at Mesa was dedicated to the Lesbian Trinity (Zeus, Hera, Dionysos). It is identified with the relief representation on the copper coins of the *Koinon* of Lesbians. Reconstruction drawing and aerial photograph of the temple.

118 | NORTH AND EAST AEGEAN

152

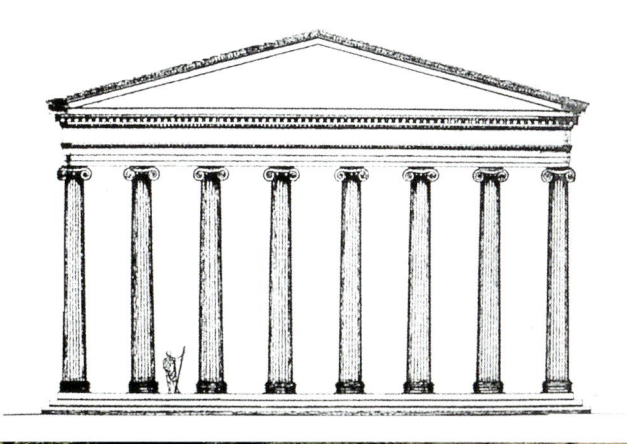

153

154

Lesbos | 119

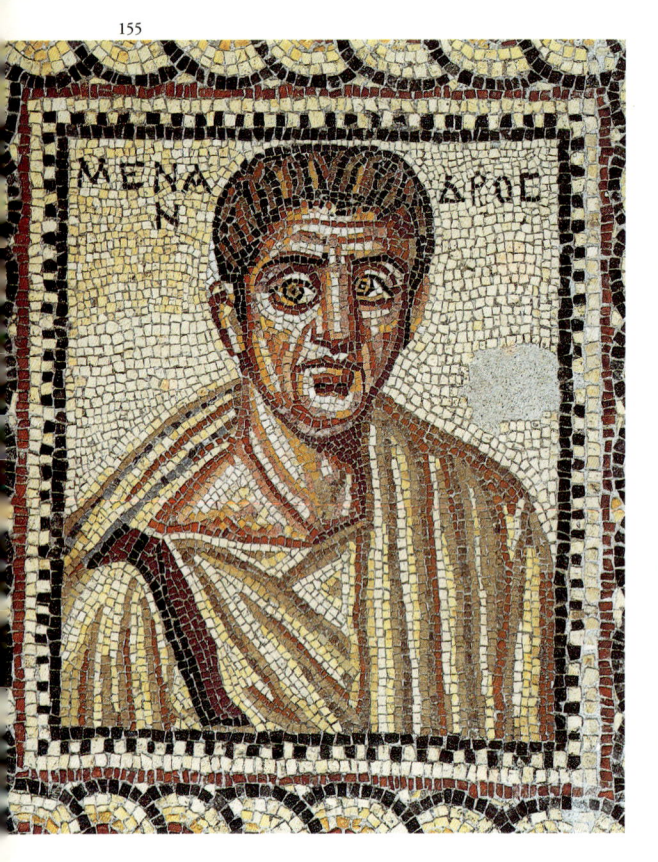

155. Lesbos. The mosaic from the so-called "House of Menander", which is dated to the late 3rd or the early 4th c. AD, is rare for its subject and its quality. Characteristic is the portrait of the poet, while uncommon are the inscribed representations with scenes from his plays. Mytilene Archaeological Museum.

156. Lesbos. On a mosaic floor from an opulent residence in Mytilene, the Euripos is personified as a beardless youth with luxuriant hair, bedecked with lobster pincers and dolphins. Dated to the 2nd-3rd c. AD. Mytilene Archaeological Museum.

times, wheat continued to be grown in the lowlands and vines tended in the highlands, as is apparent from the terraces with retaining walls built in the polygonal system, which survive to this day. The remains of fortified farmsteads bear witness to the cultivators' and residents' need of protection, while the organized small cemeteries within the boundaries of the estates, such as that investigated in Mytilene, give an insight into social structure and stratification. At the centre are the richly-furnished graves of the "landlords" (fig. 151) and around them are the burials of the poor farm-labourers and slaves. The luxurious red-figure vases in the roadside necropolises of Mytilene in Classical times point to its relations with Athens. However, extant architectural remains of this period are scant.

Sole example of monumental architecture in the second half of the fourth century BC is the Ionic pseudo-dipteral, octastyle temple at Mesa, with exquisite vegetal decoration on its sima (figs 153, 154). The pottery workshops produced Attic vase shapes, but also continued the tradition of *bucchero* technique, copying Attic black-glaze vases. Large-scale sculpture has not been found. Sculpture on Lesbos in Classical times can only be followed through contemporary coroplastic art (fig. 150).

For Mytilene the campaign of Alexander the Great in Asia Minor and the Persian reprisals brought Persian attacks and tyranny. Alexander liberated it in 324 BC, together with other Aegean islands. His announcement at Olympia of the return of the exiles who had been exposed as friends of the Persians brought to an end the political strife that troubled the life of the city for centuries. Indicative is the spirit of the decree of Mytilene, regulating the details of the deserters' homecoming and the restoration of their real-estate property.

In the period of Alexander the Great's successors, the island's cities entered the sphere of influence of Lysimachos and from 289 BC that of the Ptolemies, with a brief interlude of Syrian sovereignty imposed by Antiochos II in the middle years of the century.

In the early second century BC the Lesbian cities formed a coalition with other cities in the East Aegean islands and the Hellespont, with which they had mercantile and maritime interests in common. The direct association of the sanctuary at Mesa, which is attributed to the Lesbian Trinity (Zeus, Hera, Dionysos), with the *Koinon* of Lesbian cities is manifested by the representation of the Ionic eight-columned temple on the coinage of the *Koinon*.

Mytilene, Methymna and Eresos continued to flourish in Hellenistic times, while the other cities merged or were destroyed by natural phenomena or military events. After the earthquake in 231 BC, Pyrrha declined and its territory was merged with the Mytilenaia in 167 BC. Antissa was laid waste by the Romans, in the reprisals after the Third Macedonian War and then ceded to Methymna, while Eresos was under the influence of Mytilene.

Lesbos also prospered under Roman rule. Opulent villas have come to light in Mytilene, with wonderful mosaic floors. Outstanding is the so-called "House of Menander", in which scenes from the poet's plays, portraits of him (fig. 155) and the Muse of Theatre Thaleia are the predominant representations. A conspicuous position is accorded to Orpheus, who is depicted playing his lyre beneath an olive tree, surrounded by animals enchanted by his music.

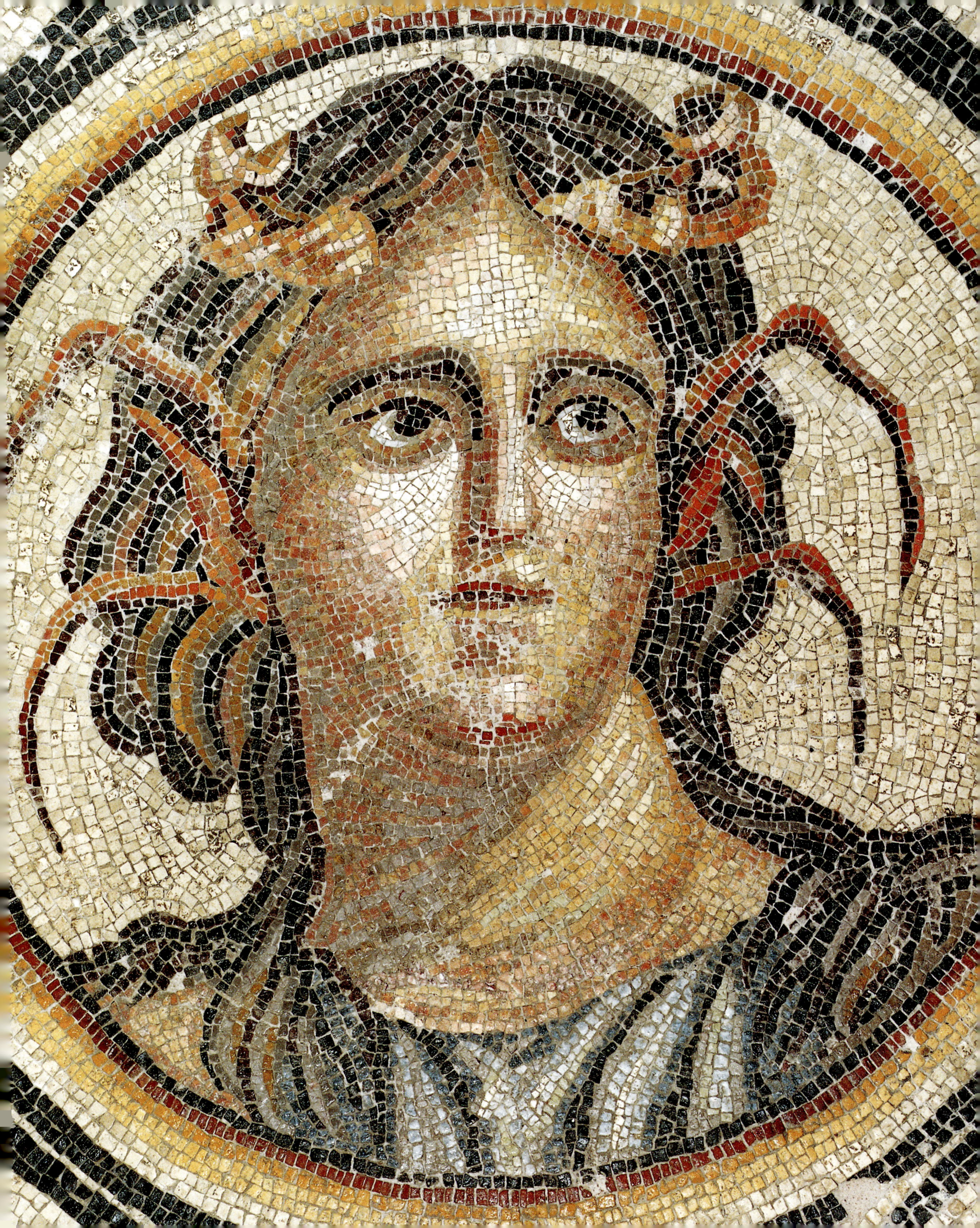

157. Lesbos. The *piscina*, built in the pseudo-isodomic system, on the south coast of Mytilene, was used in the 1st c. BC. When its use stopped, probably due to a sudden event, it filled with vases and vessels for preparing food, and symposium vases, that were used by the owners of the fish tank.

158. Lesbos. The arcades of the Roman aqueduct in the village of Moria. The aqueduct brought drinking water a distance of 30 km. (from Ayasos) to the city of Mytilene. The ravines and dells were spanned by arcades, the best-preserved of which are at Moria and Lampou Myloi.

The architectural remains of public buildings of the Hellenistic and Roman periods bespeak wealth and power. According to the literary sources, the city of Mytilene was considered one of the loveliest of the age. The first city of Lesbos, it is compared with Ephesos and Rhodes. The economic affluence can be seen in its well-organized harbour with the large spacious quays to facilitate the loading and unloading of cargoes, always busy with arriving and departing ships. Marble bridges linked the two banks of the Euripos, while the luxurious stoas with shops, along the east bank at least, had tessellated pavements (fig. 156). The Euripos played a seminal role in the life of the city, securing communication between the two harbours. Lining its banks were the most important civic buildings and sanctuaries, and it was the focus of business activities.

The economy of Lesbos enjoyed a sustained heyday in Hellenistic and Roman times. This is imprinted in the splendid residences, the bathhouse complexes in the north commercial harbour, the mints, the pottery and coroplastic workshops (fig. 157). Impressive was the production of a particular category of relief pottery and coroplastic works with glazing, which imitates the analogous expensive gold and silver symposium vessels (fig. 159).

A monument of outstanding importance was the ancient theatre, constructed after the final expansion of Mytilene on the western outskirts of the city, close to the entrance in the fortification wall, on the slopes of the highest hill hereabouts. Remnants of the last building phase survive, including the circular orchestra, 24.20 metres in diameter, and part of the horseshoe-shaped cavea, 107 metres in diameter. The retaining wall, 1 metre high and defining the orchestra, bears traces of revetment. Preserved is an inscribed part of the marble crowning course with information on the inspector (*epimeletes*) of works in the theatre, Julius Leontus, during the generalship (*strategia*) of Marcus Claudius Triphonianus. The importance of the theatre of Mytilene in the citizens' life is reflected in the host of figurines of actors, in the representation of scenes from New Comedy plays in the mosaics in the so-called "House of Menander", and in literary tradition. Its uniqueness lies in the fact that it was the model for the theatre of Pompey in Rome, which influenced the architecture of theatres in the Italian Peninsula.

Although Lesbos is mountainous with abundant and excellent water sources, the settlements had a severe water-supply problem. With the population increase in Hellenistic and Roman times there was insufficient water to cover the inhabitants' needs. The water-supply system of Mytilene seems to have included not only wells but also a central network already in the Hellenistic period (fig, 158). This system was perfected in Roman times at Methymna, with the aqueduct that brought water from Lepetymnos to Mytilene, and with a second monumental aqueduct that brought water from the springs on Olympos.

Research on the island's mineral resources in Antiquity is fullest for the period from the second century BC onward. Knowledge of the situation in earlier times is limited to the quarrying and working of the stones trachyte and liparite. The greyish white limestone, the red trachyte and other igneous rocks found on the surface were used by the inhabitants of Lesbos either for the polygonal-masonry retaining walls of the Archaic period, or for building farmhouses and houses generally. More systematic exploitation of the Lesbian quarries commenced in the time

158

of the successors to Alexander the Great, with the enormous realms, the free trafficking of goods and the increased needs for constructing large and luxurious buildings. Materials from the quarries at Moria, with the golden grey limestone, have been identified in columns at Pompeii and Rome, in the odeum of Smyrna and the monuments of Pergamon (fig. 161).

The traveller Cyriacus of Ancona, who visited Lesbos at the invitation of the Gatelusi in the fifteenth century, notes that they owed much of their wealth to the production and circulation of alum, production centres of which were Lesbos and Phokaia. The principal applications of alum were medicinal as an astringent and haemostatic agent, in leather working, as a mordant when dyeing wool, and so on. According to a recent study, the processing, production and trade of alum on Lesbos dates back to as early as the end of the second century AD. The workshop in the creek of Kalloni Bay consists of a complex of conical and rectangular storerooms, with simple ovens, a monumental entrance, lintel and jambs (fig. 162). The product was transported and traded in amphorae, as in other production centres in the Western Mediterranean, such as the island of Lipari near Sicily.

Mytilene mainly, but the other Lesbian cities too, experienced the harshness of the Romans in reprisal for allying with Mithridates and the massacre of Romans in Asia Minor. Julius Caesar and the general Lucullus campaigned on Lesbos in 88 BC, besieging the city of Mytilene, which they finally captured and sacked, as attested by the archaeological evidence over its entire area. Peace and tranquility were secured in the region after Pompey's defeat of Mithridates and the Parthians. The triumphant general celebrated his victory in the theatre of Mytilene, where the people accorded him a warm welcome that contributed to their reconciliation with Rome. The Lesbian historian Theophanes, who accompanied Pompey, was instrumental in the final normalization of relations between Mytilene and Rome.

All the deities in the Greek pantheon were worshipped on Lesbos. A special place was held by the so-called Lesbian Trinity, comprising Zeus Antiaos, Aioleia, who is identified with Hera, protectress of the Aeolian clans, and Zonnysos Omystas, who is associated with orgiastic cult and is identified with Dionysos, protector of the old inhabitants. He seems to represent the local element, whereas Hera and Zeus represent the main clans on the island. Cult centre of the Lesbian Trinity was the pan-Lesbian sanctuary at Mesa. Cult centres of Dionysos have been located at Methymna, where he is mentioned with the epithet Phallen, Bresa as Bresigenes, Antissa, Eresos and Mytilene.

Apollo was one of the most important gods of Lesbos (fig. 160). He is represented on silver coinage of Mytilene, of 450-400 BC. Centres of his worship have been identified at Methymna, where he is referred to with the epithet Smintheus, Eresos, the southern Mytilenaia, with the epithet Killaios, *extra muros* of the city of Mytilene, with the epithet Malloeis, and according to some scholars in the sanctuary at Klopedi (fig. 152).

159. Lesbos, Mytilene. Skyphos with reddish brown glaze and greenish brown olives, from the deposit of the workshops producing relief pottery, of the 1st c. BC. Mytilene Archaeological Museum.

160. Lesbos. Electrum stater of Mytilene, with head of Apollo, 428/7 BC. London, British Museum.

124 | NORTH AND EAST AEGEAN

The sanctuary of Demeter and Kore, uncovered inside the Kastro of Mytilene, and of Aphrodite, brought to light on the plot now occupied by the new Mytilene Archaeological Museum, date to Hellenistic and Roman times.

From Antiquity the mints played an important role in the economy of Lesbos. To them are ascribed billon coins issued and in circulation from the sixth century to 480 BC. After the end of the Persian Wars until the mid-fourth century BC, the billon coins were replaced by electrum hektai, a denomination of the stater, which is called "*chrysion*" in the inscription of the contract between Mytilene and Phokaia for the issue and circulation of coins of this category. From 440 BC the mints of Mytilene and Methymna began to issue silver and copper coins, while the smaller cities apparently did not issue their own coins until the fourth century BC. Their needs were covered by the coins of Methymna and primarily Mytilene, which had greater political and economic influence on them.

In the Byzantine Age Lesbos belonged to the Thema of the Aegean, until 1355 when it was presented to Francesco Gateluso, after his marriage to Maria, sister of the Palaiologan emperor. In 1462 Lesbos fell to the Ottoman Turks, who remained until 1912. Since that year Lesbos, Lemnos and Aghios Efstratios constitute a prefecture of the free Greek State.

161. Lesbos. The quarry at Moria with the golden grey limestone was one of the most important on the island. Preserved *in situ* are unfinished products and on the rock faces are traces of quarrying.

162. Lesbos, Apothika. Alum workshop. The material was used in dyeing and tanning. In medicine it was used as an astringent and haemostatic agent.

LESBOS | 125

Chios

AGLAIA ARCHONTIDOU-ARGYRI

According to myth, Chios owes its name to the Nymph Chion, daughter of Oinopion, or to Chios, son of Poseidon, whose birth was accompanied by severe snowfalls on the island. According to the historian Isidoros, however, the name is Phoenician and is associated with mastic.

Human activity on Chios can be dated back to the early sixth millennium BC, as indicated by the finds from the cave at Ayio Galas, near the northwest coast. Several prehistoric sites have also been identified near the north and the south coast, but only Emporio has been excavated, revealing settlement remains dating from the Final Neolithic to the end of the Mycenaean period (5th-2nd millennium BC). The privileged geographical position, the natural harbour, the fertile hinterland and the source of potable water were the basic reasons why the settlers who arrived from Asia Minor opted for this site (fig. 163). They evidently considered the water source the most basic good and protected the ovoid well they sunk with a mighty wall, with exedras and embankments throughout the duration of habitation.

Ten settlement phases have been distinguished at Emporio, of which the phase III settlement, dated to the late third millennium BC, was provided with a strong defensive wall. The houses were single storey, of rectangular plan – in rare cases apsidal –, with flat roofs and compacted clay floors. The occupants were herdsmen, agriculturalists, fishermen, potters, metalworkers and weavers. They had trading contacts with the Asia Minor coast, the nearby islands and the Cyclades, as is deduced from the obsidian debitage. The scant settlement remains of the Late Mycenaean (Late Helladic III) period show that life at Emporio continued until the end of the Late Bronze Age.

After the demise of the Mycenaean world, Ionians from Histiaia in Euboea migrated to Chios, under the leadership of Amphikles, who is mentioned as the island's first king. The new colonists merged with or expelled the Pelasgians from Hymettos, Abantians from Euboea and Molossians from Attica, who had preceded them. By the early eighth century BC Aeolians and Ionians were living in dispersed villages (*kata komas*) in the central part of the island. Later, the Aeolians were confined to the northern part of Chios and the Ionians to the southern.

The earliest excavation evidence of the settlement of colonists from Euboea and the northern Cyclades are the Protogeometric graves of the city of Chios (10th-9th century BC) (figs 167, 168). The tholos tomb at Vourlidia, the few Geometric sherds from Phana and Emporio attest to the subsequent spread of the Ionians in southern Chios, with which the settlement of early historical times on Prophitis Ilias Hill at Emporio is associated. On the terrace formed a little way below the summit, the colonists built the walled acropolis with the megaron and the sanctuary of the patron goddess Athena, which were marked off by a special precinct wall (*peribolos*). In the sixth century BC the temple of Athena was built, a simple edifice of rectan-

126 | NORTH AND EAST AEGEAN

gular plan with prodomos and cella, in which the earliest altar was housed (figs 164, 165). Next to it was placed the statue of Athena, in the type of the Promachos, with shield, spear and a circlet of griffins on the helmet (fig. 166). The so-called "altar B", on a terrace north of the temple, is from the same building phase.

The official sanctuary of the settlement, which has been identified as the large cemetery of Artemis, was founded *extra muros* of the acropolis on a lower hill near the harbour. It has a big Ionic temple with column capitals of exceptional art, a richly decorated cornice and benches at the ends of cella walls, which are set on lions' paws. This sanctuary was more cosmopolitan in character, but the small sanctuary on the acropolis had greater longevity, as it was linked with the protection of the settlement, the vestal gods and the origin of the ancestors.

The settlement at Emporio, without any preconceived layout and without defensive wall, spread over the south slope, from the entrance in the acropolis wall down to the harbour. The houses were one-roomed with small courtyard in front of the entrance, had a flat roof supported by timber posts on stone bases and a doorway with stone threshold. In almost all there was a small hearth that was not only used for cooking food but also provided light and heat.

163. Chios. General view of Emporio. The prehistoric settlement occupies the promontory overlooking the harbour.

164. Chios, Emporio. The temple of Athena after the recent restoration works.

165. Chios, Emporio. Aerial photograph of the temple of Athena with the terrace and "altar C" to the north.

166. Chios. Lead griffin from the helmet of the statue of Athena at Emporio, 6th c. BC. Chios Archaeological Museum.

167, 168. Chios. Protogeometric pottery from the city of Chios, with influences from Euboea and the northern Cycladic islands, 900-850 BC. Chios Archaeological Museum.

After the abandonment of the settlement and the destruction of the temples, which is connected with the Ionian Revolt, life continued in the more lowland areas until about 324 BC, when favourable conditions for developing activities near the sea appeared once again. The temple of Athena was repaired, "altar A" was enlarged and the earlier "altar B" was replaced by the so-called "altar C" (fig. 165).

The regime of the early colonists was the monarchy, since there is reference to names of kings, whose seat was the city of Chios. The system was feudal, with semi-autonomous families in the countryside, and the local lords were dependent on the central administration. By the seventh century BC, the regime on Chios had begun to be transformed into a democracy. A "*boule demosie*" already existed in the sixth century BC, while concurrently there functioned the boule of the deme and the basileis, that is, the boule of nobles, while the elected archons were the basileus and the demarchos.

After the Mycenaean Age, in those cities where the Greek element was predominant federal relations of ethnic and political character were developed. The Ionians belonged to a federal organization with seat at Ephesos, which was established in the ninth century BC, although the prevailing view is that the Panionion resulted from the coalition of many cities against rich and powerful Melie, *circa* 700 BC.

In the eighth century BC, a period of political upheavals and of colonization, Chios established trading relations first with Smyrna and Erythres, and then with Egypt and the Euxine Pontus. From the mid-seventh century BC it developed commercial contacts and activities in the Aegean islands, the Asia Minor hinterland, the Thracian coast, the Propontis and the Euxine Pontus. Chian merchants sold the choice "*ariousion*" wine, and in return obtained timber, metals, slaves and grain from Egypt, with intermediate port of call Naukrates. Clashes between Chios and Erythraia, over the fertile region of Leukonio, in the seventh century BC, ended with the final imposition of Chios over Erythraia. Despite the disputes, the two cities joined forces in the colonization of Maroneia in the Thracian littoral, and of Naukrates in North Africa.

Henceforth, and because of the colonization, the island enjoyed considerable economic and political progress. The main harbours, Chios, Volissos and Emporio, were of great importance for maritime communications. Shortly after 650 BC the Greek cities of Asia Minor were subjugated by the King of Lydia, Croesus, which whom Chios maintained amicable relations, while at the same period the formation of a new aggressive power in the East, Persia, commenced. In 546 BC Persia dissolved the Lydian State and captured the Greek cities in the East Aegean.

For Ionian Chios the Archaic period (7th-6th century BC) was a heyday. The refinement of Ionian art is reflected in the "school" of sculpture, which is represented by outstanding works found outside the island, mainly in major sanctuaries of the Hellenic world. These include the Nike in *Knielaufschema* on Delos, by the sculptor Archermos (fig. 54) and the superb kore known as the "Chian Maiden" on the Acropolis of Athens. Because information on this wonderful school is drawn mainly from literary and epigraphic testimonies, the very few pieces from the island itself are

166

128 | NORTH AND EAST AEGEAN

167

168

CHIOS

169. Chios. Marble torso of a kore, with the hands below the hair locks that fall on the bosom and the back. She wears an Ionic chiton with incised undulating folds. Found in the city of Chios and dated to 580-570 BC. Chios Archaeological Museum.

170. Chios, Phana. Gilded silver figurine of a warrior in helmet and breastplate, from the sanctuary of Apollo at Phana, second half of 6th c. BC. Chios Archaeological Museum.

invaluable for the peculiarities of Chian sculpture. That is why the two korai in the Chios Archaeological Museum (fig. 169), the torso of a kouros found recently at Emporio, the torso of a small kouros from Nagos and the small silver kouros from the sanctuary at Phana acquire special significance (fig. 170).

A special pottery workshop developed on Ionian Chios, which belongs in the general framework of the Ionian workshops and has its roots in the Protogeometric period (figs 167, 168). From the late seventh century BC, the kylix, a familiar type of drinking vessel with high foot and horizontal handles, played a leading role. Distinctive is the buff slip coating the surface of all vase shapes from the Chian workshops, upon which was painted the main subject, which could be a vegetal motif, an animal or a human figure (fig. 174).

The Persian conquests, with their expansion into Egypt in 526 BC and to the Hellespont in 513 BC, restricted the trade of the Greek cities, Chios among them, and contributed to their decline. The conflict between Greeks and Persians came to a head with the Ionian Revolt in 499 BC, which ended to the detriment of the Greek cities. Chios suffered the heaviest losses in the naval battle of Lade in 494 BC. In 481-480 BC, Chios, Lesbos and Samos, as significant naval powers, were accepted in the alliance of Greek cities, which was already breaking up because Sparta withdrew. Then the preconditions were created for the new alliance, headed by Athens, which promoted the argument of the Ionian cities' common origin. This was the ideological mantle of the Athenian League, of which Chios became a member in 478 BC, untaxed and independent. In these circumstances, with peace guaranteed by the Athenian Navy and the curbing of piracy, Chios was able to concentrate on transit trade and its citizens became the "wealthiest of the Hellenes". Alongside trade, the inhabitants of Chios promoted their own products, mainly the excellent wine, in the principal ports of the Mediterranean and the Euxine Pontus (fig. 73). Thus they secured not only food supplies but also a luxurious lifestyle, to the degree that expressions such as "Chian laughter" and "Chian life" became proverbial.

Chios, the "greatest of the allied cities in Ionia", remained a loyal ally of Athens even in the difficult years of the hegemony. It joined forces with the Athenians to suppress the apostasy of the Samians in 440 BC, it followed the Athenian Navy to Sicily and it took part in the destruction of Melos in 415 BC. When, after the Athenians' defeat in Sicily, the role of the oligarchs in the East Aegean was reinforced and a climate of instability held away, with serious effects on the economy, Chios broke away with the help of Alcibiades, who had in the meanwhile defected to the Spartan camp. The uprising failed, with severe consequences. According to the textual sources, the Athenians captured Oinouses, landed at Kardamyla, Phana and Leukonio, and fortified themselves at Delphinio, where they remained until 406 BC. After the Athenians were vanquished at Aigos Potamoi, Sparta acquired sovereignty in many Aegean cities, including Chios, where garrisons were installed and a decarchy was appointed. As part of their imposition and control, the Spartans demolished the shipyards, took away the ships and sent the democrats into exile. Until the third quarter of the fourth century BC the state of war in the Aegean was virtually permanent, exhausting the battling cities and resulting in the loss of the islands' *peraia* to the Persians, in 386 BC. Chios allied with Athens in 383 BC and joined the Second Athenian League, but with the aid of Mausolos it seceded in 357 BC and, following the defeat of the Athenian Navy between Chios and Erythraia, gained its autonomy.

After the synedrion of Corinth and the Greek cities' decision to unite against the Persians (337 BC), Chios was beset by internal strife between the pro-Macedonian and the pro-Persian factions, given that it allied with Athens in the clash with Philip II of Macedon. It is indicative that when Alexander began his campaign, the pro-Persian group of oligarchs in power in Chios facilitated the installation of the Persian garrison, which the Macedonians expelled. Alexander restored the democratic regime in 332 BC, imposed the handing over of twenty trieremes and in his epistle ordered the return of the political exiles (fig. 171). In the time of his successors Chios continued to have a flourishing economy due to trade. At first it was part of the realm of Antigonos, and subsequently of that of Lysimachos. From 281 BC until the mid-third century BC it passed to the State of the Ptolemies and then to the ambit of influence of the kings of Pergamon.

During the Classical and Hellenistic periods the development of art on Chios followed the current of the other Greek cities and received the influences of artists with whom it came into contact. Among the rarest monuments in Greece, which is housed in the Chios Archaeological Museum, are the pillars of pale grey Chian limestone with incised decoration in a technique used in metalwork. The pillars, many of them inscribed, have been interpreted as altars or grave monuments. The subjects of the representations vary and included dancing girls in short chiton and bearing a kalathos, aquatic birds, a seated female figure playing a lyre, Sirens with double-flutes or lyre (fig. 175). The earliest pillar, with the dancing girls, is dated to the late fifth or the early fourth century BC (fig. 66) and has been associated with works by the well-known sculptor Kallimachos or his pupils.

During the period of Roman rule Chios enjoyed economic privileges, as it was declared free and exempt from taxes under the terms of the Treaty of Apameia in 188 BC. It attracted Roman merchants and the Roman fleet used the shipyards for repairs. Chios adopted a pro-Roman policy in the Mithridatan Wars and in 86 BC suffered terrible destruction at the hands of Mithridates' general Zenobios. On the now desert island Mithridates settled colonists and an army from Pontos, which were finally expelled by Sulla's treasurer and later general Lucullus. In 85 BC Sulla himself declared Chios free and an ally of Rome. The sack of the island by Mithridates, the earthquakes that followed and the civil strife in the Roman Empire impeded economic recovery. Even so, Chios kept its laws to the end and continued to mint its own coinage until the reign of Galienus (AD 253-268). With the administrative reforms of Diocletian (AD 284-305) it was included in the *Provincia Insularum* and subsequently, with the split of the empire, became part of the Eastern Roman State.

170

171. Chios. Epistle from Alexander the Great to the deme of Chians, 332 BC, in which he demands the return of the political exiles, sets the time for resolving the issues of their return and installs a garrison on the island. Chios Archaeological Museum.

Sculpture in Roman times is distinguished not only by the copies of important Classical and Hellenistic originals, the votive or grave stelai, the sarcophagi and altars, but also by portraits, such as those recovered from civic buildings close to the harbour. The most notable of these are of Sabina, wife of Emperor Hadrian, and of Herennia Etruscilla, wife of Trajan Dacius. These works confirm the textual sources, which refer to the excellent relations between Rome and Chios, and concurrently emphasize the development of Roman portraiture from the Julio-Claudian dynasty to the era of the tetrarchs.

According to the sources, the epigraphic testimonies and the archaeological evidence, the cult of Cybele, which reached the Aegean islands from Asia Minor, was very widespread on Chios from the Archaic period into Late Antiquity. In Archaic times the goddess was represented seated within a small temple with her hands on her knees. From Early Hellenistic times she is represented seated on a throne with a lion cub on her knees and a phiale in her left hand (fig. 172). The best-known sanctuary of the goddess is at Vrontados. It is located on a terrace on a rock and preserved at the centre are the remains of the seated goddess's throne and the relief

132 | NORTH AND EAST AEGEAN

lions. In folk tradition this sanctuary has been linked with Homer and his origin, and it is popularly known as Homer's Stone or *Daskalopetra* (Teacher's Stone) because the formed rock was believed to have been intended for the poet's pupils and the remnants of the small oikos for Homer himself.

The worship of Apollo held an important place on the island, as is apparent from the magnificent Archaic temple at Phana, which was associated with the god's birth and the wanderings of Leto, while according to the sources, in northern Chios worship of Apollo was combined with worship of Dionysos.

Artemis too was a significant deity for the Ionians of Chios. The goddess worshipped in the sanctuary by the harbour at Emporio has been identified as Artemis from the votive inscription on a kylix by the painter Nikesermos, which was found in the fill removed in excavation.

The patron goddess Athena, had her most important sanctuary on the acropolis (Prophitis Ilias Hill) at Emporio, while she was also worshipped in the city of Chios, where there was said to be a seated statue of the goddess.

Between myth and reality, first settler (*oikistes*) of Chios was Oinopion, who is associated with tending the vine and making wine, the island's principal source of wealth. Oinopion's tomb was guarded by the Sphinx, the most enduring symbol of the city, which was the obverse type on Chian coins. According to myth, epigraphic testimonies and archaeological evidence, worship of Dionysos, who is associated directly with the vine and wine, was widespread on the island into Late Antiquity, in combination with the cult of Herakles or of Apollo Xenios. The attributes of Dionysos – who is referred to on Chios with the epithets Omadios and Pleus –, a vine branch and a bunch of grapes, together with the transport amphora for wine and more rarely the kantharos, appeared on the reverse of the coins (fig. 173).

The city of Chios was one of the earliest Greek cities to mint coins. Production of the first issues, which were electrum staters with the Sphinx within a vine wreath on the obverse, stopped in the fifth century BC. From around 500 BC the amphora was added on Chian coins and henceforth the mints followed the development of its typology. From the sixth century BC Chios also issued silver staters (fig. 61), production and circulation of which continued after the

172. Chios. Marble votive relief with representation of Cybele with the lion, accompanied by Attis and a Korybant. Found in the city of Chios and dated to Roman times. Chios Archaeological Museum.

analogous electrum coins ceased. Concurrently, silver tetradrachms and didrachms began to be issued. In the closing years of the fifth century BC copper coins appeared, which represented fractions of lesser value. From 350 BC the Chian mints stopped production until 190 BC, when they resumed operation issuing coins on the basis of the type of the Attic silver tetradrachm of the reign of Alexander the Great.

Oinouses

The small island group of Oinouses lies between Chios and the Erythraia Peninsula and was presumably named after the excellent quality wine (*oinos*) it produced in Antiquity. The largest islet is Oinousa (14 sq. km.), whose fate was always bound up with that of Chios. It is mentioned already from the sixth century BC by Hekataios and later by Thucydides. Herodotus recounts that when the Phokaians asked the Chians whether they could settle there, after the Persians had destroyed their city, Chios refused to sell the island, so as not to lose the commercial privileges. No systematic excavations have been conducted on Oinousa but a few antiquities have been located (settlement remains, mosaics, etc.).

173. Chios. Chian silver coin of the Classical period, with representation of the Sphinx on the obverse and an amphora with the inscription ΧΙΟΣ on the reverse. 475-450 BC. London, British Museum.

174. Chios. Chian kylix with depiction of a Sphinx. On the inside is the familiar Chian lotus flower. Found at Marion on Cyprus and dated to the late 7th/early 6th c. BC. Nicosia, Cyprus Museum.

175. Chios. Marble pillar (grave stele) with incised representation of a Siren with lyre, framed by running spiral pattern in relief. 3rd c. BC. Chios Archaeological Museum.

134 | NORTH AND EAST AEGEAN

175

CHIOS | 135

Psara

AGLAIA ARCHONTIDOU-ARGYRI

The seven rocky islets of the Psara complex, lying 10 nautical miles from the west coast of Chios, are Psara, Antipsara, Kato Nisi, Aghios Nikolaos – known as Aghionikolaki – Daskalio, Prasonisi and Nisopoula. Their total area is 67 sq. km., with Psara, the biggest, covering 42 sq. km. Psara is essentially a mountain (fig. 176), the highest peak of which is Prophitis Ilias (531 m. a.s.l.).

Settlement remains from Antiquity and from recent times have been located on the small tracts of low land near the coast, with arable soil and potable water. This island group is known from the Greek War of Independence and the total destruction of Mavri Rachi in 1824, sung for posterity by the poet Dionysios Solomos.

In the ancient literary sources it is considered a poor, barren isle with not even enough wine for the libations to Dionysos. It is also mentioned as a satisfactory harbour capable of sheltering some twenty ships, and as a place swept by strong winds. The earliest textual reference is in Homer's *Odyssey*, where it is called "Psyrie", in Nestor's narrative in the episode of the Nostos.

Archaeological research has brought to light at the site of Archontiki remains of unbroken human activity from the Final Neolithic period (5th-4th millennium BC) to the fifth century BC, reaching its zenith in the Late Bronze Age (14th-12th century BC), and evidence of hero worship from the eighth to the fifth century BC. According to recent sources, Psara was deserted several times, mainly after incursions or other martial events. Surface survey on the island has shown that there was no interruption in habitation until Late Roman times. At Archontiki evidence for use of the site after the fifth century BC is scant. In other areas, however, settlements and cemeteries of Hellenistic and Roman times have been identified: at historic Mavri Rachi there is a Hellenistic settlement, at Ftelio and Limnos there is pottery of the same period, at Xirokampos there are remains of a Roman installation and in the present village there is a Late Roman cemetery with grave stelai.

The Mycenaean settlement of the Late Helladic III period (14th-12th century BC) can be interpreted as an emporion, with trading relations throughout the Eastern Mediterranean, as deduced from the imported goods, such as sard, steatite, bars of glass paste, faience and gold. There were workshops on the island producing objects intended for local use or for trade, as indicated by the steatite moulds for rings and seal stones, and the *in situ* making of seals from glass paste or faience.

The flourishing society of Psara in this period is reflected in the spacious houses with storage spaces and pithoi, found *in situ*, and the prestige artifacts accompanying the burials in cist graves: bronze weapons, excellent-quality imported pottery (fig. 179) and local figurines (fig. 178), jewellery of faience, steatite and sard (fig. 177), as well as the impressive number of one hundred and ten seal stones.

At the edge of the Mycenaean cemetery (fig. 180), burials of the Early Bronze Age (3rd millennium BC) and of Protogeometric times (10th-9th century BC) were found, as well as a small altar of *eschara* type with votive offerings around it, almost all of them vases dating from the eighth to the mid-fifth century BC (figs 181, 182). They are mainly examples of Chian pottery, but also included skyphoi from Lesbos, aryballoi from Corinth, black-figure and superb red-figure wine vases from Attica (figs 183, 184), as well as bronze swords and bars of glass paste. Many vases bear dedicatory inscriptions "to the hero" ("τῷ ἥρωι") and the name of the dedicator, but the name of the hero who was worshipped so piously there eludes us.

176. Psara. The rocky coast.

177. Psara, Archontiki. Faience necklace from the Mycenaean cemetery. The burials were accompanied by jewellery of semiprecious stones, faience and glass paste. Chios Archaeological Museum.

178. Psara, Archontiki. Clay figurine of Phi (Φ) type from the Mycenaean cemetery. These figurines possibly represented deities or handmaidens, in which capacity they accompanied the dead in the grave. Chios Archaeological Museum.

179. Psara, Archontiki. Mycenaean cemetery. Outstanding among the imported and local pottery are the stemmed kylikes. Chios Archaeological Museum.

PSARA

180. Psara, Archontiki. Mycenaean cemetery with cist graves (14th-12th c. BC). Burials and grave goods *in situ*.

181, 182. Psara, Archontiki. The *apothetes* around the altar of the hero, with the finds *in situ*.

183. Psara, Archontiki. Red-figure cup with representation of Satyrs, from the altar of the hero. *c.* mid-5th c. BC. Chios Archaeological Museum.

184. Psara, Archontiki. Black-figure kylix with representation of schematic eyes (eye cup) and a Dionysiac scene, from the altar of the hero. Early 5th c. BC. Chios Archaeological Museum.

PSARA | 139

Samos

CONSTANTINOS TSAKOS

Dorysa, Dryousa, Kyparissia, Melamphylos, Melanthemos, Phyllis, Anthemis, Hydrele, are just some of the epithets used in the ancient literary texts to qualify the verdant East Aegean island with its dense woodlands and abundant water. The official name of Samos is attributed to a very ancient root *sama*, which relates to heights and is vindicated by the island's high mountains.

The crucial location of Samos on the sea routes linking the West with the East of the early civilizations, and the rich lands of the North with Egypt and the South, had a decisive effect on the island's historical development.

Tradition has it that *oikistes* and *ktistes* (founder-hero) of the island was Ankaios, son of Poseidon and the Nymph Astypalaia, King of the Lelegians who dwelt on Samos before the arrival of the Ionians. He is accredited with introducing viniculture here.

Shortly before 1000 BC Ionian colonists from the Epidauria, led by Prokles son of Pityreus, brought a new spirit to the island, whose inhabitants had been part of the Mycenaean world since the second half of the second millennium BC. The incomers brought with them the cult of Hera, which readily took root on the island and in the Heraion, since the great prehellenic Mother Goddess had been worshipped on the same site since time immemorial (fig. 186).

The earliest traces of habitation have been found on Kastro tou Lykourgou Hill, which should probably be identified with Astypalaia, the ancient acropolis of the city (fig. 191). The finds date back to the Final Neolithic period (late 4th millennium BC) and display affinities with the contemporary culture in the Cyclades.

Mycenaean finds from the Heraion, a tumulus with built burial chamber (13th century BC) to the north of the great temple, and the rock-cut tomb found intact in the village square at Myloi, confirm the Mycenaean presence in the region, even though no traces of a settlement have yet been uncovered.

Prokles' descendants ruled Samos until the end of the eighth century BC, when the wealthy landowners, the *geomoroi* (those among whom the fertile lands were shared) took power.

During the first two centuries after their arrival, the Ionians apparently lived dispersed in the plains in the southeast part of the island. From the eighth century BC the city began to develop rapidly, whereas the Heraion was confined gradually to its religious role, as principal sanctuary of Hera, patron goddess of Samos. The turn of the population to the sea, with the growing interest in shipping and maritime trade, was of de-

185. Samos. The small ivory figure of a youth, a masterpiece of what is believed to be Cretan art, was a fitment on a lyre, late 7th c. BC. Samos Archaeological Museum.

186. Samos. View of the Heraion. The sanctuary of Hera, patron goddess of the island, with the impressive remains of her huge temple with in the verdant landscape of the Imbrassos Estuary, is the most important and best-studied archaeological site on Samos. The rich finds, of unique artistic and historical value, are housed in the Samos Archaeological Museum in the island's capital.

187. Samos. The colossal kouros, pride of the Samos Archaeological Museum, was originally about 5 m. tall. Found in 1980, to the east of the Heraion, this statue in Samian marble is the work of a Samian artist (580 BC). Thanks to its enormous size, the accomplished modelling of the flesh and the brilliant expression, this splendid youth with the inscription on his left thigh proclaims the unprecedented economic and social status of the wealthy dedicator.

cisive significance for the progress of Samos. The organizing of a harbour in the vicinity of the city served more effectively its contacts with the East, source of products as well as ideas. From the late eighth century BC, as the finds from the Heraion and the city indicate, there was a proliferation of objects from the Orient and Egypt. After the mid-seventh century BC Cypriot figurines predominated, ousting the local products. In these same years, the Samians had already embarked on their first long voyages, which were to take them to the ends of the then-known world.

Circa 630 BC the mariner Kolaios sailed through the Pillars of Herakles (mod. Gibraltar) and reached Tartessos in Spain, whence he returned with a cargo of silver valued at 60 talents. His votive offerings in the Heraion from the tithe (*dekate*) of his profits evoked the admiration of Herodotus. The Samians' trading relations now spread as far as the distant regions of Caucasus and Iran, Mesopotamia and the Middle East, Egypt and Libya, the Euxine Pontus and Spain, from which they brought back not only earnings and experiences, but also precious and exotic gifts for the patron goddess of the Heraion. Concurrently, they forged stable relations with the Aegean islands (fig. 185) as well as with Eretria, Corinth, Sparta and Athens, which was to dominate the island commercially and politically in the ensuing centuries.

Already from the eighth century BC bridgeheads had been created to the rich tracts of land on the opposite coast of Asia Minor. However, the Samians often had to defend these from the expansionist designs of the neighbouring cities of Priene and Miletos, paying a high price not only in blood. From the early seventh century BC the Samians showed interest in the Northeast

SAMOS | 141

Aegean, while towards the end of the century they founded colonies on the shores of Thrace. The trading stations (emporia) established on the coast of Cilicia facilitated communications with the East and Cyprus. The founding of Minoa on Amorgos, the colonists of which were led by the poet Simonides, strengthened the Samians' position in the Aegean and their participation in the settling of Ionians at Naukrates reinforced trading relations with Egypt.

The accumulation of wealth and the advancement of the lower classes, of tradesmen, seamen, craftsmen, were to create tensions with the rich *geomoroi*, who had a monopoly on power. The clashes provided an opportunity for able and ambitious individuals to install tyrannical regimes. One of the tyrants, Demoteles, was assassinated around 600 BC and power reverted once more to the *geomoroi*. At the same period the Megarians, rivals of the Samians in the region of Propontis, moved against Perinthos, but were defeated. After their victory, however, the Samian generals and the ranks, in connivance with the Megarians, succeeded in dissolving the authority of the *geomoroi*. To commemorate the event, the chains of the Megarian captives were dedicated in an *oikos* in the agora of Samos, which was called "*Pedetes*" (after the *pedes* (fetters) of the prisoners).

188, 189. Samos. Terracotta figurines, one of a seated deity and the other of a Siren, from the large Archaic *apothetai* of the Artemision (550-525 BC). Pythagoreio Archaeological Museum.

Around 560 BC the tyrant Syloson began building the first big "temple of Rhoikos". His son Aiakes, who is probably represented in the large sculpture in the Mouseion of the ancient city, which he himself dedicated to Hera at the time he was warden (*epistates*) of her sanctuary. Polykrates, grandson of Syloson and son of Aiakes, whom Herodotus particularly admired, controlled the city's fortunes from 538 until 522 BC, when he was assassinated by the Persian satrap Oroites. That moment, with the involvement of the Persians and later the Athenians, signalled the city's gradual wane.

The economic growth of Samos from the late eighth century BC, with the maritime and mercantile expansion of the city, continued unabated until the end of the sixth century BC (fig. 195). The close contacts with the intellectual powers of the East and Egypt, but above all with Ionia, Athens and the rest of the Hellenic world, brought an outstanding floruit in Arts and Letters, which reached its peak in the first half of the sixth century BC. The major public works ascribed to Polykrates may well have started earlier, but whatever the case they bespeak the wonderful heyday the island enjoyed in Archaic times.

There were three particular projects that Herodotus admired: the great temple of Hera, the Eupalineion Aqueduct and the harbour installations, "the earth in the sea". Luckily, all three are preserved satisfactorily, so that we can appreciate why the historian was so fulsome in his praise.

The Heraion, the sanctuary of the goddess at the west edge of the plain of Chora, on the silt and the marshes of the Imbrassos estuary (fig. 186), an old sanctuary of the great pre-Hellenic Mother Goddess, was dedicated to Hera after the arrival of the Ionians. Nonetheless, local tradition prevailed, which is why the Samians believed that the goddess had been born in this place, at the root of a willow that still existed in the time of the traveller Pausanias. On the same site, where the Sacred Marriage, the union of Hera with Zeus was placed, the cult statue not made by human hand, the "*axoos sanis*" of the poet Kallimachos, was found. The lyric poet

190. Samos, Heraion. Among the most impressive *ex-votos* in the sanctuary is the sculptural group representing members of a wealthy family of ancient Samos, a work by the great Samian sculptor of the mid-6th c. BC, Geneleus. Replicas of the surviving statues have been put in the place of the originals, which are exhibited in the Samos Archaeological Museum and the Pergamon-Museum in Berlin, giving some idea of the effect they created in their natural setting.

191. Samos. Partial view of Pythagoreio, built on the site of ancient Samos and named in honour of the island's most famous son, the mathematician and philosopher Pythagoras. Visible on the hill is the castle of Lykourgos Logothetis, built at the time of the 1821 War of Independence, upon the remnants of an early Byzantine fortress. In all probability the palace of Polykrates stood on the same hill, but archaeological remains found there so far are from Hellenistic and Roman buildings.

Alkaios in the early sixth century BC names the goddess "*panton genethlan*", she who gives birth to all goods, and the early votive offerings in the sanctuary, imitation fruits with lots of seeds, which symbolized fertility, or small bovine figurines, were appropriate to this quality.

Excavations in the Heraion were begun essentially in the early twentieth century by the Archaeological Society at Athens and were continued by the German Archaeological Institute. As a result, the Heraion is among the most important and best-studied ancient Greek sanctuaries.

In its early form the sanctuary had a simple little temple to house the *xoanon* (wooden cult effigy), a small altar and beside it the osier, reminder of a very ancient tree cult. In the eighth century BC the altar was given a rectangular shape and to the west of it was built the first *hekatompedon* (a temple 100 feet long), one of the earliest Greek temples, as well as some other small edifices of Π-shaped plan. A second *hekatompedon* followed, with the toichobate of carefully worked ashlar blocks of Samian limestone and a wooden peristasis, while the altar was reshaped yet again, acquiring a more monumental form towards the end of the seventh century BC. The south stoa was also constructed, an interesting building with wooden columns in a precursor form of the stoa that was later to dominate in Greek architecture. Concurrently, work commenced on the large marble *ex-votos* with the first "Daedalic" figures, fragments of which are housed in the Samos Archaeological Museum. In the early sixth century BC the colossal statues appeared, mainly kouroi, which were set up in the sanctuary and along the sacred way linking the city with the Heraion (fig. 187). These were followed by a host of *ex-votos*, outstanding among which is the statue group by Geneleus (fig. 190).

Before the middle of the sixth century BC building of the poros "temple of Rhoikos" had started. Of unprecedented dimensions for a Greek temple, this was the wonder of Ionic architecture. At the same time, the final form of the altar was elaborated. This too was of exceptionally monumental dimensions and had lavish relief decoration which remained unaltered until the reign of Augustus.

However, within the space of a generation, the great temple with the columns and their superb bases of sensitive Samian limestone had to be replaced because of the alluvial ground. The new temple, the so-called "temple of Polykrates", was even larger and built 40 metres further west of its predecessor, so that a large esplanade, essential for festivals and sacrifices, could be arranged in front of it. The dimensions of the temple (55.16 x 108.63 metres), the double and triple colonnades on its fronts, and its enormous height rightly earned the admiration of

192, 193. Samos. Eupalineion Aqueduct. Among the most important creations of ancient technology is the "two-mouthed tunnel", the gallery opened through the rocky heart of the mountain of the acropolis, in order to bring water to the city from the Agiades springs. The successful solutions that the engineer of the work, Eupalinos son of Naustrophos from Megara, gave to the problems confronted, so that the two galleries would meet, astonishes specialist scientists to this day.

194. Samos. Tower in the wall of the second phase of fortifications (*c.* 300 BC). The city's Archaic fortifications had been largely demolished under the terms of the armistice of 439 BC. The new fortification, of ashlar stone blocks built in the isodomic system and reinforced with 40 mighty towers, which survive in excellent condition, was constructed after the exiled Samians returned home, in accordance with the edict of Alexander the Great on the repatriation of refugees.

195. Electrum stater of Samos, 600-550 BC. Athens, Numismatic Museum.

Herodotus (fig. 186). This temple was actually never finished, even though works continued for centuries, since events after the death of Polykrates (522 BC), the Persian Wars and the island's adventures with Athens and its hegemony, prevented progress on the project. Edifices of lesser dimensions, serving the needs of the sanctuary, continued to be erected from Archaic into Roman times, when a new temple of Hera was constructed between the old abandoned temple and the altar.

The unique Eupalineion aqueduct with the "two-mouth tunnel" that so impressed Herodotus, would never have been known without the testimony of the Father of History, since its two entrances had been buried under masses of earth (figs 192, 193). The difficult task of clearing the tunnel and then studying it revealed one of the greatest technical achievements of Hellenic Antiquity and enhanced the genius of the engineer who designed it, Eupalinos. The aqueduct was constructed in the mid-sixth century BC, in order to bring water to the city from the Agiades springs, behind the mountain of the acropolis. In order to protect the conduit from enemy attacks it was decided to cut it through the mountain, at a depth of 180 metres from the summit. Water was collected in a perfectly constructed tank, which is preserved at the site of the source, under the later church of St John, and then channelled in an underground conduit 900 metres long, as far as the mountainside. The tunnel, 1.036 km. in length and of dimensions 1.80 x 1.80 metres, was opened through the mountain in a north-south direction. To speed up the project, work began simultaneously on both entrances, creating serious difficulties for the success of the undertaking and the coinciding of both sections of the tunnel at the midpoint of its length. Difficulties that appeared once works had begun led to the cutting of a second channel in the tunnel, with the appropriate slope to ensure the smooth flow of water. Last, a built subterranean conduit brought water into the city, where it was distributed along pipes at right angle to fountains in the agora and at other points. One such fountain was discovered recently, next to the impressive "building of the lion-griffins" with its superb mosaic pavement (fig. 199).

The aqueduct remained in use for almost one thousand years. In the last few centuries, however, either because it was not sufficiently effective or because of increased needs caused by the creation of large thermae complexes during Roman imperial times, a new aqueduct was built, possibly in the reign of Hadrian (mid-2nd century AD). This monument, with its magnificent arched bridges, conveyed water over a huge distance, spanning vales and torrents, from an abundant source in the vicinity of the village of Myloi to the city of Samos.

The third major public work to which Herodotus refers is the "earth in the sea around the harbour", with the enormous mole 360 metres long, founded at a depth of 20 fathoms, which protected the harbour.

The Eupalineion aqueduct and the harbour installations would have been of little use without the fortifications of the city. For this reason the Archaic walls must have been constructed around the mid-sixth century BC and certainly before the campaign of the Lacedaemonians who camped outside the west walls when the came to the aid of the Samians persecuted by Polykrates (524 BC). These fortifications, of polygonal masonry in the lower parts and the gateways, and

146 | NORTH AND EAST AEGEAN

of mud bricks in the upper structure, still survive in many places, despite their destruction after Pericles entered the beleaguered city in 439 BC. After their forced demolition they must have been repaired before 365 BC, since Samos was able to withstand the second Athenian siege, led by the general Timotheos. The new fortification, which is preserved in good condition, was organized in the late fourth century BC and is attributed to Demetrios Poliorketes, to whom Samos was subject in this period (fig. 194). He is also accredited with the gymnasium complex, of impressive dimensions, with the stadium and the palaestra, which have been found in he southwest corner of the city (fig. 196).

The site of the ancient agora has been located in the city and remains of buildings belonging to it have begun to be uncovered. The majority, however, date from Roman times.

On the contrary, more is known about the city's sanctuaries, thanks to excavations in recent years. The sanctuary of Artemis was identified in the marshes of Mikri Glyphada, outside the west wall. An Archaic temple, a simple oikos with timber columns inside, upholding the roof, has survived in fragmentary condition, possibly because of its devastation by the Persians in 522 BC. However, very rich sacral repositories (*apothetai*) have been found in ditches cut in the marshes, containing destroyed votive offerings (precious vases and vessels, numerous terracotta figurines, etc.), dated around 560-525 BC (figs 188, 189, 197). The identification of the sanctuary of Artemis also explained the hitherto puzzling discovery on this site, which is associated with the west necropolis, of the huge kouros which – according to the inscription incised on its thigh – had been dedicated by Leukios to Apollo (fig. 58).

On the hill higher up, immediately inside the west wall, the thesmophorion, a sanctuary of Demeter and Kore, has been excavated. This includes a small temple and interesting ancillary buildings, protected by a precinct wall (*peribolos*) at the edge of the city, as befits mystery cults. Many of the vases, female figurines and animal figurines, mainly of pigs, characteristic of the cult of these two deities, were found in hollows in the ground.

In the lower part of the city, towards the harbour, part of the impressive crepis of a large temple has been revealed. According to the epigraphic finds, this should be identified as the temple of Dionysos, god of the vine and protector of vegetation, who was worshipped particularly on Samos with peculiar epithets.

At the city centre, at "Stathmos", in the area of the ancient agora, ruins of an important sanctuary that is ascribed to Aphrodite have been exposed. The small temple set upon a high solid podium is considered the Roman remodelling of the goddess's temple, while a small Archaic *apothetes* on the opposite side of the street suggests the existence of cult hereabouts from the sixth century BC. Recently, the foundations of a magnificent temple have been found at this site. Similar to the temple of Dionysos, it could be attributed to the worship of Aphrodite. The front of the temple faces east, onto the agora square where a large stoa and parts of an altar of Classical times have been located. So, the Roman temple, on account of its position in the agora and on the sacred way, could be associated more plausibly perhaps with the temple of Augustus and Roma,

196. Samos. View of the archaeological site at Tria Dontia. The impressive athletics facilities of Hellenistic times were partially revealed at the southwest edge of the city in the 1970s. These include a stadium, gymnasium, palaestra, in the spaces of which were founded later the most complete Roman thermae installations found to date in the city (mid-2nd *c.* AD). Later, the Early Christian basilica at Tria Dontia was erected on the site, with extensive mosaic floors, and corresponding basilica of the thermae (5th-6th c. AD).

197. Samos. Laconian bossed bowl (*omphalos phiale*) with decorative zone of birds and animals, from the Artemision. The vase is an example of the close relations between Sparta and Samos in the 6th c. BC. Pythagoreio Archaeological Museum.

SAMOS | 147

which is mentioned in the sources. Another similar Roman temple has been uncovered a few dozen metres to the east, while a monumental marble staircase even further east, in the small civic square, has been attributed to Isis, whose majestic altar had been found in the same area earlier.

The worship of other deities in the city, such as Hera, Ammon Zeus, God of Syria, Hermes, Aphrodite *en elei* (in the marshes), etc. is attested in the textual sources but has not been confirmed by archaeological evidence. On the contrary, it is certain that the Nymphs were worshipped inside the Spiliani Cave and in the valley of the stream at Pyrgos, which is perhaps identified as Amphilyssos, the other river of Samos.

Particularly interesting data on settlement and urban planning have also emerged from excavations. An impressive Hellenistic edifice has been excavated recently on the margins of the city, below the modern road leading towards the ancient theatre and the Spiliani monastery, which separates the residential quarter of the city from the uninhabited acropolis. The "building of the lion-griffins", with the beautiful mosaic floor in the andron (fig. 199), has a row of rooms facing onto the central atrium. The history of this building must have been long and interesting, spanning the Archaic period into Early Roman times, as is deduced from the successive repairs made to it.

Another interesting Hellenistic complex with extensive Roman alterations stands on Kastro tou Lykourgou Hill and seems to have accommodated generals and emperors, Anthony and Cleopatra, Augustus and Hadrian, and other distinguished foreign visitors who came to Samos at various times for diverse reasons.

Roman villas with mosaic floors and mural paintings have also been found on the west side of the hill. In the area of the ancient agora, particularly on the site where the new Museum of Ancient Samos is being constructed, buildings and shops have been uncovered, as well as workshops of bronze-smiths, marble-carvers and so on, lining a paved main street.

Continuous habitation from Geometric times into at least the seventh century AD, hostile attacks as well as, primarily, natural disasters (earthquakes, etc.) have obliterated many remains from the periods of heyday (fig. 198). Apart from the temples of Aphrodite and of Dionysos, which can be dated to at least the fourth century BC, and the stylobate of a temple of Archaic times, most of the buildings brought to light in excavations date to later phases, when the city was in the sphere of influence of the Ptolemies initially and of the Romans subsequently. More remains have survived from Early Christian times, when the zealous converts to the new religion, by raising large Early Christian basilicas in the ancient sanctuaries and temples, in the agora and the athletics installations (fig. 196), strove to exorcize memories of a splendid life that lasted over a thousand years.

198

198. Samos. The large votive or grave relief from Chora. Despite its fragmentary condition, this superb creation of Ionian art, with influences from the styles of Pheidias and Polykleitos, charms with the radiant beauty of the nude youth and the sensitive drapery of the garment of the seated figure, unfortunately not preserved whole. Late 5th c. BC. Samos Archaeological Museum.

199. Samos. Detail of a tessellated floor from the andron of the "building with the lion-griffins", the reception rooms in which are adorned with wonderful mosaics (2nd c. BC). Excavated in recent years, this building in the upper city is the most interesting Hellenistic edifice found so far in the ancient city of Samos.

Ikaria

Maria Viglaki-Sophianou

Ikaria, an island in the eastern Sporades, between Samos and Mykonos, shares features of the Cyclades and of the East Aegean islands, yet has several elements that are unique. The highest peak is on Mount Atheras (1042 m. a.s.l.) at the centre of the island. The coasts, rocky and rugged, are punctuated by some sandy bays. In Antiquity the island was known as Makris or – according to Apollodoros – Dolichi, because of its elongated shape, Ichthyoessa because of its rich fishing grounds, Anemoessa because of the strong winds that blow there.

According to mythology, the name Ikaros or Ikaria derives from Ikaros, the son of the mythical artisan Daidalos. After both escaped from the Labyrinth in the Minoan palace in Crete, wearing wings of wax and feathers, he defied his father's instructions as to how high he should fly. The wax melted and Ikaros fell and was drowned in the sea named after him ever since. Pausanias attests that Herakles found Ikaros' corpse, which had been washed up on the island, and buried it close to a cape thrusting into the waters of the Aegean.

The earliest traces of human activity date from the Neolithic Age and have been found at the site of Palioperivolo, in the village of Glaredo, as well as at Kataphygi, while at the site of Propezoulopi, north of Drakano and overlooking Iero Bay, there are remnants of megalithic monuments. In the same area of Iero, whose name is certainly not fortuitous (*hiero* = sacred, sanctuary), indications of an installation in Roman times at least have been noted.

The earliest historical information on Ikaria is given by Anaximenes of Lampsakos, who mentions that before the end of the eighth century BC Miletos, which faced geomorphological impediments to its development in a continuous space, proceeded to colonize Ikaria. On the west coast of the island, on the banks of the River Chalaris in the idyllic landscape of Nas, stand the ruins of a sanctuary dedicated to Artemis Tauropolos. The cult of the goddess was of considerable longevity, from the seventh century BC to the fourth century AD, according to an inscription built into the altar table of the church of the Dormition of the Virgin, near Yaliskari, and the sanctuary must have been a religious centre of ancient Ikaria (fig. 201). Rectangular constructions in the creek of the bay, perhaps belonged to the quay of the ancient harbour of Istoi, which is mentioned as the sole good harbour on the otherwise harbourless island.

A decree of the fourth century BC confirms the identification of the present village of Kampos, in the north part of the island, with the ancient city (according to Strabo "*polismation*") of Oinoe or Oine, which excavations are showing was important. The Oinaians are known from the tax lists of the Athenian League, from their entry as debtors to the Amphictyony of Delos, from three honorary decrees of the Delians for specific Oinaians, as well as from the decree of the Parians accepting games of Artemis Leukophryene as equal to the Pythian Games (*isopython*). Ruins of public buildings, the agora, bathhouses, a stadium and private houses in the area point

200

200. Ikaria. An inscribed marble relief of unique art (475-450 BC) was found in the mountain village of Kataphygi. Work of the sculptor Platthis or Palion (depending on the reading of the inscription), it represents a family performing rituals in front of a seated deity, which has been interpreted as Kourotrophos. Aghios Kirykos Archaeological Collection.

201. Ikaria, Nas. Ruins of the sanctuary dedicated to Artemis Tauropolos, an epithet given to the goddess because "she was brought from the Taurus Peninsula" or because "bulls [*tauroi*] were sacrificed to her", or because "she slew the monster in the form of a bull", which Poseidon had sent to tear up Hippolytos. The ruins of a small rectangular temple and of a rectangular altar, a short distance from it, have been revealed. The finds, which date from Archaic into Roman times, attest that the building was in use for some five centuries.

202. Ikaria, Kampos. On the west slope of the ancient city of Oinoe part of the ancient cemetery has been excavated. The moveable finds document its use from the 6th c. BC into Hellenistic times. Cist graves with rich grave goods yield significant evidence on the Oinaians' burial habits as well as on the existence of local pottery workshops, whose products imitate Attic models.

to settlement from Archaic times into Late Antiquity. The city circulated its own coinage, with the head of Dionysos or of Artemis on the obverse and a bunch of grapes, a bull and other representations, together with the inscription ΟΙΝΑΙΩΝ, ΟΙΝΑΙ or ΟΙ, on the reverse.

Of seminal significance for study of the ancient city are the finds from the excavation in the cemetery on the west slope of Kampos. These document the long use of the site from the sixth century BC into Late Hellenistic times and attest the existence of a local pottery workshop (fig. 202). Some of the grave goods are exhibited along with other artifacts, of clay, metal and marble, in the one-room Archaeological Collection of Kampos.

In the fifth century BC, Ikaria, which belonged to the Ionian region, joined the First Athenian League, paying tax, as is deduced from Attic inscriptions found on Delos and fiscal lists of the members of the League for the years 454/3 BC to 410/9 BC. These include the Ikarian cities of Thermes and Oinoe. In 411 BC, during the period of the Peloponnesian War, the Persian satrap Tissaphernes sought refuge on Ikaria in a great storm that started as soon as he had set sail for Miletos, intent on sailing to the Hellespont, where the allied ships were at anchor. He calculated that in this way he would cut off the Athenians' grain supplies from the northern shores of the Euxine Pontus. The end of the Peloponnesian War brought Spartans to Ikaria (405-395 BC).

Burials of the Geometric and Archaic period, and remains of an acropolis of the fifth century BC, as well as an excellent relief of 475-450 BC, found in the mountain village of Kataphygi, bear witness to a settlement of some cultural sophistication hereabouts (fig. 200).

Graves dated to the second half of the fifth century BC and to Hellenistic times, at Proespera on the west side of the island, point to the existence of a few scattered farmsteads.

Of outstanding importance in Antiquity was the city of Thermes, in the southeast part of the island, with organized facilities for thermal therapeutic baths, which operated at least from 400 BC. Patients from the surrounding islands as well as from the coast of Ionia came to these installations, which were submerged by the sea after landslides in Late Hellenistic times. Remnants of the ancient spa survive in the area of Chalasmena Therma, where dozens of springs still burble. From the fourth century BC onwards the Thermaians, who are present in the tax lists of the First Athenian League, were named Asklepieians and were under the protection of the healing god Asklepios.

203. Ikaria. An inscribed colonnette of the Roman period, from an *ex-voto* of the Samians living on Ikaria. When the island was deserted of its inhabitants, between the early 2nd c. BC and 130 BC, Samians used the fields there. Of interest for the history of Ikaria in this period are the inscriptions with which the Samians honoured various Roman emperors: Nerva (AD 96-98), Hadrian (shortly after AD 117) and Antoninus (AD 138-161). Kampos Archaeological Collection.

204. Ikaria, Drakano. Hellenistic fortification. The acropolis is encircled by a wall still standing 6-7 metres high, reinforced by square towers. At its highest point is a circular tower, standing to a height of 11.50 metres, with three storeys and arched entrance, making the area a highly important fort.

205, 206. Ikaria, Kampos. An important Roman monument of ancient Oinoe is the odeum, upon the ruins of which a secular building known as "Palatia" was built in the Middle Ages. The odeum comprised a cavea and an orchestra but no proscenium because of its small dimensions – in the view of its excavator Nikolaos Zapheiropoulos. It has a mosaic pavement decorated with confronted griffins, a galloping horse, a running deer, guilloche and rinceau.

207. Phournoi. A marble sarcophagus found in excavation in a house plot in the village. Its inscription records that it is the funerary monument of Epameinon, son of Telon and Philte, who died at the age of 25 years.
The sarcophagus of Alexandrian type, decorated with floral garlands, ivy leaves and rosettes, is dated to the Roman period and defines the site of the Roman cemetery of ancient Korseai.

208. Phournoi, Petrokopio. Unfinished architectural members on the beach of the ancient quarry, waiting to be loaded on a ship and transported to the Asia Minor coast opposite. On present evidence it seems that this quarry is the provenance of a major part of the architectural members of the monuments in ancient Ephesos.

In the period of the successors to Alexander the Great, the Ikarians passed to the sovereignty of the Ptolemies, which was challenged by the Macedonian kings. During the reign of Demetrios Poliorketes a notable fortification was organized on Cape Drepano or Drakano, where there is evidence also of a homonymous ancient town.

"Farewell to Dionysus, whom Lord Zeus set down
on snowy Dracanus when he had opened his mighty thigh"
wrote Theokritos in his *Idylls*.

The first mention of the cult of Poseidon Helikonios on Ikaria is in an inscription of the second century BC. The god was also worshipped at the Panionion of Mykale, gathering place of the Ionians in Asia Minor.

After the beginning of the second century BC and before 130 BC, according to Strabo and to epigraphic testimonies, Ikaria was uninhabited and its lands were used by the Samians (fig. 203). Subsequently, like other Greek regions, it came under the domination of Rome, remaining so until the end of Antiquity. Dated to this period are remains of public buildings and houses at Kampos, and well-preserved ruins of a Late Roman bathhouse and of other buildings in the vicinity of Proespera. The most important monument of the Roman period in Oinoe is a small odeum, upon the ruins of which a secular building known as "Palatia" was erected in the Middle Ages (fig. 206). An oracle incised on a stone of the fifth/sixth century AD attests the existence of an ancient temple dedicated to a female deity, on Aghia Irini Hill at Kampos, on the site of the Early Christian basilica. In the ninth/tenth century AD, the domed cruciform church of St Irene was built on exactly the same spot. A new era began for the island with the advent of Christianity.

Phournoi

The Phournoi of Ikaria are a cluster of 13 islets, barely mentioned in the ancient sources. Evidence of habitation from ancient times on the largest islet, known in Antiquity as Korseai, as well as of the significant role it played in the historical development of the region, exists on the acropolis, on Aghios Georgios Hill in the main village. Carved on a rock there is the interesting inscription: ΕΠΙΓΟΝΟΝ ΠΟΘΩΝ ΦΥΛΑΤΤΩ ΚΟΡΣΙΗΤΩΝ ΑΚΡΟΠΟΛΙΝ (Yearning for Epigonos I guard the acropolis of the Korseaians). Life on the island is dated between the third century BC and the second/third century AD, as indicated by a Hellenistic tower at Chrysomilia, ruins of a settlement of the Roman and Early Christian periods at Kamari, now submerged in the sea, an impressive quarry at Petrokopio, with many unfinished architectural members *in situ* (fig. 208), and an inscribed marble sarcophagus of Roman times (fig. 207).

PSATHOURA

YOURA

KYRA PANAYA   PIPERI

ALONNISOS

PERISTERA

SKIATHOS

SKOPELOS

SKYROS

SKYROPOULA

SPORADES

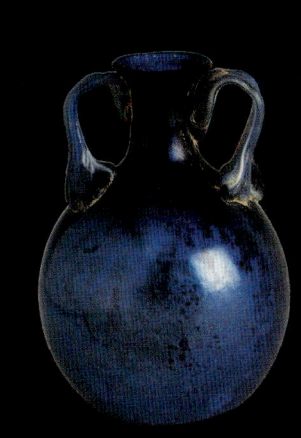

Northern Sporades

ARGYROULA DOULGERI-INTZESILOGLOU

From the time of Homer (*Hymn to Apollo* 32) the ancient authors make frequent but sporadic reference to the Northern Sporades. Strabo (IX 5,16) calls them the islands "off the country of the Magnetans" and specifically mentions Skiathos, Peparethos, Ikos, Halonnesos and Skyros, with homonymous cities.

In general these islands have a common historical course, with determinant factor their geographical location at a nodal point on the important sea routes, which from the early days of seafaring and the mythical voyages linked Thessaly and Central Greece with Asia Minor and the Euxine Pontus, as well as the southern and the northern Aegean. According to the testimonies of the so-called Skymnos of Chios (*Periegesis* 578-586) and of Diodorus Siculus (*Library* V 7,4), from the domination of the Minoan thalassocracy with Staphylos son of Dionysos and Ariadne, and the Pelasgians of Thrace, the islands passed into the hands of the Mycenaeans, with the Thessalian Pelias son of Poseidon and Tyro, and subsequent King of Iolkos.

In the period of the second Greek colonization (8th century BC), Chalkideans founded in the then desert islands colonies that were subsequently organized as independent city-states. During Classical times these became members of the Athenian League, which proved decisive for the substantial progress and prosperity they enjoyed, reflected in the minting of coins. In the fifth century BC they contributed to the treasury of the First Athenian League sums commensurate with their economic standing: Peparethos three talents, Ikos one thousand five hundred drachmas and Skiathos one thousand drachmas. After the end of the Peloponnesian War the islands were under Lacedaemonian occupation for a few years, but Chabrias returned them to the sphere of influence of Athens when they joined the Second Athenian League. Consequence of their close relations with Athens was their embroilment in the latter's conflict with Philip II of Macedon, who captured Halonnesos (Demosthenes VII, *On Halonnesos*, and XII 12-15), not the island so named today but one of the desert islands to the northeast of it, possibly Kyra-Panaya. Finally, after the capture of Peparethos too, the whole region came into the possession of the Macedonians. During the Hellenistic and Roman periods the islands of the North Sporades followed the fortunes of the less favoured regions of the Hellenic world. They were an arena of war between Greeks and Romans, and sunk into decline. By the end of Antiquity they had waned completely. They experienced some brief intervals of recovery and affluence, particularly after 42 BC when the Roman Mark Anthony restored them to the Athenians once again, together with other islands in the Aegean (Appian V I,7), in whose ambit they remained until at least the second century AD.

Today this entire region belongs to the National Sea Park of the North Sporades, which is intended to protect and enhance the rare natural wealth of its environment as well as its particularly noteworthy cultural heritage.

209. Skiathos. The Kephala Peninsula on the northeast coast of the island, site of the ancient city of Palaiskiathos. Around Xanemo Bay is a necropolis of Classical times. The evidence from surface pottery indicates that the city was abandoned in Hellenistic times and was never resettled. Consequently, it has remained more or less untouched by later interventions.

Skiathos

The island that keeps to this day its ancient name Skiathos is mentioned by Herodotus (VII 176, 179, 183 and VIII 7) in his account of the episodes between Greek and Persian forces that took place hereabouts, shortly before the naval battle of Artemision (480 BC). Skiathos had two cities and a harbour, according to Skylax of Karyanda (*Periplous* 58). Its first city, Palaiskiathos, was located on the small Kephala Peninsula, which was inhabited from at least Geometric times until the Hellenistic period and is the earliest known settlement on the island (fig. 209). The city's name was identified thanks to an Athenian decree of 408/7 BC, in which a Palaiskiathian, Oiniades, is honoured for his benefactions to the Athenians. No excavations have been conducted at this site, but parts of a fortified enceinte built of rubble masonry and ruins of buildings are visible.

The second ancient city of Skiathos occupied the site of the present homonymous town and is covered almost entirely by the later urban tissue. Some small-scale excavations have indicated that the site was first inhabited in Classical times, most probably in the fifth century BC, and continued to thrive into Late Byzantine times, when it was abandoned and not resettled until the nineteenth century. Several fortuitous stone finds, such as reliefs, inscriptions, architectural members, which have been collected from the area of the ancient city, are kept in the Volos Archaeological Museum and the Skiathos Town Hall. These are valuable documents of the island's historical course (fig. 210).

Round towers, which probably belonged to fortified farmsteads or to military installations of the Classical period, survive at the sites of Anastasa-Pyrgi (fig. 212) in the northwest and Pounta in the southwest, in the area of Koukounaries. Similar contemporary monuments, particularly of the fourth century BC, have been located on all the islands in the North Sporades and it is possible that they constituted an organized network of *phryktoria*, for transmitting signals with lighted torches.

In the early centuries of Roman imperial times Skiathos enjoyed a brief heyday, attested by inscriptions as well as by ancient authors. Athenaeus (*Deipnosophistae* I 4c, I 30f, IX 390c) mentions its choice produce, particularly its wine. A building boom in Roman times was confirmed recently by the identification of many small farmhouses and installations, as well as of villas at various points on the island (sites of Mandraki-Xerxes' Harbour, Aghioi Asomatoi, Kechria, Pounta to the east of the city, Aghios Ioannis at Pyrgo-Loutraki, and elsewhere). At the site of Vasilias, southwest of the city and near the coast, a large building complex of this period has been excavated, most probably thermae or a villa with baths (fig. 211). The existence of a balneum on Skiathos is recorded in an inscription in honour of Emperor Nerva.

210. Skiathos. Marble grave stele of Lykophronides son of Pelyesios from Samos, which was set up by Leukon in memory of their friendship. This fortuitous find possibly comes from the second ancient city of Skiathos, on the site of the present capital. The text of the inscription is metrical, obviously an epigram, and dates to the 5th c. BC, making it the earliest known epigraphic testimony from the Northern Sporades. Volos Archaeological Museum.

211. Skiathos. View of the interior of the water cistern belonging to the large building complex of Roman imperial times, uncovered recently on the coast at Vasilias, southwest of the city of Skiathos. In all likelihood the remains are of thermae or a villa with baths.

212. Skiathos. The lower part of a round tower of the Classical period at the site of Anastasa-Pyrgi, on the north west side of the island, where there is a chapel of Saint Anastasia. This is the best-preserved monument of its kind on Skiathos and most probably belonged to a fortified farmstead or was a military installation, perhaps a *phryktorion* for transmitting signals with lighted torches. Herodotus (VII 183) records an incident of contact by torch signals between Skiathos and Cape Artemision in Euboea, during the Persian Wars.

Skopelos

The island of Peparethos, now called Skopelos, was perhaps the most important in the region. The earliest traces of human habitation have been found at Staphylos and date from the Mycenaean period (16th-14th century BC). The Mycenaean settlement perhaps stood atop a rocky headland. In 1936, the archaeologist N. Platon excavated a rectangular built tomb of this period, on the narrow strip connecting it to the rest of the coast. Among the rich grave goods were a gold sword hilt (fig. 214) and a bronze double axe. These finds allude to the mythical founder-hero (*oikistes*) of the island, Staphylos, and confirm the testimony of Diodorus Siculus (V 79,2) that Rhadamanthys gave Peparethos as a gift to the prince of Crete. Indeed, the island owes its name to Staphylos' brother, Peparethos.

Homeland of the Olympic victor Hagnon (6th century BC) and of the historian Diokles (3rd century BC), the island had three cities and a harbour in historical times, according to Skylax from Karyanda (*Periplous* 58). Notable ruins of the three cities are visible today, but very little has been done towards their excavation and enhancement.

Peparethos, the homonymous city of the island occupied the site of the modern town of Skopelos, which has been inhabited continuously since Archaic times (fig. 213). In the Classical period the acropolis was fortified with a mighty wall, a small part of which survives in the Kastro, the highest point of the settlement. Thucydides (III 89,4) records that part of the city wall, the prytaneion and a few houses were destroyed by earthquake (426 BC). Founded upon the ruins of the ancient wall is the fortification of the Medieval town, confirming historical

213. Skopelos. The present town of Skopelos, a listed traditional settlement, occupies the site of the ancient city of Peparethos, homonymous with the island. Many ancient architectural members (*spolia*), sculptures and reliefs, inscriptions and sarcophagi are built into the walls of houses and churches. In the background left is the Kastro quarter, where the acropolis was located from Classical into recent times.

214. Skopelos. Gold sword hilt with intricate decoration, from the rectangular built tomb of the Mycenaean period (15th c. BC) at Staphylos. Athens, National Archaeological Museum.

215. Skopelos. The Asklepieion of ancient Peparethos, with the exceptionally careful masonry belonging to a stoa of the 4th c. BC. The sanctuary of Asklepios was discovered in the early 1960s. Works are in progress on enhancing the monument and arranging the site for visitors.

216. Skopelos. Torso of a marble statue of a boy, of Late Classical or Early Hellenistic times (late 4th c. BC), an *ex-voto* in the Asklepieion of Peparethos. Skopelos Town Hall Archaeological Collection.

217. Skopelos. Torso of a marble statue of the goddess Aphrodite, Hellenistic period. It was found by chance in the area of the ancient city of Selinous and handed in to the authorities by C. Dentis. Volos Archaeological Museum.

continuity. Preserved higher up, to the west and northwest of the Kastro, at Kanaki Lakka and Raches-Aghios Constantinos, are parts of well-built retaining walls that underpinned the terraces, on which stood respectively a temple of Athena, attested epigraphically, and a temple of Dionysos, worship of whom is inferred by the representations on coins of Peparethos and other indications. Among the important sanctuaries of Peparethos was the Asklepieion, on the south side of Skopelos Bay at Leivadi-Ambeliki, which was identified thanks to the discovery of an inscribed base of an *ex-voto* to Asklepios. Excavations conducted here revealed a Classical stoa (fig. 215) as well as marble votive offerings, such as statues of children (fig. 216) and reliefs. There is a small Archaeological Collection in Skopelos Town Hall, housing mainly finds from the Asklepieion as well as from other areas of the island.

The city of Panormos lay on the site of the homonymous modern settlement, which was created only twenty years ago and as its name implies has an excellent natural harbour. The acropolis, on Palaiokastro Hill, was fortified with a well-built wall in Classical times (fig. 220). At the highest point of the fortification are the ruins of two round towers, not contemporary with each other, and possibly a gateway, while inside the acropolis are visible remains of buildings and retaining walls. The lower city was located further south, in a small valley on the east side of which is the only cave on Skopelos, which was used for worship in Antiquity, most probably of Pan. The city was short-lived, spanning the Classical and Early Hellenistic periods. As Polyainos (*Strategemata* VI 2,1-2) and Diodorus Siculus (XV 95,1-3) relate, Panormos was involved in a military episode between Alexander of Pherai and Athenians (361/0 BC).

The city of Selinous, on the site of the modern village of Loutraki near Glossa (fig. 217), was also fortified with a mighty wall in Classical times. Large parts of the fortification survive on Palaiokastro Hill, which was presumably the acropolis. Walls of ancient buildings are visible inside the acropolis, where the existence of a temple of Athena is suspected, because a statue of the goddess and its inscribed base were found there (now in the National Archaeological Museum in Athens). Important are the ruins of buildings in the lower city of Roman imperial times, some of which will soon be visitable. Particularly noteworthy are the thermae, with walls standing to a considerable height and tessellated marble floors. The monument was uncovered in 1980, beside the sea at Katakalou, southeast of the ancient city. Indeed, the settlement of Loutraki, created in recent times, was perhaps named in memory of its existence.

Peparethos owed its flourishing economy during Archaic, Classical and Early Hellenistic times to export trade of its famous wine, mainly to the Euxine Pontus, as is attested by Demosthenes (XXXV 35): "… wine imported to Pontus from our lands, from Peparethos and Kos, and Thasian and Mendean …", as well as to markets in the Eastern Mediterranean. The wine-producing activity of the Peparethians has been confirmed recently by the discovery and the study of three extensive and most probably organized farmsteads in the areas of Staphylos,

216

217

SKOPELOS | 163

Agnontas and Panormos, which included among other installations pottery workshops producing amphorae in which the wine was transported. Indeed, two types of local amphorae have been identified, numerous examples of which have been found in cities on the north shore of the Euxine Pontus, verifying Demosthenes' information (figs 218, 219). In the countryside of Peparethos, mainly to the north of Selinous (sites of Elliniko, Mavragani, Sentoukia, Priounos, and elsewhere), as well as at other points (Ditropo), there are dispersed fortified farmhouses with round or rectangular towers of Classical and Hellenistic times, which served and protected the cultivators and the production process, although the possibility of their use for military purposes cannot be precluded.

On the highest mountain of Skopelos, at the site of Karya, there is a cluster of rock-cut tombs known by the characteristic name Sentoukia (= chests). A similar tomb has been found also at Alykias, on the south side of the island.

218, 219. Skopelos. Examples of the two types (I and II) of local amphorae of the 4th c. BC, common in the pottery workshops of Peparethos and Ikos. These were used for exporting the islands' wine to markets in the Eastern Mediterranean and especially to cities on the north coast of the Euxine Pontus. The capacity of type I amphorae ranged between 16 and 20 litres. Volos Archaeological Museum.

220. Skopelos. View of the north wall of the acropolis of the ancient city of Panormos, with characteristic masonry of Classical times preserved in very good condition on Palaiokastro Hill.

221. Alonnisos. On Kokkinokastro Peninsula, on the east coast, is the site of one of the two ancient cities of Ikos. Preserved here are a small section of the Classical wall and ruined houses, while the necropolises lie on the slopes west of the peninsula. Although Skylax of Karyanda does not mention a harbour on the island, this city was located between two bays suitable for mooring ships.

Alonnisos

On the island of Ikos, now called Alonnisos, traces of prehistoric habitation dating back to the Palaeolithic Age have been found. At many places on mainly the southeast coast, among them the Kokkinokastro Peninsula and the islet of Mikro Kokkinokastro, the sites of Leptos Yalos, and elsewhere, finds dating from the Middle Palaeolithic to the Mesolithic period have been noted. Remains of settlements of the Neolithic Age and the Early and Middle Bronze Age also exist on the islet of Mikro Kokkinokastro and at other sites, while a tomb of the Geometric period uncovered on the north side of the island at Aghios Constantinos was the possible provenance of an intact oinochoe with painted decoration, a rare find from the area.

According to Skylax of Karyanda (*Periplous* 58), Ikos had two cities in the historical period. One city was located on the Kokkinokastro Peninsula (fig. 221), where part of a Classical wall and ruins of buildings survive. The other city was at the site of Aghios Ioannis, close to Palio Chorio, but no significant building remains are visible. Fortunately, both ancient cities lie outside the present villages on the island. At the coastal site of Tsoukalia, on the southwest side of Alonnisos, there is an important wine-making installation of Classical and Early Hellenistic times. This farmstead included among other things at least one farmhouse, as well as pottery

ALONNISOS | 165

workshops producing amphorae, with extensive pits full of broken pots and wasters. These workshops yielded several stamped amphora handles with the inscription IKION, thanks to which the island was identified as ancient Ikos (fig. 222). There was an analogous wine-making installation at Kalamakia-Vamvakies, on the east coast. Recent research has identified two types of local transport amphorae from Ikos, which are the same as those of neighbouring Peparethos (Skopelos). These amphorae, as has been noted, are abundant in the cities of the northern Euxine Pontus, where stamped handles of amphorae from Ikos have been found too.

Several villages, fortified farmhouses with round towers and other rural installations, mainly of the Classical period but also of the Hellenistic, have been identified at various points in central and north Alonnisos, such the sites of Raches, Kastraki, Karbitses (fig. 223) and elsewhere.

It seems that Ikos had fallen into decline by the end of the Hellenistic period. According to the testimony of Philostratos (*Heroic* 8,9-10), around the end of the second and the beginning of the third century AD the entire island was an immense vineyard owned by the Peparethian viticulturalist Hymnaios.

222. Alonnisos. Stamped handle of a local amphora of the 4th c. BC, with the inscription IKION, that means product of Ikos. Similar stamps have been found in cities on the north coast of the Euxine Pontus as well as in Athens, Pella and Eastern Mediterranean regions, irrefutable witnesses to the scope of wine exports from Ikos.

223. Alonnisos. The east face of the round tower of the Classical period, at Karbitses, to the northeast of the Kokkinokastro Peninsula. It probably belonged to a fortified farmhouse or to a military installation.

224. On the islet of Aghios Petros, in the homonymous bay on the southwest coast of the deserted island of Kyra-Panaya, a particularly important Neolithic settlement has been excavated, from which excellent-quality finds were recovered, such as pottery and clay figurines. Illustrated here is the upper part of a characteristic clay figurine of the Early Neolithic period (6500-5800 BC), 6 cm. high. Volos Archaeological Museum.

225. The Cyclops' Cave on Youra is an important locus of diachronic human presence from the Mesolithic and the Neolithic Age, one of the earliest known cases in the Aegean. The view from the site of the cave southwestwards includes the rocky islets of Grammiza (left) and Strongylo or Koumbi (right), while visible in the distance is the island of Kyra-Panaya.

Deserted islands of the Sporades

Scattered to the east and northeast of Alonnisos are numerous islets that no longer have permanent residents but which in Antiquity were settled already by the Middle Palaeolithic period. The most important of these deserted islands are Peristera, Kyra-Panaya, Youra, Psathoura, Skantzoura and Piperi. Many installations of prehistoric and historical times have been identified on these, the best known of which is the Neolithic site on the islet of Aghios Petros of Kyra-Panaya, the earliest excavated site in the Aegean. Investigated by Dimitrios R. Theocharis (1970-1971), it yielded local pottery of excellent quality and distinctive clay figurines (fig. 224). On Youra is the well-known Cyclops' Cave, used seasonally as a dwelling place from the Mesolithic and the Neolithic Age until Roman times, which too has been systematically excavated (figs 19, 20, 225). Significant is the ascertainment that the area constituted a particular cultural space in prehistoric times.

Many shipwrecks of various periods have been discovered close to the shores of the deserted islands. In recent years some have been investigated systematically. One shipwreck, just off the islet of Phagrou (fig. 674), southwest of Kyra-Panaya, contained fifth-century BC amphorae from the city of Mende in the Chalkidike. Another shipwreck explored near the islet of Peristera (fig. 673), to the east of Alonnisos, contained a cargo of local amphorae of Ikos or Peparethos, as well as amphorae of Mende.

DESERTED ISLANDS OF THE SPORADES | 167

Skyros

Amalia A. Karapaschalidou

Skyros in the open sea lying by Euboea
Dionysios Kalliphon, *"Description of Greece"*, lines 148-150

Stony Skyros (Sophocles, *Philoktetes*, line 459) is the largest island in the Sporades and is the southernmost of the group. Lying northwest of Chios and 20 nautical miles from the east coast of Euboea, it dominates the Central Aegean. In a particularly important nodal position on the sea routes of Antiquity, the island was indeed the crossroad linking mainland Greece – via Euboea – with Asia Minor and the East, as well as with the Euxine Pontus.

There is nothing fortuitous in the myth that Achilles set sail from here – possibly from the site of Achili – for Troy. His mother Thetis had sent the hero, disguised as a girl, to the court of the island's king. Lykomedes, in order to avoid the sufferings of war. But there the boy was discovered by Odysseus, who used a cunning ruse to expose Achilles' true identity. Skyros, tradition has it, was also the burial place of King Theseus.

The island is earthquake-prone and its soil barren, according to the relevant passage in Aelian (*De Natura Animalium* IV 59), who notes too that it was for the most part bereft of people. The ancient authors refer especially to its hard ground, which is of limestone and schist (fig. 226). Hesychios speaks characteristically of "Skyros city and island rocky". The northern and central parts of the island are mountainous with some plains, the southern part is barren and only the north tip is fertile.

Skyros is a windswept isle, which explains the epithets "*enemoessa*", "*anemoessa*" and "*anemodes*", given by Dionysios Periegetes (*Oikoumenes Periegesis* 521), on which goats were reared, as mentioned by Diodorus Sardianus (*Anthologia Graeca*, Θ. 529). It was also home to ponies, descendants of which are the today's small-breed horses. On the lowland and cultivated areas, such as Trachy, Kampos and Kallikri, olives and cereals were grown.

Skyros was inhabited already in the Neolithic Age, as remains found at various places attest. It flourished during the Early Bronze Age (3rd millennium BC), when there were close relations with the Cycladic Culture, and enjoyed its heyday in the Mycenaean Age (16th-12th century BC), from which several sites are known. The finds from graves, such as a twelfth-century BC stirrup jar with representation of a ship (fig. 228), bear witness to contacts with the northern Cyclades, Attica and Euboea, while relations with Thessaly have also been ascertained.

Early settlement of the island is associated with the Pelasgians and the Dolopians. Skyros was evidently significant in Geometric and Archaic times (9th-6th century BC). In 475 BC it was conquered by the Athenians and in 323/2 BC it passed into the hands of the Macedonians. In 197 BC the Romans captured the island and by the second century AD Christianity had reach it.

226. Skyros, Pouria. An ancient quarry for poros stone, in which the chapel of St Nicholas was cut in the living rock in recent times.

227. Skyros, Kastro. The modern settlement and part of the fortification of the Classical acropolis.

SKYROS | 169

228. Skyros. Mycenaean stirrup jar with painted decoration. Represented on one side is a ship with prow ending in a bird head, and on the other an octopus, one of the most popular subjects on stirrup jars in this period. Late Helladic IIIC (12th c. BC). Skyros Archaeological Museum.

229. Skyros, Palamari. Aerial photograph (November 2003) of the settlement with the monumental fortification and the building remains of the Early and the Middle Bronze Age (3rd and first half of 2nd millennia BC).

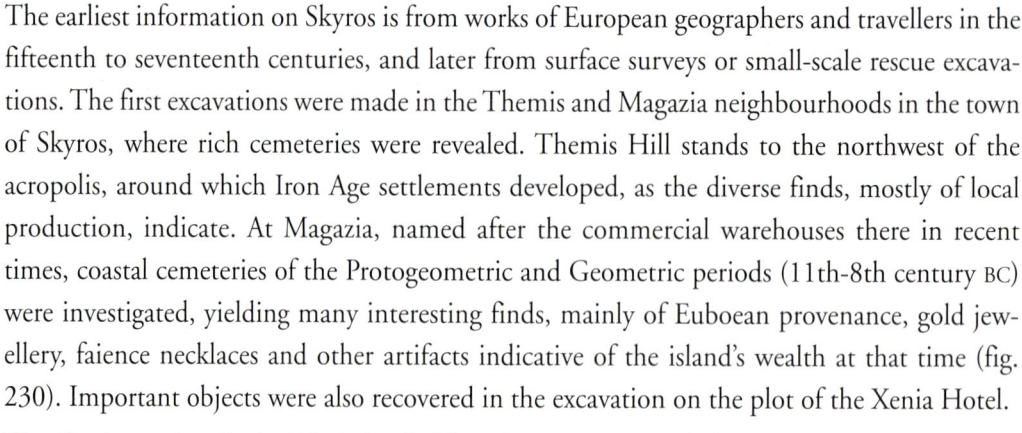

The earliest information on Skyros is from works of European geographers and travellers in the fifteenth to seventeenth centuries, and later from surface surveys or small-scale rescue excavations. The first excavations were made in the Themis and Magazia neighbourhoods in the town of Skyros, where rich cemeteries were revealed. Themis Hill stands to the northwest of the acropolis, around which Iron Age settlements developed, as the diverse finds, mostly of local production, indicate. At Magazia, named after the commercial warehouses there in recent times, coastal cemeteries of the Protogeometric and Geometric periods (11th-8th century BC) were investigated, yielding many interesting finds, mainly of Euboean provenance, gold jewellery, faience necklaces and other artifacts indicative of the island's wealth at that time (fig. 230). Important objects were also recovered in the excavation on the plot of the Xenia Hotel.

The Skyrian archaeologist Dimitrios R. Theocharis was particularly involved with surface surveys and excavations on his native island. He excavated in the area around the Kastro, at Papa to Chouma, Achili and other sites, making a major contribution to Skyrian archaeology. In the past few decades, excavation activity has been continued by the Archaeological Service, and is ongoing.

Nonetheless, the only systematic excavation to date is that at the coastal settlement site of Palamari (fig. 229), in northwest Skyros. There a prehistoric fortified settlement has been revealed, the main phase of which dates to the Early Helladic III period (late 3rd millennium BC). Located in a strategic position, it controlled maritime communications with the Northeast Aegean and its most important centres, Lemnos and Troy. Inside the settlement, two complexes of houses have been uncovered either side of a street. These have stone-paved floors, built hearths, storage and other spaces. Nearby is a water source. The east sector of the settlement has fallen into the sea, due to earthquakes and erosion by the waves over the millennia. The monumental fortification, which protected the landward side of the settlement, is preserved to the northwest and the southwest. Consisting of a strong defensive wall reinforced with horseshoe bastions, this exceptional example of the art of fortification in the third millennium BC enjoyed considerable longevity, until the Middle Bronze Age (mid-17th century BC).

The settlement at Palamari, a well-organized centre with proto-urban elements, was an important port of call for Aegean transit trade, particularly the trafficking of metals. The inhabitants were involved mainly with fishing, stock-raising and agriculture, and had developed craft-industrial and trading activity, making obsidian tools, clay vases and vessels, and distributing pottery and other products.

A large part of the present town of Skyros is surrounded by the Classical wall (fig. 227), known as the Kimoneion, which is dated to the second half of the fourth century BC, or according to other researchers between 370 and 356 BC, that is to the period when Athens regained hegemony at sea, after the naval battle of Naxos (376 BC). The existence of ancient temples has been verified at Magazia, Phourka, Markesi, Aghios Phokas, Aghios Mamas and Ari. Cemeteries have been identified in various places and so the picture of the ancient city is being filled in gradually by notable finds, such as those from recent investigations on the Primary School plot

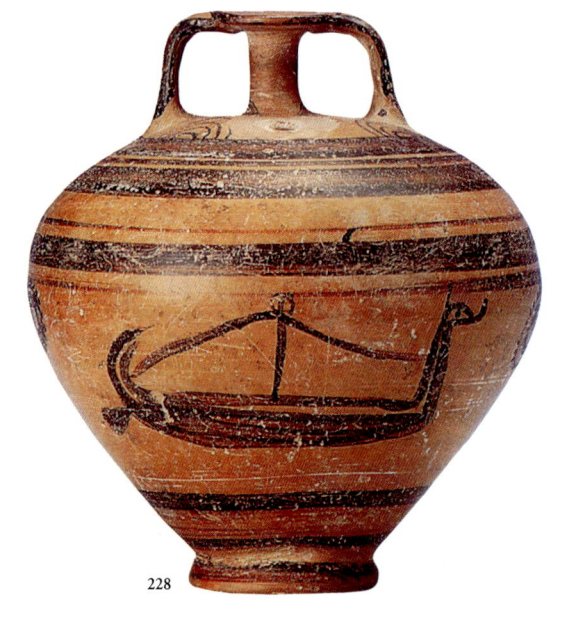

170 | SPORADES

229

230. Skyros, Magazia. Imported Attic pyxis of the Geometric period (8th c. BC). Skyros Archaeological Museum.

231. Skyros, Tourkomnimata. Glass vase from the recent excavation of the ancient cemetery on the Primary School site. Skyros Archaeological Museum.

232. Skyros. Clay plastic vases from the excavation on the Primary School site. Skyros Archaeological Museum.

233. Skyros. Gold disc-shaped pendant with serrated circumference embellished with granulation. At the centre is a repoussé representation of Aphrodite Epitragia. 1st c. BC. From a cist grave on the Primary School site. Skyros Archaeological Museum.

(fig. 232), enriching our knowledge of the island's history. The discovery in 2003, in the playground of the Skyros Primary School, of a richly-furnished grave dated to the late second-early first century BC is especially important because this is a closed assemblage from a period for which information was hitherto scant and fragmentary (fig. 233).

The agora of the ancient city was most probably situated at Brouk. The mole of the harbour has not been found, presumably because it has been destroyed by the elements. It is thought to have existed in the small harbour of Aghios Dimitrios, which the Venetians called San Giorgio. Ships arriving from the East Aegean anchored here.

The Skyros Archaeological Museum houses numerous objects (vases, sarcophagi, sculptures, jewellery) that bear witness to the island's long history.

233

SALAMIS

ANGISTRI
AEGINA

POROS

YPSILI

DOKOS
SPETSES
HYDRA
SPETSOPOULA

KYTHERA

PRASONISI
ANTIKYTHERA

ARGOSARONIC ISLANDS
KYTHERA – ANTIKYTHERA

Salamis

Yannos G. Lolos

Salamis, the Saronic island closest to Attica, is mentioned in Antiquity by other names too, such as Kychreia, Skiras, Pityoussa and Kolouris. The name Salamis is attested already in the Homeric epic (*Iliad* II 557-558).

Human presence on Salamis is attested from the Late Neolithic period. The Neolithic food-producing stage was first documented there by the large assemblage of pottery and other finds (stone tools, minor objects and jewellery) found in the excavations conducted by the University of Ioannina (1994-1997) in the historic Cave of Euripides at Peristeria, at the south tip of the island (figs 234, 236).

This cave, "a breath away from the sea", is now eponymous thanks to the combined interpretation of the related references in four ancient sources and one epigraphic testimony of decisive importance, from the 1996 excavation (fig. 235). It had many and varied functions during six different periods of Greek prehistory and history. Particularly significant, due to recent systematic studies, are the testimonies on the use of the Cave of Euripides in the Late and early Final Neolithic periods (late 5th-4th millennium BC), as point of mythical connotations and locus of cult visits. The peculiar morphology, with the very narrow entrance and the long winding passage, may well have contributed also to the emergence of the myth of Kychreus, first hero and "spectre" of the island.

Surface finds offer valuable evidence of very early settlement organization on Salamis at four sites (three in the hinterland), which were occupied, permanently or occasionally, in Late and Final Neolithic times.

Habitation in southern Salamis during the Early Bronze Age (3rd millennium BC), a period of impressive development in seafaring, communications and maritime trade in the wider geographical region, is indicated by the host of coastal settlements and related iconographic evidence, in conjunction with invaluable underwater testimonies. Intensive research in recent years has led to the identification of three sites on the coast, two on small promontories, at Maroudi and Kolones, and one at Kanakia, a citadel in continuous use in the Middle and Late Bronze Age (2nd millennium BC), as well as another three sites inland.

The function of the settlements and the anchorages in southern Salamis should be considered in the framework of an early Helladic thalassocracy, founded in the Argosaronic and the Myrtoo Sea during the second half of the third millennium BC. The first two settlements, at Maroudi and Kolones, along with many others in the wider region, project the special dimension of Early Helladic II culture (2800-2300 BC) as a culture of the capes.

During the Middle Helladic period (2000/1900-*circa* 1600 BC), the fortified citadel at Sklavos Maroudi on the south coast, dominates by virtue of its size, layout and ambit. There is also suf-

234. Salamis, Peristeria, Cave of Euripides. Ring pendant of hammered silver sheet, of accomplished workmanship and excellent art. It belongs to a Balkan or "international" type of pendant, deeply rooted in the ideology and aesthetic of the Neolithic Age, which enjoyed an impressive circulation, mainly during the 5th and 4th millennia BC, over a very wide geographical region extending from Carpathia to Crete. Piraeus Archaeological Museum.

235. Salamis, Peristeria, Cave of Euripides. Part of an Attic black-glaze skyphos of 430-420 BC, with the name Euripides incised upside down and in reverse, as a dedication. The honorific incising of the name should be dated to Roman imperial times, during which the cave was enhanced as a place of sight-seeing and pilgrimage, a kind of "*heroon*" of the poet, known beyond the borders of the island. Piraeus Archaeological Museum.

236. Salamis, Peristeria. View of the interior of the Cave of Euripides, with its strange heavy atmosphere and morphology, "unpleasant and frightening" (*spelunca taetra et horrida*), to use the expression of Aulus Gellius, a Roman author of the 2nd c. AD who visited it. In the depths to the right is Gallery 8, which functioned as a burial chamber in the Late Mycenaean period.

ficient documentation, thanks to recent pottery finds, of continuity of habitation from the Early Helladic to the Late Helladic or Mycenaean period, on the citadel at Kanakia, while there was very probably similar continuity of settlement on the precipitous citadel of Kastelli in the Saterli area, west of Kolones Bay. All three sites on Salamis are now added to the map of the Middle Helladic Saronic Gulf, among the well-known centres at Eleusis, Kolona on Aegina and Corinth.

From the early phases of the Mycenaean Age, the settlement in the vicinity of Kanakia set its seal on organized life in southern Salamis. It developed into a major urban centre on the island, undoubtedly playing a leading role in the wider region of the Saronic Gulf during the Late Mycenaean period. Like the other Mycenaean political centres, it enjoyed its heyday in the thirteenth century BC and was abandoned in the early phase of the troubled twelfth century BC (before 1150 BC).

Until the discovery of the Mycenaean city of Salamis on the southwest coast, in 1999, our knowledge of Mycenaean Salamis was based exclusively on finds and data from the excavation and publication of rock-cut chamber tombs, found in five or six places on the island, and the grave goods accompanying the burials in the deepest chamber of the Cave of Euripides at Peristeria.

The extensive Mycenaean settlement at Kanakia, where the University of Ioannina has been conducting systematic research since 2000, includes a nucleus-citadel (with estimated inhabited area of 4.5-5 hectares on two contiguous heights), as well as smaller satellite villages, and had direct access to two natural harbours. This nucleus has a clear urban layout, densely built and with a street network, basic axis of which is the ascent ("*Kychreia Hodos*") on the north side of the first hill, which led from the main harbour to the highest terraces of the citadel.

Although the citadel is not protected by mighty Cyclopean walls, it has a markedly fortified aspect, due to the natural boulders on top of the first hill, successive terraces with houses in stepped arrangement on the slopes, an external defensive enceinte for an appreciable length on the lower part of the south slope and a network of towers, guardhouses and lookout posts.

Over a considerable area on the uppermost levels of the citadel, large building complexes with peculiar fortified entrances have been uncovered (the public craft-industrial complex ΙΑ-ΙΒ-ΙΔ, consisting of 41 spaces, and Buildings Δ and Γ, with residential spaces and an incorporated twin megaron). These were founded on the basis of a building programme and controlled by the local princely house, during the phase of their zenith (13th century BC) (fig. 239). Apart from the building complexes on the summit, which played a dominant role, and the big autonomous Building ΙΓ high up on the north slope, smaller isolated houses of various types have been investigated or identified at neighbouring points, as well as parts of the lower city.

It is noteworthy that the material from recent research on the coastal citadel includes finds documenting communication between the Mycenaean centre of Salamis and other island centres in the Aegean and Cyprus, even in the years of crisis and decline in the early decades of the twelfth century BC (fig. 238).

The Mycenaean urban centre of Salamis, now coming to light, with its own formation and ambit, betwixt the mightier palatial powers of Athens and the Argolid, should be identified

237. Salamis, Ambelakia. Part of a marble grave stele dated *c.* 420 BC, with a rare representation of an actor. It is not certain whether the deceased was shown standing or sitting. The young actor ("charioteer of tragic art", according to the ancient verse), contemporary of Euripides, holds opposite him a tragedy mask, perhaps commemorating his distinction in a drama contest in Athens or Salamis. The stele was one of those set up on tombs in the Classical cemetery of Salamis. Piraeus Archaeological Museum.

238. Salamis, Kanakia, Mycenaean citadel. A black steatite spindle whorl of Cypriot or Oriental provenance, decorated all over with incised motifs. This artifact (souvenir, gift, heirloom-amulet or prestige object) as well as other Cypriot finds and elements bespeak a particular dimension in relations between the major centre in the Saronic Gulf with Cyprus, within the complex environment of generalized upheavals and migrations in the early decades of the 12th c. BC. Piraeus Archaeological Museum.

239. Salamis, Kanakia. The mighty twin triangular gate with adjoining tower-like construction, designed to control access to the inside of Building IB. The building was part of an extensive complex with workshops, storerooms and ancillary spaces, which stood on the uppermost levels of the Mycenaean citadel of Salamis and was in use during the 13th and the early 12th c. BC.

240

241

unreservedly with the "ancient city" of Salamis, that is the earlier capital in the south of the island, which the geographer Strabo (IX 1,9) mentions as being deserted in his day and which has been sought since the nineteenth century. Its abandonment and total desolation after the early twelfth century BC is confirmed by the finds in all sectors of the excavation. This mass exodus of its inhabitants may well be echoed in the ancient traditions of the flight of the last legendary representatives of the island's dynastic house: Teuker to Cyprus, Eurysakes and Philaios to Attica.

After the desertion of the coastal city at Kanakia, with the movement of part of the population into the hinterland, the succeeding settlement in southern Salamis, of the so-called Dark Age and the Geometric period (*circa* 1050-700 BC) was on the hidden Ginani Plateau. This lies on the south side of Akamas (mod. Malieza) and is flanked by two small fortified acropolis sites at Kastro and Aspri Rachi. In the northern part of the island, excavated cemeteries of the Post-Mycenaean period, one at the entrance to the Salamis Naval Station (about 100 graves of the Submycenaean period) and part of another in the Tsami neighbourhood, near the city of Salamis (consisting of 11 graves, pits and pyres, with rich grave goods of the Protogeometric and the early Middle Geometric period), point to the existence of nearby settlements that have not yet been found.

From the late sixth century BC and perhaps earlier, urban life on the island was concentrated in an area of the east coast, opposite Attica, that is at a geographical point diametrically opposite to the Mycenaean settlement at Kanakia, specifically on the Pounta Peninsula and the inner coastal zone of Ambelakia Bay. This development should be associated with important political events: the annexation of Salamis to the city-state of Athens, perhaps after arbitration in the closing decades of the sixth century BC, following a protracted dispute with the Megarians, the possible installation on the island of a peculiar cleruchy and the creation of an unofficial Athenian deme whose fortunes largely followed those of Athens until the end of Antiquity.

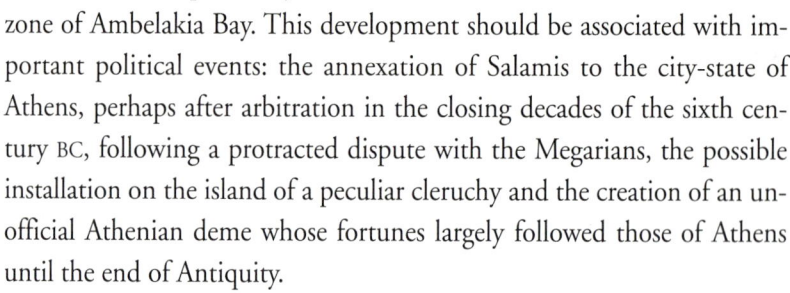

The city of historical times, also known as Kolouris, with its harbour, is mentioned by Skylax of Karyanda, Strabo and Pausanias. Indeed, the last refers to ruins of an agora there and a temple of Ajax.

Ruins of the historical city, with elements of the Hippodamean urban plan, have been brought to light in recent decades in excavations by the Archaeological Service, and earlier by Professor Antonios Keramopoullos, at various points on the south slope of Pounta and at Ambelakia. Inside the city limits, carefully constructed houses with organized interiors, and other buildings of Classical, Hellenistic and Roman times (in Evrysakou St, the Gioka and Zougris plots, etc.) have been investigated. Interesting evidence has been revealed, in some cases regarding the management and exploitation of water, while the area of the sanctuary of Bendis has been determined. Sections of the course of the wall, reinforced with large rectangular towers, have been traced, which seems to have enclosed the city and its harbour (fig. 240).

180 | ARGOSARONIC ISLANDS

The major cemetery of Salamis extended to the west and northwest of the city, and included isolated tombs and tombs set within enclosures, some with grave stelai and marble lekythoi.

Beyond the area of historical Salamis, other monuments of Classical and Hellenistic times on the island have been excavated or identified (fig. 241). Among these are the Hellenistic sanctuary of Dionysos at Peristeria, at a point on the ascent to the historical cave, most probably intended for the co-worship of Dionysos and Euripides. An early fourth-century BC building of circular plan containing three sarcophagi, and a site with a large retaining wall of careful masonry of the fourth century BC and other architectural elements, have been uncovered in the area of Kolones. Two forts are known at Peristeria and Danili, as well as towers, both round and rectangular, on the tops of mountains, hills and rocky islets (Kanakia, Perani, Lagousa).

Psyttaleia

Psyttaleia is a small rocky isle, 1,500 metres long, situated between the Kynosoura Peninsula and Piraeus (fig. 242). Dominating its highest point is an old stone-built lighthouse.

This inhospitable islet earned a place in the annals of history thanks to the role it played in the naval battle of Salamis (480 BC). It is mentioned by Aeschylus, Herodotus, Plutarch, Strabo, Pausanias and other authors as a place of worship of Pan, where a wooden cult effigy (*xoanon*) of the deity existed.

Psyttaleia became a reference point for the Greeks because of the terrible events enacted there, when at an advanced stage of the naval battle of Salamis, Athenian hoplites under the command of Aristeides disembarked on its shores and annihilated to a man a Persian force stationed there. Precisely for this reason, one of the trophies commemorating the Greek victory over the Persians was erected on the isle.

Excavations conducted on Psyttaleia in 1986 uncovered a building complex of Late Roman (Early Byzantine) times, on a headland on its northwest coast. Another installation was identified recently on the neighbouring rocky islet of Atalanti or Talantonisi, a refuge in the period of the barbarian incursions into Greece (6th-7th century AD).

Psyttaleia no longer has its ancient configuration. The greater part of it has been levelled in order to accommodate the construction and the progressive expansion of the biological waste-processing plant for the sewerage from the Athens Basin.

240. Salamis, Ambelakia. Remains of submerged harbour installations and other constructions, in the inner sector of Ambelakia Bay, which was the harbour of the city of Salamis in historical times. The first moveable nautical find (a small stone anchor) associated with the ancient harbour was discovered in an adjacent house plot during recent rescue excavations.

241. Salamis. The manmade tumulus (known as the *Tymvos ton Salaminomachon*), on top of Magoula Hill on the north side of the Kynosoura Peninsula, is about 20 m. in diameter and consists of a circular cairn and a mound of earth. Graves of the late 5th c. BC were found outside the circumference of the tumulus, while visible on the hillside are enclosures, constructions, cuttings in the bedrock and poros stone blocks. Although there is no decisive evidence for identifying the tumulus with the *polyandrion* or common grave of those slain in the naval battle of Salamis, in 480 BC, the information that a layer of ash and burnt bones was found in an excavation made in 1856 is critical.

242. Psyttaleia. Aerial photograph.

Aegina

EVA SIMANTONI-BOURNIA

At the centre of the Saronic Gulf, at the junction of sea routes, with a mild climate and sufficient arable – if not particularly fertile – land, Aegina was inhabited by man already in the Late Neolithic period (*circa* 5000 BC). This is attested by two anthropomorphic figurines, fortuitous finds from the east part of the island, as well as by scant sherds of Urfurnis pottery from Cape Kolona. This naturally fortified site to the northwest of the modern town (figs 245, 246), which rises 12 metres above the sea, is spacious enough for habitation and is flanked to north and south by sheltered bays/harbours. It was enhanced as the main settlement on the island from the end of the Neolithic and during the Chalcolithic Age (4th millennium BC). Some traces of settlement have been noted also on the east coast of the island (Aghia Marina Bay). Appreciable quantities of deep red pottery with linear burnished decoration have survived from this period, but primarily clay anthropomorphic figurines, both female and male, several of the latter with helmet, perhaps denoting the Aeginetans' turn towards martial activities and piracy, so closely connected with maritime trade.

The flattening of Kolona Hill, in the mid-third millennium BC, presumably to create living space, ushered in intensive building activity in virtually all phases of the Bronze Age. The rich architectural remains of houses and fortifications (distinguished by the excavators as "cities I-XII") have yielded extremely important information and establish the settlement as one of the most prominent in Greece during the Early and Middle Helladic periods (3000-1600 BC).

Noteworthy in particular are a two-storey building of rectangular plan, of the mid-third millennium BC, which has been dubbed "White House" because of its white plaster coating ("city III"), and the earliest securely identified fortification wall, which protected the settlement ("city V") (fig. 35) from the landward side in the closing years of the millennium (Early Helladic III period). A small hoard of gold and silver jewellery found at the centre of the settlement confirms the prosperity of Aegina in a period of generalized economic decline, as well as the extent of overseas trade, since contacts are attested with the Northeast Aegean, Crete and the Near East. "City V" and its wall were destroyed by fire, perhaps during an incursion.

From the end of the Early Helladic period and all through the Middle Helladic, continuous re-buildings and re-arrangements of the settlement are observed ("cities VI-IX"), but primarily of its fortified enceinte, which acquired impressive dimensions. Abundant excellent-quality pottery, local (figs 243, 244, 247, 248) and imported, points to the Aeginetans' artistic abilities and the scope of their trading transactions (Argos, Cyclades, Crete).

The restructuring on the hill in the Archaic period (6th century BC) destroyed a large part of the archaeological levels of the end of the Middle Helladic and of the Mycenaean period (*circa* 1600-1200 BC). Nonetheless, what has remained from the enlargements and repairs of the

243

walls, and the recently ascertained development of the Mycenaean settlement on the south slope of the hill, almost down to the harbour, bear witness to a heyday in this period. During the twelfth century BC (Late Helladic IIIC period) the settlement at Kolona ceased to exist. The picture of a flourishing Aegina in the Late Bronze Age is supplemented by the rich finds from the Mycenaean cemetery, which spreads on the hill opposite Kolona, as well as from some other sites in the south and southeast of the island (possible Mycenaean installation on Mount Hellanion, quite well-preserved Mycenaean settlement and graves at Lazarides).

Human activity is documented again during the tenth century BC, while the earliest evidence of cult on the hill dates from the eighth century BC. From the first half of the seventh century BC, when the city of Aegina was transferred to its present site, Kolona was devoted exclusively

243. Aegina. Aeginetan pithos with representation of four ships and their crew, of the Middle Bronze Age (18th c. BC). From the prehistoric settlement at Kolona. Aegina Archaeological Museum.

244. Aegina. Sherd of an Aeginetan pithos of the 18th c. BC, with representation of a human figure standing on a fish or a ship. From the prehistoric settlement at Kolona. Aegina Archaeological Museum.

245. Aegina. The column of the opisthodomos of the Doric poros temple of Apollo (c. 520 BC), which gave its name to Cape Kolona. To the left, part of the prehistoric settlement.

246. Aegina. Aerial photograph of the archaeological site of Kolona. Visible are the foundation of the temple of Apollo and the prehistoric settlement.

247. Aegina. Middle Bronze Age (18th c. BC) vase with highly-burnished surface, from the prehistoric settlement at Kolona. Pottery of this category is characteristic of the local workshops and was exported systematically to many parts of the Aegean. Aegina Archaeological Museum.

248. Aegina. Recent excavations in the prehistoric settlement at Kolona have brought to light a Middle Bronze Age pottery kiln. A similar and more or less contemporary kiln had been uncovered earlier in the area of the "inner suburb", west of the temple of Apollo.

to religious activities. Literary and epigraphic testimonies refer to a host of deities, heroes and rulers whose sanctuaries stood on the hill, transforming it into a veritable sacred acropolis, analogous to that of Athens. Of these sanctuaries, the temple of Apollo (6th century BC), the principal god worshipped, has been identified securely. To it belongs the sole standing column (Gr. *kolona*), after which the area is named (fig. 245). Recent excavations have brought to light the Thesmophorion, mentioned by Herodotus (VI 91,2), the Thearion, a space for ceremonial banquets on the north slope of the hill (6th century BC), two "*oikoi*" – one could be identified with the Attaleion (2nd century BC), dedicated to the cult of the King of Pergamon –, a tholos and in all probability the temple of Artemis.

Very interesting creations in sculpture and vase-painting found in the excavations here are housed in the local museum (fig. 249) to the southeast of the hill, and are incontrovertible witnesses to the island's importance and thriving economy (fig. 251). On the site of the museum are the foundations of the city's theatre, comparable in size to that of Epidauros. Already from the late sixth century BC the acropolis of Aegina was girt by a strong wall, which with continual repairs and remodellings remained standing and functioning until the sixth century AD.

The ancient capital occupied the same site as the modern one. Parts of the wall of the late sixth-early fifth century BC have survived, which together with the wall of the acropolis and the fortifications of the city's two harbours, the commercial and the military or "secret harbour", remains of which are visible to this day, provided adequate protection. At various points the course of the complicated ancient water-supply system has been located, while around the city spread the cemeteries of historical times, from the eighth century BC into the Roman imperial period, with graves of various types (mainly chambers cut in the soft bedrock, but also cists and even "Macedonian" tombs), which have yielded rich grave goods. Part of the street network of the ancient city has also been uncovered, while in the northern part of the island extensive quarries have come to light, which supplied poros stone for constructing public and private buildings not only of Aegina but also of Attica and possibly Kea.

On the northeast side of the island, on the top of a wooded hill with a superb view, is the sanctuary of Aphaia (fig. 252). Here was worshipped even in Mycenaean times a *kourotrophos* goddess, whom myth identifies as the Cretan Nymph Britomartes or Diktynna, who was renamed Aphaia. Worship on the hill began in the Mycenaean period, around the end of the fourteenth century BC, and must have been in the open air. It continued thus, that is without a temple building and with successive formations of the rocky terrace and its *peribolos*, until at least the early sixth century BC, when the first temple of the goddess was built (570-560 BC). This Doric prostyle edifice of poros stone, which preserves its original polychromy to an appreciable degree, was destroyed by fire in 510 BC. A total remodelling of the sanctuary followed and was constructed of a new temple on the site of the old one. This second temple of Aphaia (510-500 BC), which still stands in very good condition, is also Doric and of poros stone, but

249. Aegina. Jug of the second quarter of the 7th c. BC, with representation of Odysseus' companions escaping from the Cyclops' Cave, strapped under the bellies of rams. The eponymous work of the "Ram jug" Painter. Aegina Archaeological Museum.

250. Aegina. The monumental staircase and the strong retaining wall at Sphyrichtres on Mount Hellanion.

251. Aegina. Silver stater with turtle on the obverse, *c.* 480 BC. Aegina was one of the first cities in the Hellenic world to mint coinage (early 6th c. BC), henceforth using the turtle (and the tortoise) as distinctive symbol. Athens, Numismatic Museum.

252. Aegina. Temple of Aphaia, of the late 6th c. BC. It succeeded the earlier temple of 570-560 BC, which stood on the same site. Fragments from this temple are exhibited in the local museum. The second temple is built of Aeginetan poros stone and is the clearest expression of the Doric order. It is peripteral with deep pronaos and shallower opisthodomos, while the internal colonnades dividing the cella into three aisles supported a second row of smaller columns.

is peripteral, with 12 x 6 columns. It was decorated with exceptional pedimental sculptures (490-480 BC), displayed today in the Glyptothek in Munich (figs 254, 255), while a few fragments are in the National Archaeological Museum in Athens (fig. 253). These remarkable works are irrefutable proof of the importance of the Aeginetan school of sculpture in the late sixth and the first half of the fifth century BC. The sanctuary was in total decline by the Hellenistic period.

In the south of the island rises Mount Hellanion, the highest peak in the Saronic Gulf, which is linked with the cult of Zeus Hellanios or Panhellenios, giver of rain. On its summit was founded the altar and possibly the small cult "*oikos*" of the god, while on the north slope, at Sphyrichtres, recent excavations have redefined the form and function of constructions brought to light in earlier investigations. A monumental staircase leads to two large terraces (fig. 250), the earliest phases of which date back to the sixth century BC, whereas their present aspect is from Hellenistic times. Founded on the upper terrace is a Hellenistic Π-shaped stoa suitable for ritual meals. This seems to have replaced an Archaic hestiatorion, the foundations of which have been located in front of the entrance to the Hellenistic one. Pilgrims attending festivals were supplied with water from two rock-cut cisterns, the bigger of which was probably coated with impervious hydraulic plaster.

The documents of human activity from very early times dispersed all over the island are today "arks" in which, alongside man's creations, the natural environment of Aegina has also remained intact. The archaeological sites are among the very few places where the island's character has "remained undisturbed, like an icon which however much it has frayed, you should not touch it, you should just approach it as a venerator", as Rallis Kopsidis wrote in 1965, in a small booklet entitled *Pilgrimage to Aegina*.

252

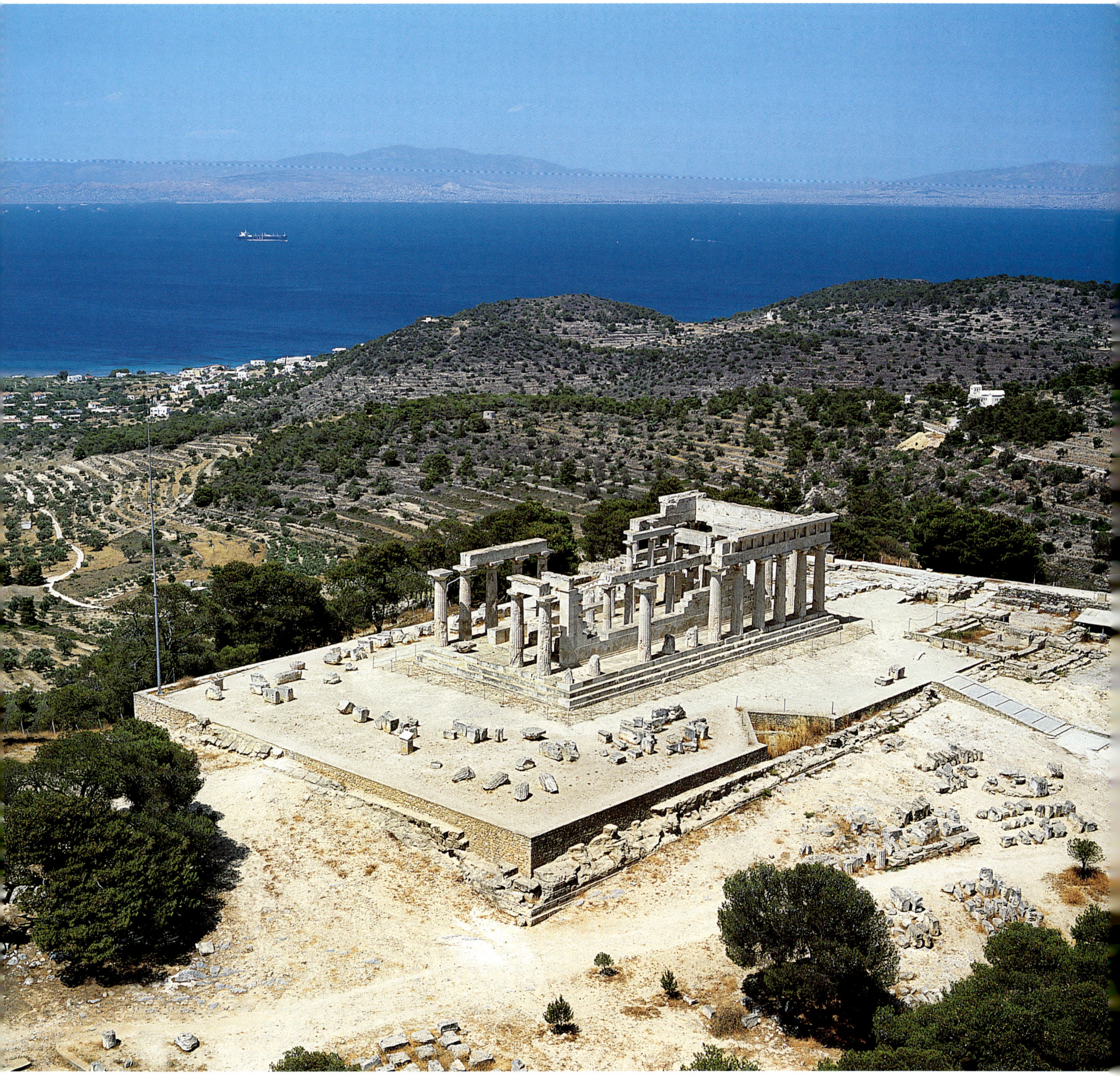

253. Aegina. Head of a warrior from the earlier east pediment of the Aphaia temple. The hole in the chin was most probably for inserting a beard. Athens, National Archaeological Museum.

The earlier east pediment of the temple has survived in very fragmentary state; it probably represented a myth associated with the abduction of Aphaia by Zeus (or Minos). This pediment was replaced by the later one, but the figures on it were exhibited in a special place on the east side of the temple. Represented on the west pediment of the earlier phase was the Amazonomachy.

254. Aegina. The "dying" hoplite from the left cuneus of the east pediment of the Aphaia temple (c. 480 BC). Munich, Glyptothek.

The later pediments of the temple of Aphaia bore sculptural compositions of exquisite art, carved in Parian marble. The west pediment predates the east one by a decade (c. 490 and c. 480 BC respectively), which interval corresponds to the transition from the Archaic to the Classical period. Central figure in both representations is the goddess Athena, flanked by figures of warriors and heroes who participated in the two falls of Troy, the Homeric with Ajax and Teuker (west pediment), and the mythical with Herakles and Telamon (east pediment).

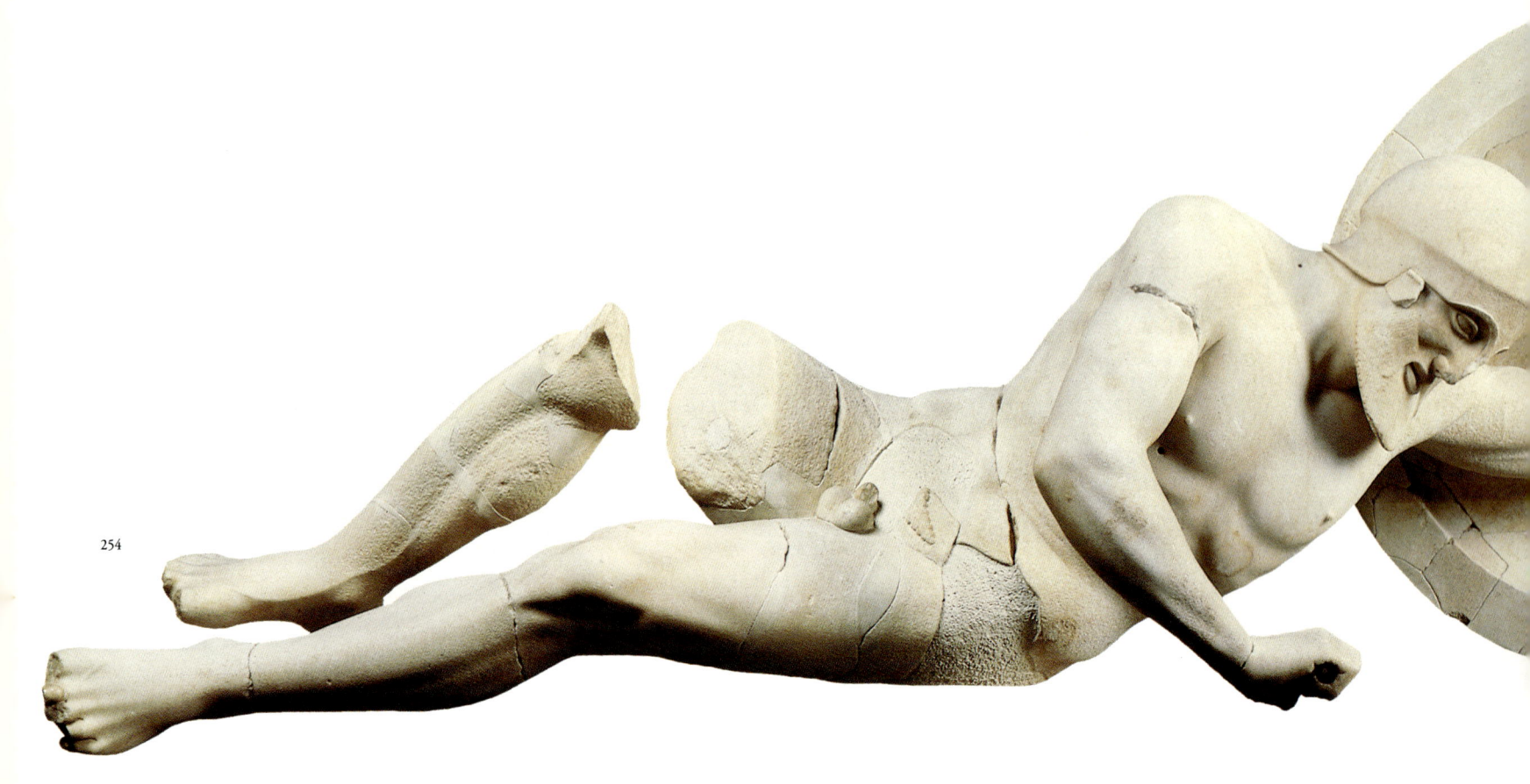

255. Aegina. Herakles archer. A figure from the east pediment of the temple of Aphaia (*c*. 480 BC). Munich, Glyptothek.

Through the mythical hero's expedition against Troy and its king Laomedon, the Aeginetans projected their origin from Aiakos, who had helped to build the walls of Troy, and his son Telamon, who took part in the war, so enhancing their island's historic role. The choice of subjects for the new pediments of the temple is considered to reflect the desire of the oligarchs of Aegina to promote their island in the face of the growing naval power of democratic Athens.

Poros

EVA SIMANTONI-BOURNIA

Poros lies to the south of Aegina and just 200 metres from the coast of the Peloponnese, to which it was joined until Late Antiquity, when it was separated due to subsidence of the ground. It actually comprises two islands joined together by a narrow isthmus, the smaller Sphairia and the bigger Kalaureia. On Sphairia is the temple of Athena Apatouria, to which are attributed several of the ancient architectural members dispersed in the modern town.

The settlement of ancient Kalaureia, of which some traces of the fortified enceinte and a few graves survive, was located on a hill in about the centre of the island, directly southwest of the temple of Poseidon, the patron god (figs 256, 257). The sanctuary (site of Palatia) was famous in Antiquity as a place of refuge (sanctuary) for suppliants, the most eminent of whom was the Athenian orator Demosthenes. The Kalaureians honoured his tomb. Only the foundations of the buildings in the sanctuary are preserved, as most of the stones were removed and transported by caiques to the neighbouring islands to cover building needs, prior to the Greek War of Independence, of 1821. As the meagre evidence uncovered in excavation indicates, the temple of Poseidon Kalaureatas was Doric, peripteral with 6 x 12 columns, and can be dated to 520-510 BC. It was enclosed by a strong rectangular precinct wall (*peribolos*) with two propyla, a large one on the narrow east side and the small one on the long south side. Recent investigations west of the peribolos have shown that the space was probably used for worship from the end of the Mycenaean period (first half of 11th century BC) and during historical times, from the eighth century BC onwards.

On the large flat area southwest of the peribolos of the temple extends a complex of stoas and other buildings (A-F) that surround a quadrilateral court entered through a propylon. The buildings obviously served the needs not only of pilgrims but also of the host of suppliants who sought asylum in the sanctuary. A case in point is Building D, which was a hestiatorion (fig. 258). Southwest of the propylon is another stoa of Π-shaped plan (building F), which several scholars considered to be a bouleuterion for representatives of cities of the renowned Kalaureian Amphictyony. A very probably square building excavated southwest of the bouleuterion, part of which has been destroyed by the opening of a new road (building G), was thought to be the xenon (guest house) in which the representatives of the federation were accommodated, or priests' houses or an Asklepieion, because a headless torso of Asklepios was found inside it.

Extremely important is the Early Helladic II settlement (mid-3rd millennium BC) discovered recently at Kavo Vasili, on the northeast coast. Clusters of houses with well-preserved stone-built walls and abundant excellent-quality pottery, local and imported, attest to the significance of the site.

To the east of Poros lies the deserted islet of Modi, where a notable Late Mycenaean (12th century BC) installation has been identified.

256. Poros, Kalaureia. Coin with representation of Poseidon on the obverse and a sea monster, perhaps Triton, on the reverse. It was found in the sanctuary of Poseidon. The letters KA on the reverse indicate that the coin was minted in Kalaureia, which in that period was an independent city.

257. Poros, Kalaureia. The sanctuary of Poseidon from the west, with Aegina beyond. It was first excavated in 1894 by the Swedish Archaeological Institute; investigations in the sanctuary were resumed in 1997 and are still in progress.

258. Poros, Kalaureia. Building D, which is identified as the hestiatorion of the sanctuary, from the west. Recent excavations have brought to light a triangular *peribolos*, within which had piled the remains of some major festival celebrated in the early 2nd c. BC.

257

258

POROS | **191**

Hydra, Dokos, Spetses and islets

Yannos G. Lolos

Hydra

Hydra (ancient Hydrea), the island-spearhead at the entrance to the Argolic Gulf, rugged, imposing, many-peaked, barren and famed for the beauty of its harsh rocky landscape, is mentioned in few ancient sources, which speak of its inhabitation by the Dolopians. "Hydra, a poor island of Dolopians", according to the Alexandrian lexicographer Hesychios. Early settlement by Dryopians from the area of Hermione is also deduced.

As is the case with nearby Spetses, Hydra's fame in recent history is due mainly to the major contribution of its fleet to the Greek War of Independence. The archaeology of the island, particularly its prehistory, remained largely unknown until recently and has been enhanced remarkably by the extensive explorations and studies of the researcher Adonis Kyrou and the excavations and surveys of the Archaeological Service.

The earliest human presence on Hydra is documented by sherds in the so-called "Cave of Kolokotronis" on the slope of a rocky height above the present town, which was in use at least from the Final Neolithic period. The use of the cave must be related to the existence of a permanent settlement at a lower level, with access to the natural harbour, as attested by the fortuitous finds of Neolithic stone tools at various points in modern Hydra.

Impressive is the dispersal of sites (settlements and small maritime installations) all over the island, from Zourva to Bisti, which are dated on the basis of surface remains and potsherds to the Early Bronze Age (3rd millennium BC). There are at least twelve confirmed settlement sites of the Early Helladic II period (2800-2300 BC), most of them founded on small headlands or steep cliffs overlooking the coast of Hydra. The largest and most important settlement of the period is located on the relatively fertile Episkopi Plateau, in the southwest part of the island. Recognizable among the extensive Early Helladic ruins are remains of enclosures and retaining walls, foundations of apsidal and rectangular houses, and other architectural evidence. It appears to have been a proto-urban centre that was probably about the same size as other early island centres, such as Poliochni on Lemnos.

Outstanding among the settlements of the Late Bronze Age (1600-1100 BC) on the island is the fortified Late Mycenaean citadel at Choriza, overlooking Vlychos Bay and controlling the vital sea channel between Hydra and the coast of Hermione (figs 259, 261). The advantageous position of the high fortified hill on the northwest coast explains, to a degree, the continuity of habitation there during historical times, including its use as a pirates' lair in Late Archaic times as well as during the Peloponnesian War (431-404 BC) and the Chremonideian War (266-263 BC).

259. Hydra, Vlychos. "The Hydriot", head of a large clay male figurine, height 6 cm., from the Mycenaean citadel at Choriza. This little-known find was collected by the archaeologist Vana Hadjimichali some forty years ago and is now exhibited in the Hydra Historical Archive and Museum. A notable example of minor sculpture in the 12th c. BC, it displays striking morphological similarities with clay heads from Asine, Mycenae, Mani, Crete and Ephesos.

260. Hydra, Aghios Nikolaos (Bisti). Water-collecting work of the Mycenaean Age, of impressive aspect, constructed on the rocky slopes of a hill where springs must have existed. It is developed on a succession of manmade terraces underpinned by mighty retaining walls, surviving to a height of 4.20 m. There are also indications of the existence of incorporated built cisterns or wells. This important and complex hydraulic project of the 13th c. BC can be included in the category of works that the ancients called "*Agamemnoneia phreata*" and ascribed to the king of Mycenae, sovereign not only of the Argolic coasts and hinterland, but also of the islands in the Argolic Gulf. The presence of water sources on Hydra seems to explain convincingly the etymology of the ancient name (Gr. *hydor* = water) of the now waterless island.

A monument of unique value from Hydra's Mycenaean past is the major technical hydraulic work in Aghios Nikolaos Bay at Bisti, one of the most important water-management projects in Greece during the late thirteenth century BC, as yet unknown in the specialist bibliography (fig. 260). Located at a crucial geographical point in correlation to the sea routes of the period, at the west end of Hydra, and most probably controlled by the dominant power of the Argolid – rather than by the local shepherds and stock-raisers –, it must have functioned as a basic station for supplying the crews of passing ships with water rations. The direct surveillance and technical supervision of the work could have been entrusted to a district governor or inspector, perhaps residing in the big building complex that has been located at the neighbouring site of Stani tou Nyklioti and falls within the same temporal horizon.

The clusters of rock-cut chamber tombs at Kamini near Choriza, Palamidas and Episkopi, can be included in the cemeteries of Mycenaean Hydrea. Some were remodelled and reused perhaps in Early Christian-Byzantine times.

It is noteworthy that on Choriza Hill a battlefield from a dramatic chapter in Archaic history has been identified. Specifically, a martial episode in the latter years of the sixth century BC, which is recounted by Herodotus (III 57-59), has been documented archaeologically by surface finds (bronze arrow heads and coins, displayed in a temporary exhibition in the Spetses Museum). This was the surprise and victorious attack by the Aeginetans, *circa* 526 BC, against a garrison of Samian refugees installed on the hill. The Samians, at that time owners of Hydrea, had established a fort on Choriza, which they used as a base for piratical raids in the Argosaronic waters. The Aeginetan assault resulted in the expulsion of the Samians to more distant places.

At Episkopi a notable continuity of life is observed from prehistoric into historical times, including the Late Roman period. Later habitation on the plateau is attested by building remains, cairns, architectural members, coins and surface sherds.

The existence of an important settlement of Late Roman and Early Byzantine times in the vicinity of the present town of Hydra is verified by finds (graves, columns, column capitals and other architectural members, grave stones, tiles, copious coins) from these years, which have been mentioned from time to time at various points in the flourishing later settlement.

In contrast to the area of the later and modern settlement of Hydra, where the dense urban tissue has developed almost solidly as far as Kamini, Choriza Hill and the still "virgin" Episkopi Plateau, the most important archaeological sites on the island, and with the greatest longevity, are promising fields for future excavations.

Last, the only figure from the prosopography of ancient Hydrea who is known from Greek literature is Euages, a shepherd and a comic poet.

261. Hydra, Vlychos. Part of the fortified enceinte with the gateway, on the northwest and west side of the rugged summit of the Mycenaean citadel on Choriza, which dominates the coast of Vlychos. The wall, almost Cyclopean in construction, protected *inter alia* the water source inside a rock formation on the hilltop. The settlement developed on the main level area of the hill and other smaller terraces on the downward slopes. Among the surface finds of Mycenaean date from Choriza are sherds, lead fishing-net weights and fragments of clay figurines.

Dokos

Dokos (ancient Aperopia), smaller than Spetses, mountainous and rocky with a few springs, lies between Hydra and the coast of Hermione, on the sea route linking the Saronic with the Argolic Gulf. It has a large safe bay, Skintos Bay, on the north coast, winter anchorage for the Hydriot fleet in the years of the Greek War of Independence, and summer haven for thousands of modern pleasure craft.

The earliest evidence of human habitation on Dokos is from the two permanent settlements founded in the Early Helladic II period (2800-2300 BC) on the north coast, on Cape Myti Kommeni and at Ledeza. These can be interpreted in the framework of the intensive maritime activity of the bearers of Early Helladic Culture and of the flourishing sea trade in the Argosaronic Gulf and the Myrtoo Sea during the second half of the third millennium BC. Tangible

262. Dokos. Building B40 of megaroid type is one of the largest in the central part of the Late Mycenaean walled settlement on Cape Myti Kommeni, on the north coast. The extensive settlement, founded at a crucial point on a basic sea route along the south Argolic coast, is situated between the Mycenaean installation on Choriza, Hydra, and Magoula, Hermione, visible in the background left.

testimony of major importance for seafaring in the wider region is the wreck of a merchant ship with a cargo of pottery, dated to 2200 BC and discovered a short distance from the south cliffs of Cape Myti Kommeni (figs 667-669). A large part of the cargo was brought up from the seabed and studied by the Hellenic Institute of Marine Archaeology in 1989-1992. In Late Mycenaean times, a fortified settlement of considerable size flourished on the same cape (fig. 262), while at neighbouring Ledeza a mighty Mycenaean enclosure of almost elliptical form has been identified, intended to protect a water source and for the penning of flocks and herds.

A notable event in the history of Dokos was the founding of a burg in the mid-seventh century AD, on top of the highest hill and visible from afar on the northeast side of Skintos Bay. It appears to have been created by refugees from near and far, and was probably destroyed by the Arabs in the autumn of AD 673.

Over the centuries and to this day, Dokos was a seasonal and occasional place of stay for shepherds and fishermen, as well as of quarrymen (at intervals in recent times).

Islets and rocky islets

Of the many islets and rocky islets in the wider expanse of sea, which preserve traces of diverse human activities and adventures in ancient times (among them Ypsili near Cape Iria in the Argolid, Spetsopoula, Trikeri, the rocky islet in Limnioniza Bay and Aghios Ioannis Theologos Vlychou, off the coast of Hydra), of particular archaeological interest is the islet of Parapola or Velopoula, 24 miles from Spetses, at the centre of the Myrtoo Sea, feared by mariners in all eras. Like Kastri on Kythera, it is the furthest outpost of the Early Helladic thalassocracy, on which an important installation of the Early Helladic II period (2800-2300 BC) has been identified. This includes a large central building with a row of rooms, occupying the top of a precipitous promontory, as well as smaller buildings on the lower slope (fig. 263). The relatively permanent character of this settlement is evident from the existence of a contemporary cemetery a short distance away on the opposite slope, overlooking the small bay, with cist graves and built graves of elliptical and circular plan.

As is deduced from the abundant surface finds from Parapola and neighbouring Phalkonera (Gerakouli), which are in the Spetses Museum, as well as from observations *in situ*, this outpost seems to have been a base from which Early Helladic seafarers and miners, perhaps coming from Episkopi on Hydra during the heyday of the centres on the Argolic coast, set forth to extract copper ores from inhospitable Phalkonera. It was also a place where these ores were smelted.

263. Parapola. Rocky height in the northwest part of the islet in the middle of the Myrtoo Sea, where remains of an Early Helladic settlement of seafarers and miners has been identified (3rd millennium BC), with access to a small natural harbour.

Spetses

The two earliest known settlements on Spetses (ancient Pityoussa = pine-wooded) are located on the coast, on the capes of Aghia Marina and Aghia Paraskevi, and date from the Early Helladic II period (2800-2300 BC). Specifically, on Cape Aghia Marina excavations have revealed architectural remains of a flourishing settlement with rich pottery deposits, which undoubtedly had frequent contacts with the Early Helladic settlements and ports of call on the neighbourng islands and in the western Cyclades (figs 264, 265). There is evidence of considerable settlement activity in the same area during the Early and Late Mycenaean periods too, while another Mycenaean settlement has been located at Aghioi Anargyroi on the southwest coast, on a nearby hill close to a water source.

During the Classical and Hellenistic periods Pityoussa probably belonged to the territory of the Hermionians, who could use its closed safe harbour. There does not seem to have been an important town on the island in these years. From the scant remains of historical times found on Spetses, some isolated towers of makeshift construction, of the late fourth century BC, have been noted at Zogeria and on the summit of Prophitis Ilias, in communication with the city of Halieis (modern Porto Cheli); they were possibly related to the organization of local defence, in order to cope with Macedonian attacks in this period.

In the troubled years of successive foreign incursions (of Visigoths, Vandals, Slavs, Avaro-Slavs, Arabs) into southern Greece, from the late fourth to the advanced seventh century AD, Pityoussa and most of the islets in the Argolic Gulf received waves of refugees from the populations in the southern Argolic regions, who established settlements, some temporary and some more permanent in character.

264. Spetses, Aghia Marina. Sauceboat, one of the many found in the settlement. This is the most characteristic vase in Early Helladic fine ware, widely used in central and southern Greece, and appearing sporadically in the Cyclades in the mid-3rd millennium BC. Spetses Museum.

265. Spetses, Aghia Marina. On the small cape whose form has been altered by erosion, remains of a flourishing settlement of the Early Helladic II period (mid-3rd millennium BC) have been found, with traces of habitation in later (Mycenaean) times too. This is a typical Early Bronze Age settlement founded on a headland, with rudimentary natural fortification, a double harbour and the possibility of surveying the surrounding area. It belongs in a dense network of coastal settlements and ports of call of the mid-3rd millennium BC, which have been identified on the southern shore of the Argolid and the neighbouring islands and islets. These define to a considerable degree the main sea lanes of the region.

Kythera, Antikythera

ARIS TSARAVOPOULOS

Kythera and Antikythera, the two islands to the south of the Peloponnese, lie on the route of ships travelling from Laconia to Crete, as well as of those sailing from the Aegean and the Euxine Pontus to the Western Mediterranean. Because of this strategic position, they were from prehistoric times the object of dispute between powers claiming hegemony in the waters of the Aegean and in the Eastern Mediterranean in general. However, the history of the two islands was different, prior to the Ottoman conquest of Crete (1669). Kythera was linked more closely with the Peloponnese and Laconia, despite the relatively long Minoan presence on the island during the second millennium BC (Middle and Late Bronze Age), while Antikythera, on account of its geographical position, was bound organically to Western Crete throughout Antiquity and until the mid-seventeenth century AD.

Kythera

The island of Kythera seems to have "emerged" from the sea three times, in three different geological eras. The last emergence was completed two million years ago, during the Pleistocene. These emergences, which are recorded in the ubiquitous fossils, visible from the beaches to the mountain peaks, possibly influenced the linking of the island with the myth of Aphrodite "*anadyomene*", according to which the goddess was born of the foam whipped up in the sea off Kythera when the genitalia of Uranus were cast into it.

There are very few safe anchorages on the island today: at Kapsali at the south end, the bay of Palaiopoli on the southeast coast, Diakophti on the northeast and Limionas Bay on the west. In ancient times the bay of Palaiopoli thrust deeper into the island, the main harbour of which, Skandeia, was located there.

The earliest known evidence of human presence on Kythera dates to the Late Neolithic period (late 6th millennium BC). Vases of this period have been found at Kalamos, in the Aghia Sophia Cave (fig. 266), while surface surveys conducted in recent years have identified settlements at several other sites. Antiquities of the Final Neolithic period (4th millennium BC) have come to light at Palaiopoli and Diakophti.

There was an increase in installations on the island during the Early Bronze Age (3rd millennium BC). Evidence has been noted in the north (on Cape Spathi, at Aghia Pelagia, Diakophti), the east (Avlemonas, Palaiopoli, Katochori Alexandrades) and the south (Vani near the monastery of St Kosmas, in the southwest of the island, and Manitochori). The pottery of this period reveals the close relationship between Kythera and the Peloponnese.

From the early second millennium BC and particularly during the Middle Bronze Age, when the Cretan palatial economy was at its zenith, the Minoan thalassocracy extended as far as Kythera, which was for the Minoans an intermediate port of call *en route* to Laconia, from where they imported various raw materials. The island was also used as a base and lookout post in the Minoans' campaign to rid the Aegean of piracy, as has been perceptively pointed out. In the 1990s a Minoan peak sanctuary was excavated at Aghios Georgios sto Vouno, at the east end of Kythera, revealing the function of the first peak sanctuary outside Crete. Noteworthy among the finds are the many bronze adorant figurines (more than those found in all the other sanctuaries on Crete) and other votive offerings, which show its particular importance (figs 268, 269). The sanctuary ceased operating after the destruction of the Minoan world, towards the end of the sixteenth century BC. From the hill of Aghios Georgios the Minoans controlled the eastern passage to Crete, while at Kataphygadi in Mermygari a sacred cave has been located, ideal for surveillance of the western passage. The main harbour of the island in the time of the Minoan presence was at Palaiopoli, where excavations were conducted by the British School at Athens. At the site of Kastri, overlooking the harbour, parts of Minoan installations were uncovered, while many graves were excavated in the environs (fig. 267).

Towards the end of the fifteenth century BC the Minoans evidently abandoned the island, while indications of a Mycenaean presence proliferate. During the fourteenth and thirteenth centuries BC (Late Helladic IIIA-B period), when Mycenaean Civilization was at its zenith,

266. Kythera. The earliest human presence on the island is dated to the end of the 6th millennium BC, the Late Neolithic period. The vase here was found in the Aghia Sophia Cave at Kalamos, in the south, and points to Kythera's relations with the Cyclades. Kythera Archaeological Museum.

267. Kythera. Polychrome jug of Kamares Ware, imported from Crete (Middle Minoan III period). From the early 2nd millennium to the mid-15th c. BC, Kythera was in the sphere of influence of Minoan Crete. Chamber tombs containing important finds have been investigated at many spots on the island. Kythera Archaeological Museum.

268, 269. Kythera, Aghios Georgios sto Vouno. Finds from the peak sanctuary, bronze figurine of a female worshipper and a stone spoon with Linear A inscription. Late Minoan IA period (16th c. BC). Temporary exhibition in the Piraeus Archaeological Museum.

270. Kythera. Cape Maleas as seen from the new harbour of Kythera at Diakophti. In 424 BC, during the Peloponnesian War, Athenians landed at Diakophti and captured Kythera. Traces of human habitation here date back to the Early Bronze Age (3rd millennium BC), while in the Classical period it was a place for mooring ships. In the subterranean "hidden" cave, the "Chousti", there was a sanctuary of a deity of unknown identity.

Mycenaeans were evidently settled all over the island. Installations and cemeteries of this period have come to light in the wider area of Palaiopoli, at the centre of the island, as well as at Lazarianika in the west, Mermygari, and the area of Aghia Moni in the east. The use of caves in Mycenaean times is attested at Aghia Sophia at Aghia Pelagia, Kataphygadi at Mermygari – which was used from Minoan times – and Aghia Sophia at Kalamos – with continuous human presence from Neolithic times.

When exactly the worship of Aphrodite began on the island is not known, but it is very possible that it was introduced in the period of the break up of the Mycenaean kingdoms on the Greek Mainland (1200 BC), when the Phoenicians, taking advantage of the power vacuum, set up trading stations (emporia) on the island. It is possible that worship of Aphrodite was incorporated in the earlier Minoan cult of the Great Goddess, whom the Phoenicians worshipped as Astarte. The Phoenicians on Kythera were involved with fishing for murex and processing the purple dye (porphyra) extracted from the mollusc. The island was also called Porphyris.

In the early first millennium BC the Dorians captured the island, although when and how elude us. The texts mention Argeian sovereignty over Kythera in this period. The few sporadic archaeological finds, mainly from the area of Palaiokastro, a naturally fortified hill west of Palaiopoli Bay, indicate that their presence may have commenced in the early eighth century BC. In the middle years of the sixth century BC, after Sparta's victory in the war against Argos for domination of the region of Parnon and the Malea Peninsula, the island passed into the hands of the Lacedaemonians (fig. 274).

From the eighth century BC the island's fortified capital developed on Palaiokastro Hill. Parts of the walls survive to a considerable height mainly on the east side. On the flat rocky top of

271. Kythera. Metrical inscription of the late 1st c. AD, revealing the Kytherians' orientation towards Laconia in the period of Roman rule. A physician who had learnt his profession in Sparta and was practising successfully at Boies in Laconia, complains because the "earth" of his homeland, Kythera, bore no fruits: "οὐκ ἔλαβεν καρποὺς τῶν ἰδίων καμάτων". Kythera Archaeological Museum.

272. Kythera. The island's capital from Archaic times was on the naturally fortified hill of Palaiokastro. The two churches there are built on the ruins of ancient sanctuaries. In the church of St George, pictured here, remains of an ancient peribolos were revealed, as well as foundations of buildings and many moveable finds dating from the Geometric to the Hellenistic period. The other church, of Sts Cosmas and Damian, stands in a sanctuary dedicated to the Dioskouroi.

273. Kythera. Outstanding among the votive offerings in the "Chousti" Cave at Diakophti is the fragment of a clay tablet incised with the syllables ΚΑ, ΚΕ, ΚΗ, ΚΙ, ΚΟ, ΚΥ, ΚΩ, / ΛΑ, ΛΕ, ... ΛΩ, ΜΑ, ΜΕ etc. The tablet was used to practise learning to write and had been dedicated to the deity by a pupil. Kythera Archaeological Museum.

the hill, west of the chapel of St George a sanctuary of a female deity, which dates from the eighth century BC into Late Hellenistic times, has been excavated (fig. 272). Lower down, inside the walled city, the little church of Saints Cosmas and Damian has been built on the ruins of an ancient temple dedicated to the Dioskouroi. The outport of the city was Skandeia in Palaiopoli Bay.

In the early years of Spartan rule the worship of many deities in the Laconian pantheon was added to the earlier established cult of Aphrodite. Apart from the sanctuary of the Dioskouroi, a sanctuary of Halea has been found in a rock-shelter at Palaiopoli, a sanctuary of an unknown deity in the "Chousti" Cave at Diakophti (figs 270, 273), a sanctuary of Poseidon Gaieochos, as the god was worshipped at Sparta, on the islet of Mikri Dragonara (Antidragonera) to the east of Kythera, a sanctuary of Asklepios with the Laconian name of Aiglapios at Aghios Theodoros, Aroniadika in the interior of the island, a small sanctuary of Herakles in the area of the large quarry at Skaphidaki next to Avlemonas. Very interesting are the finds on the islet of Mikri Dragonara, which include numerous votive vases and amphorae of Hellenistic times, as well as many gemstones and coins from 54 different cities and kingdoms in the Mediterranean and the Euxine Pontus, from the coasts of Spain to the Crimea Peninsula and Ptolemaic Egypt.

With two brief interruptions, during and shortly after the end of the Peloponnesian War, when it was captured by the Athenians, the island remained under Spartan authority almost until the second century BC. It seems that then Kythera became autonomous, after the insurrection of the "*Eleutherolakones*" (Free Laconians). There are few archaeological remains from this period, mostly from excavations in the area of Palaiopoli, although some have been gathered from the surface at Livadi.

The sources are mute on the island's history in the period when the Peloponnese was subjugated to the Romans. After the naval battle of Actium (21 BC), Augustus ceded Kythera to his friend Gaius Julius Eurykles, whom he had appointed *epistates* of the Lacedaemonians, while from inscriptions of the period the island's close relationship with Laconia until late imperial times can be surmised (fig. 271).

274. Kythera. The "Lion of Kythera", as this statue is popularly known, was most probably found in the area of Palaiokastro, built into the walls of the Kastro of Chora, from where it was smuggled to Germany during the Nazi Occupation. It was returned to Greece in the 1960s and since 1985 has been the showpiece of the Kythera Archaeological Museum. Dated to the mid-6th c. BC, that is just after Kythera was captured by the Spartans, it is considered by many scholars as an excellent example of the Laconian sculpture workshop.

KYTHERA | 201

Antikythera

Antikythera (ancient Aigila or Aigilia) lies 22 nautical miles from Kythera and 18 from Crete, controlling the passage from the open sea of the Aegean to the Western Mediterranean. Today there is no suitable anchorage on the island, except Potamos Bay which is exposed to the north winds. In Antiquity, when sea level was 2.5 metres higher, the cove at Xiropotamos insinuated deeper inland, providing a small but sheltered "hidden" harbour.

Antikythera became known in the early twentieth century when a Roman shipwreck was discovered off the north coast. Divers recovered from wreck the important bronze sculptures of the Late Classical and Hellenistic periods (4th-3rd centuries BC), which are exhibited in the National Archaeological Museum in Athens (fig. 680).

There are only scant references to the island in the ancient sources. The sole known event, which is mentioned by Plutarch, is that King Kleomenes III of Sparta sought refuge there *en route* to Egypt, after his defeat at Sellasia. Inscriptions of the mid-third century BC from Rhodes refer to operations of Rhodian warships against the "brigands" of Aigilia, revealing the piratical activities of the island's inhabitants.

275. Antikythera. Lead sling shots with the inscription: ΠΑΡΑΦ [ΑΛΑΣ] Α[Ρ]ΝΙΩΝ. Kythera Archaeological Museum.

276. Antikythera. Stone catapult missile used in the first half of the 3rd c. BC, against the city of Aigila. Contemporary Rhodian inscriptions refer to a Rhodian attack, using catapults, against the "brigands" of Aigila. Excavations have revealed that serious damage was inflicted inside the fortification, with a destruction level dated to the early 3rd c. BC. Kythera Archaeological Museum.

277. Antikythera. In the cove of Xiropotamos, which went much further inland in Antiquity, behind the Kastro Hill, was the harbour of Aigila, with a sanctuary of Apollo.

278. Antikythera. In 1880, in the area of the harbour, a statue of Apollo citharode was discovered, dated to the early 3rd c. BC. In excavations conducted by V. Stais immediately afterwards, its inscribed base was found, revealing that it was a votive offering of a Pherraian, a Thessalian and an Athenian to the sanctuary of Apollo Aigilieus. Athens, National Archaeological Museum.

The archaeological data show that the island was inhabited during the Late and /Final Neolithic periods and in the Early Bronze Age (5th to 3rd millennia BC), although related finds are so far minimal. A few surface sherds give a limited picture of human activity in the Minoan Age, even though the island's position imposed the presence of Minoans to control the Aegean region.

Well-preserved is the walled ancient city that existed in Hellenistic times in the northern part of the island, at Kastro, overlooking the Xiropotamos Bay where the harbour was located (fig. 277). There was a sanctuary of Apollo in the harbour, which was located and excavated in the late nineteenth century by Valerios Stais. It was then that the statue of the god was found, with a dedicatory inscription from an Athenian and a Thessalian (fig. 278).

The entire city survives, covering an area of about 30 hectares and with an estimated population of 800-1,000. In many places its walls stand to a height of 6 metres. Also in good condition is the ship-shed (*neosoikos*), entirely cut in the bedrock. On present excavation evidence the fortification was constructed in the late fourth century BC. Two destruction levels have been identified. The first is dated to the second quarter of the third century BC, shortly after the construction of the fortification, and coincides chronologically with the Rhodians' campaign (fig. 276). The second, dated to the early first century BC, refers to the Romans' suppression of the Cretan "revolt". Life in the city ceased in the first century BC.

It seems that from early on Antikythera was under the authority of Phalasarna, the well-known "pirate" city in western Crete, of which it was the surveillance outpost. Between 69 and 67 BC, it followed Phalasarna's fate when the Romans decided to eradicate piracy. Over the entire extent of the city there are obvious signs of the island's checkered martial history (figs 275, 276).

After the Roman destruction of Antikythera it was inhabited again in the closing years of the Imperial period, around the fourth century AD, as indicated by finds from the coast at Xiropotamos and at Charchaliana. It appears that a permanent settlement was established there, which continued until at least the end of the Early Byzantine period.

278

MAKRONISOS
KEA
ANDROS
YAROS
TENOS
KYTHNOS
SYROS
MYKONOS
RHENEIA
DELOS
SERIPHOPOULA
SERIPHOS
PAROS
NAXOS
DONOUSA
ANTIPAROS
SIPHNOS
DESPOTIKO
KOUPHONISIA
KEROS
PHALKONERA
KIMOLOS
KITRIANI
HERAKLEIA
SCHINOUSA
AMORGOS
ANTIMELOS
POLYAIGOS
IOS
MELOS
ANYDROS
PRASONISI
SIKINOS
OPHIDOUSA
PHOLEGANDROS
THERASIA THERA
ANAPHE
CHRISTIANA
PACHIA

CYCLADES

Kea

Yanna Venieri

Kea or Tzia (anc. Keos), the northernmost island in the western Cyclades, lies southeast of the coast of Attica and Makronisos, and north of Kythnos.

It is mostly mountainous, with small fertile valleys formed between the massifs, and has a rocky coastline indented with many coves. Kea is located at the crossroad of the Aegean sea-lanes and from prehistoric times developed into and important port of call and bridge between the Cyclades and the Greek Mainland. The farming economy of the island is based on cultivation of the vine, the olive tree and the oak tree (until the mid-20th century), stock-raising and bee-keeping. The lodes of iron and lead ores and red ochre-ruddle (iron oxide used in vase-making, shipbuilding and pharmaceuticals) were important natural resources for Kea in Antiquity.

Myth has it that the Nymphs were the first to come to live on the island, which was named Hydrousa (= watery). However, they were pursued by a lion and forced to abandon it. After their flight, the island suffered terrible drought and aridity. The inhabitants then sought the help of Aristaios, son of Apollo and Kyrene, who led a group of Arcadians to settle there. He built an altar on the mountaintop and sacrificed to Seirios and to Zeus Ikmaios, god of coolness. And northerly winds then blew for forty days. It was Aristaios who brought the arts of animal husbandry and apiary to the island.

Kea was apparently named after the hero from Naupaktos, Keos, who captured the island as head of the Locrians. According to the ancient historians, Pelasgians, Karians, Lelegians and Phoenicians were among the tribes who inhabited the island prior to its colonization by Ionians, which took place when Thersidamas settled people from Attica there.

The extensive archaeological investigations and rescue excavations conducted on Kea from the late nineteenth and throughout the twentieth century have brought to light two highly important prehistoric settlements, at Aghia Irini and Kephala, the ancient city of Karthaia and part of the ancient settlement of Koresia. In parallel, systematic surface surveys, which have essentially covered the entire island, identifying new sites and mapping the ancient cities already known, as well as a large number of ancient towers, have filled in the archaeological map that was first drawn in the second half of the nineteenth century by the local antiquarian Constantinos Manthos, in his book *Archaeology and History of the Island of Kea* (in Greek).

The earliest finds date from the end of the Neolithic Age and come from the settlement at Kephala. This was founded in the Final Neolithic period (3300 BC), on Cape Kephala on the northwest coast of the island. The cemetery of the settlement, with small cist graves, was at the foot of the headland. The site was inhabited for about one hundred years and subsequently abandoned. Nonetheless, this relatively brief period represents a significant developmental stage in Aegean prehistory, namely the transition to the Early Bronze Age in the Cyclades (3rd millennium BC).

279

206 | CYCLADES

During the Bronze Age (*circa* 3000-1100 BC) a settlement was established at Aghia Irini on a small peninsula in the bay of Aghios Nikolaos, which is a natural sheltered harbour on the northwest side of Kea. This was to develop into an important centre of Cycladic Culture (fig. 280). The earliest evidence of human presence at the site dates from the transition from the Final Neolithic period to the Early Bronze Age (*circa* 3000 BC). The first permanent installation dates to the Early Cycladic II period (2800/2700-2300 BC). During the Middle Bronze Age (*circa* 2000/1900 BC) the settlement expanded and acquired a fortification wall. To that period date the cemeteries and the first phase of the "temple", one of the most important buildings in the settlement (fig. 281).

In the Late Cycladic I and II periods (*circa* 1600-1450 BC) an extensive building programme was implemented. Most of the buildings with large storerooms, which are visible today, were constructed then. House A, a two-storey building decorated with wall-paintings, with many rooms and basement storerooms, may well have been a central building of administrative function for the settlement. Dated to this period are the large clay statues of bare-breasted female figures in characteristic bell-shaped skirt, standing or dancing, which were discovered in the

279. Kea, Aghia Irini. Clay statue of a female figure from the Bronze Age temple. Excavations uncovered parts of about fifty similar statues, which probably represent deities, priestesses or worshippers (15th c. BC). Kea Archaeological Museum.

280. Kea. Aerial photograph of the prehistoric settlement at Aghia Irini. Visible are the fortification of the north side, houses and the temple, as well as the city wall – now submerged in the sea.

281. Kea. The shrine in the prehistoric settlement at Aghia Irini. The excavations at this site were conducted by the University of Cincinnati, under the direction of Professor John Caskey, between 1960 and 1976.

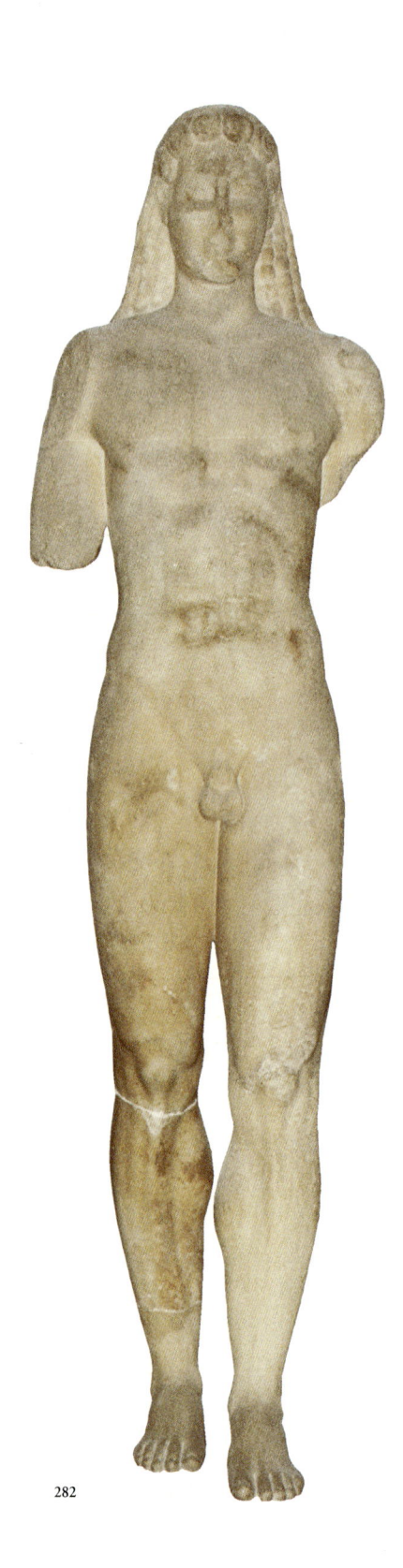

course of excavating the temple (fig. 279). Unique in size and kind, these products of a local workshop display peculiarities that differentiate them from the figurines of deities that have been found in other regions of the Cretan-Mycenaean world. They are dated to the fifteenth century BC and not later than 1450 BC, when they were destroyed together with the building.

The city at Aghia Irini has an excellent network of paved streets linking the neighbourhoods and a sewerage system. During this period the settlement at Aghia Irini was enjoying its heyday and continued to be an important port of call in the Aegean world. It was destroyed by a severe earthquake around 1450 BC, but some of the buildings were repaired in the ensuing Late Helladic IIIA period (*circa* 1400 BC).

Very little is known about Kea in Geometric times (mid-11th-8th century BC). It seems that in the prehistoric settlement at Aghia Irini the area of the temple was reused as a place of worship. The first phase of settlement at Karthaia is dated to the eighth century BC. In this period Kea participated, along with other Cycladic islands, in the sanctification of Delos as a religious centre.

During the Archaic period (7th-6th century BC) four city-states were founded: Ioulis, Karthaia, Koresia and Poieessa. With the exception of Ioulis, which was inland, the other three cities were coastal and had good harbours. All four cities were fortified. The territory of each was controlled and protected by constructing towers at crucial points. A dense road network connected the city-states to each other, and the urban centre (*asty*) to the rural territory (*chora*) of each. The boundaries between the cities are not absolutely clear, although many proposals have been made, based on the geomorphology and the natural limits as well as epigraphic testimonies.

In Classical times (5th-4th century BC), there was an increase of rural installations in the countryside. At the time when the Piraeus developed as the port of Athens, the harbour cities of Kea prospered, due to their advantageous position, which fact is also linked with the intensification of mining and exporting ruddle and argentiferous lead. In the fourth century BC the cities of Kea formed a federation (*sympoliteia*). At about the same time the Athenians took over and monopolized the exploitation of ruddle. In the mid-fourth century BC, on the intervention of Athens, the federation was dissolved and the cities became autonomous once more. From then until the early third century BC several of the towers that have been identified at various points on the island were erected. These were of defensive and military function or were associated with large farmsteads.

Karthaia, on the southeast coast of Kea, in the bay known today as Poles, was apparently settled first in the eighth century BC. The first excavations were carried out in the nineteenth century but surveys and excavations made over the last twenty years have enriched our knowledge of the city's history.

At the south end of the range of hills known as Aspri Vigla, on the acropolis of Karthaia, are the most important buildings: the temple of Apollo (530 BC) to the south (fig. 287) and the "temple of Athena" (late 6th/early 5th century BC) to the north (figs 285, 286). It is deduced from the preserved decoration of the so-called "temple of Athena" – sculptures and fragments of the pediments (torso of Athena, legs of horses, etc.) – that the subject of the composition was

282

208 | CYCLADES

the Amazonomachy. Represented on the south akroterion was Theseus' abduction of the Amazon Antiope. During the fourth/early third century BC, a temple-shaped building, the so-called Building D, was constructed on the terrace of the "temple of Athena". On the southern lower slopes of Aspri Vigla, in the Vathypotamos Valley, the theatre of the city was uncovered, as well as a section of the water-supply system. The cemetery of Karthaia lies in the Kalamitsios Valley, to the east of the acropolis. Life in the city of Karthaia continued throughout the Late Roman period and into the seventh century AD.

Ioulis is the only city in the island's interior, situated on a height overlooking the north side of Kea and the sea beyond, as far as the shore of Attica. It was founded in the Archaic period on a site which was later occupied by the Medieval Kastro (castle) of Ioulis and where an active settlement still exists. Two lines of fortifications circumvallated the ancient city: the outer wall, which is low down on the hill slope and the inner enceinte, which surrounded the acropolis, that is the area of the present castle. Part of the walls is preserved on the west and east sides of the Kastro.

There is scant archaeological evidence from Ioulis, as no systematic excavations have been conducted. The ancient authors refer to the existence of a temple of Apollo and of Aphrodite, and it is surmised from inscriptions that Athena, Artemis, Apollo, Hermes and Dionysos were worshipped there. According to the ancient sources, Ioulis was the native city of the lyric poets Symonides (6th-5th century BC) and Bacchylides (481-431 BC), the orator Prodikos (2nd half of 5th century BC) and the physician Erasistratos (4th-3rd century BC) (fig. 283).

In the southeast part of the city, opposite the Kastro and close to the modern cemetery of Ioulis, is a colossal lion carved in the bedrock. This unique sculptural creation of the Early Archaic period is dated to the late seventh/early sixth century BC.

Ancient Koresia was located above the modern village of Livadi (Koresia), at the west end of the bay of Aghios Nikolaos. It had two acropolises, occupying two hilltops, of Aghios Savvas to the north and of Aghia Triada to the south. The city was founded, like the others, in Archaic times. Initially only the area of

282. Kea. The Kea Kouros. Found on the eastern lower slopes of the acropolis of Koresia and dated 530-520 BC. Athens, National Archaeological Museum.

283. Kea. The Lion of Ioulis. A colossal lion carved from the living rock. A unique sculptural work of the Early Archaic period. Late 7th/early 6th c. BC.

KEA | 209

284. Kea, Poieessa. The five-storey tower at Aghia Marina, a defensive building of the 4th c. BC.

285. Kea, Karthaia. Restoration drawing of the terrace with the "temple of Athena" after completion of the first phase (500-490 BC). Drawing by the architect A. Papanikolaou.

286. Kea, Karthaia. The so-called "temple of Athena" (late 6th-early 5th c. BC). Discernible in the distance is Kythnos.

287. Kea, Karthaia. The temple of Apollo.

the lower acropolis (Aghios Savvas Hill) was walled and included a system of four towers. In Classical times the fortification was extended by constructing a wall enclosing both acropolises. House remains are visible on the lower acropolis, while it is speculated that the upper acropolis (Aghia Triada Hill) was not a permanent place of residence. Excavations here (upper acropolis) have brought to light a temple, although it is not known to which deity it was dedicated. However, Strabo mentions that there was a temple to Apollo Sminthios at Koresia.

It is suspected that there was a cemetery of the city at the bottom of the east slope of Aghia Triada Hill, because it was there that the renowned Kea Kouros was discovered, today exhibited in the National Archaeological Museum, Athens (fig. 282). There was a second cemetery close to Yaliskari, which began to function – on present evidence – in the seventh century BC.

In the early second century BC Koresia was annexed to Ioulis. In Roman times there was probably limited habitation on the lower slopes of both hills.

Poieessa is situated on the west coast of Kea, on the hill of Phyra or Panaya tis Soteras, which rises on the north side of a fertile valley. It was founded in the late sixth century BC and like the other cities on the island was walled. Inside the fortification the remains of houses and retaining walls are visible. On the south shore of the bay, harbour installations have been found, possibly ship-sheds. The city's cemeteries lay in the northern part of the valley, on the slopes of Tourkos Hill. In Hellenistic times Poieessa was annexed administratively to Karthaia.

A noteworthy example of defensive architecture of the fourth century BC is the tower at Aghia Marina, thus named after the monastery of St Marina which was built on the same site around 1600. It stands at the junction of the roads leading from Koresia and Ioulis to Poieessa. Of square plan (10 x 10 m.) and originally five-storeyed, it is estimated to have been about 20 metres high; it is preserved today to 19.632 metres (fig. 284). According to the bibliography, the tower survived virtually intact until the mid-nineteenth century and the greater part of it collapsed in the great earthquake of 1858.

In Early Byzantine times Ioulis became capital of the island, and remains so to this day.

285

286

287

KEA | 211

Makronisos

EVANGELOS CH. KAKAVOYANNIS

Long, narrow and for the most part rocky, this virtually waterless island in the south Euboean Sea has a few poor patches of cultivable ground and a coastline devoid of any safe coves. 12.5 km in length and 1.5 km in width, it lies parallel to the Attic coast, about 3 miles distant, opposite Thorikos, and Sounion. Its bedrock consists of strata of marbles and schists, with pockets of argentiferous metal ores in places, such as galena (lead sulphide, PbS). Its metal lodes are the same as those of the Laureotike, but much smaller. According to all indications, the island was used occasionally as a seasonal dwelling place for shepherds, who also grew some crops. In same periods its metalliferous deposits were exploited. On account of its proximity and geological affinity, Makronisos belongs to the Laureotike, rather than to the Cyclades.

The island undoubtedly owes its name to its shape (*makros* = long, *nesos* = island). In Antiquity it was known also as Helene, because the wife of King Menelaus of Sparta disembarked here, *en route* for Troy, after her abduction by Paris. Our knowledge of the history of ancient Makronisos is generally scant, due to the lack both of ancient testimonies and of archaeological research.

According to D. Theocharis, Cycladic graves containing marble vessels and clay vases of the Early Helladic period (3rd millennium BC), including some "sauceboats", were uncovered on Makronisos, although their findspot is not mentioned. In 1966 the archaeologist N. Lambert discovered in the north part of the west coast, on a small headland at the locality Leontari or Provatsa, a prehistoric settlement with remains of stone-built walls and deposits some 4 metres thick. She also found, *inter alia*, a lead spool, two small lumps of litharge (lead oxide, PbO) and a quantity of scoria from the smelting of argentiferous metal ore. These last three finds attest that the inhabitants of the settlement were exploiting the island's argentiferous metal lodes and producing silver and lead.

In 1981 the archaeologist with the Belgian Archaeological Mission, P. Spitaels, conducted a small excavation in order to study the stratigraphy of the settlement. She confirmed the existence of three stone-built houses, of which only the central one was partially investigated (fig. 289). The settlement dates to the Early Helladic-Early Cycladic II period (*circa* 2700-2300 BC) and is contemporary with the mine no. 3, which was then operating at Thorikos opposite. Other finds were a seal impression on clay (fig. 288), a sherd of a "sauceboat" with lead clamp indicating repair of the vessel in Antiquity, and some pieces of litharge. This last substance is produced during the cupellation of argentiferous lead, which is the process of separating its two main components, i.e. silver and lead. In the lower reaches of the fill at the settlement there was an archaeological level dating from the period of the transition from the Neolithic to the Bronze Age (late 4th millennium BC), while in the upper reaches Mycenaean levels were located. In neither were there indications of metallurgical activities.

288. Makronisos. Seal impression made on damp clay, from the settlement at Leontari. Early Helladic-Early Cycladic II period (2700-2300 BC).

289. Makronisos. Photograph of the excavation of the Early Bronze Age (3rd millennium BC) settlement at the locality Leontari or Provatsa.

Remnants and traces of antiquities of various periods are preserved at other places on Makronisos, but have yet to be studied. Some of these possibly relate to ancient mining. However, there is indirect evidence of metallurgy and metalworking on the island in historical times, in the form of the scoria, the waste from smelting metal ore. The ancients kept the argentiferous lead but discarded this sinter as useless, even though it had a small argentiferous lead content, sometimes as much as 12% of its weight, which could not be extracted because of imperfections in their technology. The intensive working of the mines in the Laureotike during Classical times resulted in the accumulation of enormous quantities of scoriae, where the smelting workshops operated. The exploitation of the Laureotike in modern times, from 1865 onwards, began with the systematic smelting of the ancient scoriae by the mining companies of Greece, because they had a more sophisticated technology than the ancient Greeks.

According to the Athenian newspapers of the day, there were mounds of ancient scoriae on Makronisos too, which from 1871 onwards were transported systematically to   , where they were smelted to remove their argentiferous lead content. The existence of heaps of scoria on Makronisos bears witness to significant mining and metallurgical activities locally, especially in Classical times. Moreover, since these continued over a long interval there must have been houses too. The various ancient ruins that N. Petris claimed to have seen in the vicinity of Aghios Georgios, when he visited Makronisos in 1884, are most probably associated with the practice of metallurgy.

In view of the aforesaid, we conclude that whenever there was intensive mining and smelting activity in the Laureotike in Antiquity, the situation was usually similar on the neighbouring island of Makronisos.

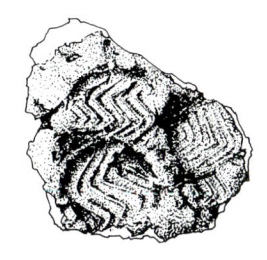

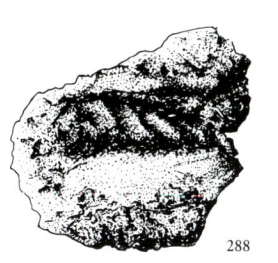

MAKRONISOS | 213

Andros

Christina A. Televantou

Andros, the northernmost and the second largest of the Cyclades (374 square kilometres in area), lies in a strategic geographical position, constituting a natural bridge between Euboea, Attica and the Cyclades.

The earliest mention of its name is in the fifth century BC, in Aeschylus' tragedy *Persians* (line 886). According to mythological tradition, which alludes to earlier times, it was named after the founder-hero, Andros or Andreas, who was of divine origin and a general of King Rhadamanthys of Crete, who gifted him the island. Father of Andros was King Anios of Delos, son of Apollo, or Eurymachos, and his mother was Kreousa or the nymph Rhoio, daughter of Staphylos, son of Dionysos and the Bacchant Chryseis. For this reason these gods and their attributes are represented on the coinage of Andros.

The island was settled by prehellenic tribes already in the Late Neolithic period (5th millennium BC) and enjoyed a heyday during the Final Neolithic or Chalcolithic period (4500-3200 BC), as borne out by the settlements at Strophilas, Vriokastro and Mikroyali.

Strophilas is so far the biggest Neolithic settlement in the Aegean, covering an area of at least 2 hectares on a naturally fortified plateau and protected by a mighty wall (fig. 292). The buildings are of quadrilateral or apsidal plan and of large dimensions. Particularly important is the organized sanctuary, the earliest known in the Aegean. It comprises a spacious hall, approximately 100 square metres, arranged on two levels, the larger one with monumental rock-art of pictorial and schematic/symbolic motifs on the floor, and the smaller with a sizeable circular construction of stone at the centre. Particularly significant is the extensive rock-art – in some cases carved and in some pecked – adorning blocks of the fortification wall, the floor of the sanctuary and parts of the rock along the base of the fortification wall, with representations that are both naturalistic (ships, animals, fish) and symbolic (spiral motif in the shape of Neolithic ring-idols) (fig. 292).

The representation of ships in the rock-art (fig. 291) bears witness to the high level of shipbuilding and seafaring. The numerous moveable finds – clay vases (fig. 290), ground stone tools, obsidian tools, jewellery, figurines, one gold bead and bronze objects (daggers, awls, fibulae, etc.) – indicate the wealth as well as the advanced technical know-how, particularly in the sectors of metallurgy and metalworking.

The settlement at Strophilas, with its pre-urban structures and collective works (fortification wall, sanctuary), attests that already from the fourth millennium BC there were in the Cyclades organized communities with a high standard of culture and developed technology, on which the Cycladic Culture of the third millennium BC was based.

During the Early and the Middle Bronze Age (2700-1750 BC) there was a thriving settlement at Plaka, on the east coast of the island (fig. 293). Well-preserved buildings with careful masonry, belonging to at least two constructional phases, survive. The moveable finds, mainly pottery, are uncovered *in situ*, virtually intact, and it is possible that the settlement suffered destruction from earthquakes. The Late Bronze Age finds are very limited, due to circumstance. In the Geometric period (11th-8th century BC), two cities, were founded at Zagora and Ypsili, on the west coast, while a small rural installation has been identified in the area of Palaiopoli. A group of vases, now in the Chora Archaeological Museum (fig. 294), which probably comes from the cemetery at Zagora, as well as sherds from the city, bear witness to human activity from the tenth century BC. The city, which flourished in Late Geometric times (second half of 8th century BC), extends over a naturally fortified plateau and is protected by a robust defensive wall (fig. 298). The open-air sanctuary was located at the centre of the plateau. The city was abandoned in the late eighth century BC. Later, in the sixth century BC, the gateway in the wall was reconstructed and a temple was built. Dedicated most probably to Athena Polias, it functioned until at least the fifth century BC (fig. 297).

The city at Ypsili spreads over the upper part of the homonymous hill, which dominates the mid-point of the island's west coast. It is estimated to have covered an area of 4 hectares in the Geometric period, whereas it appears to have been confined to the acropolis in the Archaic period. Buildings of the Middle Geometric period (925-850 BC), in the area of the acropolis, indicate that the city was founded in the tenth-ninth century BC and enjoyed a considerable heyday in the Late Geometric period (second half of 8th century BC). In the late seventh century BC, when the city at Zagora was deserted, that at Ypsili shrank to the bounds of its acropolis, until the end of the sixth century BC, when it too was abandoned. A small-scale and short-lived reoccupation is observed in the Hellenistic period.

290. Andros. Late Neolithic jug (4500-3300 BC), from the Neolithic settlement at Strophilas. Andros Archaeological Museum.

291. Andros, Strophilas. Restoration drawing of a ship carved on a block of the fortification wall of the Neolithic settlement. Final Neolithic period (4500-3300 BC).

292. Andros. Neolithic settlement at Strophilas. The fortification wall is the earliest example of defensive architecture known in the Aegean. Built of large roughly-dressed stone blocks and 1.5-2 m thick, it is reinforced with curved bastions, one of them protecting the gateway. Represented on its external face, either carved or pecked, are ships, single or in flotilla, echoing the maritime activity and economic power of the inhabitants.

293. Andros. Buildings in the Middle Bronze Age (2000-1700 BC) settlement being excavated at Plaka in recent years.

In Geometric times the acropolis and the city were protected by a mighty rampart, as much as 6.5 m thick in the final phase. Its course followed the configuration of the ground, forming recesses at large intervals and incorporating the bedrock in places. A rectangular construction on the southeast side, integral with the wall, seems to have been some kind of tower. Here, among other things, numerous pebbles were found, perhaps missiles.

The buildings are stone-built with benches inside, on which vases were placed. The moveable finds are many and varied: clay vases decorated with geometric motifs and figural representations (fig. 295), minor objects, jewellery, and others. The acropolis was densely built up during all periods, while in the final phase of occupation, the Archaic, there were buildings with several rooms.

At the centre of the acropolis is the sanctuary, which is defined to the north by a large precinct wall (*peribolos*). It was founded in the Late Geometric period (second half of 8th century BC) and the votive offerings show that it functioned until at least the fifth century BC. During the Archaic period (first half of 6th century BC) a megaron-type temple was constructed (fig. 296), possibly dedicated to Demeter, as deduced from the architectural features in combination with the kore and pig figurines discovered here.

The temporal co-existence of the cities at Zagora and Ypsili, in conjunction with their size and prosperity, attests that Andros was a power to be reckoned with in the Late Geometric (second half of 8th century BC) Aegean. The finds point to relations with Attica and, primarily, Euboea, with which the cities collaborated in founding colonies in the North (Stageira, Sane, Akanthos, Argilos), in the Chalkidike Peninsula. From the end of the eighth century BC the inhabitants of

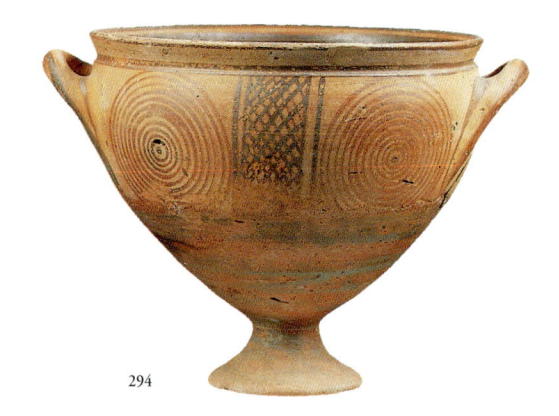

294. Andros, Zagora. Small footed krater, product of an island workshop of the Late Protogeometric period (925-850 BC). Found in 1899 in a grave near Zagora, perhaps in the cemetery of the city there. Andros Archaeological Museum.

295. Andros, Ypsili. Sherd of a pictorial vase with depiction of warriors (2nd half of 8th c. BC). Discernible are three soldiers, marching in battle formation and holding their spear on high. They are armed in the characteristic manner of the Geometric period, with figure-eight shield, boars'-tusk helmet with plume, sword at the waist and spear. Andros Archaeological Museum.

296. Andros, Ypsili. Archaic temple (1st half of 6th c. BC). View from the west. The temple is of megaron plan with prodomos and cella (temple proper). The walls and the votive offerings of the earlier Geometric temple were enclosed and sealed by the floor in the prodomos. The plan and the masonry are analogous to the temple at Zagora. Offerings were found in the rock-cut cavity in the prodomos. In the cella are the altar, two built rectangular trapezas and benches along the walls, features denoting chthonic cult.

297. Andros, Zagora. Restoration model of the Archaic temple (575-500 BC). It was built on the site of the open-air sanctuary of the Late Geometric period (2nd half of 8th c. BC) during the Archaic period, long after the abandonment of the city. It is of megaron plan with closed pronaos and cella (temple proper), which enclosed the ancient altar (or pedestal of a cult statue). The inscription ΠΟΛΙΑΣ incised on a clay lekanis found here indicates that the temple was most probably dedicated to Athena Polias.

298. Andros, Zagora. General view of the settlement with Gyaros in the background. Along the length of the plateau runs the wall, one of the best examples of Geometric fortification in the Aegean (2nd half of 8th c. BC).

ANDROS | 217

299. Andros. Hellenistic tower at Aghios Petros. The tower was most probably built to protect the mines in the area, and also as a lookout post. It is 9.40 m in diameter and survives to a height of some 21 m. An opening in the vaulted ceiling of the first storey led to a spiral staircase with reached the uppermost part of the tower, which seems to have had five storeys.

300. Andros, Palaiopoli. Tower in the wall of the acropolis (4th-3rd c. BC). During Classical and Hellenistic times a strong wall, 2-3 m thick, protected ancient Andros, both the city together with its cultivated fields and the acropolis, in which a cross-wall provided even greater security. At intervals the wall is indented – particularly obvious on the west branch –, reinforced with square towers and provided with gateways.

these cities moved towards the fertile area of what is now Palaiopoli, where they founded the city of Andros. From the sixth century BC until the sixth/seventh century AD this was the political and cultural hub of the island. Smaller settlements, such as at Aghia Eleousa and Phellos, the settlement at Ypsili, the harbour of Gaurion (mod. Gavrio), the towers, such as the circular tower of Aghios Petros (fig. 299) and the quarries of marble and of green stone at Phellos, Pelekitis, Trochalia and Strongylo were subject to it.

The city of Andros was not built to a preconceived urban plan, which is due in part to the nature of the terrain, the large area it covered – from the church of St Demetrios to the seashore – and possibly to the gradual arrival of inhabitants. In the fourth century BC this entire area was protected by a mighty wall (fig. 300). The site was arranged in terraces, underpinned by large retaining walls, on which buildings were erected and fields were cultivated.

The private houses spread to the southwest of the cross-wall, the public edifices and major sanctuaries on the plain as far as the coast, and the cemeteries *extra muros*.

The centre of the city's public life, political, mercantile and commercial, developed in the littoral zone. Here were located the agora and – as inscriptions and ancient sources indicate – the bouleuterion, possibly the prytaneion and in all probability the sanctuary of Artemis Tauropolos. Close by, on the shore, were the bathhouses, while the mole of the harbour is still visible, half sunk under the sea (fig. 681). Higher up are the gymnasium and the temple of Apollo, while there are clues to the position of the theatre.

From Archaic times, the public buildings and the cemeteries of Andros were decorated with abundant sculptures, such as the "Hermes of Andros" (fig. 302) and the statue of Artemis (fig. 301). Rich too is the corpus of honorary and dedicatory decrees, as well as of funerary inscriptions. In Early Byzantine times some public edifices and temples were converted into basilicas, many of which are decorated with important mosaics.

301. Andros, Palaiopoli. Marble torso of Artemis. Roman copy of a work of the 2nd c. BC. Andros Archaeological Museum.

302. Andros, Palaiopoli. The Hermes of Andros (1st c. BC). A larger than life-size statue of a naked young male, a Roman copy of an earlier Praxitelian model. It was set up in second use on a built pedestal of a heroon, together with a statue in the type of the "Matron of Herculaneum", in a class of monument known from Thera to Macedonia. The statues were found in 1833, in the area of the agora of the city of Andros. Brought to Athens on the initiative of King Othon, they were exhibited in the National Archaeological Museum until 1981. They were then returned to the island and are now displayed in the Andros Archaeological Museum.

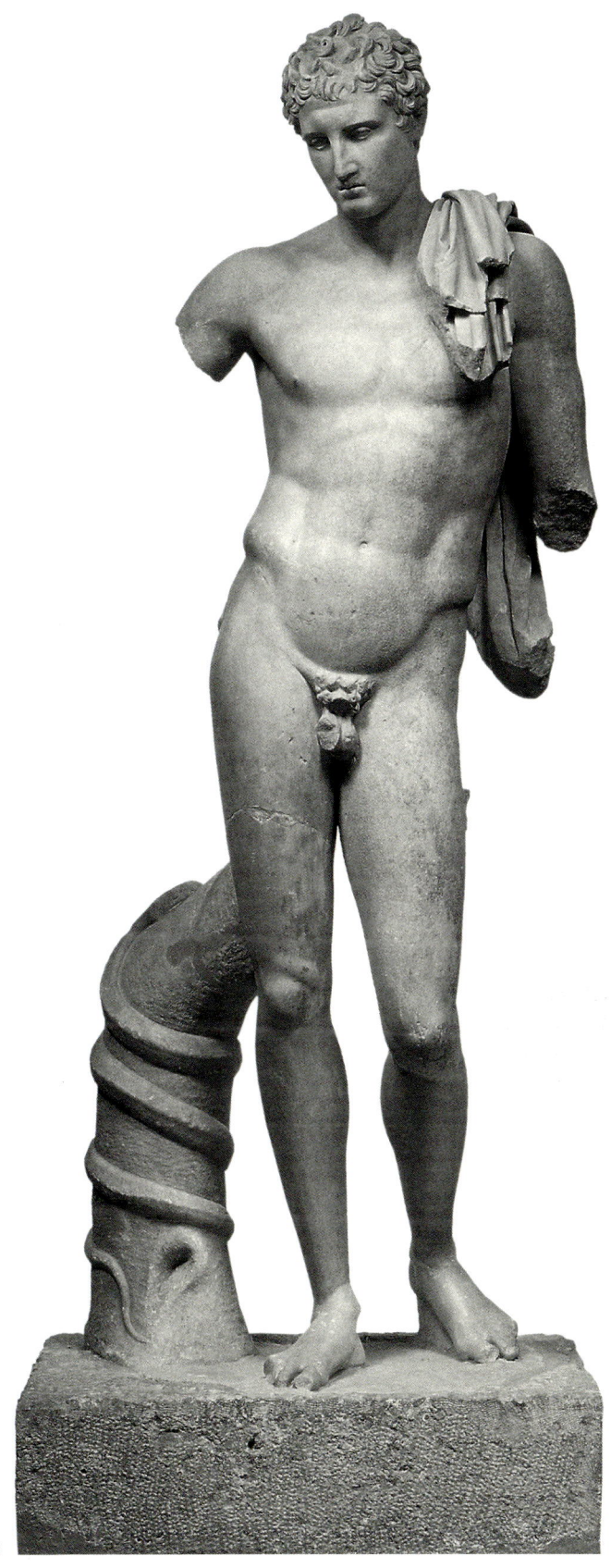

ANDROS

Gyaros

ALEXANDROS P. GOUNARIS

303. Gyaros. General view of Panaya Bay.

304. Gyaros. Fragment from the sole inscription, to date, that comes from an archaeological context and mentions the deme of Gyarians. A recent find from the excavation in the ancient city of Andros.

305. Gyaros. General view of the coast of Panaya Bay, towards the island's hinterland, where the ancient settlement of the Gyarians was possibly located.

When, as dusk is falling, the visitor looks out to sea from Andros to the southwest or from Tenos to the west, or at daybreak from Kea to the east or from Kythnos to the northeast, he wonders what is the tiny islet that cuts the horizon, at which no ships call and which has no lights. A Syran looking to the north recognizes it immediately: it is Gyaros of the Greeks, Gyara of the Roman period. The island rises at the centre of an imagined curve, open towards Karystia; it is formed from these islands and encloses a sea surface of radius approximately 12 nautical miles. Does the island's name derive from "*gyalon*", the cube, the square stone? Or is its etymology perhaps from the Homeric "*gyalon*", the half breastplate of the warrior's armour?

The first reliable information on the island in Antiquity comes from Aristotle, via Aelian: here the rats eat even the iron ore. The wildness of the landscape haunts the references to ancient Gyaros, such as that of Antigonos from Karystos: here grows the deadly *acherdos*, a bush – possibly a species of wild pear (*Pyrus amygdaliformis*) – which if pushed into a tree causes it to shrivel. Some three hundred years after the Stageiran philosopher, Strabo visited the island. He mentions that the fishermen inhabitants sent an ambassador to Caesar in Corinth, requesting a reduction in the tribute of one hundred and fifty drachmas levied on them when they could only with difficulty pay one hundred drachmas. Again in the Roman period, there are the first references to Gyara as a place of exile of eponymous citizens. In the reign of Tiberius, Gyara was suggested as place of exile for Gaius Silanus, proconsul of Asia and for Vibius Serenus, proconsul of Further Spain. In the reign of Gaius Caligula, it was likewise suggested for Flaccus Avillius, prefect of Alexandria and Egypt. In the reign of Nero, the Stoic philosopher Musonius Rufus was banished here; he discovered a spring and survived. The island became a place visited by his disciples and the fountain was sung of by the Greeks. The island's lack of water was tantamount to death. But all three aforementioned officials were lucky. It was decided for each respectively that Kythnos, Amorgos and Andros replace the "rocky, unfit for corn or vine or tree" Gyara. The Romans showed a rudimentary logic: they sent them into exile, not to death, even though the Stoic philosopher Epictetus asked: What Rome, what Gyaros, what Athens, what prison …? Lucian, in his short story *Toxaris or Friendship* seems to second him: when Deinias is exiled here, his friend Agathokles follows him. Lacking the essentials, he dives together with the murex fishers in order to feed himself and indeed "when [Deinias] died, [he] did not care to return again to his own country, but remained there in the island, ashamed to desert his friend even after his death". Even in this wretched place there is evidence of observance of the cult of Aphrodite Mychia, in the form of an inscription incised on a marble slab. It is possible that Artemis was worshipped and that Perseus was honoured, as their figures are represented on the bronze coins of the Gyarians. Possibly Zeus was worshipped too, since part of a terracotta head portraying the god was found on the island. A terracotta piglet from Gyaros, in the Syros Archaeological Museum, also suggests the worship of Demeter or the existence of a Thesmophorion. However, the cult of the goddess on the island is not to be taken for granted. The figurine could be associated with domestic cult, a child's toy or a grave good.

Do ancient houses and burials exist on Gyaros? Already from 1870 Klon Stefanos recognized that the inscription about Aphrodite Mychia comes from the ruins of the ancient town on the island. Was this the village of Plutarch's fishermen or of Lucian's murex divers? Can the site of the settlement be identified in the east, in the area of Panaya Bay (figs 303, 305)? Was this perhaps the seat of the Deme of Gyarians, as attested in an inscription from Samos or in the inscription found at Palaiopoli on Andros (fig. 304)? All the indications are that until the legendary persecution of the inhabitants by the iron-eating rats and before the commencement of its history as a place of martyrdom, another world existed on the island. Was it perhaps this that prompted Sappho – or Alkaios? – to put the name Gyaros in a somewhat equivocal line? It refers to a woman. It is strange that her pupil, the fleetly-running maid, Hero, should have Gyaros as her homeland …

To this day, in the absence of systematic excavations, the island keeps its well-guarded secrets.

Tenos

OLGA PHILANIOTOU

The winds blowing down from the Hellespont (mod. Dardanelles) beat against the northeast heights of Tenos and then swoop even stronger on its entire southwest side. Tenos is the island of the *tramontana*, for, according to myth, the Boreads (north winds) slain by Herakles are buried on its highest mountain, Tsiknias. Tenos is also "Hydrousa", island of abundant springs and elegant fountains, while the abandoned terraces scrambling up to the mountain peaks are a reminder that until a few years ago not an inch of land was left uncultivated.

Due to circumstance and coincidence, the wheel would seem to have come full circle for Tenos, which ostensibly differs little from ancient times: there is one city with its harbour in exactly the same place and one *locus sanctus* of panhellenic fame: in Antiquity this was the sanctuary of Poseidon and Amphitrite, today it is the church of the Virgin Evangelistria. In reality, however, from Antiquity to the present day, Tenos has experienced many upheavals and changes.

The most important prehistoric site known so far on the island is Vryokastro (fig. 307), a hill on the coast 2 kilometres south of Chora, which surveys a wide expanse of sea, the surrounding islands and part of the hinterland of Tenos. Defensive walls built of boulders enclose one of the characteristic settlements founded in the Cyclades during the Early Bronze Age, on naturally fortified sites near the sea. Such settlements flourished in the Middle and the beginning of the Late Bronze Age (*circa* 2800-1500 BC), developing a complex network of communication and reciprocal exchanges with Minoan Crete and the Greek Mainland. Vryokastro was contemporary with Akrotiri on Thera, Mikri Vigla on Naxos, Aghia Irini on Kythnos, Phylakopi on Melos and Aghia Irini on Kea.

At present no major Mycenaean urban centre, such as Grotta on Naxos or Phylakopi, has been located on Tenos. Nevertheless, a Mycenaean tholos tomb with rich grave goods (fig. 306), found on the northeast side of the island, between Aghia Thekla and Kyra Xeni, points to the existence of a settlement, most probably associated with the harbour of Panormos, between 1250 and 1200 BC.

Later, *circa* 1000 BC, when the Cycladic islanders withdrew from the coast and founded new settlements on hilltops or returned to fortified sites, analogous new settlements were established on Tenos, as the cemeteries at Kardiani, Chtikado and elsewhere (fig. 308) attest. At Xobourgo was the ancient *polis*, with a mighty wall of granite boulders (fig. 49). Many centuries later, the advantages of this naturally fortified site led the Venetians to

306. Tenos. Mycenaean krater with scale decoration (13th c. BC), from the tholos tomb at Aghia Thekla. Tenos Archaeological Museum.

307. Tenos, Vryokastro. A naturally fortified site surveying a wide area of sea, the surrounding islands and the hinterland of Tenos. The settlement, founded on the hilltop in the Early Bronze Age, flourished during the Middle Cycladic and the early Late Cycladic period (*c.* 2800-1500 BC), exploiting its protected position, its proximity to arable land and its two natural harbours.

308. Tenos. Kantharos (left) and trefoil-mouth oinochoe (right) from Kardiani, one of the mountainous settlements characteristic of Tenos in the Geometric period. Tenos Archaeological Museum.

222 | CYCLADES

found the island's capital there too. Recent investigations have revealed an earlier, Mycenaean, presence at Xobourgo, although its precise date and character have yet to be clarified. However, it is certain that Xobourgo continued to be inhabited and to prosper during the seventh and sixth centuries BC. The city expanded and its enceinte was adjusted accordingly. A building complex uncovered *extra muros* has been interpreted as a Thesmophorion, a sanctuary dedicated to Demeter (fig. 309), while further east, at the site of Vardalakkos, lies the cemetery of the Classical and Hellenistic periods.

Numerous relief pithamphorae, with a diverse thematic repertoire that includes both known and unknown mythological scenes, such as the Birth of Athena or the Wooden (Trojan) Horse, bear witness to an important workshop of long duration in which the entire evolution of these vases can be followed, from the earlier Geometric stage into Archaic times (fig. 310).

Life continued at Xobourgo until the fourth century BC and possibly later, but the administrative centre had been transferred to the area of the present Chora. Reasons that are not entirely clear apparently impelled the inhabitants to return to the sea.

During the fourth century BC the lower city, the *asty*, was fortified with a strong enceinte (fig. 314), large sections of which survive north of the church of the Virgin Evangelistria and probably continued down to the sea. At this time too a large aqueduct was constructed, a collective and costly work, the tunnel of which with the ventilation shafts can still be traced from Linopi as far as Chora. The *asty* had an organized urban plan, with public buildings and sanctuaries. The agora and the prytaneion were in the vicinity of the Evangelistria church, while the gymnasium was a little to the west and the theatre perhaps to the southwest. Still to be located is the sanctuary of Dionysos, where the Dionysia festival was held, with drama contests, and where in Roman times the honours accorded benefactors of the city were announced.

However, the city's major sanctuary was further west, at modern Kionia. Dedicated to the sea deities Poseidon and Amphitrite (figs 311-313), its history more or less reflects the history of the *asty*. In its building phases can be distinguished the passage of the Macedonians, the Ptolemies, the Rhodians, the rise and fall of the Roman Empire. For an interval during the second century BC it was the seat of the *Koinon* (Federal Organization) of Islanders. Perhaps because of the sanctuary's reputation, but also because of the importance of its harbour, the city of Tenos developed vigorous external relations. Inscriptions speak not only of the presence on the island of people from all over the Mediterranean, from Syracuse to Arabia, but also of the activity of Tenians abroad.

TENOS | 223

309. Tenos, Xobourgo. The rocky massif of Xobourgo, visible also from the sea, was a refuge in many difficult periods, as well as the site where the earliest city (*polis*) developed on Tenos, with a strong fortification wall and a sanctuary dedicated to Demeter (Thesmophorion).

310. Tenos. Large pithamphora from Xobourgo, on which is depicted the birth of Athena from the head of Zeus, 7th c. BC. Large relief pithamphorae, richly decorated with mythological and other representations, are the most distinctive creations of Tenian art in the Geometric and Archaic periods. Tenos Archaeological Museum.

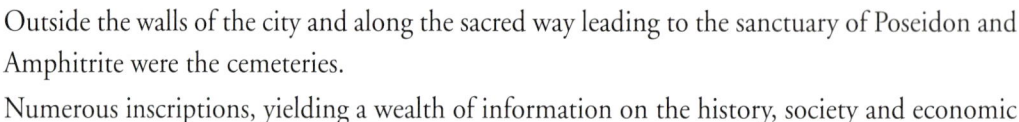

Outside the walls of the city and along the sacred way leading to the sanctuary of Poseidon and Amphitrite were the cemeteries.

Numerous inscriptions, yielding a wealth of information on the history, society and economic fortunes of the island and the wider insular milieu, have been found on Tenos. Particularly valuable for knowledge of life in the countryside, the demographic pattern and social structures is the "inscription of sales and purchases", which was taken to the British Museum along with the "Elgin Marbles". This refers to houses, fields, tracts of fallow land, farmsteads with towers, isolated towers and towers with "pithoi storerooms".

Towers, of rectangular and circular plan, have been found at various points on Tenos, at Ai Yannis Porto, Avdos, Aghioi Anargyroi, Samantla, Panormos and elsewhere. These defensive constructions bear witness in general to insecurity and dangers from piracy, as well as to the affluence during the fourth century BC. Perhaps, however, they were not all exactly contemporary and did not all serve the same purpose.

In addition to the *asty*, there were rural settlements during the fourth century BC, such as those identified at Kokkina Petradia and Ai Yorgis in northern Tenos, as well as rural sanctuaries. At Evangelistria Grammatikou, close to the Aghia Thekla tholos tomb, there is epigraphic testimony of the existence of a sanctuary dedicated to Gaia and to other deities, while Steno, opposite Andros, was protected by a large building of rectangular plan, a tower or perhaps a sanctuary.

After 88 BC and following a long period of prosperity, Tenos, like all

224 | CYCLADES

the islands, suffered the adverse effects of piracy and of the wars between Rome and King Mithridates of Pontus. Some bright-spots can be pinpointed, such as the erection of a portrait statue of Emperor Claudius and statues of other members of the imperial family in the sanctuary of Poseidon, in the first century AD (fig. 311). Nevertheless, the island's physiognomy underwent a gradual change, especially noticeable in the second century AD: wealth and authority had been concentrated in the hands of few, and public works were undertaken by individual benefactors rather than the deme. In the third century AD the population once again withdrew into the hinterland, after six centuries of life on the coast. The sanctuary was abandoned at the time that the new religion of Christianity appeared. Hundreds of years later, in the nineteenth century, the major Christian pilgrim shrine was to revive life in the harbour.

Archaeological investigations on Tenos commenced about one hundred years ago, with excavations in the sanctuary of Poseidon and Amphitrite at Kionia, conducted by the French Archaeological School. A team from the University of Athens, led by Professor N. Kontoleon, explored Xobourgo. The Mycenaean tholos tomb at Kyra Xeni/Aghia Thekla was excavated by G. Despinis, the Geometric cemetery at Kardiani by D. Levi and other Geometric cemeteries by N. Zapheiropoulos. The Archaeological Service is also engaged in archaeological research and excavations.

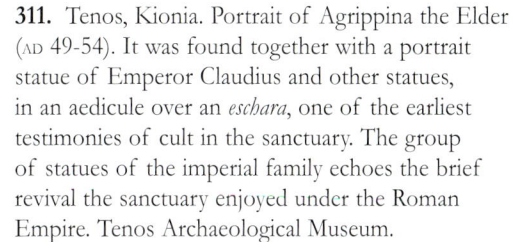

311. Tenos, Kionia. Portrait of Agrippina the Elder (AD 49-54). It was found together with a portrait statue of Emperor Claudius and other statues, in an aedicule over an *eschara*, one of the earliest testimonies of cult in the sanctuary. The group of statues of the imperial family echoes the brief revival the sanctuary enjoyed under the Roman Empire. Tenos Archaeological Museum.

312. Tenos, Kionia. The sanctuary of Poseidon and Amphitrite. In the foreground is the temple, with foundations of gneiss and upper structure of white Tenian marble. In the Doric order and most probably amphiprostyle tetrastyle, it housed the cult statues of Poseidon and Amphitrite, works by the Athenian sculptor Telesinos. In the background is the fountain, an austere yet elegant Doric building of the 4th c. BC, in white and greyish Tenian marble.

313. Tenos, Kionia. Metope with relief representation of dolphins, from the sanctuary of Poseidon and Amphitrite. The dolphin, attribute of the sea god, dominates the sculptural decoration of the sanctuary and the votive offerings. Tenos Archaeological Museum.

314. Tenos, Poles. One of the imposing rectangular towers in the fortification wall of the 4th c. BC, which stands for a length of some 800 m, north of Chora. The wall surrounded the ancient *asty* and probably descended as far as the sea.

Syros

MARISA MARTHARI

Syros, 88 square kilometrs in area, lies at about the centre of the Cyclades. Its northern part, Epano Meria, is mountainous with rocky coasts, whereas its southern part is lower and gentler, with deep bays and small coastal vales. Archaeological research on the island has important moments to its credit. It began in the second half of the nineteenth century, with the publication of inscriptions found there by Klon Stephanos and the excavations made by Christos Tsountas at the significant Early Bronze Age sites of Chalandriani, Kastri and Aghios Loukas. In the early 1960s, the German archaeologist E.-M. Bossert excavated at Kastri, while during the 1970s and 1980s François Aron conducted surface surveys at several sites all over the island. The excavations carried out by the Archaeological Service, which has been particularly active in the past decade, have brought to light an ancient city at the site of Galissas and an undisturbed part of the cemetery at Chalandriani.

Data collected from surface surveys show that Syros was inhabited in the Late (5300-4500 BC) and Final Neolithic (4500-3200 BC) periods. The most notable Neolithic installations are in southern Syros, namely at Chondra in the Bay of Vari, Talanta on the plateau above Hermoupolis and Atsiganokastro in a cove to the west of Phoinikas.

Syros continued to be inhabited during the Early Bronze Age (3rd millennium BC) and enjoyed particular development in its mature period. Interest shifted to the rocky north, where significant settlements were established initially at Chalandriani, on the homonymous plateau (Early Cycladic II period, 2700-2300 BC) and subsequently at Kastri, on a nearby precipitous cliff-top site ("Kastri phase", 2300-2200 BC). Soundings made in the area in recent years indicate that the settlement at Chalandriani was large by Cycladic standards for the third millennium BC, covering in excess of 1 hectare. Kastri was smaller, no more than 0.5 hectare in area, but with impressive fortifications, comprising an outwork and a main wall with horseshoe bastions, all built of marble (fig. 317). The layout of the walled settlement is concentric, with building *insulae* separated by narrow radial streets, frequently stepped (fig. 316). Some buildings have walled courtyards and built hearths. Metalworking was particularly developed at Kastri, as borne out by the clay crucibles for smelting metals and the clay and stone moulds for casting bronze tools and weapons, the considerable number of metal artifacts and the identification of one area as a bronze-smith's workshop.

The extensive cemetery of both settlements spreads to the north of Chalandriani and includes graves corresponding to all chronological phases of the settlement there and some contemporary with the later settlement at Kastri. The Early Cycladic graves are dug into the ground and corbelled, a type so far encountered only on Syros. The grave goods are clay vases (fig. 315) and stone vessels, objects of metal and of bone. The most impressive of all are the clay "frying-pan"

315. Syros. Clay zoomorphic jug of extraordinary artistry, in the shape of a small sitting bear holding a bowl. From the cemetery at Chalandriani (2700-2300 BC). Athens, National Archaeological Museum.

316. Syros. Most of the buildings in the Early Cycladic settlement at Kastri (2300-2000 BC) are arranged in *insulae* around the contours of the hilltop. Of trapezoidal plan, usually with rounded corners, and comprising one or two rooms, they are constructed in the same manner as the fortification, using small, thin slabs of marble.

317. Syros. Although the settlement at Kastri is small, the impressive fortifications, in combination with the moveable finds, point to the relative affluence of its inhabitants and their particular relations with the Asia Minor littoral. The type of fortification, which includes an outwork and a wall with horseshoe bastions, possibly originates from that region, as the recent excavation of a large settlement at Liman Tepe (anc. Klazomenai) in Asia Minor indicates.

vessels with impressed or incised decoration depicting oared ships (fig. 318), reflecting the maritime activities of the people of Chalandriani.

The settlements at Chalandriani and Kastri are in a strategic position in the communication networks linking the Greek Mainland with the Asia Minor littoral and this is surely one of the main reasons for their notable development. Moreover, the period of habitation at Kastri coincides with an intensification of contacts between the Cycladic islanders and the islands and coasts of the East Aegean.

Towards the end of the Early Bronze Age (Early Cycladic III period, 2200-2000 BC) life continued at some sites, as attested by a grave of this period found at Aghios Loukas. The grave goods accompanying the burial show relations between Syros and the Greek Mainland.

Sporadic finds show that life did not cease on Syros during the Middle and the Late Bronze Age (2nd millennium BC). In the *Odyssey* (xiv 403ff.) Homer refers to the island *Syrie*, which some scholars identify as Syros. *Syrie* is described as fertile, with two cities and ruled by King Ktesios Ormenides, father of Eumaios.

Syros was one of the Ionian Cyclades and its first settler (*oikistes*) was believed to be the Athenian Hippomedon. In the sixth century BC it was captured by the Samians. During the Persian Wars it allied with the Persians, but afterwards participated in the First and the Second Athenian League. Among the personalities associated with Syros are the philosopher Pherekydes, mentor of Pythagoras. In Hellenistic times the island was a member of the *Koinon* (Federal Organization) of Islanders, in the period when this was a Rhodian Protectorate.

During Roman times, and after the destruction of neighbouring Delos in the late first century BC, Syros evidently enjoyed a heyday and played an important role in the region as a centre of transit trade. This is borne out by the portrait statue of Emperor Hadrian, an *ex-voto* of the Syrans, which stood in the city (its pedestal survives in the church of the Transfiguration), the imperial decrees relating to Syros and the unusually rich – for a Cycladic island – coinage. Particularly interesting are the silver *stephanephora* (wreath-bearing) tetradrachms of the second century BC, with the goddess Demeter on the obverse and the Kabeiroi within a wreath on the reverse, which echo the existence of a Kabeirion on Syros.

The ancient city of Syros occupied the same site as Hermoupolis, the building of which destroyed it almost completely. Preserved on the Katailymata hillock is a small part of the fortification wall. In Moraitini Square an honorary decree of Berenice and an epistle of emperors Septimius Severus and Caracalla were found, as well as the inscription Αθηνάς Φρατρίας (Phratry of Athena) on a rock. These testimonia led K. Stephanos to suggest that this

318. Syros. Clay "frying-pan" vessel from the Early Cycladic cemetery at Chalandriani (2700-2300 BC). The representation includes a many-oared ship voyaging on the sea and the female pubic triangle. Diverse interpretations have been offered for the "frying pans", among them that they symbolize a female deity. The fact that vessels of this type with ship representations come almost exclusively from the cemetery at Chalandriani suggests that this settlement played a special role in maritime transport in the Aegean during the Early Bronze Age. Athens, National Archaeological Museum.

319. Syros. An impressive silver diadem 0.47 m. long, with pointillé decoration, from the Early Cycladic settlement at Kastri. The representation is composite and echoes beliefs, now difficult to interpret, of the Cycladic islanders in the 3rd millennium BC. Interposed between three rosettes encircling stars are two confronted male animals. At the ends of the diadem are possibly anthropomorphic figures with bird-shaped head. Athens, National Archaeological Museum.

was the location of the city's agora and prytaneion. Further east, in the basement of a house, seats from the city's theatre are preserved. The cemetery extended over the southwest foot of Katailymata Hill.

Excavations conducted by the Archaeological Service between 1994 and 1997, in Galissas Bay in the southwest of the island, brought to light a second ancient city. Most probably called Galessos, this existed from Geometric times into the fourth century BC, when it was abandoned. The city included two fortified acropolises, the present heights of Aghia Pakou and Vounaki (fig. 322), a settled area inside and outside the acropolises, and a street network linking the two acropolises with each other and the city with its two harbours, in Galissas and Armeos bays. The development of the city from Geometric times is echoed in the interesting Geometric pottery. During the Archaic period Corinthian pottery was imported and vases of various Cycladic workshops, among them the Naxian. During Classical times the imports of Attic pottery were substantial, which fact confirms the close relationship between Syros and Athens (figs 320, 321).

Travellers and earlier researchers placed a third city in Phoinikas Bay in southern Syros, because some graves and a mosaic floor were brought to light there in the nineteenth century.

320, 321. Syros, ancient city of Galessos. Attic black-glaze vases of the early 4th c. BC. They were found in a repository (*apothetes*) in the environs of a large building, possibly a sanctuary, of Classical times, on the west slope of Vounaki Hill, *extra muros* of the acropolis. In addition to abundant pottery dating from Geometric times to the early 4th c. BC, the *apothetes* contained figurines, loom-weights, spindle-whorls and metal objects, included a bronze vessel, bronze hooks and a bronze saw, as well as stone vessels and tools, and food residues. Syros Archaeological Museum.

322. Syros. The bays of Armeos and Galissas, in which were located the harbours of ancient Galessos, and Aghia Pakou Hill, which was one of the two acropolises of the city, as seen from the west slope of Vounaki Hill. The acropolis was fortified on the seaward side, by a wall with semicircular bastions. On the top of the hill stood a circular tower, upon the ruins of which the chapel of St Pakou was built.

Mykonos

PHOTEINI N. ZAPHEIROPOULOU

Mykonos is a small island to the northeast of Delos, exposed to the northerly winds of the Aegean, which is why Chora, the present capital, is located in a relatively sheltered harbour about half way along the west coast, opposite Delos. The entire island, with a few cultivable lowland tracts, is rocky and stark. The highest point is no more than 392 metres a.s.l. and the coast is indented by numerous tiny havens and coves – "*remezza*" in the sailors' patois. These are the essential refuges for seafarers in this usually tempestuous stretch of sea.

Mykonos seems to have been inhabited earlier than Delos, as traces of human presence dating from at least the fifth millennium BC have been found in several locations on the north coast of the island, where there is a large, deep natural harbour, Panormos. Here, in the inner reaches at the site of Ftelia (fig. 324), a settlement is currently being excavated. In addition to building remains (fig. 23), interesting household effects and various small objects have come to light, the most important of which are two clay female figurines dating from the Final Neolithic period (5th millennium BC) (figs 29, 323).

A tumulus, almost overhanging the sea, has been excavated in the same area and may well have covered the burial of the Trojan hero Ajax of Locris, who tradition has it was drowned in the

323. Mykonos. Head of a clay figurine, possibly of a female, from the Neolithic settlement at the site of Ftelia. Final Neolithic period (5th millennium BC). Mykonos Archaeological Museum.

324. Mykonos. General view of Ftelia, where an important Neolithic settlement is being excavated.

230 | CYCLADES

straits between Tenos and Mykonos, and cast ashore by the waves on the north coast of Mykonos, where he was buried in a tumulus beside the sea. This Neolithic settlement is one of the very few discovered to date in the Cyclades. Other sites in the countryside of Mykonos have yielded information on the continuity of life on the island in the Early Cycladic and Middle Cycladic periods (3rd-first half of 2nd millennium BC), as well as in Mycenaean times, around the end of the fifteenth century BC.

Of Mycenaean date is the tholos tomb brought to light recently on a hilltop in the locality Angelika, a short distance to the south of Chora. This is an impressive funerary construction, consisting of a circular chamber 5.80 metres in diameter, to which leads a dromos 2 metres wide and 14 metres long (fig. 325). The tomb, which survives to a height of about 3.70 metres, had a low Π-shaped bench built on the floor, upon which the deceased was placed. On top of this bench, three rock-crystal seal-stones with intaglio devices of animals, and parts perhaps of two gold necklaces (fig. 326) were found; there was also copious painted pottery in the fill of the burial chamber. The tomb was possibly of a noble or even a Mycenaean king who was buried on the island.

In the late sixth century BC Mykonos was referred to as *dipolis*, but only scant remnants of the two cities exist in the island's hinterland. On the contrary, in Chora there is much more archaeological evidence dispersed within the modern settlement, such as the ancient city which must have occupied the area of the present Kastro as far as the shore, where Late Antique buildings have been uncovered near the harbour. An impressive find is the funerary pithos with relief decoration of subjects inspired by the Fall of Troy, with the Wooden Horse and the massacre following the capture of the city (fig. 327). Found in the summer of 1961, in the centre of Chora, about 300-400 metres from the seashore, this unique work by a Tenian potter complements the excellent collection of pottery from the Purification Deposit (*bothos*) in Rheneia. The discovery of this last material was the main reason why the now "historic" Mykonos Archaeological Museum – one of the oldest museums in Greece – was built.

325. Mykonos. Mycenaean tholos tomb at the site of Angelika, close to Chora. View from the south. The monument is dated to the late 15th c. BC.

326. Mykonos. Gold necklace of beads in the form of papyrus flowers and shells. From the Mycenaean tholos tomb at the site of Angelika. Late 15th c. BC. Mykonos Archaeological Museum.

327. Mykonos. Pithamphora with relief scenes of the Fall of Troy, from Chora. On the neck, the Wooden Horse and warriors inside and around it; in three zones on the shoulder and belly, scenes of slaying and looting in the captured city. Was the vase made for someone who fought or fell in similar battles? Product of a Tenian pottery workshop, it is dated c. 675 BC. Mykonos Archaeological Museum.

Delos

Photeini N. Zapheiropoulou

In the archipelago of the central Aegean, Delos would have been an insignificant reef lost betwixt the restless sea and the sheltering sky, had it not been fated to be the birthplace of Apollo, the most splendid god – as figure and as idea – in the Olympian pantheon. It is no accident that Delos was chosen for the birth of the new god, who expresses the bounty and the clarity of the Hellenic spirit. There the schistose rocks, particularly the gneiss, almost bare of earth, shimmer in the midst of the immense blue waters that surround them, so that the land is virtually indistinguishable from the sea.

Myth refers to the island as Asteria, which was unseen (*a-delos*) from its wanderings, and with the birth of Apollo became visible – *Delos* – henceforth remaining immobile in the same place, indeed fixed to the seabed by diamond chains. As soon as the Titaness Leto, "turned towards Kynthos, the mountain of Zeus" and brought the new god into the world, close to the "wheel-shaped lake", embracing the palm tree that stood at its hub, the immense Gaia laughed (Theognis, *Elegies* I, 5-10), all around was flooded in light, filled with flowers. And the newborn Phoebus, with his long hair, cast off the swaddling bands and began wandering around with his beloved kithara and arched bows (*Homeric Hymn to Apollo*, line 131). So, in this place that was brilliant by nature, the new god acquired traits absolutely in keeping with the environment: Apollo Delios is the god of joy and of life; in his festivals music and dance had pride of place.

Delos is a narrow strip of land, 5 kilometres long and 1,300 metres wide, with low hills and one conspicuous rocky eminence, Kynthos, which rises no more than 112 metres a.s.l. at the island's centre (fig. 330). This is the sacred mountain of Delos, which dominates the surrounding plain through which runs a permanent torrent, the Inopos, which has its wellspring on Kynthos and flows into the sea in the northwest bay at Skardanas. At about the midpoint of the west coast there is a large harbour with two deep bays (figs 75, 331), which is protected to the west by two insular reefs, Megalos and Mikros Rematiaris. Further to the west spreads Rheneia, the large Delos as it is called by the locals, in contradistinction to Delos proper, which is the smaller of the two. To the east of this harbour spreads the only plain on the island, which continues between hills as far as the northwest edge of Delos, opposite Mykonos. In its lowest part, which was formerly flooded with waters, a lake used to form. "Wheel-shaped", as it is called in

328. Delos. Corinthian alabastron from the Heraion (drawing). On the front a representation with a *Potnia Theron* (Mistress of Animals), identified with Artemis: a large winged female deity in polos (sacerdotal headdress) and chiton stands between two heraldic swans, which she holds from the head. Late 7th c. BC. Delos Archaeological Museum.

329. Delos. Colossal lions standing in a row on the levelled terrace to the west of the Sacred Lake. Represented semi-sedent on the hind legs, they have a small head, an open mouth and turn the head eastwards, gazing at the Sacred Lake with the palm tree beneath which Apollo first saw light of day. *Ex-voto* of the Naxians. Late 7th c. BC.

330. Delos. The hill of Kynthos with the Theatre Quarter just in front.

331. Delos. General view of the archaeological site from Kynthos, with the Theatre Quarter (left), the Sanctuary (right), the ancient harbour, Mikros Rematiaris and Rheneia in the distance.

329

330

331

Delos | 233

the ancient sources, this too was considered sacred, along with Kynthos and the Inopos.

In a privileged location in the central Aegean, half way along sea routes, Delos developed from early on as a commercial harbour, which became one of the most important ports in the Eastern Mediterranean. Preserved on Kynthos are remains of habitation (circular houses-huts) dating from the third millennium BC, while later, in the mid-second millennium BC, in the Mycenaean period (fig. 45), when fear of pirates had been eradicated, installations were transferred to the plain close to the harbour, where an organized settlement was established. It was on this site that the sanctuary of Apollo was founded, after the arrival of the Ionian tribes and the prevailing of the gods of the Olympian pantheon, such as Artemis. The sanctuary also included the earlier Mycenaean sanctuary of Artemis, whose cult continued in the same *locus sanctus*, but as sister of the new god (fig. 328). In the *Odyssey* and the *Homeric Hymn to Apollo*, which were written *circa* 700 BC, Delos is mentioned as a renowned religious centre of the Ionians. Ships that dropped anchor here carried not only pilgrims but also commodities, and the island consequently developed rapidly into a commercial port (fig. 47). However, what is important is that the "great assembly" of the Ionians was the particular manifestation of worship in a common sacred centre, where they were united by common interests.

When a place gains fame as an important religious centre, then many cities and rulers appear, laying claim to spiritual domination, because such a place is ideal for exercising political influence. The Naxians were the first Ionians who tried to impose their domination in the Apollonian sanctuary, and by extension in the Aegean region; from the late seventh century BC they offered a host of *ex-votos* (fig. 329), while concurrently they adorned the sanctuary of Apollo with splendid edifices. In the sixth century BC, Paros also came on the scene, but offered only works of art, not monuments (fig. 332). However, of old the Athenians had laid claim to precedence on Delos in all manner of ways, in order to dominate the Ionians and the Aegean. Athenian influence on the island was inaugurated by the tyrant Peisistratos, with the building of the Archaic temple of Apollo. In parallel, the Athenians, with sights on the economic control of the island, carried out the first purification (*catharsis*) of Delos in 540 BC, removing all the graves from that part of Delos which was visible from the temple of Apollo. The fall of Peisistratos and the Persian Wars were the pretext for Delos to extricate itself from Athenian domination; at the same time, however, the *theories* (sacred embassies to Delos) and the festivals lost their original splendour, because the Greek cities in Asia Minor and the neighbouring islands were subjugated by the Persians, causing the break up of the old Ionian Amphictyony of Delos. After the Greeks' victory over the Persians, due in large part to the

234 | CYCLADES

332. Delos. Kore statue. The figure wears a chiton and a multi-pleated himation falling from both shoulders onto the back and forming a sheaf of folds. The long hair falls on the back and on the chest, where metal ornaments embellished the tips of the locks. A Parian work with Attic influence. *c.* 500 BC. Delos Archaeological Museum.

333. Delos. Bronze mask of horned Dionysos, representing the god with a thick curly beard, a fillet on the forehead and an ivy wreath on the head; behind the fillet are two small horns. The mask, found in the south of the Agora of the Competaliasts, was a votive offering. Late 2nd c. BC. Delos Archaeological Museum.

334. Delos. Statue group of Aphrodite and Pan, from the Lesche of the *Koinon* of Berytian Poseidoniasts. The goddess is represented naked, threatening with her sandal the horned, goat-legged Pan who assaults her and tries to embrace her with both arms. An infant Eros figure flying behind the goddess comes to her aid, grabbing Pan's right horn and pushing him away. The inscription on the base records that the sculpture was commissioned by Dionysios son of Zenon from Berytos (mod. Beirut), one of the most important benefactors of the Lesche of Berytian Poseidoniasts. *c.* 100 BC. Athens, National Archaeological Museum.

335. Delos. House in the Theatre Quarter. Tessellated floor with checkerboard pattern framed by a zone of spirals, giving the impression of a carpet.

336. Delos. Clay seal impression (*rypos*) from the Skardanas Quarter. Stamped on the sealing is the head of a youth with idealized features, in profile right, with a leafy wreath and rays in his hair. Represented is Apollo-Helios in the type of portrait heads of Alexander the Great. Second half of 2nd-early 1st c. BC. Delos Archaeological Museum.

337. Delos. The Inopos House, one of the opulent private residences in the Theatre Quarter. In the background left is the four-storey Hermes House.

338. Delos. The street running between the wealthy private houses in the Theatre Quarter.

339. Delos. Set of cooking vessels (brazier with grid, frying pan and cooking pots) from the House of Sealings. Hellenistic period (2nd c. BC). Delos Archaeological Museum.

Athenians, the First Athenian League was founded in 478 BC, with the participation of almost all the Greek cities in the Aegean and Delos as seat. The treasury of the League, with the contributions of its members, was kept on the island. Delos became once again the centre of the Ionian Amphictyony, but the alliance gradually developed into a hegemony of the Athenians. In 456 BC they transferred the League's treasury to the Acropolis of Athens, supposedly for safety's sake, and in 426/5 BC they decided on the second purification of Delos. Delians were forbidden not only to die on the island but also to be born there; all existing graves and tombs were opened and their contents removed to the opposite isle of Rheneia, where they were deposited in a communal grave, the "purification *bothros*", as Thucydides calls it. This act was taken on the basis of an oracle, after a plague, according to which the isle of Apollo should remain uncontaminated by miasmas. In reality, this purification meant that for the Delians Delos ceased to be their homeland, since they could not be born there or have the tombs of their ancestors there.

The second purification ushered in a new period of prosperity on Delos: the old festival took on another form and alongside the annual celebration, another one, quinquennial – held every four years – was established. A new temple was built too, in the Doric order and amphiprostyle, with six columns on front and back. It was constructed of Pentelic marble, another element that was a reminder of the hegemony of the Athenians. The temple was erected between the two other temples of Apollo, the Archaic one of poros stone, to the north, and the unique peripteral temple (with 13 x 6 columns) in the sanctuary, which is known as the "temple of the Delians", to the south. Building of this last temple commenced with the founding of the First Athenian League in 478 BC, was interrupted in the fifth century BC and was then continued by the Delians in the late fourth century BC, although the final processing of the architectural members was never finished.

These three temples of Apollo stood at about the centre of the sanctuary, as this had been laid out already in Archaic times. The Sacred Way passed in front of the revered Archaic Oikos of the Naxians, with the colossal statue of Apollo, as well as in front of the three temples to the east and the temple of Artemis to the west. It then continued northwards, passing between the row of Naxian lions (fig. 329) and the "wheel-shaped" lake, having left on its east side the Archaic temple of Leto, mother of Apollo and Artemis, and terminating at the present Skardanas Bay. The Sacred Way started from the sacred harbour (figs 75, 331) – the northernmost of the two creeks, the southernmost was the commercial harbour –, led first in an easterly direction and then in a northerly, as far as the south main entrance to the sanctuary. From here it traversed the area as far as the northwest bay of Skardanas, which was almost certainly a second, auxiliary harbour giving access to the site.

In Archaic and Classical times the sanctuary was surrounded by gardens, especially to the north and northeast. These were dispensed with, however, during the expansion from the fourth century BC onwards, to make room for various public buildings and later for huge

236 | CYCLADES

stoas (*ex-votos* of powerful rulers, to display their might), which gave the principal part of the sanctuary the form of an enclosed space.

Athenian sovereignty over Delos lasted throughout the fourth century BC. At the end of the century, however, Athens lost her naval supremacy and domination of the Greek cities passed into the hands of the Macedonians. On the initiative of Antigonos and his son Demetrios Poliorketes, the *Koinon* (Federal Organisation) of Islanders was founded, with Delos as religious centre. In 314 BC the island was declared free and independent. Henceforth, until 166 BC, Delos enjoyed a new heyday. At first, until 250 BC when the *Koinon* of Islanders was dissolved, rulers vied with one another to offer the most donations and monuments to Apollo, and the island profited from this. Later, however, from the mid-third to the early second century BC, the harbour of Delos opened to large-scale trade and became one of the main transit ports for grain and other commodities, from Noumidia in Cherrhonesos of the Euxine Pontus (mod. Black Sea), as well as Asia Minor, Syria and Egypt. Strabo (X 5,4) records that it was an important centre of the slave trade. Characteristic too of the commercial activity was the creation and development of banks, public and private.

In 168 BC the new super-power of the age, Rome, defeated Perseus, last king of the Macedonians, at Pydna. The Macedonian kingdom was dissolved and Delos passed once again to the domination of the Athenians, to whom the Romans ceded it. This time the Athenian masters finally expelled the Delians, who at first sought refuge in Achaea and whose traces were subsequently lost. Delos was now an Athenian colony, under the direct control of Rome.

In the beginning the island was populated by poor Athenian cleruchs, who were allotted parcels

Delos | 237

340

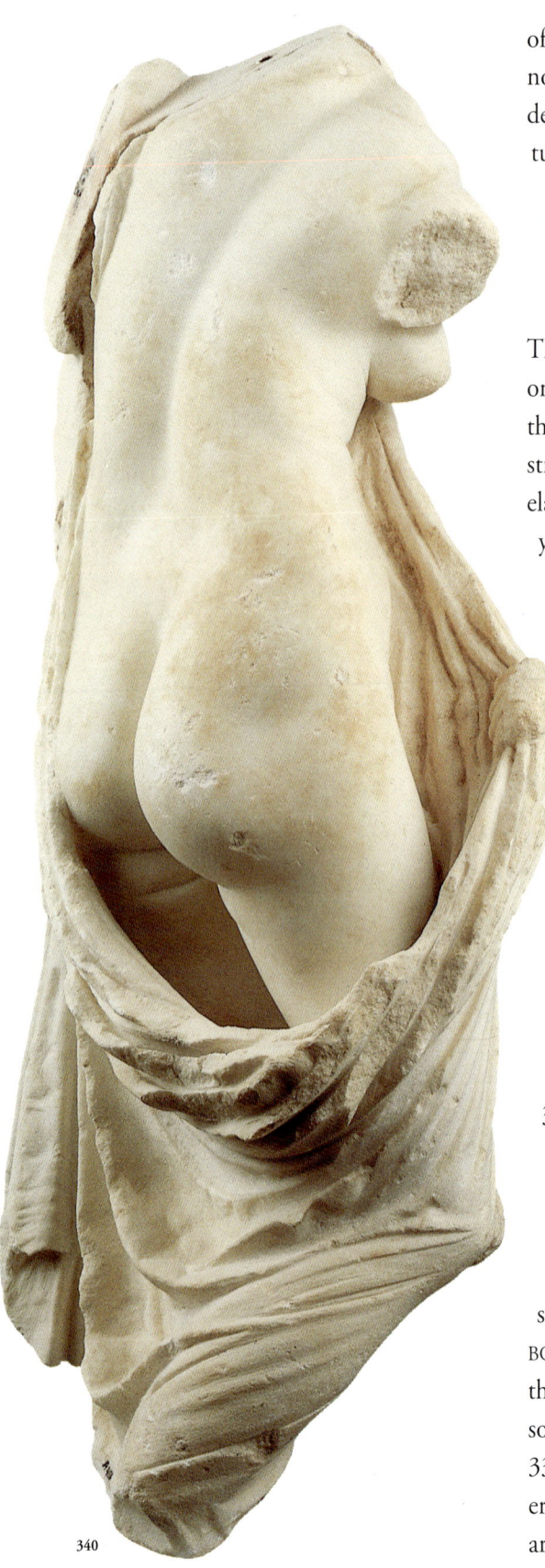

of land, and by city-dwellers who settled as officials or merchants. However, the inordinate economic development brought a corresponding population increase in its wake, altering the demographic composition of the city. In the second half of the second and the early first century BC, there was a large thriving city, home to an estimated 30,000 persons who came to settle in this wealthy port from all over the Mediterranean basin, from the Greek Mainland and Asia Minor, Italy, Egypt, Syria, Phoenicia and Palestine (figs 334, 344, 345). It is only natural that within this cosmopolitan clime a host of foreign, non-Hellenic, religions appeared and flourished, particularly from the East. As a result the old religious character of Delos was lost.

This great city made up of various quarters had spread to the margins of the sanctuary and not only in the lowland areas but also onto the slopes of the surrounding hills. The architecture of the private houses on Delos in the Hellenistic period is the best preserved and the most instructive ensemble in the whole of the Hellenic world (figs 335, 337, 338). The house types were elaborated during the second and the early first century BC, and together with their contents yield an abundance of information on private life in these years. The organic centre of the residence was the court, around which the various rooms were ranged, without openings onto the street, so that the usual exterior aspect of the Delian house is blank walls punctuated by one or two doors. Light entered the rooms from the court, which in the wealthy houses had a peristyle, normally with Doric columns, fluted towards the top. The use of the rooms is difficult to determine precisely, but some large and richly decorated ones must have been reception rooms, *oikoi* or *andrones*, in which symposia were also held. The ancillary rooms included lavatories, while very often on the sides facing the street there were separate rooms, accessible from outside, which accommodated workshops for trade or manufacturing. In general the houses were single-storey, although the larger ones had two storeys and examples exist of four-storey residences, such as the "Hermes House" (fig. 337). The masonry of the walls was mainly of local gneiss coated with lime plaster, which was sometimes coloured monochrome and sometimes in imitation of marble, through variegated coloration and modelling of the stuccoes. The court and the rooms usually had mosaic floors with geometric patterns, still-lifes or figural representations (fig. 335, 341, 343). The water supply was from wells or cisterns, inside the houses under the tessellated pavement of the court, and in public buildings, such as under the theatre (fig. 80).

The most important of the city's quarters (which have been given conventional names) was the Theatre Quarter (fig. 330, 338). Recent excavations have revealed that houses were built here from the early fifth century BC. Over the centuries architectural reforms were made, resulting in the conversion of one of these into an industrial olive-oil press, in the first century BC. In this early quarter the streets follow the contours of the terrain, which is a hill slope, and the building *insulae* (residential sectors) are bisected by a main street artery running north-south, that is from the harbour towards the highest point of the theatre (figs 330, 331 left, 337, 338). Here resided the wealthy (fig. 345, 347), shipowners (?), merchants, bankers (?) and others, while in the lower commercial quarter to the south, along the shore, were the houses of artisans, tradesmen and other professionals.

341▶

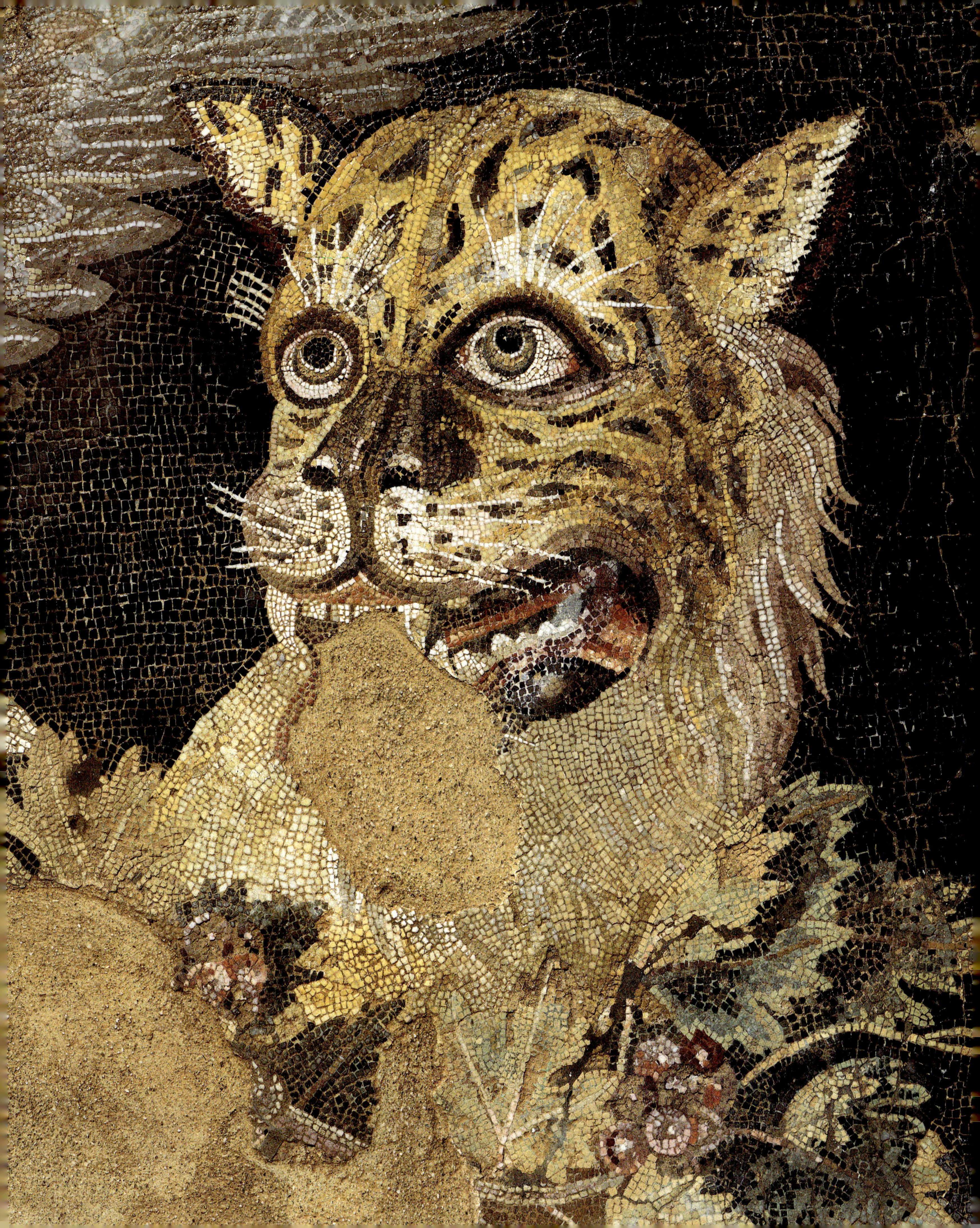

340. Delos. Statue of a female from an erotic group, represented resisting a male attempting to disrobe her, pushing away his hand that has grasped her himation. The figure is shown in three-quarter pose from behind, naked to the thighs, with her himation slipping down and exposing her back and buttocks and covering only part of the front; the male will have been represented in profile or three-quarter pose to the front, on the female's left (his hand is preserved on the himation). The group could perhaps be interpreted as the sacred marriage between the Nymph Amymone-Beroe and Poseidon, according to a local myth of Berytos, although in the view of other scholars it shows simply an erotic assault on the Nymph, not by a god but by someone she wards off. Hellenistic period (3rd c. BC). Delos Archaeological Museum.

341. Delos. Detail of a mosaic floor from the Dionysos House in the Theatre Quarter. Dionysos is depicted mounted on a panther, around the neck of which is a wreath of vine leaves and grapes. Late Hellenistic period (2nd c. BC).

Later is the Skardanas Quarter, to the north of the sanctuary, with a regular urban plan according to the Hippodamean system of a grid of streets intersecting at right angles. Here too the houses were large and luxurious (fig. 343), and among them were public buildings, such as palaestrae, the Lesche of the Poseidoniasts (fig. 344), and so on. It was in this area that some 15,000 seal impressions were found, that is oblong nodules of unfired clay which served much the same purpose as sealing wax, to seal confidential documents (fig. 336). For this reason these "*typoi*" (as such sealings are called in the ancient sources) are considered the remnants of the archive of a wealthy merchant or banker. The Stadium Quarter, at the southeast end of the island, opposite the west coast of Mykonos, included not only residences but also cult edifices associated with non-Greek religions, such as the Synagogue, which means that many foreigners lived in this third quarter. In recent years investigations in one house here have confirmed the

earlier hypothesis that a perfumery functioned in it. On the basis of this ascertainment and in conjunction with other related evidence, the existence of a developed perfume-making industry on Delos, to the famed perfumes of which there is reference in the sources, can be considered certain. Together with the processing of the renowned Delian copper (Pliny, *Naturalis Historia* XXXIV 34, 9) this was one of the sources of wealth and fame for the Hellenistic city.

This splendid mercantile city-sanctuary failed to survive until the end of Antiquity. In 88 BC Mithridates Eupator, King of Pontus, in his efforts to strike a blow to the Romans at a critical point, attacked flourishing Delos, principal regulators of which were the Romans since it was essentially a Roman colony. Terrible destruction followed, with 20,000 dead according to con-

342. Delos. The theatre from the east, a construction of the 3rd c. BC, which could accommodate 5,000 spectators.

343. Delos. Detail of a mosaic floor from a house in the Skardanas Quarter, with depiction of a female mask surrounded by ivy leaves and flowers. Second half of 2nd c. BC-first half of 1st c. BC. Delos, Archaeological Museum.

344. Delos. The Lesche of the Poseidoniasts in the Skardanas Quarter. Hellenistic period (3rd c. BC).

DELOS | 241

temporary historians. Even though the Romans reinstated the Athenian regime, the Mithridatan Wars continued. In 69 BC pirates under Athenodoros, an ally of Mithridates, utterly destroyed the island, which ceased forever to be a sacred commercial centre for seafaring peoples. None of the various historical events that ensued succeeded in restoring to the isle of Apollo even an echo of its ancient glory. As a result, travellers in the late fifth century AD characterized Delos as "*adelos*".

In the Middle Ages, Delos, which was a vast expanse of ruins littered with marbles, was for the surrounding islands a seemingly inexhaustible source of materials for construction, or even worse for producing quicklime. As a result, all that remains of the sanctuary and the city is, in the best of cases, the lower courses of the buildings and usually only the foundations.

In AD 1445, Cyriacus of Ancona visited Mykonos and Delos, where he was impressed by the colossal statue of the Naxian Apollo, which despite its dismemberment continued to dominate the site.

In 1872, Greek and French archaeologists began excavations, which from the following year onwards – to the present day – were conducted by the French Archaeological School. From 1960 the Archaeological Service has been involved with the conservation and restoration of the ancient monuments, as well as with arranging the archaeological site for visitors.

Excavations have brought to light not only architectural monuments but also a large number of sculptures, terracottas, minor objects of various materials and pottery, spanning a long period, mainly from the fourteenth to the first century BC, as well as traces of Christian edifices – small basilicas – constructed on top of the ancient ruins up to the fifth century AD. The first large sculptures brought to light were taken to the National Archaeological Museum in Athens, but the wealth of finds made the need to establish a museum on Delos imperative. The small building erected in 1904, at the expenses of the Archaeological Society at Athens, underwent several alterations and additions, acquiring its present aspect in the mid-1960s. The then newly-appointed Ephor of Antiquities for the Cyclades, Nikolaos Zapheiropoulos, began to organize the exhibition (which was completed in 1994), conserving and positioning the truncated sculptures so as to enhance to the maximum their lost splendour (figs 332, 340, 346, 347). He was assisted in this task, particularly the display of the Hellenistic sculptures, by the researches and studies of the French archaeologist J. Marcadé, who devoted many years to identifying and mending the dispersed members of each sculpture in the storerooms of Delos.

I hope that this brief historical review has conveyed the highly important character of a unique site, from almost the dawn of ancient Greek civilization – late second millennium BC – to almost its dusk – end of the first millennium BC. Under the shelter of the splendid young Olympian god, it gathered and united the Hellenic tribes and subsequently the Mediterranean world, and all around it, in a cosmopolitan ensemble without precedent, which over the centuries left a lasting legacy of superb works of art in all sectors of human creation.

345. Delos. Bronze male portrait head from the granite palaestra. Represented is the head of a mature beardless man, inclined towards the left shoulder and gazing slightly upwards, which belonged to a bronze statue and was cast separately from the body. The eyes are of enamel. Possibly an important person is portrayed, perhaps a wealthy oriental (Syrian?) merchant. The work is one of the loveliest portrait heads of the Late Hellenistic period. Post mid-2nd c. BC. Athens, National Archaeological Museum.

346. Delos. Hand from a colossal bronze statue of a ruler or a general. Impressive is the rendering of the veins. 2nd c. BC. Delos Archaeological Museum.

347. Delos. Statue of Artemis *elaphebolos* (striking a deer) from the Theatre Quarter. The goddess wears a short chiton, high girdled and with *apoptygma*, preserving painted bands on its hem. Traces of red and blue pigment indicate the thongs on the high boots. A multi-pleated himation is draped around her left forearm and hangs down. In her left hand she grabs the kneeling animal by the horns, while her right is posed to deliver the mortal blow, as she digs her left knee into its back. The vigorous movement of the statue transmits to the beholder the distress of the huntress and of the prey. Second half of 2nd c. BC. Delos Archaeological Museum.

DELOS | 243

Rheneia

PHOTEINI N. ZAPHEIROPOULOU

Rheneia or Megali (Large) Delos, the island lying to the west of Delos, beyond the two Rematiaris islets, consists of two parts joined by an isthmus. Its indented coastline forms coves and havens with wonderful little beaches (the islanders call then "*angalies*", which means hugs or embraces). There is more cultivable land on Rheneia than on Delos and it seems to have been inhabited since at least the sixth century BC. There are settlement remains in the Ambelas Plain on the west coast, south of the Aghia Triada bays where retaining wall of terraces also exist, one of them 600 metres long and up to 3 metres high in places.

In the area of Aghia Triada, which is about half way along the west coast, slightly to the north, a sanctuary though to be dedicated to Herakles, since his statue was also found, was revealed in 1900 (fig. 349). In the sanctuary there is a strange oblong building, 16 x 9.50 metres, terminating on its east side in a small semicircular water tank with mosaic floor depicting dolphins (fig. 348); the walls are coated with stucco with lacustrine representations and the spout is in the form of a huge cockleshell. Two statue pedestals, on the long sides Panathenaic amphorae (now in the Mykonos Museum) and another building, possibly a small temple, were also brought to light. In 1994, in the course of works on consolidating and arranging the site, a well – probably associated with worship – was revealed at the northwest corner of the little temple, conduits and a row of pillars.

In contrast to the west side of the island, which was a residential area with a life of its own, independent of sacred Delos, the east side and particularly the part opposite Megalos Rematiaris became the official cemetery of the city after the purification (*catharsis*) in 426/5 BC. The "purification *bothros*", a trench some 500 square metres in area, in which the bones and grave goods of the dead of Delos were deposited, is under the small church of St Kyriaki. The *bothros* was excavated by the Archaeological Service in 1898-1900, bringing to light one of the most important assemblages of pottery spanning the period from the early first millennium BC until 426/5 BC. These vases, now exhibited in the Mykonos Archaeological Museum, helped to identify various pottery workshops, mainly in the island region, and to define their distinctive traits. In addition to the purification deposit, burials of all kinds were made in this area until the Hellenistic period. There are even complexes with rows of cist graves – one is underground with a stairway leading to a corridor, on both sides of which are graves, 14 and 16 respectively, in two overlying rows. However, as well as the inhumations on this side of the island there are also fields with farmhouses (as on Delos too), which belonged to the sanctuary of Apollo. On Glaropounta, the north cape of Rheneia, there is a monument, of which the high stepped base has survived.

348. Rheneia. Mosaic floor with representation of dolphins, from the sanctuary of Herakles. The dolphins would appear as if swimming in the water in the cistern, the floor of which they decorate (2nd half 2nd c. AD).

349. Rheneia. The sanctuary of Herakles, from the east; front right is the cistern with the mosaic floor with dolphins.

RHENEIA | 245

Kythnos

ALEXANDROS MAZARAKIS AINIAN

According to Herodotus (VI 90; VIII 46), Kythnos was settled originally by Dryopians and later by Ionians. The island is of particular archaeological interest, even though many known sites await excavation. At Maroulas, on the northeast coast, near Loutra, is the earliest known settlement in the Cyclades. Laboratory analyses of samples of organic remains confirm its dating to the ninth and eighth millennia BC, that is to the Mesolithic period. Excavations have brought to light remnants of circular constructions which may have been dwellings, as well as a few burials.

The role played by Kythnos in the development of early metallurgy has been known for some time. An important site of the Early Cycladic II period (2800-2300 BC) has been investigated at the site of Skouries, on the precipitous northeast coast. Some twenty circular constructions were identified, which are associated with furnaces for smelting copper.

There are several installations dating from historical times. Noteworthy are over thirty towers, of circular and of rectangular plan, primarily of the Classical period. Two circular towers still stand in satisfactory condition, the "Pyrgos" close to Chora and the Paliopyrgos at Aspra Spitia, at the northwest end of the island.

The impressive fortified acropolis on the sheer north edge, known today as Kastro tis Orias or Katakephalou, is identified as the island's capital in the Byzantine Age and during the Latin occupation. However, there are indications that it existed as a citadel in Mycenaean times. On the contrary, another fortified acropolis on the west coast, Kastellas, seems to have been founded in early historical times but was abandoned towards the end of the Archaic period.

The most important site of historical times is undoubtedly Vryokastro or Rigokastro, on the northeast coast, site of the ancient capital of the island, also called Kythnos, according to the ancient sources (fig. 350). Surface surveys in recent years have yielded rich finds and have contributed considerably to understanding the urban organization of the city, which was evidently inhabited continuously from the tenth century BC into the seventh century AD.

The city is enclosed by mighty fortification walls, which are preserved in excellent condition in places. On the basis of their masonry, they are dated to Classical and Hellenistic times, although some sections, particularly in the Upper City, perhaps date from the Archaic period.

Opposite the acropolis, southeast of the city on a neighbouring hilltop, are the remains of a small independent Hellenistic fort. There are some indications that this was the billet of the Macedonian garrison that Philip V installed on Kythnos in 201 BC and which contributed decisively to the city withstanding the siege in 199 BC by the allied forces of the Rhodians, Pergamenians and Romans. Dominating the summit of the acropolis is an important sanctuary, which surface finds show was in use from the eighth century BC to the first century AD. The quantity and the

350. Kythnos, Vryokastro. View of the ancient city. The walled city covered an area of 2.85 hectares, including the small rocky islet which in Antiquity was joined to the coast but is now cut off from the main island, due to the significant rise in sea level. Visible on the seabed are the foundations of coastal walls as well as a breakwater that delimited the south entrance to the harbour.

351. Kythnos. Vryokastro. Bronze lotus flower from the undisturbed adyton of the Archaic temple (7th c. BC) in the Upper City of ancient Kythnos. Kythnos Archaeological Collection in Chora.

352. Kythnos. Vryokastro. The Archaic temple (7th c. BC) stood upon a terrace underpinned by mighty retaining walls. Constructed of schist, it was probably in the Doric order and has a small shallow adyton and cella. Due to the poor preservation of the monument, it is not clear whether it had a pronaos. The external dimensions of the foundation of the temple measure 14.65 x 8.65 m. The transverse buttresses connecting the temple proper with this foundation were added in Hellenistic times. The overall picture that emerges from the excavation suggests that there was a sudden destruction, possibly caused by earthquake.

kind of finds, as well as an inscription found at Eleusis in Attica, lead to the preliminary conclusion that the sanctuary was dedicated to the worship of Demeter.

Lower down, on a narrow terrace formed along the crest, are two monumental buildings of rectangular plan (fig. 357). The south one comprises two rooms opening onto a Doric stoa facing east. Touching the stylobate is a cistern cut in the bedrock, the mouth of which communicates with a built basin, as well as a semicircular exedra. Adjacent to it are the foundations of a small rectangular altar. The north building is larger and more imposing – the retaining wall stands to a height of 3 metres – but the layout of its interior is not visible on the surface. On the basis of the masonry of both buildings they can be dated to Late Classical or Hellenistic times.

In recent years excavations have begun in one of the sanctuaries of the Upper City, which is at the northernmost edge of the terrace (figs 352, 353). The level of destruction and abandonment covering the temple and its environs has yielded numerous votive offerings dating from the Archaic to the Hellenistic period. The temple was uncovered north of the two altars and was probably constructed in Early Archaic times (7th century BC).

The adyton was found undisturbed with the many votive offerings still *in situ* (figs 351, 354, 355). Most of these 1,500 or so precious objects are pieces of jewellery and intact vases, mainly of the Archaic period. Although it is too early to make a documented proposal

353. Kythnos. Vryokastro. View of the sanctuary. Visible in the foreground (middle and left) are the two altars and on the right is the fortification wall. In the background is the temple.

354. Kythnos. Gold rosette from the undisturbed adyton of the Archaic temple (7th c. BC). Kythnos Archaeological Collection in Chora.

355. Kythnos. Vryokastro. View of the adyton of the Archaic temple (7th c. BC) in the course of its excavation. Here were found gold, silver, bronze and bone jewellery and minor objects, decorated metal sheets, necklace beads and pendants of various types, of rock crystal, glass paste, faience and semiprecious stones. Other finds included relief discs and cut-out plaques of ivory, Egyptian scarabs, Phoenician small bearded heads, terracotta figurines of the type of the enthroned female, numerous intact decorated vases imported from different parts of the Aegean region. Also recovered were many seashells and several pieces of coral (some with a suspension hole or silver wire), bones and knucklebones (*astragala*) of small animals.

on the identity of the deity worshipped, on the basis of the kind of the dedications and the individual characteristics of cult, it can be argued that it was a goddess. The wealth of the finds and the variety of their exotic provenances, primarily the East (fig. 60), prompt a reconsideration of the picture of ancient Kythnos as a relatively poor city, as assumed from the few available literary and epigraphic testimonies.

A stepped street led from the Upper City to the harbour. Several underground cisterns for collecting rainwater have been located (some still in use), while water from the spring at Trypio, a few kilometres outside the city, flowed through an underground conduit into the central aqueduct (fig. 356).

The earliest finds from Vryokastro date from the tenth century BC. Important among them are the fragments of pithoi with relief decoration and the Attic pottery of Archaic and Classical times, as well as the stamped handles of transport amphorae of the Hellenistic period. Surface finds indicate that the city was abandoned in the seventh century AD, when the inhabitants moved to the fortified settlement of Kastro.

356. Kythnos. Vryokastro. Preserved from the central aqueduct of the ancient city of Kythnos are three parallel tunnels in the bedrock, which communicate at the far end with a fourth tunnel that intersects transversely, as well as the orthostats of the fountain that occupied the space in front of the cisterns.

357. Kythnos. Vryokastro. One of the two temples on the Middle Terrace. The hypothesis that both buildings were intended for cult is supported among other things by a dedicatory inscription found built into a nearby farmhouse: ΣΑΜΟΘΡΑΚΙΟΝ ΘΕΟΝ (Samothracian god), as well as the fragment of a marble sculpture which, according to one view, comes from the calf of a colossal statue of Aphrodite. The statue is possibly a work of the Messenian sculptor Damophon, who, according to a decree of the Kythnians, which was found in Messene, made a statue of the goddess and dedicated it himself in her sanctuary on Kythnos, in the early 2nd c. BC. The worship of Aphrodite on Kythnos is confirmed by the discovery, near the ancient harbour, of a small inscribed base of the 4th c. BC, mentioning the name of the goddess.

Seriphos

ALEXANDROS MAZARAKIS AINIAN

The "rough and stony" Seriphos of the ancient lexicographers is still largely unexplored. The island was known in Antiquity for its iron and copper mines. Indeed, it has been suggested that its name derives etymologically from the Phoenician route *sareph*, which means foundry. Mining and metallurgical activities date back to the Early Cycladic period (3rd millennium BC). Mining installations have been identified on the Kephala Peninsula, while considerable deposits of scoriae can be seen in the wider are of Avesalos Bay.

Apollodorus (I 88.2, II 36.1ff.) mentions that the first settlers on the island were Polydektes and Diktys, Aeolians from Thessaly. According to Herodotus (VIII 48.4-5), Seriphos was colonized later by Ionians from Athens.

The ancient city probably occupied the same site as the present Chora (fig. 360), which is why archaeological evidence is scant. A few remains of the fortification of the acropolis survive, as well as dispersed antiquities, among them an inscription recording that the agora was repaired in Roman times, and other inscriptions referring to the *balneum* (public bathhouse) and the *peripatos* (circuit walkway). The city's outport was presumably the sheltered bay at Livadi.

The best-preserved towers are on the west side of the island. Outstanding are the marble round tower known as Aspros Pyrgos, in Koutalas Bay (fig. 359), the rectangular Psaropyrgos (or Kanapes tou Kyklopa) on the Kyklopas headland southwest of Megalo Livadi, and a round tower constructed of marble and gneiss, on the col of the Kephala Peninsula. Some of these towers appear to have been associated with mining and metallurgical activities.

According to Pausanias (I 22,7 and II 18,1), one of the Seriphians' foremost cults was of Perseus. The earliest coins of the island are silver staters, dating from the sixth century BC, the obverse of which features the "Seriphian frog", who is linked with the local cult of Perseus, and the reverse the incuse square (fig. 358). Represented on bronze issues of the Hellenistic period are Perseus on the obverse and Medusa or the *harpe*, the scythe with which the hero beheaded the Gorgon, on the reverse.

There is a small archaeological collection in Chora, where fortuitous finds from all over the island are gathered.

358. Seriphos. Silver stater, *c.* 530 BC, with the "Seriphian frog" on the obverse. Athens, Numismatic Museum.

359. Seriphos. The marble Aspropyrgos, northeast of Koutalas Bay. On the basis of the isodomic masonry it is dated to Late Classical times.

360. Seriphos. The island's Chora, beneath which the ancient city of Seriphos probably lies.

Siphnos

ALEXANDROS MAZARAKIS AINIAN

The island owes its name to the homonymous founder Siphnos, son of Sounios. An Ionian colony "of Athenians" (Herodotus VIII 48, 4-5), Siphnos was renowned in Antiquity for its wealth, which evidently came from exploiting the mines of gold and silver ores (Herodotus III 57, 4-6; Pausanias X 11, 2). This prosperity, mainly in Archaic times, is reflected in the excellent quality Siphnian silver coins of the period, such as the staters with the head of Apollo on the obverse and an eagle on the reverse (fig. 361). Impressive too are the Archaic marble walls of the acropolis at Kastro (figs 366, 367) and, above all, the marble treasury with the superb sculpted decoration (fig. 362), which the Siphnians dedicated in the sanctuary of Apollo at Delphi (Pausanias X 11,2), in 525 BC.

In the late sixth century BC the Siphnians were obliged to pay 100 talents to Samian refugees who plundered the island. Later, in the framework of the Delian League, the Athenians milked Siphnos of its resources. Gradually, the metalliferous lodes were worked out, and the island fell into decline. Indeed, tradition has it – although this is not confirmed by archaeological finds to date – that the sea flooded the galleries in the mines, on account of Apollo's rage because the Siphnians no longer paid the due tithe of their income to the god (Pausanias X 11.2). However, the reasons for the island's decline must have been more complex, and even today scholars disagree over what happened and when. Although the piratical attack by the Cretans, most probably in 153 BC (Diodorus Siculus XXXI 45), led to further decrepitude, the sarcophagi and the grave goods of imperial times, from the ancient cemetery at Kastro, indicate that the Siphnians enjoyed relative affluence during the Roman Age.

Several ancient mines have been located on the island, but none can be associated securely with the extraction of gold (the mine at Aghios Sostis was for silver). Some of the numerous round towers seem to be linked with mining and metallurgical activities (fig. 368). Some 70 towers, dating mainly from the Classical period, have been identified in all, a considerable number for such a small island. The use of these constructions remains uncertain: some must have served as *phryktories* (for bonfire signals), others for protecting the rural population and the harvest. However, it is not known whether the towers were included in a state-organized defence network.

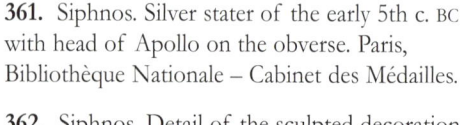

Stephanos Byzantios refers to two other cities in addition to Siphnos – which is usually identified with Kastro –, Apollonia and Minoa, but so far these have not been identified with certainty. It has been suggested recently that the Aghios Andreas citadel might be identified with Minoa, but this is no more than a hypothesis.

On the top of Aghios Andreas Hill, in about the middle of the island, is an important fortified settlement of the Mycenaean period

361. Siphnos. Silver stater of the early 5th c. BC with head of Apollo on the obverse. Paris, Bibliothèque Nationale – Cabinet des Médailles.

362. Siphnos. Detail of the sculpted decoration of the Treasury of the Siphnians at Delphi. In the words of Herodotus (III 57.8) "So wealthy were they that the treasury dedicated by them at Delphi, which is as rich as any there, was made from the tenth of their revenues". Through this monument the Siphnians sought to aggrandize themselves. The conspicuous display of their wealth verged on hubris and the ancient Greeks associated their decline with divine punishment. Delphi Archaeological Museum.

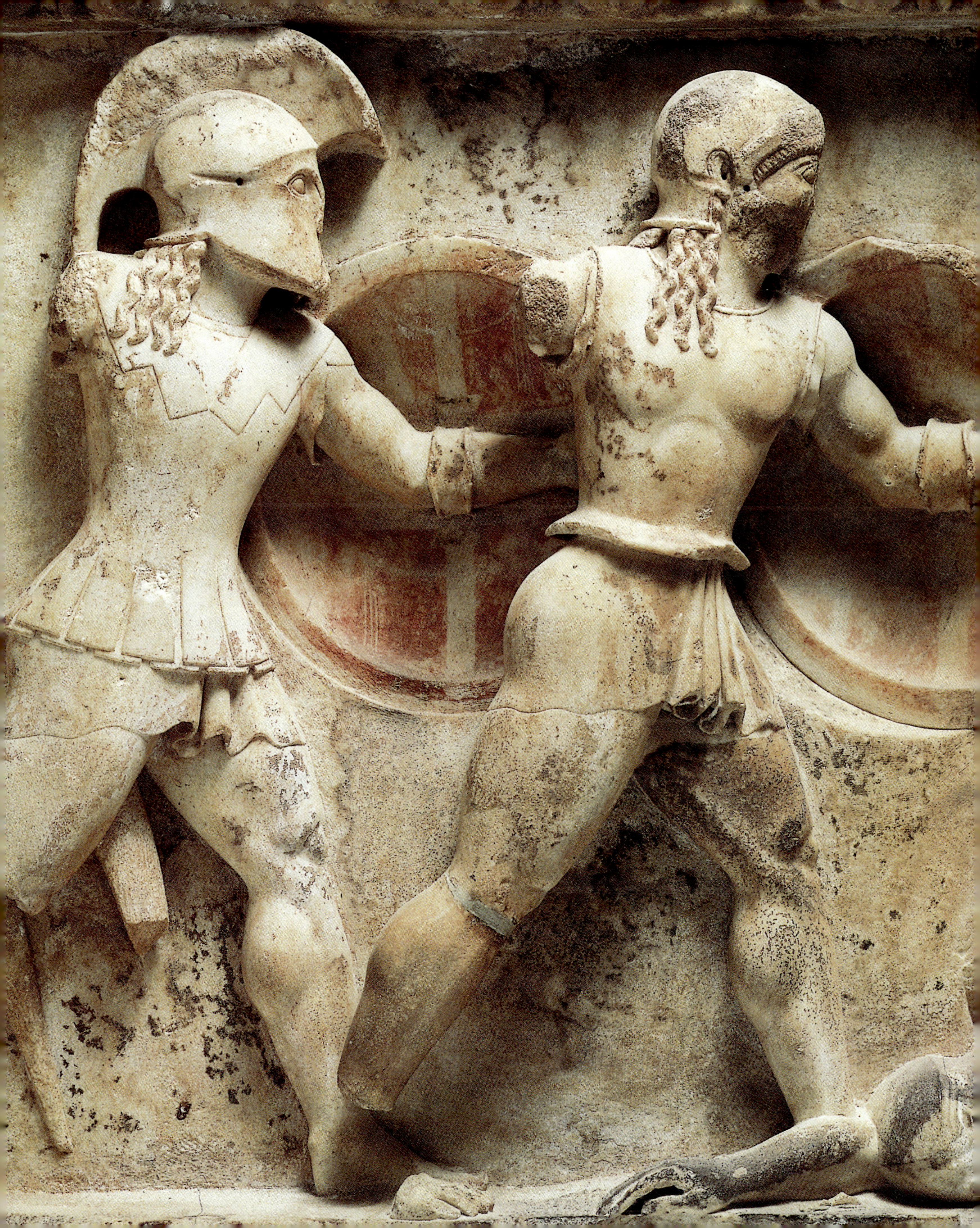

(fig. 365). The walled citadel seems to have been founded in the second half of the thirteenth century BC (Late Helladic IIIB period) and was inhabited until the end of the Bronze Age (12th century BC). The site was deserted for several centuries and was settled anew towards the end of the Geometric period (second half of 8th century BC). Life continued there uninterrupted into Hellenistic times.

Prehistoric Siphnos is little explored. An Early Cycladic cemetery (3rd millennium BC) has been investigated at Akrotiraki, a hillock south of Platys Yalos, and a significant Late Mycenaean installation (12th-11th century BC) has been located on the steep rocky height at Froudi tis Baronas.

The precipitous and naturally fortified site of Kastro, on the east coast of the island, has been identified convincingly with the ancient city of Siphnos, the *asty* of Herodotus (fig. 367), which was inhabited already in prehistoric times, as surface sherds of Middle Cycladic pottery (first half of 2nd millennium BC) indicate.

At several points on the acropolis imposing marble walls of the Late Archaic period (late 6th century BC) are preserved, in some places to a height of 4.5 m. (fig. 366).

The schist fortification wall enclosing the city is dated most probably to Hellenistic times. Very few building remains have come to light, mainly of the Geometric-Early Archaic and Hellenistic periods, since the city of historical times lies beneath the modern town. The ancient

363, 364. Siphnos. Among the interesting votive offerings from the Early Archaic sanctuary on the acropolis at Kastro are two unique large figurines of females with bell-shaped skirts painted with elaborate decoration. The same *apothetes* has also yielded a terracotta headdress, which may have bedecked one figurine or may have been an independent offering. Siphnos Archaeological Museum.

365. Siphnos. Houses of the Geometric period, inside the fortified acropolis at Aghios Andreas. The wall, 330 m. in perimeter and 4 m. thick, consists of two concentric circuits. The earlier inner enceinte of the 13th c. BC was reinforced by nine quadrilateral bastions. The main gateway was on the east side; two posterns had been opened in the south and west sides. The outer crenellated circumvallation, which included a large bastion on the west side, was constructed in the 12th c. BC and is weaker. With the addition of the external wall a narrow passage was created between the two fortifications, a kind of defensive ditch. Numerous residences of Mycenaean, Geometric and Classical times have been excavated in the interior of the walled zone.

254 | CYCLADES

cemetery was in continuous use from the seventh century BC into Roman times (most of the excavated graves are of this last phase) and extended over the south slope, opposite the city, in the Seralia Valley. At the northwest end of the acropolis a deposit (*apothetes*) of a sanctuary, of Geometric and Early Archaic times (700-550 BC), was found. This belonged most probably to the sanctuary of Artemis Ekbateria, mentioned by Hesychius, or to a sanctuary of Athena situated nearby, perhaps on the site of the church of the Panaghia Eleousa (Virgin of Mercy).

Hesychius also records the cults of Apollo Enagros and Pythios (the second epithet is attested in Hellenistic inscriptions, and of Zeus Epibemios, who is represented on Siphnian coins. Another sanctuary has been found in excavation, in the south corner of the acropolis of Siphnos, and is dated to the late sixth century BC. It is mentioned that the city had an agora and a prytaneion of Parian marble (Herodotus III 57, 16-17). Inscriptions record that there was also a theatre, where drama contests were held in Classical and Hellenistic time, and a sanctuary dedicated to Dionysos.

The ongoing surface survey of Siphnos has already identified a host of new sites (many new towers among them), which show that the island was flourishing throughout Antiquity and had relations with the wider Aegean region and the Greek Mainland.

366. Siphnos, Kastro. Part of the acropolis wall. This is the unique example of a marble fortification wall in the Cyclades and is incontrovertible testimony of the Siphnians' prosperity during the Archaic period (6th c. BC).

367. Siphnos. View of Kastro. The modern settlement occupies the site of the acropolis of the ancient city.

368. Siphnos. The round Aspros Pyrgos. Siphnos and Kea are the two islands in the Cyclades where the largest number of towers has been identified.

SIPHNOS | 255

Islets of the Western Cyclades

Peggy Pantou – Zozi Papadopoulou

According to myth, the Sirens who fell into the sea were metamorphosed into rocks, which today seem to be condemned, we could say, to eternal silence. Researchers rarely concern themselves with these rocky islets, while the few visitors are content with the magic of their crystal-clear waters. However, a different approach reveals their particular role in the culture and history of the Aegean.

Lying on important sea routes, the islets of the Western Cyclades were not always deserted and neglected as they are today. They were used for seasonal or permanent settlement, providing grazing land and cultivable fields for the neighbouring larger islands, serving as points for surveillance and communication, and above all anchorages and ports of call on the difficult maritime voyages. This is attested also by the little chapels of later times, built close to harbour coves, which are frequently associated in tradition with mariners' adventures.

Seriphopoula

Seriphopoula, a rocky islet northeast of Seriphos (see map p. 250), is waterless, harbourless, with extremely steep cliffs and very few anchorages. Human presence there is attested from the Late Neolithic period, as shown by the finds of recent surface surveys (obsidian blades and débitage, obsidian arrowhead, parts of stone tools, sherds of prehistoric vases) at the sites of Dasos, Tsouni and Kofto.

Atop the highest hill on the islet (191.62 m. a.s.l.) are the ruins of a marble round tower (external diameter 6.80 m. and maximum preserved height 1.40 m.), built of large rectangular blocks in a rudimentary isodomic system (fig. 370). Inside the tower is a built basement cistern of elliptical plan, coated with plaster. On the basis of the masonry and the potsherds found on the surface around the cistern, it is dated to the late fourth-early third century BC.

A second underground cistern (in the east part of the islet), at the site called "tou Diakou i sterna" by the locals, may also be correlated with the construction of the tower. This cistern is coated inside with durable plaster and is roofed with irregular pieces of marble set in mortar.

Incontestable witness to man's presence on Seriphopoula is the life-size right "footprint" at Kofto (fig. 369). Whether it was carved by some traveller or whether it expresses a wish for safe return remains an unanswered question.

369. Seriphopoula. Footprint carved in the rock at Kofto.

370. Seriphopoula. The tower from the northeast. On account of the strategic position of this isolated monument, it is thought to have served as an outlook tower or for transmitting signals.

Kitriani

Kitriani lies off the southeast tip of Siphnos (see map p. 252), from which it is separated by a narrow channel (fig. 371). On account of its location, far away from the settlements on the neighouring island, Kitriani was used in Antiquity as an anchorage and as a refuge for pirate ships, as is deduced from a first-century BC inscription in which it is referred to as the "opposite island of the rural territory (*chora*) of the Siphnians". The straits between Siphnos and Kitriani must have been on at least one important maritime route, linking the southwest with the central and the northeast Aegean. This assumption is reinforced by the fact that two ancient shipwrecks have been located in the area – the earlier wreck is of the fourth century BC and the later of the late second century BC.

Furthermore, more recent traditions associated with the building of the Byzantine church of the Panaghia (Virgin) Kitriani or Kypriani appear to echo memories of a busy sea passage (fig. 372). Marble architectural members in second use (columns and parts of columns, bases and capitals, parts of closure slabs), inside and outside the church, have prompted suggestions that an Early Christian basilica or an earlier temple existed on the same site, or that this construc-

ISLETS OF THE WESTERN CYCLADES | 257

tion material was brought from the opposite coast of Siphnos. The notable density of obsidian and of potsherds from prehistoric into later times, in the environs of the church, is a strong indication of the continuous use of the site.

Traces of human activity are evident on the top of the hillock to the east of the church. The scant remains of a circular construction of larger stone blocks are correlated with the foundations of an ancient tower, which could have controlled the Siphnos-Kitriani channel and would have been in visual contact with the numerous towers in southern Siphnos.

At the locality Stavroudaki, on the south entrance to the Siphnos-Kitriani channel, where the only natural coves suitable as havens are formed, there is an exceptionally large concentration of obsidian, mainly flakes and débitage. The toponym "Yalia", for the wider area, should be associated with the presence of obsidian in this place.

Polyaigos

Polyaigos, also known as Poly(i)vos or Nipolyvos in more recent times, forms together with Melos and Kimolos an island complex at the southwest edge of the Cyclades (see map p. 304), on an important maritime crossroad in the Aegean (fig. 373). Arid and with havens only on its west coast, it is covered for the most part by volcanic rock. One of the largest uninhabited islets in the Aegean today, it was a "desert island" already from the time of the geographer Claudius Ptolemy (second century AD).

According to a now lost inscription dated shortly after 338/7 BC, Melians and Kimolians were embroiled in a dispute over possession of the islet. It was awarded to the Kimolians after a trial heard by Argeian judges. A similar dispute arose in later times, presumably due to the use of the islet's resources, since Polyaigos has a rich subsoil and notable tracts of arable land, which were essential for the subsistence of the neighbouring islands.

Although all indications are that Polyaigos was uninhabited in Antiquity, a recent surface survey has shown that it hosted human activities or seasonal installations for centuries; on the west coast at the site of Pano Mersini, where two small coves form a safe anchorage, a large concentration of obsidian, chert and pottery has been found, spanning prehistoric into Byzantine times.

371. Kitriani. View of the islet from the southeast tip of Siphnos.

372. Kitriani. The church of the Virgin from the southwest.

373. Polyaigos. View of the islet from the northeast tip of Kimolos. Evidence of human activity in prehistoric times has been located on the west side of the island.

ISLETS OF THE WESTERN CYCLADES

Paros

Photeini N. Zapheiropoulou

Those who have shown interest in the importance and the quality of the contribution of each Greek place to the creation of the artistic civilization of ancient Greece know that the contribution of Paros was not insignificant. In the domain of poetry it gave Archilochos. The ancients persistently placed him alongside Homer ... Of late, several scholars of ancient art have been involved with enhancing the artistic contribution of Paros to vase-painting and sculpture, from the eighth century BC into Classical times ... We shall try to express, albeit provisionally, in a few phrases, the essence of this art. A strong desire for movement and some special elasticity nests within its forms ... Parian paintings or sculptures always show clean lines or planes, with definite borders between them – some soft and supple, capable of flexing but also of springing back taut. Their ease of movement (whether ornament or organic figure) is strange, has something of the sudden jolt of the spring. And from very early on the Parian artists applied themselves to representing movement, even if only with external signs, at the time when other schools were not even thinking about it.

I begin with this very vivid text by the great archaeologist Christos Karouzos because I consider that it truly expresses all the power of Parian artistic creation and the "essence of this art", as he says characteristically. A text written in 1938, on the basis of the still scant finds, it lacks nothing in the correct assessment of Parian works, even today when the earth of Paros, primarily in the past few years, has yielded some veritable masterpieces of ancient Greek art.

Lying at the centre of the Aegean, Paros, the third largest island of the Cyclades after Naxos and Andros, is distinguished by its soft outlines and the tranquility of its landscape; Paros and neighbouring Naxos are the two most important islands in the Cyclades, from around the fourth millennium BC to the present day. Paros owes its diachronic cultural heyday as well as its economic development not only to its strategic position on the sea lanes linking mainland Greece with the islands and with Asia, but also to the precious raw material available in abundance: the famous "Parian stone", that is the marble of wondrous whiteness and translucence (Strabo X 5, 7; Pindar, *Nemean Ode* IV 81). Parian marble is of better quality than even the renowned Carrara marble, which is translucent to a thickness of 2.5 mm., whereas Parian lychnite, a special type of marble, is translucent to a thickness of 3.5 mm., to which property it owes its name (*lychnites* = that which gives light or which allows light to pass through it). The ancient quarries are in the foothills of Mount Marpissa, at Marathi in the island's hinterland, and the marble was extracted from subterranean galleries, at the entrance to one of which a relief of Nymphs has been carved.

Traces of human presence on Paros date from the Early Cycladic period (3200-2300 BC). Very few remains of settlements have come to light, while on the contrary many cemeteries have been

374. Paros. Early Cycladic marble male figurines of Plastiras type (1st half of 3rd millennium BC). Stolen from the Paros Archaeological Museum in 1992.

excavated, bearing witness to the existence of settlements in almost all areas of the countryside (Dryos, Avyssos, Galana Gremna, Kampos, Aghia Irini, Plastiras) and more on the southeast coast, opposite Naxos (fig. 374). At the end of the Early Bronze Age it seems that the preference for settlement on the west coast returned, a preference still evident today. On the site of the modern capital, Paroikia, in the northwest part of the island, next to a deep harbour well sheltered from the prevailing winds, a settlement existed already in the late third and the second millennium BC, on the hill now topped by the Medieval Kastro (castle). However, the east side of the island was not abandoned. On another sheer cliff on the north coast, to the west of modern Naousa, there was an important settlement at the site of Koukounaries (fig. 51), from the mid-second millennium BC until almost the end of the sixth century BC. This was a key site for controlling the sea route to the southeast. During the final period of the Mycenaean Age (Late Helladic IIIC, 12th century BC) (fig. 375), an important building was constructed on the naturally fortified rocky height of Koukounaries (fig. 376), which was possibly left desolate after an enemy attack.

With the advent of the first millennium BC, a time of great upheavals and significant changes in Greece, with the movements of populations, Ionians settled on Paros as well as on its closest neighbours, Naxos, Siphnos, Mykonos and Delos. From the outset, the Geometric period – as recent finds demonstrate –, artistic activity commenced, due of course to the thriving economy of Parian society. This affluence is attested moreover in the colonization of Thasos in the far north Aegean, *circa* 680 BC, a bold expedition to an unknown and dangerous place in those early years when no other Cycladic island had dared to embark on such an adventure. Paros was the only one to attempt, without any assistance from elsewhere, to found a colony close to the gold-bearing regions of the North. And she enjoyed complete success, as Thasos emerged as a politically and culturally flourishing city that remained loyal to its metropolis during virtually the whole of Antiquity, without this preventing its developing an identity of its own.

Paros advanced significantly during the Archaic period (6th century BC), acquiring power and wealth. It became a major cultural and commercial centre, remaining so into Roman times, that is until the demise of the ancient world. From the sixth century BC the city was encircled by a wall 2.5 kilometres in diameter, two gateways in which survive with antae standing to an appreciable height. In a commanding position on the coastal hill now crowned by the Venetian Kastro, on the site of the prehistoric settlement, stood the principal sanctuary of the city, which was built around 525 BC and dedicated to the patron goddess Athena. The urban centre (*asty*) developed around the sanctuary and a little beyond were the various outlying areas of a city, such as the workshops of the marble-carvers and the potters, which have come to light in excavations in recent years, to the southeast. There were, of course, many public build-

375. Paros. Large krater painted with symmetrical spirals and other linear motifs, from the Mycenaean settlement at Koukounaries. 12th c. BC. Paros Archaeological Museum.

376. Paros. The Mycenaean settlement on the rocky hill of Koukounaries, in the Bay of Naousa, enjoyed a heyday in the 12th c. BC (Late Helladic IIIC period) although habitation at the site goes back the Early Cycladic period (3rd millennium BC). Outstanding in the settlement is a building of large dimensions, which was destroyed around 1150 BC, possibly in an enemy raid. Later, in the 6th c. BC, a sanctuary dedicated to the goddess Athena was founded here.

377. Paros. Krater-shaped vase of height 1.08 m. from a Parian workshop (2nd half of 7th c. BC), originally made as a grave marker and subsequently used for a child burial. Depicted on the front is a mythological scene with three female deities led by a male figure holding a Chimaera(?), all walking towards a male figure who receives them. Paros Archaeological Museum.

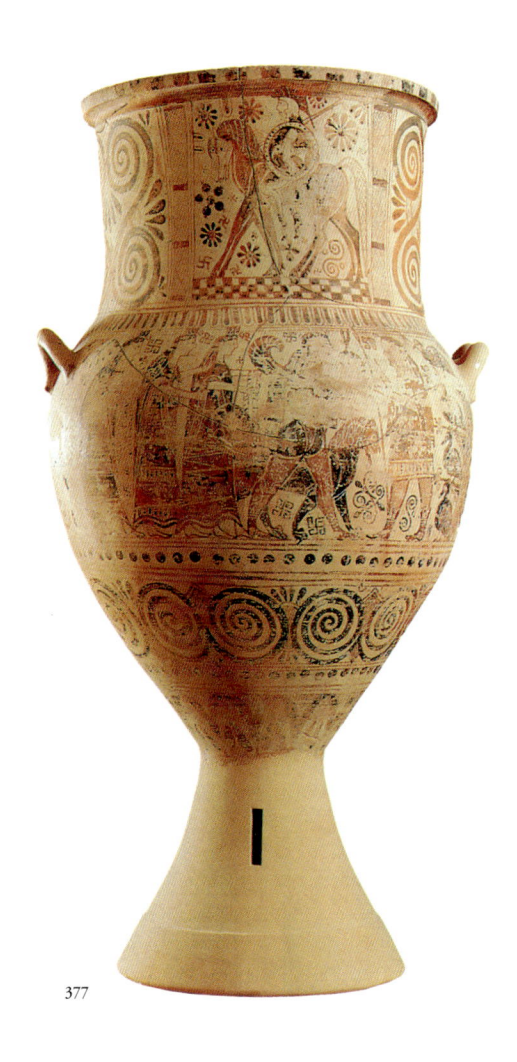

ings, stoas, agoras, prytaneion, agoranomeion, temples, and so on, the sites of which are impossible to identify because the modern town unfortunately covers the ancient city. Nonetheless, many architectural members have survived, because these *spolia* were used as building material, particularly in the Venetian tower of the Kastro (fig. 378) as well as in most of the houses and churches in Paroikia. As a result it is possible to reconstruct graphically some of the edifices, although these cannot be identified with specific monuments of ancient Paros. Sanctuaries also existed *extra muros*, in the countryside, the most important among them being the sanctuary of Apollo Delios and Artemis, to the north of the city, on a bluff facing Delos. To the south, on a hill by the shore, was the sanctuary of Apollo Pythios, in the Archaic period, and an Asklepieion – on the same spot – during the fourth century BC.

Rich *ex-votos* were dedicated in the Delion, which functioned from the ninth-eighth century BC into Classical times. These included colossal sculptures, such as the cult statue of the goddess or statues of smaller dimensions, such as Artemis donated by young Aries, daughter of Teisenor, terracotta protomes and a plethora of terracotta figurines, works in the minor arts in various materials, and pottery. Quite recently, another large, probably open-air sanctuary, has been revealed to the northeast of the city, just outside the wall and contiguous with it. The surrounding area served as a cemetery for members of the higher echelons of Parian society, which has yielded some sculptures that are extremely important for our knowledge of the Parian sculpture workshop (figs 385, 386).

The cemeteries too were *extra muros* and the main burial ground has been uncovered close to the ancient harbour, northeast of the city (fig. 381). It was in use from the late eighth century BC until the third-fourth century AD and included all manner of burials: in large jars (*enchytrismoi*) of the seventh century BC, in cist graves of the Archaic period, in marble cinerary urns-kalpides with the name of the dead of Classical times – in one case a disc painted with a representation of a discus-thrower (discobolus) had been placed as a grave marker (fig. 379) –, in huge marble sarcophagi of Roman times, which were used as family graves with inscriptions and relief decoration. According to the excavation data, use of the area as a cemetery began sometime in the closing decades of the eighth century BC, after a martial engagement with some 150 slain. After the cremation of the dead, as was the custom of the time, the burnt bones were kept in amphorae, which were placed all together in two large pits (fig. 382). These two *polyandria* (mass graves) are unique in Greece at such an early date. Most of the vases were decorated with geometric motifs, except two unparalleled examples, which carried scenes of battle and of burial (figs 52, 380, 383).

A fertile island by Cycladic standards, agriculture developed in the lowlands of Paros, which by the end of the eighth century BC had acquired an urban society of clans and closed families. One of the Parians' main occupations was seafaring and they in fact designed a new type of small, light ship, the "*paron*". The founding of the colony on Thasos and the relations that were subsequently established with the cities opposite led to the exploitation of the gold mines in these regions, which brought wealth to Paros. The city also collaborated with the important Ionian city of Miletos, engaging in trade from Egypt as far as the Propontis, where it participated in the founding of another colony, Parion. However, the island's paramount source of income was without doubt its marble, which, as has been said, was the best quality marble in the Hellenic world.

The number of free citizens on Paros during the fifth and fourth centuries BC is estimated to have reached 12,000. In the fifth century BC Herodotus relates (VIII 112) that the Athenian general Themistocles collected "great sums" of money from the Parians in 480 BC, while in 489 BC the other Athenian general and victor at Marathon, Miltiades, set sail to campaign against Paros, on the pretext that the Parians had sided with the enemy during the Persian Wars. However, it seems that in reality the Athenians were more interested in the wealth of the Parians, as Herodotus again narrates (VI 133).

From the early fifth century BC Paros began to lose its autonomy and was obliged to follow the more general historical and political developments, like other Greek cities, until 145 BC, when it was subjugated by the Romans. However, this did not mean that the island fell into oblivion, as is deduced from an inscription of the fifth century AD, which refers to the *asty* of Paros as "the most splendid city of the Parians", as well as from the fact that Justinian chose it as an appropriate place to found the Katapoliani basilica, a uniquely important monument after Aghia Sophia at Constantinople.

For most of Antiquity, the regime that held away on Paros was the oligarchy, but not in its extreme version, since there was a relatively just division of goods. The dissemination of Pythagorean philosophy in the early fourth century BC attests to the predominant political spirit. The Samian philosopher Pythagoras (580-500 BC), one of the founding-fathers of mathematics, set up a school at Kroton in South Italy, where several Parian philosophers and mathematicians studied. However, the greatest intellectual figure of Paros and one of the most significant of early Greek Antiquity, was the first lyric poet, the iambographer Archilochos, who lived in the first half of the seventh century BC. Son of the noble Telesikles and a slave girl, he was an irascible personality who led an unconventional life. In his work, of which unfortunately only fragments have survived, he tries for the first time to liberate man from the shackles of tradition and to confront consciously his insecurity in the world and his fate, helping not only the individual but also society as a whole. In appreciation of Archilochos' contribution, the Parians heroized him right from Archaic times, constructing a small temple-like edifice, the Archilocheion. This was most probably a cenotaph where cult honours were rendered, which concurrently housed a gymnasium, that is, a venue of public education. Mention should be made here of a marble inscribed stele, known as the "Parian Chronicle", the 134 lines of which record significant events in Greek Antiquity, as well as dates of deaths or births of the most important intellectual figures from 1582 BC until 264/3 BC, but with no mention of events connected with Paros or the Cyclades; it is suggested, therefore, that the stele was intended to be read as a history lesson.

In addition to Letters, the Arts too flourished on Paros, with pottery and the minor arts in various materials, mainly bronze, already from the Geometric period. From the opening decades of the sixth century BC, thanks also to the existence of the excellent marble, an im-

378. Paros, Paroikia. The Venetian tower into which are built architectural members from the temple of Athena (*c.* 525 BC), patron goddess of the city.

379. Paros. Marble funerary disc (1st half of 5th c. BC) with depiction of a *discobolus* at the moment of throwing the discus. The figure is painted in red and the blond hair in gold, as was the discus he held in his right hand. Paros Archaeological Museum.

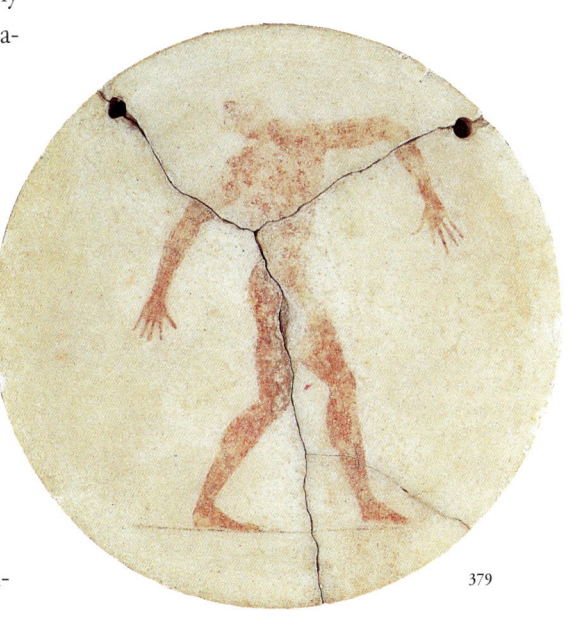

PAROS | 263

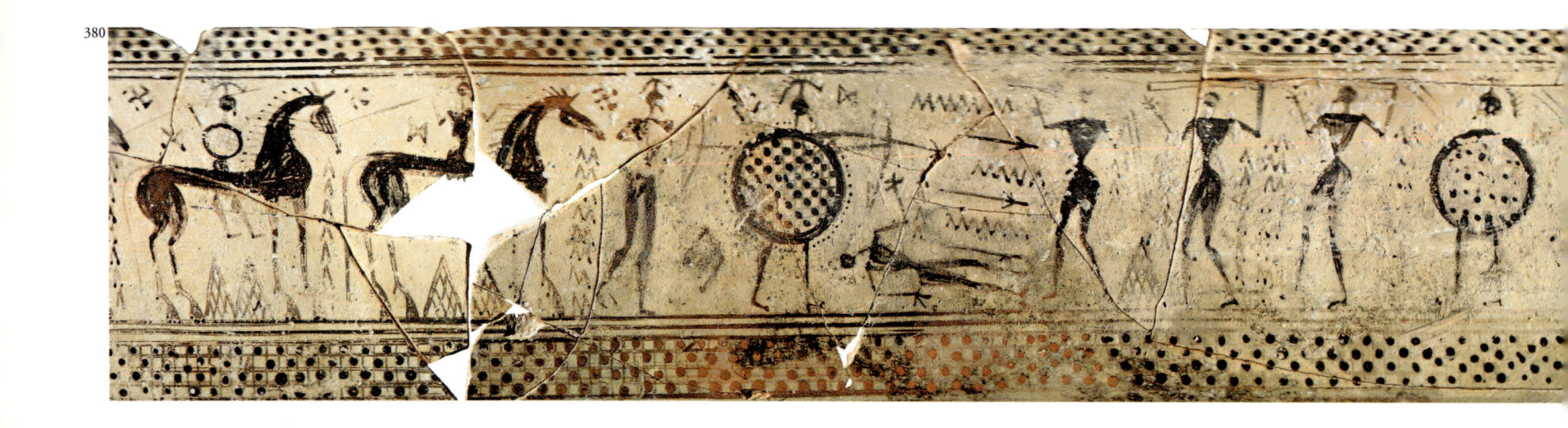

380. Paros. Outfold of a representation of battle between archers and sling-throwers, and in the middle the corpse of the deceased; the scene is completed by hoplites and horsemen. The depiction decorated the body of a Geometric amphora from a Parian workshop, which was found as a cinerary urn inside the *polyandrion* in the cemetery of ancient Paros. 725-700 BC. Paros Archaeological Museum.

381. Paros. The cemetery of ancient Paros, which has been arranged as a visitable archaeological site, near the harbour. In use from the 8th century BC to about the 3rd/4th century AD, it include many kinds of burials: in simple cist graves in the early periods, to even monumental marble sarcophagi with relief decoration in Roman times; the two standing stelai on the left were set up on graves of the Classical period, while the largest stele on the right was positioned as a boundary marker of the Geometric cemetery.

382. Paros. Photograph of the excavation of the Geometric *polyandrion* (2nd half of 8th c. BC). Visible in the right half of the picture are the amphorae in figs 380 and 383, unique works which have transformed our knowledge about the beginnings of ancient Greek painting.

383. Paros. Geometric amphora from the *polyandrion*. Represented on the upper body are battle scenes: the leader with Homeric figure-eight shield, as well as attacking warriors on horseback (750-725 BC). Paros Archaeological Museum.

382

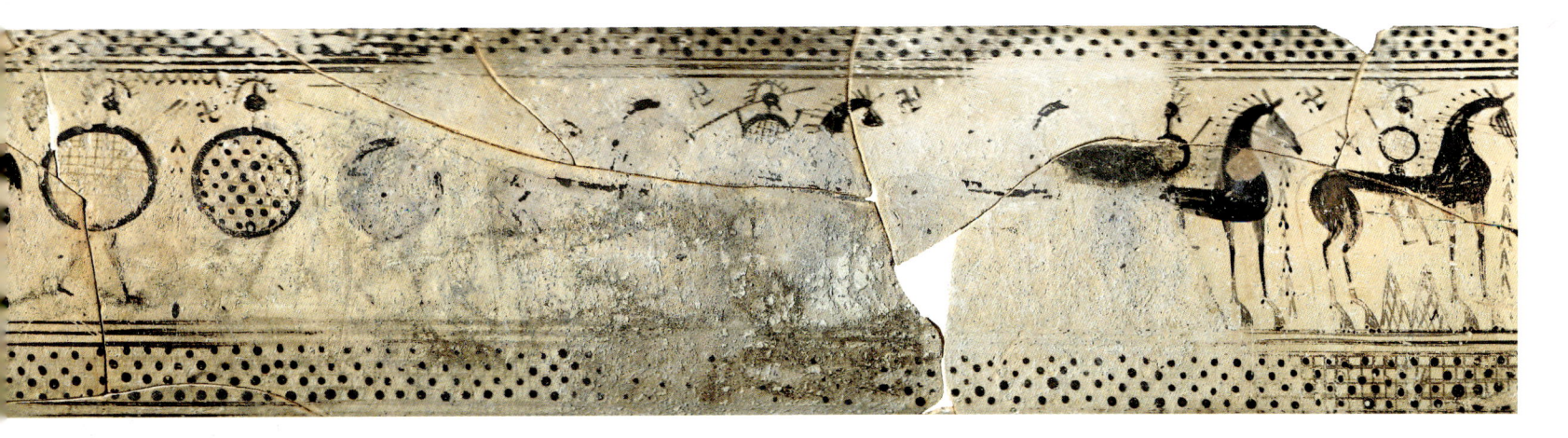

383

PAROS | 265

portant school of sculpture developed on Paros. Belonging to the Ionian cycle of art, it developed into one of the largest and most important centres of sculpture in the Hellenic world, its creations reaching many major sanctuaries of the period, from nearby Delos (fig. 331) to distant Delphi. Furthermore, Parian artists themselves circulated throughout Greece, very often together with the raw material from their island. The names of several Parian sculptors of the sixth and fifth centuries BC are preserved in various ancient sources. Well-known is Agorakritos, favourite pupil of Pheidias, who collaborated with him on the Parthenon. But the most famous of all was Skopas, who lived in the fourth century BC and who worked, *inter alia*, on the Artemision at Ephesos and the renowned Mausoleum of Halikarnassos. With such a legacy, it is hardly surprising that the work of Parian sculptors is distinguished by boldness, movement, innovative and avant-garde elements, which in other places they "were not even thinking about". Characteristic example is the superb statue representing Gorgo alighting on a roof (fig. 386). This was most probably a statue set atop a tall column in a public place. A work of the early sixth century BC, it is the first and unique example of a three-dimensional statue of Gorgo moving correctly in space, that is the two parts of her body. The upper and the lower represented in the same direction. This means that the artist had moved away from the two-dimensionality of relief, conquering depth for his sculpture and the real movement of a living figure.

The great heyday of the Parian school of sculpture, with the most of kouroi (fig. 385) and korai statues of the Archaic period (6th century BC) and the reliefs in Paros and in many other sanctuaries, seems to have continued in the fifth century BC, particularly its first half, from which there are some outstanding works of art: life-size and larger statues of gods and mortals (fig. 387), small-scale and monumental reliefs. In most of the sculptures the artists strive to render momentary movement (fig. 387), concurrently inventing audacious solutions and creating new forms and shapes, many of which are bold in conception and execution; of course, the existence of the precious raw material, the wonderful "Parian stone" that offers the sculptor the possibility of artistic creation provided he is inspired, should not be overlooked. Even so, the recent ceramic finds alter the parameters, since these show that even without their excellent marble the Parians were capable, much earlier than anywhere else, of producing pioneering works in terms of composition and execution (fig. 380, 383), opening new horizons in all sectors of art, horizons that led to the perfection of Classical times.

384. Paros. Excavation of an open-air(?) sanctuary *extra muros* of the ancient city, probably dated to Archaic times. In one wall the torso and possibly the base of a kouros have been used as building material.

385. Paros. The kouros torso of fig. 384. The life-size statue of a nude young man displays the suppleness of the body structure, distinctive of Parian kouroi, as well as the superbly harmonious proportions. Late 6th c. BC. Paros Archaeological Museum.

386. Paros. Statue of Gorgo descending swiftly from the heavens. The mythical monster has just set foot on earth, her body still vibrating from the impetuous movement which is emphasized by the vertically raised powerful wings, while the firm body with the elastic curvatures throbs with the pulse of youth. *c.* 580 BC.
Paros Archaeological Museum.

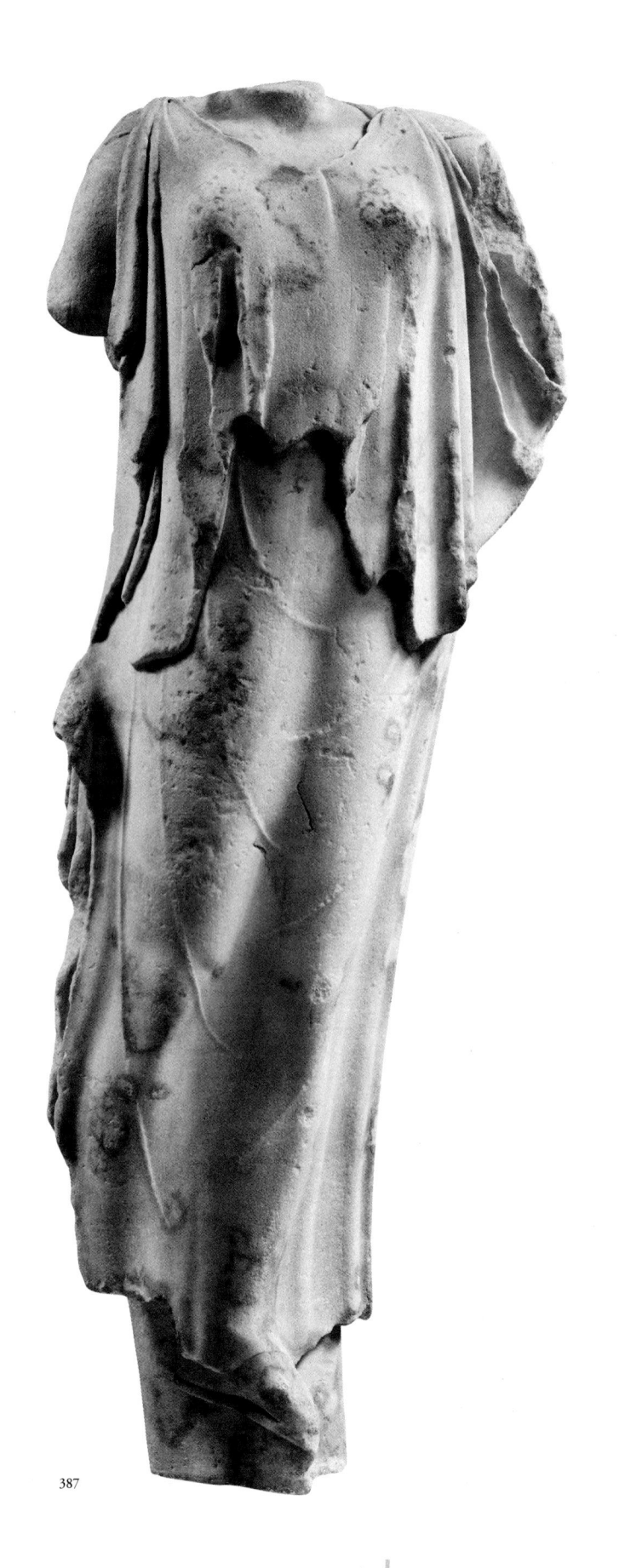

387. Paros. Torso of a statue of Nike, who has just alighted on a steady point, her right leg still in the air. The diaphanous garment clings to the vibrant young body and flutters behind her; the wings that will have further enhanced the airiness of the figure are missing. *c.* 480 BC. Paros Archaeological Museum.

388. Paros. Palmette from the crowning finial of a grave stele, 5th c. BC. Paros Archaeological Museum.

Antiparos, Saliagos

PHOTEINI N. ZAPHEIROPOULOU

Antiparos, the ancient Oliaros, lies between the southwest shore of Paros and the islets of ancient Prepesinthos – now Despotiko – and Strongylo to the southwest. The channel between Paros and Antiparos is also dotted with numerous tiny islets, or rather reefs that barely project above sea level and offer safe anchorages for ships. For this reason tradition has it that the Phoenicians used Oliaros as a centre of transit trade. It is named "colony of Sidonians" in the literary sources, which link it with the Asia Minor peoples (Phoenicians and Karians) even linguistically, considering the suffix -*aro* as possibly Karian.

Antiparos along with many of the surrounding islets, particularly Despotiko, was inhabited from the third millennium BC, as the host of Early Cycladic burials (fig. 390) attest, mainly in the southern part, at the sites of Apantima, Soros, Petalida, Krasades. These did not belong to poor populations, judging from the grave goods, some of which were of very valuable materials for the time, such as bronze and silver. In later times the island's fortunes were bound with those of Paros, almost as if it were just another settlement in the rural territory of ancient Paros, and it developed no particular political or cultural characteristics.

Nonetheless, the earliest settlement in the area is attested on Saliagos, today an islet-reef between the southern part of the west coast of Paros and the northeast coast of Antiparos. Excavations there brought to a light a settlement of the Late Neolithic period (5300-4500 BC) with highly important finds of excellent workmanship and artistic quality. Among them are the very lovely clay kylikes with high conical foot and white-painted decoration (fig. 389), as well as an unfinished marble figurine of a female, given the sobriquet "the fat lady of Saliagos" (fig. 30).

389. Saliagos. Deep kylix with high foot and white-painted decoration of geometric motifs, from the Neolithic settlement. Late Neolithic period (5300-4500 BC). Paros Archaeological Museum.

390. Antiparos. Early Cycladic violin-shaped figurine of the early 3rd millennium BC. Athens, National Archaeological Museum.

Despotiko

YANNOS KOURAYOS

To the west of Antiparos lie three small uninhabited islands, Despotiko, Tsimintiri – between Antiparos and Despotiko – and Strongylo – west of Despotiko. Despotiko is identified as the ancient Prepesinthos. The first excavations were conducted on the island in the nineteenth century by Christos Tsountas, who discovered Early Cycladic cemeteries. In 1959 N. Zapheiropoulos excavated at the sites of Zoumbaria and Mantra on the northeast coast, where architectural members of an Archaic Doric temple, dated *circa* 500 BC, were brought to light.

Since 1997 excavations at Mantra have revealed a large part of the ancillary spaces of a sanctuary (fig. 394). Specifically, a building complex of oblong plan, 35 metres long and comprising five adjacent parallel rooms. The three rooms on the south side form an independent building unit, thanks to a Doric prostoon, with stylobate 18 metres long, along their length. The two rooms on the north side have a kind of closed prodomos 17 metres to the east of them. The preservation of the building's façades is excellent. Two courses of marble ashlar blocks in the isodomic system survive, set on an euthynteria of large schist slabs. The gradual removal of the

391. Despotiko. Restoration drawing of the Daedalic figurine of a deity, found on the floor of room A1 of building A. Preserved is the upper torso and the head, on which is a polos. It is identified most probably with the earliest cult effigy in the temple (680-660 BC). Paros Archaeological Museum.

392. Despotiko. Part of an Archaic kouros. Preserved is the head and part of the torso. It was found upside down and wedged with stones, propping up a doorway. The facial features and the hairstyle recall products of East Greek workshops. *C.* 580 BC. Paros Archaeological Museum.

393. Despotiko. Lower bodies of two Archaic kouroi, in second use as jambs of a double door. The legs of both statues have the characteristic stride of kouroi, with the left leg to the fore.

394. Despotiko. View from south of the rectangular room of building Θ, which was uncovered in 2005. The floor is paved with rectangular schist slabs and there is a marble bathtub. Traversing the room is a conduit, which, via a closed sluice, ends outside the space.

391

sheepfold revealed 520 new architectural members, column drums, column capitals, triglyphs and cornices.

To the southeast a host of later buildings was found, constructed of architectural members from the Doric temple. In the lower levels, beneath the Medieval buildings, the continuation of the south wall of the ancient complex was exposed for a length of 60 metres. Under the floor in the north room of the Archaic building A, very important finds of the Archaic period were discovered, of East Greek, Rhodian, Cypriot and Egyptian provenance. Protocorinthian and Corinthian aryballoi, alabastra, cups (kotyles), terracotta figurines, various objects and statuettes of faience, seals of semiprecious stones, bronze and ivory spectacle fibulae, an ostrich eggshell, stone, glass and gold beads, metal artifacts such as daggers, sword and farming implements were recovered. A unique find is the large figurine of a female deity in the Daedalic style, dated *circa* 680-660 BC (fig. 391), the original height of which is estimated at 0.45 m.

Many fragments of marble sculptures have been found on the excavation site, such as heads and parts of torsos of Archaic kouroi (figs 392, 393), torso of a nude male statue, and part of an Archaic perirrhanterion bearing the inscription: ΜΑΡΔΙΣ ΑΝΕΘΗΚΕΝ (Mardis dedicated [it]). A very important find is the Classical altar, which is square and built of marble, and dedicated to ΕΣΤΙΑ ΙΣΘΜΙΑ (Hestia Isthmia). This is not only a testimony of one of the deities worshipped but also confirms the existence of an isthmus. In addition to building A, another five buildings have been uncovered (Β, Γ, Δ, Ε, Ζ, Η, Θ) as well as the so-called "south complex", excavation of which is still in progress.

Building Γ is bipartite, measures 12.5 x 10 metres and is dated to the sixth century BC. Building B, of dimensions 20 x 8 metres, occupies a conspicuous position 5 metres away from building Γ.

East of building A, building E was revealed, which preserves its plaster floor. Last, east of building E is another building of large dimensions, named building Z, which dates to Late Classical-Early Hellenistic times (late 4th century BC).

The discovery of five incised sherds dating from the sixth to the third century BC and all inscribed ΑΠΟΛΛ confirms that the sanctuary was dedicated to Apollo. The moveable finds and the architectural members from Despotiko display remarkable similarity to those from the Delion sanctuary on Paros, which was dedicated to Apollo and Artemis.

The plan of the temple, which is dated on the basis of the architectural members *circa* 500 BC, is impossible to determine at present because the foundations have not been found.

The sanctuary on Despotiko is a unique case in the Aegean. On one of the loveliest uninhabited and virgin little islands in the Aegean is an untouched Archaic sanctuary, which functioned from the seventh century BC into Roman times.

392   393

394

DESPOTIKO | 271

Naxos

Prehistoric times

OLGA PHILANIOTOU

The fate of Naxos was determined to a degree by its central location in the Aegean, its geomorphology and its natural resources. It is the largest and most fertile island in the Cyclades, with small plains or semi-mountainous valleys suitable for agriculture. The mountain massif, of which the highest summit is Zas, traverses Naxos from North to South, virtually dividing it into two. It is rich in marble and emery, minerals exploited from prehistoric times, while at the same time it provides grazing for sheep and goats. Dominating the northwest coast is a hill of flint, Stelida. Highland Naxos had dense woodlands in Antiquity, indeed it seems that there were deer in the area of Kleidos even in the eighteenth century. The bays all around the island, but especially on its southeast and south coasts – the sea off Kalantos is one of the calmest parts of the Aegean – offered safe havens for the small prehistoric boats.

The leading cultural role of Naxos in the Early Bronze Age (3rd millennium BC) became known from the first archaeological investigations in the early twentieth century. Much later, however, two excavations that coincidentally were conducted at the same time, in the Zas Cave and at Kokkinovrachos, at the west edge of Grotta, revealed that this cultural role was based on a strong Neolithic substrate.

At Kokkinovrachos were found the remains of a large coastal settlement, destroyed by continuous habitation and erosion, which is dated on the basis of the pottery and the Carbon-14 method to the Late Neolithic period, *circa* 4500 BC. Clay vessels and stone tools, as well as food residues, shells and bones of sheep, goats and fish, compose the picture of the Neolithic island economy, which was not based solely on mixed farming but also turned towards the sea. The obsidian and the pottery point to external contacts extending from the Cyclades to the East Aegean, mainland Greece and possibly the Balkans.

There was also human habitation in the Zas Cave in the same period. There, however, continuity of occupation is attested in the succeeding phases, Late Neolithic II or Final Neolithic, during the fourth millennium BC. The pottery of this phase, unslipped or with plain burnished decoration, belongs to the so-called "Attica-Kephala" culture, which is encountered throughout southern Greece from Euboea to the Peloponnese. The early development of metallurgy in the Cyclades is evidenced in this phase, by bronze tools, axes, awls and pins. A gold strip (fig. 24), for which there are parallels in Macedonia and the shores of the Black Sea, indicates contacts with distant centres, remarkable for a mountainous inland site.

The Early Bronze Age, at the dawn of the third millennium BC, appeared timidly at first, dynamically a little later, with an increase and dispersion of the population, as is deduced from

395

395. Naxos, Aplomata. Marble figurine of a female seated on a throne. Mid-3rd millennium BC. Naxos Archaeological Museum.

396. Naxos. Pecked slab from Korfi t'Aroniou, with representation of a human figure and animals. Apeiranthos Archaeological Collection.

397. Naxos. The Early Cycladic (3rd millennium BC) citadel at Korfari ton Amygdalion, Panormos, on the southeast coast. Visible in the distance are the small islands of Schinousa and Kato Kouphonisi.

398. Naxos. Marble figurines of Louros type, named after the Early Cycladic cemetery at Louros in southern Naxos, where they were found. Athens, National Archaeological Museum.

399. Naxos. Marble footed bowl, an outstanding example of Early Cycladic stone-carving. Mid-3rd millennium BC. Apeiranthos Archaeological Collection.

400. Naxos. Clay burnished vessel ("incense-burner") with intricate decoration. Mid-3rd millennium BC. Apeiranthos Archaeological Collection.

the number of cemeteries that have been excavated or were found plundered (figs 401, 402). In the heartland of the island, not only the fertile valleys of Sangri, Engares, Melanes were inhabited, but also mountainous regions from Apollonas to the southern foothills of Mount Zas.

The coastal hills, close to arable land and sheltered coves that secured communication with the outside world, combined those factors that determined habitation in the Aegean during the Early Bronze Age (fig. 397). The greater density of settlement in southeastern and southern Naxos was perhaps due to the region's particular terrain: the large massif of Mount Zas impeded communication with the hinterland, whereas the sea gave direct access, as today, to the islets opposite: Kouphonisia, Keros, Schinousa, Herakleia and, via these, to the east and south Aegean, as far as Crete.

The main source of information on Early Cycladic Naxos (3rd millennium BC) is its cemeteries. The stone-built houses, destroyed by ploughing or erosion, were a ready source of construction material in later periods and have been lost, with very few exceptions. The host of Early Cycladic cemeteries, in contrast to the absence of graves of the Neolithic Age, perhaps reveals a change in burial habits and mortuary beliefs: in the Neolithic levels of the Zas Cave there are indications of burials below living spaces, whereas all the Early Cycladic cemeteries have been found outside settlements. The graves were usually small cists of trapezoidal plan (fig. 402), but there are also other types, such as the "chambers" on Aplomata Hill near Grotta.

The dead were interred in acutely contracted pose and the grave was covered with one or more capstones, upon which a "marker" was usually placed, in the form of a cairn of stones mixed with potsherds or even whole vases. This evidence and the rituals that are apparent from the finds (fig. 403) bespeak belief in an afterlife. Some graves were richly furnished with marble vessels (fig. 399) and clay vases (fig. 400), marble figurines (figs 395, 398), jewellery, bronze and stone tools and weapons. Others were poorer. Those graves found without goods perhaps contained objects of perishable materials (wood, matting or offerings of foodstuffs, flowers) now lost. Nonetheless, these inequalities along with other evidence, such as the grouping of the graves in clusters in the earliest cemeteries, perhaps echo social differences. The existence of complex social organization on Naxos in the Early Cycladic period is also suggested by the seals, of silver or semiprecious stones, found at various sites, as well as by clay seal impressions from the Zas Cave, since these are associated with the need to certify personal property.

The demographic growth characteristic of the zenith of Early Cycladic Culture, in the middle years of the third millennium BC, is evidenced on Naxos by the marked increase and dispersion of settlements. In the same period there was a notable widening of the repertoire of pottery shapes, which continued the tradition of burnished surfaces but with different incised and impressed decoration (fig. 400), while painted vases of fine fabric also appeared. Metal technology is conspicuous, with diverse bronze weapons and tools, lead objects, silver jewellery and miniature vases, while carpentry and boat-building, crafts closely connected to seafaring and the expansion of external relations, are inferred.

However, the greatest contribution of Naxos to the Cycladic Culture is in the domain of stone-carving and sculpture, which is the most distinctive and discussed aspect of its artistic expression (figs 395, 398, 399). Early Cycladic figurines have been interpreted as toys, *"psychopompoi"* (conductors of souls), effigies of specific individuals which accompanied their owner in the grave. The few larger examples – over one metre high – have been considered images of deities or heroes. Naxos is thought to have been the largest production centre of marble figurines in the Cyclades. The figurine types named after Naxian toponyms depict the evolution of forms during most of the third millennium BC, from the early Louros variety to the classic Spedos type and the schematic Apeiranthos variety. All the rarer types are represented on Naxos, such as the seated figures, male figurines, figurine groups, figurines of pregnant women and of musicians.

The abstract austerity, the clarity of line and the sense of proportion characteristic of the figurines are qualities also encountered in Early Cycladic vessels of marble or other stones. These creations, in their technical perfection, reflect a society with refined taste and needs beyond those of day-to-day survival.

No cult sites have been identified securely. Korfi t'Aroniou, an excellent vantage point surveying almost the entire east coast of the island and out to sea as far as Amorgos, has been considered a shrine, on account of its situation and the nature of the finds – a series of limestone slabs with pecked pictorial representations (figs 32, 396). It is noteworthy that representations in the same technique have been found recently in the much earlier settlement at Strophilas on Andros, prompting a similar interpretation.

During this particularly creative period and shortly before the transition to the final phase of the Early Bronze Age, the founding of citadels, such as Spedos, points to circumstances that were not entirely peaceful. Concurrently, some settlements, such as Panormos (fig. 397) and Kastraki, reinforced their defences by building walls, while for others the natural fortification seems to have sufficed, as at Mikri Vigla and Rizokastellia.

This obvious need for defence, in conjunction with imports or local imitations of pottery and bronze objects from the East or the Northeast Aegean, suggest that Naxos was affected by the wider changes and upheavals that marked the end of the Early Bronze Age all over the Aegean, in the Asia Minor littoral and Cyprus, upheavals that brought, among

401. Naxos. The Early Cycladic cemetery at Tsikniades, in the area of Sangri.

402. Naxos, Tsikniades. Early Cycladic cist grave lined with vertically placed schist slabs and preserving skeletal remains of numerous dead.

403. Naxos. Hat-shaped vase from the Early Cycladic cemetery at Aghioi Anargyroi (*c*. 2800-2700 BC). On account of the large number of these vessels and the position in which they were found, they have been interpreted as associated with rituals to commemorate the dead. Naxos Archaeological Museum.

NAXOS | 275

other things, radical changes in population distribution. By the beginning of the next period, the Middle Bronze Age, in the first half of the second millennium BC, very few Early Cycladic settlements continued to be inhabited on Naxos. These were located close to the sea or at naturally fortified sites, such as Grotta or Kastro in Chora, Rizocastellia and Mikri Vigla.

Mikri Vigla, clinging to a windswept rock on the west coast of Naxos, between two coves, had obvious contacts with Melos, an important Cycladic centre of the time, and with mainland Greece, while it received gradually increasing influences from Minoan Crete. These last are particularly apparent in the pottery as well as in other artifacts, among them some fragments of wall-paintings. If the stone construction and the clay figurines found in a conspicuous position on the hilltop bear witness to the existence of some kind of shrine, it is not unlikely that this contributed to the radiating influence of this flourishing settlement.

Whatever its significance, Mikri Vigla did not manage to keep it for long after 1500 BC. From the fifteenth century BC, historical circumstances that remain vague led to the development of the north coastal area, of modern Chora, where there is clear evidence of urbanization. There, by around 1450 BC, Grotta exploited fully its two harbours, as is surmised from the massive constructions and a paved street uncovered at its west edge (fig. 405). Domestic pottery and fine decorated vases reveal not only intimate knowledge of the products of Minoan Crete and the emergent centres of mainland Greece, but also the ability to produce locally artifacts of corresponding quality. In general, it seems that at the beginning of the Late Bronze Age Naxos, continuing the Middle Cycladic tradition, participated in a complex network of communications between other Cycladic islands, the Greek Mainland and Crete.

In this period, and even more so during the fourteenth and thirteenth centuries BC, the trend apparent from the early second millennium BC, that is for the concentration of population from small villages in larger settlements, was crystallized. Final outcome of this was the gradual development of Grotta into the largest, if not the sole, urban centre on the island, a phenomenon observed both on the Greek Mainland and in other islands, such as Melos, Kea and Rhodes. The rest of Naxos was by no means devoid of population. Rizokastellia, Mikri Vigla and the Zas Cave continued to be inhabited, at least occasionally, while new Late Bronze Age settlements have been identified from finds dispersed over the island, from Chosti at Komiaki in the north to Kalantos at the southernmost tip.

After the beginning of the Late Bronze Age (14th century BC), Grotta appears to have been more Mycenaean than Minoan in character. The same situation is observed on other islands, such as Delos, Kea and Melos, which is why their progress was linked to a degree with the consolidation of the Mycenaean presence in the Aegean. This presence became gradually more intensive, while Grotta flourished, benefiting from the expansion of Mycenaean trade beyond the Aegean, as far as Egypt and the Levant (fig. 404), the routes of which certainly passed through the Cyclades.

Circa 1250-1225 BC, Grotta was destroyed by an earthquake or some other cause. A new city was built on top of the old one, but with a different orientation and extended to south and east. These developments coincide with a major turning point, when relations with mainland Greece waned to vanishing point, while for a long interval, lasting until the early twelfth century BC, conditions in the Aegean, the Cyclades and the Dodecanese appear to have necessitated fortifications. Following the general trend, the Mycenaean city on Naxos was girt with a wall. The Kastro, which had most probably been settled from Middle Cycladic times if not earlier, was perhaps the site of the Mycenaean citadel, while the lower city spread in the coastal zone. This city was fortified shortly after 1200 BC with a wall of unusual construction that had a stone socle and an upper structure of mud bricks.

The turbulent times in mainland Greece and the consequent dissolution of the Mycenaean palaces are reflected, among other things, in the creation of local pottery styles at various Mycenaean centres in the Aegean. Among these was Naxos, favoured by natural wealth and its role in maritime communications. The finds from the settlement and the rich grave goods from the cemeteries on the hills of Aplomata and Kamini (figs 46, 406, 407) compose a picture of an affluent society with a powerful ruling class. Apart from original creations, the material culture attests contacts with Attica, Crete, the Dodecanese and Cyprus. These were not limited to imports or similarities of local pottery to imported, or to the debts of jewellery-making to the earlier tradition of the Eastern Mediterranean (fig. 407). As indicated by the unusual mud-brick wall, which is extremely rare in Greece but echoes similar constructions in Cyprus, these contacts extended to a much wider community of ideas.

With the end of the Mycenaean world the coastal area of the city was abandoned for reasons that are still unclear. The inhabitants seem to have moved to the site of Kastro for security, but kept alive, as we shall see below, the memory of the "old splendid picture".

404. Naxos. Faience flask from the settlement at Grotta, 13th c. BC. This type, the closest parallels for which are from Cyprus, echoes, like the gold sheet in fig. 407, the very wide external relations of Naxos in this period. Naxos Archaeological Museum.

405. Naxos, Grotta. Paved street linking the north with the west harbour of the city in the 15th century BC.

406. Naxos. Hydria with strainer spout, with painted decoration of a scene of fishing. From the Mycenaean cemetery at Aplomata, 12th c. BC. Naxos Archaeological Museum.

407. Naxos. Gold sheet, 0.06 m. high, with embossed representation of a human figure. From the Mycenaean cemetery at Kamini, 12th c. BC. Naxos Archaeological Museum.

Historical times

VASSILIS LAMBRINOUDAKIS

Constant factors in Naxian history during the first millennium BC were the island's size and its central position in the Aegean, its wealth in agricultural and stock-raising produce, secured by the alternating mountains and plains of its landscape, as well as the potential for exploiting the rich deposits of marble and emery in its earth. This combination provided an enduring basis for greater or lesser self-sufficiency in the insular community of Naxos. Characteristic is Herodotus' phrase (V 28,5): "For Naxos surpassed all the other islands in prosperity".

The worldview of Naxian society, which was based on the functioning of a self-sufficient microcosm, was expressed characteristically by the mythology and the religious beliefs of the ancient Naxians: the father of the gods, Zeus, was said to have been raised on the island. He was Zeus Melosios, protector of flocks of sheep, who was worshipped (a relevant inscription has survived) on the island's highest mountain, Zas, which bears the god's name to this day. Apollo too, son of Zeus, widely known as god of prophecy and music, had a strongly rustic character on Naxos and was worshipped in the island's interior as Anthokomes (= curator of flowers), Tragios and Poimnios (= of the goats, of the flocks).

However, incarnation of the precious benevolent powers of nature for Naxos was Dionysos, who became its patron deity and whose attributes were represented on the city's coinage (fig. 409). Zeus left Dionysos on Naxos after his birth and there the mountain Nymphs brought him up. There he married Ariadne, whom Theseus abandoned on Naxos, where he dropped anchor when homeward bound from Crete. The festivals celebrated on Naxos for Ariadne, a pure hypostasis of the Great Mother Goddess, are characteristic of the hibernation of Nature in winter and the rebirth in Spring. A mourning festival recalled Ariadne's sleep, which allowed Theseus to abandon her, and her death from her grief, while another happy ritual celebrated Ariadne's awakening and resurrection, and her fruitful marriage to Dionysos.

The importance of marble and of emery is also reflected in the religious beliefs of Naxos. Two fabulous creatures, Otos and Ephialtes, both sons of Nature fathered by Haloeus, that is the Thresher, multiplied excessively each year and were soon able to put the mountains one on top of the other, and to reach the seat of the gods on Mount Olympus. They pursued Ares and imprisoned him in the bowels of the *iron-eating stone*, that is, emery. In the end they perished, like all suitors of the Nature Goddess, when they tried to unite with Artemis, and they became protectors of the quarries of marble and of emery.

It is characteristic that in contrast to the neighbouring island of Paros, no important poets, historians or philosophers are known from Naxos. The textual testimonies on ancient Naxos come from other ancient authors and a host of inscriptions found on the island. However, the most eloquent witnesses to the importance of the civilization that developed on Naxos in the first millennium BC, and especially in its first half, are the monumental remains and the Naxian works of art that have been discovered on the island or elsewhere. Invaluable for experiencing the history of the Archaic period on Naxos are the Archaeological Museum in the Kastro, the

In-situ Museum in Metropolis Square in Chora, the unfinished works in the ancient quarries at Melanes and Apollonas, and the sanctuaries at Yria and Gyroulas, which have been enhanced for the public.

The character of the self-sufficient microcosm described above functioned in such a way that in periods when there was no great power on either side of the Aegean this island society flourished and wielded influence in its region. This seems to have been the case in the first half of the first millennium BC. During the difficult times that came after the eleventh century BC, the prosperity that had prevailed for some three hundred years, with the "*pax Mycenaeaca*" controlled by the powerful centres of the Mycenaean world, when the economy and the state shrank to the boundaries of many local groups, Naxos quickly emerged as a leading regional power, thanks to its potential.

Memories preserved in the genealogies of Naxian mythology concerning the settlement of Ionians of Attica on Naxos, in the course of their migration towards the coasts of Asia Minor, indicate that this large central island in the Aegean was a node of contact with the more easterly regions towards which the bearers of Mycenaean civilization moved in its twilight years. Excavations have shown that the strong Mycenaean centre of Naxos, the large settlement on the site of the present capital, did not cease to exist. For safety reasons the inhabitants withdrew from the seashore to Kastro Hill, but they began to bury their dead in their traditional hearths, in the area occupied by houses on the shore. In the ninth century BC family grave enclosures were created, in which the first dead were honoured as ancestors of founding clans (fig. 410). Towards the end of the eighth century BC the honours for the ancestral genarchs were organized around a tumulus that covered such enclosures, next to the remnants of the Mycenaean city wall, with the clear social and political symbolism of the continuity of the city-state, the formation of which was completed in this period, from the glorious Mycenaean past. In fact, the pottery of Naxos in this Geometric period (1050-700 BC), which mainly comes from the cemeteries on the outskirts of the ancient settlement in the area of the present town (Grotta, Aplomata, Plithos, South Cemetery), is of very good quality, akin to corresponding products of Attica and Euboea, regions in which the watershed from Mycenaean to historical times was likewise without disjuncture. It bears witness to a society that always has sufficient potential to sustain its momentum.

It seems that in the island's wealthy interior more traditional social groups of an earlier Aegean population, which the Greeks in Classical times conventionally called "Kari-

408. Naxos. Geometric amphora (9th c. BC) from the coast at Grotta, the area of the Mycenaean city of Naxos, within the ruins of which extensive burials were made during the early centuries of the 1st millennium BC. Naxos Archaeological Museum.

409. Naxos. Coin of Naxos, 500-490 BC. The head of Dionysos and his attributes, the bunch of grapes and the kantharos, the cup for wine, bearer of Dionysiac potency, were constant motifs on the coins of the island city. Athens, Numismatic Museum.

410. Naxos. The interior of the In-situ Museum in Metropolis Square, Naxos. Preserved here are visible parts of the wall and workshops of the Mycenaean city, and three phases of the evolution of burials in the 10th century BC, into a tumulus of the genarchs of Naxos in historical times.

NAXOS | 279

411. Naxos. Unfinished statue of a young man (kouros), of the early 6th century BC, in the quarry at Melanes. The overall height of the figure was approximately 5.5 m. It was abandoned most probably because the legs broke as it was being moved.

412. Naxos. Unfinished statue of Dionysos in a long garment, 10.5 m. high, in the quarry at Apollonas in northern Naxos. The most likely date is *c.* 540 BC and the statue is thought to have been commissioned to adorn the sanctuary of Dionysos at Yria.

ans", lived on. And such was the island's dynamism that this section of the population thrived too, as is attested by cemeteries with monumental family tombs, such as the tumuli at Tsikalario. However, the wider use of simpler vases with incised decoration points to differences between these rural areas and the city.

In contrast to the other smaller islands in the Aegean, Naxos was not divided into several city-states. The entire island was one state, a *polis*, with its urban centre, the *asty*, on the site of the present capital town, while the rest of the island was the *chora* of the *polis*, that is the rural territory in which the population of cultivators and stock-raisers lived dispersed in small installations and organized in demes. This structure secured the island's dynamism, but at the same time, on account of the cultural diversity, it also created deep and chronic divisions. Outcome of these divisions during the development of the *polis* was the dispatching of colonists to Naxos in Sicily, together with the Chalkideians in 734 BC, and to Arkesine on Amorgos not long after, which in all probability gave a way out to undesirable or discontented sections of the Naxian population.

Nevertheless, Naxos entered the seventh century BC in a great heyday, which enjoyed a sustained peak for one hundred years, from 650 to around 550 BC, lasting until the Persian Wars. In addition to being self-sufficient in agriculture and animal husbandry, the development of monumental architecture and large-scale sculpture endowed the Naxian landowners with a new source of wealth, through the exploitation of the marble quarries (figs 411-412). Naxos became a leading power in the Central Aegean, having the greatest influence on the religious centre of Delos, as shown by the central edifices (Oikos of the Naxians, most probably the first temple of Apollo, Stoa of the Naxians) and the major *ex-votos* of the period (colossal Apollo of the Naxians, Artemis votive offering of the Naxian lady Nikandre, fig. 416) in this sanctuary. Works of art show that Naxos had a particular impact on Thera and exported works and possibly craftsmen to Paros (temple buildings corresponding to Naxian ones), Boeotia (statues in the sanctuary of Apollo Ptoios) and Attica (marble roof tiles and sculptures on the Acropolis).

The founding of the colony in Sicily, the relations with Euboea more generally, Egyptian influences in Naxian works, information on the invention in Naxos of a type of ship known as the *kantharos*, and on Naxos's sovereignty over the seas in the late sixth century BC, all reinforce the view that during this period the farming island acquired naval power. In the early panhellenic war triggered by the rival claims of Chalkis and Eretria to the Lelantian Plain, Naxos played an important role, siding with the more conservative Chalkis.

This heyday is reflected in the island's art of the period. Already from the first half of the seventh century BC vase-

412

NAXOS | 281

413. Naxos. Fragment of a mid-7th century BC vase with representation of a chariot race. Apart from the use of a simple but vivid polychromy, noteworthy is the painter's signature (ΕΓΡ]ΑΦΣΕΝ), one of the first known in Greek works. Naxos Archaeological Museum.

414. Naxos. The sanctuary of Demeter at Gyroulas, near the village of Sangri. The marble temple of 525 BC, which has been restored recently (1995-2001), housed an earlier cult (8th-6th c. BC), the remnants of which are visible around the building.

415. Naxos. The ruins of the temple of Apollo Delios on Palatia (the tiny islet at the harbour entrance), of *c*. 530 BC. It was designed as a peripteral temple but the peristasis was never built. On the contrary, the gigantic portal remained standing and popularly known as Portara is the emblem of Naxos. Visible in the background is Kokkinovrachos, at the west edge of Grotta.

painting advanced, with polychrome pictorial representations of considerable power, from myth and the animal or the plant kingdom, which are distinguished by a majuscule plasticity and austerity (fig. 413).

However, the island was mainly a pioneer in its contribution to the development of monumental Greek sculpture and architecture. Recent investigations have brought to light monuments which demonstrate that it was on Naxos that the first steps were taken and that here great marble Ionic architecture was developed (fig. 417). In the sanctuary of the patron god of Naxos, Dionysos, at Yria (figs 55, 56), a series of four successive temples (800-550 BC) documents the passage from humble materials to marble, from the simple single-space oikos to the three-aisle prostyle temple, from the flat roof to the pitched marble one (tradition accredits the Naxian Byzes with constructing the first marble roof, *circa* 570 BC), from the plain functional wooden post to the articulated Ionic column. And in the sanctuary of Demeter at Gyroulas, near the village of Sangri (fig. 414) in the interior of Naxos, an all-marble temple constructed around 525 BC shows that already by these years Naxian craftsmen had devised the large portals, the refinements of curvatures in temple buildings and the visual augmentation of the interior space by obviating the ceiling and applying a pitched roof-ceiling, all features that were utilized later and are admired in Attic architecture of Classical times.

The temple of Demeter at Gyroulas was a religious centre for farming communities scattered in the island's hinterland. The cult of Demeter was central to the character of these communities. However, according to inscriptions, Apollo was worshipped in this sanctuary too, most probably as Anthokomes and Tragios, mentioned at the beginning of this chapter.

After the mid-sixth century BC, the island began to wane. The more modern quarries on Paros had become a victorious rival to Naxian marble and domestic enmities between various strata of the population brought political upheavals. Lygdamis, a progressive noble, was placed as head of the dissatisfied farmers in the countryside and seized power as a tyrant.

Despite the setbacks such an upheaval brought (the Naxian influence on Delos receded), the rule of Lygdamis until 524 BC, year of his overthrow, seems to have been a good period still for the island. It was then that the large temple of Apollo Delios was built at Palatia (fig. 415), on the islet in front of the natural harbour of Naxos. It was then that the same craftsmen must have worked on Paros (under the domination of their tyrant?) on similar buildings. It was then that the temple of Demeter at Gyroulas must have been constructed. Ground-breaking sculptural works also continued to be produced, such as a naturalistic statue of a runner, found at Grotta and now in the Naxos Museum.

415

416. Naxos. Artemis, votive offering on Delos of Nikandre, a lady of an aristocratic family. This life-size statue is one of the earliest known works of Greek monumental sculpture and is dated *c.* 660 BC. Athens, National Archaeological Museum.

417. Naxos. Remains of two single-space temples of the 8th and the 7th century BC, in a sanctuary discovered recently at Flerio, inside the quarries in the area of Melanes. This place was frequented by the pioneering quarrymen, whose work can be seen through the finds in the sanctuary.

After Lygdamis Naxos enjoyed a precarious prosperity. Following a brief oligarchy, democracy was established on the island, which in 506 BC withstood the four-month siege by Aristagoras, Tyrant of Miletos, and Megabates, the Persian general, whom the exiled oligarchs of Naxos encouraged. The ten-year thalassocracy of Naxos, preserved in tradition, perhaps refers to this period. A major technical project demanding centralized organization and social consensus is dated to the time of Lygdamis or to the Democracy. This is the 11-kilometre aqueduct which brought water from Melanes to the city of Naxos, in its course also distributing water for cultivation purposes. However, characteristic of the period are the words related by Herodotus as having been uttered by Aristagoras to persuade the Persians to attack Naxos: Naxos stood out among the islands for its prosperity, it had great wealth and many slaves, Paros, Andros and other islands of the Cyclades were dependent on it and the island had 8,000 hoplites.

The Persian Wars brought the acme of Naxos to a sudden end. With the new attack by the Persians in 490 BC, the inhabitants fled to the mountains. Those who stayed in the city were taken captive and enslaved, the city was destroyed and the sanctuaries were burnt down. Naxos did not recover from this catastrophe, because although it joined the Delian League in 479 BC, it was the first city in the alliance to feel the hegemonic oppression of the Athenians, against whom it revolted unsuccessfully in 473/2 BC. The Athenians subjugated the island and settled 1,000 cleruchs there. But even after the fall of Athens, in the late fifth century BC, the Naxians fared no better under the hegemony of the Spartans. In 378/7 BC, after the crushing defeat of the Spartan navy in the straits between Paros and Naxos, the beleaguered Naxians were forced to capitulate once more to the Athenians. Nevertheless, the works of the period, such as a small fifth-century BC marble kore in the Naxos Museum, or the handsome marble tower of the fourth century BC on an estate in the Cheimarros region, show that the old noble tradition in the arts had not vanished from the island. And the erection of the large *xenon* (= hostel) in the sanctuary of Zeus at Olympia, by the Naxian Leonidas in about 330 BC, reveals that there was no shortage of resources on Naxos.

The island enjoyed a new limited prosperity when it joined the *Koinon* of Islanders in 315 BC. Characteristic is the city's reoccupation of the shore at Grotta, where the agora developed with four perimetric marble stoas and a host of monuments in front of them. While maintaining a basic autonomy, with deme, boule, archons and its own coinage, Naxos passed at intervals into the sphere of influence of the Egyptian Ptolemies, then of the Macedonians and lastly of Rhodes. But the island's significance dwindled over time and the Romans used it as a place of exile.

Some of the surviving works from this period document that the old tradition lived on, such as the impressive statue of the Roman general Mark Anthony as New Dionysos (fig. 419), which was set up inside the temple of Dionysos at Yria, or the superb head of a man with the portrait features of the Roman emperor Gallienus, of the third century AD.

The transfer of the capital of the Roman Empire to Constantinople brought a final flickering for the ancient society of Naxos. The houses of the city spread over a large area, which shows an upsurge in activity and an increase in population. Some of these residences were decorated with interesting mosaics and murals (fig. 418). However, here too the advent of Christianity set its seal on a new era.

418. Naxos. Nymph riding a sea-taurus. Mosaic floor from a Late Antique house in the city of Naxos. Naxos Archaeological Museum.

419. Naxos. Statue of Mark Anthony from the temple at Yria. Anthony was worshipped on Naxos as New Dionysos after 41 BC. Represented on the cuirass are: above the sculptural group of the Punishment of Dirke, which Anthony had taken from Rhodes to Rome, in the middle Anthony's ancestor Hercules with the Nemean Lion, and below Dionysos with the panther. After Octavian came to power, the statue was dedicated to him, by changing the head. Later, when the temple was converted into a church, it remained standing and was interpreted as the soldier-saint, St George. Naxos Archaeological Museum.

Lesser Cyclades

OLGA PHILANIOTOU

Ranged like a protective arc facing the south coast of Naxos are Herakleia, Schinousa, Kouphonisia and Keros with Antikeria, while Donousa appears to have escaped eastward.

Small and stony, these islands were in various periods home to societies which exploited all their natural potential: every inch of cultivable land, the rich fishing grounds and, primarily, their central position in the Aegean. With their safe anchorages, sometimes serving as pirates' lairs, they lie on the sealanes linking North and South, East and West. Archaeology has revealed the important role they played in eras when the Cyclades opened up to the outside world. Particularly interesting, for example, is the relationship between the Early Cycladic pottery on Pano Kouphonisi and the finds from Aghia Photia in Crete, as well as the Minoan-Mycenaean influences on the early Late Cycladic pottery found on Kato Kouphonisi. Interesting too is the existence of a Late Geometric settlement on this same island and of a contemporary trading station on Donousa, on routes of communication with the east and south Aegean, in the period (8th century BC) when Naxos joined the Chalkideans in founding the first colony of Naxos in Sicily.

However, the smallness of these island was a counterweight to their advantageous location. They were unable to tolerate protracted periods of drought or external pressures, as a result of which they were almost totally abandoned for some intervals of time. In eighteenth- and nineteenth-century documents they are referred to as "*Eremonisia*" (desert islands), grazing land for the Chozoviotissa monastery on Amorgos, while foreign travellers in the same period comment on the rare plants of Donousa and observe that Schinousa – and not Schoinousa as its name is usually but erroneously spelt – supplied Amorgos with timber. Relations between these small islands and their larger neighbours – Naxos and Amorgos – were ambivalent. It is in the Lesser Cyclades that one appreciates more than anywhere else both the singularities and the dynamism of Early Cycladic Culture.

Donousa

At the borderline of the Aegean with the Ikarian Sea, about 10 miles east of Naxos, Donousa appears isolated from the rest of the Cyclades and exposed to all weathers. Nevertheless, precisely because of its position it was at times an obligatory port of call on various maritime crossings: Virgil mentions it on Aeneas' route from Troy to Italy, while travellers in the eighteenth and nineteenth centuries, sailing from Naxos to Patmos or vice-versa, always passed by way of Donousa.

On his rock that rises to the impressive height, for its size, of 489 metres a.s.l., there was more than one Early Cycladic settlement. Excavations have revealed that upon the ruins of one of them, at Vathy Limenari (fig. 421) on the southeast coast of the island, on a steep headland with a deep

420

haven protected from the north wind, a very interesting but short-lived fortified settlement was founded later, dated between the ninth and the eighth century BC. The Dodecanesian traits in its pottery (fig. 420), in addition to the Cycladic-Naxian ones, indicate that this was a trading station on a maritime route linking Attica and Euboea with the east Aegean. This was the same route as on which lay Zagora and Ypsili on Andros, Kardiani, Chtikado and the better preserved and of greater longevity Xobourgo on Tinos.

In the first century BC Mark Anthony ceded Donousa to the Rhodians, while in imperial times it was, like other small islands in the Aegean, a place of exile.

Kouphonisia (Pano and Kato Kouphonisi)

Pano Kouphonisi, one of the smallest islands in the complex, is today the most densely populated and prosperous, thanks to fishing, tourism and its proximity to the southeast coast of Naxos, to where it sends its produce immediately and from where it imports what it needs. The Kouphonisians' absolute control of the local maritime communications inevitably recalls, *mutatis mutandis*, the Cycladic islanders' activity in this sector in the Early Bronze Age (3rd millennium BC).

On this island a large Early Cycladic cemetery with peculiar chamber graves has been excavated at the site of Agrilia, and another two cemeteries in the vicinity of Pano Mylos and Loutra. In addition to small farmsteads, there was one Early Cycladic settlement on the east side of the modern village and a second, unfortunately almost totally destroyed by erosion, to the west, close to the chapel of St Nicholas at the site of Potamia (figs 422, 423).

The present village appears to have been built on the site of a large Roman settlement that spread as far as Loutra Bay. There are various Early Christian remains, marble closure slabs, etc., in the churches of St George and of St Nicholas, while the foundations of Early Christian basilicas are visible in at least two places on the island.

420. Donousa. Peculiar Geometric vase with strong Dodecanesian influences, from the settlement at Vathy Limenari, 8th c. BC. Naxos Archaeological Museum.

421. Donousa. Vathy Limenari on the promontory where the important Geometric settlement was excavated.

422. The sea passage between Pano and Kato Kouphonisia, as seen from the Early Cycladic settlement at the site of Potamia.

423. Pano Kouphonisi. Excavation of an Early Cycladic settlement at the site of Potamia, mid-3rd millennium BC.

LESSER CYCLADES | **287**

424. Keros. Early Cycladic marble figurine, height 0.58 m. A classic example of the Spedos variety, most probably carved in Naxos, it represents the heyday of Early Cycladic art. Mid-3rd millennium BC, Naxos Archaeological Museum.

425. Keros. Marble figurine of a flute-player, mid-3rd millennium BC. Athens, National Archaeological Museum.

426. Pano Kouphonisi, Aghios Nikolaos-Potamia. Visible in the background is Keros, with Kato Kouphonisi in between.

Although no traces of settlement between Early Cycladic and Roman times have been located on Pano Kouphonisi, on the now deserted Kato Kouphonisi (fig. 422), as mentioned above, remains from the early Late Cycladic period (15th century BC), with strong Minoan/Mycenaean influences, have been uncovered, as well as a Late Geometric settlement on a site with exceptional visibility over a wide area of sea.

Keros

Uninhabited today, despite its size – only Herakleia is bigger –, Keros has been associated with the zenith of the Early Cycladic period (the so-called Keros-Syros culture, 2700-2300 BC). In the popular imagination it is almost legendary for the remarkable number and quality of Early Cycladic finds from there, which include some of the loveliest examples of stone-carving and sculpture, such as the figurines of the harpist (fig. 33) and the flute-player (fig. 425), in the National Archaeological Museum. Even the shape of Keros, as seen from Kouphonisi or Naxos, brings to mind a Cycladic figurine of a reclining pregnant female.

Habitation on Keros during the Early Bronze Age is documented by dispersed remains on the main island and an important settlement on the islet of Daskalio, which was a peninsula in Antiquity. Recent geological surveys have discovered copper ore. A tragically looted and obscure Early Cycladic

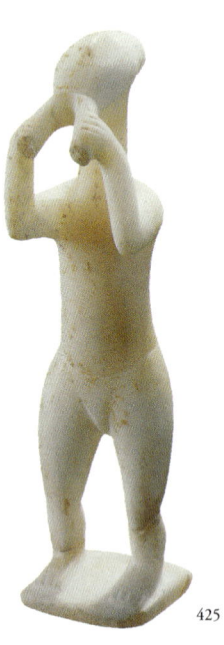

288 | CYCLADES

site on the north coast at Kavos, from which multitudinous fragments of marble figurines (fig. 424) and vessels have enriched museums and private collections worldwide, has contributed considerably to disseminating the island's myth. It is not known whether this is a cemetery of exceptional wealth or a sanctuary, like Delos in historical times, or an ossuary for bones removed from burials and a place for cult of the dead.

In the fifth century BC Keros appears in the ancient sources as paying tax to Athens. Fortifications of the historical period have been identified at Gerani, possibly built on the site of an Early Cycladic citadel, and on the south side at the locality Megalo Kastro.

Schinousa

Schinousa is small and almost flat, with one hill on which stands a fort (Kastro) of Late Classical times, perhaps built on the site of an Early Cycladic citadel. Although inland, the Kastro, which continued in use into Roman times, is not very far from the sea. A large Hellenistic and Roman settlement has been located at the coastal site of Tsigouri, as well as an Early Christian basilica, while marble architectural members of Early Christian and Byzantine date, from various parts of the island, have been gathered together in the village. The archaeologist Ludwig Ross had observed ancient terraces and it is tempting to see a direct reflection of Antiquity in the later, purely rural character of Schinousa, where traditional oil-presses and flourmills operated until recently.

427. Herakleia. Spirals of the Early Cycladic period (3rd millennium BC) carved on rocks in pecking technique, in the area of Aghios Athanasios.

428. Herakleia, Kastro. Part of a tower of the 4th century BC, incorporated into a later rural construction.

Herakleia

Protected from the north winds by the landmass of Naxos, Herakleia is the westernmost, the biggest and the highest island in the southern complex of the Lesser Cyclades (18 km^2, max. altitude 418 m.).

A large Early Cycladic settlement has been identified at Aghios Mamas, while on the site of the Kastro of historical times, overlooking Leivadi Bay, there may have been an Early Cycladic citadel. Prehistoric habitation is also indicated by the spirals carved on the rocks by pecking technique (fig. 427), a characteristic of the Early Cycladic period, in the area of Aghios Athanasios and elsewhere on the island. Early Cycladic objects exhibited in museums and private collections, among them a head of an Early Cycladic marble statue, if indeed found on Herakleia as reported, give a picture of a flourishing island in this period.

The Herakleia Cave perhaps corresponds in the longevity of its habitation to the Zas Cave on Naxos. Long-lived too was the settlement at Aghios Mamas, where surface pottery includes not only Early Cycladic but also Mycenaean, Geometric and later material. In addition to the small fortification of Kastro (fig. 428) and the scattered finds, it seems from an inscription of the third century BC that Herakleia had a thriving and autonomous society which, judging by its archaeological remains, evidently lived on into Hellenistic and Roman times.

Amorgos

Lila Marangou

Of the several ancient names by which the easternmost island in the Cyclades was known, the name Amorgos, the provenance and exact meaning of which are unknown, has prevailed.

Archaeological finds, the sole source of information for eras without script, have shown recently that the earliest human habitation of the island goes back to the so-called Late or Final Neolithic period (late 5th millennium BC). On the basis of material and organic remains, humble artifacts of obsidian, the shiny black volcanic stone from Melos – blades, flakes, cores and numerous arrowheads –, handmade clay vases and vessels for everyday use, and one figurine, as well as seeds of cereals, seashells and bones of sheep and goats from the later sanctuary on the summit of the ancient city of Minoa, the earliest permanent installation on the island has been identified securely. The few other finds attest to relations between Amorgos and Naxos, Paros and other more distant regions, as well as to the substrate of the culture that flourished in the Cyclades during the Early Bronze Age, known as Cycladic.

The island's history during the third millennium BC is the most fully documented. Old and new archaeological finds confirm that Amorgos, surely because of its privileged geographical location and the wide harbour at Katapola, as well as to the many bays-anchorages on the south coast, was one of the most important centres of the Cycladic Culture. From the early nineteenth century Amorgos is known as the provenance of significant artefacts, such as the famed Cycladic marble figurines – some veritable statues – which are displayed in the National Archaeological Museum in Athens (figs 429, 430), as well as many museums and private collections in Europe and America.

However, apart from the old archaeological finds, some fortuitous and some from the excavations conducted by Christos Tsountas, many new ones from excavations and surface surveys, from settlements and cemeteries, have enriched our knowledge of the demographic pattern of the island in the third millennium BC. In order to reconstruct the picture of life in those times, reliable information can be drawn from objects for daily use from the settlement being excavated at Markiani, where remains of houses and of the fortification wall with semicircular bastions have been revealed. However, new evidence on burial habits has come from recent chance finds and, primarily, from the rescue excavation of a cluster of graves at Aghios Pavlos, Aigiale, opposite the islet of Nikouria. Human skeletal remains were recovered, as well as grave goods, objects that accompanied the dead in their last resting place.

Very little is known about life on Amorgos in the first half of the second millennium BC, the Middle Bronze Age, the so-called Middle Cycladic period, certainly because of gap in systematic archaeological research.

From the final cultural phases in the late second millennium BC, the Late Bronze Age, the so-called Late Cycladic period, important testimonies have survived, such as the rock-cut chamber

429

290 | CYCLADES

tombs at Xylokeratidi on the north shore of Katapola harbour (figs 431, 432). Although the tombs had been looted, the remaining sherds of painted vases, beads, etc., are among the usual grave goods of the latter years of Mycenaean Civilization (14th-13th century BC). The area awaits systematic investigation, but the few building remains and many vase sherds point to the existence there of an important Mycenaean installation.

Knowledge of life in the Cyclades after the break up of the Mycenaean kingdoms, in early historical times, the so-called Protogeometric and Geometric periods (11th-8th century BC), is based primarily on material cultural remains, because of the lack of contemporary written sources. These are finds documented by excavation and more rarely later information and traditions, frequently mythical in character.

Until twenty years ago, before systematic archaeological research commenced on Amorgos, very little was known about the Iron Age and the Early Archaic period (7th century BC). Both the building remains of the island's three cities, Aigiale, Arkesine and Minoa, the sites of which had been identified by L. Ross in 1837, and the insriptions were from later periods, from the fourth century BC to the third century AD.

Nevertheless, serious indications of earlier habitation were a few epigraphic testimonies, such as the Archaic funerary inscriptions at Aigiale, as well as isolated finds, fortuitous or from the "excavations" made in the three cities by G. Deschamps, on behalf of the French Archaeological School at Athens, in 1888.

The picture of the island in Classical times (5th-4th century BC) was likewise extremely patchy. It is known from Attic inscriptions with the names of the vassal allies of the Athenians, in which the inhabitants of the three cities are referred to by the common ethnic name Ἀμόργιοι (Amorgians), that Amorgos participated in the First Athenian League in the year 434 BC and in the Second Athenian League in 357 BC.

In contrast, valuable information for reconstructing the political history, the regime and the daily life in the three cities in Hellenistic time (late 4th-2nd century BC) and under Roman rule (1st century BC-4th century AD) is preserved in the numerous inscriptions, of public and private character. The public documents of the cities, primarily the decrees of the deme, record the alternations of κηδεμόνες (guardians) in the third and second centuries BC, the dependence of the cities on the prevailing powers in the Aegean – Macedonians, Ptolemies, Samians, Rhodians and Romans – as well as the settling of foreigners, of Samians in Minoa, of Naxians in Arkesine and of Milesians in Aigiale.

From 133 BC, the τρίπολις νήσος (three-citied island) of Amorgos was subject to the newly instituted Province of Asia, and in the first century AD, according to the Roman historian Tacitus (*Annales* IV 13, 30), it was a place of banishment for Roman politicians. In AD

429. Amorgos. Cycladic marble figurine from Dokathismata, 3rd millennium BC. Athens, National Archaeological Museum.

430. Amorgos. Head of a Cycladic marble figurine, 3rd millennium BC. Athens, National Archaeological Museum.

431. Amorgos. The harbour of Katapola and in the background the site of Xylokeratidi, where the Mycenaean cemetery of chamber tombs is located.

AMORGOS | 291

294, in the reign of Diocletian (AD 284-305), Amorgos was included in the Province of the Islands (*provincia insularum*), capital of which was Rhodes.

Since the 1970s, thanks to surface surveys and reconnoitering of the island, and mainly thanks to systematic excavations carried out since 1981 at Minoa, under the auspices of the Archaeological Society at Athens, new highly important evidence has come to light, of early historical times (1100-700 BC) and the Archaic period (7th-6th century BC), and of the ensuing centuries until the final abandonment of all three cities in the fourth century AD.

According to recent archaeological data, all three cities were founded around the eleventh century BC on high, naturally fortified hills, close to or distant from the sea, and all were abandoned in the fourth century AD.

Aigiale (fig. 434), whose name lives on in the corrupted form Giali, preserves not only the fortification wall but also important building remains in now uncultivated fields and meadows, as well as inscriptions carved on the rocks. The public buildings mentioned in the inscriptions, such as the agoranomion (market inspectors' headquarters), the archeion (archive), the gymnasium, and the sanctuaries and temples, such as of Zeus Polieus and Athena Polias, of Hera and Apollo, of Poseidon, of Eileithyia, of the Mother of the Gods, of Tyche, of Isis and Sarapis, etc., remain unknown. Although the city awaits excavation, inscriptions and coins, mainly the "coppers" Aigiale issued during the third and second centuries BC, towers in the countryside and moveable finds help in part to reconstruct the history of the body politic and the religious life, from Hellenistic times (3rd century BC) until the fourth century AD.

However, several marble sculptures of Archaic (fig. 433), Classical and Hellenistic times, inscriptions from the ancient city and from G. Deschamps's "excavations", as well as others from the wider area and the harbour at modern Ormos, fortuitous finds or looters' spoils – today in museums in Greece and abroad, as well as in the Amorgos Archaeological Collection – add significant evidence on the daily life, the cultural relations, commercial contacts and aesthetic preferences of the citizens of Aigiale.

According to textual testimonies, Arkesine was a Naxian colony. Here too the monumental wall encircling the city (fig. 438), the double gateway known as "Portes" (fig. 437) and copious building remains of mainly Classical and Hellenistic times are visible beneath the high field

432. Amorgos. Xylokeratidi. Mycenaean chamber tomb with dromos cut in the bedrock, at the locality Katiphorida.

433. Amorgos. Palmette finial of a grave stele from Aigiale. Made of Parian marble, it dates from the Late Archaic period (510 BC). Amorgos Archaeological Collection.

434. Amorgos. View of ancient Aigiale at the locality Vigla, close to the village of Tholaria.

walls, built of ancient blocks, architectural members and fragments of monumental statues. Because the city has not been excavated systematically, its layout and the position of the public and religious buildings referred to in inscriptions are unknown. These include the agora, the theatre, the gymnasium, etc., the temples of Apollo Delios, of Hera, and the sanctuaries of Artemis, Aphrodite Ourania "en Aspidi", Demeter, Zeus Apotropaios, Eileithyia, Dionysos, and others. The city's history is documented not only by the inscriptions of diverse content and the copper coins issued in the third and second centuries BC, but also by many moveable finds, such as the marble sculptures in the National Archaeological Museum, Athens (fig. 435) and in Syros, as well as several new fragments from Archaic, Classical and Hellenistic works, in the Amorgos Archaeological Collection.

Important information on the exploitation and the protection of the agricultural "*Lebensraum*" in Hellenistic times is provided by the towers, the isolated fortified multi-purpose buildings that stand in the rural territory of Arkesine. Outstanding among them is the tower at Chorio (figs 436, 439), adjacent to the chapel of the Holy Trinity (Aghia Triada), which is the sole ancient monument on Amorgos that survives in excellent condition (25.31 x 11.40 m.) to a maximum height of 5.60 m. In fact, it is the best-preserved rectangular tower in the Cyclades. Although known since 1843, the first rescue works commenced in 1993.

Minoa, about half way along the north coast, overlooks the harbour at Katapola, which is identified as the ancient Limen, on the south slope of Mountoulia Hill. (fig. 445).

The name Minoa, widely diffused from Sicily to the Asia Minor littoral, the coast of the Levant and Arabia, is encountered as the name of a city on Crete, Paros, Siphnos and Samos. The only city whose site had been identified securely is Minoa on Amorgos. Although its name had been forgotten, memories of the old inhabitants lived on in local lore about the palace of Minos on Mountoulia, the impressive Roman cistern (2nd century AD) that dominates in the midst of the ruins, the tomb of Minos in the rocky crevice on the summit of the hill, and the throne of Minos in the rock shelter. The kernel of truth in these fanciful narratives was confirmed by inscriptions in which, from the third century BC, the word is written as the name of the city, as an adjective, demotic name of the inhabitants, Μινωίτης (Minoan, the resident of Minoa) and as epithet of the god worshipped in the city, Dionysos.

Excavations ongoing at Minoa since 1981 have revealed building remains that are important for reconstructing the earlier settlement nucleus, as well as the various forms of the city's urban tissue. The thousands of datable moveable finds of various periods and diverse categories, in particular the stratified finds (fig. 444), yield manifold and invaluable information on habitation in prehistoric times and on the newly-founded settlement of early historical times, as well

435. Amorgos. Marble head of Sarapis from Arkesine, Early Hellenistic period. Athens, National Archaeological Museum.

436. Amorgos. The tower at Chorio-Aghia Triada, Arkesine.

437. Amorgos. Arkesine. The double gateway: "Portes".

438. Amorgos. Arkesine. Partial view of the wall of the ancient city.

439. Amorgos. Aerial view of the tower at Chorio-Aghia Triada (4th c. BC).

as for reconstituting the picture of the walled city from the Archaic period (7th-6th century BC) to the third century AD. Marble sculptures dated from the sixth century BC to the third century AD, inscriptions, architectural members and above all countless utilitarian and votive objects, of clay and of metal, and also of precious materials such as gold, ivory (fig. 440) and glass, sketch a picture of everyday life and bring the building remains to life

On the lowest terrace of the south side of the hill, remains of the settlement nucleus from the eleventh century BC to the years of the city's abandonment in the third century AD, coexist harmoniously.

As a consequence of continuous habitation on the same site from the eleventh century BC to the third century AD, extensive building remains of early historical times (10th-8th century BC) have not survived. The excavation has uncovered important remnants, such as the grave enclosure, the later Ἱερό τῶν κεκμηκότων (sanctuary of the dead), the stepped street cut in the bedrock and leading to the upper terraces and the earliest cult area with the ash deposit (*apothetes*) and the enclosure wall with the foundation sacrifice.

There is no testimony in the ancient sources and inscriptions on the history of Minoa in Homeric times, but this can be documented by new archaeological evidence, such as the manmade fortification of the acropolis and the old settlement, which acquired the aspect of a fortified city. An important cult building complex of the eighth century BC has been revealed on the summit of the hill (255 m. a.s.l.), on the acropolis overlooking the harbour at Katapola (fig. 445) and at the very edge of the cavernous chasm near the gateway and the northeast bastion of the wall.

In Classical times, in the years of the Athenian hegemony, the old fortification wall was repaired in places, reinforced with bastions and extended to the southwest slope and on the north side as far as Kato Akrotiri, in order to protect land on which there were no buildings but which was of vital importance for the city's self-sufficiency.

Impressive are the cult and public buildings of the Hellenistic period (late 4th-1st century BC): the central monumental gateway (fig. 442), the marble temple (fig. 443) and the gymnasium, which is mentioned in inscriptions (fig. 441), with the excellently preserved latrine

439

house. The theatre, the bouleuterion, the stoa of the agora, the Metroon, the temple of Dionysos Minoites and other buildings referred to in inscriptions have not been revealed so far.

Among the few constructions of the Roman period (1st-4th century AD), outstanding are the "Palatia" (= palace), the very high well-built wall and the collapsed vault of the cistern (2nd century AD), which in the fertile imagination of Amorgians was associated with Minos, the legendary founder of the city that bears his name.

In Roman times, as the inscriptions and the abundant building remains attest, life shifted gradually towards the harbour, Limen, present Katapola. From the fourth century AD, when Christianity had prevailed, the city of Minoa was finally abandoned, after one thousand four hundred years of continuous life there. Its ruins were a ready source of construction material for the dry-stone walls of the arable tracts, which for centuries discreet "kept buried in the fields, wells and cisterns, treasure troves" of precious information.

296 | CYCLADES

440. Amorgos. Ivory relief head of a female, Hellenistic period, from Minoa. Amorgos Archaeological Collection.

441. Amorgos, Minoa. The discovery of storage jars for olive oil, in the course of excavating the gymnasium, permitted identification of the space as the *pitheon* (pithoi storeroom), *elaiothesion* (olive oil store) of the gymnasium.

442. Amorgos, Minoa. The marble gateway in the fortification wall, which is dated to Early Hellenistic times (late 4th-early 3rd c. BC). The wall became redundant in the Roman period (1st c. BC), when the city lost its autonomy and liberty.

443. Amorgos, Minoa. All-marble Doric temple with pebble floor. Preserved is the headless cult statue, possibly of Apollo, product of an Asia Minor workshop of the early 2nd c. BC.

444. Amorgos, Minoa. Amphora containing a child burial (*enchytrismos*) and grave goods (8th c. BC). Amorgos Archaeological Collection.

445. Amorgos, Minoa. Aerial view of the acropolis and the lower city.

Ios, Sikinos, Pholegandros

MARISA MARTHARI

Ios

Ios (107 km²) is a mountainous island with many small plains, at the centre of the southern Cyclades. The sole excavation conducted before the 1980s was by the Belgian P. Graindor, in 1904, in the area of the temple of Apollo Pythios in the ancient city of Ios, which occupied the same site as the present Chora. Recent archaeological research on Ios was begun by the Archaeological Service in the 1980s, under the pressure of the island's rapid development as a tourist destination, and continues to this day. Surface surveys, collecting of fortuitous finds, rescue and systematic excavations have yielded important information on the island's cultural course in both prehistoric and historical times.

Archaeological evidence shows that Ios was inhabited by man from at least the Early Bronze Age (3rd millennium BC). It appears as flourishing, densely populated and with a wide-ranging network of contacts in the mature period of this era (Early Cycladic II, 2700-2400/2300 BC), when communications in the Aegean were at their peak. Thriving settlements existed mainly on the promontories and the coastal hills, at Plakotos, Aghia Theodoti, Psathonisi, Plakes, Manganari and Skarkos.

Skarkos is not only the largest and most notable settlement on the island, but also one of the most important Cycladic settlements of the third millennium BC. Particularly significant is the unique state of preservation, with walls up to 3 and 4 metres high, and two-storey buildings, since the preservation of the very few other contemporary Cycladic settlements is extremely poor.

The size of the settlement, which is in a privileged location at about the midpoint of the west coast of Ios (fig. 447), is estimated at about 1.1 hectares. A considerable part of it was revealed in a decade of excavations seasons (1986-1996). The settlement tissue is dense and the plan is pericentric. Interposed between the building *insulae* are 2 metre-wide streets and quadrilateral squares. As a rule, the impressive stone-built buildings comprise a ground floor and an upper storey (fig. 448), as well as courtyards enclosed by high walls.

Abundant moveable finds were brought to light. The pottery includes tableware, storage jars (fig. 449) and cooking vessels, which can be restored complete – exceptionally rare for pottery from an Early Cycladic settlement. There is a variety of stone vessels and tools, of schist (fig. 446) and of marble. Obsidian technology was sophisticated and a few objects of lead or bronze have also come to light.

The economy of the settlement at Skarkos was based on agriculture and stock-raising, as is deduced from the archaeo-botanical remains and the bones of sheep and goats found, as well as on seafaring. There is archaeological

446. Ios. Stone ellipsoid grinder and grinding stone with traces of red pigment, as well as a lump of red mineral, from the Early Cycladic settlement at Skarkos. Several such grinders with traces of red and more rarely blue pigment, which were obviously used for pulverizing solid pigments, have been found. One use of these materials was for face and body painting, as is apparent from the coloured decoration of some anthropomorphic figurines and from other evidence. Ios Archaeological Museum.

447. Ios. The Early Cycladic settlement at Skarkos stands on a low hill in about the centre of the fertile Kato Kampos valley, in the creek of one of the largest and safest natural harbours in the Cyclades. The harbour is opposite Sikinos and is also a nodal point for important sea routes.

448. Ios, Skarkos. Detail of a room of a two-storey building which stands to a height of 4 m. The room has two cupboards in the north wall of the ground floor, in which vessels were stored.

449. Ios. Pithos 1.07 m. high from the Early Cycladic settlement at Skarkos. This is the largest restorable clay vase known from a settlement of the 3rd millennium BC in the Cyclades. It was found in a storage space in the upper storey of a big building, together with other vases of large capacity. Ios Archaeological Museum.

450. Ios. Conical cups from the Middle-Late Cycladic cemetery at Skarkos (mid-2nd millennium BC). They were grave goods accompanying, along with other vases, the burial of a child. The cups are locally-produced imitations of Minoan models. Conical cups, some containing sheep and goat bones – obviously food residues –, and cooking pots were brought to light around and outside certain graves, indicating that rituals of some kind (*nekrodeipna* = meals for the dead) took place in the cemeteries. Ios Archaeological Museum.

IOS | 299

evidence of the import of raw materials, stone, clay and metal vessels or tools, as well as of organic substances, which were transported to the island in appropriate vessels. Contacts are attested with nearby and far-off Cycladic islands, with mainland Greece, Crete and Asia Minor. Last, the coexistence of both large and humble buildings, and the discovery of seals and an appreciable number of clay objects with seal impressions point to the existence of a rather complex social organization.

Life on Ios continued throughout the Middle and the Late Bronze Age (2nd millennium BC). Of importance for this period is the cemetery covering some parts of the Early Cycladic settlement at Skarkos. The grave goods supplement our knowledge of society in the southwest Cyclades from 1700 to 1400 BC, in the sector of burial habits (fig. 450), since this knowledge is based mainly on the excavation of cities such as at Akrotiri on Thera and Phylakopi on Melos, the cemeteries of which have not been explored. The finds from the cemetery at Skarkos also show that Ios followed the fortunes of the other Cycladic islands in this period, which came

451. Ios. Upper part of a Late Archaic grave stele (late 6th c. BC) of preserved height 1.06 m., from a cemetery of the ancient city of Ios. Represented is the head and torso of a warrior who steadies his helmet with his right hand, while with the left he holds the hilt of his sword. A fortuitous find, as is the lower part of a grave stele in fig. 452. The two stelai of high artistic quality are products of a choice Cycladic workshop, perhaps the Parian. Ios Archaeological Museum.

452. Ios. Lower part of a Late Archaic grave stele in white marble, of present height 0.80 m., from a cemetery of the ancient city of Ios. The stele, an outstanding work of island art, preserves the calves of a male figure turned left. Late 6th c. BC. Ios Archaeological Museum.

within the sphere of influence of Crete and subsequently belonged to the periphery of the Mycenaean world.

The transition to historical times remains obscure for Ios, since investigations have produced no evidence associated with the Protogeometric and Geometric periods. The only link between the two eras is the ancient tradition that Ionians led by Neleus son of Kodros, a hero connected with the Mycenaean kingdom of Thebes, were the founding settlers (*oikistai*) of the island. Ancient tradition also associates Ios closely with Homer (fig. 453).

Already from the Archaic period Ios was a small city-state, which because of its weakness was obliged to accept the hegemony of the maritime powers that successively dominated the Aegean. During the Classical period it was a member of the Athenian League. In Hellenistic times it participated in the *Koinon* of Islanders. During the interval 246-220 BC it was in the sphere of influence of the Macedonian realm, while from 220 until at least the mid-second century BC it was linked closely with Rhodes.

Principal urban centre on Ios, at least from Archaic times onwards, was the homonymous city, the existence of which is also attested by the geographer Claudius Ptolemy (III 15, 28): "Ios island and city". As excavations have revealed, the city was organized around the hill of the Kastro, from the Archaic period into Late Antiquity, and overlooked the harbour. This naturally fortified site was reinforced by a wall, encircling the entire hill. Chance finds collected from the area of the city and its cemeteries, and now housed in the Ios Archaeological Museum, include architectural members, numerous inscriptions, fragments of three-dimensional sculptures and of reliefs (figs 451, 452).

Outside the ancient city, ruins of temple-like edifices and a Roman aqueduct exist in the coastal zone of Psathi-Aghia Theodoti, on the east of the island. On summits suitable for lookout posts, in the interior and on the shore, ruins of round or rectangular towers are visible (Mersynia, Psaropyrgos, and elsewhere), while at the site of Ellinika in Epano Kampos, stands a Hellenistic two-storey rural building, in very good condition. At the site of Magazia, in the north, lie the ruins of a Roman coastal (town *vicus*).

The regime of Ios was democratic, as is surmised from the rich corpus of epigraphic testimonies. In Hellenistic times at least, Ios had a class of wealthy citizens whose members held offices and were in a position to assume administrative responsibilities. Sources of their wealth were agriculture, stock-raising and trade. Ios had mercantile and economic relations with other Cycladic and Aegean cities, as is borne out by the presence of *proxenoi* on the island. Under Roman rule, Italian merchants (*negotiatores*) were present in Ios, as in most Cycladic islands.

453. Ios. Inscribed stele declaring a date of sacrifice, of height 0.42 m., found at Aghia Theodoti, close to the homonymous church. It emerges from the inscription that the calendar of Ios included the month *Homerea*. The ancient city of Ios was one of the seven cities that claimed to be the birthplace of Homer, while several ancient authors refer to the death and burial of the poet, and of his mother, on the island. Indeed, from the mid-4th c. BC the idealized portrait head of Homer features on the coins of Ios, along with the legend ΟΜΗΡΟΣ on the reverse, for propaganda reasons. The tradition continued on the island's coinage during Roman imperial times. Ios Archaeological Museum.

Sikinos, Pholegandros

Sikinos (41 km.2) and Pholegandros (33 km.2) are two small, rocky and barren islands between which lies the islet Kardiotissa (Lagousa in Antiquity, where inscriptions have been found). Pholegandros was called "*sidereie*" (of iron) by the ancient Greeks, an epithet coined by the poet Aratos, because of its rugged terrain. Only limited fieldwork has been carried out on Sikinos and Pholegandros, and our knowledge of these islands' history is filled out by epigraphic testimonies and literary sources.

Both islands were settled at least by the Early Bronze Age (3rd millennium BC), as is apparent from the surface scatter of pottery sherds and obsidian artifacts at several sites. Noteworthy settlements of this period developed on Sikinos at Palaiokastro, on the north tip, and Katergo, in the middle of the east coast. On Pholegandros there is evidence of important installations on Panaghia Hill in Chora and on the Kastellos Peninsula on the northeast coast. Indeed, at this latter site there are visible building remains of an Early Cycladic II period (2700-2400/2300 BC) settlement, possibly walled.

Continuity of settlement on Pholegandros during the Middle and the Late Bronze Age (2nd millennium BC) is evidenced by surface finds of these periods, mainly pottery, observed at Pountaki in the area of Karavostatis. According to ancient tradition, which may well echo the Minoanization of Pholegandros in the mid-2nd millennium BC, the founder-hero (*oikistes*) of the island was Pholegandros, son of Minos.

Although there is a dearth of finds from the second millennium BC on Sikinos, it is possible that the mythological tradition referring to the advent there of King Thoas of Lemnos, son of Dionysos and Ariadne, hints at settlement on the island in Mycenaean times. Sikinos, son of Thoas and the nymph Neida, is considered the founder-hero (*oikistes*). Certainly the myths echo

302 | CYCLADES

Sikinos's association with viticulture, from which its earlier name, Oinoe, also derives, as well as with the worship of Dionysos. It should be noted that the coins of Sikinos in the third century BC include the head of Dionysos and the bunch of grapes among their thematic repertoire.

In historical times both islands were inhabited by Dorians, although they clearly received Ionian influences because of the strong Athenian presence in the region. As a result, the Ionian dialect prevailed from the beginning of the Hellenistic period. Like the rest of the Dorian Cyclades, Pholegandros and Sikinos joined the First Athenian League as soon as it was founded (478/7 BC). After the Athenians' defeat at Aigos Potamoi (404 BC), they came into the Spartans' sphere of influence. Sikinos became a member of the Second Athenian League from the beginning (376/5 BC), whereas there is no information about Pholegandros.

The ancient city of Sikinos is located in the southwest of the island, on Aghia Marina Hill, overlooking a small bay. Building remains are visible, while a cemetery, which extends mainly on the south slope, has been identified. A fair distance to the east of city is an excellently-preserved Roman sepulchral monument that has been converted into a Christian church, as part of the monastery complex at Episkopi (figs 454, 455). There are remnants of an ancient city at Palaiokastro, in the north.

The ancient city of Pholegandros spreads over the Palaiokastro Hill in Chora, as far as the church of the Virgin. Building remains are visible and architectural members are dispersed over the entire area, while part of the defensive wall still stands. The cemetery must have been close by, as is surmised from the grave statues of Roman times found there, while others are still built into the walls of later constructions. On the seaward slope of Palaiokastro Hill is the Chrysospilia Cave, on the walls of which are many ephebic inscriptions, mainly of the fourth century BC (figs 456, 457).

454, 455. Sikinos. Heroon in the form of temple *in antis*, in the Doric order, with vaulted crypts, converted into a domed Christian church of the Mother of God (Theotokos), as part of the monastery complex at Episkopi. Dated to the 2nd c. AD.

456, 457. Pholegandros. Ephebic inscriptions on the walls of the Chrysospilia Cave, in which excavations have been conducted in recent years. The inscriptions are written in natural iron oxides. Pottery of historical times, Roman cisterns and evidence of phallic cult have been found in the cave.

Kimolos

ISMINI TRIANTI

Kimolos, the small island in the western Cyclades, to the northeast of Melos, is renowned since Antiquity for its chalk (*kimolia ge*), a white clay mineral used as soap and powder, as well as in medicine. Strabo (X 5,1) writes of "Cimolos, whence comes the Cimolian earth". Kimolos was also known for its figs (*kimoliai ischades*) and for its sea urchins, as it was also known as Echinousa, and a sea urchin (*achinos*) was represented on its coins.

Little is known about the prehistoric age on the island. A marble violin-shaped figurine, of unknown provenance, exhibited in the National Archaeological Museum in Athens (fig. 458), is claimed to be a characteristic example from the first phases of the Early Cycladic period (early 3rd millennium BC). A few vase sherds from the Mycenaean cemetery at Ellinika indicate that Kimolos was a port of call in the Mycenaean expansion in the Aegean, *circa* 1200 BC.

Ellinika or Limni, in the southwest of the island, was the site of the ancient city, which spread onto the island of Aghios Andreas, now 200 metres from the shore but once joined to the land. Today the city is submerged and only the extensive cemetery is visible on the coast (fig. 460). All the graves are looted, some have been washed away by the waves, while a few have been investigated and yielded finds dating from Mycenaean to Hellenistic times. Particularly rich are the graves of the Geometric period. This cemetery must be the provenance of one of the earliest grave stelai, dated around 700 BC and bearing a representation of a female figure with only

458. Kimolos. Marble violin-shaped figurine with traces of red pigment on the neck. The figurine had broken in Antiquity and was repaired, possibly using lead wire passed through the holes. Early 3rd millennium BC. Athens, National Archaeological Museum.

459. Kimolos. Grave stele with relief female figure. *C.* 700 BC. Kimolos Archaeological Museum.

460. Kimolos. The coast at Ellinika, site of the ancient city of Kimolos and the cemeteries.

461. Kimolos. Cycladic oinochoe in the Orientalizing style. Depicted in the shoulder zone is a winged horse between two winged griffins. In front of one griffin sits a small deer. The representation is complemented by geometric filling motifs, lozenges and zigzag lines in columns. Dated *c.* 700 BC. Kimolos Archaeological Museum.

462. Kimolos. Subgeometric krater (late 8th c. BC). In the handle zone are meander pattern and two six-petalled rosettes. Kimolos Archaeological Museum.

the upper body in relief (fig. 459). The head must have been attached in some way, while the body was perhaps painted on the flat surface of the lower part of the stele. A grave in the same cemetery was presumably adorned with a now headless female statue, life size and sculpted in coarse marble, which is dated to the Hellenistic period and is closely akin to the statues found in the ancient city of Melos.

Not far from Ellinika, in a well in the Deka Valley, Subgeometric and Orientalizing vases, of excellent quality and in good condition, were brought to light (figs 461, 462).

Kimolos is known to have joined the Athenian League in 425/4 BC and to have paid dues of 1,000 drachmas. In the fourth century BC the Kimolians claimed from the Melians the surrounding islets of Polyaigos, Eteireia and Lybeia (pres. Polivos, Aghios Efstathios and Aghios Georgios), which they were awarded after a trial at which Argeians were judges, as recorded in a now lost inscription. There is mention of a temple of Athena Polias on Kimolos in a third-century BC inscription found at Kastri (near Karystos) on Euboea. The inscription contains two honorary decrees of the Kimolians for a judge named Charianthos from Karystos. One copy was set up in the temple of Poseidon at Geraistos in Euboea and the other in the temple of Athena on Kimolos.

It is possible that Kimolos was later deserted, as is hypothesized from the total absence of information until the sixteenth century AD, when the Kastro was built on the opposite side of the island from Ellinika. This is a burg of fortified houses that could accommodate about one thousand persons, far more than the present population of Kimolos. The new museum, opened recently, may perhaps stimulate further investigation of the island's antiquities and history.

Melos

Ismini Trianti

Melos is the westernmost island in the Cyclades and the closest to the east coast of the Peloponnese. It owes its name either to Melos, the founder-hero (*oikistes*), or, more probably, to the apple (*melos*), which fruit is represented on its coins.

Striking features of the island's geomorphology are the deep Adamas Bay, the low hills and small plains in the eastern part, and the mountainous massif of Chalakas in the western. Melos is a volcanic island, rich in minerals, such as Melian earth (kaolin), aluminium, chalk, pumice, sulphur and others, which were known in Antiquity and are extracted to this day. The characteristic mineral, which also constitutes the principal reason for the island's development in prehistoric times, is obsidian, a black volcanic glass (fig. 463). Obsidian – stone of Opsios, who, according to Pliny, was the first to discover it in Aethiopia – is present in igneous rocks in nodules of differing size, from which conchoidal blades can be struck by pressure flaking. These were used as tools and weapons not only by the locals but also by other inhabitants of the prehistoric Aegean. Obsidian can be quarried at two places on the island, Demenegaki and Nychia.

Melos was densely inhabited in Antiquity, as is borne out be the 111 archaeological sites that were identified and recorded in a systematic surface survey conducted in 1982. Settlement on the island goes back to the Neolithic Age, when seafaring was already known, since from as early as the sixth millennium BC Melian obsidian was present at sites from Knossos in Crete to Nea Nikomideia in Macedonia. The Early Cycladic period (3rd millennium BC) on the island is attested mainly by cemeteries of rock-cut chambers. The cemetery at Rivari in Adamas Bay is the most recently excavated. There, deposited in hollows in the bedrock, piles of vases and other grave goods were found, the most important among which is a vessel in the form of a house.

Melos enjoyed a great heyday in Mycenaean times, when the main centre was at Phylakopi on the north coast (fig. 465). The settlement existed throughout the Bronze Age, from 2300 to 1100 BC, and four phases of life can be distinguished there. In the early phases Minoan influence is pronounced, whereas in the later ones it is Mycenaean, although local production and creation is much in evidence, especially in iconography (fig. 464). The walled city dates to the Late Helladic or Mycenaean period (1600-1100 BC) and had a megaron and a shrine, finds from which include a large clay female figurine, known as the "Lady of Phylakopi" (fig. 44), which is exhibited in the Melos Archaeological Museum.

Information on the Dorian inhabitants of Melos in historical times is given by Herodotus (VIII 48) "… the Melians (who are of Lacedaemonian stock) …") and Thucydides (V 84,2-4): "Now the Melians are colonists of the Lacedaemonians …" and (V 89): "… because you were colonists of the Lacedaemonians". Tradition has it that the first settlers were Minyans from Lemnos and Imbros. The Amyklaians had conceded them places in which to settle, but some left from there for Crete and in the course of their voyage remained on Melos.

463. Melos. Obsidian core and blades. The exceptionally hard shiny volcanic stone of Melos was used from the Mesolithic Age for making small tools, usually in the form of long blades.

The city of Melos, at the site of Klima, was founded in Geometric times (9th-8th century BC). Only its cemeteries are known, which are located on the upper terraces at Trypiti, where Geometric vases have been found. Precious objects of the Archaic period are also said to have been found in graves at Trypiti, such as seal-stones now in museums abroad and considered to be of Melian provenance, gold jewellery of exquisite quality and possibly from a Melian workshop, such as the gold rosettes of the second half of the seventh century BC, in the National Archaeological Museum (figs 469, 470), and large amphorae with mythological representations, also in the same museum, which recent research has shown to be products of a Parian workshop (fig. 468). Terracotta reliefs with mythological scenes, the well-known Melian reliefs, have also been found. The majority of these pieces were looted in clandestine excavations in the nineteenth century.

No buildings of the Archaic period have been identified. The ancient city has not been excavated systematically but the mighty walls still stand in several places and some parts are dated to Archaic times. The well-known Melos kouros, considered to be the creation of a Naxian workshop, dates from mid-sixth century BC (fig. 466) and is a funerary statue which probably

464. Melos, Phylakopi. Clay vessel, perhaps a lamp base, with painted representation of fishermen. A characteristic example of Cycladic iconography in the Middle Bronze Age (mid-2nd millennium BC). Athens, National Archaeological Museum.

465. Melos, Phylakopi. This is the site of one of the most important Bronze Age settlements in the Aegean. Today a large part of it is submerged, due to the erosion of the cliff by the sea. The site was excavated by the British School at Athens in the late 19th-early 20th c. and again during the 1970s. Very little is known about the Early Bronze Age settlement (Phylakopi I, 2300-2000 BC), but the contemporary cemetery was well organized and the graves were richly furnished. Phylakopi II, in the Middle Bronze Age (2000-1600 BC) flourished in the period when Crete was increasing its power and influence in the Aegean; at the end of this period the settlement was destroyed by fire. The new settlement (Phylakopi III, 1600-1400 BC) was protected by mighty walls, 6 m. thick. Its urban layout included two-storey buildings of rectangular ground plan, decorated with wall-paintings. After a new destruction, possibly due to Mycenaeans from the Greek Mainland, who were expanding into the Aegean at that time, the inhabitants of Phylakopi IV (1400-1100 BC) strengthened the fortification. There are clear signs of Mycenaean influence, with the erection of a megaron and the founding of a sanctuary of Helladic type. The city was abandoned at the end of the Mycenaean era. A project to arrange the archaeological site of Phylakopi, by the XXI Ephorate of Antiquities, is in progress.

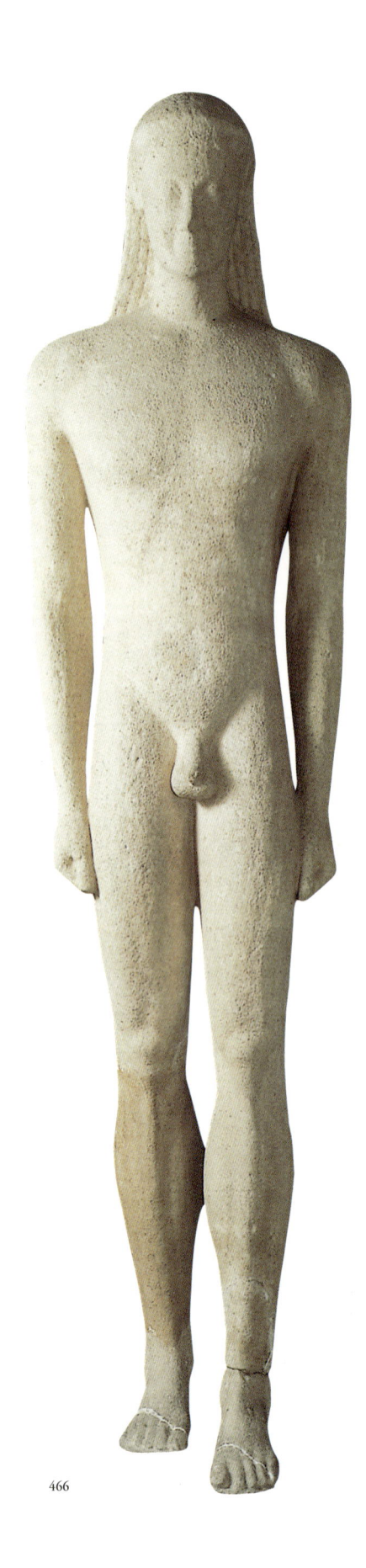

466. Melos. Marble kouros. The nude male figure has a slim torso, a smiling face and long hair falling on the back. The larger than life size statue (h. 2.14 m.) probably stood on the tomb of a young man. Product of a Cycladic workshop, it is dated *c.* 550 BC. Athens, National Archaeological Museum.

467. Melos. Marble disc with relief bust of a goddess, possibly Aphrodite. The long neck, determined chin, half-open lips and relatively small eye, as well as the smooth hair devoid of details and drawn behind into a snood (*sakkos*), and the pervasive severity of the work date it to the years around 460 BC. Athens, National Archaeological Museum.

468. Melos. Large Cycladic pithamphora from a Parian workshop, with representation of Apollo kitharode on a chariot drawn by winged horses. Accompanying him are two female figures, Muses or Hyperborean Maidens, while he is received by his sister Artemis, holding with one hand a deer by its horns and in the other a bow. Is the god returning from the land of the Hyperboreans? Depicted on the neck of the vase are two armed male figures and a female at the edge of the representation. Dated to the decade 540-530 BC. Athens, National Archaeological Museum.

308 | CYCLADES

stood on the tomb of a young man of that period. Last, a peculiar monument in the form of a marble curved disc with a female head in profile, possibly of the goddess Aphrodite, must have been sculpted in the years of the Severe Style (fig. 467).

Almost nothing is known about the output of artworks in Classical times. This is probably due to the total destruction of the city of Melos by the Athenians in 416 BC, a catastrophe recounted by Thucydides (V 84,11-13), who also records the dialogue between the Melian archons and the Athenian ambassadors, which preceded it. In recent times this was the inspiration for the poem by Yannis Ritsos, "The extermination of Melos" (1973).

A hero relief from Trypiti, with representation of "*nekrodeipno*" (fig. 473), showing the hero reclining right and a woman on a throne left, was perhaps made in the late fifth century BC by Athenian cleruchs who had settled on the island, or in the fourth century BC by the surviving Melians whom the Lacedaemonians reinstated after the victory at Aigos Potamoi in 405 BC and the defeak of the Athenians in 404 BC.

The organization of the city in Hellenistic times is surmised chiefly on the basis of the places where large marble statues were found.

In 1829 a farmer discovered by chance the famous statue of Aphrodite, the "Venus de Milo", together with three herms. All these sculptures were removed from the island and are now the pride and joy of the Musée du Louvre in Paris (fig. 474). The find-spot is thought to have been the gymnasium of the ancient city. The stadium lay to the south of the gymnasium, as a polygonal retaining wall preserved for a considerable length indicates. In 1877 another peasant found other statues close to the beach at Klima. These now grace the National Archaeological Museum in Athens. A sanctuary of Poseidon is believed to have existed here, as is implied by the

469, 470. Melos. Gold rosettes decorated with granulation. On each of the six petals is a second tiny double rosette, and at the centre is a lion head, again within a rosette. These rosettes, together with another three, possibly decorated a diadem. Dated between 650 and 600 BC. Athens, National Archaeological Museum.

471. Melos. The ancient theatre. The cavea has seven rows of seats and six stairways. All that remains of the destroyed skene building are large richly decorated architectural members.

MELOS | 309

larger than life size statue of the god, with raised hand which held a trident, and the dolphin next to his right leg (fig. 77). In 1896, in systematic excavations by the British School at Athens, at Saranta Ekklisies eight statues were brought to light, which are exhibited in the Melos Archaeological Museum. It is estimated that the ancient agora of Melos was hereabouts.

Of particular interest is a semicircular statue base bearing an inscription recording that the deme of Melians set up a bronze statue of Roma, with a gold wreath. Incised on the lower part of the base is the signature of the sculptor: *Πολιάνθης Σωκρατεὺς ἐποίησεν* (Polianthes son of Sokrates made [it]). The base is dated to the second century BC and the statue of Roma must have been one of the first erected in Greece. This is indicative of the great heyday the Melos enjoyed during the period of Roman rule.

These were the years in which the ancient theatre of Melos was possibly built, with two diazomata, which was revealed for the first time by King Ludwig of Bavaria in 1836 (fig. 471). Last, to the north of the ancient city, at the site of Tramythia, a large hall with an enormous mosaic floor was excavated. It contained an altar inscribed: *Διονύσῳ Τριετηρικῷ*(To Dionysos Trieterikos) (triennial) and a herm representing Marios Trophimos, priest of the initiates of Dionysos (fig. 472).

In other parts of the island, such as at the locality Komia, farmhouses have been located, while trade in minerals was possibly conducted from installations at the sites of Aghia Kyriaki and Paliochora, in the south of the island.

Not far from the theatre are the catacombs of Melos, a large complex of graves cut in the soft volcanic rock. They comprise three big tunnels and other smaller ones. Opened in the walls are the arch-shaped tombs, the arcosolia, while in the floor are pits covered with slabs. The catacombs were an extensive subterranean cemetery and place of worship in Early Christian times.

472

473

The existence of a baptistery at Treis Ekklisies, where the marble statues were found and the ancient agora of Melos is thought to have been located, indicates that the area continued in use as a place of worship during Early Christian times.

Significant event in the history of Melos in the Middle Ages was the founding of the Kastro or burg, the outer circuit of houses in which formed the fortification. This took place in the years when Marco I Sanudo was Duke of Naxos. The Frankish Duchy was dissolved in the late sixteenth century and succeeded by the administration of an Ottoman regional governor, through Greek representatives. At that time a second settlement was founded at Zephyria, which prospered particularly in the seventeenth century. Information on this period is given by the traveller J. Pitton de Tournefort, who visited Melos around 1700.

472. Melos. Herm with a bearded male figure wearing a short chiton girdled at the waist and a panther skin, the head of which is visible right, below the girdle, and the leg to the left, over the folds of the garment. A small himation is folded over on the shoulder and falls around the right arm. On the head is a wreath of ivy leaves. According to the inscription carved on the stele, above the acanthus leaves, it was a portrait of the priest Marios Trophimos, in whose honour the herm was erected by initiates in the mysteries. Melos Archaeological Museum.

473. Melos. "Banquet relief" (*Nekrodeipno*). The hero reclines on a couch, in front of which is a table laid with offerings. Seated on a throne in front of him is a female figure, while between them slithers a large snake, its head reared towards the bowl held by the male. One of the earliest examples of a "banquet relief", it is dated *c.* 400 BC. Melos Archaeological Museum.

474. The "Venus de Milo". Aphrodite is represented with naked torso, her himation swathed round her lower limbs. On the bent right leg the garment folds over, forming fine oblique folds. The upper body, with its almost living flesh, turns to the left, possibly towards an object the goddess held at her side with both hands. Her head too is turned in this direction, with the characteristic small mouth, dreamy eyes, fine wavy hair locks framing the face and tied behind in a chignon. The contrast between the drapery of the lower part with the nudity of the movement-filled upper body, the smooth rendering of the skin and the lovely face have all contributed to making the "Venus de Milo" a model and an ideal of feminine beauty. Dated *c.* 130 BC. Paris, Musée du Louvre.

474

MELOS | 311

Thera

Prehistoric times

CHRISTOS DOUMAS

The earliest evidence of human presence on the island of Thera comes from Akrotiri. This is pottery akin to that from the Neolithic settlement on Saliagos, between Paros and Antiparos, which dates settlement at Akrotiri to at least the fifth millennium BC. This Neolithic coastal village was destined to evolve into the most cosmopolitan port of the Bronze Age.

During the third millennium BC, the settlement at Akrotiri developed in the sphere of the Cycladic Culture, as the related pottery and abundant marble figurines and vessels attest. Neither the exact site nor the extent of the settlement of this period has been confirmed. However, its cemetery of large underground burial chambers spread beneath the later city. After this cemetery had fallen into disuse, a "cenotaph" monument was founded, inside which grave goods such as marble figurines and vessels, and obsidian blades, were kept (fig. 476).

Although Akrotiri seems to have been the site of the most important Early Cycladic settlement on the island, small installations of the same period have been located elsewhere. Early Cycladic graves have been uncovered in the quarries at Phira, at Aghios Ioannis Eleemon (Karageorgis quarry) and Kalamia, close to the Akrotiri lighthouse. An underground stone construction was discovered at Ftellos, again in the quarries near Phira. This building brings to mind a corresponding one of the same period on the nearby islet of Christiana (fig. 477). These finds document the gradual development not only of Thera but also of the wider region.

475. Thera. Panoramic view of the caldera, the large basin formed by the volcanic eruption that shook the island in about 1630 BC.

476. Thera, Akrotiri. Early Cycladic figurine from the "cenotaph" (3rd millennium BC), a makeshift stone construction of trapezoidal plan, presumably in imitation of a typical Early Cycladic grave, in which a hoard of marble figurines and vessels was found. This construction remained visible until the final phase of life in the city, when it was buried under the pumice ejected by the volcano. Museum of Prehistoric Thera.

477. Islet of Christiana. A circular well-like construction carefully lined with dry-stone walling. 3rd millennium BC.

During the last centuries of the third millennium BC the settlement at Akrotiri had begun to forge relations and contacts with places further afield, as the presence of pottery from the Northeast Aegean islands indicates. It is well known that these islands were in the vanguard of practising metallurgy, and the bearers of this pottery may well have played their part in introducing the new technology to Thera. There is significant evidence at Akrotiri for the local development of metallurgy. Certainly, immediately after the appearance of these innovative elements developments at Akrotiri were rapid. The Early Cycladic cemetery was abolished and those burial chambers that were not used as storage areas under the new houses were filled in deliberately with stones and earth up to their ceiling, in an effort to rehabilitate the ground on which the monumental buildings of the Middle Cycladic period were constructed.

The decision to abolish the Early Cycladic cemetery and to extend the settlement over it was a political one, while the ambitious building programme and the urban planning presuppose centralized organization and a sound economy. In other words, by the end of the third millennium BC the settlement at Akrotiri had already developed into a wealthy and well-organized city. Circumstances at that time appear to have been propitious for its further growth. For reasons still unknown, the settlement at Poliochni on Lemnos was abandoned in precisely this period and its dealings with the region of the Euxine Pontus, primarily the import of metals, evidently ceased. The new inexhaustible source of copper in the second millennium BC, and indeed for the whole of the Mediterranean, was Cyprus. So, from the moment Crete entered its palatial phase and the demand for metals increased vertically, Thera was ready to undertake the role of transporter/supplier. Of course, the island's strategic geographical location on the new metal route – Cyprus-Rhodes-Thera-Crete – was a prime contributor to this development.

The Middle Cycladic city at Akrotiri, which is buried under the ruins of the Late Cycladic city, is difficult to investigate. Nonetheless, it is certain that most of the buildings of the final period, and particularly the large monumental constructions, were founded in the area of the abolished Early Cycladic cemetery. The city suffered several earthquakes, but after each one it was rebuilt and quickly got back on its feet. In the debris from these seismic destructions, evidence has come to light that confirms the wealth and the urban character of the city at Akrotiri during the Middle Cycladic period (*circa* 2000-1650 BC). Paved streets and squares, drains and sewers, are typical features of Middle Cycladic Akrotiri, while associated with its large and monumental buildings is pottery that points to the sensitivity and the artistic preferences of their residents. The potters and the vase-painters succeeded their sculptor ancestors and with humbler materials, clay and pigment, produced works of "simple beauty" that covered everyday needs. Vases of elegant shapes for diverse uses were painted with representations of plants, animals and even human figures. Continual inquiries led to production of the so-called bichrome style, in which plants animals and humans compose scenes, frequently of narrative content (fig. 478). These scenes perhaps conceal popular tales and myths of Middle Cycladic society. Fragments of wall-paintings with mainly geometric motifs, found in deeper levels, may date to the end of the Middle Cycladic period.

Several of the smaller Early Cycladic installations, such as at Phira, Aghios Ioannis Eleemon, continued in existence at least until the beginning of the Middle Cycladic period (20th-19th century BC), while others (Megalochori) were created towards its end. However, all these were of secondary importance, as a rule small farmsteads.

478. Thera, Akrotiri. Middle Cycladic jug in bichrome style, with two narrative scenes. On one side an eagle lifts up its eaglet, apparently initiating it into the technique of flying; on the other side two male figures in a scene of "pouring from a jug"(?). The subject perhaps alludes to the myth of Ganymede. Akrotiri, excavation storeroom.

479. Thera, Akrotiri. Triangle Square with the West House on the north side and Complex Delta on the east.

Around the end of the eighteenth-the beginning of the seventeenth century BC a major earthquake razed the city at Akrotiri to the ground yet again. The debris was collected together and what could not be recycled as building material was laid in the streets and squares, thus raising their level and transforming the ground floors of the Middle Cycladic houses into semi-basements. With very few modifications to the urban plan, the city was rebuilt, virtually upon the foundations of its predecessor. Radical interventions were made mainly in the entrances to the buildings, so as to bring them up to the new height of the streets. The city of the Late Cycladic I period (*circa* 1650 BC), with its imposing (figs 479, 480) and richly furnished buildings (fig. 481), and unique mural decorations (figs 482, 487-490), represents the final phase of life on Thera, prior to the enormous eruption of the volcano sometime in the second half of the seventeenth century BC.

314 | CYCLADES

Although some of the mixed-farming installations (e.g. at Megalochori) were abandoned in the Late Cycladic I period, others were established, if they did not already exist. Among them are the settlement at the south edge of Therasia and perhaps a small installation north of Oia. However, the city at Akrotiri had grown into a cosmopolitan port, as the exotic objects brought to light in its ruins (figs 483-486) attest. The rich and well-travelled merchant-mariners of the city vied with one another to decorate their houses with wall-paintings whose subjects proclaimed their occupation (figs 482, 488) and their status (fig. 487). The exotic landscapes with flora and fauna unknown in the Aegean evoked the admiration of the craftsmen and the tillers of the soil, while at the same time enhancing the prestige of those who contributed to the city's wealth: the traders and seafarers. This wealth gradually changed the character of the city's inhabitants. The archaeologist who explores and interprets the ruins of the city has the strong feeling that he is reading the history of a consumer society.

An earthquake that preceded the eruption caused serious damage to the thriving city and perhaps claimed victims. After the event, the inhabitants, who were presumably encamped temporarily outside the city, set about clearing the ruins and rescuing furniture and goods that might be useful to them. Presumably they also removed from the ruins any earthquake victims. Concurrently, they began to separate from the heaps of debris the reusable building materials – stones, wood and earth –, as had been done after every previous severe earthquake.

Whilst these rescue and preparatory operations for rebuilding were in full swing, the volcano began to erupt. This is a serious indication that the island's population did not manage to move away and probably lies buried in the temporary encampments, under the thick layers of volcanic ejecta. The layers of pumice and pozzuolana (volcanic ash) that covered the entire island reach 60 metres in places, while its overall volume is estimated as approximately 30 cubic metres. The winds blowing at the time of the eruption were westerly, as deduced from the deposits of volcanic ash on Thera itself – the entire plain from Akrotiri to Perissa and from Kamari to Oia is created from these – and from the eastwards dispersal of this ash. With main axis in the direction of Rhodes, Theran ash covered the entire angle between eastern Crete and the southern shores of the Euxine Pontus.

Westerly winds blow mainly in early summer and given that the storage jars (pithoi) in the cellars of the houses at

480. Thera, Akrotiri. The north face of Xeste 2, a three-storey building, and the southeast corner of Complex Delta with the entrance and the window of the vestibule, still unexcavated. A narrow street runs between the two buildings and the square is arranged in terraces.

481. Thera, Akrotiri. Plaster cast of an elaborate tripod table, retrieved from the imprint (negative) of the original in the volcanic ash. The carved decoration was complemented by inlaid rings of ivory. Museum of Prehistoric Thera.

THERA | 315

482. Thera, Akrotiri. Part of the miniature frieze from the West House, with scene of a flotilla returning from a long voyage to foreign harbours. It sails into an Aegean harbour (possibly Akrotiri), as indicated by the architecture, to a tumultuous welcome. Museum of Prehistoric Thera.

483. Thera, Akrotiri. Bronze ewer, after conservation. Still preserved on its handles are remains of the plaited reed or palm leaves which covered them. Akrotiri, bronze conservation laboratory.

484. Thera, Akrotiri. The same ewer as found in the pumice layer. It had already been recovered from the ruins caused by the earthquake that preceded the great volcanic eruption.

485. Thera, Akrotiri. The gold ibex figurine, as found in the excavation. It was kept in a wooden box, that had perished but traces of the red paint on which remained. This box and its precious content had been put inside a clay larnax, close to which was found a pile of double horns, of sheep, goats and deer. From the unexplored House of the Benches, perhaps a public building like the adjacent Xeste 3.

486. Thera, Akrotiri. Gold ibex figurine made in cire-perdue technique and finished with hammering. Without parallel in Aegean art, the figurine was perhaps an import from the East. Museum of Prehistoric Thera.

Akrotiri are usually found empty, it is estimated that the volcanic eruption took place shortly before the Therans harvested their crops to fill their storerooms, that is in June.

The ejection of enormous quantities of volcanic materials created an immense magma chamber, the roof of which collapsed, taking a large part of Thera with it and leaving in its place the present caldera, some 85 square kilometers in area (fig. 475). The sea rushed into the void of the caldera, generating tidal waves, the effects of which scientists are now seeking on the north coast of Crete.

On the basis of Carbon-14 dates for organic materials from Akrotiri, of the dendrochronology of Irish oak in Europe and of a species of pine in America, the eruption episode is dated to the middle years of the seventeenth century BC. This dating seems to be corroborated by discoveries of molecules of Theran ash in a Greenland ice layer corresponding to the year 1646 BC +/- 20 years.

After this date the island of Thera was deserted for several centuries, until vegetation took root and suitable conditions were created for its settlement anew. It is not known exactly when this took place. However, it is known that shortly before the end of the Mycenaean period, around the twelfth century BC, there was already a small installation at Monolithos, as the scatter of Mycenaean sherds around the hill attests.

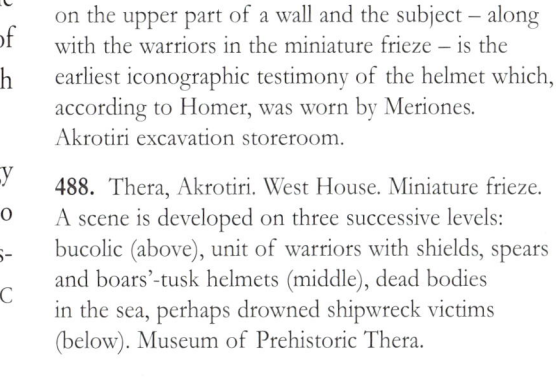

487. Thera, Akrotiri. Part of a wall-painting with depiction of a life-size boars'-tusk helmet with plume. It was found in Xeste 4, a monumental building at least three storeys high. The representation comes from a decorative zone on the upper part of a wall and the subject – along with the warriors in the miniature frieze – is the earliest iconographic testimony of the helmet which, according to Homer, was worn by Meriones. Akrotiri excavation storeroom.

488. Thera, Akrotiri. West House. Miniature frieze. A scene is developed on three successive levels: bucolic (above), unit of warriors with shields, spears and boars'-tusk helmets (middle), dead bodies in the sea, perhaps drowned shipwreck victims (below). Museum of Prehistoric Thera.

489. Thera, Akrotiri. The wall-painting of the Saffron-gatherers from Xeste 3. In a rocky landscape a young girl (right) and a mature woman (left) pick the stamens of the saffron crocus, a plant valuable in Antiquity for its pharmaceutical properties and also as a condiment and a dye. The mature figure appears to be instructing the young girl, who – also bedecked in colourful garments and elaborate jewellery – is perhaps participating in an activity that was a stage of initiation into the adult woman's world. The wall-painting is part of the great composition in the central room of Xeste 3, a public building for rituals. The representation reaches its climax in the offering of crocus to the goddess (*Potnia*), which is depicted on the next wall. Museum of Prehistoric Thera.

490. Thera, Akrotiri. The wall-painting of the Potnia, from Xeste 3. The revered goddess, seated on a special stepped construction and flanked by two creatures, one exotic (monkey) and the other fantastic (griffin), presides over the females gathering the crocus stamens. Her head can be interpreted as crowned by a snake, which, clearly distinct from the hairstyle, flows down the back like a braid. Two of the three necklaces are of beads in the form of ducks and of dragonflies. Thus, the creatures depicted represent the entire animal world (exotic, fantastic, chthonic, aquatic and of the sky), justifying the figure's characterization as *Potnia Theron* (Mistress of Animals). Akrotiri excavation storeroom.

490

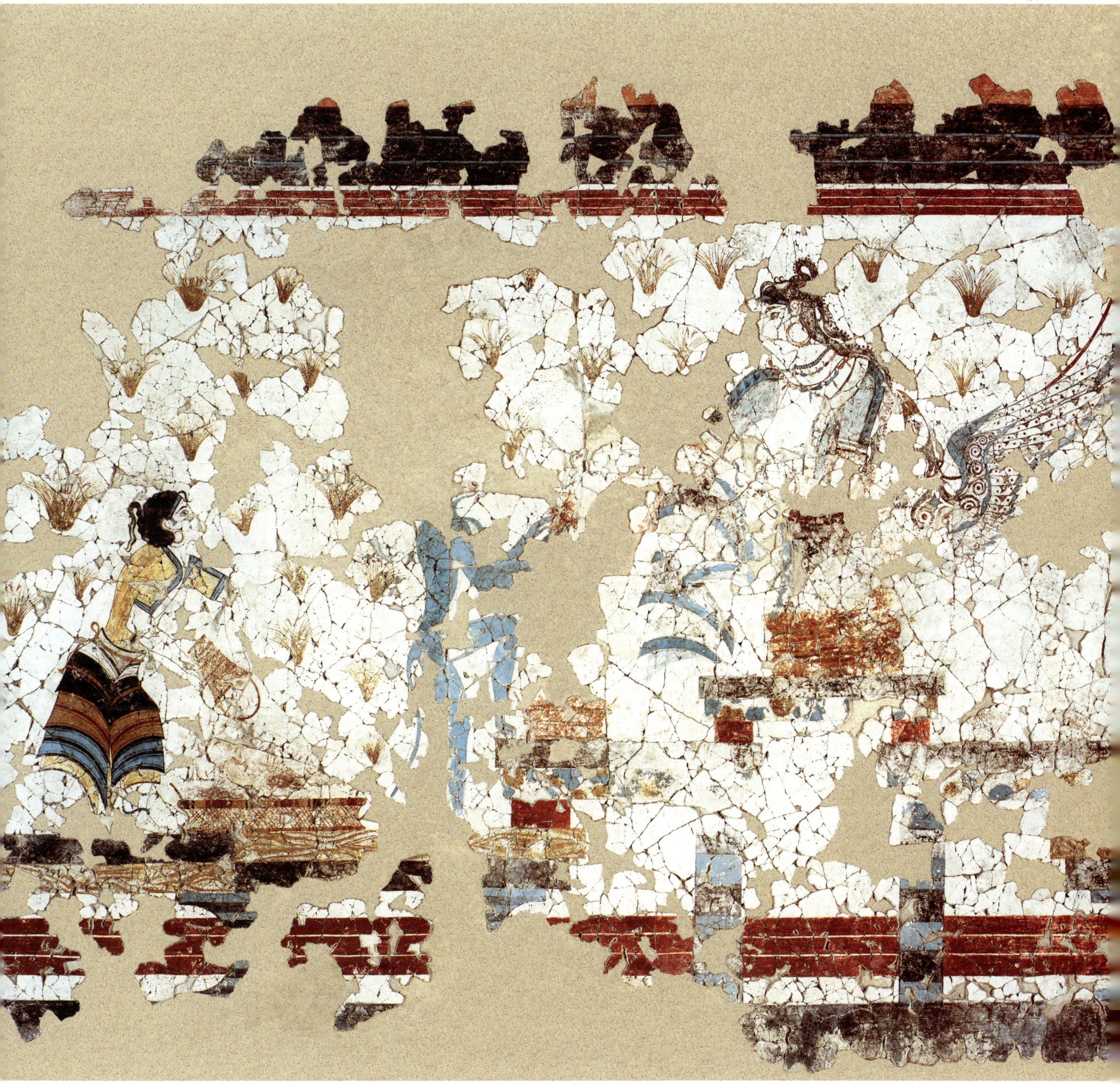

491. Thera. Terracotta figurine of a female figure in the Daedalic style, with painted decoration. On account of the characteristic movement of the hands towards the head, the figure has been interpreted as a lamenter. Late 7th c. BC. Thera Archaeological Museum.

492. Thera. Terracotta figurine of a Negro, sitting and resting in total nudity, from the cemetery of ancient Oia. The Therans were particularly fond of subjects deriving from the region of North Africa, after their colonization of Cyrene. 520-500 BC. Thera Archaeological Museumn.

493. Thera. The city of ancient Thera, on the summit of Mesa Vouno, the precipitous cape that interrupts the continuity of the southeast coast, between the seaside villages of Kamari and Perissa. Visible on the right, below, is part of Kamari, site in Antiquity of the north outport of ancient Thera, Oia.

Historical times
MAYA EFSTATHIOU

In historical times, in the eighth century BC, Thera was colonized by Lacedaemonians, as Herodotus relates. Leader of the colonists was Theras son of Autesion, descendant of Kadmos, who ruled in Sparta as *epitropos* of Eurysthenes and Prokles, sons of Aristodemos. When the boys came of age and assumed power, Theras, together with numerous Lacedaemonians and a few Minyans, departed for the island then known as Kalliste, where he founded a colony to which, as *oikistes*, he gave his name, Thera.

Herodotus also informs us that, after a Delphic oracle, a chosen band of Therans sailed to the coast of North Africa where, in 631 BC, they founded Cyrene, the sole colony of Thera (fig. 492).

For the succeeding centuries information on Thera in the literary sources is limited and sporadic. It is deduced from Attic taxation lists that at the outbreak of the Peloponnesian War, in 431/30 BC, the island was forced to join the First Athenian League, paying tribute of three to five talents. After the Athenians' defeat at Aigos Potamoi (404 BC), it returned to the Spartan sphere of influence, but later became a member of the Second Athenian League, established in 376/5 BC, apparently remaining so, like the other Cyclades, until the battle of Chaironeia (338 BC). After 288 BC Thera entered the sphere of influence of the Ptolemies, who in the second half of the third century BC made it a Ptolemaic possession, installing a garrison there and organizing it as an occupied territory. The particular importance the Ptolemies attached to Thera was due, of course, to its strategic location. The period of Ptolemaic sovereignty, well known from several inscriptions yielding information on its administrative and military structure, was a heyday for the island, which lasted until 145 BC, when the garrison was withdrawn after the death of Ptolemy VI. Information is scant indeed on the years that followed, until the end of Antiquity. During Roman imperial times the island was incorporated administratively in the Province of Asia, while around the mid-third century AD it evidently suffered an incursion by Goth tribes; not long after, with the administrative reforms of Diocletian, Thera became subject to the newly-founded *Provincia Insularum*, along with most of the Cyclades.

The reticence of the literary sources is compensated for by the rich archaeological testimonies. Archaeological research on Thera was essentially begun by the German philologist and epigraphist Hiller von Gaertringen – previous investigations were occasional and restricted – who, accompanied by a team of scholars, systematically explored the island's antiquities and excavated the city of ancient Thera and its cemeteries, over a wide area (1895-1903). The results of their researches were published in a pioneering *magnum opus*, and led to the founding of an archaeological museum on the island as early as 1902. Since then, no systematic research was conducted for over fifty years. In 1961 a fortuitous find, made in the course of widening the road leading to ancient Thera, prompted the Ephor of Antiquities

320 | CYCLADES

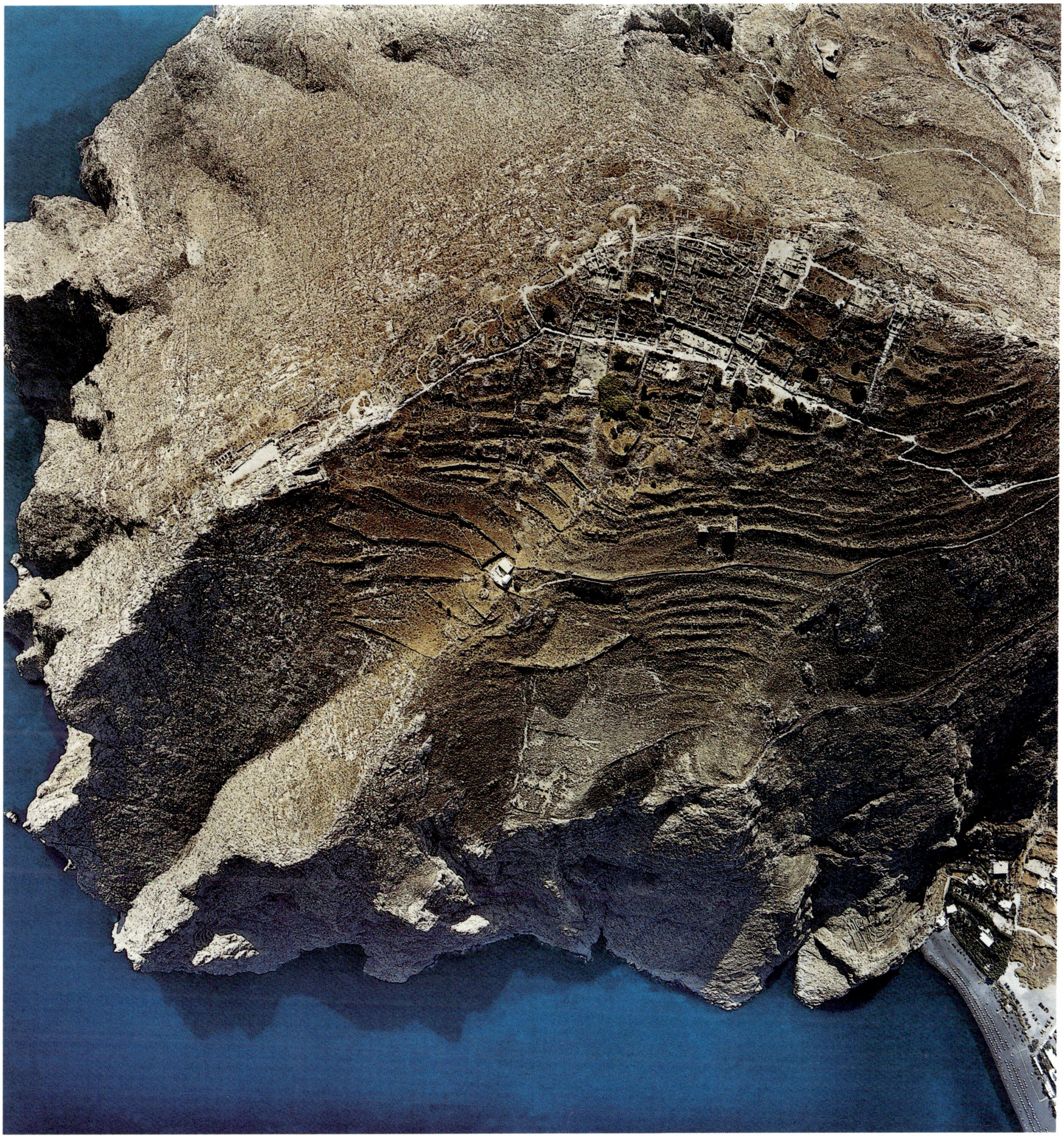

494. Thera. A large amphora with handles on the belly. Product of a Theran workshop, dated to the 7th c. BC. Thera Archaeological Museum.

495. Thera. A large amphora with handles on the belly. Product of a Theran workshop, with strong orientalizing traits. Dated to the 7th c. BC. Thera Archaeological Museum.

496. Thera. View of part of the cemetery of ancient Oia, with burials of the Archaic period. Visible are pits for cremation burials, some lined with walling, as well as simple rectangular cists, which are the above-ground part of others.

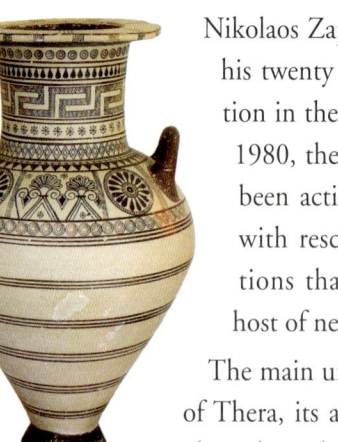

Nikolaos Zapheiropoulos to commence his twenty years of systematic excavation in the cemetery of the city. Since 1980, the Archaeological Service has been active continuously on Thera, with rescue and systematic excavations that have brought to light a host of new finds.

The main urban centre of the city-state of Thera, its administrative and religious nucleus throughout Antiquity, was the city homonymous with the *oikistes*, which was founded in the eighth century BC on the summit of Mesa Vouno, a high hill difficult of access at the southeast edge of the island (fig. 493). In addition to the city there were other installations all over the island, as the diverse archaeological remains at many sites eloquently attest.

From Herodotus' account of the colonization of Cyrene we learn that seven territories existed on Thera. It seems that this division of the island was for administrative reasons and the existence of a main settlement in each territory, as well as smaller installations, is implied. Herodotus does not name the territories and in the absence of related epigraphic testimonies all that is possible is the hypothetical identification of some of the sites where antiquities have been found, with the settlements in the territories. The only sites at which the existence of organized settlements, apart from ancient Thera, is deduced from present data are its outports Oia and Eleusis, on the site of the modern villages of Kamari and Perissa respectively. Although the settlement of Eleusis cannot be dated on existing evidence to earlier than Late Hellenistic times, recent research has shown that Oia was founded in the same period as ancient Thera and that habitation there was continuous; the building remains revealed date to Early Byzantine times, but the cemetery, which has been excavated almost entirely, includes burials from the eighth century BC to the seventh century AD, when the settlement was abandoned. Oia and Eleusis are also the only settlements that are mentioned as cities of Thera by the geographer Claudius Ptolemy, in the mid-second century AD, who actually fails to mention the city of ancient Thera.

The German excavations brought to light the city of ancient Thera as it was in the second century AD, that is the final phase of its existence. Because of the many centuries of habitation on the same site, the preservation of building remains of the early periods is limited. Most of the buildings date from Hellenistic and Roman times (figs 499-503) and many of these bear witness to the boom in construction during the period of domination by the Ptolemies, when the city expanded considerably and magnificent public and private edifices were erected, as well as sanctuaries to foreign deities. The last also bespeak the high-profile presence of foreigners, who settled on the island in these years and who introduced the new cults. In the Roman period building activity was substantially curtailed. Nevertheless, the city evidently prospered and the sculptures found point to a relative flourishing of the arts.

Information on the preceding periods is drawn mainly from the extensive cemetery of ancient Thera (fig. 491), in which numerous burials of the eighth, seventh and sixth centuries BC, as well as of the Classical period and later, have been uncovered. The burials in the cemetery of Oia (modern Kamari) mostly date from the second half of the eighth to the early fifth century BC (fig. 496). Only recently have finds of the Geometric and Archaic periods been discovered in excavations of building remains. These indicate the existence of two sanctuaries in ancient Thera, one of which is identified as a sanctuary of Aphrodite, as well as of a heroon of Achilles in the plain of Episkopi, Gonia. At the south edge of the city of ancient Thera, is an area dedicated to the principal cult of the Dorian colonists, the cult of Apollo Karneios, as well as to the worship of other deities. There are many inscriptions on the rocks, which are the earliest examples of the Greek alphabet in the Aegean.

In the Late Geometric period, perhaps *circa* 720 BC, a local vase-making workshop developed, with pronounced provincial character. Faithful to the Geometric tradition and with no particular stylistic evolution, it continued its Subgeometric production well into the seventh century BC, without ever exporting its products (figs 494, 495). On the contrary, the plethora and the provenance of all manner of imported products – vases, figurines, works in the minor arts, etc. – indicate that from the eighth century BC Thera had trading relations with the major centres of the time, while the kind and quality of several of these artifacts reveal the preferences and economic standing of the Theran aristocracy.

Indeed, their taste and affluence is borne out by the parts of colossal grave kouroi of the second half of the seventh century BC, found in Thera, which are among the most monumental works of Archaic large-scale sculpture, as well as the creation from as early as the second quarter of the sixth century BC of a local workshop in the tradition of Naxian sculpture, capable of serving the local needs. Among its creations is the kouros known as the Thera Apollo, dated to 580-570 BC (fig. 498). The larger than life-size marble Daedalic kore of the second half of the seventh century BC has been added recently to the corpus of large-scale sculptures found on Thera. Discovered by Charalambos Sigalas in November 2000, in the cemetery of ancient Thera, on south Sellada, this is a work of unique artistic and historical importance.

So, despite the voluntary political isolation of its landowners, Thera, as recent finds in particular demonstrate, was from the eighth century BC already in contact, direct or indirect, with all the leading centres of the age, from Corinth and mainland Greece, the islands of the North Aegean, the Cyclades and Crete, as far as East Greece and Cyprus, the Levant (Syria and Phoenicia) and North Africa (fig. 492). Although the finds from recent investigations still await systematic study it is certain that they will yield valuable information about the society of Thera in Geometric and Archaic times, which although somewhat conservative in its structures and devoted to Dorian traditions, was apparently receptive to the influences of other regions, particularly after the domestic upheavals that led to the colonization of Cyrene.

497. Thera. Pithos with relief decoration. Represented on the neck metope is a swan, and on the shoulder are two chariots drawn by winged horses. From the cemetery of ancient Thera. Dated *c.* 675 BC. Thera Archaeological Museum.

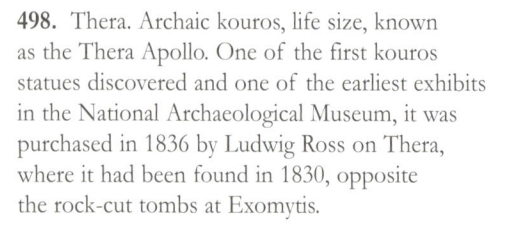

498. Thera. Archaic kouros, life size, known as the Thera Apollo. One of the first kouros statues discovered and one of the earliest exhibits in the National Archaeological Museum, it was purchased in 1836 by Ludwig Ross on Thera, where it had been found in 1830, opposite the rock-cut tombs at Exomytis.

499. Ancient Thera. Sacred precinct (*temenos*) of Artemidoros. A relief eagle for Oympian Zeus, on the smoothed face of the rock. Detail of fig. 500.

500. Ancient Thera. Sacred precinct (*temenos*) at the northwest edge of the city, dedicated to the worship of several deities: Zeus, Apollo, Poseidon, Homonoia, the Dioskouroi and others. On the smoothed face of the rock, which is filled with inscriptions, attributes of the aforesaid gods are carved in relief. The temenos was founded by Artemidoros of Perge in the mid-3rd c. BC.

501. Ancient Thera. View of part of a stepped street in the city centre. The city of ancient Thera developed on the top of Mesa Vouno, following the configuration of the ground. Because of the steep slope along the east-west axis, most of the streets are stepped.

502. Ancient Thera. The Basilike Stoa, the most impressive public building in the city. Inscriptions of the 2nd c. AD refer to it as an old and special building that graced the city. Of rectangular plan (41.50 x 10.10 m.), it has a colonnade of nine Doric columns without flutes, along its central axis and an exedra for statues in its north part. According to Fauvel, one column, with its capital, still stood *in situ* in 1788; it consisted of three drums and was 3.11 m. high, including the capital.

503. Ancient Thera. The theatre. Its earliest stone construction, a skene building of Hellenistic type, which left the orchestra free, dates to the 3rd c. BC. Later, possibly in the first half of the 1st c. AD, a higher skene building of Roman type was erected, occupying the orchestra.

500

501

502

503

THERA | 325

Anaphe

Christina A. Televantou

Anaphe, at the southeast extremity of the Cyclades, is 38.35 square kilometres in area and has a terrain consisting of mountains, hills, ravines and sandy beaches. Myth has it that the island was first inhabited by Phoenicians led by Membliaros, to whom it owes the prosonyms Membliaros or Bliaros. The name Anaphe is due to an intriguing episode in the Voyage of the Argonauts, according to which the island emerged from the sea when Jason beseeched Apollo to save the *Argo* from a tempest during the return from Colchis, as they were sailing across the Cretan Sea, bound for the Aegean. The Argonauts dropped anchor on the island and founded there an altar in honour of Apollo Aigletes, for the salvationary burst of light (*aigle*) he sent in the midst of the storm.

Anaphe was probably settled by Dorians in the eighth century BC, like neighbouring Thera. It was, however, a member of the Athenian League, paying tax of one thousand drachmas. The ruins of buildings and the mighty fortification wall of the ancient city of Anaphe extend on the summit of Kastelli Hill (327 m. a.s.l.) on the east side of the island. During the Hellenistic period (300 BC et seq.) Anaphe minted its own coinage, with the head of Apollo Aigletes on one side and on the other a krater, usually with a bee flying above it, symbol of the flourishing practice of apiary. Impressive are the remains of the cemetery that spreads over the southeast slope of the hill. The tombs combine large chambers underground with built monuments above ground, and have niches adorned with statues and sarcophagi, mainly of Roman times. The large marble sarcophagus close to the church of the Virgin at Dokari has relief decoration on all four sides with representations of griffins, Eros figures, a Siren, Bellerophon and Pegasos (fig. 506).

The city was linked by road, a branch of the sacred way, to its outport in Katalymatsa Bay. The sacred way commenced at the east edge of the city and following the col led to the sanctuary of Apollo Anaphaios or Aigletes (fig. 505), located on the site of the monastery of the Life-bearing Source (Zoodochos Pigi). The sanctuary was enclosed by an impressive precinct wall (peribolos), built of local stone in isodomic masonry (fig. 507). It includes not only the temple of Apollo but also an extensive building complex to serve the cult and the worshippers, while there were also altars of other deities worshipped jointly, such as Artemis, Aphrodite, Asklepios and Zeus Ktesios.

On the west side of the island is Pyrgi Hill, which surveys the sea and Thera, as well as a large part of the hinterland, from Chora to Prasas Bay. Here stands a notable ancient building complex, constructed of large blocks, possibly a kind of lookout tower.

No systematic excavations have been conducted on the island. The antiquities that have been collected systematically in recent years (fig. 504) are kept in the local Archaeological Collection.

504. Anaphe. Kastelli. Roman statues of himation-clad male figures in the cemetery of the ancient city, before their collection and removal to the island's Archaeological Collection.

505. Anaphe. Temple of Apollo at the monastery of the Panaghia (Virgin) Kalamiotissa.

506. Anaphe. Kastelli, Panaghia sto Dokari. Roman sarcophagus in the cemetery of the ancient city.

507. Anaphe. Peribolos of the sanctuary of Apollo, at the monastery of the Panaghia (Virgin) Kalamiotissa.

AGATHONISI
ARKIOI
PATMOS MARATHI PHARMAKONISI
          LEIPSOI
        LEROS
KINAROS LEVITHA   IMIA
        TELENDOS PSERIMOS
        KALYMNOS
              KOS
            YALI STRONGYLI
ASTYPALAIA   SYME
        PERGOUSA NISYROS
OPHIDOUSA   PACHIA   SESKLI
        KANDELIOUSA TELOS
    SYRNA   ALIMIA
                CHALKE
                    RHODES

        SARIA
    ASTAKIDA

        KARPATHOS

        KASOS

DODECANESE

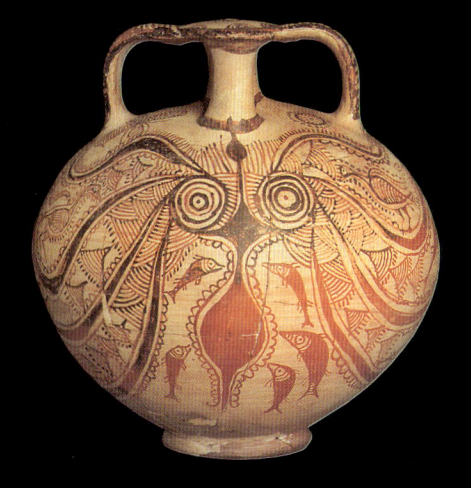

Milesian islands

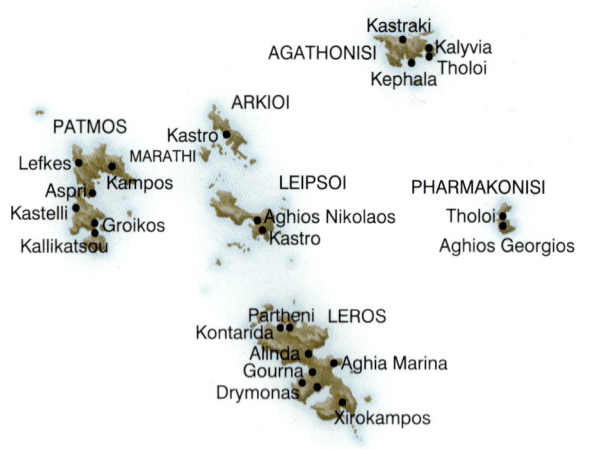

The Ionian islands of the northern group of the Dodecanese are known also to archaeological scholarship as Milesian islands, because in Antiquity they belonged to the great metropolis of Ionia, Miletos, which in the Archaic period was the largest city of Hellenism. The present Dodecanesian islands of Agathonisi, Arkioi, Marathi, Patmos, Leipsoi, Pharmakonisi, Leros and some islets are considered to have been possessions of Miletos, which facilitated her free and safe access to the Aegean. Of these, Leros was the most important.

Agathonisi

ANASTASIA DRELIOSSI-HERAKLEIDOU

Agathonisi, lying southeast of Samos and northeast of Leipsoi, is the northernmost island in the Dodecanese, with an area of 13.417 square kilometres. It lies opposite Miletos, to which it was subject politically in Antiquity, together with the neighbouring islands. Its ancient name was Tragia, Tragaiai, Atragia or Tragiai. As Thucydides (I 116) relates that in 440 BC Pericles "they fought at sea-fight at the island of Tragia against seventy ships of the Samians". According to Stephanos Byzantios, Tragia was the birthplace of the philosopher Theogeiton, disciple of Aristotle.

The earliest traces of habitation on the island, surface finds from the sites of Kephala and Kalyvia, date from the Final Neolithic period (4th millennium BC). Remains of a fortification and a fortified enceinte of the Hellenistic period survive at the site of Kastraki, on the homonymous cape on the north coast of the island. An important monument of Late Antiquity or possibly the Byzantine Age is the built bathhouse complex preserved in good condition at Tholoi, on the east coast.

Arkioi, Marathi

MARIA MICHALAKI-KOLLIA

The Arkioi lie north of Leipsoi and northeast of Patmos, to which they belong administratively. They comprise a cluster of 13 islets and 10 rocky islets, named the Arkioi after the largest isle. In Antiquity they belonged to the city-state of Miletos. Pliny mentions them by the name Argiae, while the third-century AD geographer Agathemeros calls them Arkitis. Prehistoric pottery and obsidian débitage have been found in the highest part of the modern settlement, which was built in the innermost creek of a deep bay on the west coast of the island and is also the modern harbour of Porto-Avgousta. On the top of the rocky hill to the left of the harbour entrance stand the remnants of a rectangular tower constructed of large polygonal blocks, in the

508. Marathi. General view from the air. Visible on the hill slope is the site of the old and the modern settlement.

509. Arkioi. View of the tower dated to the 4th c. BC.

510. Marathi. Vaulted-roofed construction.

Lesbian system of masonry (fig. 509). Two walls transverse to the tower end at the steep rocky coast, while successive retaining walls descend to the hinterland. Access to the fort was probably from the side of the bay, as indicated by a wide path terminating in the area of Piso Patelia, where later building remains are still visible on the beach. The fort can be dated to the late fourth century BC, on the basis of dispersed pottery in the vicinity and the kind of masonry, while various constructional interventions and corresponding potsherds confirm its use in later times. On the northwest side of Arkioi there is a cave with stalactites and columnar stalagmite formations, which must have been used as a place of worship, while sherds of a Melian vase of the sixth century BC were found on the surface.

The second inhabited island in the group, and the third largest in size, is Marathi, today home to two families. On the west coast is an open bay with a lovely sandy beach (fig. 508). On the hillock above the beach, on the site of the old ruined settlement with the chapel of St Nicholas, is a stone-built vaulted-roofed construction, possibly a cistern, which should be dated to the Early Christian period. The vault is revetted inside with parallel rows of pieces of tiles, while at the centre of the ceiling these tiles form decorative triangles that form a rectangle (fig. 510). On the northeast side of Marathi, on the rocky shore at the site of Elliniko, are remains of buildings and another Early Christian vaulted cistern, eroded by the sea, while traces of prehistoric settlement survive at the site of Vigla, at the south end of the island.

MILESIAN ISLANDS | 331

Patmos

Anastasia Dreliossi-Herakleidou

Patmos, 34.05 square kilometres in area, lies to the northwest of Leipsoi and Leros. It is known as the holy island where St John the Theologian wrote The Revelation. The earliest mention of the island's name is by Thucydides, in connection with the pursuit of the Spartan fleet by the Athenian General Paches, in 428 BC. It is also referred to by Pliny and Strabo. The earliest traces of human habitation date from the Final Neolithic period/Early Bronze Age (4th-3rd millennia BC), attested by sherds of clay vases and stone tools found at the sites of Kastelli, Kallikatsou, Aspri, Lefkes and Kampos.

During the Hellenistic period, at least, Patmos belonged to Miletos, as is deduced from inscriptions on the island and testimonies from the metropolis itself.

The island's acropolis, which is also its most important ancient monument (fig. 511), is at Kastelli, an imposing site overlooking three bays, of Skala, Chochlakas and Merikas. Surface sherds dating from prehistoric, Classical, Hellenistic and Roman times bear witness to continuous occupation of the hill. At Kastelli stand impressive remains of Late Classical fortifications (late 4th century BC). Significant parts of the defensive wall are preserved to a considerable height, with careful masonry and rectangular towers, one provided with a staircase and a gateway (fig. 512). The main settlement of the island must have extended to the east of the acropolis.

Principal deity of Patmos was Artemis Patnia, whose worship is perhaps associated with Amazonion, a site mentioned in the Late Antique treatise "*Stadiasmos of the Great Sea*". The goddess's sanctuary is believed to have been located in the area where Hosios Christodoulos later founded the renowned monastery of St John the Theologian. In an inscription of the second/third century AD there is mention of Artemis Scytheia, who is linked with the myth of Orestes; after his cure, he brought the effigy of the goddess from Tauris in Scythia to Patmos.

In addition to Artemis, Apollo Didymaios was also worshipped on the island, while the cult of Hermes is mentioned in an honorary decree of an association of "torch-bearers (*lampadistai*) from Patmos and participants in the *aleimma*", of the second century BC. Moreover, in the apocryphal text on the life of St John there is reference to a sanctuary of Apollo and of Zeus.

The open-air sanctuary at the site of Kallikatsou, with staircase and niches carved in the imposing living rock on the south side of Groikos Bay, was perhaps associated with Aphrodite.

511. Patmos. Ancient acropolis at Kastelli. View from Chora. At the foot of the hill is the modern settlement of Skala, the main harbour of the island.

512. Patmos. Steps of a built staircase leading to the large rectangular tower on the acropolis at Kastelli.

Leipsoi

Anastasia Dreliossi-Herakleidou

Leipsoi, 16 square kilometres in area, lies between Leros and Patmos. Its ancient name was Lepsia, as recorded in inscriptions found on the island. Pliny also refers to it as Lepsia. Lepsia was inhabited from the Final Neolithic period/Early Bronze Age (4th-3rd millennia BC), as indicated by pottery from the sites of Kastro and Aghios Nikolaos.

The island's geographical location determined its historical course, linking it with Miletos. The political relationship between Leipsoi and Miletos during the Hellenistic period is evidenced by decrees of the island in which there is reference to "Milesians residing in Leipsia".

The most important monument of Leipsoi is the Kastro (fig. 513), on the hill close to the present settlement, southeast of Tarsanas. This was the site of the ancient acropolis, on which are preserved remnants of the fortified enceinte with bastion, gateway and indentations. On the south slope of the hill, outside the enceinte, traces of terraces and abundant pottery indicate the existence of the ancient settlement there.

The official sanctuary of Lepsia, where decrees were set up, was dedicated to Apollo Lepsieus and was situated in the vicinity of the little church of St Nicholas. The entire area between Aghios Nikolaos and the church of the Virgin at Kouselio, is littered with potsherds dating from prehistoric to Early Christian times, architectural members and ruined buildings, among them a tetraconch of Late Antiquity. A marble corner akroterion, from the architrave of an altar of "Milesian" type was found at Aghios Nikolaos. Decorated with well-executed volutes with oculi and palmettes, it is dated to the mid-fifth century BC. There is a similar marble akroterion in the old refectory of the Patmos monastery of St John the Theologian.

In addition to the cult of Apollo Lepsieus, Apollo Didymaios was also worshipped on Lepsia, while dedicatory inscriptions on small altars from the ancient acropolis refer to Zeus Genethlios and Artemis Soteira.

513. Leipsoi. General view of the settlement with the harbour and the Kastro, site of the ancient acropolis.

514. Pharmakonisi. Partial view of one of the two built towers on Aghios Georgios Hill. Late 4th c. BC.

Pharmakonisi

Anastasia Dreliossi-Herakleidou

The islet of Pharmakonisi or Pharmako lies east of Leipsoi, opposite the Bay of Iasos on the Asia Minor coast. Its ancient name was Pharmakoussa, the root of which – preserved in the present name – derives from a medicinal herb that grew here. Pliny mentions the islet as belonging to the Sporades. It was one of the small group of the so-called Milesian islands, which belonged to the territory of Miletos and secured that city's free and safe access to the Aegean.

515. Leros. Inscribed stele from Partheni, 2nd c. BC. It records a decree "of the inhabitants on Leros", in honour of Aristomachos son of Dromon. Leros, Archaeological Museum.

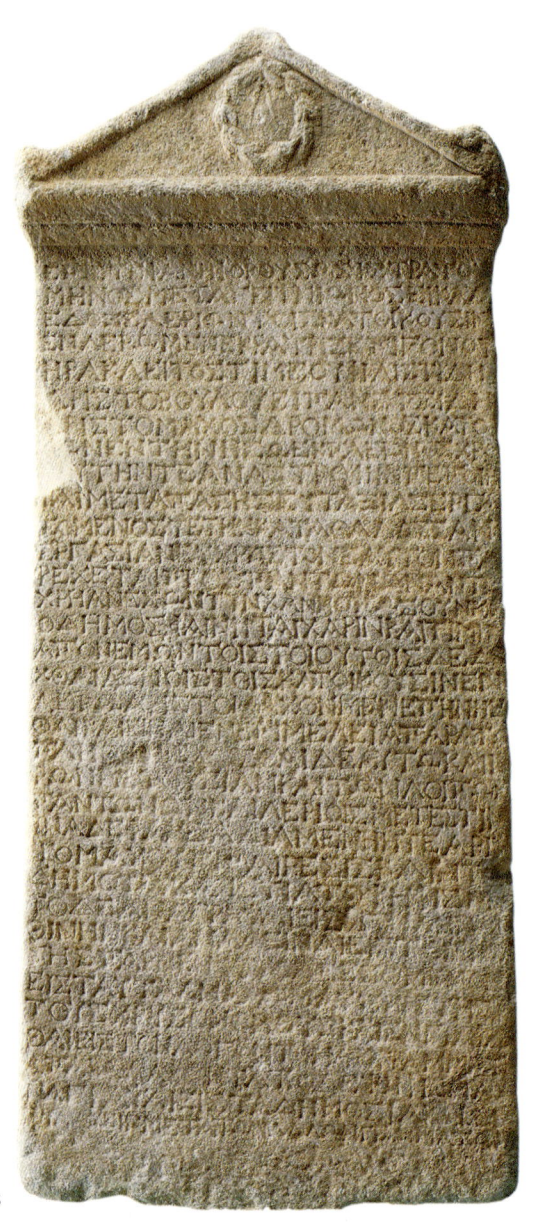

Surface finds, potsherds and stone tools, indicate that the islet was already inhabited in prehistoric times. On Aghios Georgios Hill, which surveys the sea routes, stand the ruins of two built towers (fig. 514). From Tholoi Bay, the main natural harbour, to Paliomantra there are traces of buildings and mosaic floors dating from the Late Roman and Early Christian periods.

Pharmakoussa is associated with a major historic figure, Julius Caesar, who in 74 BC, as a young man, was taken captive by Cilician pirates "near the island of Pharmakoussa". However, as Plutarch relates, when the pirates demanded twenty talents as ransom the hostage laughed because they had no idea who he was. He promised them fifty talents and sent his men to collect the money. Caesar remained a prisoner on Pharmakoussa for 38 days, "among Phoenician men from Cilicia … and he wrote poems and orations", and used the pirates as an audience. Because they did not admire what he read to them, he called them "… uneducated and barbarians", and laughing heartily he threatened that he would hang them. As soon as the ransom arrived from Miletos and Caesar was freed, he chartered a ship in the city's harbour and pursued the pirates. After capturing them he sent them to jail in Pergamon, where he crucified them all, as he had told them often on Pharmakoussa, seemingly in jest (Plutarch, *Parallel Lives, Gaius Julius Caesar*, 1, 2).

Leros

ANASTASIA DRELIOSSI-HERAKLEIDOU

The southernmost Ionian island, "fair-bayed" and "fair-harboured" Leros, 53 square kilometres in area, is separated by a narrow channel from nearby Dorian Kalymnos. The earliest reference to Leros is in the *Iliad*, "Calydnian islands", which according to some scholars included both Kalymnos and Leros. The earliest mention of the name of the island's inhabitants is in the derisory epigrams of the gnomic poet from Miletos, Phokylides, *circa* sixth century BC.

Leros was inhabited from at least the Final Neolithic period (4th millennium BC), as attested by prehistoric remains at several sites around the sheltered bays of Partheni and Gourna. On the north coast, at the site of Kontarida, in the south creek of Partheni Bay, remains of a prehistoric settlement have come to light. This is the first known installation of this period in the northern Dodecanese, which is not in a cave. Obsidian tools, unpainted domestic vessels, bowls, storage jars, all handmade and of coarse clay, some with imprints of matting, leaves and grain on their walls, as well as sandstone grinders and querns, give an insight into the activities of the settlement's inhabitants.

Early sea routes and trading relations with the nearby islet of Yali, off Nisyros, and distant Melos in the central Aegean, are attested by the significant quantity of obsidian tools and débitage found scattered at Drymonas, on the south rocky side of Gourna Bay, where the raw material was probably worked *in situ*.

Ancient tradition attests an early colony of Milesians on Leros: "Milesians settled on the islands of Ikaros and Leros". It is also connected to Miletos by events of the Ionian Revolt; according to Herodotus, the speech-writer Hekataios advised the Tyrant of Miletos, Aristagoras, to seek refuge on the island if forced to quit Miletos. The earliest secure testimony of Leros's dependence on Miletos is in the Athenian fiscal lists for 454-453 BC, in which there is reference to Milesians from Leros. Towards the end of the Peloponnesian War, the fleets sallied forth from the safe harbours of Leros. In the fourth century BC Leros appears as a deme of Miletos and its public texts are dated on the basis of the eponymous archon of that city, the *stephanephoros*. An authority appointed by the central administration of Miletos, the garrison commander, was also responsible for the island's security.

The main settlement centre on the island was in the area of Aghia Marina, where representative examples of pottery from the Geometric period (8th century BC) to Late Antiquity have been found. Characteristic are the terracotta masks of Dionysos, in excellent style, the terracotta female protome and the figurine of a symposiast, of the fourth/third century BC, from Bourtzi, now in the Leros Archaeological Museum.

At Partheni, the island's official religious centre, was the sanctuary of Parthenos Iokallis, who is identified with Artemis. The area has kept not only its ancient name but also its unspoilt landscape, as described by the peripatetic philosopher Klytos in the first book of *On Miletus*: "the place is marshy". The Meleagrids, sisters of the Theban hero Meleager, took refuge in the sanctuary. The goddess transformed them into birds, because she was saddened by their incessant lament over their brother's death whilst hunting the Calydonian boar (Antonius Liberalis, *Metamorphoses*). The sanctuary of Parthenos was also the place where decrees of the Lerians were set up, as attested by the island's inscriptions (fig. 515).

On the north side of Leros, on a hill in the Partheni valley, is a rectangular fortification with well-constructed masonry, of the fourth century BC (figs 516, 517). At Xirokampos, at the south end of the island, in a naturally fortified position dominating the area between Lakki and Lepida, is an impressive enceinte with rectangular tower, contemporary with the fort at Partheni. Remains of an earlier wall of "Cyclopean" construction are preserved on the south side of the enceinte. These two fortification works must be linked with the measures taken by Miletos on the islands in her territory, to control the sealanes and to protect the islands from pirates.

In addition to the official worship of Parthenos, there were probably cults of Apollo, Dionysos and Asklepios on Leros. The island was the home of the poet Demodokos or Demodikos (*circa* 550 BC) and the historian Pherekydes (75th Olympiad or Hellenistic period, according to other scholars), who was the author of *On Leros*, *On Iphigeneia*, *On Festivals of Dionysos*, and other works.

516. Leros. View of the Partheni valley from the hill with the ancient fort. In the distance, the islet of Archangelos, which protects Partheni Bay from the north.

517. Leros. Remains of an ancient fort at Partheni, in the north part of the island. The fort was built in the late 4th c. BC, on the hill overlooking the Partheni valley.

Kalymnos

ANASTASIA DRELIOSSI-HERAKLEIDOU

"... and that Kalydnai islands also known as the Sporades, one of them is called Kalymnos ..."
(Eustathios II 677)

Kalymnos, 109.67 square kilometres in area, known today as the sponge-fishers' island, lies northwest of Kos and south of Leros. Its ancient name was Kalydna. From the fourth century BC the type Kalymna is encountered, while in the "list of ships" in the *Iliad* (II 676), which is the earliest mention of the island, there is reference to "the Calydnian islands", which some scholars consider included not only Kalymnos but also the islets of Telendos, Pserimos, Kalolimnos and Plati, while according to another reference the Calydnian islands also included Leros. Pliny and Ovid mention it as Calymne; indeed, the latter describes it as "*silvis umbrosa*". Well-known and lauded by ancient authors was "Kalymnian honey", which vied with that of Attica in quality and is still produced.

The earliest traces of habitation on Kalymnos date from the Final Neolithic period (4th millennium BC) and were found in the Choiromandres and Aghia Varvara caves, in the vicinity of Pothia, present capital of the island, and Daskaleio, in the natural harbour of Vathys Bay. The rich material recovered from the cave sheds light on the everyday life of those cave-dwellers, their activities and cult practices: Neolithic burnished clay vases, Early Bronze Age (3rd millennium BC) handmade vases with incised and painted decoration, storage jars, notable examples of stone tools and works in the minor arts, such as figurines. In the cave at Daskaleio and at Aghia Varvara artifacts of the Minoan (fig. 518) and Mycenaean periods were found. Mycenaean remains have also been identified on the site of the Medieval castle of Chrysocheria, where there was possibly a citadel, as well as at other sites, Vathys, Pothia, Chora and elsewhere.

According to Diodorus Siculus, Karians lived on Kalydna and Nisyros. Herodotus relates that Dorians from Epidauros came and colonized the island. Kalymnos took part in the Trojan Campaign, with two ships under the command of Antiphos and Pheidippos, the Herakleid kings of Kos. In the sixth century BC Kalymnos minted its own coinage, a silver stater with the head of a bearded and helmeted male on the obverse and a seven-stringed lyre on the reverse. During Xerxes' expedition to Greece the island sided with the Persians, under the leadership of Artemisia, together with Halikarnassians, Koans and Nisyrians. After the Persian Wars were over, Kalymnos joined the First Athenian League and later the Second. In fourth-century BC inscriptions from the island there is

518. Kalymnos. Bronze figurine of an adorant, Late Minoan IA period (17th c. BC). Fortuitous find from the Daskaleio Cave at Vathys. It is possibly associated with the use of the cave for worship in this period. Similar figurines of the Minoan adorant type have been found on Rhodes.

519. Kalymnos. Intricate gold earrings with pyramidal pendant, articulated female figures, dancing girls and Nike "*sandalizousa*", third quarter of 4th c. BC. Grave good from the cemetery at Elies, Panormos. Kalymnos Archaeological Museum.

520. Kalymnos. Christos tis Ierousalim. An Early Christian basilica with built in architectural members and inscriptions from the sanctuary of Apollo Dalios.

reference to four tribes: Theugenidai, Hippasidai, Periphidai and Kydreleioi. Around the mid-fourth century BC the island was ruled by the Karian dynasty, while in the time of the Successors to Alexander the Great it came under the influence of the Ptolemies. In the latter years of the third century BC Kalymnos contracted a *homopoliteia* with Kos, that is, it was subject politically to the latter. The *homopoliteia* brought essential changes in the island's regime, including its division into the three traditional Dorian tribes and the re-articulation of the demes, which were reduced from seven or eight to three: Pothaia, Panormos and Orkatos. In Roman times Kalymnos belonged to the Province of Asia, while in the reign of Diocletian it was subject to the Province of the Islands.

The most important monument on Kalymnos and one of the most significant in the surrounding island region is the sanctuary of Apollo Dalios, located between the sites of Limniotissa and Pigadia. This was the official religious and political centre of the island. In Early Christian times two basilicas were built on the site of the sanctuary of Apollo. In the construction of the larger basilica, known today as Christos tis Ierousalim, abundant epigraphic and architectural material from the ancient edifices was used (fig. 520). The *temenos* of Apollo was set within a sacred grove of bay trees and included a theatre with skene and proscenium, where music and choric contests were held. The sanctuary was adorned with a host of *ex-votos*, attesting to both its prestige and its longevity, from Geometric into Roman times. An impressive array of marble sculptures has come to light recently at the sanctuary site. Outstanding among them is the noble figure of a dressed kouros, in marble, which was dedicated as a "tithe" to Apollo in the late sixth century BC. The earliest *ex-votos*, which include vase sherds with inscriptions in the Argeian alphabet and Karian script, as well as a series of terracotta bull figurines with painted decoration, dating from the Geometric and Archaic periods, were recovered from a sacral repository (*apothetes*) in the sanctuary, in the course of researches by the Italian archaeologist M. Segre in 1937. The sanctuary is also the provenance of two colossal – probably cult – statues of Asklepios and Hygieia. Its significance as the official religious and political centre of the island is emphasized by the numerous inscriptions found there. Removed from their original position when the sanctuary's splendour ceased, some were incorporated in the walls of the Early Christian basilica of Christos tis Ierousalim and many were dispersed over the site. These were discovered by C. Newton in his investigations in 1854-1855, who transferred them to the British Museum, while a few remained on Kalymnos and will be exhibited in the new Archaeological Museum, presently under construction. These are decrees of the deme of Kalymnians, lists of citizens of the island, inscribed dedications of Kalymnians and foreigners, texts of arbitration to resolve legal disputes, as well as of manumissions of slaves.

519

520

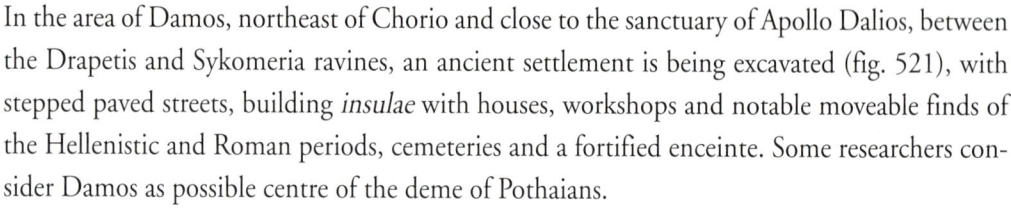

In the area of Damos, northeast of Chorio and close to the sanctuary of Apollo Dalios, between the Drapetis and Sykomeria ravines, an ancient settlement is being excavated (fig. 521), with stepped paved streets, building *insulae* with houses, workshops and notable moveable finds of the Hellenistic and Roman periods, cemeteries and a fortified enceinte. Some researchers consider Damos as possible centre of the deme of Pothaians.

Tombs and funerary monuments have been uncovered at other sites too, such as Flaska, Archangelos at Chorio, Elies at Panormos. These have yielded rich grave goods, outstanding among which are a gold myrtle wreath dated to the second half of the third century BC (fig. 522) and a pair of gold earrings with pyramidal pendant and Nike "*sandalizousa*" (Victory adjusting her sandal), of the third quarter of the fourth century BC (fig. 519). Kalymnos is cited as the provenance of a similar pair of gold earrings of comparable style and beauty in the Berlin Archaeological Museum, which also possesses another piece of jewellery from the island, a gold ring with intaglio representation of Aphrodite showing Eros how to draw the bow.

At Pothia, the modern capital town and main harbour, are remains of a fort, while building material used in an Early Christian basilica is considered to have come from a temple of Artemis. A Roman bathhouse (thermae) has come to light northeast of the church of St Anthony at Panormos. On Kastri Hill at Emporeio, the island's northernmost bay, there is a fortified farmstead of Hellenistic times, with two rectangular towers, water cisterns and an olive-oil press.

On the east side of Kalymnos, on the range of high hills north of Vathys, are remains of a settlement that spread on the slopes of the imposing height of Kastellas and is associated with the presence of Karians. Human habitation in the area goes back to prehistoric times and con-

521. Kalymnos. Damos. View of part of the settlement that developed between the two ravines in the area of Panormos, during the Hellenistic and Roman periods.

522. Kalymnos. Gold myrtle wreath from a grave, second half of 3rd c. BC. Handed in by Emmanuel Koutouzis. Kalymnos Archaeological Museum.

tinued into the Classical period. South of Kastellas, on a low terrace at Empolas, is a fortified enceinte built according to the isodomic system with massive stone blocks and with a gateway, which is dated to the fourth century BC. On the north side of this same valley, between the harbours of Rina and Empolas, at the site of Phylakai, is a built look-out tower of Hellenistic times.

There is evidence that in addition to Apollo Dalios and Asklepios, there were cults of Dionysos and Poseidon, Demeter and Kore, Panakeia, Aphrodite and Homonoia on Kalymnos, as well as a temple and statues of the Dioskouroi.

Thanks to the wealth of moveable finds, monuments and epigraphic testimonies, in conjunction with ongoing archaeological research, various aspects of the culture and the long history of Kalymnos are being elucidated. Even so, its earth and the surrounding sea still hold many secrets.

Telendos

Telendos, a rocky islet 6.5 square kilometres in area, lies to the west of Kalymnos, a short distance from Myrties (fig. 523). Its name, which it keeps to this day, is thought to be prehellenic. The island was included in the "Calydnian islands" mentioned in Homer's "list of ships", along with the others on the periphery of Kalymnos. During Antiquity Telendos probably belonged to the Kalymnian deme of Panormos. Abundant remains from the Late Roman period, such as bathhouses (thermae) and an olive-oil press, have been identified on the east coast of Telendos, between the large Early Christian basilicas on the outskirts of the modern settlement. West of Pefki or Tholaria, where there are underground vaulted tombs of the Early Christian period, is the site of the ancient theatre. On the majestic precipitous hill of Aghios Constantinos with the Byzantine burg, are remains of a guardhouse. At the coastal site of Vlychada are remains of a Late Roman pottery workshop.

523. Telendos. The islet west of Kalymnos.

Pserimos

Pserimos, an islet 14 square kilometres in area, lies between Kalymnos and Kos. It was included, along with Telendos and the other islets around Kalymnos, in the "Calydnian islands" mentioned by Homer in his "list of ships". The islet is referred to by Pliny (*Natural History* V 36, 134) as Pserema, among the islands of the Cerameicus Gulf. The name Pserimos (Ψήριμος) was preserved in a now lost inscription seen by W.R. Paton in 1888, in the village church: "ἐν κάποις ἐν Ψηρίμῳ… / in gardens on Pserimos". The inscription also mentioned archons of Kos (*monarchoi*, *gerephoros*, *pregistos* and *hieropoioi*), pointing to Pserimos's dependence on Kos in the third century AD, to which the inscription is dated.

Kos

DIMITRIOS BOSNAKIS

The exceptionally rich and systematic excavations conducted on Kos have been yielding results for over a century. First came the German classicist and archaeologist R. Herzog, who between 1900 and 1905 – when Kos was still part of the Ottoman Empire – brought to light the Asklepieion, the island's most splendid monument, which enjoyed panhellenic appeal in Antiquity. From 1912 until 1943, before the unification of the Dodecanese with Greece, the competent archaeologists of the Italian Archaeological Mission continued investigations on Kos, making an essential contribution to knowledge of the history and monumental topography not only of the capital city Kos-Meropis (fig. 524), but also of the other ancient demes.

The catastrophic earthquake of 23 April 1933 gave archaeologist L. Morricone the opportunity to undertake large-scale excavations in the city centre, result of which are the spacious archaeological sites-parks now incorporated in the urban tissue of the modern town. After the liberation of the island from the Italians in 1947, the local Ephorate of Antiquities, which was established in the 1970s in response to the building boom triggered by the development of tourism, has carried out mainly rescue excavations. These offer new evidence on the island's history, which has either prompted a revision of earlier views or filled in gaps in the record of its phases.

The earliest traces of human habitation date from the Final Neolithic period/Early Bronze Age (later 4th millennium BC) and are found all over the island (Troulli, Tsilibiri at the north end, Amaniou in central mountainous Kos, and the Aspri Petra Cave at the southwest end, to cite only the most important). The tradition that the first inhabitants of Kos were Karians and Lelegians can perhaps be detected in the mortuary habits and the pottery accompanying the burials of this period, which have been found in the area of Askloupi (environs of the Asklepieion), Mesaria and Antimacheia. These are *enchytrismoi*, in which the dead are inhumed in large jars with few grave goods, mainly domestic vases, which are encountered also in settlements in Asia Minor, such as Karian Iasos.

There has been continuous occupation on the site of the modern town since the Early Bronze Age (3rd millennium BC), which is attested on Seraglio Hill. Parts of a fortified settlement have been revealed and the pottery bears witness to open routes of communication with the East and with the Cyclades. The settlement flourished and expanded during the Middle Bronze Age (2000-1600 BC), and because of the existence of a good natural harbour and the proximity of the Asia Minor littoral, it was an important port of call on the maritime routes, mainly during the Late Minoan I period (16th century BC). During this period of the so-called "Minoan Thalassocracy", there

524. Kos. Silver tridrachm. On the obverse, a discobolus poised to throw the discus, beside his prize (tripod); on the reverse a crab. *C.* 480-450 BC. Athens, Numismatic Museum.

525. Kos. Mycenaean tholos tomb excavated recently on the Yorgaras plot.

526. Kos. Stirrup jar of the final Mycenaean period (12th c. BC), decorated with an octopus and linear motifs. From the cemetery of chamber tombs at Lagada. Kos Archaeological Museum.

are obvious Minoan elements in the thriving settlement, characteristic among which is the pier-and-door partition (*polythyron*), uncovered in a complex of house remains.

The tremendous eruption of the Thera volcano evidently covered the city with volcanic ash (pozzuolana), a layer of which has been identified in excavation, but life there was not interrupted and continued until around 1450 BC. Two tholos tombs have been found recently in isolated locations, one not far outside the town of Kos on the district road and the other southeast of the town limits. Dated to the thirteenth-twelfth century BC (Late Helladic IIIB-C period) and on account of their rarity in the Aegean region and their wealth (multiple burials with rich grave goods of pottery and gold jewellery), these have added new data on the scope of the Mycenaean Civilization on Kos (fig. 525).

Although no settlement from the Geometric period has yet been discovered, between 950 and 700 BC an extensive Protogeometric-Geometric cemetery occupied the greater part of the Mycenaean settlement. The wealth of finds (excellent quality local pottery and imported Cypro-Phoenician unguentaria, as well as talismanic amulets of Egyptian provenance) attests the presence of a dynamic community which, according to Herodotus, was due to the settlement of Dorian colonists from the Argolid. Recently, the *par excellence* Dorian funerary customs associated with the cremation of the dead have been confirmed on Kos, by clusters of pits containing primary cremations of males, which have come to light in the town and the wider area of Kardamaina.

Recent investigation have overturned earlier views that, in the absence of evidence, the settlement was abandoned in the Archaic period (6th century BC) and transferred to the south end of the island, which is identified as the old capital Astypalaia, according to Strabo. Significant parts of the settlement, with its sanctuaries and cemeteries, have been uncovered on the southwest outskirts of the town, indicating the unbroken continuity of habitation on the hill beside the harbour throughout the Archaic and Classical periods. In addition to one of the city's sanctuaries close to the harbour, the remains of a large temple (fig. 527) and possibly an enormous altar with impressive votive offerings (swords, Egyptian scarabs, Corinthian aryballoi and figurines of female deities), discovered in the area of Iraklis, east of the town, have given new momentum to research on Kos prior to the synoecism (figs 528-531). Among the important new finds that shed light on this period is a strong wall, 60 m. long, which has been identified with the fortification works carried out by Alcibiades when he used Kos as an operations base against Rhodes, in 410 BC.

In 366 BC, after synoecism, the new city of Kos was founded as capital of the entire island, inaugurating a long heyday in building activity and economic development. Characteristic is the testimony of Diodorus Siculus (XV 76,2), who praises the splendid fortification, the harbour, the public and the private prosperity of the new capital, visible to those approaching by sea and beholding the city, which although not particularly large was well appointed and well built, and therefore distinguished among other Hellenistic urban centres.

KOS | 341

The new city was organized according to the basic principles of the Hippodamean system. It was surrounded by a defensive wall, on the inside of which ran a wide perimetric street. Streets running from north to south and from east to west crossed at right angle, creating a grid of building *insulae* in the city's interior. The imposing fortification, four kilometres in length, was protected outside by circular, rectangular and polygonal towers. The harbour was protected by two long breakwaters. An islet at the harbour entrance created two narrow channels for the entry of ships. The ship-sheds used for hauling the warships ashore, have been uncovered in recent years.

The first building phase of the city, from the founding by synoecism and throughout the third century BC, was dubbed the "Travertine period" by the Italian excavator L. Morricone, because local travertine was used extensively in the buildings. During the second century BC, dubbed the "Marble period", the city enjoyed a considerable economic and building boom, which is reflected in the new edifices, this time constructed of local marble from the Dikaios quarries. Important public buildings came to light in both the large archaeological sites excavated by Italian archaeologists. Visible on the site of the agora and the harbour are part of the wall of the first period (preserved to a height of 2.50 m. and length 80 m.), constructed of large ashlar blocks in the isodomic system, part of the east breakwater and, contiguous with this, a rectangular stoa of the late fourth century BC, for the commercial needs of the port. Three sanctuaries of the second century BC were arranged *extra muros*, facing the harbour. These are the temple of Herakles (fig. 533), principal deity on Kos prior to the introduction of the cult of Asklepios, to the west a smaller temple of an unknown god, and even further west a third temple of the Aphrodision. A sacred precinct (*temenos*) on a podium, which included a large double temple dedicated to the cult of Aphrodite with the hypostases of Pandemos and Potnia.

527. Kos. View of the Archaic temple in the area of Iraklis.

528-531. Kos. Votive offerings from the Archaic temple in the area of Iraklis. Kos Archaeological Museum.

342 | DODECANESE

530

531

KOS | 343

Inside the walled city three building *insulae*, 33 metres wide, have been exposed, as well as the north part of the impressive complex of the ancient agora (fig. 532). The agora was Π-shaped and comprised a large internal court, 50 metres wide, surrounded by stoas. On the east and possibly the west side there were shops, while the north side abutted the fortification wall. Recent excavations have shown that the monument was over 300 metres long, creating one of the largest known agoras in the ancient world. In the south part there was a workshop producing pigments, mainly the Egyptian blue used in wall-paintings, and a workshop processing litharge.

At the southernmost end of the agora stood a Doric temple and altar to Dionysos, of the mid-second century BC (fig. 534), built according to Hellenistic models, like the temple of Zeus at Pergamon. The frieze of this temple, with relief representations from the Dionysiac cycle, has survived. The similarity in both architecture and iconography, such as the battles between Dionysos' thiasos and the Galatians, strongly suggest that the monument was a gift of the last Attalid kings.

The second large archaeological site in the town of Kos, known as the west site because it occupies part of the western sector of the city, includes the stadium, thermae, Vespasians and luxurious Roman villas. The intersection of the two main paved streets of the city in Roman times, the *decumanus maximus* and the *cardo*, has been uncovered here (fig. 535).

The stadium is of rectangular plan, without the horseshoe sphendone as was the norm, and preserves to this day the starting line (*apheses*), where the automatic starting mechanism was installed. Further south is one of the three gymnasia of Kos, 200 metres long and with an internal peristyle court. The Doric east stoa, known as the *xystos dromos*, is where athletes trained for track events when the weather was bad, mainly in the winter months. Constructed abutting

532. Kos. East stoa of the building in the ancient agora. 2nd c. BC.

533. Kos. View of the *temenos* of Herakles Kallinikos, in the vicinity of the harbour. 2nd c. BC.

the monument were the opulent bathhouse complex (thermae) and east of these the public lavatories, known as Vespasians, now restored. This is a building with cement walling, internal peristyle court and elaborate architectural decoration.

North of the *decumanus* are the Roman villas, lavishly decorated with mosaic floors and painted murals, and adorned with statues (fig. 543). Outstanding is the tessellated pavement with representation of the "Rape of Europa", as well as another in the northeast part of the site, central scene of which is the "Judgement of Paris", and with complementary scenes of combat with wild beasts (fig. 537).

South of the west archaeological site are two restored monuments of Roman imperial times. The Casa Romana, a villa erected upon a Hellenistic residence – the foundations of which are visible. Its impressive interior is arranged around three internal courts and is richly decorated with polychrome marble dadoes, *opus intersectile*, mosaics and frescoes.

The Roman odeum, a roofed building that held an audience of 750 persons (fig. 538), accommodated the activities of the senate as well as musical events and recitals of encomia for the Roman emperor. The odeum has a peculiar pentagonal skene, while under the cavea are porticoes and rectangular tabernae.

The Hellenistic theatre, which the Italian excavators identified at the southeast edge of the city, remains essentially unexcavated and therefore unknown.

Even in Antiquity, the Asklepieion was the most renowned monument on Kos. According to the relevant passage in Strabo (XIV 2,19), it was situated a short distance from the city and was full of famous *ex-votos*, such as the panels by the great painter Apelles, "Antigonos" and "Aphrodite Anadyomene". Another ancient literary source, the third-century BC poet Heron-

534. Kos. The altar of Dionysos. Monumental building arranged after Pergamene architectural models. Its frieze bears relief representation from the Dionysiac cycle. Mid-2nd c. BC.

535. Kos. View of the Roman *cardo* (main street running northeast-southwest). Roman imperial period.

KOS 345

das, refers in his fourth mimiamb to statues by the sons of Praxiteles, Kephisodotos and Timarchos, representing the family of Asklepios, that adorned the homonymous altar. During the third and second centuries BC worship of Asklepios was enhanced as one of the most important public cults of Kos.

If Epidauros claimed to be the paramount place where the myth of the healing god Asklepios and his miracles developed, Kos, as birthplace of Hippokrates, vied with it as the paramount place where medical science developed. Indeed, according to the testimony of Strabo (VII 6, 15), *ex-votos* recording cures were set up in the sanctuary at Epidauros, as well as at Kos and at Trikke in Thessaly. Although the Asklepieion of Kos has yielded numerous inscriptions of religious and political content, nothing has survived of the "*iamata*" (inscriptions recording cures) and the characteristic votive reliefs for therapies. This is extremely odd, as according to Pliny (*Natural History* XXIX 2, 4) Hippokrates himself had gathered much information from the archived case histories of the sick persons who visited the Asklepieion.

The inclusion, by law, of the cult of Asklepios in the sacred grove on the slopes of a low hill with unimpeded view towards the Asia Minor shore, created a monumental installation extending over three terraces (fig. 539). Excavations have shown that the sanctuary was designed and developed during the third century BC as a single complex of buildings with ultimate conscious aim to continue and to promote the worship of Asklepios. The year 242 BC is a *terminus ante quem* for the completion of the construction of the main monuments, since it was then that the Koans claimed the right of asylum for the sanctuary and concurrently organized the quinquennial festival of the Asklepieia, of panhellenic appeal.

The earliest building was an altar of the mid-fourth century BC, on the middle terrace, which according to an inscription was dedicated jointly to Helios, Hemera, Hekate and Machaon, son of Asklepios. In the mid-second century BC the altar, the position of which remained the same, was rearranged after the model of the magnificent altar of Zeus at Pergamon.

In the early third century BC, the temple of Asklepios (fig. 540) was built opposite the altar. This was a small temple in the Ionic order, two-columned *in antis*, with rectangular pronaos and cella of equal size. The wide base of the statues of Asklepios, Hygieia and Machaon was found inside the cella, as well as the marble box, gift of the city of Kos according to the founding inscription (shortly after 300 BC), for the safe-keeping of the sanctuary's monies, known as *thesauros* (treasury). The elegant, though somewhat academic, architectural form of the temple, to the decoration of which radical changes were made in the second century BC, is reminiscent of the temple of Zeus in Magnesia.

In the early third century BC, an almost square building-*abaton*, with two spaces intended as *enkoimeteria* (dormitories) for men and for women, was added south of the temple.

The so-called Lesche, built east of the altar, is a portico with the bases of five votive statues preserved in front of its back wall. In later times the *ex-votos* offered by suppliants to the sanctuary were stored here. Behind the altar is another temple, now partially restored, which in the time of the Antonine emperors (2nd century AD) acquired a pteron with columns in the Corinthian

536. Kos. Part of an Archaic grave relief (6th c. BC) with representation of a child holding a cockerel and an aryballos (small vase for perfumed oil). Kos Archaeological Museum.

537. Kos. View of the mosaic with representation of the "Judgement of Paris". 2nd c. BC. West archaeological site.

ΠΑΡΙС ΕΡΜ

ΠΟΘΟС

KOS | 347

538. Kos. View of the Roman odeum in the ancient city. 3rd c. AD.

539. Kos. View of the Asklepieion. Roman arrangement of the retaining wall on the lower terrace, in the niches of which stood statues. Visible left is the fountain, and in the middle the monumental staircase leading as far as the upper terrace. On the middle terrace are the temple of Asklepios (right) and the Roman temple in the Corinthian order, possibly dedicated to Apollo (left).

540. Kos. Asklepieion. The Ionic temple of Asklepios on the middle terrace. 3rd c. BC.

KOS | 349

order. This is believed to have been dedicated to Apollo, father of Asklepios, who with the epithet Kyparissios was the first lord of the sacred grove. A semicircular exedra, possibly constructed for assemblies of the priesthood, and a fountain complete the installations on the middle terrace, which served primarily cultic needs.

Sometime in the second century BC a low terrace with peristyle stoas on three sides was created. Behind this shady Π-shaped passage of stoas were 26 cubicles for the needs of the sick. The lateral stoas reached as far as the retaining wall of the middle terrace, but left two wide passageways. The space was entered from the lower terrace, through a majestic tetrastyle propylon leading to a splendid open-air staircase.

The sanctuary was supplied with water through three fountains, which were incorporated in the retaining walls reinforced with arches, right and left of the second staircase leading to the middle terrace. Water was brought to the Asklepieion from two springs on the slopes of Horomedon, one southwest of the Asklepieion, the Kokkinonero, with the reddish iron-rich waters, and one southeast, the Vourinas source, which still supplies water to the town.

In the first century AD lavatories were built behind the right stoa. In the same period, a large thermae complex was constructed on the left side of the terrace. The bathhouse and the water conduit are considered to have been donated by a famous Koan doctor, Gaius Stertinius Xenophon, who lived in Rome and was personal physician to Emperor Claudius. Among the other probable benefactions of this renowned medical man to the sanctuary is the little temple (naiskos) to the right of the staircase leading to the middle terrace, which was dedicated to Asklepios, Hygieia and Hepione, as well as a library.

Although a third higher terrace had been created already by the third century BC, the space only acquired the monumental installations appropriate to the rest of the terraces in the second century BC, when the Asklepieion was placed under the protection of Eumenes II of Pergamon (197-159 BC). A larger monumental staircase leads to the last terrace, on the central axis of which is placed the large Doric peripteral temple erected in 170/160 BC. The new peripteral temple, copy of the temple of Asklepios at Epidauros but of larger dimensions, is orientated north-south and has no altar. Doric stoas with rooms, which replaced earlier wooden ones, for accommodating the numerous pilgrims, were constructed on three sides of the third terrace.

As far as the rest of the island is concerned, six demes are known from inscriptions of the Hellenistic period. In the deme of the Phyxeotai or Pyxeotai, possibly in the wider area of modern Asphendiou, traces of fortification of a settlement and part of a necropolis have been identified. In the deme of the Hippiotai, possibly between Zipari and

541. Kos. Kardamaina. General view of building Γ-Early Hellenistic temple of ancient Alasarna.

542. Kos. Kardamaina. Inscribed stone block of an anta with wreaths, from the temple-building Γ. The inscriptions inside the wreaths honour the members of a family who were perhaps benefactors of the temple and date to the 3rd c. AD.

543. Kos. Statue of Hermes. The god wears the winged cap (petasos) and winged sandals, and holds a *kerykeion*. Beside him stands a ram. Found in the "House of the Europa mosaic". 2nd c. AD. Kos Archaeological Museum.

Mastichari, a temple of Hera has been located at the site of Ai-Yorgis Liizos. In the deme of the Halentiai, in the area of modern Pylio, Mycenaean tombs, the Hellenistic heroon of Charmylos (the underground chamber with the many funerary niches and architectural members from the overlying naiskos have survived) and a temple of Demeter have been found at Kyparissi Amaniou.

In the deme of the Alasarnitai, in the vicinity of the modern coastal village of Kardamaina, the religious centre of the deme with the sanctuaries has been found (figs 541, 542), as well as the site of the Hellenistic theatre. In the wider area of modern Antimacheia, was the deme of the Antimachidai, Archiadai and Aigeliai, well-known centre of the worship of Herakles, where part of the Hellenistic necropolis has been found. Last, in the deme of the Isthmiotai, at the south end of the island, in the environs of modern Kephalos, which is also considered the seat of the ancient capital Astypalaia, a small Doric temple of the fifth century BC, possibly of Demeter, has come to light (in the foundations of the church of the Virgin Palatiani), as well as a Hellenistic theatre with two Doric temples, one associated epigraphically with the cult of Asklepios, Hygieia and Homonoia.

543

KOS | 351

Astypalaia

Maria Michalaki-Kollia

Completely isolated from the other larger islands, Astypalaia "lying in the open sea", as Strabo says, forms a bridge between the Dodecanese and the Cyclades. Surrounded by numerous islets and with a coastline indented by many coves and bays, it was inhabited already by the Early Bronze Age (3rd millennium BC), as attested by archaeological finds mainly from the sites of Vathy, Vai and Ai-Yannis. The pottery found there displays similarities with that of the Early Cycladic period, while part of a Cycladic violin-shaped figurine was discovered at Vathy. The Mycenaean presence on the island is indicated by chamber tombs in the hinterland at Armenochori and on the coast at Sygairo.

During historical times the island was inhabited by Dorians. Astypalaia is mentioned as a colony of the Megarians, while an inscription at Epidauros links it with the Argolid. Other historical sources record its participation in the Greek colonization. Astypalaia was apparently the birthplace of Phalaris, Tyrant of Akragas, and the historian Onesikritos. In the fifth century BC it appears in the fiscal lists of the First Athenian League. Nonetheless, it remained an independent polity throughout its history.

The island's capital has occupied the same position as today's Chora since the seventh century BC, with the acropolis on the same site as that of the Venetian castle built by the Querini overlords. In its heyday, from the fifth century BC onwards, Astypalaia was an organized city-state with a boule, deme, senate, prytaneion, agora, theatre, stadium and harbour, as is known from inscriptions and ancient authors. There are also testimonies of the existence of treasury officials (*tamiai*, *logistai*) and market inspectors (*agoranomoi*), as well as of a "*damiorgos*", as eponymous archon. The numerous inscriptions found on the island – some of which are exhibited in the small local museum – also reveal the existence of temples: of Athena and Asklepios, of Apollo, of Artemis Lochia, of Eileithyia or Diktynna, of Sarapis and Isis. There is mention of an "oikos" of Zeus Soteras, as well as of several cults, such as of Dionysos, Aphrodite, Hera, the Nymphs, Kore (Persephone), Roma, Achilles and the athlete Kleomedes.

Of particular interest is the inscription-dedication to Helios and Rhodes, by the head of a Rhodian expeditionary force, Kleinombrotos, which testifies to the good relations between Astypalaia and the Rhodian State. Another two noteworthy inscriptions refer to the Syrian deity Atargatis. The island has two caves with wonderful stalagmite and stalactite formations, as well as finds dating at least from the Archaic period. The "Negro's" Cave was associated with worship of the Nymphs, as confirmed by the discovery there of an inscription incised on the base of an Attic vase.

The ancient cemeteries extended on the outskirts of the modern settlement of Chora, on Katsalos Hill, opposite the Kastro. The graves uncovered there are mainly pits containing primary

352 | DODECANESE

cremations and date from the Late Geometric and Archaic periods (fig. 545), while inhumations and jar-burials (*enchytrismoi*) of adults and children are also represented, continuing into Roman times. On the contrary, on the southwest lower slopes of the Kastro and below the houses of the settlement, in the area of southwest Kylindra, which has not yet been built on (fig. 544), a cemetery of jar-burials exclusively of newborn infants is being excavated (fig. 546). Over 2,000 *enchytrismoi* have been recovered so far. The physical anthropological study of some 500 skeletons, conducted by a team of British specialists, has revealed that with the exception of four or five cases all the remains are of newborn infants. This find, unique in Greece, possibly alludes to some kind of cult, particularly if it is associated with the two inscriptions relating to Artemis Lochia and Eileithyia (the goddess of child-bearing), which were found many years ago built into the walls of houses in Chora.

The important location of Astypalaia on the sea routes attracted the interest of the Romans, who in 105 BC signed with the city the alliance known from an inscription as "*foedus aequum*", that is alliance on equal terms. Astypalaia still kept its autonomy, helping the Romans in their efforts to eradicate the scourge of piracy, while also enjoying their friendship into later imperial times. From this period too a considerable number of inscriptions has been found on the island, including three interesting "epistles" of Roman emperors.

Syrna

Syrna lies southeast of Astypalaia, to which it belongs administratively. Atop the hill overlooking the deep bay are the foundations of an ancient fort and enclosures. The wider area is scattered with obsidian débitage and potsherds dating from prehistoric into Hellenistic times. Virtually the whole area from the sea to the hill is arranged with retaining walls, creating terraces for cultivation. One tiny sherd of a Minoan vase found in the hinterland recalls the mythical tradition, recorded by Ovid, linking Astypalaia with the Minoan Civilization. Recently, a fisherman found – and handed in to the authorities – a small Cycladic figurine on the seashore. A huge hoard of coins found in the sea off Syrna and dating from the reign of Diocletian in the third century BC, points to the existence of a Roman shipwreck.

544. Astypalaia. General view of the settlement of Chora. Visible on the southwest side of Kylindra is the excavation of the site with the jar-burials of newborn infants.

545. Astypalaia. Incised miniature vases from a cremation burial in the cemetery in the Katsalos area, Chora. Astypalaia Archaeological Museum.

546. Astypalaia. Jar-burials of newborn infants from the excavations on the southwest side of Kylindra, Chora. 6th c. BC.

Nisyros

Melina Filimonos-Tsopotou

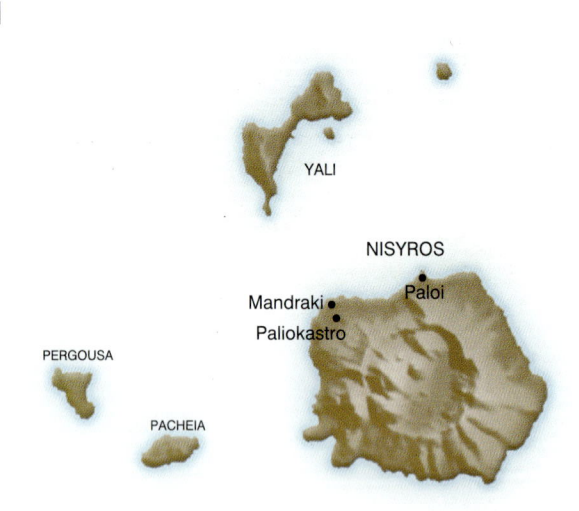

Strabo's account of the creation of Nisyros is as follows (X 5,16): "They say that Nisyros is a fragment of Cos, and they add the myth that Poseidon, when he was pursuing one of the giants Ponybotes, broke off a fragment of Cos with his trident and hurled it upon him, and the missile became an island, Nisyros, with the giant lying beneath it". There is no doubt that the myth alludes to the volcanic activity on the island, manifest from Antiquity.

Nisyros, approximately 41 square kilometres in area, is one of the smallest islands in the Dodecanese. Strabo describes it as "round, high and stony". There are few finds from the prehistoric period, among them a Cycladic figurine in the Berlin Museum.

In the "list of ships" in the *Iliad*, Homer recounts that Nisyros, together with Kos, Karpathos, Kasos and Kalymnos, took part in the campaign against Troy with thirty ships, under the command of the two sons of Thessalos, Pheidippos and Antiphos. The island's Dorian character is apparent also in Herodotus' testimony (VII 99) that its inhabitants came from Epidauros. The Persian expansion and conquest of the cities in the Asia Minor littoral was decisive for the island's fate. Thus, in 480 BC, Nisyros along with Kos and Kalymnos were subject to Artemisia, female dynast of Halikarnassos, and participated in the naval battle of Salamis with five ships. After the end of the Persian domination of the island the Nisyrians joined the First Athenian League, paying tax, as did the neighbouring islands.

Nisyros flourished during the fourth century BC, as an autonomous city-state that minted its own coinage. Its territory encompassed the nearby islets, notable among which is Pergoussa, where two rectangular towers survive in good condition. Around 200 BC Nisyros was subjugated to the great Rhodian State, henceforth following its fortunes until it came within the sphere of influence of the Roman Republic and subsequently became part of the Roman Empire.

The island's most important monument is undoubtedly the wall of the ancient city, which crowns the low hill southwest of Mandraki and is called Palaiokastro by the locals. This is one of the most impressive and best-preserved fortification works of the ancient world (fig. 548). It is constructed of black volcanic stone in the pseudo-isodomic trapezoidal system of masonry on both faces, with rubble fill. Carved on the outside, north of the gateway that survives intact, is the inscription: "Δαμόσιον τό χορίων πέντε πόδες από τό τείχος", which defines the width of the public zone of five feet that must remain free of any use, for defensive purposes. On the inside of the wall built staircases led to towers and the parodos. The ancient harbour, mentioned by Strabo, must have been situated low down, in the fertile region of Mandraki now known as Limnes, and has been silted up for centuries.

No excavations have been made in the settlement itself, which spread on the flat hilltop as well as on the steep west slope down to the sea. Nonetheless, the island's heyday in both Archaic and

547. Nisyros. Plate from the Archaic cemetery of the island, first half of 6th c. BC. Nisyros Archaeological Museum.

548. Nisyros. Tower on the south side of the defensive wall, which was reconstructed in the Hellenistic period. Visible in the distance is the islet of Pergousa.

Classical times is attested by the rich finds from the cemetery which covered the hillside *extra muros* as well as the height of Ai-Yannis opposite, above Mandraki. Here, systematic excavations by Italian archaeologists in 1932 and by the Greek Archaeological Service in recent years have brought to light an extensive cemetery that was in use from the seventh century BC until Early Roman times.

During the Archaic period funeral pyres for adults were the norm. These have yielded abundant pottery with painted decoration, characteristic of the region of eastern Doris (fig. 547). Jar-burials (*enchytrismoi*) were reserved for infants and children. In contrast, from the fifth and mainly in the fourth century BC all the dead were buried in large pithoi or clay sarcophagi. The grave goods accompanying them on their post-mortem journey included a preponderance of imported Attic vases. Two relief grave stelai were found in the cemetery; one of them, with a representation of an athlete and dated to the mid-fifth century BC, is in the Istanbul Archaeological Museum.

The thermal baths, of which Strabo writes in the first century AD, were on the site of the Roman thermae at Paloi. Preserved here is a large vaulted-roofed rectangular hall, where a small single-aisle Post-Byzantine church has been built, known characteristically as the Virgin Thermiani.

The official god of Nisyros was Poseidon, whose attributes, the dolphin and the trident, appear on the city's coinage. Inscriptions found on the island also attest to the worship of Apollo Dalios (there is a locality Dali), Aphrodite, Ares, Artemis, Dionysos and Hermes. A sanctuary of Zeus Meilichios must have existed close to the Holy Trinity church at Mandraki, as deduced from four inscriptions of the Roman period, referring to the purifying god of the Underworld and of fertility.

Yali

Excavations on the volcanic islet of Yali (figs 25, 26), northwest of Nisyros, have revealed significant remains of human occupation in the Final Neolithic period (4th millennium BC), notable among which are a building of elliptical plan, as well as moveable finds such as two crucibles for smelting copper, pointing to the early practice of metallurgy. Habitation on Yali was seasonal and probably associated with agriculture and animal husbandry, rather than with the working of obsidian, which is abundant in the northwest part of the isle.

Telos

Melina Filimonos-Tsopotou

The geographer Strabo (X 5,15) describes Telos, a small island approximately 63 square kilometres in area, lying between Rhodes and Kos: "Telos extends alongside Caria, is long, high, narrow, has a perimeter of about one hundred and forty stadia, and has an anchoring-place", and ascribes it to the Sporades group.

Investigations by the Palaeontological and Geological Laboratory of the University of Athens, in the Charkadio Cave, below the Medieval castle of Mesaria, have brought to light fossils of dwarf elephants that lived on the island 45,000 years ago. The disturbed archaeological levels in the cave bear witness to human presence there from the Final Neolithic period (4th millennium BC), while stone tools and potsherds date from the Early Bronze Age (3rd millennium BC). Traces of Neolithic habitation have been noted in the area of Lakkia, on the Megalo Chorio plain, while at Garipa moveable finds indicate the existence of a Late Bronze Age settlement (second half of 2nd millennium BC).

Telos appears dynamically on the forestage of history in the seventh century BC, participating with Lindos, already a strong naval power, in the colonization of Gela in Sicily. Herodotus (VII 153) recounts that Telines ancestor of Gelon, "was of the island of Telos, that lies off Triopium". During the fifth century BC the island joined the First Athenian League. The naval battle of Knidos in 394 BC, which expelled the Spartan fleet from the islands of the East Aegean, marked the beginning of the happiest period in the history of Telos. Historical testimonies, inscriptions and coins attest to the independence of the island and its democratic regime, at least until the second half of the third century BC, when it was annexed to the Rhodian State, whose fortunes it subsequently followed.

The most important archaeological site on Telos is the ancient settlement above Megalo Chorio. Clinging to the east side of the steep hill and unseen from the sea, it had two safe harbours,

549. Telos. Detail of a gold diadem with Herakles knot and two winged Eros figures. Found in a Hellenistic grave (1st half 3rd c. BC). Rhodes Archaeological Museum.

at Eristos and Aghios Antonios, where remains of ancient harbour installations have been identified. The houses in the ancient city were founded on terraces underpinned by mighty retaining walls, behind which were cisterns in which rainwater was collected for domestic needs. The walls visible today date from Classical and Hellenistic times, although recent research has shown that the terraces were perhaps laid out in the Archaic period. The centre of settlement on the island today is lower down, at the foot of the hill.

Dominating the summit of the hill is the fortified acropolis, where stood the temple of Zeus Polieus and Athena Polias, which was covered over in the fourteenth-fifteenth century by the church of the Taxiarchs. Scant remains of the ancient buildings survive inside the Medieval castle, as there was continuous occupation of the site in Byzantine times and the Middle Ages (fig. 551). The city was surrounded by a wall, the best-preserved part of which is visible low down in the village, behind the new church of the Taxiarch (fig. 550).

The cemeteries of the Classical and Hellenistic periods, with underground chambers cut in the bedrock, spread in the fertile plain below the city and on the rocky shore of Aghios Antonios. An important ensemble of gold jewellery dated to the third century BC, recovered from a grave in the area of the plain, is indicative of the wealth this small island enjoyed during its heyday (fig. 549).

On Kastellos, a rocky hill overlooking Leivadia, are remnants of fortified enceinte and a tower. Early Bronze Age sherds here point to habitation also in prehistoric times.

Although no systematic archaeological research has yet been conducted on the island, the numerous inscriptions from the Classical and Hellenistic periods are irrefutable witnesses to the social and political organization of the ancient Telians, as well as to their private life.

550. Telos. The ancient fortification behind the church of the Taxiarch at Megalo Chorio.

551. Telos. The acropolis and the ancient settlement above Megalo Chorio. Visible in the foreground is the ancient defensive wall.

Syme

Eleni Farmakidou

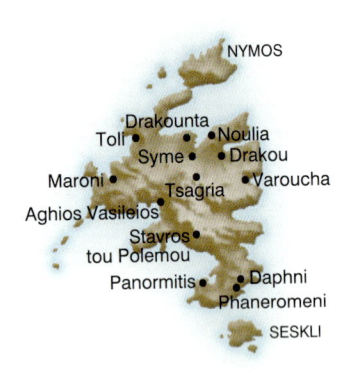

In the Gulf of Doris, formed by the deep embrace of Asia Minor between Rhodes and Kos, lies the small rocky island of Syme. Its geographical location determined its historical course, as the scant ancient textual sources also demonstrate.

The island's name is lost in the mists of mythical time and is attributed to its first settlers: to Glaukos who abducted Syme, daughter of Ialysos and Dotis, and brought her to this desert isle (Athenaeus VI 1.296.b.8-c.9-11), or to Chthonios, son of Poseidon and Syme, founder-hero (*oikistes*) who came to the region with Triops (Diodorus Siculus V 53,1-3). The reference to the King of Syme, Nireus, in the list of ships that took part in the Trojan War (*Iliad* II 671-675) links the island with Mycenaean Greece.

Surface surveys have identified at various sites in the hinterland and on the surrounding islets (Drakounta, Drakou, Varoucha, Aghios Vasileios, Stavros tou Polemou, Panormitis, Daphni, Seskli, and elsewhere) traces of human presence dating from the Late Neolithic (4th millennium BC) to the Late Bronze Age (second half of 2nd millennium BC). This evidence places Syme in the cultural group of the Southeast Aegean during the Early Bronze Age (3rd millennium BC), whereas strong Minoan influences exist from at least the beginning of the Late Bronze Age (16th century BC), as ascertained from remains in the area of Drakounta.

For early historical times the ancient sources recount that in one of the later phases of the Dorian migrations Syme was colonized by Argeians and Lacedaemonians. First to settle was a group led by Nausos, who was followed by Xouthos with colonists from Rhodes and Knidos (Diodorus Siculus V 53.1-3). As an "island close to Karia" it must have been in the territory of the Dorian hexapolis, an amphictyony centred on the sanctuary of Apollo Triopios near Knidos (Herodotus I 144). It was incorporated politically in the group of Dorian cities in the Southeast Aegean, which during the Persian Wars were forced to provide Xerxes with forty ships.

Later, Syme paid tax to the Athenian League, as is deduced from the latter's fiscal lists. During the Peloponnesian War the island was occupied by the Athenians, who used it as an arsenal (*skeuapotheke*) of the Athenian Navy and perhaps as a billeting station for military forces. Thucydides records that in the twentieth year of the war (412/11 BC), the fleets of the Lacedaemonians and the Athenians fought a sea battle between Syme and Knidos. After their victory, the Spartans came ashore on the island and set up a trophy there (Thucydides VIII 41-43). Doubtful, though not impossible, is the identification of this trophy with the tumulus known as Pontikokastro on Noulia Hill (fig. 552), east of the windmills in the present capital. The earliest surviving phase of the fortification on the acropolis of Syme (fig. 553) can be dated to the fifth century BC. An inscription records the existence of a temple of Athena inside the acropolis.

In Hellenistic times, under the sovereignty of the Rhodian State, Symeans are mentioned in inscriptions as: "κοινὸν τῶν ἐν Σύμᾳ κατοικούντων" (*koinon* of those residing on Syme) and

552. Syme. Pontikokastro, Noulia. Ancient tumulus with circular stone crepis.

553. Kastro of Syme (ancient acropolis), seen from the southwest. An ancient fortification with Medieval additions. The best-preserved part of the ancient wall with rectangular tower, immediately west of the modern staircase to the church of the Virgin of the Castle (Panaghia tou Kastrou).

it is argued that they belonged to one of the Rhodian demes of the Peraia, perhaps the deme of Kasareoi.

Most of the monuments dispersed on the island and the nearby islets, which are known locally as "Kastra" (of Syme, Tsagria, Phaneromeni, Nymos, Seskli, etc.), date to this last period. The monuments in the countryside should be interpreted as farmsteads, rural towers or signal towers (*phryktoria*), military guard-posts.

In Roman times Syme's fortunes were yoked to those of Rhodes, with alternating periods of "liberty" and annexation to neighbouring provinces. In the reign of Emperor Vespasian (AD 69-79) it became part of the *Provincia Insularum*, which was subject to the Diocese of Asia, with which it was united finally in the reign of Diocletian, in AD 279.

The exhibits housed in the Syme Archaeological Museum are mainly from donations of small private collections and finds from surface surveys, since systematic archaeological research on the island has yet to commence.

Rhodes

TOULA MARKETOU – IOANNIS CH. PAPACHRISTODOULOU

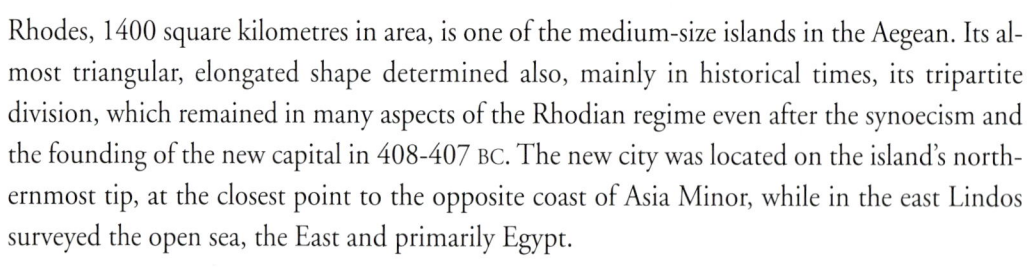

Rhodes, 1400 square kilometres in area, is one of the medium-size islands in the Aegean. Its almost triangular, elongated shape determined also, mainly in historical times, its tripartite division, which remained in many aspects of the Rhodian regime even after the synoecism and the founding of the new capital in 408-407 BC. The new city was located on the island's northernmost tip, at the closest point to the opposite coast of Asia Minor, while in the east Lindos surveyed the open sea, the East and primarily Egypt.

The fertile soil of Rhodes favoured the development of agriculture, while its strategic position on the maritime routes from the Aegean to the East and vice-versa favoured trade and seafaring. The proximity to Asia Minor played a special role in the history and culture of the Southeast Aegean islands at various times, and the ties with the Aegean world and the metropolis on the Greek Mainland were close and continuous, particularly during the Minoan and Mycenaean periods (2nd millennium BC).

The earliest traces of human presence on Rhodes are dated, on present evidence, to the Late and Final Neolithic period (5300-3400 BC). These were seasonal installations in fertile parts of the island, mainly in caves in the area of Erimokastro and of Kalythies, at Kolympia, in the rocky environs of Archangelos, around Lindos and Pefkoi. There are also sporadic traces of habitation in the southernmost part of the island and to a lesser degree in the west part. Domesticated animals – sheep, goats, dogs, pigs and cattle – were kept for their meat and their produce, while wild animals – deer, hares and birds – were hunted as game. The inhabitants, who usually chose areas close to the coast, were engaged also in fishing and collecting molluscs, while they grew wheat, barley and vetch.

In the course of excavating the Aghios Georgios Cave at Kalythies, three successive occupation levels were identified in the Late Neolithic period, from 5300 to 4000/3700 BC. The Koumelo Cave at Archangelos, which has also been excavated, was inhabited from the phase of later occupation at Kalythies into the Final Neolithic period (3400 BC). The pottery used in this phase, is contemporary with the settlement at Kephala on Kea. Other finds, such as tools of obsidian from Melos, Yali and Anatolia, bear witness to reciprocal influences with islands in the Cyclades and the Northeast Aegean, as well as with Asia Minor, in the Chalcolithic Age, transitional to the Bronze Age.

Rhodes, like the rest of the Dodecanesian islands, kept several of the Final Neolithic characteristics until the early third millennium BC. A few fortuitous finds from southern Rhodes, displaying traits of the wider cultural group of southern Asia Minor, and some Cycladic ones, are dated to the Early Bronze II period (2800-2300 BC).

At Asomatos, between Kremasti and Paradeisi, in the part of the island closest to Asia Minor, the earliest known settlement on Rhodes was discovered, with large buildings of rectangular

554

plan (fig. 555), which date from the Early Bronze IIB period (2400/2300 BC) to the end of the Early Bronze Age (2050/1950 BC). The buildings of the later phase at the settlement are of megaron plan and on the floors of one of them, which has been uncovered completely, were many intact vases, tools and animal bones. The variety of vessels (fig. 556), such as elegant duck vases and jugs, well-made cups, amphorae with potters' marks, incised spindle whorls similar to those at Troy, bear witness to aesthetic sophistication, while their spatial distribution points to excellent organization. Both architecture and material culture display cultural affinity with Heraion on Samos, Troy and Western Anatolia, with reciprocal influences from the Northeast Aegean, the Cyclades and the northeastern Peloponnese.

At the end of the Early Bronze Age (2050/1950 BC) the inhabitants suddenly abandoned the settlement. Sporadic Middle Bronze Age installations have been located on the hill at Philerimos, Trianda – under parts of the large Late Bronze Age city – while further north and east groups of Middle Bronze Age houses have been revealed, as well as a space with many loomweights, similar to those found in the area of Akantia harbour in the city of Rhodes. The local pottery is wheel-made and includes carinated cups, jugs, kalathos-shaped vases, amphorae and pithoi. During this period the economy was evidently based more on agriculture and domestic manufacturing activities, such as textile weaving.

At the beginning of the Late Bronze Age (*circa* 1700/1650 BC), one of the largest cities in the Aegean, covering an area of over 17 hectares, was founded at Trianda (Ialysos), on the founda-

554. Rhodes, Ialysos. Wall-painting fragment with depiction of red lilies on a white ground. Dated to the 17th c. BC. Found in 1936 during the Italian excavations directed by G. Monanco. Rhodes Archaeological Museum. Prehistoric Collection.

555. Rhodes. The Early Bronze III period (late 3rd millennium BC) building of megaron plan at Asomatos, Kremasti. View of the excavation from the south. The excavation has yielded valuable evidence on the spatial distribution of the finds, the rich economy of the settlement and the cultural interaction with the Northeast Aegean, the Cyclades, the northeastern Peloponnese and Asia Minor.

556. Rhodes. Anthropomorphic amphora of the Early Bronze III period (late 3rd millennium BC), from Asomatos, Kremasti. The facial features modelled on the shoulder of the vase are picked out in red paint. Rhodes Archaeological Museum. Prehistoric Collection.

tions of the earlier settlement. On account of its location and the culture that had developed on the island from the Early Bronze Age, the new city forged relations during the Late Bronze IA period (*circa* 1630 BC, according to the new dating of the eruption of the Thera volcano) with the major palatial centres of Minoan Crete, Seraglio on Kos, Miletos and Iasos in Asia Minor, Aghia Irini on Kea and Akrotiri on Thera. Particularly close also were its ties with Cyprus and Egypt.

In the early phases of this period the architecture (fig. 558) and the pottery retained the local character, but towards the end models of Minoan pottery were adopted, together with architectural features such as pier-and-door partitions (*polythyra*) and decorative "sacral horns". The new buildings were founded on strong walls, frequently with upper storeys and ashlar façade, and were decorated with wall-paintings with lilies (fig. 554), double axe with sacred knot and elaborate rosettes, parts of larger compositions of high art. Three bronze figurines of adorants, of Minoan type, found in one of the ashlar buildings, hint at the practice of domestic cult (fig. 557).

The end of the Late Minoan IA city was sealed by the fall of volcanic ash after the eruption of the Thera volcano, after a destructive earthquake *circa* 1630 BC. By this time habitation had spread randomly into the countryside of Ialysos, as far as Paradeisi, further east to Kolybia, Siana in the southwest part of the island, as well as the site of the present city of Rhodes, on the hill of the neighbourhood of Aghioi Anargyroi. On the surface of the volcanic ash layer, a smaller city was built in the Late Bronze IIB period, on the outskirts of the northernmost part of the ruined earlier city. It kept contacts with various sites in the Aegean, Cyprus and the Eastern Mediterranean (fig. 559). The Mycenaean phase of the settlement covers the period 1440-1340 BC, in parallel with the Mycenaean chamber tomb cemetery at Moschou and Makria Vounara,

557. Rhodes. Bronze adorant figurine of Cretan type, dated to the Late Bronze IA period (17th c. BC). It was found with another two figurines of the same type outside an ashlar building in the central part of the city at Trianda. These figurines not only hint at domestic cult inside the imposing buildings but also offer information on the dress and hairstyles of the period. Rhodes Archaeological Museum. Prehistoric Collection.

558. Rhodes. View of the excavation in the south sector of the 17th c. BC city at Trianda. Visible are two pier-and-door partitions (*polythyra*) destroyed by the earthquake and deposits of debris from clearing the ruins, which were covered subsequently by pozzuolana from the eruption of the Thera volcano.

559. Rhodes. Fragment of an imported vase with dense reed decoration (17th c. BC). Found at Trianda, above the level of volcanic ash (pozzuolana). Rhodes Archaeological Museum. Prehistoric Collection.

560. Rhodes. Wheel-made equine figurine loaded with vases. Late Helladic IIIC period (1180-1065 BC). Offering in a Mycenaean grave in the cemetery at Moschou Vounara, Ialysos. Rhodes Archaeological Museum. Prehistoric Collection.

Ialysos (fig. 567), until its final abandonment after a catastrophic flood which reduced the area to marshland for several centuries.

Graves at Paradeisi and Lardos, the Mycenaean installation at Aghios Minas near Kattavia and Apsachtira, and Angeio at Vati date to the same period (Late Helladic IIB-IIIA).

During the second half of the fourteenth century BC (Late Helladic IIIA period) there was an increase in the number of graves at Ialysos, while Mycenaean cemeteries have been excavated virtually all over the island. The decrease in graves at Ialysos and the northwest part of the island during the succeeding Later Helladic IIIB period (*circa* 1340-1180 BC) coincides with the corresponding increase of sites in southern Rhodes. During the next period, Late Helladic IIIC (1180-1065 BC), an increase in graves is observed at Ialysos, as well as in many sites on the island, and the pottery is in the spirit of the so-called "Aegean Koine", with lots of local features (fig. 560). The following century, at least until the late Protogeometric period (9th century BC), is a "dark age" for Rhodes and the Dodecanese as a whole, which picture is perhaps due to the lack of excavation evidence.

Rhodes in historical times was Dorian, like most of the Dodecanese. The earliest literary record of its three cities, Lindos, Ialysos and Kamiros, is in rhapsody II of Homer's *Iliad*. The cities later participated in a union, the Dorian hexapolis, corresponding to the Ionian dodecapolis, the centre of which was the sanctuary of Apollo Triopios on the Knidos Peninsula.

In the Geometric period (*circa* 900-700 BC), known from archaeological finds at Lindos, Ialysos and Kamiros, as well as other smaller sites, Rhodes followed the general trends in the Hellenic world in its pottery and works in the minor arts. Certain peculiarities are due to the island's geographical position, such as the influences from Cyprus and the rest of the East, regions with which Rhodes had special contacts, as a gateway to the Hellenic world proper. There are, however, influences from Greece, especially Attica, while a "softness" in the Late Geometric vase-painting style (second half of 8th century BC) is due to the more general influence of the East Greek/Ionian environment on the early art of the Dorian islands located within this (fig. 562).

Although there are literary and archaeological indications of a Rhodian presence outside the island at least by the eighth century BC, if not earlier, the colonization movement, in which maritime Lindos was trailblazer, reached its peak in the early seventh century BC with the founding, together with Cretans, of Gela in Sicily, in 688 BC. From there Akragas was founded, a city with strong Rhodian influences even in later times. In the East, the Rhodian colonies of Phaselis and Soloi existed in Asia Minor. Important too was the Rhodian presence at Naukratis in Egypt.

In the sixth century BC the dominant personality in Lindos was Kleoboulos – one of the Seven Sages of Antiquity –, who ruled as a moderate "tyrant" for forty years. He is associated with the first monumental arrangement of the sanctuary of Athena Lindia. Most of our information on the art of the Archaic period on Rhodes comes from the sanctuaries of Athena on the acropolises of the three old cities and from the finds from the cemeteries. There are many imports

RHODES | 363

561

from Ionia and later from Corinth, Laconia and Attica. The finds (now in museums abroad and in the Rhodes Archaeological Museum) include a wealth of pottery and vase-painting, coroplastic art (fig. 563), jewellery and works in the minor arts (fig. 561).

The prosperity of the three flourishing cities is also attested by the issue of coinage from the sixth century BC. There is no doubt that the artistic centre for the vase-painting styles prevailing in Rhodes during the seventh and sixth centuries BC, such as the so-called "Wild Goat Style" and the vases of "Fikelloura Style", existed in Ionia, and indeed in the metropolis Miletos. Although views on the essential contribution of Rhodes to forming these styles and their diffusion to other regions are tending to be revised, the last word has yet to be said and future archaeological investigations in the hinterland of the island will help to provide answers.

The high standard and tradition of local monumental sculpture, of which there are very few examples from the Archaic period, is evident in some Rhodian works from the fifth century BC. Two from the second half of the century are the grave relief of Krito and Timarista, from the necropolises of Kamiros and in the Rhodes Archaeological Museum, and the votive relief with pronounced Attic influence, representing the rape of a Nymph, from northeast Ialysia and in the Berlin Museum. A third recent find of a funerary relief with representation of a young man and a boy, in the Severe Style (pre mid-5th century BC) completes the picture of this art (fig. 570).

With the Greek victory in the Persian Wars, in 480 BC, Rhodes along with the other Greeks in the East Aegean and Asia Minor cast off the Persian yoke, imposed after the Persian conquest of Asia Minor in the sixth century BC. It joined the First Athenian League, soon to become an Athenian hegemony. As a result of experiences during this period and the destructive Peloponnesian War, in 411 BC the Rhodians decided to join forces in a single state of federal type and in 408/7 BC they founded the new pan-Rhodian capital at the northernmost tip of the island, "on the eastern promontory" as Strabo relates. How apposite this decision was for the subsequent splendid heyday of the island, particularly in Hellenistic times after the death of Alexander the Great, was proved by the events themselves. The design of the new city expressed the *Zeitgeist* and applied the urban plan and street system devised in the fifth century BC by Hippodamos of Miletos. This system foresaw a strict geometric division, with straight streets intersecting at right angle, regular building *insulae* and a rationalized allocation of space into zones with public edifices and sanctuaries, with private houses, with harbour and commercial installations, and so on.

The Italian excavations in the interwar years revealed part of the acropolis, which was "filled with plains and groves" and free of residences. There were located the sanctuaries of Zeus Polieus and Athena Polias, and Apollo Pythios, the stadium and the large gymnasium of the city (fig. 565). Since the time of the Italian Occupation of the Dodecanese

562

364 | DODECANESE

561. Rhodes. Small electrum plaques with representation of the Mistress of Animals (*Potnia Theron*) in the form of winged Artemis, from Kamiros. These characteristic examples of a Rhodian workshop with oriental and Cretan influences belonged to a necklace. Second half of 7th c. BC. Paris, Musée du Louvre.

562. Rhodes. Rhodian krater of the Late Geometric period (2nd half of 8th c. BC). The Rhodian Geometric style belongs in the climate of East Greece, with influences from other regions (Orient and Greek Mainland). Rhodes Archaeological Museum.

563. Rhodes. Characteristic terracotta female protome with traces of coloration, from Kamiros. It belongs in the long tradition of Rhodian coroplastic art (1st half of 5th c. BC). Rhodes Archaeological Museum.

564. Rhodes, Kamiros. View of the excavation of the lower city of Kamiros, from the south (Hellenistic and Roman periods). In Hellenistic times and later the lower city was traversed by a street running north-south, intersected at right angle by other streets and ending at the acropolis. Among the buildings uncovered in the lowest part are the remains of a temple orientated north-south, a square with a fountain that was reconstructed later and a sacred precinct with altars of many deities, outstanding among which is the altar of Helios. In the lower city there are also remnants of private houses, some with peristyle court. On the acropolis are a large Hellenistic stoa of Π-shaped plan, which made redundant an early water cistern (6th-5th c. BC), and scant remains of the sanctuary of Athena Kamiras.

565. Rhodes, acropolis of Rhodes. View of the restored remains of the stadium and the sanctuary of Apollo Pythios. Visible here is the terraced arrangement which gave the city its distinctive theatrical aspect. At the level of the stadium, at its north edge and lower than the level of the *temenos* of Apollo, stand the restored remains of a small marble theatre. East of the stadium (out of range of the picture) are the remains of the partially excavated large gymnasium, while in the same area was the library, known from inscriptions.

566. Rhodes. Silver tetradrachm, post-350 BC. Obverse: head of Helios, reverse: rose (Gr. *rhodos*), *type parlant* of the city. Athens, Numismatic Museum.

567. Rhodes. View of Ialysos from the acropolis (Philerimos), where stood the remains of the temple of Athena Ialysia, and the restored monastery from the period of the Hospitaller Knights of St John of Jerusalem, while in the lower city are the hills of Moschou Vounara and Makria Vounara (Mycenaean chamber-tomb cemeteries).

568. Rhodes, Lindos. Aerial view of the restored acropolis and part of the traditional settlement. Visible on the acropolis, from top to bottom, are the remains of the temple of Athena Lindia, of the so-called propylaia, the monumental staircase, the Hellenistic Π-shaped portico and the Late Hellenistic vaults. (1st c. BC).

568

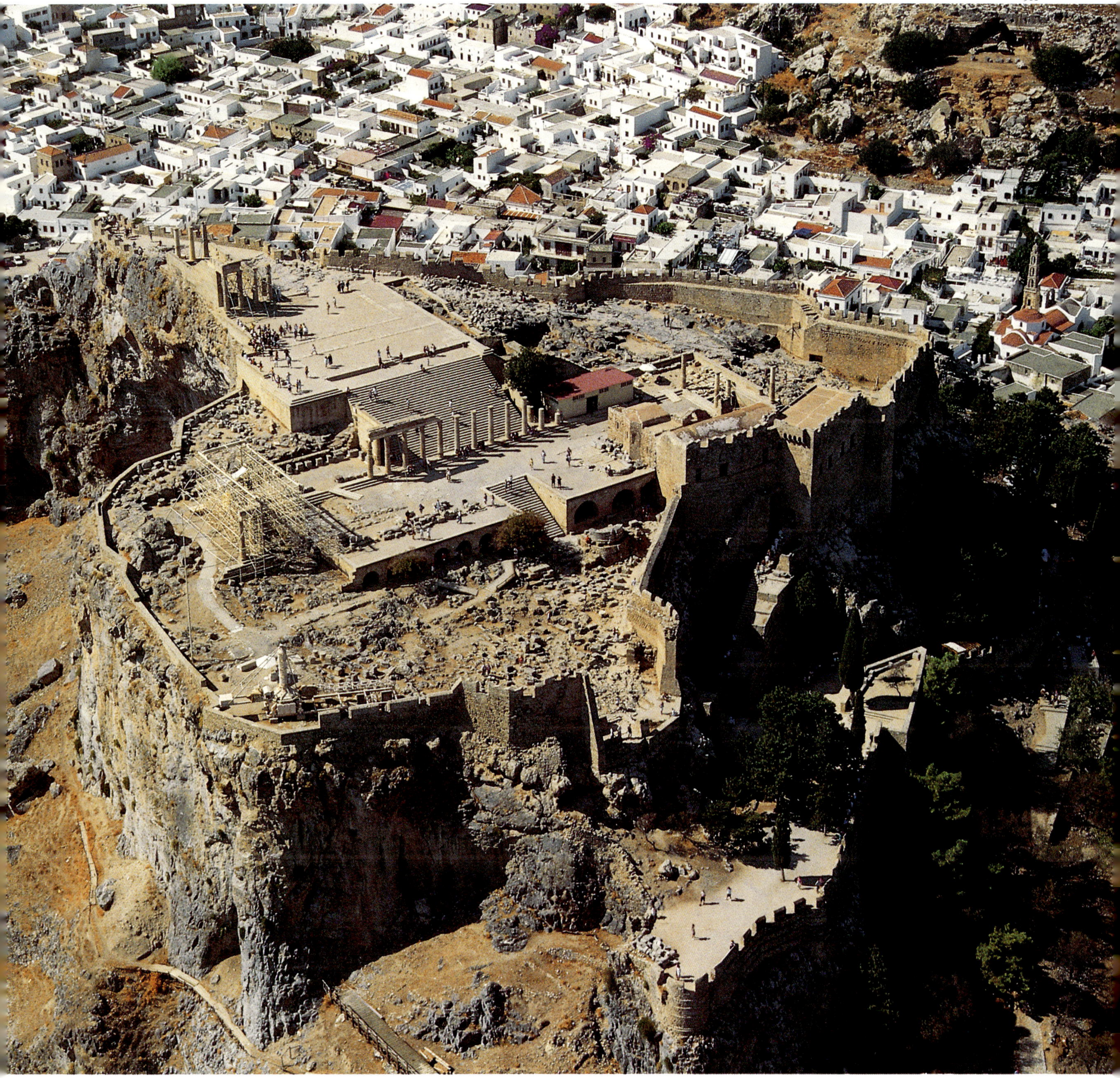

569. Rhodes. The restored Doric fountain of Ialysos, on the steep southwest slope of Philerimos (see fig. 567). On one of the antae is an interesting, barely legible inscription defining the rules of the fountain's operation and use.

(1912-1947), the area of the acropolis has been kept and widened as an extensive archaeological zone. The mainly rescue excavations of the Greek Archaeological Service in the lower city, in the postwar years, have revealed not only the Hippodamean urban plan and grid of streets, but also many residences, some of them quite magnificent with lovely mosaic floors, moulded stucco and painted decoration, important public buildings and sanctuaries, such as the sanctuary of Demeter, the "sanctuary of all gods" (Pantheon), the Asklepieion and the second large gymnasium-Ptolemaion.

Two important events in the history of the city of Rhodes were the siege by Demetrios Poliorketes (305-304 BC) and the destructive earthquake of 227-226 BC. It seems that after the siege the mighty Hellenistic walls were built, surrounding the eastern expansion of the city, while after the earthquake the economic aid from the great powers of the period was used to rebuild an even more magnificent city which acquired its final Hellenistic aspect with a preponderance of large and impressive private houses.

The necropolises surrounding the city over a wide area was of comparable importance and luxury, as revealed by excavations mainly in the last two decades, occasioned by the expansion of the modern town. Many of the significant moveable finds from the necropolis have been displayed since 1993 in the permanent exhibition entitled "Ancient Rhodes. 2400 Years", in the Palace of the Knights (Castello), while outstanding among the hundreds of ordinary graves and grave complexes are some monumental tombs, such as the tomb-mausoleum with the karyatids. Thus the Rhodian necropolis takes its place among the necropolises of other major Hellenistic centres.

During the Hellenistic period Rhodes was one of the greatest political, commercial and economic centres in the Mediterranean. The scope of the mercantile activities is attested, *inter alia*, by the Rhodian amphorae, the majority stamped, examples of which have been found not only on the island but also throughout the Mediterranean and the Euxine Pontus. Particularly noteworthy too are the Rhodian coins, which bear witness to the island's economic and artistic heyday (fig. 566).

Life continued in the three ancient cities even after the synoecism, on a much-reduced scale in Ialysos (figs 567, 569), the closest to the new capital, but thriving in Kamiros (fig. 564) and Lindos. At Lindos in particular there is continuity into the Middle Ages and recent times to the present, with periods of considerable development and acme. Epicentre of Lindos (fig. 568) was the acropolis with the sanctuary of Athena Lindia, the most important pan-Rhodian *locus sanctus* on the island; other sanctuaries of pan-Rhodian appeal were those of Apollo Erethimios in the Ialysia and of Zeus Atabyrios on Mount Atabyris (mod. Atavyros).

After the synoecism and especially during the Hellenistic period Rhodes became a major centre of artistic production, thanks to the contribution of local artists and of foreign ones who flocked in large numbers to the flourishing city of Helios. In painting, already from the early fourth century BC there were works by Parrhasios from Ephesos in Rhodes, and particularly in Lindos, while in the latter years of the same century the great painter Protogenes from Kaunos, on the opposite coast of Karia, was living and creating in Rhodes. Two famous works by him, "Ialysos" (eponymous hero of Ialysos) and the "Resting Satyr", adorned the Dionysion, the sanctuary of Dionysos, which must have been close to the big harbour, in the area of the Medieval town, as was the city's agora. The other towering painter of the period, Apelles, was associated with Protogenes.

Reference has been made already to the mosaics, murals and stucco mouldings that decorated the private houses. Vase-making and vase-painting also flourished, in the fourth century BC and in the Hellenistic period (3rd-1st century BC). All the known styles are represented on Rhodes, either by imports or by local variations: vases of "West Slope Style", vases with relief decoration (Megarian), various local styles and above all the hydrias of "Hadra" type with white ground, which imitate Alexandrian models.

Notable foreign sculptors were active in Rhodes in the fourth century BC, such as Bryaxis and primarily Lysippos, the father of Hellenistic art. One of his pupils was Chares from Lindos, creator of the famous Colossus. This was a bronze statue some 30 metres high, of the patron deity Helios, which the Rhodians set up in gratitude for their city's deliverance from the siege by Demetrios Poliorketes. In general there was a preference for colossal works, while there were also accomplished bronze-casters. Only a few examples of bronze sculpture survive on Rhodes, several casting pits for statues have come to light in recent years. Indeed, two such installations are of enormous dimensions, for colossal works such as the Colossus. Two important Rhodian bronze statues are now in museums abroad, the "Praying Child" in Berlin and the "Eros" in New York. Rhodes also bequeathed important sculptural works in stone. Irrefutable testimonies of the formidable output of statues of all kinds by a large number of artists, mainly from the fourth century BC to the first century AD, are the surviving inscribed pedestals. Many marble sculptures, some very important, now grace the Rhodes Archaeological Museum and the exhibition "Ancient Rhodes. 2400 Years", while others, some masterpieces among them, are abroad.

One of the best-known Hellenistic sculptures, the Nike (Victory) of Samothrace (fig. 114), an *ex-voto* in the sanctuary of the Kabeiroi on that island, is considered a Rhodian work. Its pedestal in the form of a ship, as was popular on Rhodes, is of local Rhodian stone (*lartios lithos*). Most probably a dedication of the early years of the second century BC, after a Rhodian naval victory, it is a representative work of the Middle Hellenistic period, a "triumphant

570. Rhodes. Grave relief stele from the purlieus of the city of Rhodes, with representation of a young man offering a cockerel to a boy. A work in the Severe Style (*c.* 460 BC). Grand Masters' Palace (Castello). Exhibition "Ancient Rhodes. 2400 years".

571.

571. Rhodes. View of the site of the Roman tetrapylon, which was built in the second half of the 2nd or the early 3rd c. AD on redundant remnants of ship-sheds in the naval harbour (Mandraki). A characteristic example of the monumental articulation of the city centre in the Roman period.

572. Rhodes. The Laocoon group. Laocoon, priest of Apollo in Troy, was punished by the goddess Athena for his impiety. Whilst he was sacrificing to Poseidon two terrible snakes attacked him and his two sons, and killed them (or according to another tradition, only the father and the younger son). There is a sophisticated gradation in both the rendering of the bodies of the three figures and in the expression of pathos, which attains its climax in the father. By today's standards, however, this surpasses the bounds of realism in conveying pain and suffering, despite the technical perfection, the variety and the contrasts in individual details which led to this work being considered in ancient and in later times as a masterpiece *non pareil* of Greek art. Notwithstanding its excesses, the Laocoon group remains one of the choicest creations in art worldwide, which left artists of the stature of Michelangelo ecstatic on first seeing it. Rome, Musei Vaticani.

reveille of Hellenistic baroque", according to Christos Karouzos. Many scholars accredit it to Pythokritos, a Rhodian citizen, but whose father was from Eleutherna in Crete. Pythokritos is known also from the Roman author Pliny, but mainly from the host of his signatures on statue bases, one of which is on the relief-base in the form of a ship, carved on the rock on the acropolis of Lindos.

Crowning glory of the period of grand sculpture on Rhodes, as well as of great Greek art in general, is the Laocoon complex, a work of Early Roman times which is housed in the Vatican Museum. For centuries this sculpture had a profound influence on the art and the culture of modern Europe and was admired to excess (fig. 572). Today judgements on the Laocoon are more sober, because despite the artistic excellence and the remarkable rendering of the movement of the bodies, it contains elements of academicism that herald the end of deep-seated inspiration and led to the classicism that prevailed in Roman times. The Laocoon group was rediscovered in Rome in 1506, but it is known from elsewhere, primarily from the renowned sculptural ensemble in the Sperlonga grotto, that its Rhodian creators, Polydoros, Athanodoros and Agesandros, worked also in Italy.

During these years Rhodes, a close ally of Rome, also a major centre of culture in the Hellenistic period, of poetry, literature, rhetoric, philosophy and the positive sciences, was one of the main hearths from which the torch of Greek civilization was passed on via Rome to the West. The consciousness of this fact exists in modern Europe to this day, with main symbol the Colossus of Rhodes, one of the Seven Wonders of the Ancient World.

The city of Rhodes continued its tradition as a typical free state also in the Roman world. This applied both to the appearance of the city and its inhabitants. After the terrible earthquake in the mid-second century AD a change in the spirit of the new times appeared at least in the monumental centre of the city, principal example of which is a Roman tetrapylon and a paved avenue on the course of a pre-existing street. This possibly led to the agora, which as recent finds indicate was also renovated in Roman times (fig. 571).

In Early Christian times Rhodes continued to be important. The end of Antiquity came in the seventh century AD, when the city was confined to around the later Grand Masters' Palace, in the area of the Medieval town, which was also the nucleus of the modern one.

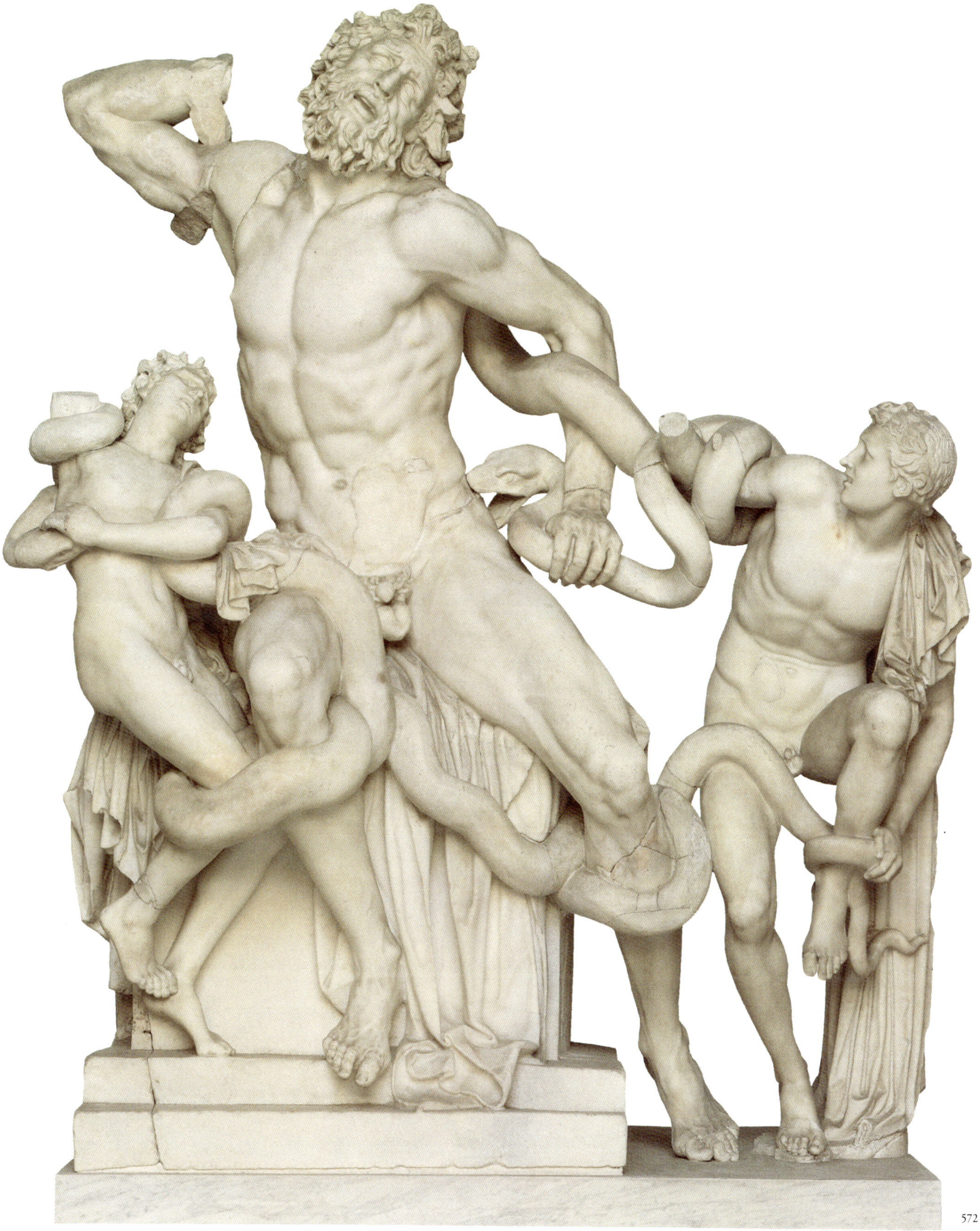

572

Chalke, Alimnia, Castellorizo, Rho

Kalliopi Bairami

Chalke

Chalke, Chalkea or Chalkeia of the ancient sources, lies 11 nautical miles west of the coast of Kamiros and together with Alimnia was an important naval station in Antiquity, first for the Athenians and later for the Rhodians.

References to the island in inscriptions and literary texts begin in the Classical period, when Chalke appears in the fiscal lists as a member of the Athenian League in the fifth century BC. According to Thucydides, during the Peloponnesian War the island played a significant role as an operations base for the Athenian fleet, against the enemy ships in Rhodes. In the late fourth century BC, after a brief interlude of independence, Chalke became part of the Rhodian State, subject to the deme of Kamirians. Its relations with Rhodes continued throughout the Hellenistic period and until the second century AD.

The geographer Strabo recounts that Chalkea: "…has also a settlement of the same name and a temple of Apollo and a harbour…". The ancient settlement is located on the site of the now deserted village of Chorio, built on a hill in the hinterland, invisible from the sea in order to protect it from pirate raids. In the foundations of the well-preserved castle of the Knights, which crowns the top of the hill, isodomic masonry of the ancient acropolis is preserved (fig. 574). Visible among the houses on the hill slope are walls with isodomic and polygonal masonry, which must have served as retaining walls of the ancient houses. Close to the acropolis is an inscription dedicated to Zeus and Hekate, carved on stone benches. In addition to the worship of Apollo, Zeus and Hekate, the cults of Asklepios, Isis and Sarapis were also important.

Retaining walls similar to those at Chorio have survived at Andramassos and Tracheia, the peninsula south of Chorio with a bay either side, east and west, suitable for mooring ships. Recent investigations at Pontamos and Tracheia have shown that habitation on the island dates back to prehistoric times. In Pontamos Bay tombs of the fourth century BC have been excavated, with interesting finds such as the red-figure plastic rhyton with the heads of Herakles and Silenus (fig. 573).

The strategic importance of Chalke is confirmed by the existence of fortified sites at various points, such as Kephali, the westernmost promontory, where stand a small tower with enceinte, remnants of an Early Christian basilica and "*kyphes*". Obviously a garrison was stationed here, which controlled the western sea routes towards Karpathos and Kasos.

Chalke followed the historical course of Rhodes until recent times. In the Middle Ages the castle of the Hospitaller Knights of St John of Jerusalem, with the church of St Nicholas (15th century), at Chorio, as well as a host of churches

372 | DODECANESE

with wall-paintings, from the ninth to the fifteenth century, all over the island, confirm the unbroken continuity of life on Chalke. Of particular interest are the "*kyphes*", stone-built beehive-like farmhouses, many of which have ancient construction material (*spolia*) in their masonry, which must belong to the Medieval and recent history of the island.

Alimnia

Alimnia, an islet between Rhodes and Chalke, is identified as the ancient Eulimnia mentioned by Pliny, whose name is due to its two harbours, Emporeio and Aghios Georgios, on the east and the southwest coast respectively. Their use in Antiquity is confirmed by the impressive rock-cut shipyards, which date from the Hellenistic period, when Alimnia, like Chalke, belonged to the Rhodian State.

Preserved on top of the hill, below the castle of the Knights (fig. 575) is the foundation of an ancient tower with external enceinte, which surveyed both harbours. Recent excavations have uncovered a small Neolithic building on the hill slope. On the shore of Emporeio, burials of Roman times have been found and ancient walls and the foundation of an Early Christian basilica are visible.

In Aghios Georgios Bay is the islet's traditional settlement, with stone-built houses and "*kyphes*", which was abandoned not long ago.

Castellorizo

Castellorizo, which lies to the southeast of Rhodes, is barely one nautical mile from ancient Antiphellos in Lycia, modern Kas, on the opposite shore of Asia Minor. The island owes its name to the red rock on which the castle of the Knights was founded (*Castello Rosso*), whereas in Antiquity it was called Megiste, because it was the largest of the islands in the Lycian Sea.

There was a permanent settlement on Megiste, as is indicated by the building remains submerged in the harbour and the dispersed graves in the hinterland. In the fourth century BC the island was part of the Rhodian State, which appointed annual military commanders there, the *epistatai*, as is revealed by dedicatory inscriptions built into the walls of the castle of the Hospitaller Knights of St John of Jerusalem and Palaiokastro. A dedicatory inscription from Kedreai in Karia records that Teisias son of Theudamos was appointed *hegemon* on the island: "καὶ ἀγεμόνα γενόμενον ἐμ Μεγίσται κατὰ πόλεμον" (first quarter of 2nd century BC). The *hegemones* were superior to the *epistatai* and were responsible for an extensive region of the Rhodian State. In this particular case, the official's appointment was dictated by critical events, probably the Third Syrian War (190 BC), when Megiste played a leading role in operations against Antiochos III, because the Rhodian fleet was stationed in its two harbours.

573. Chalke. Plastic vase (rhyton) in the shape of a head of Silenus and Herakles, with representation of Satyrs between the handles. From the cemetery at Pontamos. 450-425 BC. Temporarily exhibited in the Olympia Archaeological Museum.

574. Chalke, Chorio. View of the castle of the Knights, below the foundations of which extends the ancient settlement.

575. Alimnia. The castle of the Hospitaller Knights of St John of Jerusalem.

576. Castellorizo. The monumental façade of the Lycian tomb. 4th c. BC.

577. Castellorizo. The tower of the Knights in the modern settlement.

578. Castellorizo. Gold wreath of ivy leaves. 4th or 3rd c. BC. It was found by islanders inside a stone sarcophagus, in 1913. Athens, National Archaeological Museum.

Palaiokastro is the principal and largest fortified site of ancient Megiste. Located on the west coast, it comprises a central tower of isodomic masonry and an external enceinte reinforced on the accessible southeast side with four towers, three of which survive. Later interventions in the Byzantine Age and the time of the Hospitaller Knights strengthened the enceinte and the entrance gateway. The few houses and churches, such as St Nicholas, the Virgin and St Stephen on the south side, date to the nineteenth century.

The "Cyclopean" wall at Vigla, the highest summit on the island, was part of the Hellenistic fortification and in conjunction with Palaiokastro protected the island's interior. The castle of the Knights in the town of Castellorizo, of which one tower still stands (fig. 577), has two phases: ancient and Medieval. In the time of the Knights it was used both as a watchtower for Ottoman ships and as a prison for condemned knights.

Just below the Hospitaller castle is the Lycian tomb (fig. 576), a burial chamber with benches for the dead inside and an architectural façade with pediment, architrave and antae, all carved in the rock (4th century BC). This kind of funerary monument is common on the opposite coast of Lycia, but extremely rare in Greece. A recent study has suggested that the gold wreath of ivy leaves, found in a sarcophagus in the Aghios Georgios valley, dates to the fourth or the third century BC (fig. 578). The main deities worshipped on the island were Zeus, Apollo, Demeter and the Dioskouroi.

The wine-making installations found throughout the island and the host of amphorae point to the inhabitants' involvement with wine production in Antiquity. Viticulture was probably the main agricultural activity on the rocky, waterless island.

Rho

Rho or Aghios Georgios, the ancient Rhoge or Rhope, lies west of Castellorizo. In the ancient sources all that is noted is its position in the Lycian Sea and its distance from Megiste. The island functioned mainly as a link in the chain of military surveillance posts in the Rhodian State, as is apparent from the hilltop tower (fig. 579).

The small fort comprises a central rectangular tower, initially two-storeyed, which still stands to a height of about 4 metres, built in the isodomic system. Its walls are reinforced inside by smaller rounded stones, while there are signs of repair and maintenance in Byzantine times and the period of the Knights. A double enceinte, parts of which survive on the west, east and south sides, enclosed an area measuring 30 x 25 metres. Strong walls on the east and west sides of the hill, outside the enceinte, were used to control access to the fort, indicating that it was not merely a signal tower (*phryktorio*) but an important strategic position. In the interior is the essential cistern, which is coated with hydraulic plaster. Remains of a grape-pressing installation outside the tower and a stone conical vessel point to agricultural activities to maintain the garrison posted there. The watchtower is dated to the fourth century BC and continued in use in Roman, Byzantine and Hospitaller times.

In recent times legend has it that the fort was used as a pirates' lair by Lambros Katsonis, in the period of Ottoman rule (1788-1792).

579. Rho. Aerial photograph of the Hellenistic tower. 4th c. BC.

Karpathos, Kasos

FOTINI ZERVAKI

Karpathos

Karpathos was already inhabited in the Neolithic Age. Its geographical location between the Dodecanese and Crete determined the influences on the island during prehistoric times and explains the marked Minoan character, which remains overt even in the advanced Mycenaean period (14th-12th century BC). During historical times the memory of the Minoan past lingered on – indeed, Diodorus Siculus makes reference to a colonization by "those who joined forces with Minos".

Myth links the settlement of Karpathos with Minos and later with the Argeian Iokles, son of Demoleon. In the "list of ships" in the *Iliad*, Karpathos is associated with Kos, Nisyros and Kalymnos, which islands, under the leadership of Pheidippos and Antiphos, sons of the Herakleid Thessalos, took part in the Trojan campaign with thirty ships, whereas Rhodes participated with nine.

By the first millennium BC Karpathos was Dorian, as were most of the islands in the Dodecanese. In the fifth century BC the communities of Karpathos appear in the Athenian fiscal lists: Arkesians, Brykountians, Karpathians, Eteokarpathians from Karpathos and Sarians. In the mid-fourth century BC the geographer Pseudo-Skylax calls Karpathos three-citied (*tripolis*), while Strabo calls it four-citied (*tetrapolis*).

In the Hellenistic period (4th-3rd century BC) Karpathos was part of the Rhodian State. The aforesaid communities now appear as demes, while there is testimony of the "*ktoina*" of Potidaieis as part of the deme of Karpathiopolitans. As the cult of Athena Lindia at Potidaion, Arkasa and Brykous indicates, the demes of Karpathos had relations with the old Rhodian city of Lindos, relations that perhaps dated back to before the synoecism and the founding of the new city of Rhodes.

In Antiquity, as today, the main centre of the island was on the site of the modern capital of Pigadia, ancient Potidaion or later Poseidion. The earliest traces of human presence there date to the Late Neolithic period (5th millennium BC). A Minoan settlement existed in the area of Pigadia in the Middle Minoan and the early Late Minoan period (1700-1500 BC), when the Minoan expansion into the East Aegean was at its peak. The Minoan character remained strong in the Late Helladic III period (14th-12th century BC), as indicated by the finds from a contemporary residential-workshop installation at Pigadia and chamber tombs in the same area (on Skopi and Makelli hills), as well as at Vonies and Avlona in the north of the island (fig. 580). During Mycenaean times there was possibly a citadel on the site of the acropolis of Potidaion in historical times. Traces of retaining walls with Hellenistic-type polygonal masonry survive, while it is possible that during this period a wall girt the lower city. Hellenistic cemeteries have

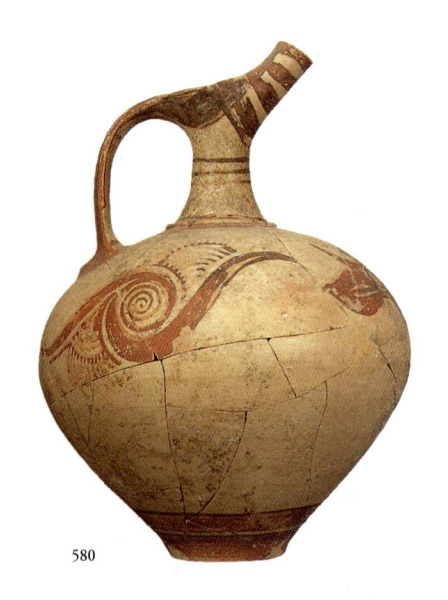

580

376 | DODECANESE

580. Karpathos, Pigadia. Beak-spouted jug from a rock-cut chamber tomb at Makelli. Late Helladic IIIA1 period (late 15th c. BC). Rhodes Archaeological Museum.

581. Karpathos, Arkasa. The ancient acropolis on the Paliokastro Peninsula and site of the Early Christian settlement with the basilicas.

582. Karpathos, Vrykous. Complex of rock-cut chamber tombs in the Late Classical-Hellenistic cemetery.

been found in the area of Pigadia, as well as a monumental tomb at Myli. Epigraphic testimonies reveal the existence of a temple of Athena Lindia. There is also evidence of cults of the Egyptian gods and the Dioskouroi, while at the site of Istia there is an open-air sanctuary.

In the wider area of Aperi, in the south-central part of the island, remains of habitation dating from prehistoric times and mainly from the Geometric period (10th-8th century BC) onwards have been uncovered, with epicentre the Kastro, where surface sherds indicate that an acropolis must have existed in Antiquity. In the area of Kouri there was a necropolis with monumental tombs-sarcophagi, while from the site of Pini comes an Athenian decree honouring the "*koinon* of Eteokarpathians" for the gift of a cypress tree from the grove of the sanctuary of Apollo on Karpathos to the temple of Athena Parthenos on the Acropolis – perhaps the sanctuary of Apollo was located here. The view has prevailed that Aperi is the site of the island's capital, Karpathos (probably the result of synoecism), continuation of which was the deme of Karpathiopolitans, to which the "*ktoina*" of Potidaionians belonged as outpost. However, it has been argued that the deme of Karpathiopolitans was located at Poseidion, while the area around Aperi belonged to the deme of Eteokarpathians.

On the southwest coast of the island, in the area of Arkasa, surface finds on Palaiokastro hill (fig. 581) date from the Late Neolithic period onwards, while remains of a Cyclopean wall and of retaining walls bear witness to the existence of a fortified acropolis, possibly from Mycenaean times and certainly during the Classical and Hellenistic periods. The settlement must have been located around the isthmus, where remnants of an Early Christian settlement survive.

583. Karpathos. "Monument of the Shields", a monumental tomb of the Roman period on the ancient road to Brykous.

584. Kasos. Minoan stone vase from Chelatros. The presence of such a characteristic Minoan artifact on Kasos indicates the island's importance during the period of Minoan expansionism. Kasos Museum.

Further north, in the area of Lefko there are traces of habitation from prehistoric times as well as from the Hellenistic and Roman periods. At the site of Ria a Roman underground cistern is preserved, with three rows of internal piers and a series of rock-cut tunnels.

On the northwest coast of the island are the fortified settlement and the cemetery of Brykous, the third of the ancient cities of Karpathos, which is dated to the Hellenistic, Roman and Early Christian periods. Preserved are remains of a fortification wall with isodomic masonry and numerous rock-cut chamber tombs, many with monumental façades (figs 582, 583).

At the site of Tristomo, which is an excellent natural harbour, was the pan-Karpathian sanctuary of Poseidon Porthmios, as attested by inscriptions found here.

On Saria, the islet north of Karpathos, on the site of the Early Christian settlement, there are traces of an earlier installation. It has been suggested that this was the city of Nisyros, to which Strabo refers.

Kasos

The earliest mention of the island is in the lines of Homer (*Iliad* II), where, together with Nisyros, Eurypoloios Kos, the Calydnian islands and Karpathos it participates in the Trojan War, with thirty ships under the command of Pheidippos and Antiphos. Stephanos Byzantios refers analytically to the island's name, calling it alternatively Amphe and Arstrabe. Pliny speaks of the island as Astrabe and Achne or Casos. The name Kasos has a Phoenician root – *kas* means sea foam or briny spray, a direct reference to the passage between Kasos and Karpathos, the most tempestuous point in the Greek seas. The geographer Strabo also calls it Astrabe.

The earliest traces of habitation have been identified in the wider area of Ellinokamara, as well as in the area between Emporeios harbour and Poli Hill. There are indications of a Middle and Late Bronze Age (2nd millennium BC) settlement – until the Late Minoan I period (17th century BC) – on the southwest coast, around the closed Chelatro Bay (fig. 584), which is also the island's only protected harbour, natural port of call on the route from Crete to Karpathos, Rhodes and the Asia Minor coast. Traces of human presence have also been noted at other sites, in the Ellinokamara Cave, as well as on the naturally fortified site of Poli, where a citadel was founded in the Mycenaean period.

During historical times the ancient capital, homonymous with the island according to Strabo, remained in the same place, at Poli, and developed around the height of the Mycenaean citadel. On the south side of the hill as well as on the opposite slope, at the site of Askelinos, lay the ancient cemeteries (fig. 585). It should be noted that the pottery dispersed on the hilltop dates from the Late Neolithic/Early Bronze Age, the Middle Minoan, Late Minoan, Geometric, Archaic, Classical, Hellenistic, Roman and Early Christian periods. Spanning the entire spectrum of Antiquity, it attests the continuous occupation of the site, which, together with the strip linking it with the harbour at Emporeios, was throughout the centuries the principal nucleus of settlement on the island.

Kasians appear for the first time in the fiscal lists of the fifth century BC, while the recording of the ethnic name *Kasios* in Hellenistic inscriptions outside the limits of the Rhodian State points to the island's independence prior to its induction to the said state in the first half of the second century BC.

From 67 BC, when Pompey dissolved the cores of piracy, until around the seventh century AD, the coasts of Kasos were relatively safe for settlement. During this period the main settlement on the island seems to have been moved to the shore around the bay of Emporeios. Preserved there are traces of an ancient quarry and between them rock-cut house foundations, water cisterns or granaries, a Roman chamber tomb, as well as clusters of rock-cut graves of Late Roman-Early Christian times. There is also scattered pottery dating from the Roman into the Early Christian period.

One of the most important monuments is the Ellinokamara Cave. Located on a terrace with unimpeded view from the mountains of East Crete as far as Karpathos, it dominates the northwest coast of Kasos. It is essentially a rock shelter, at the mouth of which is a built wall dating from Classical times, while the pottery recovered from the interior and exterior space reveals its use from prehistoric into Early Christian times.

There are indications of the existence of at least two sanctuaries on the island in Antiquity: at the site of Grammata on the precipitous northwest coast, at the tempestuous passage between Kasos and Karpathos, there are fragments of inscriptions of the second and first centuries BC, invoking the Samothracian gods and the Nymphs, protectors of seafarers, while other epigraphic testimonies mention the existence of a sanctuary of Apollo Temenites on Kasos.

585. Kasos. Part of a grave stele with relief representation of a youth holding a hare. Early 4th c. BC. Kasos Museum.

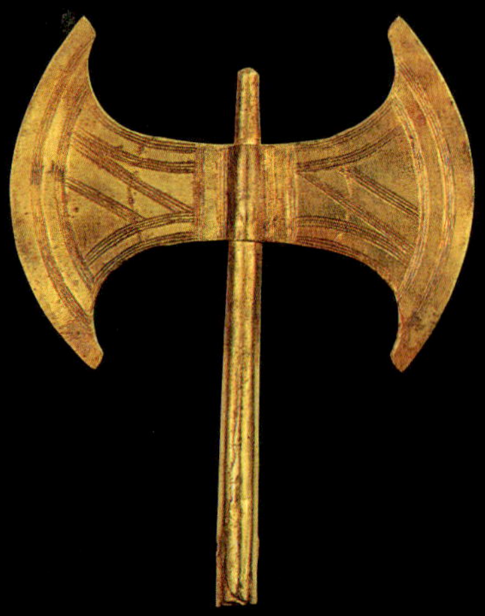

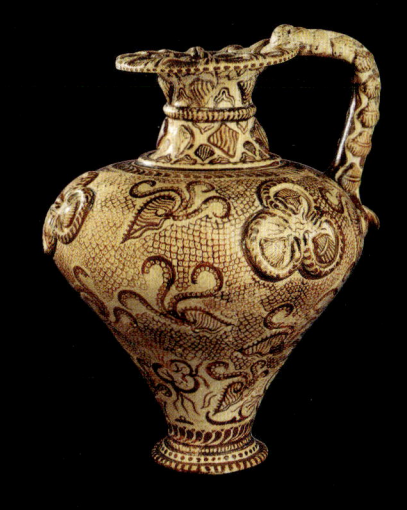

CRETE

Map of western Crete showing archaeological sites, including Cape Spatha, Diktynnaion, Ellinospilios, Arkoudospilios, Koumarospilios, Phalasarna, Kisamos, Malame, Kydonia, Perivolia, Mameloukou Cave, Polyrrhenia, Nopigeia, Vryses, Nerokourou, Aptera, Topolia, Stylos, Platyvola Cave, Stavromenos, Melidoni, Rethymnon, Chamalevri, Tsiskiana, Vrysinas, Eleutherna, LEFKA ORI, Gerani Cave, Armenoi, Axos, Hyrtakina, Goulediana, Sybritos, Zomi, Elyros, Lappa, Monastiraki, Idaion Antron, IDA, Atsipades, Ellenes, Lisos, Anopolis, Kamares C., Loutro, Sphakia, Apodoulou, Aghios Onouphrios, Aghia Galini, Aghia Triada, Phaistos, Kommos, Kamilari, Pitsidia, Matala, Odigitria, Lasaia, GAVDOPOULA, GAVDOS.

DIA
Gazi
HERAKLEION
Amnisos
Nirou
Gournes
Chersonisos
Skoteino
Poros
Knossos
Eileithyia Cave
Kalo Chorio
Malia
Milatos
Dreros
Elounta
KALYDONA
Krasi
Karphi
Lyttos
Archanes
Trapeza
Juktas
Vathypetro
Galatas
Papoura
Lycastos
Arkalochori
Dikte Cave
Prinias
Arkades
DIKTE
Viannos
Symi
Apesokari
Koumasa
Priansos
Chondros
Kophinas
Tsoutsouros
Trypiti
Lebena
Kritsa
Lato
Istron
Vrokastro
Gulf of Merabello
Mala
Myrtos
Hierapetra
Gournia
Pacheiammos
Vasiliki
Katalymata
Chalasmenos
Kavousi
Pseira
Mochlos
Myrsini
Chamaizi
Makryyalos
DIONYSADES
Siteia
Trypitos
Aghia Photia
Piskokephalo
Petras
Achladia
Zou
Praisos
Ampelos
Itanos
ELASA
Palaikastro
Petsophas
Traostalos
Zakros
Pelekita
KOUPHONISI
CHRYSI

Prehistoric times

MARIA ANDREADAKI-VLAZAKI – LEFTERIS PLATON

The discovery of the Minoan Civilization

The large-scale excavations conducted by Sir Arthur Evans at ancient Knossos – which according to Hellenic tradition was the heart of the mythical kingdom of Minos – marked the birth of a special branch of archaeology in the Aegean, which developed by leaps and bounds in the course of the twentieth century. What is still known as "Minoan archaeology" experienced its first great floruit in the period immediately following the discovery of the palace of Knossos (1900 early 1930s), mainly thanks to the extensive excavation activity of foreign archaeological schools. Within a relatively short period of time another two palaces came to light, at Phaistos in the Mesara Plain and at Malia on the north coast, east of Herakleion. Other investigations revealed some installations more or less contemporary with the above palaces and no less significant, such as at Aghia Triada near Phaistos, and at Palaikastro, Zakros, Gournia, Mochlos and Pseira, in the eastern part of the island. Smaller settlement units with interesting architecture and rich finds were explored by the first representatives of the Greek Archaeological Service, such as Amnisos, Nirou Hani, Tylissos and neighbouring Sklavokampos, sites in central Crete. During the same interval, extensive early cemeteries with abundant finds were excavated, of tholos tombs in the Mesara Plain and of built tombs on the islet of Mochlos in the Gulf of Merabello.

The discoveries in the field were accompanied by systematic presentations – ground-breaking for their time – of the finds, such as the publications of the excavations at Phaistos, Gournia, Palaikastro, Tylissos, Malia and the Mesara tombs. However, landmark for the importance of the results of researches in this first period was Arthur Evans's four-volume *magnum opus*, *The Palace of Minos*, in which the excavator of Knossos crystallizes his views on the birth, development, influence on the wider region and final demise of the early ancient Cretan civilization (fig. 587). Although today many of the views of this pioneering scholar have since been doubted, the cultural universe he described in his book continues to be a basis for discussion even in trying to understand the most recent finds (figs 588-589).

"Minoan archaeology" enjoyed a second heyday between 1950 and 1980, when the reins of research were taken up mainly by the Greek Archaeological Service and the Archaeological Society at Athens. In the then new Herakleion Archaeological Museum, in the city centre, a very rich exhibition was organized in chronological sequence, the greater part of which was devoted to objects from Minoan sites. At Chania, Rethymnon, Aghios Nikolaos, Hierapetra and Siteia archaeological museums were created to replace the earlier collections. Excavations by the foreign archaeological schools added new sites in various regions, but primarily central and eastern Crete, as did joint excavations with the Archaeological Service, mainly in western and eastern Crete. The initially sporadic investigations in relatively neglected western Crete were systematized, somewhat dilatorily, from the 1970s onward.

586. Crete. Gold votive double axe from the Arkalochori Cave (*c.* 1500 BC). Herakleion Archaeological Museum.
Representations of the double axe in religious iconography and examples of it in excavation assemblages from cult sites leave no doubt as to its function in Minoan Crete as a symbol signifying the sanctity of places, buildings and praxes.

587

CHRONOLOGICAL TABLE				
EGYPT	MINOAN CRETE			
	Dating system A. Evans	Dating system N. Platon		
Old Kingdom	Early Minoan I Early Minoan II	Prepalatial period	3000 BC	
First Intermediate period	Early Minoan III			
Middle Kingdom	Middle Minoan IA Middle Minoan IB Middle Minoan IIA Middle Minoan IIB	Protopalatial period	1900 BC	
Second Intermediate period	Middle Minoan III	Neopalatial period	1700 BC	
	Late Minoan IA Late Minoan IB			
New Kingdom	Late Minoan II	Final Neopalatial period at Knossos	1450 BC	
	Late Minoan IIIA Late Minoan IIIB Late Minoan IIIC	Postpalatial period	1370 BC	

587. Crete. One of the most important contributions of Sir Arthur Evans was the construction of a complete chronological system based on the study of the pottery found in successive archaeological levels. The Bronze Age in Crete was divided into three main periods – Early Minoan, Middle Minoan and Late Minoan – which in turn were subdivided into three phases. This division broadly followed the distinction of chronological periods in Egypt, which was based on the succession of three periods of reigns by local dynasties (Old, Middle and New Kingdom). Later, Nikolaos Platon proposed a new chronological system for Crete, based on the acceptance of simultaneity in the founding and the destruction of the first and the second palaces.

588. Crete. Snapshot of Sir Arthur Evans (left) in the excavation at Knossos. Evans's sound classical and purely archaeological education helped him to interpret most of his finds in a convincing manner, while at the same time fitting them into a much wider world of ideas and creations, essentially of his own making.

589. Crete. Much criticism was levelled at Evans of his extensive restorations at Knossos. Current concepts on the issue of interventions today in an archaeological site reject as misleading those restorations based even in part on hypotheses. However, apart from well-intentioned criticism on the correct or not restoration of individual features, and discussion on the durability of the materials used, the restorations at Knossos should also be evaluated as an educational means for understanding the function of a Minoan palace.

PREHISTORIC TIMES | 385

The new excavations uncovered inter alia some isolated buildings with notable architecture and finds, at Vathypetro near Archanes, Metropolis of Gortyn, Pyrgos-Myrtos near Hierapetra, the villages of Aghia Photia, Zou, Achladia, Piskokephalo and Tourtouli in the province of Siteia, and Nerokourou near Chania. More extensive investigations have revealed Minoan settlements and installations at Stylos in Apokoronas district, Monastiraki and Apodoulou in the Amari Valley, Vasiliki at Hierapetra, Phournou Koryphi at Myrtos and Kephali near the village of Chondros in the district of Viannos. Minoan peak sanctuaries, such as those on Juktas above Archanes, Kophinas on Mount Asterousia, Traostalos near Zakros and Vrysinas and Atsipades in Rethymnon, or hill-slope sanctuaries, such as at Symi near Viannos and Piskokephalo in the district of Siteia, have yielded a wealth of finds, the majority of which were votive offerings of ordinary worshippers. Other researches have brought to light extensive cemeteries of various periods, such as that at Aghia Photia, Siteia, with some two thousand vases, most of Cycladic provenance, at Phourni near Archanes, with tholos tombs and other tomb buildings, of all periods of the Minoan Age (fig. 598), and at Armenoi near Rethymnon, with two hundred and thirty rock-cut graves and richly furnished burials, of the period following the collapse of the Minoan palaces.

Among the most important discoveries in these thirty years (1950-1980) are the palace complex at Zakros in the prefecture of Siteia, a large part of the west wing of the old palace at Phaistos and the two palaces identified at Archanes and Chania. At Phaistos a building preserved to considerable height, buried under the foundations of the west front of the already excavated palace, came to light. Research at Zakros provided the unique – until then – opportunity to excavate *in toto* an unplundered Minoan palace contemporary with the last analogous buildings of Knossos, Phaistos and Malia (fig. 591). However, the most significant contribution to scholarship of this particular find was the systematic uncovering of a "closed archaeological level" containing thousands of artifacts buried simultaneously in the ruins caused by the great destruction that brought life to an end in all the palatial centres (fig. 590).

In the period 1950-1980, the nature of this destruction preoccupied excavators of Minoan sites. Most linked it with the eruption of the Thera volcano, which according to purely archaeological data that emerged from excavation of the prehistoric settlement at Akrotiri on the island of Thera in the Cyclades, should be dated in the middle years of the second millennium BC. However, a constant problem was that the pottery found in the excavations at Akrotiri was earlier than that found in the "destruction level" at Minoan sites.

Significant progress was made as far as the synthesis of the new scientific data is concerned. N. Platon proposed a new chronological system based on the principle of accepting simultaneity in the founding and the destruction of both the first and the second Minoan palaces. This was adopted by a large section of the scholarly community (fig. 587). In the sector of religion, A. Persson and M. Nilsson wrote important works that systematized excavation and iconographic evidence on this issue. S. Alexiou made a seminal contribution to synthesis with his monograph entitled *Minoan Civilization*, as well as with writings on more specialized but basic subjects. The uniquely important event of the decipherment of the Mycenaean script

590. Crete. The excavation of the "closed archaeological level" at Zakros brought to light thousands of objects buried in the ruins of a sudden disaster, some three and a half thousand years ago. Among the most notable finds were four elephant tusks and six copper talents (ingots cast in moulds), which apparently reached Zakros after an overseas voyage to Near Eastern shores.

591. Crete. The rock-crystal rhyton (libation vessel) found in the treasury of the palace of Zakros is counted among the supreme masterpieces of Minoan art in the Neopalatial period (1700-1450 BC). The untouched contents of the palace treasury, comprising a multitude of ritual vessels, pieces of jewellery and symbols, are to this day the richest and perhaps most important excavation ensemble from Minoan Crete. Herakleion Archaeological Museum.

known conventionally as Linear B, by M. Ventris and J. Chadwick in the 1950s, opened up a new field of research in the study of civilizations in the prehistoric Aegean. The gigantic and fundamentally important work by A. Furumark on the classification of Mycenaean pottery, according to types of vase shapes and decorative motifs, had a decisive effect on those dealing with the same issue in the kindred Minoan domain, providing solid grounding for constructing detailed chronological sequences. Last, in the early 1970s the ground-breaking book by C. Renfrew, *The Emergence of Civilisation*, came to stir up the still waters of the traditional approach to the archaeological data, offering a new theoretical model for interpreting the birth and development of prehistoric cultures in the Aegean.

Since 1980, the archaeology of Crete has been moving on multiple levels of scholarship. Excavations have continued, bringing to light important new sites with notable finds. However, research has become much more systematic and underpinned by methods provided in several cases by other disciplines. Methods of dating moveable finds and archaeological levels, such as thermoluminesence, radiocarbon (C^{14}) and dendrochronology have been mobilized to evaluate excavation data. Petrographic and chemical analyses have been used to determine the provenance of clay and metal objects, with ultimate aim of understanding the mechanisms of circulation of goods in the Aegean and the Eastern Mediterranean. Chemical analyses – by chromatography – of sediments from inside clay vases have begun to give an insight into Minoan cuisine. Measurements of geological character have helped in the examination of the environment of Minoan settlements, as well as to determine the date of the eruption of the Thera volcano. Last, the study of botanical, zoological and anthropological remains has contributed decisively to our knowledge of the dietary habits, the economy and the health of the inhabitants of Bronze Age Crete.

Another significant ascertainment of the scholars involved in fieldwork over the last twenty years was that excavation is not the only method of acquiring information hidden beneath the soil. Systematic surface surveys in various selected regions, such as the plain around Malia, the lowland strip on the isthmus of Hierapetra, the Mesara Plain, the Amari Valley, the district of Sphakia, the island of Gavdos (anc. Gaudos) and elsewhere have yielded precious data concerning the density and the dispersion of installations in different periods of ancient Cretan history. The method of surface survey consists of the detailed and systematic recording of all manner of clues gathered from the ground surface, with emphasis on the statistics concerning the number of potsherds and their concentration by area.

591

The dawn of culture (7000-3500 BC)

There is still no secure evidence of human presence on the island of Crete before the Neolithic Age. Some scholars date to the Mesolithic Age, pre-7000 BC, some carvings discovered in a rock shelter in the area of Asphendou near Sphakia, depicting wild goats, bow, arrow and other symbols.

The Neolithic Age is associated with the introduction of agriculture and animal husbandry, in contrast to the hunting and gathering (foraging) economy of the previous period. In Crete the first farmers settled at coastal sites and gradually spread into the hinterland. With the exception of Knossos, which has been investigated extensively and is considered one of the most important Neolithic settlements in Europe, information on the other known Neolithic sites (Phaistos, Lentas, Kato Zakros, Perama, Gavdos, Dia) is limited. Caves used intensively, mainly in the Final Neolithic period, are being identified almost daily, all over the island. Neolithic man's preference for caves as dwelling places is due primarily to the protection these offered from inclement weather and to the presence of water inside them. Some caves were also used for inhuming the dead. However, it has not been elucidated whether the use of caves for worship, confirmed in later times, commenced in the Neolithic Age. The best known caves are the Trapeza Cave at Lasithi, the Ida Cave (*Idaion Antron*) and the Talaion Antron (Melidoni Cave) at Mylopotamos, the Gerani Cave at Rethymnon, the Koumarospilio and the Lera and Arkoudiotissa caves at Akrotiri, Chania, the Kerameia and Therisos caves, the Ellinospilios near Kolybari and the Aghia Sophia Cave at Topolia, Kisamos.

The first settlement at Knossos is dated to the interval 7000-6500 BC and was originally a camp of some 100 people. The population increased rapidly and the temporary installation soon became a permanent settlement of 1,000-2,000 inhabitants. Knossos is so far the only known site that has produced evidence of the Pre-pottery or Aceramic and the Early Neolithic period in Crete. More is known about the Middle Neolithic period, from sites such as Katsambas Hill and Metropolis, Mesara. The Chania Plain offered ideal conditions for the activity of Neolithic man. For the Late Neolithic period there is evidence from all over the island.

Carbonized grains of barley and two varieties of wheat, as well as lentils, point to the first crops cultivated, while bones of sheep, goat, cattle and pig point to the husbandry of domesticated animals. The architecture of the Neolithic Age was simple, with mud-brick houses, with usually few rooms, pebbled open spaces and outdoor pens for the livestock. The roofs were flat and constructed of branches daubed with clay. The floors were clay and infants were often buried in them. Over time, rooms became more numerous and in the Late Neolithic period floors were equipped with permanent hearths.

Strangely, Neolithic clay vases appear from the beginning in evolved form. They are fired in a bonfire, have wide-mouthed shapes and bear pointillé, incised, pattern-burnished or plain burnished decoration. There are also clay figurines, alongside stone ones, both anthropomorphic and

592. Crete. The handmade "Partira Ware" vase belongs to a pottery group from the island of Gavdos, which from early times developed culture, functioning as a connecting link between Crete and the North African coast. This ware is dated to the transition from the Neolithic to the Minoan Age (late 4th millennium BC) and is distinguished by open shapes and black or grey surface with pattern burnish. Chania Archaeological Museum.

593. Crete. A large rectangular building of the late Prepalatial period (early 2nd millennium BC) has been investigated close to Aghia Photia, Siteia. Divided into two almost equal parts by a wide central corridor or court, the plan could be considered a precursor type of the Minoan palace. On three sides – west, north and east – it was closed by an arched wall, perhaps a fortification, reinforced by two small bastions.

zoomorphic. The minor objects – of stone, clay or bone – include beads, pendants, tools and loom-weights. Last, obsidian, a material used by prehistoric man to fashion small blades and other tools, was apparently imported from Melos to Crete even in the Early Neolithic period.

The transition from the Stone Age to the Bronze Age is called the Final Neolithic or the Sub-neolithic period (3500 BC) in Crete. Evidence for this phase comes from excavations at Phourni by the Gulf of Merabello and in the Trapeza Cave at Lasithi. In the area of the prefecture of Chania there is information from the "Mameloukou Trypa" Cave at Perivolia and the "Platyvola" Cave at Kerameia, as well as from various sites at Akrotiri. In the village of Nerokourou on the Chania Plain the first traces of an open settlement have come to light, while on Gavdos part of a grave with excellent quality intact clay vases of this period has been excavated (fig. 592).

The course towards development (3500-1900 BC): Prepalatial period

At the beginning of the Bronze Age new population groups came to the island and mixed with the local ones. There was a remarkable proliferation of coastal sites, while at the same time some settlements were established at upland sites in the hinterland (Ellenes in the Amari Valley, Aghia Galini, Debla, Nea Roumata). Although cave dwelling continued at first, organized settlements and clusters of houses at open sites were created in parallel (Palaikastro, Myrtos and Vasiliki in the district of Hierapetra, Knossos, Tylissos, Archanes, Phaistos, Aghia Triada, Chania, Nopigeia in the district of Kisamos). The widespread working and use of obsidian, and the need to import copper and raw materials, reinforced Crete's close contacts with the Cyclades. Both Gavdos and

594. Crete. The Prepalatial period settlement at Trypiti on the south coast, east of Lentas, on top of a low, steep hill, consists of one-storey houses built either side of a main street. Most houses have one rectangular room with smaller lateral spaces possibly used as storerooms. The inhabitants were engaged in agriculture and stock-raising, while the discovery of stone and bone tools points to small-scale craft-industrial activities. A few metal tools and small quantities of Melian obsidian attest to some kind of transactions with other Aegean sites.

595. Crete. The tomb complex of the Hodegetria monastery, at the west end of the Asterousia mountain range, comprises two tholos tombs and a row of long narrow rooms annexed to the largest of them. The 150 or so burials yielded a very rich assemblage of finds, among them 52 seals, about 600 necklace beads, 3 gold diadems and some 280 clay vases. The fact that they pre-date the founding of the Minoan palaces supports the existence of an economic-social – and therefore perhaps political – élite from even before the palatial system was established.

596. Crete. Figurine of "Cycladic" type, of ivory, from the cemetery at Archanes. Mid-3rd millennium BC. Herakleion Archaeological Museum.

597. Crete. This clay vase, usually called "sauceboat", from the Kerameia Cave, is an imitation of a Helladic type of the 3rd millennium BC, which was popular in the Cyclades, Attica and the Peloponnese. Relations between the northwest part of the Peloponnese and the nearby Cyclades were close throughout Antiquity. These relations were due to the geographical propinquity of the two regions and are also corroborated by myths and later traditions, as well as excavation data *per se*. Chania Archaeological Museum.

the nearby islet of Gavdopoula in the Libyan Sea served as centres of the transit trade of the period. In the second phase of the Prepalatial period (2900-2300 BC) there was not only a spectacular increase in the number of settlements but also a differentiation of their economic character, in terms of their size and architectural features. The economic differentiation of neighbouring settlements is supported by finds from the Mesara tombs (fig. 595). However, study of the relationship between architecture and finds in settlements with a theoretically different status in the hierarchy, such as at Phournou Koryphi, Myrtos and Kephali Vasilikis, Hierapetra has shown that these are relatively limited installations of less than 1000 square metres in area, consisting of a few houses (two to five) lived in by small groups, perhaps "nuclear families". On the contrary, the settlements at Knossos and Phaistos appear to have been much larger, covering an estimated area of 48,400 square metres and 10,130 square metres respectively.

In funerary architecture, predominant were the large tholos or beehive tombs of the Mesara, in which members of a clan were buried, and the rectangular tomb buildings with one, two or more rooms (Palaikastro, Mochlos, Archanes). Burials in pithoi and larnakes were also frequent, as well as jar-burials (*enchytrismoi*) (Pacheiammos, Archanes, Nopigeia). The dead were provided with jewellery, weapons, seals, clay or stone vases and figurines. Particular care was taken to clear the bones from earlier burials, to hold meals for the dead (*nekrodeipna*) and to make ritual sacrifices. In the tombs of the Mesara, at Archanes and elsewhere several figurines and artifacts have been found that indicate contacts with the Cyclades (fig. 596). The cemetery at Aghia Photia, Siteia, with the single burials inside pits of elliptical plan, cut in the limestone bedrock, contained numerous vases of Cycladic type, abundant blades of Melian obsidian and Cycladic bronze objects (daggers and tools), suggesting even the possibility of an early settlement of Cycladic islanders in Crete.

Features of tomb architecture and pottery also reveal close contacts between western Crete and both the Peloponnese and the nearby Cyclades, a phenomenon that continued throughout Antiquity. Important trading and cultural relations had been consolidated here already from Prepalatial times (fig. 597). The small tholos tomb at Nea Roumata (early 3rd millennium BC), which contained only one burial accompanied by two clay vases as grave goods, is remarkably similar to contemporary Cycladic ones.

Wonderful examples of various styles in the pottery production of the Prepalatial period have survived, which in several cases were spread over a large geographical area. The widespread use of bronze brought a thriving manufacture of specialist tools and weapons – such as double axes, knives, drills, burins and chisels, razors, tweezers, triangular daggers, spearheads and arrowheads – as well as jewellery – rings, necklaces, pendants and earrings. Men and women both wore jewellery, some pieces of which were of gold and resemble analogous ones from the greater Aegean region and Syria.

390 | ΚΡΉΤΗ CRETE

598. Crete. At the site of Phourni, close to the modern village of Archanes, perhaps the most important cemetery of the Minoan Age has been investigated. It was in use over many centuries, since the burials are dated to different periods, from the Prepalatial (3rd millennium BC) into the Postpalatial (14th c. BC). The earliest finds, such as the figurine in fig. 596, bear witness to close relations with the Cyclades, which led some researchers to argue for the existence of a Cycladic colony in this region. Most burials – in sarcophagi, pithoi or cists in the bedrock – were made inside circular tombs, which were perhaps covered by a beehive vault (tholos). Among them, Tholos A is perhaps one of the most important tholos tombs in Crete, in terms of architecture and content. The addition of a lateral burial chamber refers to the architectural type of the most magnificent tholos tombs on the Greek Mainland – the "Tholos tomb of Atreus" at Mycenae and the "Tholos tomb of Minyas" at Orchomenos, Boeotia. The main chamber was found looted, but the side room contained the undisturbed burial of a female inside a richly decorated larnax. Among the grave goods were remnants of the gold-embellished robe of the deceased, copious jewellery and other precious materials, three gold signet rings, a hoard of bronze vessels and a large number of ivory inlays that decorated a wooden "footstool" of unique art.

599. Crete. The clay Phaistos Disc, found in the homonymous palace in 1908, is considered the earliest example of "typography". Stamped on both faces, in spiralling arrangement, are 231 hieroglyphic signs, corresponding to 45 repeated symbols. The text is probably religious, but has not been deciphered, despite the efforts of specialists and amateurs. Herakleion Archaeological Museum.

From the Prepalatial period the art of seal-carving or glyptic flourished in Crete. Seals were made of various materials and display a variety of shapes and sphragistic devices, mainly abstract but also figural, such as lions, fish and scorpions. The representations of various types of ships reveal the maritime activity of the Cretans from these times, which led to the development of trade with the Peloponnese and the Cyclades, as well as with Egypt, Syria and the wider region of the East. These Eastern Mediterranean lands were sources of precious raw materials, such as ivory, noble metals and diverse kinds of stones.

Towards the end of the third millennium BC there was marked cultural recession in the Cyclades and the Greek Mainland, with the advent of new Indo-European tribes and the concurrent destruction of major centres in both Greece and the East. On Crete, in contrast, large flourishing installations were at their peak (Knossos, Archanes, Phaistos, Chamalevri, Chania, Nopigeia). Some new sites, protected by natural or manmade fortifications (Chaimazi, Aghia Photia in the district of Siteia), date to the early second millennium BC (fig. 593). The finds from the cemeteries of the period – the diachronic cemetery at Phourni, Archanes being the most characteristic example – bear witness to the great increase in wealth, which was now in the hands of specific social groups, along with the intensification of transactions with regions outside Crete. Traces of these transactions with lands such as Egypt, Syria and Mesopotamia are encountered even more frequently in the content of tombs in the Mesara and at Mochlos. The mainstays of Cretan export trade were timber, olive oil, herbs, aromatic oils and various other agricultural products.

To this same period is dated the first use of the so-called "peak sanctuaries". Recent well-documented studies have demonstrated that some of these sanctuaries were used by the inhabitants of wider regions (Juktas, Kophinas and Vrysinas), while others were of more local character, serving the population of particular communities (Petsophas, Traostalos, Atsipades).

The prevailing of the palatial system (1900-1700 BC)

According to the latest evidence, the first palaces in Crete were founded around 1900 BC, most probably by representatives of a social élite, which was distinguished from the rest of the populace by the accumulation of wealth. Most scholars believe that the idea of these large building complexes in which all political, economic and possibly religious authorities were concentrated came from the East. Nonetheless, their creation was undoubtedly the outcome of internal socio-economic development, traces of which can be observed in the previous period. Palaces were founded at Knossos, Phaistos (fig. 609) and Malia (fig. 603), but buildings of palatial type or regional centres were also constructed, as shown by recent research at Petras in the district of Siteia, Monastiraki in the Amari Valley (fig. 602) and possibly at Palaikastro in the prefecture of Siteia, Archanes, Chamalevri near Rethymnon and the town of Chania, with differences, of course, in their ambit of influence.

The Minoan palaces are always orientated North-South and the buildings are arranged around a central court, which is also their basic diagnostic feature, together with the west court and the magazines (fig. 602). The religious and political authority of each region was concentrated in these building complexes, within a pervasive religious spirit charactcristic of Minoan society. A multitudinous priesthood and administration was responsible for organizing all the activities of the palace: annual festivals, religious rituals, production, collection, storage and distribution of produce, control of exports and imports. A system of writing was essential for the bureaucratic monitoring of all the palace's activities. The first Cretan scripts were Cretan hieroglyphic (fig. 599) and Linear A. Both are syllabic and probably render the earliest form of the Minoan language. They have not been deciphered because the number of signs available to specialist scholars is very limited.

The pattern of small settlements in the countryside was organized around the "nuclei" of the first palaces (fig. 601). Road networks were created to link the different centres, while the sea was the preferred means of communication, which is why coastal settlements and harbours were established. Noteworthy water-supply networks were constructed, the most typical example of which is the Knossos aqueduct with clay pipes bringing water from the area of Archanes. The settlements founded at the beginning of the period (Gournia, Zakros, Apodoulou in the Amari Valley, Pera Galinoi in the Mylopotamos district, Stylos, Nopigeia) grew spectacularly over the years and frequently had close relations with the palatial centres.

During the period of the first palaces, worship in the peak sanctuaries continued, while comparable activities are observed also in the interior of caves (Amnisos, Dikte, Ida and Talaion, Mameloukou Trypa, Kerameia).

The high quality Minoan art was expressed mainly through the palaces, which housed well-organized specialist workshops. Its products epitomize the imposing grandeur and refined lifestyle dictated by the system of authority. New styles prevailed in pottery, such as Barbotine and Kamares Ware (fig. 600), while wheel-made vases won ground, as the tournette was replaced by the fast-rotating wheel. There were important developments too in the art of metalworking. The treasures found at Tod in Egypt and Byblos in Syria have been attributed to Cretan palatial workshops. Remarkable too are the creations of the goldsmith's art, such as the "bees pendant" from Malia and the "Aegina Treasure", which is usually ascribed to a Cretan workshop. Numerous bronze ceremonial weapons with incised, gold and ivory decoration are counted among the masterpieces of the period.

600. Crete. "Fruit-stand" from Phaistos. Herakleion Archaeological Museum. Kamares Ware, regarded by many as the most ornate pottery in the ancient world, was apparently produced exclusively in the palatial workshops of central Crete. The establishment of the potter's wheel and the introduction of polychromy in the painted decoration of the vases are the two basic factors that permitted craftsmen of the first palaces to experiment in new directions, reaching the climax of their creativity in Kamares Ware products. Some of the most elegant examples of this "display" class have walls as thin as eggshell, perhaps alluding to metal prototypes.

601. Crete. The 42 faience plaques of the so-called "Town Mosaic", from the east wing of the palace of Knossos, give a picture of the architecture of the houses on the period of the first palaces (1900-1700 BC). Used as decorative inlays on a piece of furniture or a wall, they represent façades of typical two- and three-storey houses. On some, a vertical projection at the top perhaps denotes the shelter of an internal staircase. Structural details such as doorways, wooden window frames and ashlar fronts are rendered in different colours. It has been suggested that the plaques depict houses around the palace of Knossos. Herakleion Archaeological Museum.

602. Crete. The Protopalatial settlement at Monastiraki (1900-1700 BC) was founded in the Amari Valley, between mounts Kedros and Ida, at a point controlling the road from and to the palace of Phaistos. Excavations there have brought to light a large building complex, with features encountered in the contemporary palatial centres. Many magazines have been uncovered, with a host of pithoi and smaller vases, a monumental building with structural elements suggesting use for cult, and retaining walls over a wide area. The numerous seal impressions point to a central administration with an organized bureaucratic system of monitoring the production and distribution of goods. The settlement was destroyed by a severe earthquake that brought the end of the Protopalatial period.

603. Crete. Important buildings of the Protopalatial period have been revealed recently at Malia. The so-called "Quartier Mu", a short distance to the west of the palace, essentially comprises two large buildings (A and B) with several rooms, surrounded by five smaller houses, in which specialist workshops were accommodated (of seal-engravers, potters and metalworkers). The discovery of archives of inscribed tablets, seal impressions and other objects, as well as the clear allocation of activities in sectors such as producing, inventorying, storing and redistributing goods point to a central economic management that must have operated in parallel with that of the neighbouring palace. The excavators have attributed this management to a religious authority, which during this period probably enjoyed a degree of independence from the political authority wielded by the palace.

604, 605. Crete. The "Ceremonial Hall" (above) and the "Lustral Basin" (below), in the west wing of the palace of Zakros, are two spaces that were evidently used for religious rituals. The palace of Zakros was built rather late, most probably to serve Knossian interests in the region. This is deduced from the similarities between the palaces in architecture, pottery, use of symbols and script, and from the discovery at Zakros of an archive of seal impressions, part of which was of Knossian provenance. The palatial complex replaced an earlier one, perhaps the seat of a local governor, who seems to have managed the mercantile economy of the coastal settlement.

606, 607. Crete, Palace of Malia. The way in which the main magazines for agricultural produce and the main shrines are incorporated in the west wing is reminiscent of that at Knossos, while the placement of a possible "banqueting hall" in the north wing "refers" to a corresponding arrangement at Phaistos. Of lesser importance at Malia is the east wing, which housed almost exclusively magazines for olive oil and other agricultural produce. Characteristic too is the presence of eight circular constructions that were apparently used as granaries.

608. Crete, Knossos. According to A. Evans, the "Theatral Space" to the northwest of the palace was used for celebrating rites or holding contests, in the presence of an audience.

609. Crete. The Palace of Phaistos at the west edge of the Mesara Plain, excavated in the early 20th c., is second only to Knossos in size and luxury among the analogous buildings of the Neopalatial period in Crete. An impressive stepped access from the west leads the visitor either to the opulent main apartments in the north wing, or to the spacious central court. Shrines and magazines – strangely more limited in capacity than those of Knossos – are crammed into the west wing of the building. The first palace on the site – a large part of which came to light under the west wing of its successor – had an imposing façade of massive dressed stone blocks. Outstanding among the wealth of finds recovered are exquisitely decorated clay vases and large caches of seal impressions.

396 | CRETE

PREHISTORIC TIMES | 397

610, 611. Crete. The discovery of the palace at Galatas in the district of Pediada is a recent success in the annals of excavation in Crete. The palatial complex was founded most probably in the late 18th c. BC, perhaps by Knossian incomers. Of the wings framing the large central court of the complex, more developed were the east – used mainly for preparing and holding banquets – and the north, with its impressive ashlar façade onto the central court, which seems to have housed residential apartments. The palace at Galatas is believed to have been abandoned rather early, prior to the final destruction of the other palaces. Perhaps the lack of rich moveable finds in its rooms is due to this fact. The original luxurious appointments are attested by the occasional find of wall-painting fragments of sophisticated art.

The clay pithos (fig. 610), one of the very few objects in the palace, is a characteristic example of the *par excellence* storage vessel in the palatial economy of Crete. Herakleion Archaeological Museum.

The period of Minoan domination (1700-1450 BC)

A major destruction, which most scholars ascribe to natural phenomena (earthquakes) and date to the end of the eighteenth century BC, brought the life of the first palaces and their contemporary settlements to an end. A period of reform, and very possibly of political instability, followed, during which attempts were made to rebuild the palaces with a new form. Such efforts can be seen best in the case of Phaistos and to a lesser extent of Knossos. A palace located recently in the village of Galatas, in the district of Pediada, is probably the fruit of endeavours to enhance a new socio-economic class (figs 610, 611).

As this transitional period came to an end, the building of the new palaces was completed in various parts of the island. Old sites with new palaces are Knossos, Phaistos and Malia, and on a smaller scale Petras, while new sites are Galatas and – slightly later – Zakros (figs 604, 605) at the east end of Crete. The finds from recent excavations indicate that centres such as the city of Chania (fig. 621) and perhaps Chamalevri in the prefecture of Rethymnon, Archanes and Palaikastro in the prefecture of Siteia must have been palatial in character, despite the fact that the distinctive central court has not yet been found. An important well-built building of rectangular plan and with large central court was constructed at Kommos, the site of the outport of Phaistos (fig. 613).

In the Neopalatial period worship was transferred gradually from the peak sanctuaries to inside the palaces (figs 621, 623). The religious and ceremonial role of the new palaces was paramount, determining their structure, function and use. Spaces were formed with particular features adapted to the kind of rituals that now held sway. Specific basic spaces in various variations were arranged around the central court, such as the west court, magnificent guarded entrances, ceremonial halls with pier-and-door partitions (*polythyra*), small internal courtyards and light-wells, lustral basins (fig. 605), spaces for performing blood and bloodless sacrifices (altars, *eschara*, exedras), treasuries, magazines, various workshops of lapidaries, seal-carvers, bronze-smiths, dyers and weavers, and kitchens. The walls and floors of the formal halls were frequently decorated with precious materials or impressive wall-paintings. The buildings were crowned by the so-called sacral horns or horns of consecration and the bull became a symbol of power (figs 38, 616, 617).

The cult paraphernalia and symbols included offering tables, small altars, rhyta, tubular and calyx-shaped vessels, kernoi, double axes (fig. 586), triton shells (fig. 43) and the "sacral knot". The strong religious dimension of the life of all people was combined admirably with a sense of freedom and *joie de vivre*. In such a clime – and through a probably polytheistic system – rituals invoking the deity for the rebirth of Nature were performed. Other comparable or complementary rites included worship of the sacred tree, athletics contests with seemingly religious content, ritual dances and animal sacrifices.

At several Neopalatial sites (Knossos, Phaistos, Zakros, Aghia Triada, Chania, Archanes, Tilyssos, Malia, Palaikastro) rectangular clay tablets in the syllabic Linear A script have been found, frequently accompanied by large numbers of clay discs and seal impressions. These bear witness to the functioning of an advanced bureaucratic system relating to the centralized economic system of the palace centres. The tablets record inventories of agricultural produce and censuses of persons or livestock, as is deduced from comparative study with the tablets in the deciphered Linear B script of Mycenaean times. The painted or incised inscriptions on vases or stone sacred vessels are of a different nature.

In the same period, settlements such as at Palaikastro, Gournia, Pseira, Pyrgos-Myrtos, Kastelli in the district of Pediada, Chania and Stylos, were flourishing, while an innovation is the appearance of a series of topographically independent and economically self-sufficient buildings, mostly in the countryside (Amnisos, Nirou Hani, Vathypetro, Tylissos, Aghia Triada, Sklavokampos, Achladia, Zou, Pitsidia, Zominthos, Nerokourou). The architecture of these follows the characteristics of that of the palaces, with polythyra, ashlar façades, lustral basins, light-wells, various drains and conduits, pavements and an upper storey. Such buildings, which were formerly called generically by the Roman term villa, evidently served various purposes as the occasion demanded, supportive of the major centres. They were always founded in fertile and neuralgic areas, on main road arteries (fig. 612). Characteristic is the example of a recent-

612. Crete. The building at Vathypetro near Archanes is a typical example of the so-called Minoan villa or country house. The basic building, with particularly careful architecture clearly influenced by palatial models, seems to be the nucleus of a larger installation whose rural character is revealed by the finds. A fully-equipped facility for treading grapes, some smaller installations considered to be olive-oil presses and spacious well-designed magazines with large pithoi confirm the economic orientation of the occupants. It is possible that the use of the building changed during its lifetime and from a residence for élite persons it became a centre for monitoring and managing the agricultural yields of a wider zone of farmland.

613. Crete. Kommos, on the south coast of the island, seems to have been the outport of Phaistos, which is a short distance inland. Many of the moveable finds from the excavation emphasize the commercial importance of the site and bear witness to contacts with Cyprus, the region of Canaan, the Syro-Palestinian littoral and Egypt. The most important building in the settlement (Building T) was constructed most probably in the 17th c. BC and was of rectangular outline with central court flanked by two colonnades. The impressive north façade, built of large ashlar blocks of poros stone, is the longest unbroken wall in a Minoan construction. During the 14th c. BC, a row of long narrow parallel warehouses was built on the same site, which according to the excavators were used as ship-sheds.

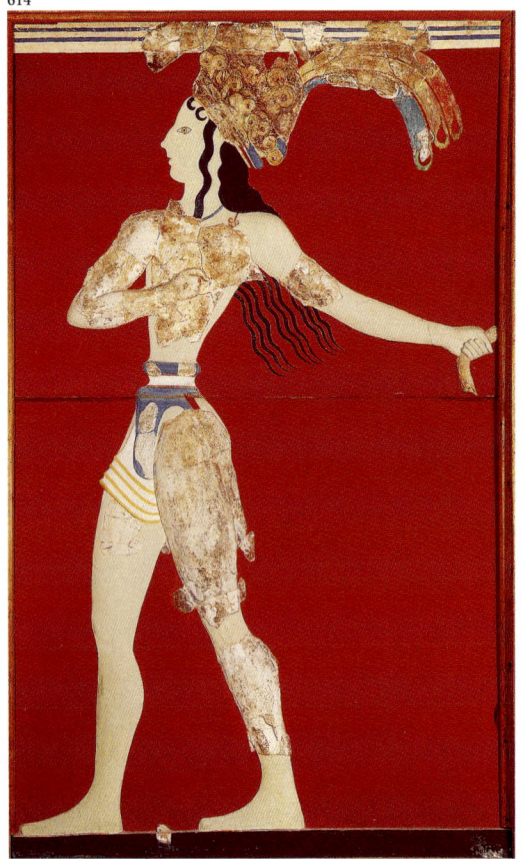

614, 615. Crete. The controversial low-relief wall-painting of the "Priest-King" or the "Prince of the Lilies" dates to the second phase of the Neopalatial period (16th c. BC) and decorated the south entrance to the palace of Knossos. Among the diverse interpretations is that the male figure is a boxer and that the crown belongs to a priest. According to the restoration proposed in fig. 615, the male figure represents a deity and the crown adorned the head of a sphinx. Herakleion Archaeological Museum.

ly excavated complex at Zominthos near Anogeia, which seems to have been intended to control the stock-raising activity in the region.

After the eruption of the Thera volcano – which some scholars now date to the last quarter of the seventeenth century BC – some signs of economic and possibly political decline appear in Crete. The palace at Galatas was abandoned, while the installations at Kommos and Petras shrunk. A slump in building activity is observed in settlements too, such as at Palaikastro, while some of the isolated buildings in the countryside, such as Amnisos, were deserted. By contrast, at other sites significant buildings were apparently erected. Among these are the palaces at Zakros, Gournia and perhaps Phaistos, and certain big buildings at Mochlos and on Pseira. The archaeological data indicate most clearly a political instability which – in the view of some scholars at least – led to the collapse of the Minoan Civilization.

Most scholars believe that in the Neopalatial period the palace of Knossos had a hegemonic role. Characteristics of Knossian cultural influence – and possibly propaganda – have been detected in many provincial centres. The discovery of caches of sealings, impressions of seals or signet rings on clay, at various sites distant from one another (Zakros, Gournia, Aghia Triada, Sklavokampos) points to the existence of a bureaucratic economic system of which Knossos was epicentre. The road network was improved. In the same period foreign trade was intensified and the Minoan presence is evident particularly in the Cyclades, the Dodecanese, Cyprus, Asia Minor, the Levant and Egypt. Imports included hippopotamus and elephant tusks from Syria, semiprecious stones from the East generally and stone vases, probably containing aromatic and therapeutic unguents, from Egypt. Correspondingly, objects and wall-paintings of Minoan art have come to light in Egypt (Tell el 'Daba on the Nile Delta) and other Eastern Mediterranean lands (Tell el Kabri in Israel, Katna in Syria). Important too is the Minoan influence in Greece, as evidenced by the finds from the royal shaft graves at Mycenae.

The Neopalatial period has splendid artistic masterpieces to its credit, including many of the wall-paintings at Knossos (figs 614, 616, 617), some of them miniature. Executed in the technique of *buon fresco*, using mineral pigments, their subjects are religious or inspired by Nature. The art of ivory-carving produced such works as the chryselephantine statuette from Palaikastro (figs 618, 619) and the bull-leaper from Knossos. Creations of metalworking include figurines of animals and of adorants, vases and a wide range of tools and weapons. In pottery, more elegant shapes began to appear and subjects from the world of nature and the sea are impressive. These influences led to the elaboration first of the "Floral Style" and then of the "Marine Style", frequently with superb examples (fig. 622). On the relief stone vases of the period some of the loveliest pictorial representations in Minoan art were produced (fig. 623), while mainly animal figures, such as the bull and the lion, were sculpted as ritual vessels. Glyptic art encompasses some exquisite compositions that vie with those executed on some unique gold signet rings. These last usually depict religious ritual scenes, borrowed from the thematic repertoire of wall-painting (fig. 620).

616, 617. Crete. The well-known wall-painting of the Head of a Bull, which is rendered in high relief, comes from the area of the north entrance to the palace of Knossos (fig. 616). Dated to the first phase of the Neopalatial period (17th c. BC), it belongs to a composition of bull-leaping, of which only this fragment has survived. Taming the bull in bull-leaping was a religious ritual in which athletes performed specific exercises on the animal's back. The bull was the paramount sacred animal in Minoan Crete, because it embodied strength and perhaps because it was associated with the chthonic deity that caused and tamed earthquakes, which often afflicted the awe-struck Minoans. In exceptional circumstances the bull was sacrificed and offered to the deity or to a distinguished dead person. The miniature frieze from the northeast part of the palace, which is dated to the early 14th c. BC, preserves the entire scene of bull-leaping (fig. 617). The bull rushes in "flying gallop", a pose that is a creation of Minoan art. Three figures, male and female, partake in the sport. It is noteworthy that females participated equally with males and indeed wore the male loincloth. The wall-paintings are exhibited in the Herakleion Archaeological Museum.

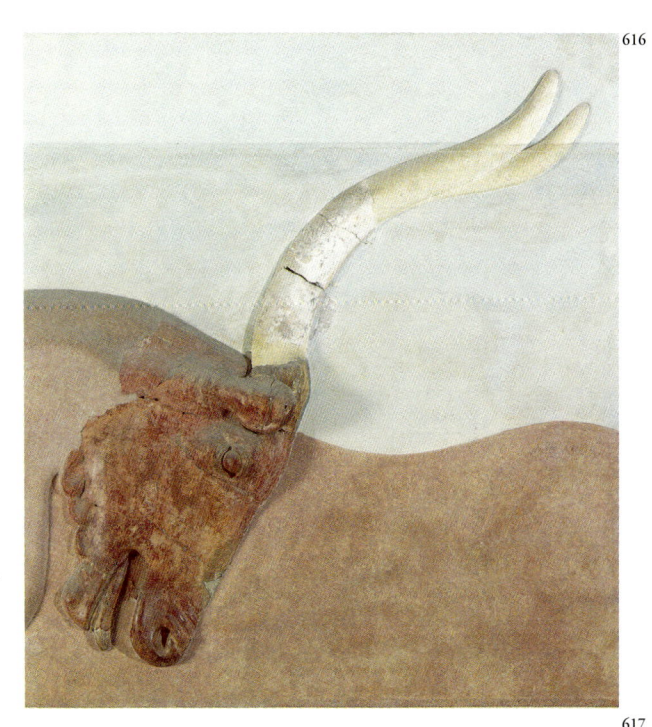

PREHISTORIC TIMES

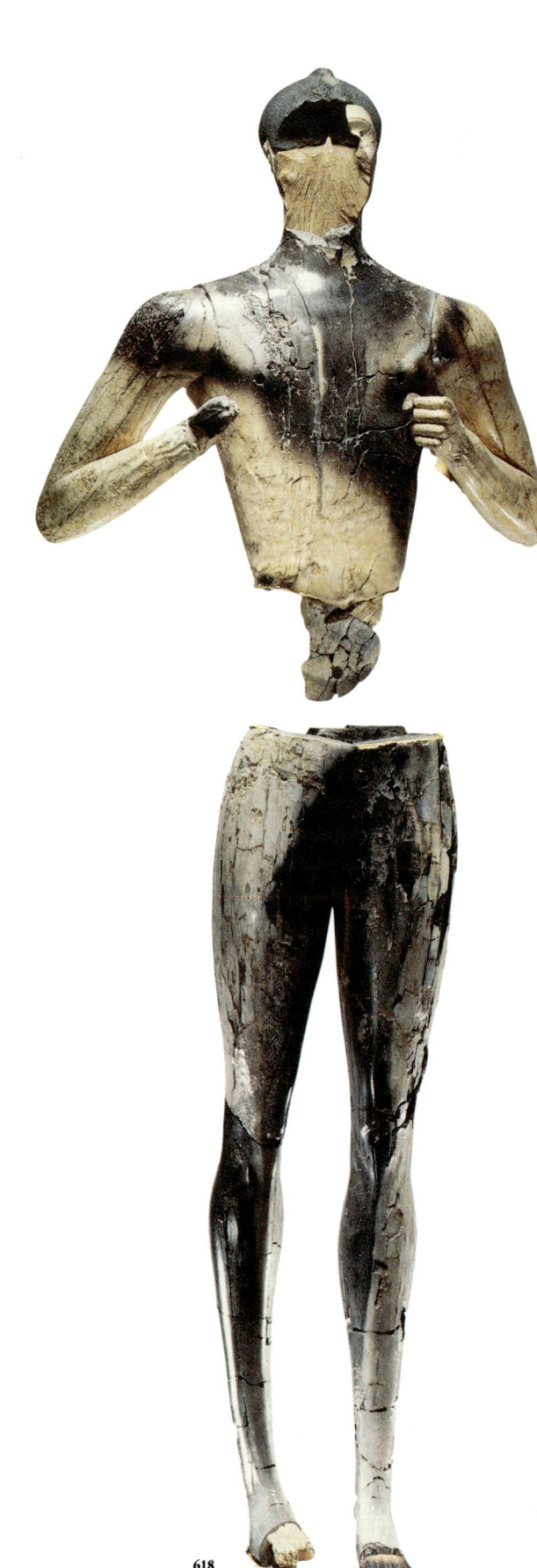

618, 619. Crete. The new excavations at Palaikastro, at the east end of the island, have filled in the picture of a flourishing Minoan settlement with economic activities clearly turned towards the sea. Even though no building has been found that could be considered the seat of a local governor, analogous with those in other contemporary settlements, the architectural remains and moveable finds are comparable to those from palatial sites. Characteristic is the recent find of a chryselephantine statuette of a young male in the pose of an adorant. In addition to the ivory and gold, other materials were used in creating this unique object, such as black steatite, rock crystal and wood. The excavators dubbed this figurine the "Palaikastro kouros" and "saw" it as representing a youthful god. The naturalistic rendering of details and the superb workmanship suggest a possible Knossian provenance. Aghios Nikolaos Archaeological Museum.

620. Crete. The scene represented on the "Master Impression" from Kastelli in the prefecture of Chania is unique in prehistoric Crete (second half of 15th c. BC). This is the imprint on clay of a seal ring with elliptical bezel. Preserved on the reverse are traces of the object it sealed, probably a document. The representation consists of a multi-storey building complex crowned by horns of consecration and standing on a rocky coastal height. Prominent at the top – and in the centre of the complex – is a robust male figure holding a spear in his outstretched right hand. The complex is interpreted as a palace, a city or a shrine, and the male figure as a master or a god in epiphany. The sealing provides hermeneutic solutions to other earlier representations and confirms the authenticity of some disputed works, such as the "Ring of Minos" (fig. 39). Chania Archaeological Museum.

PREHISTORIC TIMES | 403

621. Crete. The most important Minoan settlement in western Crete, the Kydonia (*ku-do-ni-ja*) of the Linear B tablets, lies in the heart of the Old City of Chania, beneath Venetian, Ottoman and modern constructions. Excavations over the past thirty years have brought to light various buildings on Kastelli Hill on the coast and in the neighbourhood of Splantzia, where in 1997 part of an extensive complex of the Neopalatial period, 750 sq. m. in area, was investigated. This included rooms with pier-and-door partitions (*polythyra*), light-wells, a lustral basin, an impressive stone exedra in the open air (with possible place for a sacred tree), a large court, a pyre area with burnt offerings and *eschara/bothros*, and a series of basement rooms, all in direct context with a huge number of conical cups. The constructions are linked by a system of conduits beginning inside the building, proceeding across the court and running round the exedra. These features designate the building as a *locus sanctus*, that is an urban or a palatial shrine which was most probably incorporated in the palace complex at Chania of 1600 BC. The final destruction of the building occurred at the end of the Late Minoan IB period (mid-15th c. BC), at the same time as in the other centres on the island, and was accompanied by a large-scale conflagration.

The end of the Neopalatial system (1450-1370 BC)

Around the mid-fifteenth century BC a great catastrophe reduced most of the Minoan centres to ruins. Scholarly opinions differ as the to the cause of the disaster. Some argue that it was due to natural phenomena (such as earthquakes), while others link it with military invasion from abroad or civil strife on Crete. Whatever the cause, the fact is that Knossos survived the destruction and continued to thrive under a regime with some new characteristics, which A. Evans dubbed Creto-Mycenaean. Evans detected the presence of Mycenaean incomers to the region, both in some architectural alterations inside the palace – among them the addition of the "Throne Room" to the original complex – and in the change in burial habits, in cemeteries he discovered and investigated in the environs (such as a Zapher Papoura). Today several scholars agree with Evans, supporting the presence of Achaean tribes at Knossos, Archanes, Phaistos and Chania, in this period. They base their hypothesis mainly on the appearance of new types of rock-cut graves ("warriors' tombs") in which persons of high social rank were buried, accompanied by rich and impressive bronze weaponry, precious jewellery as well as bronze and clay vases of exceptional art. It should be noted here that in the preceding Neopalatial period too some burials were furnished with the weaponry of the deceased, as evident from excavations in the cave-like tombs at Poros, Herakleion (fig. 627). Nonetheless, it is a fact that from the late fifteenth century BC onwards a different spirit prevailed in Crete, promoting a new, masculine and martial ethos.

In this period all power was apparently concentrated in just one palace, Knossos, which was repaired and decorated with wall-paintings that emit new ideas. It also seems that use of Linear B script, which has been shown to render the early form of the Greek language, began then. Linear B tablets have been found in the palaces of Knossos, Malia, Phaistos and Kydonia (mod. Chania) (figs 621, 629), on which are recorded the names of several cities that were controlled by Knossos, such as Amnisos, Tylissos, Phaistos, Siteia(?), Sybrita, Kydonia, Aptara. Recorded too is a large number of sheep (about 100,000), mainly rams, which were reared primarily for their wool, thus pointing to the great development of textile weaving, while there is also frequent mention of weavers, male and female. Other animals (goats, pigs) are recorded too, as well as agricultural produce (olive oil, herbs, perfumes, timber). Some gods are named, such as Zeus, Poseidon, Athena and Dionysos, as well as offerings to them, which include wine, honey, olive oil, barley and figs. In general, the decipherment of Linear B script opened a new window on understanding Cretan society in the second half of the second millennium BC.

Pottery in this period was dominated by the pompous "Palace Style", while there were evidently changes in drinking habits, with the Mycenaean kylikes replacing the copious Minoan conical cups of the previous period.

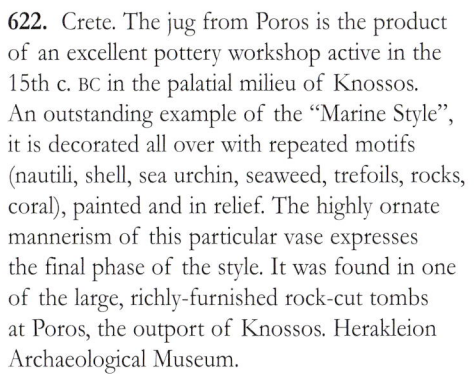

622. Crete. The jug from Poros is the product of an excellent pottery workshop active in the 15th c. BC in the palatial milieu of Knossos. An outstanding example of the "Marine Style", it is decorated all over with repeated motifs (nautili, shell, sea urchin, seaweed, trefoils, rocks, coral), painted and in relief. The highly ornate mannerism of this particular vase expresses the final phase of the style. It was found in one of the large, richly-furnished rock-cut tombs at Poros, the outport of Knossos. Herakleion Archaeological Museum.

623. Crete. Worship in peak sanctuaries, where the devotee came closer to the heavenly deity, was particularly widespread in the Protopalatial period and continued into the Neopalatial. One such sanctuary of palatial character, crowned by ibexes, is thought to be represented in relief on this chlorite rhyton of rare workmanship (c. 1500 BC), from the palace of Zakros. Initially the vessel was covered with gold leaf, traces of which still adhere to its surface. Herakleion Archaeological Museum.

PREHISTORIC TIMES | 405

The "Mycenaeanization" of Crete (1370-1200 BC)

The Achaeans are considered to have ruled the island for the next two hundred years. When the power of Knossos was broken in the early fourteenth century BC, a free field was created in which various Cretan centres developed independently under the authority of the Achaeans, within the context of the "Mycenaean *Koine*". The Mycenaeans also established emporeia at the former Minoan trading stations in the Aegean.

At the beginning of the new period relations were maintained with the New Kingdom in Egypt. From the comparison of names of cities on the base of a stele of the funerary monument of Amenhotep III, at Kom-el-Hetan in Egypt, it is surmised that Egyptian emissaries made an official visit to sites in Crete and the Greek Mainland.

The area of Chania enjoyed considerable prosperity during the fourteenth and thirteenth centuries BC, when it was associated closely with Mycenaean centres in the Argolid and Boeotia. Cypriot, Egyptian, Syrian-Phoenician and possibly Italian pottery arrived at the port of Kydonia, which played a significant role in transit trade between the Eastern and Western Mediterranean. At the same time, products from Chania were sent not only to the rest of Crete and to Greece, but also as far as Cyprus and Sardinia, as is deduced from the Kydonian clay vases identified in these places. Stirrup jars from Chania, for transporting perfumed oil or wine, have been found in Thebes, Orchomenos, Mycenae and Tiryns. The existence of a palatial centre with an organized bureaucratic system is thrown into sharper relief by the recent discovery at Chania of Linear B tablets dated to the early thirteenth century BC (fig. 629).

Another important harbour that was in its heyday was Kommos, the outport of Phaistos. A series of long narrow warehouses, or ship-sheds according to the excavators, was constructed in the period of Mycenaean rule. Aghia Triada flourished too, where the so-called "agora" also functioned as an extensive storage space. Other known sites are Zakros, Palaikastro, Gournia, Malia, Archanes, Chondros in the district of Viannos, Tylissos, Chamalevri, Perama, Stylos and Knossos itself. Much more information is yielded by the host of cemeteries that have been uncovered all over Crete.

The Mycenaean presence was now manifested overtly in architecture, pottery and the minor arts. However, the presence of Mycenaeans on the island never had a catalytic effect, nor was their sovereignty dynamic, since the Cretans were not assimilated but kept their own traditions both in life and in art. In architecture, megara of Mycenaean type have been uncovered at Tylissos, Aghia Triada and Gournia. The products of local pottery workshops, such as that of Kydonia (fig. 628), are outstanding. The bone artifacts of this period include impressive examples of decoration of wooden chests or footstools from Archanes, Knossos, Phylaki in the district of Apokoronos and Kydonia, with representations popular in the Mycenaean repertoire, such as helmeted warriors, figure-eight shields and sphinxes (fig. 626).

Cult was often practised in small domestic shrines, where figurines in the type of the "Minoan goddess with raised arms" appear together with tubular vases known as "snake tubes". These figurines and vessels dominate throughout the ensuing century. Concurrently, Mycenaean fig-

624. Crete. The cemetery at Poros near Herakleion, with cave-like tombs cut in the soft bedrock, is so far the unique example of an organized burial ground for eminent persons in the Neopalatial period. Some of the tombs appear to have been in use continuously for repeated burials, from the time of the Old Palaces until the end of the New Palaces. To date, six tombs have been explored, most of them recently, because of the intensive building activity in the area. The grave goods bespeak the high social status of the dead: rich pottery, seals of semiprecious stones, jewellery of gold, silver, glass, ivory and faience, and gold seal rings with complex religious representations on the bezel. Last, noteworthy is the presence of bronze weapons as grave goods, and of a boars'-tusk helmet. Herakleion Archaeological Museum.

625. Crete. The sphragistic devices on an overwhelming proportion of Minoan seal rings are from the religious iconographic cycle. Among them are representations of various rituals in which human (mainly female) figures participate and "epiphanies" of deities take place, funerary laments, bull-leaping and other contests. On the ring from Isopata, Knossos, a female figure hovers above the ground, while other females around her participate in a ritual dance – perhaps ecstatic. Herakleion Archaeological Museum.

urines of Phi (Φ), Psi (Ψ) and Tau (T) types appeared in Crete. In addition to handmade figurines, the use of wheel-made ones became generalized, particularly of animals. The best-known small shrine is the "Shrine of the Double Axes", inside the palace of Knossos.

New customs were introduced into tomb architecture with the founding – already from the late fifteenth century BC – of new cemeteries, such as those at Zapher Papoura, Knossos and the east cemetery of Kydonia, with graves cut in the soft limestone bedrock. The early "warriors' graves" (simple pits, with vertical or lateral ditch for single burials) were replaced in subsequent years by chamber tombs, a type suitable for family burials. The type of the tholos tomb was preferred for members of the local élite (Achladia in the district of Siteia, Archanes, Perama, Phylaki, Stylos, Maleme), frequently richly furnished with grave goods.

In the Armenoi cemetery at Rethymnon, which was founded in the late fifteenth century BC but was used mainly during the second half of the fourteenth and the thirteenth century BC, 230 chamber tombs have been excavated, while in the Kydonia cemetery over 150. The cemetery area was arranged to facilitate easy access to and movement within it, and in some cases, as at Archanes, buildings were erected to serve some functions, such as meals for the dead (*nekrodeipna*) and funerary rites. The chamber tombs invariably contain copious grave goods – weapons, tools, vessels and personal items, jewellery and seals. The norm throughout Crete, excepting the region of Chania, was burial in a larnax, in the shape of a chest or a bathtub and always lavishly decorated (fig. 631). At Chania wooden biers were the rule, also decorated with painted depictions on the plaster coating. At Archanes and Armenoi plaques used as grave stelai have survived, set up as markers as was the Mycenaean custom.

626. Crete. The plaque representing a helmeted warrior (late 14th c. BC) is from the decoration of a wooden object a casket or a footstool which had been placed as a grave good in a tholos tomb at Phylaki, Apokoronas. It is made from hippopotamus tooth, a material that was evidently more widely used than elephant ivory. The warrior with boars'-tusk helmet was a popular subject in Mycenaean art and particularly in ivory carving. The type of helmet is encountered in many parts of the Aegean, from the Early Mycenaean period onwards. An actual boars'-tusk helmet was found in a grave in the Armenoi cemetery, while similar decorative inlays were found at Knossos, Archanes and Kydonia.

627. Crete. The wall-paintings that survived best *in situ*, after the final destruction of the palace of Knossos, *c.* 1375 BC, are those that decorated the "Throne Room", with depictions of griffins. The wingless and inscrutable heraldic griffins express absolutely the spirit of the new occupants, with which the rest of the iconographic programme of the Knossian palace in this period is in accord, with subjects arranged in zones and repetitive in character.

PREHISTORIC TIMES | 407

628. Crete. The Kydonia pottery workshop enjoyed a heyday during the 14th and 13th centuries BC. Its products, of characteristic white clay, are distinguished by their excellent quality. The clay cylindrical pyxis (13th c. BC) from the area of Aptara is the most representative example of these. Painted on the front is a male figure touching a large seven-string musical instrument, a kithara or lyre. This musical representation is framed by flying birds, horns of consecration and double axes. The scene, known from examples in mainland Greece, is considered of ritual and religious content. The finding of the vase in a grave links it with funerary rites. The kitharode is interpreted as Orpheus or Apollo, but also as a simple bard or priest. Chania Archaeological Museum.

629. Crete. An important event for the history of Chania (anc. Kydonia) was the discovery of three Linear B tablets in the excavations in Aghia Aikaterini Square on Kastelli Hill. The tablet pictured here mentions a sanctuary of Zeus (Dion) with worship of the gods Zeus and Dionysos, to whom are offered amphorae of honey. The second tablet enumerates persons involved probably with textile production, with reference to two ethnic names deriving from toponyms in western Crete. The third records ten pairs of chariot wheels.

The tablets were found on the floor of a building that was destroyed in the early 13th c. BC. The necessity of scribes in this period points to the establishment at Kydonia of a central controlling authority, which presupposes the existence of an organized bureaucratic system. Chania Archaeological Museum.

From 1200 BC, and for reasons unknown – but which must be related to the destruction of the Hittite State, the extensive population movements in the Eastern Mediterranean and the appearance of the "Sea Peoples" – the power of the Aegean rulers (*anaktes*) dwindled. In the century that followed a new, single expressive language of Creto-Mycenaean Civilization prevailed on the Greek Mainland, in the Aegean region and in Crete, which can be characterized as an "Aegean *Koine*". This is obvious in architecture and mortuary practices, as well as in the various arts, such as pottery (fig. 630), metalworking, stone-carving and weaving.

Continuation or revival of cult is observed in small shrines and peak sanctuaries. There is, however, a total absence of textual testimonies, which fact has been linked with the collapse of the earlier political system, with the parallel disappearance of the large centres of authority. Nonetheless, the diffusion and adoption of new social and cultural elements (creation of new settlements, building of new houses in old settlements still in existence, introduction of new types of vessels and techniques in pottery, possible spread of the practice of cremation instead of inhumation, construction of trenches for rituals, predominance of the "goddess with raised arms") presupposes the existence of a centre in Crete, essential for their gestation.

Old settlements, which were truly flourishing – at least in the first half of the twelfth century BC – were Phaistos, Knossos, Malia, Kastelli in the district of Pediada, Chamalevri, Chania. One of these, perhaps Knossos, must have been in the vanguard of the necessary changes and innovations observed, thanks to which Crete prospered in these troubled times. In the second half of the twelfth century BC most of the aforementioned settlements were abandoned.

Concurrently, from the early twelfth century BC a gradual shift of other old settlements from lowland tracts to upland sites is observed, very often to precipitous heights and preferably in the island's interior (Lenika at Zakros, Kastri at Palaikastro, Kastrokephala, Sybrita, Aptera). New settlements were also founded gradually (Kavousi, Vrokastro, Kephala Vasiliki, Karphi, Prophitis Ilias, Chalasmenos, Katalymata). Scholars believe that the causes of these changes were the political instability, piracy and incursions that had increased at that time, the arrival of a new population element from mainland Greece, or a serious climatic change with a marked rise in temperature. Even so, the ancient tradition kept the echo of the founding of new settlements by the Achaeans, as in regions of western Crete.

630. Crete. Around 1200 BC, after the destruction of the major centres in Mycenaean Greece, a boom in building activity is observed in existing settlements in Crete, as well as the abandonment or the relocation of others, mainly to highland sites. A very interesting settlement developed at this time at Chamalevri, Rethymnon, in an area where notably human activity is attested from the Prepalatial period. A small example of the impressive early Late Minoan IIIC pottery (early 12th c. BC) brought to light in recent excavations at Chamalevri is this vase fragment with depiction of bird, which was found in a ditch cut in the bedrock. These ditches, several of which have been investigated, seem to be associated with some kind of ritual practices. Rethymnon Archaeological Museum.

631. Crete. During the 14th and 13th centuries BC it was common to bury affluent or eminent persons in larnakes, cist-shaped or bathtub-shaped, with lavish decoration. The best-known and most important example is the famous Aghia Triada sarcophagus, which is made of stone and was found in a chamber tomb. The elaborate decoration is executed in fresco technique on lime plaster, as in the wall-paintings. Depicted on one side is a standing male figure receiving gifts from three other male figures, while to their left, in the opposite direction, a ritual is taking place, in which two female figures and a kitharode participate. Represented on the second side is a bull sacrifice on an altar. Although the larnax is dated to the early years of the Mycenaean period on Crete, its iconography follows strictly Minoan models. Herakleion Archaeological Museum.

Historical times

THOMAS BROGAN - NATALIA VOGEIKOFF

The end of the Mycenaean world and the beginning of the Iron Age (12th-7th century BC)

In the late thirteenth and the early twelfth century BC the Aegean and the Eastern Mediterranean witnessed a devastating wave of violence that destroyed both the Hittite Empire and the smaller Mycenaean kingdoms. There are no historical sources to tell us what struck Crete around 1200 BC, but the archaeological record leaves no doubt that the island's inhabitants were seriously threatened. The network of coastal towns, some of which had existed for over two thousand years, was abandoned, and many inhabitants resettled in new remote sites in the mountains. This change marks the beginning of a new period in Cretan history, which is known also as the "Dark Age", during which many cultural achievements of the preceding centuries, such as writing and monumental architecture "were forgotten". Between 1100 and 600 BC Crete enjoyed a new period of development, which has its roots in the small settlements of the twelfth century BC and reached its climax in the birth of the city-states of the eighth and seventh centuries BC. This period is known on Crete as the Early Iron Age.

As written souces are not preserved before the seventh century BC, most of this period of Cretan history is reconstituted entirely from archaeological research. Field surveys have now revealed more than one hundred sites, which were first inhabited at the beginning of the twelfth century BC. Excavations in the northern Isthmus of Hierapetra are providing a detailed record of several hamlets and villages of the period. Naturally defensible situations were key factors the location of sites as with the case of Katalimata perched on the high ledges of the Cha Gorge on the east side of the Isthmus of Hierapetra (fig. 633). A path up the gravel slope (at lower left of the photograph) led to a narrow approach to the wider rock shelves on which several small houses were built overlooking the plain. The houses were supplied with a full range of clay storage, cooking, and eating vessels, suggesting that the occupation at Katalimata was permanent.

The larger neighboring settlements of Chalasmenos, Vrontas, and Vasiliki Kephala are more typical for the period, each containing the remains of small communities of five to fifteen households. Although most houses are the same size, suggesting a certain degree of equality between members of the community, there are none the less hints at that some individuals or families served a leading role, perhaps as a "big man" in the community. One such candidate is House A-B at Vrontas, which is provided with a large hall, unique storage rooms with large pithoi, and large numbers of fancy cups and foodstuffs that may represent the remains of local feasting..

From the pattern seen at Karphi, Vrontas, Chalasmenos, and Kephala, it appears that each community also had a separate built shrine housing images of a deity with raised arms and offering vessels, known as snake tubes and kalathoi. These may have been made as sets (fig. 632) for a female deity whose cult was connected with the fertility of the land and prosperity of the community.

632

410 | CRETE

632. Crete. In the Late Minoan IIIC period (12th c. BC), building G at Vrontas, Kavousi was free-standing and one-storeyed. The south room had been disturbed by a cremation burial in the 8th c. BC, but excavation of the smaller north room revealed a hoard of ritual vessels. Clay analysis has shown that the figurines of deities, the snake tubes, the plaques and the kalathoi were probably made as a set to be offered in the shrine. Hierapetra Archaeological Museum.

633. Crete. In the 12th c. BC most settlements, such as at Katalymata and Chalasmenos in the Cha Gorge at the entrance to the Isthmus of Hierapetra, were founded on sites that could be easily defended. Recent excavations at Katalymata have contributed significantly to understanding the conditions that prompted the population movements to naturally fortified areas. Evidence of a short-lived settlement of the Late Neolithic period (5th millennium BC) and brief occupations in the 2nd millennium BC was found at the site. The excavators assume that in difficult and dangerous periods people sought refuge at sites that were difficult of access, such as those in the Cha Gorge.

634. Crete. The bronze amphoroid krater that had been used as a funerary urn in the tholos tomb at Pantanassa Amari, in Rethymnon, is a rare vase type. Only seven such vases are known, five of which have been found in Cyprus. Examination of the cremated bones showed that the vase contained the remains of a middle-aged male. The use of the amphoroid krater as a funerary urn recalls the Homeric epics, where there is reference to the deposition of the ashes of Patroclus and of Achilles in gold amphorae. By analogy, it is thought that the deceased in the Pantanassa tholos tomb was an élite member in the local society. The other finds from the tomb date the burial to the late 11th/early 10th c. BC. Rethymnon Archaeological Museum.

HISTORICAL TIMES | 411

635. Crete. The faience figurine of the Egyptian deity Sekhmet was found together with a statuette of the son of Nefertum, between the pillars of the small Phoenician shrine in temple B at Kommos. The so-called "three-pillar shrine" is incontrovertible evidence of the presence of Phoenician merchants at Kommos, as well as in other Cretan harbours in the 8th and 7th centuries BC. Figurines of Sekhmet have been found elsewhere on the island, such as at Amnisos and Eleutherna. Herakleion Archaeological Museum.

636. Crete. Excavations at Kommos, at the west edge of the Mesara Plain and overlooking the Libyan Sea, have revealed the remains of an important sanctuary with three phases. The earliest, temple A, was built in the 11th c. BC upon the ruins of a Minoan settlement. Temple B with its "three-pillar shrine" was built exactly on top of temple A and is dated by the votive offerings found there to the period 800-600 BC. The photograph shows the remains of temple C, which was built on the same site around 375/350 BC. It is a single space with benches along the walls, two column bases either side of the central hearth and a pedestal for the cult statue. In the view of the excavators, the architectural evidence and the moveable finds from all three temples, among them many votive bull figurines, suggest that ritual meals were held on the temple site, perhaps in honour of Zeus, Poseidon and Athena.

Most evidence of craft is limited to household production (so-called cottage industries.) for the local subsistence economy. The inhabitants were farmers and herders living on a mixed diet of grain, legumes and meat—mostly sheep and goat. While scholars observe a sharp decline in the amount of imported raw materials and luxury goods in the this period, it highly unlikely that the island was ever completely cut off from rest of the Eastern Mediterranean. Local élites were always interested in exotic luxury items, and the appearance of iron, as knives with bronze rivets imported from Cyprus during the twelfth and eleventh centuries BC, suggests its status primarily as a prestige item.

The social position of an individual or a group and his or its access to prestige objects can also be deduced from the mortuary customs, which vary across Crete between 1200 and 1000 BC. In eastern Crete burials were mainly in small tholos tombs, as at Karphi, Vrontas, Chalasmenos and Myrsini, whereas in the North Cemetery at Knossos chamber tombs were used, mostly for inhumations and more rarely for cremations. Many tombs were reused by successive generations of one family and contained simple offerings. However, richer burials exist, such as a small cluster of tombs at Knossos (particularly tomb 200/201), tombs A and B at Myrsini-Mouliana (12th century BC), which contained weapons and jewellery – including a gold face mask – and the tomb at Pantanassa in the Amari Valley, in which there was a bronze krater of the late eleventh century BC (fig. 634).

From the beginning of the eleventh century BC, Crete witnesses a long process of consolidation during which some settlements are abandoned in favour of a smaller number of sites which expand and emerge as small towns and eventually small city-states (*poleis*). Excavations at Kastro, Kavousi provide a rare glimpse of this settlement growth from 1050-650 BC (fig. 48). During the tenth-ninth centuries the settlement was reorganized, with the construction of terraces

637, 638. Crete, Prinias. In the eastern foothills of Mount Psiloreitis, upon a peculiar height known as the "Patela tou Prinia", lie the ruins of an ancient city which historians identify as Rhizenia from the ancient sources. The hill was inhabited from prehistoric into Hellenistic times. The site is known primarily from the sculpted decoration of temple A, one of the two Archaic temples uncovered by the Italian archaeologist L. Pernier in 1906-1908. The lintel of the temple entrance was decorated on the underside with two female figures in relief, while its front held a relief frieze. The most striking feature of the lintel, however, is the decoration of the upper part, with two seated female deities (Herakleion Archaeological Museum). The architectural evidence and the Daedalic style of the sculptures date temple A towards the end of the 7th c. BC.

around the hill supporting narrow rectangular houses. Occupation of the site in eighth and early seventh centuries involved the construction of more impressive terraces supporting long narrow houses of two to five room houses with clearly defined storerooms, kitchens, and reception/dining areas with hearths between columns. The inhabitants were involved in subsistence agriculture and herding, and consumed a healthy diet of grains, legumes and meat, including sheep/goat, pig and a surprising number of cattle. The abandonment of the Kastro, probably in favour of the neighboring site of Azoria in the mid-seventh century, completed the process of consolidation in this region, with Azoria reaching the level of small Cretan polity in the seventh/sixth centuries BC (figs 647-648.)

Recent studies of Cretan Iron Age society stress its unique development, which differs in many ways from that of the rest of Greece. Cretan cities such as Knossos, Eleutherna, Kommos had early and extensive contacts with cultures in the Eastern Mediterranean. They also appear to have served as gateway communities in the network providing crucial supplies for merchants plying east-west trade routes across the Mediterranean and trans-shipment points for trading ventures with inland Cretan cities like Aphrati, Prinias, Gortyn, and Axos (figs 637-638). Luxury goods were imported from centres on Cyprus, northern Syria, Lebanon and Egypt, while artists on Crete may also have been producing local imitations of these imports, sometimes with Cretan subjects (figs 57, 641, 642, 643, 644). Interpretation of the archaeological data is confused by the fact that some of the local craftsmen were of foreign origin, immigrants to Crete from the Near East and Cyprus. What was exchanged for these imports is not clear; however, iron, a metal available on Crete, was in great demand by the powerful Assyrian Empire, which took control of the Levant, Cyprus and southern Anatolia during the course of the ninth and eighth centuries BC. In this period Phoenician and Greek traders were literally circumnavigat-

639. Crete. Eleutherna is the provenance of the upper part of a limestone statue of a seated female figure displaying all the traits of the so-called Daedalic sculptural style – thus named after the mythical sculptor Daidalos –, such as the flat head, triangular face and wig-like hair. The recent discovery in the Orthi Petra cemetery of the lower part of a female statue in the type of the "Dame d' Auxerre" (Musée du Louvre), as well as of other fragments of Daedalic sculptures, reinforces the hypothesis of the existence of a local sculpture workshop using limestone from the Eleutherna quarry. Mid-7th c. BC. Herakleion Archaeological Museum.

640. Crete. Three bronze statues perhaps representing the Apollonian trinity (Apollo, Artemis, Leto) were found at Dreros in 1935, on a stone altar in the southeast corner of the one-room building that archaeologists have interpreted as a temple of Apollo. Inside the stone altar were numerous horns of small goats, which the excavator called the "Keraton". The statuettes are made of very fine sheets of bronze that were joined together by tiny bronze nails. The male figure is just over 75 cm. high, while the female figures are shorter. The temple is dated on the basis of the excavation data to the 7th c. BC. Herakleion Archaeological Museum.

ing the Mediterranean in search of iron and other essential materials, which were then used to produce weapons and luxury items for the élites and empires of the Eastern Mediterranean.

That such Near Eastern traders and craftsmen reached Cretan cities and established residence on the island can no longer be doubted. The best evidence is the unique Phoenician altar built inside Temple B, which probably served both foreign crews and resident craftsmen at the harbour town of Kommos in the eighth century BC (figs 635-636). The discovery of Phoenician grave markers (*cippi*) at Eleutherna and Knossos, as well as the host of imported grave goods leave little doubt that immigrant craftsmen and traders were living in these Greek communities alongside the Cretans.

In contrast to central and eastern Crete, the western part of the island seems, by virtue also of its geographical location, to have turned towards the Peloponnese and mainland Greece. Study of the eighth-century BC pottery from the area of Chania, has demonstrated that Kydonia's contacts with the Argolid and Attica were close, while at the same time there was communication with the Dodecanese. By the early seventh century BC products of Corinthian workshops were reaching Kydonia in abundance. Also from Kydonia is part of a poros frieze with a representation of a shrine housing a cult effigy (*xoanon*) of a deity being attacked by horsemen and protected by archers. The subject is also represented on a bronze belt from Fortetsa and may be linked with the worship of Hera, the principal Argeian goddess, referring indirectly to the contacts between Kydonia and Argos.

Cretans' relations with the Eastern Mediterranean and the possible presence of foreigners on the island seems to have fostered the adoption of oriental decorative motifs in Cretan art from as early as the ninth century BC, almost one century before the same phenomenon is observed elsewhere in Greece. Among the Cretan works with "orientalizing" influences are the famous bronze "shields"-lids, bronze bowls, Daedalic sculptures and the large number of relief works in metal, clay and ivory. These finds come from graves at Eleutherna, Aphrati and Knossos, as well as from the large sanctuaries of Zeus at Palaikastro and in the Ida and Dikte caves, and the sanctuaries of Aphrodite at Axos and Praisos (figs 639-644).

The shrines discovered at the central Cretan cities of Prinias and Gortyn contain impressive stone temples with impressive sculptural ornament (figs 637-638), while excavation of a shrine a Dreros recovered three statues of hammered bronze sheet – perhaps representing Apollo, Leto, and Artemis (fig. 640). For some, Crete is also the likely setting for the most important Orientalizing invention – the creation of the Greek alphabet after a Phoenician model. Among the oldest examples on Crete are the stelai from Dreros (*c.* 650 B.C.) on which are written the city's laws. In Antiquity Crete was renowned for its laws and the erection of stone stelai inscribed with statutes is a particularly Cretan phenomenon.

One of the most intriguing and intangible elements of these early Cretan states is the role that various ethnic or cultural identities played on the island. That Crete hosted a mixed population is known from the ancient sources. A group known as the Eteocretans lived in east Crete and claimed to be the descendants of the Bronze Age Cretans (the Minoans). The ancient histori-

HISTORICAL TIMES | 415

an Strabo mentions Praisos as the most important Eteocretan city and inscriptions carved in Eteocretan script, which has not been deciphered, were found there. The Dorians, who were supposed to have captured the island and subjugated the Minoans, settled in most other parts of the island. According to ancient literary sources, the Spartans contributed to the colonization of Dorian Lyttos near the modern village of Kastelli in Central Crete. Evidence for the existence of mixed populations on the island may also be reflected in the wide variety of burial practices at the cemeteries of Eleutherna, Knossos, Prinias, Aphrati and in the district of Kisamos; however, attempts to associate burial forms with specific cultural or ethnic groups remain controversial.

For example, in the Orthi Petra cemetery at Eleutherna three different burial practices have been observed: cremations (usually of adult males), *enchytrismoi* (usually of infants or the very old) and simple inhumations. The discovery of grave stelai of the *cippus* type in the same cemetery suggests that there were also foreigners buried there, most probably Phoenicians (fig. 645).

Later sources suggest that conservative aristocratic families with large landholdings formed the ruling élite of Iron Age Cretan cities. It is worth noting that Crete did not participate in well-known developments elsewhere in Greece from 750-600 BC, particularly the colonization of the Mediterranean and the intra-state political upheavals that produced tyrannies. Much more puzzling, though perhaps related, is the sharp decline observed in Cretan material culture in the late seventh century BC. Suggested causes include climatic change, invasion or civil war, which may have severely disrupted the island's agricultural economy. Another explanation is the collapse of the Assyrian Empire in the late seventh century and the associated shocks to the economy of the Eastern Mediterranean during the rise of new Babylonian State. This turmoil brought an end to traditional east-west trade, running along both north and south coasts of Crete. Its collapse may have played no small role in Crete's sudden decline; however, these questions can only be answered by more systematic excavations at sites across the island.

641. Crete. Elegant clay vase (lebes) from tomb Λ at Arkades (Aphrati), dated to the 7th c. BC. Although this is a product of a Cretan workshop, both its shape and its decoration with griffin protomes may imitate bronze prototypes of Near Eastern provenance. Herakleion Archaeological Museum.

642. Crete. Cut-out gold strip found together with similar ones inside a funerary urn in grave A1K1 in the Orthi Petra cemetery of Eleutherna. Represented in the central metope is a female figure holding two animals upside down, in the type of the *Potnia Theron*, while in the two lateral panels a kind of baetyl (sacred stone) crowned by a sideways crescent is represented. Cut-out strips usually decorated the surface of wooden or bone objects Associated finds date the strip to the 7th c. BC. Rethymnon Archaeological Museum.

643. Crete. Bronze "shield"-lid from grave A1K1 in the Orthi Petra cemetery of Eleutherna. It was used as the lid of a clay funerary pithamphora of the late 9th c. BC; however, the associated finds are dated to the second half of the 8th c. BC. At the centre of the "shield"-lid is a high-relief feline head, above which, in low relief, are two antithetical sphinxes flanking a female figure. A relief frieze runs around the shield with felines attacking bovines. Similar shields with lion protomes have been found in the Idaean Cave, at Phaistos, Palaikastro and Arkades. They are considered to be products of Cretan workshops, although perhaps inspired by oriental models. According to the excavator of the necropolis of Eleutherna, the small diameter of the "shield" (40 cm.) precludes its use as a defensive weapon and it is therefore more likely that it served as the lid of a bronze vessel. Rethymnon Archaeological Museum.

644. Crete. The famous "drum" of Zeus, 55 cm. in diameter and 1 mm. thick, was found in the Idaean Cave in 1885, together with bronze shields, bowls and ivory objects, in a thick layer of ash and bones. The provenance of this piece and of the bronze shields has puzzled archaeologists. Whereas all agree that despite their pronounced "orientalizing" character the shields and the "drum" were made in Crete, views differ as to the ethnicity of the craftsmen. Some scholars maintain that the shields were made by foreign craftsmen who settled in Crete, while others argue that only Cretan craftsmen could have made objects decorated with subjects so closely linked to the island's mythology (e.g., the myth of the Curetes clashing their cymbals loudly outside the Idaean Cave so that Cronus would not hear the crying of the infant Zeus hidden inside it). Herakleion Archaeological Museum.

HISTORICAL TIMES | 417

645. Crete. On the west slope of the hill of ancient Eleutherna, at Orthi Petra, an extensive necropolis has been excavated. Its confirmed use spans the early 9th to the first third of the 6th c. BC, with indications that burials took place on the site throughout the 6th c. BC. The photograph shows the foundations of three tomb monuments, 4A, 3K and 4K, of the 7th c. BC. These were monuments that stood above ground, perhaps cenotaphs or heroa. The superstructure of 4A was decorated with a sculpted composition of stone shield-bearing warriors. According to the excavator, these warriors should be associated with the mythological Curetes, who beat their shields in order to cover the crying of Zeus, who was concealed inside a cave on Mount Psiloreitis.

They did this to prevent him from being swallowed by his father Cronus.

The "marginalization" of Crete in the 6th and 5th centuries BC

The sixth and the fifth century BC are two problematical periods in the history of ancient Crete. The decline of Knossos in the sixth century BC, which is confirmed by the lack of architectural remains, cemeteries and pottery assemblages, has led some historians to suggest that all of Crete faced a demographic, economic and cultural desolation in this period. Worship in the sanctuary on the acropolis of Gortyn and in the sanctuary of Zeus at Amnisos dwindled after the end of the seventh century BC, the votive offerings in the Psychro and Ida caves were minimal in the sixth century BC, and the rural sanctuaries at Kato Symi and Kommos waned.

The causes of the vague picture that Crete presents in these two centuries should be sought first and foremost in archaeological research itself, which has focused for almost a century on the excavation and study of the Minoan Civilization. Only in recent decades have researchers turned their attention to the historical periods on Crete, with the resultant revision of several of the earlier views. It emerges from recent research that the decline of Knossos and the desertion of Prinias are not a general phenomenon in the island's history in the sixth century BC.

In western Crete, the University of Crete excavations at Eleutherna have brought to light the remains of an Archaic necropolis (Orthi Petra) (fig. 645). The pottery accompanying the burials of the sixth century BC, which are simple in comparison with those of the eighth and seventh centuries BC, yields a plethora of information on the mercantile relations between Eleutherna and the rest of Greece at this time. A wide variety of imported pottery – Corinthian, Laconian and Attic – was found in the graves, in contrast to the absence of imported pottery at Knossos in the same period. Particularly interesting is the large quantity of Laconian pottery at Eleutherna, which shows that western Crete, because of its geographical location, was an active participant in the transit trade of the Peloponnese with the grain-growing regions of North Africa and particularly Cyrenaica. It is assumed that Cretans traded timber, since there is special mention of Cretan wood in the building inscriptions found on the Acropolis of Athens and at Epidauros. The fact that goods traded between the Peloponnese and North Africa were handled by Samian merchants explains the settling of these last at Kydonia around 525 BC. A few years later, however, the Samians were expelled by the Kydonians in collaboration with the Aeginetans, with whom their ties went back a long way. Herodotus accredits the Samians with founding the sanctuaries of Kydonia and the Diktynnaios sanctuary on Cape Spatha, which was one of the most important ancient Cretan sanctuaries.

At Gortyn, the epigraphic testimonies and pottery assemblages confirm the cultural continuity in the sixth and fifth centuries BC. The inscriptions preserve excerpts of legislative codes – the best known being the Gortyn Law Code –, the majority regulating issues of family and inheritance law, while some others refer to interstate treaties.

Knowledge of the history of the most important cities of eastern Crete (Lyttos, Lato, Praisos and Itanos) in the Archaic and Classical periods is based mainly on textual sources, since most of these cities have not been excavated systematically (Lyttos) or had been excavated in the early twentieth century with old methods (Praisos, Lato). At Lyttos the discovery of fragments of law codes, which date to the second half of the sixth century BC, confirms the existence of an Archaic *polis* for which there is no other information.

Excavations at Lato have brought to light traces of a settlement of the seventh century BC, but which was abandoned in the Archaic period. The large and mighty city that spread over the slopes of two hills developed much later, in the early fourth century BC. Surface surveys by the American School of Classical Studies, in the areas of Vrokastro and Gournia, have yielded scant indications of some significant activity in the sixth century BC. The picture of the economically and demographically weakened cities in eastern Crete during the sixth century BC has been challenged by the new excavation at Azoria, Kavousi, where a thriving Archaic settlement is being uncovered, with remains of houses and of a big public building with spaces for storage and preparation of foodstuffs, which the excavators have identified as an "*andreion*" (figs 647, 648).

Praisos, one of the most important cities of the Hellenistic period, built upon two acropolises – like Lato –, appears to have had a strong presence in the sixth century BC, judging by some fortification walls on the summit of the first acropolis, the considerable number of figurines found on the "Altar Hill" and in some smaller sanctuaries on the periphery of Praisos, as well as two fragments of Eteocretan inscriptions (figs 646, 649).

Last, the ongoing Greek-French excavations at Itanos appear to confirm the absence of archaeological finds for the greater part of the sixth century BC, with the exception of a small sanctuary of Demeter, founded in the last quarter of the century.

Archaeological investigations over the past few decades have contributed substantially to the better understanding of Cretan history in the sixth century BC. The island's cultural development did not come to a halt in 600 BC, when the Cretans' contacts with Eastern Mediterranean lands ceased. On the contrary, the Cretans – particularly those in the west of the island – apparently turned their eye on the Peloponnese. Future research at Azoria and Praisos is expected to shed more light on the position of eastern Crete in the Mediterranean in the sixth century BC.

By the end of the sixth century BC Knossos had recovered economically. Although no architectural remains of the Classical city have yet been found, there is other archaeological evidence of the upturn in its fortunes, such as the founding of the sanctuary of Glaukos and the reactivation of cult in the sanctuary of Demeter, with the construction of a small temple in the late fifth century BC. A treaty of the mid-fifth century BC, between Knossos and neighbouring Tylissos, which refers to matters of circulating goods, piracy, common sacrifices and property rights, creates the impression of an economically flourishing Knossos. At nearby Amnisos, in the sanctuary of Zeus, the big stone bird-shaped votive offerings of the late sixth century BC bear witness to Cretans' involvement with monumental sculpture.

646. Crete. Excavations on the "Altar Hill" one of the three acropolises on which Praisos was built, recovered a sacred precinct (*temenos*) which enclosed an altar for sacrifices and a host of votive offerings. The latter included large terracotta figurines, such as this male figure (pres. h. 66 cm.), parts of several bronze helmets, breastplates, shields and greaves, as well as pottery dating from the 7th to the 5th c. BC. The hill was dedicated to the worship of a deity, whose identity is unknown. Herakleion Archaeological Museum.

647. Crete. Recent American excavations at Azoria Kavousi have brought to light an extensive urban settlement of the Archaic period (c. 625-480 BC), which developed at the north end of the Isthmus of Hierapetra, at a nodal point controlling movements between the north and south coasts of the island. The discovery of a spacious dining hall with large areas for preparation and storage of food reinforces the urban character of the settlement and provides a rare illustration of the renowned Cretan messes where communal meals were consumed.

648. Crete. Archaic pottery from Azoria. Found mainly in a building on the Southwest Terrace it includes a selection of vases for storage (pithoi and amphorae), transport (pointed-base amphorae), food preparation (basins) and tableware (hydrias, amphorae, bowls and cups). Archaeobotanical analysis has shown that in several of the pithoi grapes and olives were stored.

The Cretans did not respond to the panhellenic call in 480 BC at the Isthmus of Corinth, to confront the Persians, perhaps because they did not feel seriously threatened by them. Their refusal should not be regarded as indicative of their introversion, since other Greek cities, such as Argos, took no part in the panhellenic alliance against the foe. Crete did not join the Athenian League either, and maintained its neutrality in the conflict between Athens and Sparta. Although the Cretan cities desisted from the major political alliances characteristic of Hellas in the fifth century BC, the historical sources record that the island maintained ties not only with Argos but also with Athens, Sparta, Rhodes and Cyprus.

Attic black-glaze and red-figure pottery of the early decades of the fifth century BC has been found in abundance at many sites in Crete, signifying that the cities were actively involved in transit trade in the Aegean. At Kydonia, Attic black-figure lekythoi are common grave goods in the fifth century BC. The same phenomenon is observed in burials at ancient Phalasarna in western Crete, while in graves at Eleutherna, Attic vases had been replaced by Laconian ones by the last quarter of the sixth century BC.

The comparative study of fifth-century BC pottery from Phalasarna, Kydonia, Eleutherna, Knossos and Gortyn shows that there was a drop in the import of Attic vases from shortly before 460 BC until the end of the century. This fact should not be interpreted as result of a direct rift between the Cretan cities and Athens, since other cities, such as Aegina, were involved in the trade of Attic pottery. Nonetheless, it should be mentioned that with Athenian support Kydonia was sacked by its neighbours from Polichne in 429 BC. The Athenians must have been more than eager to intervene, if the hypothesis is correct that Aeginetans expelled by them in

431 BC had taken refuge in Kydonia. The competition between Athens and Aegina, which until then was one of the most important dealers in Athenian pottery as well as in Peloponnesian products, led to the latter's decline. Consequence of Aegina's withdrawal from transit trade in the Aegean was the shrinking of Peloponnesian trade with Cyrenaica and North Africa. It appears from the historical sources that Athens in its turn aimed, through a series of strategic moves, to strike an economic blow to Sparta in the second half of the fifth century BC, during its embroilment in the Peloponnesian War. Perhaps the diminishing of communication with Crete was collateral damage of the hostilities between Athens and Sparta.

Despite the information provided by the necropolises, knowledge of the architectural remains and settlements in Crete in the fifth century BC continues to be limited. At Gortyn, the existence of the Classical city is confirmed by the Law Code, which is dated to the second half of the fifth century BC (fig. 650). However, what is at once striking and puzzling is that whereas the material culture of Crete in Archaic and Classical times is poor, it is the only region of ancient Greece in which so many inscriptions of legislative content survive. Almost all the known Archaic and Classical cities of Crete can boast some remnants of inscriptions of laws, in contrast to other archaeological finds. Was Crete in the sixth and fifth centuries BC an economically static or retarded region, or was it simply different? The law code of Gortyn, recorded on the stone walls of perhaps the largest building constructed in the city in the fifth century BC (which no longer survives), is a monument on a par with the large marble temples in mainland and island Greece in the Classical period.

649. Crete. Eteocretan inscription from Praisos. Among the many votive offerings found on the "Altar Hill", were fragments of two inscriptions in the Eteocretan language. Praisos was known in antiquity as capital of the Eteocretans (the "true Cretans"), a prehellenic tribe that withstood the Dorian conquerors in eastern Crete and in the area of Kydonia (mod. Chania) in the west. The inscriptions, incised with Ionian lettering, have not been deciphered.

650. Crete. The Great Inscription (Dodekadeltos) of Gortyn. Incised originally on the inside wall of a large circular public building of the early 5th c. BC the inscription is organized in twelve columns. The text, written in the Dorian dialect, is a legal tract covering issues of citizen status (e.g., slavery), and of inheritance and property rights of divorced or widowed women and adopted children. The circular building was dismantled in the Late Hellenistic period and the inscribed blocks were reused in the construction of the Roman Odeum of Gortyn, which was discovered in 1884 by the Italian archaeologist F. Halbherr.

651. Crete. The city of Aptera, built on a highland site, controlled the Bay of Souda with its two harbours, Minoa and Kisamos. It was enclosed by mighty fortification walls, 4 km. in length. Visible *intra muros* are the theatre and at least two Hellenistic sanctuaries, one dedicated to the goddess Demeter. The impressive vaulted-roof cisterns, the bathhouse and the prytaneion date to the Roman era, when Aptera enjoyed its greatest prosperity.

Recovery (4th-1st century BC)

By the end of the fifth century BC Crete appeared more dynamically in the Mediterranean region. The founding of new cities on the south coast (Lisos, Lasaia, Hierapytna and Ampelos) has been linked with the upturn in trading transactions between the Cretan cities and North Africa. The economic recovery of Crete should be seen in the framework of the historic changes taking place in the Aegean in the late fifth century BC, the most important being the break up of the Athenian League and the gradual retreat of Athens from transit trade in the Mediterranean.

There are signs of rapid development in all the island's cities in the early fourth century BC. Outstanding among the excavated sites in eastern Crete is the city of Lato, with important archaeological remains. Spread over two hills, with a superb view over the Gulf of Merabello, Lato preserves remnants of dozens of houses and shops, temples and sanctuaries, stoas, a theatre, bouleuterion and prytaneion (figs 652, 653). According to the ancient sources, the institution of the *syssition* (communal meals) was applied in Crete, with the city's archons, the "*kosmoi*", dining in the prytaneion and the other males in the andreion.

The prytaneion, which survives in very good condition, is divided into two central spaces: the east is occupied by a peristyle court with light-well, while the west includes the hestiatorion. Around the inside of the hestiatorion runs a wide bench, on which stood the eight couches of the "*kosmoi*" or archons of Lato. South of the prytaneion, between the two acropolises, was the site of the agora, with a long stoa and a monumental staircase, which functioned as a bouleuterion (fig. 653). The large temple, built in the second half of the fourth century BC upon a strong retaining wall, was bipartite, with prodomos and a cella in which the base of the cult statue is preserved. In Crete, temples continued to be built without the peristasis, a feature of the temples in mainland and island Greece.

At Lato, in the early twentieth century, French archaeologists revealed the ruins of hundreds of houses built on terraces on the two hills. In contrast to residences on the Greek Mainland, which were built around a central court (*pastas*), the houses in Hellenistic Crete were of linear plan, which the development of settlements on terraces dictated. Characteristic feature of most Hellenistic houses in Crete is the rectangular built hearth in the central room.

Most of the Hellenistic cities of Crete were fortified. In western Crete: Kydonia, Hyrtakina, Phalasarna, Aptera, Polyrrhenia, Elyros, Sybritos, Anopolis and Eleutherna; in central Crete: Gortyn and Phaistos; in eastern Crete: Lato, Itanos, Trypitos, Mochlos and Ampelos (fig. 651). Even though only a few of these fortifications can be securely dated (Gortyn, Phalasarna, Aptera, Trypitos), archaeologists place the construction of the majority in the Hellenistic period and associate them with the scourge of Cretan pirates in the Mediterranean as well as the civil wars between Cretan cities.

Although prehistoric cults, such as worship of the goddess Diktynna on Cape Spatha, continued on Crete until Roman times, religious beliefs were not immune to external influences. Worship of Asklepios must have been introduced in the closing years of the Classical period, at the same time as it spread in the rest of Greece. In 1957 a large number of votive offerings, in-

652. Crete. Lato, the most powerful city in the Gulf of Merabello, was built on two hills and the saddle between them. It played an important political role in the southeast Mediterranean in the 4th and 3rd centuries BC, as surmised from the treaties it signed with Miletos and Gortyn. The excavations of the French Archaeological School have revealed several public buildings of the ancient city-state, as well as numerous houses that provide unique information about architecture and everyday life in Hellenistic Crete. The photograph shows the entrance to the house on terrace IV.

653. Crete. Lato is a rare example of a Hellenistic city in Crete, where a large part of the agora has been uncovered. A monumental staircase leads to the prytaneion and was probably used as an assembly area for citizens – a type of bouleuterion. Most Cretan cities were controlled by an aristocracy. These aristocratic clans chose the archons ("*kosmoi*") who oversaw political and military affairs. The aristocratic nature of Cretan society is also apparent in its institutions such as messes (*syssitia*), associations (*hetaireies*) and herds (*ageles*), where membership depended on social status.

HISTORICAL TIMES | 423

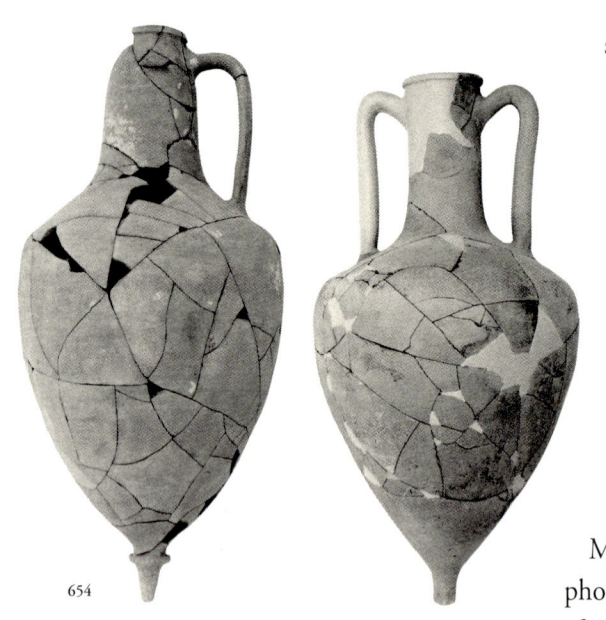

scriptions and statues, was found in the sanctuary of Asklepios at Lisos. Renowned too in Antiquity was the Asklepieion at Lebena, which flourished in particular during the Roman period. Characteristic on Crete was the joint worship of Hermes and Aphrodite, as ascertained from the sanctuaries at Lenika (near Olous), Pyrgos Myrtos and Symi Vianno. An impressive discovery is the small rural sanctuary of Poseidon in the village of Tsiskiana, on the southwest coast of Crete, where numerous terracotta figurines of bovines were brought to light (figs 656, 657).

By the late fourth century BC, Crete was in a crucial position in the new ecumenical reality created by the conquests of Alexander the Great. Recent excavations at the coastal sites of Mochlos, Trypitos, Itanos and Xirokampos Ziros (anc. Ampelos) have yielded a host of imported wine amphorae of Rhodian, Knidian and Koan provenance, which bear witness to the new strategic situation of eastern Crete in the transit trade of the Eastern Mediterranean, final destination of which was Egypt (fig. 654). The little isle of Leuke (Kouphonisi), southeast of Crete, was the apple of discord first between Praisos and Itanos, and later, after the destruction of Praisos, between Hierapytna (Hierapetra) and Itanos, precisely because of its strategic position in trade with Egypt. In order to promote their mercantile interests, the Egyptian Ptolemies installed a garrison at Itanos and on Leuke. The honours that the cities of Eleutherna and Phalasarna accorded to the Ptolemy Euergetes are a significant indication of the amicable relations between the Cretan cities and the Egyptian kings. According to Strabo, the Ptolemy Philopator met the expenses of repairing the fortification wall of Gortyn.

654. Crete. Excavations in the Hellenistic city at Trypitos have brought to light a large number of transport amphorae from important wine-producing centres such as Rhodes (right), Kos and Knidos (left), confirming the city's involvement in Eastern Mediterranean trade. Through petrographic analyses, locally produced amphorae have been identified, indicating the Cretans' interest in wine production and the possible export of Cretan wine from the 3rd c. BC.

655. Crete. The Hellenistic coastal city at Trypitos was founded in the mid-3rd c. BC, in a period when Cretans were abandoning the hinterland for settlements close to the sea, exploiting the new status quo in the Eastern Mediterranean, which followed the conquests of Alexander the Great. The city was built on the flat top of a peninsula, east of Siteia and was organized in clusters of houses divided by paved streets. The houses are small in comparison to those at Olynthos in the Chalkidike, and have no internal courtyards. The sudden abandonment of the city in the 2nd c. BC is clear from the extensive destruction horizon in which many vases and other everyday objects were found.

Crete was for Egypt one of the principal pools for recruiting mercenaries, many of whom settled there and rose to high offices in the Ptolemaic kingdom. The adoption of funerary architecture inspired by Egypt, such as that of the rock-cut tombs at Chania and Polyrrhenia in western Crete, reflects the close relations between Crete and Egypt (fig. 660). The burial of the dead in *loculi* is an Egyptian habit, encountered in the cemeteries at Fayum, Sciatbi and elsewhere. In the Hadra cemetery, in the vicinity of Alexandria, large numbers of elegantly decorate hydrias from Crete were found, which had been used as cinerary urns of Cretan mercenary officers who had died in Egypt.

Despite the prosperity that Crete enjoyed during the Hellenistic period, its cities failed to organize any type of political-military federation, after the model of the Achaian and the Aetolian *Sympoliteia*. The most important reason for this weakness should be sought in the continual rivalries between the Cretan cities, which frequently led to warfare. The *Koinon* of Cretans that was formed in the third century BC functioned occasionally, only when Knossos and Gortyn put aside their differences. The wars between Cretan cities were merciless, as evidenced by the total destruction of Lyttos by Knossos in 220 BC. The razing to the ground of omnipotent Praisos by the emergent power of Hierapytna, in 145 BC, enhanced the latter as the most important city in eastern Crete in the second century BC. This can be seen from the expansionist wars Hierapytna declared and by a series of treaties of isopolity, which secured its peaceful expansion into the territory of many neighbouring cities, such as Priansos, Lato, Mala and Arkades. Hierapytna's dispute with Itanos over exploiting the islet of Leuke (Kouphonisi) and

656, 657. Crete. Excavations at Tsiskiana, Selinos in the prefecture of Chania, have uncovered an open-air rural shrine, with successive levels of terracotta bull figurines. Fragments of a marble male statue and a small votive inscription with the name of Poseidon were also found. The god was worshipped here in his pre-Olympian form, as deity of natural destructions who was appeased by bull sacrifices. The sanctuary was founded in the 4th c. BC and functioned continuously into the 2nd c. AD. The finds are exhibited in the Chania Archaeological Museum.

the sanctuary of Zeus Diktaios led the latter into war against Hierapytna in 122 BC, which ended with the intervention of Rome and its vindication of Itanos.

Over the last decade, a series of systematic surveys in eastern Crete, in conjunction with the excavation of hitherto unknown archaeological sites, has substantially improved our understanding of the political and economic history of Hellenistic Crete in this part of the island. The excavation of Hellenistic settlements at Mochlos and Trypitos has shown that the gap on the historical map, between Istron and Itanos, is illusive. The city of Trypitos, which was founded in the third century BC and abandoned violently in the mid-second century BC, was probably an outpost of Praisos, the most important city in eastern Crete in the third century BC. Although the city is unknown in the literary and epigraphic sources, it had a mighty fortification wall and a prytaneion, minted its own coinage and played an active role in Eastern Mediterranean transit trade, as borne out by the numerous transport amphorae from Rhodes, Kos and Knidos uncovered on the site (figs 654, 655).

A short distance to the west, at the east end of the Gulf of Merabello, excavations on the islet of Mochlos, which in Antiquity was joined to the mainland of Crete, have brought to light a flourishing settlement of the second century BC (fig. 659). Study of the excavation data has shown that the settlement at Mochlos was founded to serve the trading interests of Hierapytna, the most powerful city in eastern Crete in the second century BC.

The cases of Trypitos and Mochlos, where two coastal settlements where founded in the Hellenistic period as outports or emporeia of powerful cities, such as Praisos and Hierapytna, point to the great development of Cretan seafaring and trade in this period. In western Crete there were busy harbour towns such as Kisamos and Stavromenos on the north coast, Phalasarna at the west edge and Phoinix (Loutro) on the south shore.

658, 659. Crete. Recent Greek-American excavations on the islet of Mochlos have uncovered parts of a Hellenistic settlement spanning the late 2nd until the early decades of the 1st c. BC and probably associated with the expansion of Hierapytna as far as the north coast of Crete. Finds from the 2005 season indicate that Mochlos was not deserted completely after the Roman conquest of the island in 67 BC. Fig. 659 shows a room with a square hearth, in which a bronze coin of Krassos was found, with a crocodile on the obverse (fig. 658) and a ship's prow on the reverse. The coin should be dated to the period 41-37 BC, when Crete was ceded to Egypt as a wedding gift from Mark Anthony to Cleopatra.

660. Crete. Underground rock-cut family tombs are encountered more frequently in western Crete – at least seven such monuments are known from Chania and one from Polyrrhenia. They are a local peculiarity, since they have not been identified at other sites on the island. The rock-cut tomb at Chania had nine burial chambers (*loculi*), four on each long side and one on the narrow side. Above the entrance of each loculus the names of the dead are written in charcoal. On the basis of the patronymics, five families appear, while fifteen bodies were recovered in the chamber. These underground funerary monuments reflect the cultural influence of Egypt and confirm the close relations between Cretans and the kingdom of the Ptolemies in the Hellenistic times.

660

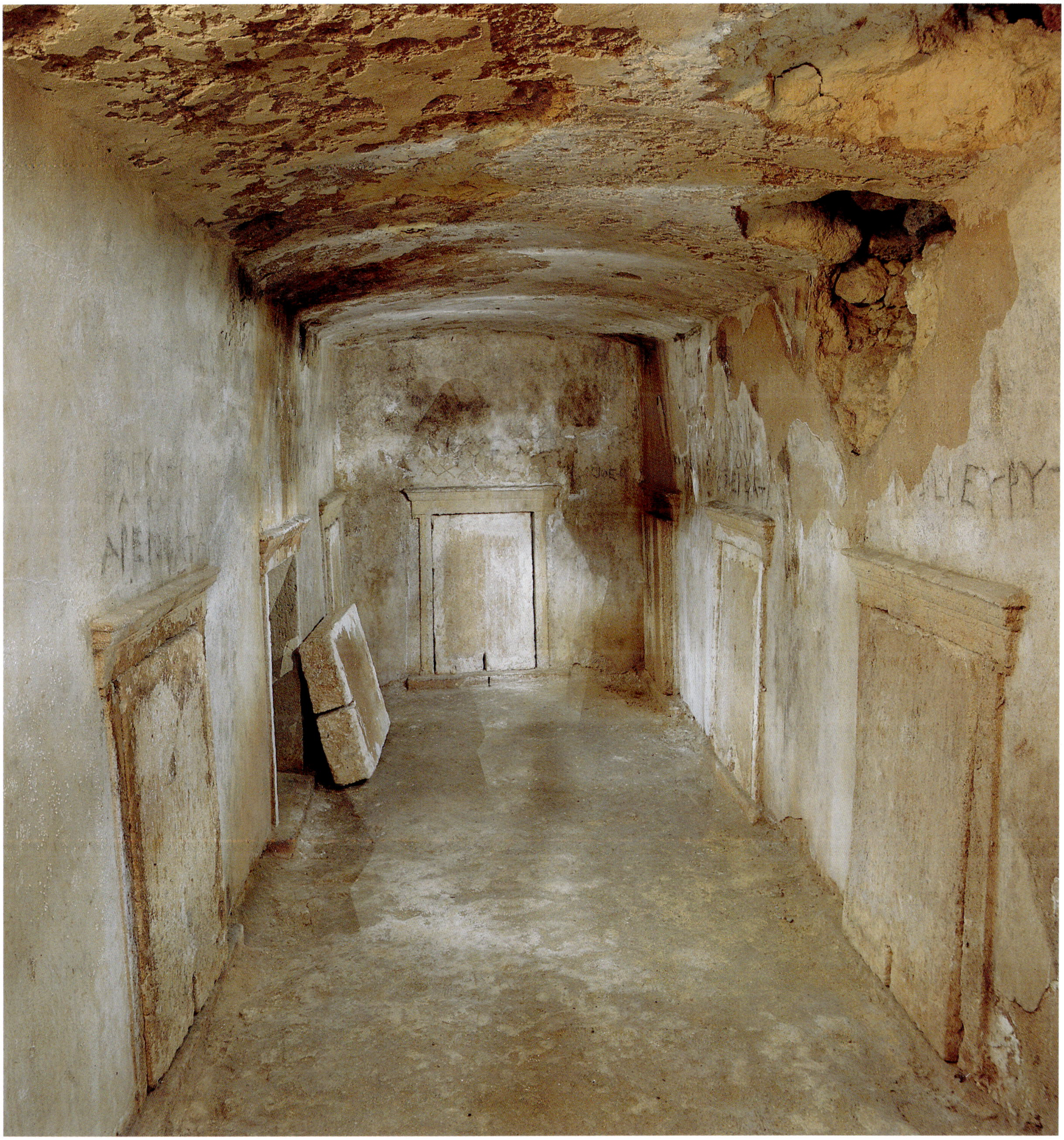

The Roman conquest (67 BC)

The end of Crete's long-lived independence, but not necessarily of its progress, came when the Roman General Metellus conquered the island in 67 BC, starting from the west. Kydonia had valiantly and successfully resisted the siege by Mark Anthony in 74 BC, but fell to Metellus in 69 BC. The activity of Cretan pirates in the Mediterranean and their alliance with the sworn enemy of Rome, King Mithridates of Pontus, were simply the pretexts for Rome to intervene in the domestic affairs of the Cretan cities from as early as the second century BC. The conquest of Crete was inevitable, on account of the island's strategic position in the *imperium* that the Romans were building. This is also the reason why Crete did not decline under its new masers but enjoyed a new heyday. In contrast to the civil strife of the previous centuries, the period of Roman rule was one of peace and tranquility. This is indicated by the fact that there was not one rebellion of Cretans against the Roman occupation. Crete was united administratively with Cyrenaica in a single province, with common governor and seat at Gortyn.

661. Crete, Aptera. The Romans were renowned for their ambitious public projects, such as roads, bridges, aqueducts and bathhouses. Today in the city of Aptera on either side of the Venetian Monastery are visible the remains of two vaulted-roof cisterns. The cistern to the west is of L-shaped plan, while that to the northeast has three-aisles. From the constructional details in the walling of the cisterns, it is suspected that both were built in Hellenistic times and renovated and enlarged during the Roman period.

662. Crete. The Roman odeum of Gortyn, in the construction of which were used the inscribed blocks with the Great Law Code. The odeum was built in the 1st c. BC for musical events. After the earthquake in AD 46, which destroyed most of the buildings in Gortyn, the Emperor Trajan rebuilt the odeum in more magnificent form.

663. Crete, Gortyn. Excavations of the Italian Archaeological School have brought to light major portions of the praetorium. The complex built between the 1st and 4th centuries AD included a large basilica, a bathhouse and a temple dedicated to the cult of Augustus.

664. Crete. In the city of Kisamos, at the west end of the island, many impressive buildings of Roman date have come to light including bathhouses, underground tombs, and urban villas with unique mosaics. Depicted on the mosaic from the so-called "House of Dionysos" is Dionysos' discovery of Ariadne on Naxos, part of a tale known from Homer, Hesiod, Plutarch and other ancient authors. On other parts of the mosaic are scenes from Menander's comedies. Chania Archaeological Museum.

665. Crete. The impressive Janiform head of Dionysos/Ariadne comes from the small Roman bathhouse on the east slope of the hill of ancient Eleutherna. It belongs to a herm found in the narthex of the nearby Early Christian basilica, where it had been re-used as a lintel. The original setting and function of the Eleutherna herms are unknown, but the excavator suspects that they were erected in a sacred precinct (*temenos*). The head is an elegant product of the Neo-Attic workshops active in Athens in the 2nd c. AD. Rethymnon Archaeological Museum.

Monumental projects were undertaken in Roman times. The vaulted-roofed cisterns, preserved to considerable height, and other impressive civic buildings at Aptera (fig. 661) led the numismatist I. Svoronos to dub the city "little Pompeii of Crete". Most impressive are the mosaic floors uncovered in rescue excavations at Kastelli Kisamos (fig. 664). Kisamos, outport of Polyrrhenia, enjoyed a sustained heyday from the first century BC into the fourth century AD, by which time the rival city of Phalasarna had been destroyed. At Eleutherna, luxurious residences and bathhouses of the Roman period have been excavated on the east slope of the city. Gortyn, as administrative seat of the new Roman province, boasts many civic buildings from this time, such as the headquarters of the praetorium, the theatres, amphitheatre and circus (figs 662, 663). The excavation of the temple of the Egyptian gods, in the early twentieth century, brought to light the impressive statues of Serapis and Isis. In Crete, in contrast to other Roman provinces, no temple dedicated to the cult of an emperor has been found, expect perhaps for a temple in the praetorium complex at Gortyn. A great deal of our knowledge of Roman Crete and its monuments is due to the Italian physician and traveller Onorio Belli, who visited the island in the sixteenth century, drawing many ruins that no longer survive. We cite indicatively the Roman theatres at Hierapytna (mod. Hierapetra), which are known only from Belli's drawings.

Crete continued to prosper throughout the imperial period, with sole exception the severe earthquakes in the second half of the fourth century AD, which resulted in the destruction of important edifices at Gortyn, Knossos and other major cities. Perhaps the most significant change observed is the gradual conversion of the island's inhabitants to Christianity, towards the end of the Roman period.

665

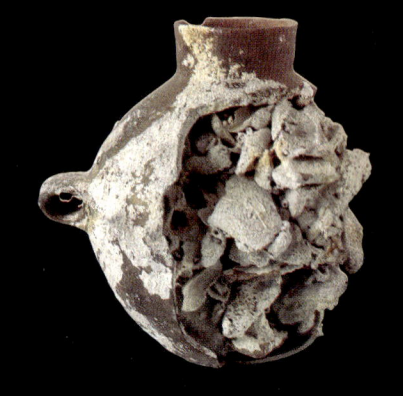

AEGEAN: AN UNDERWATER MUSEUM

Aegean: An underwater museum

Katerina P. Dellaporta

Wrecks

The ancient Egyptian chroniclers refer repeatedly to the inhabitants of the coasts or islands of the Eastern Mediterranean under the generic name "Sea Peoples". This is no fortuitous term, since for the Mediterranean populations living near the coasts the sea was the sole or principal source of supply as well as the only route of communication between them.

Within this natural environment, the inhabitants of the Aegean region had begun to venture onto the open sea already by the ninth millennium BC. Seafaring was a vital need for the small islands with barren soil and relatively arid climate, since it was the only means for the populations to maintain continuous relations and regular exchanges with other people. In the absence of nautical charts, the observation of the natural environment and of physical phenomena, experience and oral tradition enabled the early mariners to plough the entire Mediterranean basin from prehistoric times, trusting in the favourable winds. This is attested by the earliest cargo found so far in the Eastern Mediterranean, which lies off the islet of Dokos in the Argolic Gulf and dates to the Early Helladic II period (*circa* 2200 BC) (figs 667-669).

Underwater archaeology studies the historical evidence of man's relationship with the sea, the sunken archaeological remains associated with activities sometimes peaceful, such as maritime trade, and sometimes martial, such as sea battles and expeditions.

"…battle, trade, piracy, all three are inseparable", the Aegean Sea holds within it all the historical memories of Greece.

The uncovering of underwater antiquities lying on the bed of the Aegean fills in the gaps in the archaeological map and the historical mosaic of the Archipelago, both in the prehistoric era and in historical periods, adding or amplifying data in fields that are relatively poor from other sources, such as trade and shipbuilding.

Of the underwater archaeological sites in the Aegean, the most numerous and the most interesting are without doubt the wrecks. The answer to the question where are wrecks found is related directly to the conditions of navigating during Antiquity as well as to the economic history of ancient times. Wrecks are denser in areas of the seas that hold hazards for shipping, such as reefs, precipitous promontories or isolated desert islands, but mainly close to coastal cities renowned for their harbours and the development of trade (fig. 666).

Most wrecks are located by chance, thanks to indications of sponge-divers and fishermen, who literally plough the Aegean, and – particularly in the last 15 years – to systematic underwater archaeological investigations. Certainly their number has increased since diving with an independent breathing apparatus was developed, a technology that enabled man to remain on the seabed for a considerable length of time.

666. Bringing up to the surface, with the help of a balloon, one of the nine big stone anchors found on the site of a late 4th c. BC wreck at Antidragonera, Kythera. Exhibited in the Kythera Archaeological Museum.

667. Excavation on the site of concentration of the cargo of pottery of the Early Helladic wreck at Dokos (*c.* 2200 BC), using a suction machine.

668. Clay brazier (fire-box) of a rare type, from the Early Helladic wreck at Dokos. Apart from the large quantity of vases, the vessels for special use (fire-boxes, portable hearths and firedogs) formed a significant part of the cargo. Spetses Museum.

669. Typical amphora with heavy compacted contents, one of the many in the cargo of the Early Helladic wreck at Dokos. Spetses Museum.

Agent of research, rescue and scientific, on the Greek seabed is the Ephorate of Underwater Antiquities, a special regional service of the Ministry of Culture, which since 1976 has been protecting ancient wrecks and other submerged antiquities, through systematic recording and mapping of them. The Hellenic Institute of Marine Archaeology, a private research agency, is also active in the field of underwater archaeology.

The discovery of wrecks and the degree of their preservation are purely a matter of chance. Nonetheless, their geographical distribution is indicative for detecting sea routes. Characteristic example is the large number of wrecks that has come to light recently, as a result of systematic underwater investigations in the Dodecanese. The wrecks, which date from the second century BC to the second century AD are mainly of merchant vessels and are located on the sea lanes linking the islands of the East Aegean with the coasts of Cyprus and Cyrene, as well as with the shores of North Africa.

In this case too, however, the interpretation of the geographical distribution of the wrecks may be shaky, since it is determined by the chance factor of the find and the constraints of archaeological research. For example, the fact that most wrecks have been located along the coasts led in the past to the prevailing impression that ancient navigating was coastal rather than overseas. The development of technology in recent decades has permitted the exploration of the seabed that was previously inaccessible, widening our knowledge of ancient navigating and the sea routes, leading securely to the conclusion that in Antiquity seafarers were not restricted to coasting, but boldly ventured onto the open sea.

670. Excavation using a suction machine, on the site of the wreck off Cape Iria in the Argolid, at a point where two of the eight stirrup jars in the cargo were located.

671. The cargo of pottery of the wreck off Cape Iria in the Argolid (c. 1200 BC), was located on the seabed by Nikos N. Tsouchlos in 1962. It comprises mainly storage and transport vases, of Cypriot, Cretan and Argolic provenance. Pictured here are the vases after conservation and before display in the Spetses Museum.

672. The bathyscaph *Thetis* of the oceanographic vessel *Aigaio*, of the Greek Maritime Research Centre, on an exploratory dive.

673. Photomosaic of the Classical wreck of the 4th c. BC, off Peristera, Alonnisos.

674. Underwater excavation of the Classical wreck (first half of 4th c. BC) at Phagrou in the North Sporades, by the archaeologist D. Chaniotis. The cargo of ancient wrecks, mainly amphorae, is endangered by uncontrolled underwater activity. Most wrecks on the Greek seabed have been looted.

Proof of this is the wreck located recently off Castellorizo, at a depth of 3,000 metres, with a cargo of some 2,500 Rhodian and Koan amphorae of the second century BC. Moreover, the first underwater autopsy with a bathyscope, with a crew of one archaeologist, in the sea off Kythnos, located a wreck of Classical times (4th century BC) at a depth of 500 metres (fig. 672).

The event of a ship sinking in a specific place at a given moment creates a closed archaeological assemblage and offers the discipline data and study conditions that are rarely coincident in archaeological investigation on land. One such characteristic closed ensemble is the Kyrenia wreck, a merchant ship of the fourth century BC, which was transporting *inter alia* a cargo of 404 Rhodian, Samian and Koan amphorae, 29 millstones and about 10,000 almonds. This is the earliest Greek shipwreck of which both the vessel and its cargo are preserved, and was drawn up from the seabed to be conserved on the surface.

The type, the composition and the significance of the cargo of a wreck – provided these can be determined satisfactorily – enable us to define clearly the seasons and the routes, the nature, the organization and the volume of trading transactions, as well as to draw information on the route the ship followed, most probably also the ports of call it visited, even when the final destination remains unknown or hypothetical. Such is the case of the cargo of the wreck off Cape Iria in the Argolic Gulf, which confirms the trading relations of the Greek Mainland with Cyprus and Crete in the late thirteenth century BC (Late Helladic IIIB2 period), despite the fact that both the final destination of the ship and the harbour from which it set sail remain unknown (figs 670, 671).

At Uluburun on the Turkish coast of the Aegean (Kas), another wreck has been located and explored completely. Dated to the late fourteenth century BC, this is one of the most important wrecks of prehistoric times. The identification of the provenance of its cargo from various geographical regions of the Eastern Mediterranean revealed the multifaceted network of mercantile transactions during the Bronze Age, pointing out the route the ship must have taken before it sunk off the coast of the East Aegean.

The earliest Classical wreck known in Greece has been found off the islet of Phagrou in the Sporades. Its cargo consists of amphorae of Mende, a city in the Chalkidike, finer black-glaze pottery and other objects, and dates to the late fifth century BC (fig. 674).

One of the largest wrecks identified in the Aegean is that off Peristera on Alonissos, which dates from the fourth century BC and is estimated to have been carrying a cargo of 3,000 amphorae of Peparethos (Skopelos) and Mende types (fig. 673).

The most characteristic object, emblematic of underwater archaeology, is without doubt the amphora, the typical vessel for transporting and trading liquid and solid products. The easily recognizable shape of amphorae is virtually identifiable with our image of shipwrecks, since these vases accounted for the greater part – if not all – the cargo. The image of an ancient ship loaded with amphorae, on the seabed, corresponds to a fusiform arrangement of vases stuck to each other (fig. 673). This classic shape is due to the fact that amphorae remain in the same position as they had in the hold of the ship, after the wood has perished due to the action of marine micro-organisms.

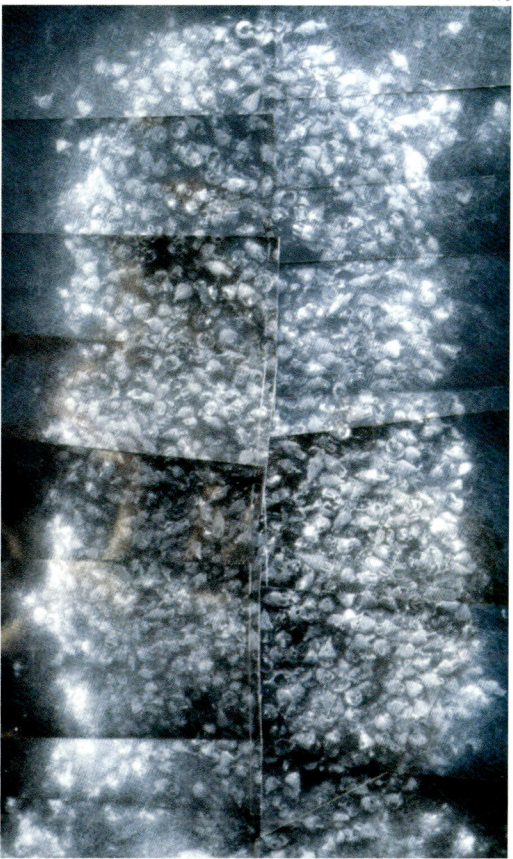

675. Leg of a bronze statue of a horseman, of the Hellenistic period (3rd c. BC), from the seabed of the Northeast Aegean area. Displayed in the exhibition "On a swift ship… past sandy shores", in the Makrygianni Bastion at Niokastro, Pylos.

676. The Ephebe of Kythnos. Bronze statue of the Late Hellenistic period (late 3rd c. BC). Found and handed in to the authorities by fishermen, in the sea off Kythnos in 2004. Although headless, the condition of the work is excellent. Kept in the conservation laboratories of the Ephorate of Underwater Antiquities.

675

Although ostensibly of little importance, the amphora (stirrup jar in the Late Bronze Age, with pointed base in Classical and Roman times) embodies all the codified information relating to seafaring and sea trade, from the prehistoric era into the Late Byzantine period, for it was used continuously for carrying commodities and as a vase had a life span of as much as two hundred years. The stamps on the handles of amphorae have led to the identification of the workshops of provenance, some of which were particularly famed, such as of Thasos, Kos, Rhodes and elsewhere. Furthermore, the decipherment of the incisions on the body of these vases contributes to the study of mercantile transactions concerning the particular products and to identifying the names of their exporters. Moreover, depending on the shape of the neck and the capacity of the amphora, their contents can be deduced, such as wine and olive oil, as well as salted fish or nuts and grain.

The results of recent underwater archaeological investigations indicate that the bulk of trading exchanges between coastal cities in the Aegean archipelago varied in Antiquity. In the Classical period transactions were on a rather limited scale, while they reached their peak in Roman imperial times.

During this period there was also a flourishing trade in marble and in architectural members, but primarily in works of art. These last were transported by sea from Greece to supply the Roman antiquities market, which from the second century AD was prominent and large-scale, with the consequent denuding of Hellenic sanctuaries of their treasures.

The recovery of works of art from shipwrecks – initially sporadic – is now more common, enabling the study of the trade of these during Antiquity. The commercialization of artworks, almost exclusively a Roman phenomenon, developed into a profitable profession for the antique-dealers of Rome, some of whom were ruthless fakers, such as Damasippos, who is mentioned in a satire by Horace. During the first century AD, Sulla shipped many works of art to Italy, as booty. Their transportation is verified by multiple wrecks with authentic works or copies of them, found along the length of the Mediterranean coasts.

Most of the bronze statues that grace museums and private collections were brought up from the sea and not the land. Many bronze masterpieces on land, some known also from the historical sources, have not survived, because the metal of which they were made was reused for diverse purposes.

The revelations of works of art and statues in recent years prompt us to wonder whether the treasures of ancient art that have not yet been discovered should be sought on the seabed rather than on land (fig. 676). The so-called Kalymnos Kore, the head of a Macedonian in the distinctive brimmed hat (fig 677), the two legs of a male from an equestrian statue (fig. 675) as well as part of a dolphin are superb works of art that have emerged of late from the waters of the Aegean, to be added to the corpus of sculptural masterpieces in bronze.

Among the first archaeological missions in the early twentieth century, which heralded underwater archaeology in Greece, those that brought up works of art hold an important place. In 1900-1901 a chance discovery by sponge-divers off Antikythera prompted the first systematic

438 | AEGEAN: AN UNDERWATER MUSEUM

676

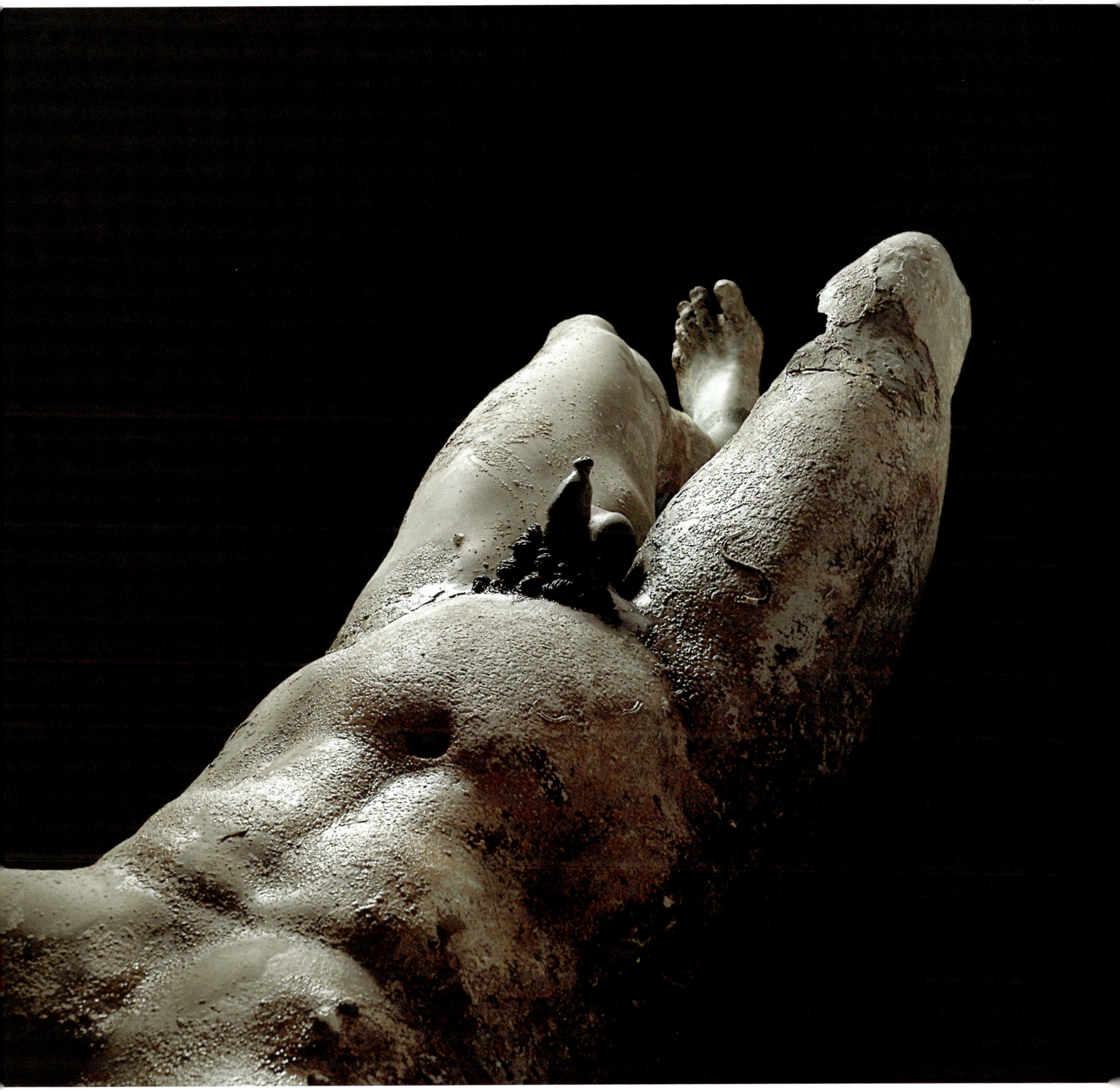

677. Head of a bronze statue of a Macedonian male with brimmed hat (*kausia*), of the early 4th c. BC. Displayed in the exhibition "On a swift ship… past sandy shores", in the Makrygianni Bastion at Niokastro, Pylos.

678. Parts of the mechanism (astrolabe) of Antikythera. This important technological instrument consists of cogs and bears inscriptions relating to the zodiacal cycle and the months. Athens, National Archaeological Museum.

679. Marble statue of Odysseus from the Antikythera shipwreck. A Roman copy of the 2nd c. AD. Although eroded by the sea, the turn of the head and the gaze convey the quick-wittedness of the cunning hero, king of the Cephalonians. Athens, National Archaeological Museum.

underwater archaeological research, undertaken by the Greek State with the support of ships of the Greek Navy.

The precious cargo, which to this day evokes the admiration of scholars and laymen alike, was brought to light by sponge fishers from the island of Syme. Thirty-six marble statues, eroded by marine organisms (fig. 679), some of which are faithful copies of works such as the Knidian Aphrodite and Herakles of the Farnese type, bronze statues of athletes, a bronze couch with relief decoration, jewellery (gold earring with representation of Eros), silver vessels, amphorae from Kos and Rhodes, glass artifacts and fine pottery, as well as the famous "astrolabe" a complex instrument for astronomical and calendrical calculations (fig. 678), were among the objects in the cargo of this wreck of the first century BC, placing it among the group of wrecks of ships carrying artworks bound for Rome. The most important artworks from the Antikythera wreck are the Ephebe of Antikythera, a work of the fourth century BC (fig. 680), and the portrait of a philosopher, a work of the second half of the third century BC, which are exhibited in the National Archaeological Museum in Athens.

The story of the chance discovery of an ancient wreck of a ship transporting works of art to Rome was repeated in 1926, off Cape Artemision in North Euboea, when fishermen drew up in their nets the arm of a bronze statue. The illicit excavation organized by antiquities-dealers intent on looting the wreck, was stopped by the Greek authorities, which undertook the underwater investigation of the wreck site. Thus were recovered from the depths of the sea the Zeus or Poseidon of Artemision, a rare work of the fifth century BC (fig. 686), the horse and the jockey, works of the second century BC (fig. 687), now exhibited in the National Archaeological Museum, as well as pottery and part of the ship, which date the wreck to the second century BC.

The Antikythera and Artemision wrecks are not unique of their kind. The sporadic handing in to the authorities of works of art such as the so-called "Marathon Boy" and the "Youth of Eleusis", as well as references in the Greek literary texts, such as Pausanias' account of the long-lived cult of the head of a god that was discovered by fishermen off Lesbos, denote the existence of many other wrecks. Those ships were carrying works of art either from workshops, such as those of Paros or Rhodes, from the sea of which come the bronze Medusa and the marble Aphrodite, or from plundering of sanctuaries or sacking of cities in Roman times.

440 | AEGEAN: AN UNDERWATER MUSEUM

In fact, the transport of Greek antiquities by sea continued even in the nineteenth century. Early in 1803 the sculptures detached from the Parthenon, on the orders of Lord Elgin were dispatched by sea to England. In the course of the voyage, the anger of the gods at the hubris of such sacrilege caused the wreck of the ship, the *Mentor*, off Avlemonas on Kythera. Three years later the precious sculptures were brought up from the seabed and continued their journey, to end up eventually in the British Museum.

680. The Ephebe of Antikythera. According to one view, the spherical object held in the raised hand was an apple, in which case the figure represents Paris. A work of the Late Classical period, *c.* 340 BC. Athens, National Archaeological Museum.

WRECKS | 441

Ancient cities on the seabed

Underwater archaeology is not only the archaeology of amphorae and ships, as is widely believed. The discipline extends to investigating and uncovering submerged settlements, very often unknown, or even forgotten ancient harbours that have suffered from modern use. The underwater archaeological sites in Greece, as in other Mediterranean countries with parallel historical courses, consist of ensembles of buildings or other remnants of constructions, which have been submerged for various reasons, such as Grotta on Naxos, Aghia Irini on Kea, the ancient city of Andros (Palaiopoli [fig. 681]), Salanti in the Argolid, Pavlopetri in Laconia, and so on.

Ancient harbours, in contrast to ancient shipwrecks, are not closed archaeological assemblages of definable date. This is because the preference over time for the same geographical locations in order to serve navigation is no coincidence. These sites kept diachronically the same geomorphological features and advantages, which in Antiquity made them suitable for serving mercantile and military purposes, as well as for establishing coastal settlements, from prehistoric into recent times.

For example, the continuous use of the closed harbour of Thasos, from the Archaic period into Early Christian times, is attested by evidence brought to light in excavations conducted by the French Archaeological School and the Ephorate of Underwater Antiquities (figs 682, 683).

Initially the anchorages served the safety of ancient seafaring, as is attested by the *Stadiasmoi*, which note for sailors the nautical advantages of the natural havens, protected by sheltered coves, reefs or islets, in Asia Minor and the African coasts.

681. General view of ancient Andros (Palaiopoli) from the acropolis. Visible in the sea is the submerged mole of the harbour.

682, 683. The submerged mole of the ancient harbour of Thasos. Ancient harbour installations are a specialized field of underwater archaeology, particularly difficult to study because of the alterations they have undergone due to diachronic use from Antiquity to today.

442 | AEGEAN: AN UNDERWATER MUSEUM

The discovery and identification of ancient anchorages is particularly difficult because the only archaeological indications that these maritime regions functioned as such on the sea routes are ancient anchors, typologically and chronologically heterogeneous (figs 666, 684, 685), as well as other kinds of disjecta, usually broken amphorae, which the mariners threw into the sea to get rid of in the case of emergency withdrawal for some reason. The first formations and improvements of the natural features of the anchorages, such as reinforcing the rocks with rubble masonry, led to the formation of the first harbours.

Ancient harbours are distinguished into two basic types, natural and manmade. The typology of their construction varies according to the physical substrate and the needs of the period in which they were made.

In Homer's descriptions the natural harbours are combined with sandy beaches, so that the ships could be pulled ashore for safety, as for example on the coast at Aghia Irini on Chios, during the third millennium BC.

On the other hand, the manmade harbours of primitive construction, with simple quays, developed into spatially planned harbour installations that served different functions, with infrastructure works such as quays, harbour basins, lighthouses, wharves and shipyards, as well as shops and warehouses, as in the case of Delos, which became very important when Rome chose it as her preferred commercial port.

The ancient Greeks quickly understood the importance of moles for tying up ships and protecting harbours. Thus, the military harbours in the Aegean are dated from as early as the sixth century BC and most belong to the category of closed harbours in which there are fortified installations and the natural or manmade harbour basin is exploited. This last is protected by the walls of the city and reinforced with fortified towers.

When economic or military conditions demanded more substantial installations, closed basins were constructed, which offered better protection and could accommodate more ships, with ship-sheds for housing the vessels and the fleet. These were associated with monumental constructions on land, which either supplemented the harbour infrastructure or were intended to protect it, such as fortified towers and acropolises connected with the defensive walls of the cities. Every large city-state had its harbour, some of which were renowned, such as Kition on Cyprus in the fourth century BC, the harbour of Hellenistic Kos, the ancient military harbour of Rhodes, at present Mandraki, and others.

The development of harbours during the Hellenistic period is linked not only with martial campaigns and the expansion of trade, but also with the building of larger ships. The Romans elevated harbour works to a high level of perfection, in terms of technical formation as well as the technique of breakwater constructions.

The most important ancient harbours have either been silted up by continuous geomorphological changes, natural or not, or are today occupied by modern installations, in which the continuous remodellings have disturbed

684. Stone anchor from the Argolic Gulf, height 50 cm. Anchors of this type were used mainly in prehistoric times, in large numbers for each ship. Kept in the laboratories of the Ephorate of Underwater Archaeology.

685. Stock (horizontal axis) of a Roman lead anchor, length 1.35 m., from the shipwreck with coins "Syrna 1", off the island of Syrna in the Dodecanese. The wreck from the reign of Diocletian (3rd c. AD) is unique because its cargo contained, among other things, a hoard of coins that were intended to pay the wages of the Roman army in the eastern provinces of the Empire, as well as a lead sarcophagus. Kept in the laboratories of the Ephorate of Underwater Antiquities.

686

444 | Aegean: An Underwater Museum

their archaeological field and only those that have been abandoned can still give some archaeological information.

Phalasarna in western Crete, the closed manmade harbour with isodomic towers linked by fortification walls, which in the Hellenistic period was used as a pirates' lair, is one of those cases in which the underwater archaeological site has been transformed totally into a land site due to geomorphological changes, the rise in ground level.

On the contrary, in Samos the harbour works of the tyrant Polykrates, whose fleet had evolved into an important naval force of 100 pentekonters, try to revive and to preserve their historical memory, under the threat of the development of a tourist marina.

Although archaeological research in ancient harbours is no easy matter, since *ipso facto* a large part of their construction is in the water and part of them on the surface of the sea or above it, they have not remained on the margins. In the Aegean islands, for example, the Ephorate of Underwater Antiquities has located in the double, military and commercial, harbour of Aegina the defensive system of manmade reefs, constructions to prevent the approach of enemy ships.

Greek history revolves around the Aegean Sea, speckled with islands, each one of which is a separate unit. Ancient shipwrecks, harbours and shipyards, sea routes and maritime trade compose a large part of the history of the Aegean, which should be sought in its depths, a unique treasure trove for archaeological research.

686. Zeus or Poseidon of Artemision. A work of the Classical period (*c.* 460 BC). One of the very few extant original bronze statues of the ancient world. Athens, National Archaeological Museum.

687. The "*keletizon pais*", popularly known as the "jockey of Artemision". It is possible that the young rider and the horse do not belong to the same statue group, even though they come from the same wreck. *C.* 140 BC. Athens, National Archaeological Museum.

ANCIENT CITIES ON THE SEABED | 445

SELECTED BIBLIOGRAPHY

Aegean Islands:
Historical and Archaeological background

Stone Age

Broodbank C., *This Small World the Great*, Cambridge University Press, London 2000.
Coleman J. E., Greece, the Aegean and Cyprus, in Ehrich R. W. (ed.), *Chronologies in Old World Archaeology. Part I: Greece and the Aegean from the Mesolithic to the End of the Early Bronze Age*, Chicago 1992, 247-288.
Efstratiou N., *Ayios Petros. A Neolithic Settlement in the Northern Sporades*, British Archaeological Reports Int. Series 241, Oxford 1985.
Evans J., C. Renfrew, *Excavations at Saliagos near Antiparos*, London 1968.
Felsch F. C. S., *Samos II: Das Kastro Tigani. Die spätneolithische und Chalkolithische Siedlung*, Bonn 1988.
Hood S., *Excavations in Chios 1938-55: Prehistoric Emborio and Agio Gala*, London 1981/82.
Sampson A., Η νεολιθική περίοδος στα Δωδεκάνησα, Athens 1987.
Sampson A., Η νεολιθική κατοίκηση στο Γυαλί της Νισύρου, Athens 1988.
Sampson A., Σκοτεινή Θαρρουνίων. Το σπήλαιο, ο οικισμός και το νεκροταφείο, Athens 1993.
Sampson A., Η εθνοαρχαιολογία του Γυαλιού της Νισύρου, Athens 1997.
Sampson A., J. Koslowski, M. Kaczanowska, Entre l'Anatolie et les Balkans: une sequence mesolithique-néolithique de l'île de Youra (Sporades du Nord), in *Préhistoire de l'Anatolie, Genése de deux mondes*, ERAUL, Liège 1989.
Sampson A., The Mesolithic and Neolithic Habitation in the Cave of Cyclope, Youra, Northern Sporades, *Annual of the British School at Athens* 93 (1998), 1-22.
Sampson A., *Ftelia at Mykonos. A Late Neolithic Settlement in Cyclades*, Rhodes 2002.
Sampson A., J. Kozlowski, M. Kaczanowska, V. Giannouli, The Mesolithic Settlement at Maroulas, Kythnos, *Mediterranean Archaeology and Archaeometry* 2 (2002), 45-67.

Bronze Age

Hägg R., N. Marinatos (eds), *The Minoan Thlassocracy. Myth and Reality. Proceedings of the Third International Symposium at the Swedish Intistute in Athens, 31 May-5 June 1982*, Stockholm 1984.
Hood S., *The Arts in Prehistoric Greece*, London 1978.
Ιστορία του Ελληνικού Έθνους, vol. A΄: Προϊστορία και Πρωτοϊστορία, Εκδοτική Αθηνών, Athens 1970.
Laffineur R., L. Basch (eds), *THALASSA. L'Égée préhistorique et la mer. Actes de la troisième Rencontre égéene internationale de l'Université de Liège, Calvi, Corse, 23-25 avril 1990*, Aegaeum 7, Liège 1991.
Marazzi M. et al. (eds), *Traffici micenei nel mondo Mediterraneo. Problemi storici e documentazione archeologica. Atti del convegno di Palermo, 11-12 maggio 1984*, Taranto 1986.
Renfrew C., *The Emergence of Civilisation. The Cyclades and the Aegean in the Third Millennium B.C.*, London 1972.
Treuil R. et al., *Les civilisations égéennes du Néolithique et de l'âge du Bronze*, Paris 1989.
Vasilikou D., *Ο μυκηναϊκός πολιτισμός*, Athens 1995.
Vermeule E., *Greece in the Bronze Age*, London 1964.
Ventris M., J. Chadwick, *Documents in Mycenaean Greek*, Cambridge 1973².

Geometric and Archaic periods

Gounaris A.P., Έρευνες οικιστικής των Πρωτογεωμετρικών - Γεωμετρικών Κυκλάδων και τα ζητούμενα της κυκλαδικής πρωτοϊστορίας, in N. Stampolidis (ed.), Φως Κυκλαδικόν. Τιμητικός τόμος στη μνήμη του Νίκου Ζαφειρόπουλου, Athens 1999, 96-113.
Ekschmitt W., *Kunst und Kultur der Kykladen. II: Geometrische und archaische Zeit*, Mainz 1986.
Lemos I. S., *The Protogeometric Aegean*, Oxford 2002.
Morris I., Archaeology and Archaic Greek History, in N. Fisher, H. van Wees (eds), *Archaic Greece*, London 1998, 1-91.
Simantoni-Bournia E., Οι Κυκλάδες από τους Πρώιμους Ιστορικούς Χρόνους μέχρι το τέλος της αρχαϊκής εποχής, in Λ. Γ. Μενδώνη, Ν. Μάργαρης (eds), Κυκλάδες. Ιστορία του τοπίου και τοπικές ιστορίες, Athens 1998, 173-207.

Snodgrass A. M., *Archaic Greece: The Age of Experiment*, London, Melbourne & Toronto 1980.
Stampolidis N., V. Karageorghis (eds), *Eastern Mediterranean. Cyprus - Dodecanese - Crete 16th - 6th cent. B.C.*, Athens 1998.
Stampolidis N. (ed.), *Ploes/Sea Routes... From Sidon to Huelva. Interconnections in the Mediterranean 16th-6th c. BC*, Athens 2003.
Stampolidis N., A. Yannikouri (eds), Το Αιγαίο στην Πρώιμη Εποχή του Σιδήρου, Athens 2004.
Syriopoulos K. Th., Η προϊστορική κατοίκηση της Ελλάδος και η γένεσις του ελληνικού έθνους, vol. B΄, Athens 1995.
Xipharas N., Οικιστική της Πρωτογεωμετρικής και Γεωμετρικής Κρήτης. Η μετάβαση από τη «μινωική» στην «ελληνική» κοινωνία (doctoral thesis, University of Crete), 2002.
Vanschoonwinkel J., *L'Égée et la Méditerranée orientale à la fin du IIe millénaire*, Louvain-La-Neuve - Providence 1991.

Classical period

Boardman J., *Greek Sculpture. The Classical Period*, London 1985.
Boardman J., *Greek Sculpture. The Late Classical Period*, London 1995.
Cargill J., *Athenian Settlements of the Fourth Century B.C.*, Leiden, New York, Köln 1995.
Figueira Th., *The Power of Money. Coinage and Politics in the Athenian Empire*, Philadelphia 1998.
Lawall M. L., *Transport Amphoras and Trademarks* (doctoral thesis, University of Michigan), 1995.
Meiggs R., *The Athenian Empire*, Oxford 1972.
Oikonomidou M., Ελληνική Τέχνη. Αρχαία Νομίσματα, Athens 1996.
Panayotaki N. (ed.), Κρήτη: Ιστορία και Πολιτισμός I, Crete 1987.
Whitbread I. K., *Greek Transport Amphorae*, Athens 1995.

Hellenistic and Roman periods
Historical outline

Gabrielsen V., P. Bilde, Tr. Engberg-Pedersen (eds), *Hellenistic Rhodes: Politics, Culture and Society*, Aarhus 1997.
Harrison G. W. M., *The Romans and Crete*, Amsterdam 1993.
Nigdelis P., Πολίτευμα και κοινωνία των Κυκλάδων κατά την ελληνιστική και αυτοκρατορική εποχή, Thessaloniki 1990.
Petropoulou A., *Beiträge zur Wirtschafts- und Gesellschaftsgeschichte Kretas in hellenistischer Zeit*, Frankfurt 1985.
Roussel P., *Délos colonie athénienne*, Bibliothèque des Écoles françaises d'Athènes et de Rome 111, Paris 1916 (reprinted 1987).
Sherwin-White S. M., *Ancient Cos: An Historical Study from the Dorian Settlement to the Imperial Period*, Hypomnemata 51, Göttingen 1978.
Vial Cl., *Délos indépendante (314-167 av. J.-C.). Étude d'une communauté civique et de ses institutions*, Bulletin de correspondance hellénique, Suppl. X, Paris 1984.

Archaeological evidence

Bruneau Ph., J. Ducat, *Guide de Délos*, Paris 1983.
Cook R. M., Ελληνική αγγειογραφία, Athens 1994³.
Gruben G., Ιερά και ναοί της αρχαίας Ελλάδας, Athens 2000.
Hermary A., Ph. Jockey, Fr. Queuyrel, sous la direction de J. Marcadé, *Sculptures Déliennes*, Paris 1996.
Kabus-Preisshofen R., *Die hellenistische Plastik der Insel Kos*, Athenische Mitteilungen Beih. 14, Berlin 1989.
Lauter H., *Die Architektur des Hellenismus*, Darmstadt 1986.
Marcadé J., *Au Musée de Délos. Étude sur la sculpture héllenistique en ronde bosse decouverte dans l'île*, Bibliothèque des Écoles françaises d'Athènes et de Rome 215, Paris 1969.
Merker G. S., *The Hellenistic Sculpture of Rhodes*, Studies in Mediterannean Archaeology 40, Göterborg 1973.
Palagia O., W. Coulson (eds), *Regional Schools in Hellenistic Sculpture*, Oxford 1998, 137-148 (V. Machaira, Ροδιακή γλυπτική)· 157-166 (I. S. Mark, Νίκη Σαμοθράκης)· 167-176 (I. Trianti, αγάλματα Μήλου)· 177-184 (Ph. Jockey, γλυπτά Δήλου).
Pollitt J. J., *Art in the Hellenistic Age*, London 1986.

North and East Aegean

Thasos

Bernard P., Céramique de la première moitié du VIIIe siècle à Thasos, *Bulletin de correspondance hellénique* 88 (1964), 77-146.

Dunant Chr., J. Pouilloux, Recherches sur l'histoire et les cultes de Thasos II, *Études Thasiennes* V, Paris 1957.

Études Thasiennes Vol. I (1944) - XIX (2002) [éd. de Boccard -Paris-Athens]. Series of the École française d' Athènes with special monographs on ancient Thasos.

Grandjean Y., F. Salviat, *Guide de Thasos*, École française d'Athènes 2000, with very important bibliography.

Kohl M., A. Muller, G. Sanidas, M. Sgourou, Ο αποικισμός της Θάσου. Η επανεξέταση των αρχαιολογικών δεδομένων, *Το Αρχαιολογικό Έργο στη Μακεδονία και στη Θράκη* 15 (2001), 57-72.

Koukouli-Chrysanthaki, Ch., G. Weissgerber, Προϊστορικά ορυχεία ώχρας στη Θάσο, *Το Αρχαιολογικό έργο στη Μακεδονία και στη Θράκη* 7 (1993), 541-558.

Koukouli-Chrysanthaki, Ch., Πρωτοϊστορική Θάσος I, Athens 1996.

Koukouli-Chrysanthaki, Ch., Οικισμός της Πρώιμης Εποχής του Χαλκού στη Σκάλα Σωτήρος, *Το Αρχαιολογικό Έργο στη Μακεδονία και στη Θράκη* 1 (1987), 389-406· 2 (1988), 421-425· 3 (1989), 507-520· 4 (1990), 531-546.

Koukouli-Chrysanthaki, Ch., A. Muller, S. Papadopoulos (eds), Θάσος, Πρώτες ύλες και τεχνολογία από τους προϊστορικούς χρόνους ώς σήμερα. Πρακτικά Διεθνούς Συνεδρίου - Λιμενάρια Θάσου 26-29/9/1995. Thasos. Matières premières et technologie de la préhistoire à nos jours. Actes du Colloque International Thasos, Limenaria 26-29/9/1995 (publication of the Hellenic Ministry of Culture [XVIII Ephorate of Prehistoric and Classical Antiquities] and the École française d' Athènes), Athens 1999.

Malamidou D., S. Papadopoulos, Ανασκαφική έρευνα στον προϊστορικό οικισμό Λιμεναρίων, *Το Αρχαιολογικό Έργο στη Μακεδονία και στη Θράκη* 7 (1993), 559-572· 11 (1997), 585-593.

Papadopoulos S., G. Aristodimou, D. Kouyoumtzoglou, Ph. Megaloudi, Η Τελική Νεολιθική και η Πρώιμη Εποχή του Χαλκού στη Θάσο. Η ανασκαφική έρευνα στις θέσεις Άγιος Ιωάννης και Σκάλα Σωτήρος, *Το Αρχαιολογικό Έργο στη Μακεδονία και στη Θράκη* 15 (2001), 55-60.

Thasiaka, Bulletin de correspondence hellénique, Supplement V, Paris 1979.

Samothrace

Burkert W., Greek Margins: Mysteries of Samothrace/Ελληνική Περιφέρεια: Τα μυστήρια της Σαμοθράκης, in A. A. Avayanou (ed.), *Λατρείες στην «περιφέρεια» του αρχαίου ελληνικού κόσμου*, Athens 2002, 31-63.

Clinton K., Stages of Initiation in the Eleusinian and Samothracian Mysteries, in M. B. Cosmopoulos (ed.), *Greek Mysteries. The Archaeology and Ritual of Ancient Greek Secret Cults*, London and New York 2003, 50-78.

Koder J., *Aigaion Pelagos (Die Nördliche Ägäis)*, Tabula Imperii Byzantini 10, Wien 1998.

Lehmann K., *Samothrace: A Guide to the Excavations and the Museum*, Thessaloniki 19986.

Matsas D., A. Bakirtzis, *Samothrace: A short cultural guide*, Athens 2001.

Matsas D., Η Σαμοθράκη στην Πρώιμη Εποχή του Σιδήρου, in N. Chr. Stampolidis, A. Yannikouri (eds), *Το Αιγαίο στην Πρώιμη Εποχή του Σιδήρου, Πρακτικά Διεθνούς Συμποσίου*, Rhodes 1-4 November 2002, Athens 2004, 227-257.

Philippson A., *Das Ägäische Meer und seine Inseln (Die Griechischen Landschaften)*, Frankfurt am Main 1959.

Imbros

Andreou I., I Andreou, Η Ίμβρος στην Πρώιμη Εποχή του Χαλκού (part b'), *Αρχαιολογία* 82 (2002), 75-83.

Araştırma Sonuçları Toplantısı 14 (1997), II, 55-60· 16 (1999), 61-5· 17 (2000), I, 123-6.

Arkeometri Sonuçları Toplantısı 15 (2000), 19-32.

Fredrich C., Imbros, *Mittheilungen des Kaiserlich Deutschen Archäologischen Instituts*, Athenische Abtheilung XXXIII, 1908, 81-112.

Harmankaya S., B. Erdoğu, The Prehistoric Sites of Gökçeada, Turkey, in M. Özdoğan, H. Hauptmann, N. Başgelen (eds), *Köyden Kente: Yakındoğu 'da İlk Yerleşimler / From Village to Cities: Early Villages in the Near East* 2, Istanbul 2003, 459-479.

Hüryılmaz H., Eine Gruppe frühbronzezeitlicher Menschenfigurinen aus Yenibademli Höyük auf Gökçeada (Imbros), *Studia Troica* 9 (1999), 475-488.

Hüryılmaz H., Silent Witnesses of Imbros: Early Bronze Age Human Figurines from Yenibademli, in R. Aslan, S. Blum, G. Kastl, F. Schweizer, D. Thumm (eds), *Mauerschau. Festschrift für Manfred Korfmann*, 1, Remshalden-Grunbach 2002, 351-362.

Hüryılmaz H., Archaeology of Gökçeada, in B. Öztürk (ed.), *Gökçeada, yes,il ve mavinin özgür dünyası...*, 83-91, Gökçeada 2002.

Kazı Sonuçları Toplantısı 19 (1998), I, 357-377· 20 (1999), I, 311-324· 21 (2000), I, 229-238· 22 (2001), I, 247-258· 23 (2002), I, 295-304· 24 (2003), I, 95-104· 25 (2004), I, 367-376· 26 (2005), I, 11-20.

Öner E., Geoarchäologische und paläogeographische Forschungen auf der Insel Gökçeada (Imbros, Siedlungshügel von Yeni Bademli, Nordwestanatolien-Nordostägäisches Meer-Türkei), *Bremer Beiträge z. Geographie u. Raumplanung* 36, 2000 (17. Jahrestagung des AK Geographie der Meere und Küsten), 23-33.

Öner E., Gökçeada Kıyılarında Holosen Deniz Seviyesi ve Kıyı Çizgisi Değişmeleri, στο E. Özhan, Y. Yüksel (επιμ.), *Türkiye 'nin Kıyı ve Deniz Alanları III. Ulusal Konferansı, Türkiye Kıyıları 01 Konferansı Bildiriler Kitabı*, İstanbul 2001, 779-790

Tenedos

Arslan N., Goldbleche aus Tenedos, *Istanbuler Mitteilungen* 53 (2004), 251-263.

Arslan N., N. Sevinç, Die eisenzeitlichen Gräber von Tenedos, *Istanbuler Mitteilungen* 53 (2004), 223-250.

Koder J., *Aigaion Pelagos (Die Nördliche Ägäis)*, Tabula Imperii Byzantini 10, Wien 1998.

Müze Kurtarma Kazıları Semineri 2 (1992) 1-9· 4 (1994) 311-320· 5 (1995) 113-127.

Philippson A., *Das Ägäische Meer und seine Inseln (Die Griechischen Landschaften)*, Frankfurt am Main 1959.

Sevinç N., T. Takaoğlu, The Early Bronze Age on Tenedos/Bozcaada, *Studia Troica* 14 (2004), 135-140.

Lemnos

Αρχαιολογία 50, March 1994.

Archontidou-Argyri A., Λήμνος, *Αρχαιολογικόν Δελτίον*, Χρονικά 41 (1986)· 51 (1996).

Archontidou-Argyri A., *Πολιόχνη. Λήμνω ἐν ἀμιχθαλοέσση*, Αθήνα 1997.

Archontidou-Argyri A. (ed.), *Αρχαίο θέατρο Ηφαιστίας*, Lemnos 2004.

Bernabò Brea L., *Poliochni. Città preistorica nell'isola di Lemno* I, Roma 1964, II, Roma 1976.

Beschi L., Cabirio di Lemno: testimonianze letterarie ed epigrafiche, *Annuario della Scuola Archeologica di Atene* 68-69 (1996-97), 7-192.

Beschi L., Arte e cultura di Lemno arcaica, *Parola del Passato* 53, 1998, 48-76 and *Egnatia* 5 (1995-2000), 151-179.

Boulotis Ch., Κουκονήσι Λήμνου. Τέσσερα χρόνια ανασκαφικής έρευνας. Θέσεις και υποθέσεις, in Ch. Doumas, E. La Rosa (eds), *Η Πολιόχνη και η Πρώιμη Εποχή του Χαλκού στο Αιγαίο - Poliochni e l'antica età del Bronzo nell'Egeo settentrionale*, Athens 1997, 230-272.

Della Seta A., Arte tirrenica di Lemno, *Αρχαιολογική Εφημερίς* 1937, 629-654.

Greco E. et al., Hephaistia, *Annuario della Scuola Archeologica di Atene* 79 (2001), 382-405· 80, II (2002), 967-1013.

Massa M., *La ceramica ellenistica con decorazione a rilievo della bottega di Efestia* (Monografie della Scuola Archeologica di Atene, V), Roma 1992.

Messineo G., *Efestia. Scavi Adriani 1928-1930* (Monografie della Scuola Archeologica di Atene XIII), Padova 2001.

Mustilli D., La necropoli tirrenica di Efestia, *Annuario della Scuola Archeologica di Atene* XV-XVI (1932-33), 3-278.

Πρακτικά της Δ' Επιστημονικής Συνάντησης για την ελληνιστική κεραμική, 1994, Athens 1997, 211-231 and E', Chania 1998, Athens 2001, 145-160.

Lesbos

Archontidou A., et al., *Αρχαιολογικός οδηγός Μουσείου Μυτιλήνης*, Lesbos 1999.

Betancourt P. P., *The Aeolic Style in Architecture*, Princeton 1977.

Bonanno-Aravantinou M., Alcuni ritratti giulio-claudi del Museo Archeologico di Mytilene, *Quaderni de «La ricerca scientifica»* 116, Roma 1988.

Charitonidis S., L. Kahil, R. Ginouvès, *Les mosaïques de la maison du Ménandre à Mytilène*, Bern 1970.

Charitonidou S., *Αἱ ἐπιγραφαὶ τῆς Λέσβου*, Athens 1968.

Kontis I. D., *Η Λέσβος και η μικρασιατική της περιοχή*, Athens 1976.

Lamb W., Antissa, *Annual of the British School at Athens* 32 (1932), 41-67.

Lamb W., *Excavations at Thermi in Lesbos*, Cambridge 1936.

Pfuhl E., Möbius H., *Die ostgriechischen Grabreliefs*, vols I, II, Mainz 1977.

Πρακτικά της Δ' Επιστημονικής Συνάντησης για την ελληνιστική κεραμική, Lesbos 1994, Athens 1997.

Shields E., *The Cults of Lesbos*, Wisconsin 1917.

Warwich Wroth F. S. A., *A Catalogue of the Greek Coins in the British Museum: Troas, Aeolis and Lesbos*, London 1894.

Chios

Boardman J., Excavations in Chios 1951-1952, Greek Emporio, *Annual of the British School at Athens* Suppl. 6, 1967, 186-202.

Boardman J., *The Greeks Overseas*, New York 1980.

Boardman J., *Annual of the British School at Athens* 51 (1956)· 58 (1963)· 59 (1964)· 56 (1961).

Εμποριό. Ένας οικισμός των πρώιμων ιστορικών χρόνων. Εργασίες ανάδειξης, Chios 2003.

Held W., Zum Athenaheiligtum in Emporio auf Chios. Eine neue Rekonstruktion und Deutung, *Archaeologischer Anzeiger* 1998, 347-363.

Kontoleon N. M., Ἀνασκαφαί ἐν Χίῳ, Πρακτικά της εν Αθήναις Αρχαιολογικής Εταιρείας 1952, 520-530.

Roebuck C., *Ionian Trade and Colonization*, Oxford 1984.

Sakellariou M., *La migration grecque en Ionie*, Athènes 1958.

Smith A. C., *The Architecture of Chios*, London 1962.

Χίος τ' ἔναλος πόλις Οἰνοπίωνος, Chios 2000 (with basic bibliography).

Zolotas G., Ἱστορία τῆς Χίου, Athens 1921-1926.

Psara

Archontidou A., Ψαρά, *Αρχαιολογικό Δελτίο* 18 (1997) (υπό έκδοση)· 19 (1998)· 20 (1999)· 21 (2000)· 22 (2001)· 23 (2002) (in press).

Archontidou A., G. Deliyorgi, *Τα Ψαρά στην αρχαιότητα, Αρχαιολογικό Μουσείο Χίου, Περιοδική Έκθεση, Οκτώβριος 1999-Δεκέμβριος 2001*, ΥΠ.ΠΟ.-Κ΄ ΕΠΚΑ, Chios 1999.

Acheilara L. A., A. Tsaravopoulos, Αρχαιολογικά Χρονικά της Χίου, *Χιακά Χρονικά* 17 (1985), 68-80.

Acheilara L. Mycenaean Events from Psara, *Atti e Memorie del Secondo Congresso Internazionale di Micenologia, Roma - Napoli, 14-20 Ottobre 1991*, Roma 1996, 1349-1353.

Charitonidis S., Ψαρά, *Αρχαιολογικό Δελτίο* 17 (1961/2), Χρονικά, 266.

Tsaravopoulos A., N. Karelli, N. Zapheiriou, S. Mouschouris, Αρχαιολογική Έρευνα στα Ψαρά, *Τα Ψαρά* 37, 38, 39 (1983), 5-11 and 51 (1984), 2-5.

Tsaravopoulos A., Ανασκαφική Έρευνα στα Ψαρά 1986, *Τα Ψαρά* 73 (1986), 2-7.

Χίος τ' ἔναλος πόλις Οἰνοπίωνος, Chios 2000 (with basic bibliography).

Samos

Kyrieleis H., *Το Ηραίο της Σάμου*, Athens 1983, with rich bibliography on researches in the Heraion.

Shipley Gr., *A History of Samos*, Oxford 1987, with full bibliography.

The results of the German excavations are published in the series *SAMOS*, vol. I-XII, 1961-1972 et seq. The results of more recent Greek investigations in *Αρχαιολογικόν Δελτίον*, Χρονικά, vol. 21 (1966) et seq.

Tsakos C., *Samos. A guide to the history and archaeology*, Athens 2003.

Walter H., *Das Griechische Heiligtum dargestellt am Heraion von Samos*, Stuttgart 1990.

Ikaria, Phournoi

Hadjianastasiou O., *Αρχαιολογικό Δελτίο* 38 (1983), Β2 Χρονικά, 1989, 348, 350.

Hadjianastasiou O., *Αρχαιολογικό Δελτίο* 43 (1988), Β2 Χρονικά, 1993, 501-504.

Ιστορία Ελληνικού Έθνους (with entry «Ικαρία»), Εκδοτική Αθηνών.

Καθημερινή, Επτά Ημέρες, «Ικαρία», 21 June 1998.

Matthaiou A P, G. K. Papadopoulos, *Επιγραφές Ικαρίας*, Ελληνική Επιγραφική Εταιρεία, Athens 2003.

Melas I., *Ιστορία της Ικαρίας*, (1st reprint), Athens 2001.

Papachatzis N., *Παυσανίου Ελλάδος Περιήγησις, Βοιωτικά-Φωκικά*, Athens 1981.

Vasileiadis Ch., *Αρχαιολογικό Δελτίο* 34 (1979), Χρονικά Β2, 1987, 367-369.

Viglaki-Sophianou M., *Αρχαιολογικό Δελτίο* 52 (1997), Χρονικά Β3, 946-949.

Zapheiropoulos N.S., *Αρχαιολογικό Δελτίο* 25 (1970), Β2 Χρονικά, 1973, 420-422.

Zapheiropoulou Ph., *Αρχαιολογικό Δελτίο* 43 (1988), Β2 Χρονικά, 1993, 503 και 508.

SPORADES

North Sporades

Skiathos, Skopelos, Alonnisos, Deserted islands of the Sporades

Doulgéri-Intzesiloglou A., Y. Garlan, Vin et amphores de Péparéthos et d'Ikos, *Bulletin de correspondance hellénique* CXIV (1990) I, 361-389.

Doulgéri-Intzesiloglou A., Φεραί, Πεπάρηθος, Σκίαθος: Μερικά στοιχεία του αρχαιολογικού έργου μιας οκταετίας, *Πρακτικά 1ης Συνάντησης για το Έργο των Εφορειών Αρχαιοτήτων και Νεωτέρων Μνημείων του ΥΠΠΟ στη Θεσσαλία και την ευρύτερη περιοχή της (1990-1998, Βόλος 1998)*, Volos 2000, 345-353.

Doulgéri-Intzesiloglou A., Η αρχαία Σκίαθος μέσα από τα κείμενα και τα μνημεία της. Τελευταία συμπεράσματα και προοπτικές της αρχαιολογικής έρευνας της νήσου, 99-120·

Efstratiou N., *A Neolithic Site in the Northern Sporades. Aegean Relationships during the Neolithic of the 5th Millennium BC*, British Archaeological Reports, Int. Series 241, Oxford 1985.

Hadjidaki E., Underwater Excavations of a Late Fifth Century Merchant Ship at Alonnesos, Greece: the 1991-1993 Seasons, *Bulletin de correspondance hellénique* CXX (1996), II, 561-593.

Picon M., Origine d'amphores du groupe dit Solocha II, trouvées en Russie, *Bulletin de correspondance hellénique* CXIV (1990) I, 390-393.

Πρακτικά Συνεδρίου «Αρχαιολογική έρευνα στις Βόρειες Σποράδες», (Αλόννησος 1996), Alonnisos 2001:

    Chaniotis Ph. C. D., D Kazianis, Υποβρύχιες αρχαιολογικές έρευνες στα νησιά του Αρχιπελάγους των Β. Σποράδων τα έτη 1994-1995, 71-77·

    Doulgéri-Intzesiloglou A., Το Ασκληπιείο της Πεπαρήθου, *Πρακτικά Συνεδρίου: 1ο Αρχαιολογικό Έργο Θεσσαλίας και Στερεάς Ελλάδας*, Volos 2003·

    Efstratiou N., Ο νεολιθικός οικισμός του Αγίου Πέτρου στην Κυρα-Παναγιά Αλοννήσου και οι νησιωτικές εγκαταστάσεις του Αιγαίου: μια επανεκτίμηση, 231-250·

    Panagopoulou E., E. Kotzabopoulou, P. Karkanas, Γεωαρχαιολογική έρευνα στην Αλόννησο: Νέα στοιχεία για την Παλαιολιθική και τη Μεσολιθική στον αιγαιακό χώρο, 121-151·

    Sampson A., Το Σπήλαιο του Κύκλωπα Γιούρων. Τα νεολιθικά και μεσολιθικά στρώματα, 41-69·

    Sampson A., Επιφανειακή έρευνα στα Ερημόνησα των Β. Σποράδων, 203-216·

    Skaphida E., Πρόσφατες αρχαιολογικές έρευνες στην Αλόννησο, Ερημόνησα και Σκόπελο, 251-266.

Sampson A., *Σκόπελος. Ιστορική και αρχαιολογική αφήγηση*, Skopelos 2000.

Skaphida E., «Από την πεδιάδα της Καρδίτσας στα νησιά των Β. Σποράδων», *Πρακτικά 1ης Συνάντησης για το Έργο των Εφορειών Αρχαιοτήτων και Νεωτέρων Μνημείων του ΥΠΠΟ στη Θεσσαλία και την ευρύτερη περιοχή της (1990-1998, Βόλος 1998)*, Volos 2000, 395-406.

Skaphida E., P Arachoviti, A. Doulgéri-Intzesiloglou, Αρχαιότητες στο Θαλάσσιο Πάρκο των Βορείων Σποράδων, in *Μνημεία της Μαγνησίας: Πρακτικά Συνεδρίου για την ανάδειξη του διαχρονικού μνημειακού πλούτου του Βόλου και της ευρύτερης περιοχής (Βόλος 2001)*, Volos 2002, 32-39.

Skyros

Antoniadi X. A., *Η Σκύρος στους περιηγητές και γεωγράφους, 1400-1900*, Αρχείο Ευβοϊκών Μελετών. Παράρτημα του ΚΑ΄ vol., 1977.

Αρχαιολογικός χώρος Παλαμαρίου Σκύρου, Leaflet of the Hellenic Ministry of Culture, Athens 2003.

Constantinidis M., Ἡ νῆσος Σκύρος, Athens 1901.

Liddell H., R. Scott, Μέγα Λεξικόν τῆς Ἑλληνικῆς Γλώσσης.

Pantazidis I., Λεξικόν Ὁμηρικόν.

Papageorgiou D., Ἡ ἱστορία τῆς Σκύρου, Patras 1909.

Parlama L., Ἡ Σκύρος στὴν Ἐποχή τοῦ Χαλκοῦ, Athens 1984.

Perdika N., Σκύρος, ἐντυπώσεις καὶ περιγραφαί, ἱστορικὰ καὶ λαογραφικὰ σημειώματα –ἤθη καὶ ἔθιμα– μνημεῖα τοῦ λόγου καὶ λαοῦ, Athens 1940.

Sapouna-Sakellaraki E., *Σκύρος* (Archaeological Guidebook), Athens 1997

Theochari M.D., L. Parlama, Παλαμάρι Σκύρου: η οχυρωμένη πόλη της Πρώιμης Χαλκοκρατίας, in Doumas Ch., V. La Rosa (eds), *Η Πολιόχνη και η Πρώιμη Εποχή του Χαλκού στο Αιγαίο - Poliochni e l'antica età del Bronzo nell'Egeo settentrionale*, Athens 1997, 344-356.

ARGOSARONIC ISLANDS

Salamis, Psyttaleia

Dekoulakou I., Ανασκαφικές έρευνες στην Σαλαμίνα, in E. Konsolaki-Yannopoulou (ed.), *Αργοσαρωνικός. Πρακτικά 1ου Διεθνούς Συνεδρίου Ιστορίας και Αρχαιολογίας του Αργοσαρωνικού, Πόρος, 26-29 Ιουνίου 1998*, vol. Β΄, Athens 2003, 29-44.

Dekoulakou I., Circular Funerary Monument at Kolones, Salamina, in E. Konsolaki-Yannopoulou (ed.), *Αργοσαρωνικός. Πρακτικά 1ου Διεθνούς Συνεδρίου Ιστορίας και Αρχαιολογίας του Αργοσαρωνικού, Πόρος, 26-29 Ιουνίου 1998*, vol. Β΄, Athens 2003, 51-61.

Dekoulakou I., Σωστικές ανασκαφικές έρευνες στη Σαλαμίνα, in the Proceedings of the Colloquium: *Β΄ Εφορεία Προϊστορικών και Κλασικών Αρχαιοτήτων: Το έργο μίας δεκαετίας, 1994-2003, Αθήνα, 18-20 Δεκεμβρίου 2003* (forthcoming).

Lolos Y. G., Late Cypro-Mycenaean Seafaring: New Evidence from Sites in the Saronic and the Argolic Gulfs, in V. Karageorghis - D. Michaelides (eds), *Proceedings of the International Symposium, Cyprus and the Sea, Nicosia 25-26 September 1993*, Nicosia 1995, 65-87.

Lolos Y., "Σπήλαιον ἀναπνοὴν ἔχον ἐς τὴν θάλασσαν": Το Σπήλαιο του Ευριπίδη στη Σαλαμίνα, *Δωδώνη* 26, 1997, 287-326.

Lolos Y. (ed.), Το Σπήλαιο του Ευριπίδη, in the periodical *Επτάκυκλος*, iss. 15, 2000, 9-66.

Lolos Y. G., Dark Age Citadels in Southern Salamis, in V. Karageorghis, Chr. E. Morris (eds), *Defensive Settlements of the Aegean and the Eastern Mediterranean after c. 1200 B.C.*, Nicosia 2001, 115-136.

Lolos Y. G., Salamis: Kanakia, in *Archaeological Reports for 2000-2001*, No 47, 14-15 and in *Archaeological Reports for 2001-2002*, No 48, 14-15.

Lolos Y., Μυκηναϊκή Σαλαμίς: Οι έρευνες των ετών 2000-2002, *Δωδώνη* 32, 2003, 17-98.

Lolos Y., Το μυκηναϊκό άστυ της Σαλαμίνος, in *Έπαθλον, Αρχαιολογικό Συνέδριο προς τιμήν του Άδωνι Κ. Κύρου*, Poros, 7-9 Ιουνίου 2002 (in press).

Mari A., *Η Νεολιθική Εποχή στο Σαρωνικό, Μαρτυρίες για τη χρήση του Σπηλαίου του Ευριπίδη στην Σαλαμίνα με βάση την κεραμεική της Νεότερης και Τελικής Νεολιθικής* (unpublished doctoral thesis, Aristotle University of Thessaloniki), 2001.

Petrakos V. Ch., Η Αρχαιολογία της Ψυττάλειας, *Ο Μέντωρ*, year 18th, iss. 74-75, 2005, 33-72.

Pritchett W. K., *Studies in Ancient Greek Topography*, Part I (1965), 94-102.

Taylor M. C., *Salamis and the Salaminioi: The History of an Unofficial Athenian Demos*, Amsterdam 1997.

Aegina

Felten F., Νέες ανασκαφές στην Αίγινα-Κολώνα, in E. Konsolaki-Yannopoulou (ed.), *Αργοσαρωνικός. Πρακτικά 1ου Διεθνούς Συνεδρίου Ιστορίας και Αρχαιολογίας του Αργοσαρωνικού, Πόρος, 26-29 Ιουνίου 1998*, vol. Α΄, Athens 2003, 17-32.

Felten F., Αίγινα-Κολώνα στην Προϊστορική Εποχή, and Αίγινα-Κολώνα. Η ακρόπολη της πόλης, *Η Αιγιναία. Περιοδική πολιτιστική έκδοση* 5 (2002), 63-87.

Goette H. R., Το Ιερό του Διός Ελλανίου στο Όρος της Αίγινας, in E. Konsolaki-Yannopoulou (ed.), *Αργοσαρωνικός. Πρακτικά 1ου Διεθνούς Συνεδρίου Ιστορίας και Αρχαιολογίας του Αργοσαρωνικού, Πόρος, 26-29 Ιουνίου 1998*, vol. Β΄, Athens 2003, 23-28.

Ohly D., *Tempel und Heiligtum der Aphaia auf Ägina*, Münich 1978².

Papastavrou E.G., Οι σωστικές ανασκαφές στην Αίγινα, *Η Αιγιναία. Περιοδική πολιτιστική έκδοση* 5 (2002), 139-143.

Schwandner E. L., *Der ältere Porostempel der Aphaia auf Ägina*, Berlin 1985.

Simantoni-Bournia E., Το Ιερό της Αφαίας στην Αίγινα, *Η Αιγιναία. Περιοδική πολιτιστική έκδοση* 5 (2002), 88-103.

Welter G., *Αίγινα* (ed. G. P. Koulikourdi), Athens 1962.

Walter H., F. Felten, *Alt-Ägina III.1, Die vorgeschichtliche Stadt*, Mainz am Rhein 1981.

Walter H., *The People of Ancient Aegina. 3000-1000 BC*, Athens 2001.

Poros

Konsolaki E., Πρωτοελλαδική εγκατάσταση στον Κάβο Βασίλη του Πόρου, in *Έπαθλον. Πρακτικά Αρχαιολογικού Συνεδρίου προς τιμήν του Άδωνη Κύρου*, vol. Α΄, Athens 2005 (in press).

Papachatzis N. D., *Παυσανίου Ελλάδος Περιήγησις*, βιβλίο 2. 33, 1-3, Athens 1976, 258-262.

Wells B., The Sanctuary of Poseidon at Kalaureia. The New Investigations of 1997, in E. Konsolaki-Yannopoulou (ed.), *Αργοσαρωνικός. Πρακτικά 1ου Διεθνούς Συνεδρίου Ιστορίας και Αρχαιολογίας του Αργοσαρωνικού, Πόρος, 26-29 Ιουνίου 1998*, vol. Α΄, Athens 2003, 337-347.

Welter G., *Troizen und Kalaureia*, Berlin 1941.

Wide S., L. Kjellberg, Ausgrabungen auf Kalaureia, *Mitteilungen des Deutschen Archäologischen Instituts. Athenische Abteilung* 20 (1895), 267-326.

Hydra, Dokos, Spetses, Islets and rocky islets

Kyrou A. K., *Στο σταυροδρόμι του Αργολικού*, vol. Α΄, Athens 1990.

Kyrou A. K., Περιπέτεια Σαμίων στον Αργολικό Κόλπο (Μία επιβεβαίωση χωρίου του Ηροδότου, ΙΙΙ 57-59), *Πρακτικά του 5ου Διεθνούς Συνεδρίου Πελοποννησιακών Σπουδών, Άργος-Ναύπλιον, 6-10 Σεπτεμβρίου 1995*, vol. Β΄, Athens 1998, 193-208.

Kyrou A. K., "Κυνήγι" χαλκού κατά την Πρώιμη Χαλκοκρατία στον Αργολικό Κόλπο. Οι νησίδες Παραπόλα και Φαλκονέρα, *Πρακτικά του 6ου Διεθνούς Συνεδρίου Πελοποννησιακών Σπουδών, Τρίπολις, 24-29 Σεπτεμβρίου 2000*, vol. Β΄, Athens 2001-2002, 257-272.

Kyrou A. K., Νησιωτικά καταφύγια στον Αργολικό Κόλπο κατά τους πρωτοβυζαντινούς αιώνες, *Πρακτικά του 6ου Διεθνούς Συνεδρίου Πελοποννησιακών Σπουδών, Τρίπολις, 24-29 Σεπτεμβρίου 2000*, vol. Β΄, Athens 2001-2002, 501-520.

Lolos Y. G., Marabea C., Myceaean Aperopia: Thoughts about working areas and producing systems, *Ενάλια* VIII (2004), 65-78.

Petritaki M., Δοκός, *Αρχαιολογικόν Δελτίον* 52, 1997 (2002), Β1, 102-105.

Petritaki M., Ύδρα: Το οδοιπορικό μίας αρχαιολογικής προσέγγισης, in Ελ. Κονσολάκη-Γιαννοπούλου (ed.), *Αργοσαρωνικός. Πρακτικά 1ου Διεθνούς Συνεδρίου Ιστορίας και Αρχαιολογίας του Αργοσαρωνικού, Πόρος, 26-29 Ιουνίου 1998*, vol. Α΄, Athens 2003, 105-128.

Theocharis D. R., Αγία Μαρίνα Σπετσών, *Αρχαιολογικόν Δελτίον* 26, (1971), Χρονικά, 84-93.

KYTHERA, ANTIKYTHERA

Kythera

Bartsiokas A., *Παλαιοντολογία των Κυθήρων*, Athens 1998.

Broodbank C., E. Kiriatzi, J. Rutter, From Pharao's feet to the Slave Women of Pylos? The History and Cultural Dynamics of Kythera in the Third Palace Period, in A. Dakouri-Hild, S. Sherratt (eds), *AUTOCHTHON: Papers Presented to O.T.P.K. Dickinson on the Occasion of his Retirement*, British Archaeological Reports, Inter. Series 1432, Oxford 2005.

Broodbank C., E. Kiriatzi, The first "minoans" of Kythera re-visited: technology demographs and landscape in the Pre-palatial Aegean, American Journal of Archaeology, spring 2007 (in press)

Coldstream J. N., G. L. Huxley (eds), *Kythera, Excavations and Studies*, London 1972.

Papatsaroucha E., Κύθηρα 1990-2000: μια πλούσια σε ανασκαφές δεκαετία, *Corpus* 21, November 2000, 10-15.

Petrocheilos I., *Τα Κύθηρα από την Προϊστορική εποχή έως τη Ρωμαιοκρατία*, Ioannina 1985.

Petrocheilos I., G. Leontsinis (eds), *Κύθηρα: Μύθος και Πραγματικότητα, Πρακτικά του Α΄ Διεθνούς Συνεδρίου Κυθηραϊκών Μελετών*, vol. Α΄, Kythera 2003:
Banou A., Τα Κύθηρα ανάμεσα στη μινωική Κρήτη και τη μυκηναϊκή Πελοπόννησο: τα μικροαντικείμενα από το μινωικό ιερό κορυφής στον Άη-Γιώργη στο Βουνό, 69-75·
Kyrou A., Ταυτότητα Μινωιτών και Φοινίκων στα προϊστορικά Κύθηρα, 51-67·
Michalakas S., Χώρος λατρείας της Αλέας στην Παλαιόπολη Κυθήρων, 91-100·
Petrocheilos I., Αρχαίο ιερό στο Παλαιόκαστρο, 77-89.

Sakellarakis Y. and E. (eds), *Κύθηρα. Το ιερό κορυφής στον Άγιο Γεώργιο στο Βουνό* (working title, forthcoming).

Tsaravopoulos A., Graffiti από τα Κύθηρα, *HOROS* 13 (1999), 261-267; Κυθηραϊκά, *HOROS* 14-16 (2000-2003), 207-211.

Waterhouse H., R. Hope Simpson, Prehistoric Laconia: Part II, Kythera, *Annual of the British School at Athens* 56 (1961), 148-160.

Antikythera

Papatsaroucha E., Αντικύθηρα, Τα αρχαία Αίγιλα στη σκαπάνη των αρχαιολόγων, *Corpus* 37, April 2002, 22-33.

Petrocheilos I., Ξεροπόταμος: μια αρχαία θέση στα Αντικύθηρα, *Αρχαιολογικά Ανάλεκτα εξ Αθηνών* 20 (1987), 31-34.

Stais V., Ἀνασκαφαὶ καὶ ἔρευναι ἐν Αἰγιλίᾳ (Ἀντικυθήροις), *Αρχαιολογικόν Δελτίον* 5 (1889), 237-242.

Tsaravopoulos A., Ενεπίγραφες μολυβδίδες από τις ανασκαφές των τελευταίων ετών στα Αντικύθηρα, *HOROS* 17 (in press).

Tsaravopoulos A. (ed.), *Αντικύθηρα, Έξι χρόνια ανασκαφών* (working title, forthcoming).

Waterhouse H., R. Hope-Simpson, Prehistoric Laconia: Part II, Antikythera, *Annual of the British School at Athens* 56, 1961, 160-163.

CYCLADES

Kea

Caskey M., *The Temple at Ayia Irini. Part I: The Statues, Keos* II, American School of Classical Studies, Princeton, N.J. 1986.

Cherry J. F., J. L. Davis, E. Mantzourani, *Landscape Archaeology as Long-Term History. Northern Keos in the Cycladic Islands*, Monumenta Archaeologica 16, 1991.

Choremi A., Ch. Vlassopoulou, Y. Venieri, *Κέα. Ιστορία και αρχαιότητες*, Athens 2002.

Coleman J., *Kephala, Keos* I, American School of Classical Studies, Princeton, N.J. 1977.

Cummer W. W., E. Schofield, *Ayia Irini: House A, Results of the Excavations*, Mainz on Rhine 1984.

Galani G., L. Mendoni, Ch. Papageorgiadou, Επιφανειακή έρευνα της Κέας, *Αρχαιογνωσία* 3, 1982 (1987), 237-244.

Georgiou H., N. Faraklas, Ancient Habitation patterns in Keos. Locations and Nature of Sites on the Northwest Part of the Island, *Αριάδνη* 3 (1985), 207-266.

Manthos C., *Αρχαιολογία και Ιστορία της νήσου Κέας* (Introduction – Transcription – Scholia: L. Mendoni), Vourkariani 1991.

Papanikolaou A., Η οικοδομική εξέλιξη της νότιας κλιτύος της Ακροπόλεως της Καρθαίας κατά τον 6ο και 5ο αιώνα π.Χ., και η στέγη του ναού της Αθηνάς στην Καρθαία, in L. Mendoni, A. Mazarakis Ainian (eds), *Πρακτικά Διεθνούς Συμποσίου Κέα - Κύθνος. Ιστορία και Αρχαιολογία, Μελετήματα* 27, Κέντρο Ελληνικής και Ρωμαϊκής Αρχαιότητος - Εθνικό Ίδρυμα Ερευνών, Athens 1998.

Psylla I., *Ἱστορία τῆς νήσου Κέας*, Athens 1921.

Makronisos

Gennadios I.: Αἱ ἐν Μακρονήσῳ σκωρίαι, *Ἐθνοφύλαξ*, iss. No 2338, Athens 5 November 1871, 1 ff.

Hope Simpson R., O.T.P.K. Dickinson, *A Gazeteer of Aegean Civilisation in the Bronze Age*, vol. I, Studies in Mediterranean Archaeology LII (1979), 210.

Lambert N., Vestiges préhistoriques dans l'île de Makronissos, *Bulletin de correspondance hellénique* 96 (1972), 873ff. [The same article was reprinted in *Αρχαιολογικά Ανάλεκτα εξ Αθηνών* VI (1973), 1ff.].

Marinos G. P., W. E. Petrascheck, *Λαύριον*, (Ινστιτούτον Γεωλογίας και ερευνών υπεδάφους, Γεωλογικαί και Γεωφυσικαί Μελέται, vol. IV, αρ. 1) Athens 1956, 125ff.

Μεγάλη Ελληνική Εγκυκλοπαίδεια (Pavlos Drandakis), Athens 1931, s.v. «Μακρόνησος».

Petris N., Η νήσος Ελένη, *Εστία*, vol. IZ΄ (1884), 125ff.

Spitaels P., The Early Helladic Period in Mine No 3 (Theatre Sector), *Thorikos* VIII (1972-1976), 151ff.

Spitaels P., Provatsa on Makronissos, *Αρχαιολογικά Ανάλεκτα εξ Αθηνών* XV (1982), 155ff.

Spitaels P., The Dawn of Silver Metallurgy in Greece, *The Illustrated London News*, July 1983, 63ff.

Spitaels P., I. Demolin, Θορικός, τα Προβάτσα και το Makronissos Project: Τα μεταλλεία της Μακρονήσου, *Πρακτικά Δ΄ Επιστημονικής Συνάντησης ΝΑ Αττικής*, Kalyvia, Attica 1993, 557ff.

Theocharis D. R., Νέοι "Κυκλαδικοί" τάφοι έν Ἀττική, *Νέον Ἀθήναιον*, vol. Α΄, iss. 2, Athens 1955, 287ff.

Andros

Cambitoglou A. (with the collaboration of S. Price, O. Segal, J. Papadopulos), *Guide to the Finds from the Excavations of the Geometric Town at Zagora*, Archaeological Museum of Andros, Athens 1981.

Kontoleon N. M., Ἀνασκαφαὶ Παλαιοπόλεως Ἄνδρου κατ' Αὔγουστον τοῦ 1956, *Αρχαιολογική Εφημερίς* 1964, 1-5.

Palaiokrassa L., Τα αρχαία γλυπτά της Συλλογής στη Χώρα της Άνδρου, *Αρχαιολογική Εφημερίς* 1980, 18-32.

Palaiokrassa-Kopitsa L., *Παλαιόπολις Ἄνδρου. Τα οικοδομικά από την προανασκαφική έρευνα*, Athens 1996.

Paschalis D. P., Ἡ Ἄνδρος, ἤτοι ἡ ἱστορία τῆς νήσου ἀπὸ τῶν ἀρχαιοτάτων χρόνων μέχρι τὴν καθ' ἡμᾶς, Α΄, Athens 1925.

Polemis D. I., Ιστορία της Άνδρου, *Πέταλον* (Παράρτημα 1), Andros 1981.

Saucius T., *Andros, Undersuchungen zur Geschichte und Topographie der Insel*, Sonderschriften des Österveichischen Archäologischen Instituts VIII, Vienna 1914.

Televantou Ch. A., *Ἄνδρος. Τα μνημεία και το Αρχαιολογικό Μουσείο*, Athens 1996.

Televantou Ch. A., Ἄνδρος. Το ιερό της Υψηλής, in N. Stampolidis (ed.), *Φως Κυκλαδικόν, τόμος τιμητικός για τον Νικόλαο Ζαφειρόπουλο*, Athens 1999, 132-139.

Televantou Ch. A., Στρόφιλας: ένας νεολιθικός οικισμός στην Άνδρο, *Άγκυρα, Δελτίο της Καϊρείου Βιβλιοθήκης*, vol. 1, Athens 2001, 203ff.

Gyaros

Brun P., *Les archipels égéens dans l'antiquité grecque (Ve-IIe siècles av. notre ère)*, Paris 1996, see Index s.v. Gyaros.

Bürchner L., A. Philippson, s.v. "Gyaros, Gyara, Gyarae", *Real-Encyclopädie der Klassischen Altertumswissenschaft* VII 2 (1912), lines 1954-1955.

Hallof Kl. (ed.), *Inscriptiones Graecae*, Fasc. VI, Pars I, Berolini, Novi Eboraci MM (2000), No 470.

Head B. V., *Ἱστορία τῶν νομισμάτων*, vol. 1: Εὐρώπη (transl. I. N. Svoronos, with completions), Athens 1898, 616.

Laumonier A., *Les figurines de terre cuite*, Exploration archéologique de Délos XXIII, Paris 1956, 106 (No 265), 121 (No 306).

Lobel E., D. Page (ed.), *Poetarum Lesbiorum fragmenta*, Oxford 1955, 293, No 11.

Mayor J. E. B., *Thirteen Satires of Juvenal*, vol. I, London 1886 (4th ed. rev.), 120-123.

Palaiokrassa-Kopitsa L., Ανασκάπτοντας την Αγορά της Αρχαίας Άνδρου, *Άγκυρα. Δελτίο της Καϊρείου Βιβλιοθήκης* 2, 2004, 128.

Rayet O., Inscriptions recueillies dans l'île de Samos, *Bulletin de l'École française d'Athènes*, No 9, Septembre 1871, 227-231 (see especially 230-231).

Stéphanos K., Ἐπιγραφαί Γυάρου καδ Θήρας, *Bulletin de correspondance hellénique* 1 (1877), 357-359.

Tenos

Barber R.L.N., *The Cyclades in the Bronze Age*, London 1987 (Greek translation, Athens 1994).

Etienne R. et aliii, *Ténos I: Le sanctuaire de Poseidon et d' Amphitrite*, Paris 1986.

Etienne R., *Ténos II: Ténos et les Cyclades du milieu du IVe siècle av. J-C au milieu du IIIe siècle après J-C*, Paris 1990.

Hadjianastasiou O., Το αρχαίο τείχος της Τήνου, *Αρχαιολογικόν Δελτίον* (1981), Χρονικά, Β2, 368.

Kourou N., Tenos - Xobourgo. From a Refuge Place to an Extensive Fortified Settlement, in M. Stamatopoulou - M. Yeroulanou (eds), *Excavating Classical Culture: Recent Archaeological Discoveries in Greece*, British Archaeological Reports, Int. Series 1031, Oxford 2002, 255-268.

Nigdelis P. M., *Πολίτευμα και κοινωνία των πόλεων των Κυκλάδων κατά την ελληνιστική και αυτοκρατορική εποχή*, Thessaloniki 1990.

Phoskolos M., Το Κάστρο της Τήνου ανά τους αιώνες, in C. Danousis (ed.), *Τήνος Εώα και Εσπερία. Πάνω Μέρη Τήνου. Πρακτικά Επιστημονικής Συνάντησης 4, 5, 6 Σεπτεμβρίου 1997*, Εταιρεία Τηνιακών Μελετών Πρακτικά Συνεδρίων 2, Athens 1999, 115-130.

Philaniotou O., Περιοδείες και Ανασκαφές στην Τήνο, *Αρχαιολογικόν Δελτίον*, Χρονικά (in press)

Simantoni-Bournia E., *La céramique grecque à reliefs. Ateliers insulaires, du VIIIe au VIe siècle avant J.-C.*, École Pratique des Hautes Études IVe Section, Sciences historiques et philologiques. Droz, Paris 2004.

Syros

Aron F., *Πτυχὲς τῆς ἀρχαίας Σύρου*, Athens 1979.

Aron F., Οι πρώτοι κάτοικοι της Σύρου, *Συριανά Γράμματα* 30, April 1995.

Barber R.L.N., A Tomb at Agios Loukas, Syros: Some Thoughts on Early-Middle Cycladic Chronology, *Journal of Mediterranean Archaeology and Anthropology* 1 (1981), 167-179.

Bossert E.-M., Kastri auf Syros: Vorbericht uber eine Untersuchung der praehistorischen Siedlung, *Αρχαιολογικόν Δελτίον* 22 (1967), 53-76.

Fragidis A. C., *Ἱστορία τῆς νήσου Σύρου*, Athens 1975.

Marthari M., Σύρος: Χαλανδριανή - Καστρί. Από την έρευνα και την προστασία στην ανάδειξη του αρχαιολογικού χώρου / Syros: Chalandriani - Kastri. From the Investigation and Protection to the Presentation of an Archaeological site, Ministry of the Aegean, Athens 1998.

Marthari M., Ο Χρήστος Τσούντας και η Σύρος: Από την ανασκαφή στη Χαλανδριανή έως την έκθεση των ευρημάτων στην Ερμούπολη, in M. E. Marthari (ed.), *1898-1998: Εκατό χρόνια από τις έρευνες του Χρήστου Τσούντα στη Σύρο. Διαλέξεις στο Πνευματικό Κέντρο Ερμούπολης, 31 Οκτωβρίου 1998*, Hellenic Ministry of Culture – XXI Ephorate of Prehistoric and Classical Antiquities – Ministry of the Aegean, Athens 2002, 101-144.

Marthari M., ΚΑ΄ Εφορεία Προϊστορικών και Κλασικών Αρχαιοτήτων, Σύρος: αρχαία πόλη Γαληνσσά, *Αρχαιολογικόν Δελτίον* 52 (1997) Χρονικά, 918-924.

Rambach J., *Kykladen I: Die frühe Bronzezeit Grab- und Siedlungsbefunde.* (Beiträge zur ur- und frühgeschichtlichen Archäologie des Mittelmeer-Kulturraumes 33), Bonn 2000.

Stephanos K., Ἐπιγραφαί τῆς νήσου Σύρου τὸ πλείστον ἀνέκδοτοι μετὰ τοπογραφικῶν καὶ ἱστορικῶν παρατηρήσεων περὶ τῆς Ἀρχαίας Σύρου, Athens 1875.

Travlos I., A. Kokkou, Ἑρμούπολη: Ἡ δημιουργία μιᾶς νέας πόλης στὴ Σύρο στὶς ἀρχὲς τοῦ 19ου αἰώνα, Athens 1980.

Tsountas Ch., Κυκλαδικά II, *Αρχαιολογική Εφημερίς* 1899, 73-134.

Mykonos

Ervin M., A Relief Pithos from Myconos, *Αρχαιολογικόν Δελτίον* 18 (1963) 1964, 37-75.

Sampson A., *Ftelia at Mykonos. A Late Neolithic Settlement in Cyclades*, University of the Aegean, Rhodes 2002.

Zapheiropoulou Ph., *Αρχαιολογικόν Δελτίον* 49 (1994) 1999, Χρονικά Β 2, 672.

Delos

Bruneau Ph., J. Ducat, *Guide de Délos*, Paris 1965.

Couilloud M. Th., *Les monuments funéraires de Rhénée*, Exploration archéologique de Délos XXX, Paris 1973. Compléments: *Bulletin de correspondance hellénique*, Suppléments 102, 1978, 879-873.

Exploration archéologique de Délos I (1909) - XLI (2003): Scientific series of volumes of the École française d' Athènes for publishing studies relating to Delos.

Hadjidakis P., *Δήλος*, Athens 2003.

Hermary A., Ph. Jockey, Fr. Queyrel, *Sculptures déliennes*, Paris 1996.

Marcadé J., *Au Musée de Délos. Étude sur la sculpture hellénistique en ronde bosse découverte dans l'île*, Paris 1969.

Tsakos C., *Delos – Mykonos. A guide to the history and archaeology*, Athens 1998.

Zapheiropoulou Ph., *Τά μνημεία τῆς Δήλου, Πρόσφατα έργα συντήρησης και στερέωσης* (Βιβλιοθήκη Αρχαιολογικής Εταιρείας, αρ. 114), Athens 1991.

Zapheiropoulou Ph., *Delos*, Athens 1998 with relevant bibliography (298-303).

Zaphiropoulou Ph., *La céramique «mélienne»*, Exploration archéologique de Délos XLI, Paris 2003.

Rheneia

Hadjidakis P., *Δήλος*, Athens 2003.
Zapheiropoulou Ph., *Αρχαιολογικόν Δελτίον* 49 (1994) 1999, Χρονικά Β2, Ρήνεια 673-676.

Kythnos

Kyrou A., D. Artemis, Ο κάπρος της Κύθνου. Αργυρά νομίσματα μιας νήσου των Κυκλάδων, *Νομισματικά Χρονικά* 17, 1998, 43-58 (see also A. Kyrou, D. Artemis, The Silver Coinage of Kythnos in the Early 5th Century BC, in *Studies in Greek Numismatics in the Memory of Martin Jessop Price*, London 1998, 233-236.
Mazarakis Ainian A., Επιφανειακές έρευνες στη νήσο Κύθνο: Το τείχος της αρχαίας Κύθνου, *Αρχαιολογική Εφημερίς* 1993, 217-253.
Mazarakis Ainian A., Επιφανειακές αρχαιολογικές έρευνες στην Κύθνο, *Πρακτικά της Αρχαιολογικής Εταιρείας* 1995, 137-209.
Mazarakis Ainian A., Επιγραφές από την Κύθνο, *HOROS* 10-12 (1992-98), 449-454.
Mendoni L., A. Mazarakis Ainian (eds), Κέα-Κύθνος: Ιστορικές και Αρχαιολογικές Έρευνες, *Πρακτικά Διεθνούς Επιστημονικού Συμποσίου, 22-25 Ιουνίου 1994*, Μελετήματα 27, Κέντρο Ελληνικής και Ρωμαϊκής Αρχαιότητας - Εθνικό Ίδρυμα Ερευνών, Athens 1998.
Ross L., *Reisen auf den griechischen Inseln des ägäischen Meeres* I, Stuttgart-Tübingen 1840, 105-124.
Sampson A. et al., The Mesolithic Settlement at Maroulas, Kythnos, *Mediterranean Archaeology and Archaeometry* 2 (2002), 45-67.
Sheedy K., The Origins of the Second Nesiotic League and the Defense of Kythnos, *Historia Zeitschrift für alte Geschichte* 45 (1996), 423-449.
Vallindas A., *Κυθνιακά*, Ἑρμούπολις 1882.
Vallindas A., *Ἱστορία τῆς νήσου Κύθνου*, Athens 1896.

Seriphos

Philaniotou O., Προϊστορικές μεταλλευτικές εγκαταστάσεις, *Η Καθημερινή, Επτά Ημέρες*, 27 Αυγούστου 2000, 8.
Ross L., *Reisen auf den griechischen Inseln des ägäischen Meeres* I, Stuttgart-Tübingen 1840, 134-146.
Samartzidou S., Η Σέριφος στην αρχαιότητα, *Η Καθημερινή, Επτά Ημέρες*, 27 Αυγούστου 2000, 6-7.
Samartzidou-Orkopoulou S., Z. Papadopoulou, Ανάδειξη-διαμόρφωση αρχαίων πύργων Σίφνου και Σερίφου, in *Η συμβολή του Υπουργείου Αιγαίου στην έρευνα και ανάδειξη του πολιτισμού του Αρχιπελάγους*, Athens 2001, 129-130.

Siphnos

Aston N. G., *Σίφνος. Αρχαίοι πύργοι*, Athens 1991.
Brock J. K., G. Mackworth Young, Excavations in Siphnos, *Annual of the British School at Athens* 44 (1949), 1-92.
Gion K. I., *Ἱστορία τῆς νήσου Σίφνου*, Hermoupolis 1876.
Matthäus H., Sifnos im Altertum, in G.A. Wagner, G. Weisgerber (eds), *Silber, Blei und Gold auf Sifnos: Prähistorische und antike Metalproduktion*, Bochum 1985, 17-58.
Papadopoulou Z., *Σιφνίων άστυ. Φιλολογικές, αρχαιολογικές και τοπογραφικές μαρτυρίες για την αρχαία πόλη της Σίφνου*, Athens 2002.
Papadopoulou Z., Ανάδειξη-διαμόρφωση πύργων Σίφνου, in *Η συμβολή του Υπουργείου Αιγαίου στην έρευνα και ανάδειξη του πολιτισμού του Αρχιπελάγους*, Athens 2001, 131.
Πρακτικά Α΄ Διεθνούς Σιφναϊκού Συμποσίου, Σίφνος 25-28 Ιουνίου 1998, Athens 2000.
Πρακτικά Β΄ Διεθνούς Σιφναϊκού Συμποσίου, Σίφνος 27-30 Ιουνίου 2002, Athens 2005.
Ross L., *Reisen auf den griechischen Inseln des ägäischen Meeres* I, Stuttgart-Tübingen 1840, 134-146.
Σίφνος, Ministry of the Aegean, Athens 1998.
Televantou Ch., Ayios Andreas on Sifnos: A Late Cycladic III Fortified Acropolis, in V. Karageorghis, C. E. Morris (eds), *Defensive Settlements of the Aegean and the Eastern Mediterranean after c. 1200 B.C.*, Nicosia 2001, 191-213.

Islets of the Western Cyclades

Hadjidaki N., Η Παναγία της Κιτριανής. Ένα άγνωστο βυζαντινό εκκλησάκι στη Σίφνο, *Πρακτικά Α΄ Διεθνούς Σιφναϊκού Συμποσίου*, vol. Β΄, Athens 2001, 197-213.
Pantou P., Z. Papadopoulou, Επιφανειακή έρευνα στις ακατοίκητες νησίδες Σεριφοπούλα και Κιτριανή, *Πρακτικά Β΄ Διεθνούς Σιφναϊκού Συμποσίου*, τ. Α΄, Αθήνα 2005, 61-70.
Reger G., s.v. «Kimolos» (496), in M. H. Hansen, Ch. H. Nielsen (eds) *An Inventory of Archaic and Classical Poleis*, Oxford 2004, 752.
Simosi A., Ένα ναυάγιο όψιμης ελληνιστικής περιόδου στην Κιτριανή της Σίφνου, *Πρακτικά Α΄ Διεθνούς Σιφναϊκού Συμποσίου*, vol. Α΄, Athens 2001, 463-467.

Paros

Berranger D., *Recherches sur l'histoire et la prosopographie de Paros à l'époque archaïque*, Clermont Ferrand 1992 (with complete bibliography until 1992).
Berranger D. - Auserve, *Paros II: prosopographie générale et étude historique du début de la période classique jusqu' à la fin de la période romaine*, Clermont - Ferrand 2000.
Costoglou-Despini A., *Προβλήματα της παριανής πλαστικής του 5ου αι. π.Χ.*, Thessaloniki 1979.
Karouzos Ch., *Ἡ Νίκη τῆς Πάρου, Μικρὰ κείμενα* (ed. V. Petrakos), Athens 1995, 150-153.
Rubensohn O., *Das Delion von Paros*, Wiesbaden 1962.
Tsountas Ch., Κυκλαδικά I, *Αρχαιολογική Εφημερίς* 16 (1898), lines. 155-161, 168-176.
Zapheiropoulos N., Αρχαϊκές κόρες της Πάρου, in H. Kyrieleis (ed.), *Archaische und klassische griechische Plastik. Akten des Internationalen Kolloquiums von 22.-25. April 1985 in Athen*, Mainz am Rhein 1986, 93-106.
Zapheiropoulou Ph., *Paros*, Athens 1998 (with bibliography).
Zapheiropoulou Ph., Recent Finds from Paros, in M. Stamatopoulou, M. Yeroulanou (eds), *Excavating Classical Culture*, British Archaeological Reports, Int. Series 1031, Oxford 2002, 281-284.
Zaphiropoulou Ph., Paros archaïque et son rôle dans la colonisation du nord de la mer Égée, in A. Avram, M. Babis (eds), *Civilisation grecque et cultures antiques périphériques, Hommage à P. Alexandrescu*, Bucarest 2000, 130-133.
Zaphiropoulou Ph., Ein Grabrelief aus Paros, in *Zona Archeologica*, S. Buzzi, D. Käch et alii (eds), *Festschrift für H. P. Isler*, Bonn 2001, 481-486.
Zaphiropoulou Ph., Un petit kouros parien, in *Identités et cultures dans le monde mediterranéen antique, Études réunies par Chr. Müller et Fr. Prost en l'honneur de Fr. Croissant*, Paris 2002, 103-112.
Zaphiropoulou Ph., Κορμός κόρης στο Μουσείο της Πάρου, in *Επιτύμβιον Gerhard Neumann*, Benaki Museum, 2nd Annex, Athens 2003, 91-99.

Antiparos

Hoepfner W., H. Schmidt, Mittelalterliche Städtegründungen auf den Kykladeninseln Antiparos und Kimolos, *Jahrbuch des Deutschen Archäologischen Instituts* 91 (1976), 291-309.
Tsountas Ch., Κυκλαδικά I, *Αρχαιολογική Εφημερίς* 16 (1898), lines 177-181.
Zapheiropoulos N., *Αρχαιολογικόν Δελτίον* 20 (1966) Χρονικά, 508.

Saliagos

Evans J. D., C. Renfrew, *Excavations at Saliagos near Antiparos*, London 1968.

Despotiko

Ernst Meyer, s.v. "Prepesinthus", *Real-Encyclopädie der Klassischen Altertumswissenschaft*, Suppl. X 1965, 666.
Kourayos Y., S. Detoratou, Πάρος, η αρχαιολογική έρευνα των τελευταίων δεκαετιών, *Περίαπτο* 2000, 47-49.
Kourayos Y., Ανάδειξη Αρχαιολογικών Χώρων της Πάρου και των μικρών νησίδων Δεσποτικό, Τσιμιντήρι, Στρογγυλό, in *Η συμβολή του Υπουργείο Αιγαίου στην έρευνα και ανάδειξη του πολιτισμού του Αρχιπελάγους*, Athens 2001, 108.
Kourayos Y., Δεσποτικό. Η Ανακάλυψη ενός νέου ιερού, in N. Chr. Stampolidis - A. Yannikouri (eds), *Το Αιγαίο στην Πρώιμη Εποχή του Σιδήρου. Πρακτικά του Διεθνούς Συμποσίου Ρόδος 1-4 Νοεμβρίου 2002*, Athens 2004, 437-450.
Kourayos Y., *Πάρος, Αντίπαρος: Ιστορία, Μνημεία, Μουσεία*, Athens 2004.
Kourayos Y., Despotiko, A Sanctuary Dedicated to Apollo, in M. Yeroulanou - M. Stamatopoulou (eds), *Architecture and Archaeology in the Cyclades*, Oxford 2006, 105-133.
Kourayos Y., B. Burns, Exploration of the archaic sanctuary of Mandra on Despotiko, *Bulletin de correspondance hellénique* 128.1 (2004), 133-174.
Petrocheilos I., Αρχαϊκό κεφάλι Κούρου από το Δεσποτικό, *Δωδώνη* 1985, 116.
Pliny, *Historia Naturalis* IV, ch. 66.
Zapheiropoulos N., *Αρχαιολογικόν Δελτίον* 16 (1960) Χρονικά, 246-247.

Naxos

Prehistoric times

Barber R.L.N., O. Hadjianastasiou, Mikre Vigla: A Bronze Age Settlement on Naxos, *Annual of the British School at Athens* 84 (1989), 64-161.
Barber R. L. N. *Cyclades in the Bronze Age*, London 1987 (Greek translation, Athens 1994).
Cosmopoulos M. V., *Η Νάξος και το κρητο-μυκηναϊκό Αιγαίο. Στρωματογραφία, κεραμική, οικονομική οργάνωση του Υστεροελλαδικού I-IIIB οικισμού της Γρόττας* (Series of publications of the periodical *Αρχαιογνωσία* No 3), Athens 2004.
Doumas C., *Early Bronze Age burial habits in the Cyclades, Studies in Mediterranean Archaeology*, Göteborg 1977.

Hadjianastasiou O., A Late Neolithic Settlement at Grotta, Naxos, in French, E. - K. Wardle (eds), *Problems in Greek Prehistory, Papers presented at the Centenary Conference of the British School of Archaeology at Athens, Manchester 1986*, Bristol 1988, 11-20.

Hadjianastasiou O., A Mycenaean Pictorial Vase from Naxos, in E. De Miro et alii. (eds), *Atti e Memorie del Secondo Congresso Internazionale di Micenologia, Roma-Napoli 1991*, Roma 1996, 1433-1441.

Lambinoudakis V., O. Philaniotou, 2001, The Town of Naxos at the End of the Late Bronze Age: the Mycenaean Fortification Wall, in V. Karageorghis, C. Morris (eds), *Defensive Settlements of the Aegean and the Eastern Mediterranean after c.1200 B.C. Proceedings of an International Workshop held at Trinity College Dublin, 7th-9th May, 1999*, Nicosia 2001, 157-169.

Philaniotou O., Naxos, Tsikniades: an Early Cycladic cemetery, in C. Renfrew, K. Boyle, G. Gavalas (eds), *Ορίζων. A Colloquium on the Prehistory of the Cyclades* (in press).

Philaniotou O., Ανασκαφές Νάξου, *Αρχαιολογικόν Δελτίον* 2001, Χρονικά (in press).

Vlachopoulos A., The LH IIIC Grotta Phase of Naxos. Its Synchronisms in the Aegean and its Non-synchronisms in the Cyclades, in S. Deger-Jalkotzy, M. Zavadil (eds), *LH IIIC Chronology and Synchronisms. Proceedings of the International Workshop held at the Austrian Academy of Sciences at Vienna*, Wien 2003, 217-234.

Zachos K., Observations on the Early Bronze Age Sealings from the Cave of Zas at Naxos, in C. Renfrew, K. Boyle, G. Gavalas (eds), *Ορίζων. A Colloquium on the Prehistory of the Cyclades*, (in press)

Historical times

Bournia E., Ανασκαφές Νάξου. Οι ανάγλυφοι πίθοι, Athens 1990.

Costa V., *Nasso dalle origini al V sec. a.C.*, 1997.

Kokkorou-Alevras G., Archaische Naxische Bildhauerei, *Antieke Plastik* 24, 1993 (1995), 37-138.

Kourou N., Ανασκαφή Νάξου. Το Νότιο νεκροταφείο, Athens 1999.

Lambinoudakis V., Αρχαία Νάξος, Ιστορία και Πολιτισμός, *Ναξιακά* I, 1985, 6-20.

Lambinoudakis V., s.v. «Νάξος», in the encyclopaedia *Πάπυρος-Λαρούς-Μπριτάνικα*.

Lambinoudakis V., N. Kontoleon, Ανασκαφή Νάξου, *Πρακτικά Αρχαιολογικής Εταιρείας* των ετών 1949-1995, Athens.

Lambrinoudakis V., Les ateliers de céramique géometrique et orientalisante de Naxos, in Rougemont, Cl. and G. (eds), *Les Cyclades. Matériaux pour une étude de géographie historique*, Lyon 1983, 165-175.

Lambinoudakis V., Veneration of Ancestors in Geometric Naxos, *Acta Atheniensia* 38 (1988), 235-246.

Lambrinoudakis V., Die Physiognomie der spätarchaischen und frühklassischen Naxischen Plastik, in H. Kyrieleis (ed.), *Archaische und Klassische Naxische Plastik* I, 1986, 107-117.

Lambinoudakis V., The Emergence of the City-state of Naxos in the Aegean, in M. Constanza Lentini (ed.), *The Two Naxos Cities. A Fine Link between the Aegean Sea and Sicily*, Athens 2001, 13-22.

Zapheiropoulou Ph., *Naxos. The monuments and the museum*, Athens 1988.

Lesser Cyclades

Broodbank C., *An Island Archaeology of the Early Cyclades*, Cambridge 2000.

Brun P., *Les archipels Égéens, dans l'antiquité grecque (Ve-IIe siècles av. notre ère)*, Institut des Sciences et Techniques de l'Antiquité. Centre de Recherches d'Histoire Ancienne, Vol. 157, Paris 1996.

Getz-Gentle P., *Stone Vessels of the Cyclades in the Early Bronze Age*, Pennsylvania 1996.

Marangou L., Amorgos and the islands around, in C. Renfrew, Chr. Doumas, L. Marangou, G. Gavalas (eds), *Keros, Dhaskalio Kavos. The Investigations of 1987-1988* (in press).

Philaniotou O., New Evidence for the Topography of Naxos in the Geometric Period, in M. Lentini (ed.), *Le due città di Naxos. Atti del Seminario di Studi, Giardini Naxos 29-31 Ottobre 2000*, Firenze-Milano 2004, 86-93.

Sotirakopoulou P., Early Cycladic Pottery from the Investigations of the 60s at Kavos-Daskalio, Keros. A Preliminary Report, in E. Álram-Stern (ed.), *Die ägäische Frühzeit, Band II. Die Frühbrozezeit in Griechenland*, Wien 2004, 1303-1342.

Thimme J., P. Preziosi (eds), *Art and Culture of the Cyclades in the Third Millennium B.C.*, Chicago and London 1977, 476, 512, 530, 586-588.

Yannouli V., Περιοδείες. Σχοινούσα, Φρούριο Προφήτη Ηλία, Ηρακλειά, Φρούριο Λειβαδιού, *Αρχαιολογικόν Δελτίον* 1991, 381-382.

Zapheiropoulou Ph., Ο Γεωμετρικός Οικισμός της Δονούσας, *Διαλέξεις 1986-1989*, Ίδρυμα Ν. Π. Γουλανδρή, Athens 1989, 43-54.

Zafeiropoulou Ph., Early Bronze Age cemeteries of the Kampos Group on Epano Kouphonissi, in C. Renfrew, K. Boyle, G. Gavalas (eds), *Ορίζων. A Colloquium on the Prehistory of the Cyclades*, University of Cambridge (in press).

Amorgos

Leventopoulou M., Female figurine from Minoa, Amorgos, in G. A. Papathanasopoulos (ed.), *Neolithic Culture in Greece*, N. P. Goulandris Foundation, Athens 1996, cat. No 245, 321.

Marangou L., Evidence for the Early Cycladic Period on Amorgos, in J. L. Fitton (ed.), *Cycladica. Studies in Memory of N. P. Goulandris*, London 1984, 99-103.

Marangou L., Κυκλαδικό ειδώλιο από την Μινώα Αμοργού, *Αρχαιολογική Εφημερίς* 1990 (1992), 159-176.

Marangou L., Νέες μαρτυρίες για τον Κυκλαδικό πολιτισμό στην Αμοργό, *Φηγός, Τιμητικός τόμος για τον καθηγητή Σ. Δάκαρη*, Ioannina 1994, 468-470.

Marangou L., s.v. «Amorgo», *Enciclopedia dell'arte antica*, Suppl. Sec. 1971-1994 (publ. 1995), 195-198 (history of Amorgos on the basis of the archaeological data).

Marangou L., *Αρχαιολογική Συλλογή Αμοργού, I. Μαρμάρινα Γλυπτά*, Athens 1999.

Marangou L., Μαρμάρινο κυκλαδικό αγαλμάτιο μουσικού από την Αμοργό, in N. Stampolidis (ed.), *Φως Κυκλαδικόν, τιμητικός τόμος στη μνήμη του Νίκου Ζαφειρόπουλου*, Athens 1999, 20-29.

Marangou L., *Αμοργός I. Η Μινώα, ο λιμήν και η μείζων περιφέρεια* (Βιβλιοθήκη της εν Αθήναις Αρχαιολογικής Εταιρείας, No 228), Athens 2002 (with full bibliography).

Marangou L., Minoa on Amorgos, in Stamatopoulou M., Yeroulanou M., *Excavating Classical Culture. Recent archaeological discoveries in Greece*, British Archaeological Reports Int. Series 1031, 2002, 295-316.

Marangou L., C. Renfrew, Ch. Doumas, G. Gavalas, *Markiani on Amorgos*, Annual of the British School at Athens, Suppl. 2005 (with extensive summary in Greek, in press).

Nigdelis P. M., *Πολίτευμα και κοινωνία των πόλεων των Κυκλάδων κατά την ελληνιστική και αυτοκρατορική εποχή*, Thessaloniki 1990 (with earlier bibliography).

Ios

Graindor P., Decret d'Ios, *Bulletin de correspondance hellénique* 27 (1903), 394-400.

Graindor P., Foulles d'Ios, *Bulletin de correspondance hellénique* 28 (1904), 308-333.

Mantis A., Υστεροαρχαϊκή επιτύμβια στήλη από την Ίο, in D. Pantermalis, M. Tiverios, E. Voutyras (eds), *Άγαλμα: Μελέτες για την αρχαία πλαστική προς τιμήν του Γιώργου Δεσπίνη*, Thessaloniki 2001, 67-78.

Marthari M. E., Σκάρκος, ένας Πρωτοκυκλαδικός οικισμός στην Ίο, in *Ίδρυμα Ν.Π. Γουλανδρή - Μουσείο Κυκλαδικής Τέχνης. Διαλέξεις 1986-1989*, Athens 1990, 97-100.

Marthari M. E., Από τον Σκάρκο στην Πολιόχνη: Παρατηρήσεις για την κοινωνικο-οικονομική ανάπτυξη των οικισμών της Πρώιμης Εποχής του Χαλκού στις Κυκλάδες και τα νησιά του βορειοανατολικού Αιγαίου, in Ch. Doumas, V. La Rosa (eds), *Η Πολιόχνη και η Πρώιμη Εποχή του Χαλκού στο Βόρειο Αιγαίο. Poliochni e l'antica età del Bronzo nell'Egeo settentrionale*, Athens 1997, 262-82.

Marthari M. E., Το Αρχαιολογικό Μουσείο της Ίου: Σύντομη περιήγηση στις αρχαιότητες της Ίου μέσω των εκθεμάτων του Μουσείου, ΚΑ΄ Εφορεία Προϊστορικών και Κλασικών Αρχαιοτήτων, Athens 1999.

Marthari M. E., Ίος: Από την Πρωτοκυκλαδική περίοδο στην ύστερη αρχαιότητα, *Καθημερινή, Επτά Ημέρες*, 3 August 2003, 3-6.

Marthari M. E., Ios, Archäologisches Museum: Skarkos, in *Kleinere Griechische Sammlungen: Neufunde aus Griechenland und der westlichen Türkei*, ed. I. Pini (CMS V, Supplementum 3), Berlin 2004.

Marthari M. E., Aspects of Pottery Circulation in the Cyclades During the Early EB II: Fine and Semi-fine Imported Ceramic Wares at Skarkos, Ios, in C. Renfrew, K. Boyle, G. Gavalas (eds), *Ορίζων. A Colloquium on the Prehistory of the Cyclades*, University of Cambridge 2004 (in press).

Nigdelis P. N., *Πολίτευμα και κοινωνία των πόλεων των Κυκλάδων κατά την ελληνιστική και αυτοκρατορική Εποχή*, Thessaloniki, 1990.

Sikinos

Burchner L., s.v. «Sikinos», *Real-Encyclopädie der Klassischen Altertumswissenschaft* E II, A.2, 1923, 2523-26.

Frantz A., H. Thompson, J. Travlos, The Temple of Apollo Pythios on Sikinos, *American Journal of Archaeology* 73 (1969), 397-422.

Pholegandros

Bechraki E., A. Vavylopoulou-Charitonidi, Το "ανέγγιχτο νησί": Μικρό χρονικό από την αρχαιότητα έως τις αρχές του 2ου αι., *Η Καθημερινή, Επτά Ημέρες, Φολέγανδρος*, 28 July 1996, 3-7.

Philaniotou O., Κάστελλος: μια προϊστορική θέση στη Φολέγανδρο, *Η Καθημερινή, Επτά Ημέρες*, 28 July 1996, 4.

Vasilopoulou V., Η Χρυσοσπηλιά, *Η Καθημερινή, Επτά Ημέρες, Φολέγανδρος*, 28 July 1996, 16-17.

Kimolos

Hoepfner W., H. Schmidt, Mittelalterliche Städtegründungen auf den Kykladeninseln Antiparos und Kimolos, *Jahrbuch des Deutschen Archäologischen Instituts* 91 (1976), 310-339.

Felten W., Ein geometrischer Krater aus Kimolos, *ΣΤΗΛΗ, τόμος εις μνήμην Ν. Κοντολέοντος*, Athens 1980, 394-401.

Insriptiones Graecae XII, 3, 1259· XII, 9, 44.

Journal of Hellenic Studies 74 (1954), 165.

Jacobsen T., P. M. Smith, Two Kimolian Dikast Decrees from Geraistos in Euboia, *Hesperia. Journal of the American School of Classical Studies at Athens* 37 (1968), 184-197.

Kontoléon N., Eine Grabstele aus Kimolos, in F. Eckstein (ed.), *Theoria: Festschrift für H. Schuchhart*, Baden Baden 1959, 129-137.

Kontoleon N., Ἐπιτύμβιος στήλη τῆς Κιμώλου, *Κιμωλιακά* Β´ (1972), 3-21.

Moustakas Ch., Kimolos, *Athenische Mittheilungen* 69/70 (1954/55), 153-158.

Polychronakou-Sgouritsa N., Η Κίμωλος στη μυκηναϊκή Περίοδο, *Αρχαιολογικόν Δελτίον* 49/50 (1994-95) Μελέτες, 1-11.

Zapheiropoulou Ph., *Αρχαιολογικόν Δελτίον* 21 (1966) Χρονικά, 389-393.

Zapheiropoulou Ph., Περὶ τοῦ ἀρχαίου νεκροταφείου εἰς τὸν ὅρμον Λίμνης τῆς Κιμώλου, *Κιμωλιακά* Γ´ (1973), 89.

Melos

Hadjidakis I., *Ἡ ἱστορία τῆς νήσου Μήλου*, Athens 1972².

Jacobstahl P., *Die melischen Reliefs*, Berlin-Wilmersdorf 1931.

Karouzos Ch., An Early Classical Disc Relief from Melos, *Journal of Hellenic Studies* 71 (1951), 96-110.

Kontoleon N., Ἀρχαϊκά γλυπτά της Μήλου, *Επιστημονική Επετηρίς Φιλοσοφικής Σχολής καί Πανεπιστημίου Αθηνών* 1958, 218-35.

Pasquier A., *La Vénus de Milo et les Aphrodites du Louvre*, Paris 1985.

Renfrew C. (ed.), *An Island Polity*, Cambridge 1982 (with earlier bibliography).

Televantou Ch., The Early Cycladic Cemetery at Rivari on Melos, in C. Renfrew, K. Boyle, G. Gavalas (eds), *Ορίζων. A Colloquium on the Prehistory of the Cyclades*, University of Cambridge (in press).

Trianti I., Ελληνιστικά αγάλματα της Μήλου, in O. Palagia, W. D. E. Coulson (eds), *Regional Schools in Hellenistic Sculpture. Proceedings of the International Conferecne held at the American School of Classical Studies at Athens*, 1996, Oxford 1998, 167-175

Trianti I., Τρία ανάγλυφα από τη Μήλο, in *Επιτύμβιον Gerhardt Neumann*. Benaki Museum. 2nd Annexe, 2003, 163-167.

Yerousi E., *Μήλος. Τα χριστιανικά μνημεία του νησιού*, Athens 1999.

Zapheiropoulou Ph., *Προβλήματα της μηλιακής αγγειογραφίας*, Athens 1985.

Zapheiropoulou Ph., *La céramique «mélienne»*, Exploration archéologique de Délos, XLI, Paris 2003.

Thera

Prehistoric times

Doumas C. (ed.), *Thera and the Aegean World* I, London 1978, II, London 1980.

Doumas C., *Thera: Pompeii of Prehistoric Aegean*, London 1983.

Hardy D. et alii (eds), *Thera and the Aegean World*, vols I-III, The Thera Foundation, London 1990.

Marinatos S., *Ἀνασκαφαί Θήρας*, Excavations at Thera I-VII, Athens 1968-1976.

Michailidou A., Ἡ μελέτη τῶν ὀρόφων στὰ κτήρια τοῦ οἰκισμοῦ (Βιβλιοθήκη τῆς ἐν Ἀθήναις Ἀρχαιολογικῆς Ἑταιρείας ἀρ. 212), Athens 2001.

Doumas Ch. (ed.), *Ἀκρωτήρι Θήρας 1967-1987. Εἴκοσι χρόνια ἔρευνας: Συμπεράσματα - Προβλήματα - Προοπτικές*, Ἡμερίδα γιὰ τὸ Ἀκρωτήρι 19/12/ 1987, Athens 1992.

Doumas Ch., *The Wall-Paintings of Thera*, "Petros M. Nomikos" Foundation, Athens 1992.

Palyvou C., *Ἀκρωτήρι Θήρας. Οἰκοδομικὴ τέχνη* (Βιβλιοθήκη τῆς ἐν Ἀθήναις Ἀρχαιολογικῆς Ἑταιρείας ἀρ. 183), Athens 1999.

Sherratt S. (ed.), *The Wall-paintings of Thera*, Thera Foundation Petros M. Nomikos, Athens 2000.

Sotirakopoulou P., *Ἀκρωτήρι Θήρας: Ἡ Νεολιθικὴ καὶ ἡ Πρώιμη Ἐποχὴ τοῦ Χαλκοῦ ἐπὶ τῇ βάσει τῆς κεραμεικῆς* (Βιβλιοθήκη τῆς ἐν Ἀθήναις Ἀρχαιολογικῆς Ἑταιρείας, ἀρ. 191), Athens 1999.

Televantou A. Ch., *Ἀκρωτήρι Θήρας. Οἱ τοιχογραφίες τῆς Δυτικῆς Οἰκίας* (Βιβλιοθήκη τῆς ἐν Ἀθήναις Ἀρχαιολογικῆς Ἑταιρείας, ἀρ. 182), Athens 1994.

Historical times

Efstathiou M., Το νεκροταφείο της αρχαίας Οίας στη Θήρα. Ταφές καύσης, in N. Chr. Stampolidis (ed.), *Πρακτικά του Συμποσίου «Καύσεις στην Εποχή του Χαλκού και την Πρώιμη Εποχή του Σιδήρου»*, Ρόδος, 29 Απριλίου-2 Μαΐου 1999, Athens 2001, 301-320.

Hiller von Gaertringen F., *Thera. Untersuchungen, Vermessungen und Ausgrabungen in den Jahren 1895-1902*, I-IV, Berlin 1899-1909.

Pfuhl E., Der archaische Friedhof am Stadtberge von Thera, *Mitteilungen des Deutschen Archäologischen Instituts. Athenische Abteilung* XXVIII (1903), 1-290.

Sigalas Ch. I., Un sanctuaire d'Aphrodite à Thera, *Kernos* 13 (2000), 241-245.

Sperling J. W., Thera and Therasia, *Αρχαίες ελληνικές πόλεις* 22, Αθήνα 1973.

Stavridi A., Η ρωμαϊκή τέχνη στη Θήρα: πορτραίτα και αγάλματα, in I. M. Danezis (ed.), *Σαντορίνη*, Athens 2001, 241-245.

Trianti I., Νέα αρχαϊκά γλυπτά από τη Θήρα, in N. Chr. Stampolidis (ed.), *Φως Κυκλαδικόν, τιμητικός τόμος στη μνήμη του Νίκου Ζαφειρόπουλου*, Athens 1999, 190-199.

Anaphe

Guliano A., *Il commercio dei sarcophagi attici*, 1962, αρ. 127.

Hiller von Gaertringen F., *Die Insel Thera in Altertum und Geqenwart mit Ausschluss der Nekropolen*, Berlin 1899, 351-358.

Ross L., *Reisen auf den griechischen Inseln des ägäischen Meeres* I, Stuttgart-Tübingen 1840, 64-65.

Televantou A. Ch., *Αρχαιολογικόν Δελτίον* 52 (1997), Χρονικά, Β3, 954-955.

Televantou A. Ch., Εργασίες διαμόρφωσης αρχαιολογικών χώρων Αγ. Ανδρέα Σίφνου, Υψηλής Άνδρου και Ανάφης, in *Η συμβολή του Υπουργείου Αιγαίου στην έρευνα και ανάδειξη του πολιτισμού στους Αρχιπελάγους*, Ministry of the Aegean 2001, 101-103.

Zapheiropoulou Ph., *Αρχαιολογικόν Δελτίον* 26 (1968), Χρονικά, Β2, 382.

Dodecanese

Milesian islands

Agathonisi

Herbst R., s.v. «Tragia», *Real-Encyclopädie der Klassischen Altertumswissenschaft* II, 6 (1937), 1895.

Kotorros C., *Αγαθονήσι*, Athens 1995.

Rehm A., *Die Milesischen Inseln*, Milet II 2, Berlin 1929, 22.

Skandalidis M., *Ο νησιωτικός μικρόκοσμος του Δωδεκανησιακού Αρχιπελάγους*, Athens 1994.

Triantaphyllidis P., Αρχαιολογικοί περίπατοι στο Αγαθονήσι, *ΙΓ´ Πολιτιστικό Συμπόσιο Στέγης Γραμμάτων και Τεχνών Δωδεκανήσου*, Λειψοί 27-29 August 2003 (proceedings in press).

Volanakis I., Τα νησιά Αγαθονήσι και Αρκιοί της Δωδεκανήσου και τα μνημεία των, *Πατμιακές Σελίδες* 26 (1990), 18-23· 27 (1991), 20-22.

Arkioi, Marathi

Hope Simpson R., J. F. Lazenby, *Annual of the British School at Athens* 65 (1970), 51.

Michalaki-Kollia M., Αρχαιότητες σε λιλιπούτεια νησιά, *ΙΓ´ Πολιτιστικό Συμπόσιο Στέγης Γραμμάτων και Τεχνών Δωδεκανήσου*, Leipsoi 27-29 August 2003 (proceedings in press).

Pikoulas Y. A., Argiae: Αρκίτις-Αρκιοί Δωδεκανήσου, *HOROS* 13 (1999), 201-211.

Patmos

Haussoullier R., Les îlles milésiennes Leros-Lepsia-Patmos-Les Korsiae, *Revue de philologie, de littérature et d'histoire ancienne* 26 (1902), 131ff.

Hope Simpson R., J. F. Lazenby, Notes from the Dodecanese, *The Annual of the British School at Athens* 65 (1970), 48-51.

Manganaro G., Le Iscrizioni delle isole Milesie, *Annuario della Scuola Archeologica di Atene* 41-42 (1963-64), 329-346.

Pace B., Ricordi classici dell'isola di Patmos, *Annuario della Scuola Archeologica di Atene* 1 (1914), 370-372.

Papachristodoulou I., A. Dreliosi-Irakleidou, Τα ιωνικά νησιά της βόρειας Δωδεκανήσου στην αρχαιότητα, *ΙΓ´ Πολιτιστικό Συμπόσιο Στέγης Γραμμάτων και Τεχνών Δωδεκανήσου*, Leipsoi 27-29 August 2003 (proceedings in press).

Rehm A., *Die Milesischen Inseln*, Milet II 2, Berlin 1929, 23-24.

Ross L., *Reisen auf den griechishen Inseln des Ägäischen Meeres*, II, Stuttgart 1843, 123-139.

Schmidt J., s.v. «Patmos», *Real-Encyclopädie der Klassischen Artertumswissenschaft* 18 (1949), 2174-2191.

Leipsoi

Bean E. G., J. M. Cook, The Carian Coast III, *The Annual of the British School at Athens* 52 (1957), 135-8.

Bürchner L., s.v. «Lepsia», *Real-Encyclopädie der Klassischen Artertumswissenschaft* 12 (1925), 2070.

Dreliossi-Herakleidou A., Λειψία: το νησί των Λειψών στην αρχαιότητα, *ΙΓ΄ Πολιτιστικό Συμπόσιο Στέγης Γραμμάτων και Τεχνών Δωδεκανήσου*, Λειψοί 27-29 Αυγούστου 2003 (proceedings in press).

Hope Simpson R., J. F. Lazenby, Notes from the Dodecanese II, *The Annual of the British School at Athens* 65 (1970), 51-52.

Manganaro G., Le Iscrizioni delle isole Milesie, *Annuario della Scuola Archeologica di Atene*, 41-42 (1963-4), 317-329.

Rehm A., *Die Milesischen Inseln*, Milet II 2, Berlin 1929, 22-23.

Volanakis I., *Ιστορία και μνημεία των Λειψών Δωδεκανήσου*, Rhodes 2002.

Pharmakonisi

Dreliossi A., *Αρχαιολογικόν Δελτίον* 49 (1994) Χρονικά, 798-799.

Manganaro G., Le Iscrizioni delle isole Melesie, *Annuario della Scuola Archeologica di Atene* 41-41 (1963-4), 294.

Rehm A., *Die Milesischen Inseln*, Milet II 2, Berlin 1929, 21-22.

Schmidt J., s.v. «Pharmakussa», *Real-Encyclopädie der Klassischen Altertumswissenschaft* 19 (1938).

Skandalidis M., *Ο νησιωτικός μικρόκοσμος του Δωδεκανησιακού αρχιπελάγους*, Athens 1994, 39-42.

Leros

Bean E. G., J. M. Cook, The Carian Coast III, *The Annual of the British School at Athens* 52 (1957), 134-5.

Benson J., *Ancient Leros*, Durham 1963.

Bürchner L., s.v. «Leros», *Real-Encyclopädie der Klassischen Altertumswissenschaft* 12 (1925), 2094-2098.

Dreliossi-Herakleidou A., M. Michailidou, *Λέρος: από την Προϊστορία έως τον Μεσαίωνα* (in press, publ. Archaeological Receipts Fund).

Haussoullier R., Les îlles milésiennes Leros-Lepsia-Patmos-Les Korsiae, *Revue de philologie, de littérature et d'histoire anciennes* 26 (1902), 125-143.

Hope Simpson P., J. F. Lazenby, Notes from the Dodecanese II, *The Annual of the British School at Athens* 65 (1970), 52-54.

Manganaro G., Le Iscrizioni delle isole Melesie, *Annuario della Scuola Archeologica di Atene»*, 41-42 (1963-4), 296-317.

Oikonomopoulos D., *Λεριακά, ήτοι χωρογραφία τῆς νήσου Λέρου*, Κάϊρο καὶ Ἀθῆναι 1888.

Ross L., *Reisen auf den griechishen Inseln des Ägäischen Meeres*, II, Stuttgart 1843, 116-123.

Rehm A., *Die Milesischen Inseln*, Milet II 2, Berlin 1929, 24-26.

Sampson A., *Η Νεολιθική περίοδος στα Δωδεκάνησα*, Athens 1987, 87-92, 109-113.

Kalymnos, Telendos, Pserimos

Bean E. G., J. M. Cook, The Carian Coast III, *The Annual of the British School at Athens* 52 (1957), 127-133.

Bürchner L., s.v. «Kalymna», *Real-Encyclopädie der Klassischen Altertumswissenschaft* 10 (1919), 1768-1771.

Diamantis N., Μια πρώτη παρουσίαση των αρχαιολογικών ανασκαφών στο Δάμο Καλύμνου, *Καλυμνιακά Χρονικά* 1999, 301-312.

Dreliossi A., s.v. «Calimno», *Enciclopedia dell'arte antica, secondo supplemento 1971-1994*, 820-823.

Koukoulis G., *Κάλυμνα της Ιστορίας*, Αθήνα 1980.

Lissi E., s.v. «Calimno», *Enciclopedia dell'arte antica*, II, Roma 1959, 275-276.

Maiuri A., Esplorazione di grotte con avanzi preistorici nell'isola di Calimno, *Clara Rhodos* I (1928), 104-117.

Newton C. T., *Travels and Discoveries in the Levant*, London 1865, 226-227, 285 ff.

Paton W. R., Insriptions de Myndos, *Bulletin de Correspondance Hellénique* 12 (1888), 282-3, αρ. 7.

Ross L., *Reisen auf den griechishen Inseln des Aegaeischen Meeres*, Stuttgart, II, 1843, 92-115.

Segre M., Relazione preliminare sulla prima campagna di scavo nell'isola di Calino, *Memorie* III (1938), 33-55.

Segre M., Tituli Calymnii, *Annuario della Scuola Archeologica di Atene* 22-23, Nuova Serie VI-VII (1944-45).

Zervoudaki E., Kalymnos, in E. Melas (ed.), *Die griechischen Inseln*, Köln 1976, 240-263.

Kos

Herzog R., P. Schatzmann, *Kos I. Asklepieion*, Berlin 1932.

Kantzia Ch., Recent Archaeological Finds from Kos. New Indications for the Site of Kos-Meropis, in S. Dietz, I. Papachristodoulou (eds), *Archaeology in the Dodecanese*, Copenhagen 1988, 175-183.

Kantzia Ch., C. Kouzeli, Εργαστήριο παραγωγής χρωμάτων στην αρχαία αγορά της Κω. Το αιγυπτιακό μπλε, *Αρχαιολογικά Ανάλεκτα εξ Αθηνών* XX (1987), 211-238.

Kantzia Ch., Το ιερό του Απόλλωνα στην Αλάσαρνα της Κω, *Αρχαιολογικόν Δελτίον* 39 (1984) Μελέτες, 140-162.

Kokkorou-Alevra G., Πανεπιστημιακή ανασκαφή στο Ιερό του Απόλλωνα στην Καρδάμαινα (αρχαία Αλάσαρνα) της Κω: ένδεκα χρόνια ανασκαφικής έρευνας in G. Kokkorou-Alevra, A.A. Lemou, E. Simantoni-Bournia, *Ιστορία, Τέχνη, Αρχαιολογία της Κω* (Publications of the periodical *Αρχαιογνωσία*, No 1), Athens 2001, 91-107.

Livadioti M., G. Rocco, *La presenza italiana nel Dodecaneso tra il 1912 e il 1948. La ricerca archeologica, la conservazione, le scelte progettuali*, Atene 1997, 77-188.

Marketou T., Marine Style Pottery from the Seraglio in Kos, *Annual of the British School at Athens* 82 (1987), 165-169.

Morricone L., Scavi e ricerce a Coo (1935-1943). Relazione preliminare, *Bolletino d'Arte* 1950, 54-75, 219-331.

Morricone L., Eleona e Langada. Sepolcreti della tarda età del Bronzo, *Annuario della Scuola Archeologica di Atene* 43-44, N.S. 27-28 (1965-66), 5-311.

Morricone L., Sepolture della prima età del Ferro a Coo, *Annuario della Scuola Archeologica di Atene* 56, N.S. 40 (1978), 6-427.

Preliminary conclusions on researches conducted by the XXII Ephorate of Prehistoric and Classical Antiquities are published in the Χρονικά of the *Αρχαιολογικού Δελτίου* from 1980 onwards.

Skerlou E., Ένα ιερό της γεωμετρικής και αρχαϊκής περιόδου στην περιοχή Ηρακλής του Ψαλιδιού, in N. Stampolidis, A. Yannikouri (eds), *Το Αιγαίο στην Πρώιμη Εποχή του Σιδήρου, 1100-600 π.Χ., Ρόδος 1-4 Νοεμβρίου 2002*, Athens 2004, 177-188.

Stampolidis N., *Ο βωμός του Διονύσου στην Κω*, Athens 1987.

Swerwin-White S. M., *Ancient Cos. An Historical Study from the Dorian Settlement to the Imperial Period*, Hypomnemata 51, Göttingen 1978.

Astypalaia

Astypalaia (Chora), in *The Princeton Encyclopedia of Classical Sites*, 1976, 105-106.

Dawkins R. M., A. J. B. Wace, Notes from the Sporades, *Annual of the British School at Athens* 12 (1905-6), 151ff.

Doumas Ch., *Αρχαιολογικόν Δελτίον* 30 (1975), Χρονικά Β2, 372.

Hope Simpson R., J. F. Lazemby, Notes from the Dodecanese III, *Annual of the British School at Athens* 68 (1973), 156-157 (with earlier bibliography).

Michalaki-Kollia M., Céramique incisée de tradition géométrique, trouvée dans l'ile d'Astypalée, in S. Dietz, I. Papachristodoulou (eds), *Archaeology in the Dodecanese*, Copenhagen 1988, 225-243, with earlier bibliography.

Michalaki-Kollia M., Μουσείο Αστυπάλαιας, *Αρχαιολογία* 87 (2003), 101.

Michalaki-Kollia M., Αρχαίες λατρείες στην Αστυπάλαια, *ΙΑ΄ Πολιτιστικό Συμπόσιο της Στέγης Γραμμάτων και Τεχνών Δωδεκανήσου, Αστυπάλαια*, 26-29 August 1999, with supplementary bibliography (in press).

Oberhumme E., *Real-Encycopädie der Klassischen Altertumswissenschaft* II 2 (1896), 1873-1875.

Pharmakidou E., Καύσεις στην Αστυπάλαια, in N. Chr. Stampolidis (ed.), *Καύσεις στην Εποχή του Χαλκού και στην Πρώιμη Εποχή του Σιδήρου, Rhodes, 29 April-2 May 1999*, Athens 2001, 321-330.

Zervoudaki I., *Αρχαιολογικόν Δελτίον* 26 (1971), Χρονικά Β2, 549· 27 (1972), Χρονικά Β2, 676ff.

Syrna

Della Seta A., *Bollettino d'arte* 4 (1924-5), 87-88.

Michalaki-Kollia M., Αρχαιότητες σε λιλιπούτεια νησιά, *ΙΓ΄ Πολιτιστικό Συμπόσιο Στέγης Γραμμάτων και Τεχνών Δωδεκανήσου. Λειψοί, 27-29 Αυγούστου 2003* (in press).

Touratsoglou I., A. Dellaporta, Το ναυάγιο Σύρνα I/2000: "Θησαυρός" Αντωνιανών των χρόνων του Διοκλητιανού, *Το νόμισμα στα Δωδεκάνησα και στην Μικρασιατική τους Περαία. Κως, 30 Μαΐου-2 Ιουνίου 2003*, Αρχαιολογικό Ινστιτούτο Αιγαιακών Σπουδών (proceedings in press).

Nisyros

Bean G. E., J. M. Cook, The Carian Coast III, *The Annual of the British School at Athens* 52 (1957), 118-119.

Buchholz H. G., E. Althaus, *Nisyros, Giali, Kos*, Mainz 1982, 14-20.

Dawkins R., A. Wace, Notes from the Sporades, *The Annual of the British School at Athens* 12 (1905-1906), 165-171.

Filimonos-Tsopotou M., Νισυριακά I, *Αρχαιολογικόν Δελτίον* 35 (1980), 60-86.

Herbst R., s.v. «Nisyros», *Real-Encyclopädie der Klassischen Altertumswissenschaft* XVII 1 (1936), 761-767.

Jacopi G., Scavi e ricerche di Nisiro, *Clara Rhodos* VI-VII, 469-552.
Oikonomaki R., *Νίσυρος. Ιστορία και αρχιτεκτονική*, Athens 2001.
Pantelidi P. A., Περὶ τῶν ἀρχαίων θειούχων Θερμῶν ἐν Νισύρῳ τοῦ Ἀρχιπελάγους, *Bulletin de correspondence hellénique* 15 (1891), 488-490.
Papacostas V., Ἱστορία τῆς Νισύρου, *Νισυριακά* 3 (1969), 49-141· 4 (1972), 95-238.
Papachristodoulou I., Σχέσεις Νισύρου και Ρόδου στην αρχαιότητα. Ο δήμος Νισυρίων στα πλαίσια της ενιαίας ροδιακής πολιτείας, *Νισυριακά* 12 (1993), 39-50.
Ross L., *Reisen auf griechischen Inseln des Aegaischen Meeres* II, Stuttgart 1843, 67-81.
Sampson A., *Η νεολιθική κατοίκηση στο Γυαλί Νισύρου*, Athens 1988.

Telos

Bent T., The Islands of Telos and Karpathos, *Journal of Hellenic Studies* 6 (1885), 233-235.
Charitonidis S. I., Δύο νέαι τηλιακαὶ ἐπιγραφαί, *Ἀρχαιολογικόν Δελτίον* 16 (1960), 94-100.
Dawkins P. M., A. Wace, Notes from the Sporades», *The Annual of the British School at Athens* 12 (1905-1906), 159-165.
Fiehn, s.v. «Telos», *Real-Encyclopädie der Klassischen Altertumswissenschaft* V (1934), 427-431.
Filimonos M., *Ἀρχαιολογικόν Δελτίον* 51 (1996) Χρονικά, 693-697.
Hoepfner W., M. Filimonos, Telos. Eine Stadt mit Turmhäusern, in W. Hoepfner (ed.), *Geschichte des Wohnens* 1, Stuttgart 1999, 170-189.
Hope Simpson R., J. F. Lazenby, Notes from the Dodecanese II, *The Annual of the British School at Athens* 65 (1970), 65-68.
Kollias I., Ἰχνογράφημα τῆς Τήλου, *Δωδεκανησιακά Χρονικά* Γ´ (1974), 1-32.
Koutelaki Ch., *Τῆλος*, Athens 1988.
Sampson A., Μινωικά από την Τήλο, *Αρχαιολογικά Ανάλεκτα εξ Αθηνών* 13 (1980), 68-73.
Susini G., Supplemento epigrafico di Caso, Scarpanto, Saro, Calchi, Alimnia e Tilo, *Annuario di Scuola Archeologica di Atene* 41-42 (1963-1964), 261-292.

Syme

Chaviaras D., F. Hiller v. Gaertringen, Inschriften von Syme, Teutlussa und Rhodos, I. Syme, II. Teutlussa, in *Jahreshefte des Österreichischen Archäologischen Institutes*, Band VII, Βιέννη 1904, 81-92.
Farmakidou E., Η προϊστορική περίοδος στη Σύμη, in A. Vlachopoulos, K.Birtacha (eds), *Αργοναύτης. Τιμητικός τόμος για τον καθηγητή Χρίστο Γ. Ντούμα*, Athens 2003, 292-299.
Grigoropoulos M., *Ἡ νῆσος Σύμη. Πραγματεία ἀπὸ γεωγραφικήν, ἱστορικὴν καὶ στατιστικὴν ἔποψιν*, Athens 1877.
Hope Simpson R., J. F. Lazenby, Notes from the Dodecanese, *The Annual of the British School at Athens* 57 (1962), 154-175.
Hope Simpson R., J. F. Lazenby, Notes from the Dodecanese II, *The Annual of the British School at Athens* 65 (1970), 47-77.
Maiuri A., Viaggio di esplorazione in Caria. Parte II-B, *Annuario della Scuola Archeologica di Atene e delle Missioni Italiane in Oriente* 4-5 (1921-22), 1924, 424-459.
Papachristodoulou Ch., *Ἡ ἱστορία τῆς Ρόδου. Ἀπὸ τοὺς προϊστορικοὺς χρόνους ἕως τὴν ἐνσωμάτωσῃ τῆς Δωδεκανήσου*, Athens 1972.
Ross L., *Reisen auf den griechisen Inseln*. Band III, Stuattgart und Tübingen 1845.
Sampson A., *Η Νεολιθική Περίοδος στα Δωδεκάνησα*, Athens 1987.

Rhodes

Αρχαία Ρόδος-2400 χρόνια, Σύντομος Οδηγός (publ. Hellenic Ministry of Culture – XXII Ephorate of Prehistoric and Classical Antiquities), Athens 1993.
Benzi M., *Rodi e la civiltà micenea* (Incunabula Graeca. No XCIV), Roma 1990.
Constantinopoulos G., *Ἀρχαία Ρόδος*, Athens 1986.
Dietz S., I. Papachristodoulou (eds), *Archaeology in the Dodecanese*, Copenhagen 1988.
Enciclopedia dell Arte Antica, s.v. «Camiro, Ialiso, Rodi» (1959-1965), Secondo Supplemento IV (1996), s.v. «Rodi» και «Rodia Arte Ellenistica».
Höpfner W., E. L. Schwandner, *Haus und Stadt im Klassischen Griechenland*. 2, München-Berlin 1994².
Karouzos Ch., *Ρόδος*, Athens 1973².
Knell H., *Die Nike von Samothrake*, Stuttgart 1997.
Marketou T., Excavations at Trianda (Ialysos) on Rhodes: New Evidence for the Late Bronze Age I Period, *Atti della Accademia Nazionale dei Lincei. Rendiconti*. s. IX, vol. IX, Fasc. 1, Rome 1998, 39-82.
Marketou T., Ασώματος Ρόδου: Τα μεγαρόσχημα κτήρια και οι σχέσεις τους με το βορειοανατολικό Αιγαίο, in Ch. G. Doumas, V., La Rosa (eds), *Η Πολιόχνη και η Πρώιμη Εποχή του Χαλκού στο Βόρειο Αιγαίο. Poliochni e l'antica età del Bronzo nell'Egeo settentrionale*, Athens 1997, 395-413.
Papachristodoulou Ch., *Ιστορία της Ρόδου*, Athens 1997.
Sampson A., *Η Νεολιθική περίοδος στα Δωδεκάνησα*, Athens 1987.

Chalke, Alimnia

Antoniou E., Ἐπισκόπηση τῆς Χάλκης τῆς Δωδεκανήσου κατὰ τὴν ἀρχαιότητα, *Δωδεκανησιακά Χρονικά*, vol. Ε´, 1976, 97-150.
Fraser P. M., G. E. Bean, *The Rhodian Peraea and Islands*, Oxford and London 1954, 144-145.
Hope-Simpson R., J. F. Lazenby, Notes from the Dodecanese III, *The Annual of the British School at Athens* 68 (1973), 156-157.
Inscriptiones Graecae XII,1, 158-161 ap. 956-976.
Jacopi G., La Necropoli di Pontamo (Calchi), *Clara Rhodos* II, 117-164.
Katsioti A., Το Ευρετήριο Βυζαντινών Τοιχογραφιών Χάλκης Δωδεκανήσου, in *Δέκατο Τέταρτο Συμπόσιο Βυζαντινής και Μεταβυζαντινής Αρχαιολογίας και Τέχνης, Περιλήψεις Εισηγήσεων και Ανακοινώσεων, Αθήνα 22, 23 & 24 Ἀπριλίου 1994*, Athens 1994, 19-20.
Papachristodoulou I. Ch., *Οι Αρχαίοι Ροδιακοί Δήμοι*, Athens 1989, 43-44.
Real-Encyclopädie der Klassischen Altertumswissenschaft III (1899), s.v. «Chalke» (Bürchner), 2066.
Sampson A., *Η Νεολιθική περίοδος στα Δωδεκάνησα*, Athens 1987, 79-86, 106 (Alimia), 113-114 (Chalke).
Sampson A., *Ἀρχαιολογικόν Δελτίον* 35 (1980), B2 Χρονικά, 561-563.
Stephanidou A., Χάλκη, Κάστρο Χωριού. Αλιμνιά, Κάστρο Αλιμνιάς, in *Ενετοί και Ιωαννίτες Ιππότες. Δίκτυα οχυρωματικής αρχιτεκτονικής*, Athens 2001, 221-224.
Susini G., Supplemento epigrafico di Caso, Scarpanto, Saro, Calchi, Alinnia e Tilo, *Annuacio della Scuola Archeologica di Atene e delle Missioni Italiane in Orieute* 41-42 (1963-1964), 247-261.

Castellorizo, Rho

Ashton N. G., Ancient Megisti, *The Forgotten Kastellorizo*, West Australia 1995.
Fraser P. M., G. E. Bean, *The Rhodian Peraea and Islands*, Oxford and London 1954, 54ff., 85ff., 97 n. 4.
Himmelmann N., *Der «Sarkopaphag» aus Megiste*, Wiesbaden 1970.
Hope Simpson R., J. F. Lazenby, Notes from the Dodecanese II, *The Annual of the British School at Athens* 65 (1970), 73-77.
Kaninia E., Χρυσά στεφάνια από τη Νεκρόπολη της αρχαίας Ρόδου, *Ἀρχαιολογικόν Δελτίον* 48-49 (1994-1995) Μελέτες, 97-132.
Kyparissis N., Περὶ ἀνασκαφῆς γενομένης ἐν Καστελορίζῳ, *Ἀρχαιολογικόν Δελτίον* 1 (1915), Παράρτημα 63.
Papachristodoulou I. Ch., *Οι Αρχαίοι Ροδιακοί Δήμοι*, Athens 1989, 44-45.
Peek W., Inschriften von den dorischen Inseln, *Abhandlungen der sächsischen Akademie der Wissenschaften zu Leipzig Philologisch-Historische Klasse*, Band 62, Heft 1, Berlin.
Pirazzoli P. A., Submerged Remains of Ancient Megisti in Castellorizo Island (Greece): A Preliminary Survey, *The International Journal of Nautical Archaeology and Underwater Exploration* XVI (1987), 57-66.
Real-Encyclopädie der Klassischen Altertumswissenschaft XV 1 (1931), s.v. «Megiste», 331-332 (Zschitzchmann)· IV, A1 (1931), s.v. «Στρογγυλή», 371 (Ruge).
Stephanidou A., Καστελλόριζο, Παλαιόκαστρο, Castell Rosso, in *Ενετοί και Ιωαννίτες Ιππότες. Δίκτυα οχυρωματικής αρχιτεκτονικής*, Athens 2001, 218-220.
Susini G., Iscrizioni greche di Megiste e della Licia nel Museo di Mitilene, *Annuario della Scuola Archeologica di Atene e delle Missioni Italiane in Oriente* 30-32 (1952-1954), 341-350.
Vardamidis E., *Ἱστορία τῆς νήσου Μεγίστης*, Ἀλexandria 1948.
Wuster W., Bauten auf Kastellorizo und Rhos, *Athenische Mitteilungen* 94 (1981), 209-235.
Zimmermann M., Bemerkungen zur rhodischen Vorherrschaft in Lykien (189/88-167v.Chr.), *Klio* 75 (1993), 110-130.

Karpathos

Charitonidis S., Θαλαμοειδής τάφος Καρπάθου, *Ἀρχαιολογικόν Δελτίον* 17A (1961-1962), 32-76.
Frazer P. M., G. E. Bean, *The Rhodian Peraea and Islands*, London 1954.
Melas E. M., *The Islands of Karpathos, Saros and Kasos in the Neolithic and Bronze Age*, Studies in Mediterranean Archaeology LXVIII, Göteborg 1985.
Melas M., *Ποτίδαιον Καρπάθου*, New York 1991.
Michailidis-Nouaros M. G., *Ἱστορία τῆς νήσου Καρπάθου*, iss. II, Athens 1940.
Moutsopoulos N., Κάρπαθος, *Επιστημονική Επετηρίς της Πολυτεχνικής Σχολής του Πανεπιστημίου Θεσσαλονίκης*, vol. Ζ´, 1975-1977, 39-744.
Papachristodoulou I. Ch., *Οι Αρχαίοι Ροδιακοί Δήμοι*, Athens 1989.
Ross L., *Reisen auf den griechischen Inseln des ägäischen Meeres*, Stuttgart 1845.
Segre M., Iscrizioni di Scarpanto, *Historia* XII, No 4, 1933, 577-588.
Susini G., Supplemento epigrafico di Caso, Scarpanto, Saro, Calchi, Alinnia e Tilo, *Annuario della Scuola Archeologica di Atene e delle Missioni Italiane in Oriente*, vol. 41-42 (1963-1964), 203-225.

Kasos

Beaudouin M., Inscriptions de Kasos, *Bulletin de correspondance hellénique* 4 (1880), 121-124.

Evangelidou T., M. Michailidou-Nouarou, *Ιστορία τῆς νήσου Κάσου*, Athens 1935.

Frazer P. M., G. E. Bean, *The Rhodian Peraea and Islands*, London 1954.

Μεγάλη Ελληνική Εγκυκλοπαίδεια, vol. ΙΓ', Athens, s.v. «Κάσος», 937-939.

Melas E. M., *The Islands of Karpathos, Saros and Kasos in the Neolithic and Bronze Age*, Studies in Mediterranean Archaeology LXVIII, Göteborg 1985.

Papachristodoulou I. Ch., *Οι Αρχαίοι Ροδιακοί Δήμοι*, Athens 1989.

Ross L., *Reisen auf den griechischen Inseln des ägäischen Meeres*, Stuttgart 1845.

Simpson Hope R., J. Lazenby, Notes from the Dodecanese II, *Annual of the British School at Athens* 65 (1970), 71-72.

Susini G., Supplemento epigrafico di Caso, Scarpanto, Saro, Calchi, Alinnia e Tilo, *Annuario della Scuola Archeologica di Atene e delle Missioni Italiane in Oriente*, vol. 41-42 (1963-1964), 203-225.

Zervoudaki I., *Αρχαιολογικόν Δελτίον* 28 (1973) Χρονικά, 640-641.

CRETE

Prehistoric times

Betancourt Ph. P., Village Life in Minoan Crete: New Evidence, *Πεπραγμένα του Η' Διεθνούς Κρητολογικού Συνεδρίου*, vol. Α1, Herakleion 2000, 91-95.

Chaniotis A. (ed.), *From Minoan Farmers to Roman Traders*, Stuttgart 1999.

Driessen J., C. Macdonald, *The Troubled Island. Minoan Crete before and after the Santorini Eruption*, Liège 1997.

Driessen J., I. Schoep, R. Laffineur, *Monuments of Minos. Rethinking the Minoan Palaces*, Aegaeum 23, Liege 2002.

Evans A. J., *The Palace of Minos at Knossos*, vols. I-IV, London 1921-1935.

Evely D., H. Hughes-Brock, N. Momigliano (eds), *Knossos. A Labyrinth of History. Papers in Honour of Sinclair Hood*, Oxford and Northampton 1994.

Fitton J. L., *Minoans*, London 2002.

Godart L., Y. Tzedakis, *Témoignages archéologiques et épigraphiques en Crète occidentale du Néolithique au Minoen Récent IIIB* (Incunabula Graeca, vol. XCIII), Roma 1992.

Hägg R., N. Marinatos (eds), *The Function of the Minoan Palaces. Proceedings of the Fourth International Symposium at the Swedish Institute at Athens, 10-16 June 1984*, Stockholm 1987.

Hägg R., N. Marinatos (eds), *The Function of the Minoan Villas. Proceedings of the Seventh International Symposium at the Swedish Institute at Athens*, Stockholm 1997.

Karetsou A., M. Andreadaki-Vlazaki, N. Papadakis (eds), *Crete-Egypt. Three thousand years of cultural links*, Herakleion 2000.

Rehak P., J. G. Younger, Review of Aegean Prehistory VII: Neopalatial, Final Palatial and Postpalatial Crete, *American Journal of Archaeology* 102 (1998), 91-173.

Sakellarakis Y. and E., Η νεολιθική και μινωική Κρήτη, *Κρήτη. Ιστορία και Πολιτισμός*, Α', 1-130, Herakleion 1987.

Tzedakis Y., H. Martlew (eds), *Minoans and Mycenaeans: Flavours of their time* (Catalogue of exhibition of the Hellenic Ministry of Culture in the National Archaeological Museum, Athens), Athens 1999.

Warren P., Ο καθημερινός βίος στη Μινωική Εποχή, *Πεπραγμένα του Η' Διεθνούς Κρητολογικού Συνεδρίου*, vol. Α1, Herakleion 2000, 25-37.

Watrous L. V., Crete from Earliest Prehistory through the Protopalatial Period, *American Journal of Archaeology* 98 (1994), 695-753.

Historical times

Chaniotis A. (ed.), *From Minoan Farmers to Roman Traders*, Stuttgart 1999, 181-220.

Erickson B. L., *Late Archaic and Classical Crete: Island Pottery Styles in an Age of Historical Transition, ca. 600-400 BC* (doctoral dissertaition, University of Texas at Austin), 2000.

Englezou M., *Ελληνιστική κεραμική Κρήτης*, Athens 2005.

Hoffman G., *Imports and Immigrants: Near Eastern Contacts with Iron Age Crete*, Michigan 1997.

Kalpaxis Th., A. Furtwängler, A. Schnapp, *Ελεύθερνα Τομέας ΙΙ. 2. Ένα Ελληνιστικό σπίτι («Σπίτι Α») στη θέση Νησί*, Rethymnon 1994.

Karetsou A., M. Andreadaki-Vlazaki, N. Papadakis (eds), *Crete-Egypt. Three thousand years of cultural links*, Herakleion 2000.

Lebessi A., *Η Κρητών Πολιτεία, 1100-300 π.Χ.*, Herakleion 1990.

Morris S., *Daidalos and the Origins of Greek Art*, Princeton 1992.

Nowicki K., *Defensible Sites in Crete c.1200-800 BC*, Liège/Austin 2000.

Panayotakis N. (ed.), *Κρήτη: Ιστορία και Πολιτισμός*, I, Herakleion 1987.

Perlmann P., One Hundred-Citied Crete and the "Cretan Politeia", *Classical Philology* 87 (1992), 193-205.

Stampolidis N., A. Karetsou, *Ανατολική Μεσόγειος. Κύπρος-Δωδεκάνησα-Κρήτη, 16ος-6ος αι. π.Χ.*, Herakleion 1998.

Whitley J., *The Archaeology of Ancient Greece*, Cambridge 2001.

AEGEAN: AN UNDERWATER MUSEUM

Archontidou A., A. Simossi, J-Y. Empereur, The Underwater Excavation at the Ancient Port of Thassos Greece, *International Journal of Nautical Archaeology* 18.1 (1989), 51-59.

Bass G. F. (ed.), *A History of Seafaring based on Underwater Archaeology*, London 1972.

Chaniotis D. C., Νήσος Φαγκρού ή Πελερίσσα (ναυάγιο του 5ου αι. π.Χ.), *Αρχαιολογικό Δελτίο* 49 (1994), 854, 864· 51 (1996), 724-725.

Dellaporta K. P., Το Έργον της Εφορείας Εναλίων Αρχαιοτήτων (Χρονικά 1976-1999), *Τροπίς* VII, *Πρακτικά 7ου Διεθνούς Συμποσίου Αρχαίας Ναυπηγικής, Πύλος 1999*, Athens 2002, 903-916.

Dellaporta K. P., I Spondylis, D. Evangelistis, P. Micha, Th. Theodoulou, Έρευνα της Εφορείας Εναλίων Αρχαιοτήτων και του Εθνικού Κέντρου Θαλασσίων Ερευνών στις θαλάσσιες περιοχές Καλύμνου, Λέρου και Λειψών, *Ενάλια VII*, 2003, 42-49.

Dellaporta K. P., Τα αρχαία ναυάγια, in S. Asdrachas, A. Tzamtzis, T. Charlafti (eds), *Ελλάδα της θάλασσας*, Athens 2004, 147-153.

Hadjidaki E., The Clasical Shipwreck at Alonnisos, *Bulletin de correspondance héllenique* 120 (1996), 561-593.

Karageorghis V., Y. Lolos, Y. Vichos, Ch. Agouridis, *Από την ενάλια Κύπρο στον μυχό του πολυδίψιου Άργους. Το ναυάγιο του ακρωτηρίου Ιρίων* (Catalogue of the exhibition in the Spetses Archaeological Museum), Ίδρυμα Εναλίων Αρχαιολογικών Ερευνών, Athens 1998.

Papathanasopoulos G., Y. Vichos, Y. Lolos, Δοκός: Ανασκαφική περίοδος 1992, *Ενάλια* V, iss. 1/2, 1993 (1998), 6-19 (with previous bibliography).

Parker A.J., *Ancient Shipwrecks of the Mediterranean and the Roman Provinces*, British Archaeological Reports Inter. Series 580, Oxford 1992.

Phelps W., Y. Lolos, Y. Vichos (eds), *The Point Iria Wreck: Interconnections in the Mediterranean ca. 1200 BC*, Athens 1999.

Pirazzoli P. A., Submerged Remains of Ancient Megisti in Castellorizo Island (Greece): A Preliminary Survey, *International Journal of Nautical Archaeology* 16.1 (1987), 57-66.

Simossi A., Underwater excavation research in the ancient harbour of Samos: September -October 1988, *International Journal of Nautical Archaeology* 20.4 (1990), 281-298.

BIOGRAPHICAL NOTES

MARIA ANDREADAKI-VLAZAKI
Head of the XXV Ephorate of Prehistoric and Classical Antiquities of West Crete, Director of the archaeological museums of Chania and Rethymnon, member of the Board of the Chania Cultural Centre and of the Centre for Mediterranean Architecture. She has excavated in the city of Chania and at Chamalevri, Rethymnon. She holds a doctorate from the University of Clermont-Ferrand, France, on the subject of the city of Chania in the Minoan and Geometric periods.

SOPHIA ANEZIRI
Born Athens 1967. Graduate of the Department of History and Archaeology of the National and Capodistrian University of Athens. Awarded scholarships by the Greek State and the Federal State of Baden-Wurtemburg for post-graduate studies in Ancient History-Epigraphy at the University of Heidelberg. Has collaborated with the Ionian University, the universities of Thessaly and Crete, and the Research Centre for Greek and Roman Antiquity of the National Hellenic Research Foundation. Lecturer in Ancient History-Epigraphy at the National and Capodistrian University of Athens. Basic publication: *Die Vereine der Dionysischen Techniten im Kontext der hellenistischen Gesellschaft* (Historia Einzelschriften 163, Stuttgart 2003).

AGLAIA ARCHONTIDOU-ARGYRI
Born at Moria, Lesbos. Studied Archaeology at the National and Capodistrian University of Athens. She has attended seminars in Greece and abroad on museology and underwater archaeology, organized archaeological conferences, written scientific articles and edited archaeological publications. Epimelete and subsequently Ephor of Antiquities in the ephorates of Antiquities Dealers, Underwater Archaeology, Nauplion, Mytilene. She has excavated widely in the Northeast Aegean islands, where she has organized archaeological sites, museums, collections and temporary exhibitions. She has lectured at universities and museums abroad. President of the Association of Greek Archaeologists for eight years, member of the German Archaeological Institute, the Union of European Archaeologists and the European Museum Awards. Awarded the title "Grande Officiale Ordine Della Stella Della Solidaritá Italiana" by the Presidency of the Italian Republic.

KALLIOPI BAIRAMI
Studied in the Department of History and Archaeology (1986-1990) of the National and Capodistrian University of Athens. Since 1993 she has served in the Archaeological Service, in the XXII Ephorate of Prehistoric and Classical Antiquities of the Dodecanese. She has carried out rescue excavations in the city and the necropolis of ancient Rhodes, as well as on the islands of Nisyros, Chalke, Castellorizo and Rho.

LUIGI BESCHI
Reader at the University of Padova, member and curator of the Italian Archaeological School at Athens (1961-1967), Professor of Archaeology (1972-2000) at the universities of Chieta, Napoli, Pisa and Firenze. Member of the Accademia Nazionale dei Lincei and of various other academies, and doctor *honoris causa* of the Aristotle University of Thessaloniki. Research interests include topography, sculpture, history of archaeology. Has directed excavations in Cyrene, Crete and Lemnos (Hephaistia, Kabeirion).

DIMITRIOS BOSNAKIS
Graduate of the Department of Archaeology of the University of Ioannina (1984), from which university he was awarded his PhD for a thesis entitled *Thessaly in the 5th and 4th Centuries BC*. Between 1985 and 1989 he held a Swiss State Scholarship and pursued post-graduate studies at the University of Basle. In 1989 served as scientific assistant to Professor R. Stucky. Since 2002 a collaborator of the *Inscriptiones Graecae* project of the Academy of Brandenburg, in Berlin, for the publication of a corpus of Koan inscriptions. He serves in the XXII Ephorate of Prehistoric and Classical Antiquities of the Dodecanese, with special responsibility for Kos and Kalymnos.

CHRISTOS BOULOTIS
Born at Myrina on Lemnos, 1952. Graduated "*cum laude*" from the Department of History and Archaeology of the National and Capodistrian University of Athens. Awarded a German State Scholarship and pursued post-graduate studies at the University of Würzburg, from which he received his PhD in 1979. Since 1985, archaeologist-researcher at the Academy of Athens (Centre for Greek Antiquity). Has participated in excavations on Crete (Archanes, Zakros), Thera (Akrotiri) and in ancient Elis. Director of excavations of the prehistoric settlement at Koukonisi (Lemnos). Has taught at the Ionian University, post-graduate courses at the University of Athens and at the Advanced School of Fine Arts. A specialist on issues of Aegean script, art and religion.

THOMAS BROGAN
Studied Archaeology at Wabash College and Bryn Mawr College, USA. The subject of his PhD thesis is Victory Monuments of the Antigonids, Attalids, Aetolians and Rhodians in the Hellenistic period. Since 1989 deputy director of the Greek-American excavations at Mochlos. Since 1997 director of the INSTAP Study Centre for East Crete. He is co-author (with K. Barnard) of the monograph *Mochlos IB. The Artisans' Quarter and the Farmhouse at Chalinomouri. The Neopalatial Pottery*. Recent publications focus on the victory monument of the Antigonids in Athens, and the Late Minoan settlement at Mochlos, issues relating to Minoan metalworking, metrology, pottery and architecture. Currently preparing the joint publication of diverse subjects arising from recent excavations at the same site.

KATERINA P. DELLAPORTA
Studied History and Archaeology, and French Literature, at the National and Capodistrian University of Athens. Post-graduate studies in Byzantine History at the University of the Sorbonne-Paris I. She has served in the Archaeological Service since 1979, researching on Byzantine and Post-Byzantine monuments in the Ionian Islands and underwater archaeology. Since 1998 Head of the Ephorate of Underwater Antiquities, with important underwater excavations in the prehistoric settlement at Platygiali, near Astakos, and the 16th-century Hispano-Venetian wreck in Zakynthos harbour. In recent years active in deep-sea investigations to map ancient wrecks in the Aegean, in collaboration with the Hellenic Institute of Marine Archaeology. She teaches post-graduate courses in Museology at the National and Capodistrian University of Athens and the University of the Peloponnese.

Argyroula Doulgeri-Intzesiloglou

Graduate of the Department of Archaeology in the Faculty of Letters of the Aristotle University of Thessaloniki, from where she also received her PhD. Post-graduate studies at the Université du Lumière-Lyon II, France. Served in the XIII Ephorate of Prehistoric and Classical Antiquities of Volos (1980-2003), of which she was head (1984-1994). Since October 2003, Head of the Archaeological Institute of Thessalian Studies. Involved in systematic research mainly on the area of ancient Pherai (pres. Velestino) and the islands of the North Sporades, as well as with Thessalian inscriptions in the local alphabet, which was the subject of her doctoral dissertation.

Christos Doumas

Born 1933. Graduated from the Department of History and Archaeology of the National and Capodistrian University of Athens and completed post-graduate studies at the Institute of Archaeology, University of London (PhD 1972). Served in the Archaeological Service as epimelete of antiquities in the Cyclades and on the Acropolis, as head of the department of archaeological sites, as ephor of antiquities for the Dodecanese, as Director of Antiquities and of Conservation, and as keeper of the prehistoric collections in the National Archaeological Museum. From 1980 to 2000 he was Professor in the Department of History and Archaeology at the University of Athens. Assistant to Professor Spyridon Marinatos in the excavations at Akrotiri, Thera (1968-1973) and director of the excavations since 1975.

Anastasia Dreliossi-Herakleidou

Born at Theisoa, Olympia. Graduate of the Department of History and Archaeology of the National and Capodistrian University of Athens. Serves in the XXII Ephorate of Prehistoric and Classical Antiquities, where she has conducted numerous excavations, mainly in the ancient necropolis and the city of Rhodes. Research interests include the topography of the necropolis, inscriptions and mosaics of ancient Rhodes, as well as archaeological issues relating to the islands in the northern part of the Dodecanese.

Maya Efstathiou

Born in Athens and studied Archaeology in the Faculty of Letters of the University of Crete. Holds a post-graduate diploma in Classical Archaeology from the Department of History and Archaeology in the Faculty of the Letters of the Aristotle University of Thessaloniki. Since 1986 has served in the XXI Ephorate of Prehistoric and Classical Antiquities of the Cyclades and Samos.

Eleni Farmakidou

Studied Archaeology at the National and Capodistrian University of Athens, followed by post-graduate studies at the University of Cambridge (Mphil). Serves as an archaeologist in the XXII Ephorate of Prehistoric and Classical Antiquities of the Dodecanes. Teaches prehistoric archaeology in the School of Tourist Guides, Rhodes. PhD candidate at the University of Athens, preparing a thesis on the Geometric period on Rhodes.

Melina Filimonos-Tsopotou

Born in Thessaloniki. Graduate in History and Archaeology of the National and Capodistrian University of Athens, and holds a PhD in Archaeology from the University of Ioannina. Corresponding member of the German Archaeological Institute. She serves as an archaeologist in the XXII Ephorate of Prehistoric and Classical Antiquities, of which she has been head since 2001. Her principal publications are on the street plan, the architecture and the fortification of the ancient city of Rhodes.

Alexandros P. Gounaris

Born in Veroia, Imathia, in 1955. Architect-Engineer of the National Technical University of Athens, Architect DPLG (UPA-6), PhD Faculty of Letters University of Crete, doctorate and DÉA in Regional Analysis and Regional Planning Paris I, DÉA Social and Historical Anthropology ÉHÉSS, Architect in the Plaka Office at the Ministry of the Environment, Regional Planning and Public Works, Architect in the XXI Ephorate of Prehistoric and Classical Antiquities, Member of the Archaeological Society at Athens, founder-member of the Society for the History of the City and Urban Planning, member of the British School at Athens. Teaches in the Department of History, Archaeology and Social Anthropology of the School of Human Sciences in the University of Thessaly. Research interests include ancient Greek architecture, urban planning and ekistics, particularly in the Protogeometric-Geometric period.

Evangelos Ch. Kakavoyannis

Born in Athens, 1938. Graduate of the Department of History and Archaeology in the Faculty of Letters of the National and Capodistrian University of Athens. He holds a PhD from the same university. Served for many years in the Archaeological Service, in various Ephorates of Prehistoric and Classical Antiquities, conducting excavations in many places, mainly Rhodes, Edessa, Velestino, Glyka Nera and especially the Laureotike, with systematic research on the ancient mines of all periods. Has participated in scientific conferences and has published widely in Greek and foreign periodicals.

Amalia A. Karapaschalidou

Born in Chalkida, into a family originating from Asia Minor. Graduate in Archaeology from the Aristotle University of Thessaloniki, with specialization in the Hellenistic period. The subject of her doctoral thesis is the Hellenistic grave assemblages from Chalkis. The author of articles and contributions to publications of archaeological content, periodicals and other printed matter. Serves in the Archaeological Service and is presently Head of the XI Ephorate of Prehistoric and Classical Antiquities for Euboea.

Georgia Kokkorou-Alevra

Graduate of the National and Capodistrian University of Athens and holds a PhD from the University of Munich. She has published monographs and studies on ancient sculpture, iconography, epigraphy, ancient quarries, etc. Has participated in many international conferences, excavations and research projects. A member of several scholarly societies and since 1985 co-director of the National and Capodistrian University of Athens excavation in the sanctuary of Apollo at Kardamaina (anc. Alasarna) on Kos. Professor of Classical Archaeology at the National and Capodistrian University of Athens and Director of the Programme of Post-graduate Studies of the Department of History and Archaeology.

Chaido Koukouli-Chrysanthaki

Born in the village of Kamini in the Prefecture of Kozani, 1940, and attended the Tsotylion High School, Kozani. Graduate of the Department of History and Archaeology of the Aristotle University of Thessaloniki, with post-graduate studies at the same university and the Institut für Uhr und Frühegeschichte in Heidelberg. Served in the Archaeological Service as Ephor of Antiquities in the XVIII Ephorate of Prehistoric and Classical Antiquities for Eastern Macedonia, from 1965 to 2000. She studies in particular the transitional period from prehistoric to historical times, focusing on prehistoric Thasos and the early phases of Greek colonization.

Yannos Kourayos

Studied Archaeology at the University of Florence. Since 1986 epimelete in the XXI Ephorate of Prehistoric and Classical Antiquities, with special responsibility for Paros and Antiparos. He has excavated in Paroikia on Paros, revealing important monuments of the ancient city. Since 1997 he has been excavating systematically on the islet of Despotiko, where he has uncovered a sanctuary of Apollo. He has participated in many international conferences and lectured in Greek and foreign universities and museums (USA, France, Italy). Author of scientific articles and an archaeological guide to Paros and Antiparos. Has been involved with arranging archaeological sites and exhibitions in museums, such as the Paros Archaeological Museum.

Vassilis Lambrinoudakis

Professor of Classical Archaeology at the National and Capodistrian University of Athens, corresponding member of the French Academy of Inscriptions and Letters, and of the Austrian Academy of Sciences in Vienna, member of the German Archaeological Institute. He has conducted excavations in Epidauros, Naxos, Chios and Marathon, and directs major projects for enhancing archaeological sites at Epidauros and Naxos. The author of numerous books and articles on ancient architecture and art, ancient religion, epigraphy and topography, as well as on cultural heritage management. He is President of the international foundation for the *Lexicon Iconographicum Mythologiae Classicae* (LIMC), co-editor and author in this work, as well as in the foundation's new publication, the Thesaurus of Cults and Rites of Antiquity. Awarded the Order of the Phoenix by the President of the Hellenic Republic.

Yannos G. Lolos

Born in Athens, 1953. Attended Athens College and then studied Classics and Archaeology at the University of Cincinnati (USA) and the University of London, from which he holds a doctorate (1985). Has participated in archaeological investigations, on land and underwater, in Thera, western Messenia, Kythera, the islet of Dokos, Cape Iria in the Argolid and Salamis. Since 1994 director of excavations and other research in southern Salamis (Cave of Euripides, Ginani, Kanakia). Associate Professor of Prehistoric Archaeology at the University of Ioannina, President of the Hellenic Institute of Marine Archaeology (since 2000) and member of the Archaeological Society at Athens.

Lila Marangou

Born and bred in the Cyclades. Studied in the Faculty of Letters of the National and Capodistrian University of Athens. Had the great good fortune to work with Christos and Semni Karouzos. Post-graduate studies and doctoral dissertation at the University of Tübingen. Served in the National Archaeological Museum, the Benaki Museum and the Museum of Cycladic Art. Professor of Archaeology at the University of Ioannina since 1975. Director of the systematic excavations on Amorgos since 1979.

Toula Marketou

Born in Egypt. Graduate in History and Archaeology of the National and Capodistrian University of Athens. Serves in the XXII Ephorate of Prehistoric and Classical Antiquities, where she has conducted numerous rescue excavations, mainly on Rhodes and Kos. Responsible for the excavations of the prehistoric settlements at Ialysos and Seraglio on Kos, which are the subject of her published articles. Her research interests also include the islands in the north part of the Dodecanese.

Marisa Marthari

Studied Archaeology (1973-1977) at the National and Capodistrian University of Athens, from where she was awarded her PhD for a thesis relating to the pottery from Akrotiri, Thera. Post-graduate research at the Institute of Classical Studies, London (1985-1987). Head of the XXI Ephorate of Prehistoric and Classical Antiquities of the Cyclades and Samos. Collaborator of the excavation at Akrotiri, Thera. Director of many excavations in the Cyclades and on Samos, and of the systematic excavation at Skarkos, Ios. Has organized exhibitions in the Ios Archaeological Museum, the Museum of Prehistoric Thera, and elsewhere. Supervisor of enhancement works at the sites of Skarkos, Kastri on Syros and Phylakopi on Melos. Member of the Archaeological Society at Athens and of the German Archaeological Institute. She has lectured and participated in conferences in Greece and abroad. Her publications refer to the Cyclades and the Aegean in the Bronze Age and historical times.

Dimitris Matsas

Archaeologist in the Archaeological Service since 1979. Serves in the XIX Ephorate of Prehistoric and Classical Antiquities (Komotini) and is responsible for Samothrace, dealing mainly with the island's prehistory and protohistory. He has excavated the sites of Mikro Vouni and Vychos, as well as in the sanctuary of the Great Gods. Has also participated in excavations at Paradimi and Maroneia.

Alexandros Mazarakis Ainian

Born in Athens, 1959. Studied Art History and Archaeology in the Free University of Brussels. Post-graduate studies at University College London, from which he received a PhD for his thesis on the architecture of early historical times. Assistant archaeologist in the II Ephorate of Prehistoric and Classical Antiquities (1991-1996), conducting excavations in Attica. Taught in the Department of History of the Ionian University (1992-1998). Since 1998 Associate Professor of Classical Archaeology in the Department of History, Archaeology and Social Anthropology of the University of Thessaly. Director of surface surveys on Kythnos and excavations at Skala Oropos, Kythnos (since 2002) and Soros (since 2004). Some of his publications relate to early historical times, while the rest deal with the archaeological research projects he directs.

Maria Michalaki-Kollia

Born in Athens. Graduate of the Faculty of Letters of the University of Lausanne (Switzerland) and holds a post-graduate diploma for the University of the Sorbonne, Paris. Serves in the XXII Ephorate of Prehistoric and Classical Antiquities since 1975. Her interests also include photography. Over the past decade she has been involved with museological and educational issues, and the arrangement of archaeological sites, on which she has published relevant articles.

Lydia Palaiokrassa-Kopitsa

Graduate in Archaeology from the Aristotle University of Thessaloniki (1975), from which she also holds a PhD (1983). Her doctoral dissertation entitled *The Sanctuary of Artemis Mounichia* was published by the Library of the Archaeological Society at Athens (1991). Presently in press is a monograph on the Protoattic pottery from the same site. Has taught archaeology at the University of Athens since 1983 and is currently a professor. Since 1987 she directs the systematic excavation of ancient Andros (Palaiopoli). The results of preliminary research at the site, prior to excavation (1985-1986) are published in the monograph *Palaiopoli Andros. The building remains. From the pre-excavation research* (1996).

Peggy Pantou

Born in Athens. Studied Archaeology in the Faculty of Letters of the University of Ioannina, Since 1987 serves as an archaeologist in the XXI Ephorate of Prehistoric and Classical Antiquities of the Cyclades and Samos.

Ioannis Ch. Papachristodoulou

Born in Cairo, Egypt, 1940, to Rhodian parents. Attended school in Rhodes. Studied History and Archaeology at the National and Capodistrian University of Athens, followed by post-graduate studies in Germany. He holds a doctorate from the University of Ioannina. From 1985 to 2000 was a permanent member of the Archaeological Service, serving successively in the Argolid-Corinthia, Attica, the Cyclades and primarily the Dodecanes, as ephor of antiquities. He has published widely. His mainly research interest is the ancient demes in the Rhodian countryside, fruit of which is his monograph *Ancient Rhodian Demes* (1989).

Zozi Papadopoulou

Born in Athens. Studied Archaeology in the Faculty of Letters of the National and Capodistrian University of Athens. Awarded her PhD from the Ionian University for a thesis entitled *The Place of Music and Dance in the Myths and Cults of Delos*. Serves in the XXI Ephorate of Prehistoric and Classical Antiquities of the Cyclades, and has taught at the University of Athens and the Ionian University.

Olga Philaniotou

Born in Alexandria, Egypt, where she attended the Averoff High School for Girls, and then moved to the Pancypriot High School in Nicosia. Studied History and Archaeology at the National and Capodistrian University of Athens and subsequently took post-graduate courses in prehistoric archaeology at the universities of London and Edinburgh. In 1979 she served as an archaeologist in the XI, II and III Ephorates of Prehistoric and Classical Antiquities, and since 1980 in the XXI Ephorate of the Cyclades. She is presently head of the XX Ephorate.

Lefteris Platon

Graduate in Archaeology from the National and Capodistrian University of Athens. Received his PhD from the University of Bristol, UK in 1988. From 1994-2002 taught prehistoric archaeology at the universities of Crete and the Aegean, and worked in the Archaeological Service. In 2002 elected Lecturer in the Department of History and Archaeology of the University of Athens, specializing in Minoan Archaeology. In 1992 the Archaeological Society at Athens entrusted him with directing additional conservation and publication of the excavation of Zakros.

Adamantios Sampson

From 1973 served as Curator and Ephor of Antiquities in Euboea, Boeotia, the Dodecanese, the Cyclades and the Ephorate of Speleology. Since 1999 teaches as professor at the University of the Aegean. He has conducted rescue and systematic excavations in many regions of Greece and is the author of 24 books and 140 articles.

Eva Simantoni-Bournia

Professor of Archaeology at the University of Athens. She specializes in pottery and vase-painting of the Geometric and the Early Archaic period. She has written three monographs (Greek and French) on the relief pottery of these periods, has published numerous articles in Greek and international archaeological periodicals, and has collaborated on the excavation, enhancement and restoration of the archaeological sites at Yria and Sangri on Naxos. She is currently directing the project for the "Conservation and Enhancement of Ancient Karthaia on Kea". She is a member of the Archaeological Society at Athens, the Société Française d'Archéologie Classique, the German Archaeological Institute, the Greek Archaeometry Society and the Phileducational Society.

Christina A. Televantou

Born in Cyprus, where she attended the Kyrenia High School. Studied Archaeology at the universities of the Thessaloniki and Athens. Her PhD thesis is on the prehistoric wall-paintings from the West House at Akrotiri, Thera. She is the author of many articles and studies on the wall-paintings of Thera, and the antiquities of Andros and Siphnos. Serves in the XXI Ephorate of Prehistoric and Classical Antiquities, where she is involved with diverse archaeological works (excavations, surface surveys, exhibitions in museums, etc.). She is director of excavations in the Neolithic settlement at Strophilas and the Geometric-Archaic city at Ypsili on Andros, and on the acropolis at Aghios Andreas on Siphnos.

Ismini Trianti

Born in Alexandria, Egypt, where she attended the Averoff High School for Girls. Studied Archaeology at the National and Capodistrian University of Athens, with post-graduate studies at the École des Hautes Études, Paris. She holds a PhD from the Aristotle University of Thessaloniki. She served in the Archaeological Service, in the National Archaeological Museum, at Olympia, in the Cyclades, Ikaria and Samos, as well as on the Acropolis. Since 2001 she is Professor of Classical Archaeology at the University of Ioannina.

Constantinos Tsakos

Studied Archaeology and History at the Aristotle University of Thessaloniki and subsequently attended courses on archaeology and art at the University of Munich. From 1965 to 1990 he served as epimelete and then as ephor of antiquities in the Cyclades, Epirus, ancient Olympia and the Acropolis. He has conducted numerous excavations, mainly on Samos, and has been involved particularly with the preservation of the antiquities on Delos and Samos. A life member of the Archaeological Society at Athens and corresponding member of the Archaeological Institute of Berlin. He has participated in many archaeological conferences and is the author of studies and articles in Greek and foreign periodicals, relating to finds from his excavations on Samos and subjects concerning Mykonos, Delos and Acropolis. He has also published a series of archaeological guidebooks to the Acropolis, Samos, Mykonos, Delos and elsewhere.

Aris Tsaravopoulos

Born in 1945. Graduate in Chemical Engineering from the National Technical University of Athens (1968), graduate of the department of film directing of the Stavrakos School (1972) and graduate of the Department of History and Archaeology in the Faculty of Letters of the National and Capodistrian University of Athens. Until 1980 he worked at all three professions, and since 1980 exclusively as an archaeologist in the Archaeological Service, in Piraeus, Chios, Psara, eastern Attica and for the last 11 years on Kythera and Antikythera (II and XXVI Ephorates of Prehistoric and Classical Antiquities). Member of the editorial group of the periodical *HOROS*.

Yanna Venieri

Studied Archaeology at the National and Capodistrian University of Athens and continued with post-graduate studies at the Aristotle University of Thessaloniki. Worked for several years in Crete, participating in excavations at Apodoulou and Armeni, Rethymnon, as well as in the research programme "Minoan Roads". Since 1996 she has served in the I Ephorate of Prehistoric and Classical Antiquities of the Acropolis. Until 2003 she was responsible for the island of Kea and was curator of the new exhibition in the Kea Archaeological Museum. In 2002 she became responsible archaeologist for the archaeological site of the Acropolis.

Maria Viglaki-Sophianou

Born in Athens. Graduate of the Department of History and Archaeology in the Faculty of Letters of the National and Capodistrian University of Athens. Since 1979 she has served in the XXI Ephorate of Prehistoric and Classical Antiquities, and is based on Samos. Excavated on Samos, Ikaria, Phournoi, Paros and Syros. Research focus is on Samos in the Geometric period. Director of the systematic excavation of the Geometric cemetery of the ancient city of Samos. She has presented papers at conferences and written articles published in archaeological periodicals.

Andreas G. Vlachopoulos

Born in Patras in 1965. Undergraduate and post-graduate studies in Archaeology at the National and Capodistrian University of Athens, specializing in Aegean prehistory. For his doctoral thesis (1994) on the Late Mycenaean period in Naxos he received the Michael Ventris Memorial Award for Mycenaean Studies (1997). Post-doctoral fellow at the University of Princeton (1998-1999) and visiting researcher at the Institute of Fine Arts of New York University (2001-2002). His principal research interests are the Mycenaean period in the Cyclades and the wall-paintings of Thera. Collaborator of Professor Ch. Doumas in the excavations at Akrotiri, Thera. He has taught at the University of the Peloponnese and post-graduate courses at the University of Athens.

Natalia Vogeikoff

Studied Archaeology at the Aristotle University of Thessaloniki and at Bryn Mawr College, USA. The subject of her doctoral thesis is the Hellenistic pottery from the South Slope of the Acropolis of Athens, Since 1989 she has participated in the Greek-American excavations at Mochlos, where she is responsible for publishing the historical periods. Her recent publications deal with the production and circulation of wine in Crete in Hellenistic times, as well as on the archaeology of the house and household in Crete. Since 1994 she is in charge of the Archive Department of the American School of Classical Studies.

Photeini N. Zapheiropoulou

Born in Athens, attended the Lycée St Joseph and subsequently the French Institute at Athens, in parallel with her studies in the Faculty of Letters of the National and Capodistrian University of Athens. Served in the Archaeological Service from 1960 to 1995, as epimelete and then ephor of antiquities, conducting numerous excavations in the Cyclades, Aetoloacarnania and Thessaloniki, as well as organizing museums and archaeological collections in the same regions. She holds a PhD from the Aristotle University of Thessaloniki. Author of many scholarly articles and participant in international conferences with subjects from almost all the excavations she has carried out and particularly those in the Cyclades. She has published monographs on problems of Cycladic pottery in the Archaic period and the archaeology of Delos. A long list of publications on the prehistory of the Cyclades and the sculpture of Paros over the centuries.

Fotini Zervaki

Archaeologist in the XXII Ephorate of Prehistoric and Classical Antiquities of the Dodecanese.

SOURCES OF ILLUSTRATIONS

1. Photo. Archive Italian Archaeological School • 2. Photo. Archive British School at Athens (photo. J. Brock) • 3. Photo. Archive German Archaeological Institute • 5. Photo. Archive M. Caskey • 6. Photo. Archive EfA • 7. Photo. Archive German Archaeological Institute • 8. Photo. Archive C. Renfrew • 9. Photo. Archive Archaeological Society at Athens • 10. Photo. Archive Ph. Zapheiropoulou • 11. Photo. Archive German Archaeological Institute (THERA 559) • 12. Photo. Archive Excavation at Akrotiri Thera (photo. O. Imboden) • 13. Photo. Archive XXII EPCA • 14. Photo. Archive Italian Archaeological School • 16. Photo. Archive Archaeological Society at Athens • 17. Photo. Archive Italian Archaeological School • 18. Photo. Archive Zakros excavation • 19-21. Photo. Archive A. Sampson • 22. Photo. Archive A. Sampson (photo. S. Katsaros) • 23. Photo. Archive A. Sampson • 24. Photo. Archive MELISSA publishing house • 25, 26. Photo. Archive A. Sampson • 27. Photo. Archive XVIII EPCA • 28. Photo. Archive C. Renfrew • 29. Photo. Archive A. Sampson • 30. Photo. Archive C. Renfrew • 31-33. Photo. Archive MELISSA publishing house • 34. Photo. Archive Koukonisi Excavation (photo. C. Boulotis) • 35, 36 Photo. Archive Austrian Archaeological Institute • 37. Photo. Archive Excavation at Akrotiri Thera (photo. A. Voliotis) • 38. Photo. Archive MELISSA publishing house • 39. Photo. Archive Herakleion Museum (photo. E. Eliadis) • 40-42. Photo. Archive Archaeological Receipts Fund • 43. Photo. Archive EfA (photo. Ph. Collet) • 44. Photo. Archive Archaeological Receipts Fund • 45. Photo. Archive Ph. Zapheiropoulou (photo. E. Eliadis) • 46. Photo. Archive A. Vlachopoulos (photo. Ch. Papanikalopoulos) • 47. Photo. Archive Ph. Zapheiropoulou • 48. Photo. Archive American School of Classical Studies • 49. Photo. Archive A. Vlachopoulos (photo. A. Vlachopoulos) • 50. Photo. Archive XX EPCA • 51. Photo. Archive A. Vlachopoulos (photo. A. Vlachopoulos) • 52. Photo. Archive Ph. Zapheiropoulou (photo. E. Eliadis) • 53. Le Louvre © RMN (photo. H. Lewandowski) • 54. Photo. Archive Ph. Zapheiropoulou (photo. E. Eliadis) • 55. Book *Eastern Mediterranean*, eds N. Stampolidis, A. Karetsou, Herakleion Crete 1998, 119•56. Photo. Archive V. Lambrinoudakis • 58. Photo. Archive German Archaeological Institute (1970/1042) • 59. Photo. Archive XX EPCA • 60. Photo. Archive A. Mazarakis-Ainian • 61. Photo. Archive Numismatic Museum • 62. Photo. Archive German Archaeological Institute (1972/3003) • 63. Photo. Archive NAM • 64. Le Louvre © RMN (photo. H. Lewandowski) • 65. Photo. Archive XXII EPCA • 66. Photo. Archive XX EPCA • 67. Photo. Archive XXII EPCA • 68. Photo. Archive P. Trantaphyllidi (photo. S, Mavrommatis) • 69. Photo. Archive Samothrace Museum (photo. S. Stournaras) • 72. Photo. Archive EfA (photo. A. Bon) • 73. Photo. Archive Ekdotike Athenon • 76. Photo. Archive XXII EPCA • 77. Photo. Archive NAM (photo. K. v. Eickstedt) • 78. Photo. Archive Samothrace Museum (photo. S. Stournaras) • 79. Photo. Archive NAM • 80. Photo. Archive A. Vlachopoulos (photo. A. Vlachopoulos) • 81. Photo. Archive Minoa (photo. I. Despotidis) • 82. Photo. Archive XXII EPCA (photo. M. Michalaki-Kollia) • 83, 84. Photo. Archive XVIII EPCA (photos Ch. Koukouli-Chrysanthaki, G. Weissgerber) • 85. Photo. Archive XVIII EPCA (photos Ch. Koukouli-Chrysanthaki, G. Weissgerber) • 86, 87. Photo. Archive XVIII EPCA (photo. S. Stournaras) • 88, 89. Archive XVIII EPCA (photo. Ch. Koukouli-Chrysanthaki) • 90. Photo. Archive XVIII EPCA (photo. S. Stournaras) • 91. Photo. Archive EfA (photo. A. Sérafis) • 92. Photo. Archive XVIII EPCA (photo. G. Vattis) • 93. Photo. Archive EfA (photo. J.Y. Marc) • 94. Photo. Archive A. Vlachopoulos (photo. A. Vlachopoulos) • 95. Photo. Archive EfA (photo. Ph. Collet) • 96. Photo. Archive EfA • 97. Photo. Archive EfA (photo. Ph. Collet) • 98. Photo. Archive EfA •99. Photo. Archive EfA (photo. Ph. Collet) • 100. Photo. Archive A. Vlachopoulos (photo. A. Vlachopoulos) • 101-103. Photo. Archive EfA (photo. Ph. Collet) • 104, 105 Photo. Archive Samothrace Museum (photo. S. Stournaras) • 106. Photo. Archive Samothrace Museum (photo. D. Matsas) • 107. Photo. Archive Samothrace Museum (drawing D. Sismanidis, based on a plan by J. Kurtich, mapped by XIX EPCA) • 108-113. Photo. Archive Samothrace Museum (photo. S. Stournaras) • 114. Le Louvre © RMN (photo. G. Blot) • 115. Sotheby's Picture Library © (photo. J. Ling) • 116. Photo. Archive Samothrace Museum (photo. D. Matsas) • 117, 118. Photo. Archive H. Huryilmaz (photo. H. Huryilmaz) • 119. Photo. Archive Samothrace Museum (photo. D. Matsas) • 120, 121. Photo. Archive Spyros Meletzis • 123, 124. Photo. Archive Samothrace Museum (photo. D. Matsas) • 125, 126. Book *Griechische und Romische kunst in der Turkei* E. Akurgal • 127-129. Photo. Archive Italian Archaeological School (photo. M. Querisma) • 130. Photo. Archive XX EPCA • 131m 132. Photo. Archive Italian Archaeological School (photo. M. Querisma) • 133m 134. Photo. Archive Koukounisi Excavation (photo. Ch. Boulotis) • 135, 136. Photo. Archive Italian Archaeological School (photo. M. Querisma) • 137-139. Photo. Archive XX EPCA • 140-142. Photo. Archive Italian Archaeological School (photo. M. Querisma) • 143, 144. Photo. Archive Italian Archaeological School (photo. I. Beschi) • 145-184. Photo. Archive XX EPCA • 185-187. Photo. Archive German Archaeological Institute • 188, 189. Photo. Archive XXI EPCA (photo. E. Eliadis) • 190. Photo. Archive ESPEROS publishing house • 191-193. Photo. Archive German Archaeological Institute • 194. Photo. Archive XXI EPCA (photo. E. Eliadis) • 196. Photo. Archive Archaeological Receipts Fund (photo. E. Eliadis) • 197. Photo. Archive XXI EPCA (photo. E. Eliadis) • 198. Photo. Archive ESPEROS publishing house • 199. Photo. Archive XXI EPCA (photo. Y. Patrikianos) • 200. Photo. Archive XXI EPCA (photo. G. Koukas) • 201. Photo. Archive Ph. Zapheiropoulou • 202-208. Photo. Archive M. Viglaki • 209-213. Photo. Archive XIII EPCA (photo. A. Doulgeri-Intzesiloglou) • 214. Photo. Archive NAM (photo. Miliariakis) • 215-221. Photo. Archive XIII EPCA (photo. A. Doulgeri-Intzesiloglou) • 222. Photo. Archive XIII EPCA (photo. L. Kourtzoukos) • 223. Photo. Archive XIII EPCA (photo. A. Doulgeri-Intzesiloglou) • 224. Photo. Archive XIII EPCA (photo. V. Karachristos) • 225. Photo. Archive XIII EPCA (photo. A. Doulgeri-Intzesiloglou) • 226. Photo. Archive OITYLOS publishing house (photo. Papaconstantinou) • 227. Photo. Archive MELISSA publishing house • 228. Photo. Archive Archaeological Receipts Fund • 229. Photo. Archive Project for Conservation and Enhancement of Palamari, Skyros (photo. C. Xenikakis) • 230. Photo. Archive Archaeological Receipts Fund (photo. I. Georgouleas) • 231-233. Photo. Archive XI EPCA (photo. C. Xenikakis) • 234-236. Photo. Archive University Excavation of Salamis (photo. E. Lyroni) • 237. Photo. Archive TOUBIS publishing house • 238. Photo. Archive University Excavation of Salamis (photo. E. Lyroni) • 239. Photo. Archive University Excavation of Salamis (photo. Y. Lolos) • 240. Photo. Archive Y. Lolos (photo. Chr. Marabea) • 241. Photo. Archive Y. Lolos (photo. Y. Lolos) • 242. Photo. Archive Athens Water Authority •243-246. Photo. Archive University of Salzburg, Department of Classical Studies (photo. M. del Negro) • 247, 248. Photo. Archive Austrian Archaeological Institute (photo. W. Gauss) • 249. Photo. Archive Archaeological Receipts Fund • 250, 251. Photo. Archive E. Simantoni-Bournia • 252. Photo. Archive TOUBIS publishing house • 253 Photo. Archive NAM • 254, 255. Photo. Archive Staatliche Antikensammlungen und Glyptothek München (photo. Koppermann/ Künning) • 256-258. Photo. Archive Sanctuary of Poseidon Excavation (B. Wells) • 259. Photo. Archive Y. Lolos (photo. Chr. Marabea) • 260-263. Photo. Archive Y. Lo-

462

los (photo. Y. Lolos) • 264. Photo. Archive Archaeological Receipts Fund • 265. Photo. Archive Y. Lolos (photo. Y. Lolos) • 266, 267. Photo. Archive XXVI EPCA (photo. A. Tsaravopoulos) • 272. Photo. Archive I. Petrocheilos • 273. Photo. Archive XXVI EPCA (photo. A. Tsaravopoulos) • 275. Photo. Archive XXVI EPCA (photo. A. Kontoyorgis) • 276. Photo. Archive XXVI EPCA (photo. A. Tsaravopoulos) • 277. Photo. Archive XXVI EPCA (photo. E. & . Tzinakos) • 278. Photo. Archive NAM (photo. K. v. Eickstedt) • 279. Photo. Archive XX EPCA (photo D. Xiraki) • 280. Photo. Archive M. Caskey (photo. W. & E. Myers) • 281. Photo. Archive M. Caskey • 282. Photo. Archive NAM • 283-285. Photo. Archive Archaeological Receipts Fund • 286-287. Photo. Archive Project for Conservation and Enhancement of Ancient Karthaia, Kea • 288. Photo. Archive Archaeological Receipts Fund • 298. Photo. Archive P. Spitaels (photo. I. Demolin-Osipenco) • 290. Photo. Archive XXI EPCA (photo. E. Eliadis) • 291. Photo. Archive XXI EPCA (drawing Ch. Televantou) • 292. Photo. Archive XXI EPCA (photo. Ch. Televantou) • 293. Photo. Archive XXI EPCA (photo. Ch. Televantou) • 294. Photo. Archive XXI EPCA (photo. E. Eliadis) • 295, 296. Photo. Archive XXI EPCA (photo. Ch. Televantou) • 297. Photo. Archive XXI EPCA (photo. E. Eliadis) • 298. Photo. Archive A. Vlachopoulos (photo. A. Vlachopoulos) • 299. Photo. Archive XXI EPCA (photo. G. Gesaphidis) • 300. Photo. Archive XXI EPCA (photo. Ch. Televantou) • 301, 302. Photo. Archive XXI EPCA (photo. E. Eliadis) • 303. Photo. Archive MELISSA publishing house • 304. Photo. Archive Excavation at Palaiopoli, Andros (photo. L. Palaiokrassa-Kopitsa) • 305. Photo. Archive MELISSA publishing house (photo. Ch. Mitsopoulou) • 306. Photo. Archive MELISSA publishing house (photo. S. Efstathopoulos) •316, 317. Photo. Archive XXI EPCA (photo. S. Tsoulellis) • 318. 319. Photo. Archive MELISSA publishing house • 320, 321 Photo. Archive XXI EPCA (photo. P.A. Constantopoulos) • 322. Photo. Archive XXI EPCA (photo. M. Marthari) • 323, Photo. Archive XXI EPCA • 324. Photo. Archive A. Sampson • 325. Photo. Archive XXI EPCA (photo. Ph. Zapheiropoulou) • 326. Photo. Archive XXI EPCA (photo. E. Eliadis) • 327. Photo. Archive Archaeological Receipts Fund • 328. Photo. Archive EfA • 329. Photo. Archive MELISSA publishing house • 330. Photo. Archive Ph. Zapheiropoulou • 331. Photo. Archive A. Vlachopoulos (photo. A. Vlachopoulos) • 332. Photo. Archive MELISSA publishing house • 333. Photo. Archive XXI EPCA (photo. E. Eliadis) • 334, 335. Photo. Archive Ph. Zapheiropoulou (photo. E. Eliadis) • 336. Photo. Archive XXI EPCA (photo. E. Eliadis) • 337, 338. Photo. Archive Ph. Zapheiropoulou (photo. E. Eliadis) • 339. Photo. Archive XXI EPCA (photo. E. Eliadis) • 340, 341. Photo. Archive Ph. Zapheiropoulou (photo. E. Eliadis) • 342. Photo. Archive Ph. Zapheiropoulou • 343. Photo. Archive Ph. Zapheiropoulou (photo. E. Eliadis) • 344. Photo. Archive Ph. Zapheiropoulou • 345-347. Photo. Archive Ph. Zapheiropoulou (photo. E. Eliadis) • 348, 349. Photo. Archive XXI EPCA (photo. Ph. Zapheiropoulou) • 350-357. Photo. Archive University Excavation of Ancient Kythnos (photo. A. Mazarakis Ainian) • 359. Photo. Archive XXI EPCA (photo. P. Pantou) • 360. Photo. Archive Ministry of the Aegean (photo, S. Tsoulellis) • 362. Photo. Archive MELISSA publishing house • 363. Photo. Archive XXI EPCA (photo. G. Koukas) • 364. Photo. Archive Archive XXI EPCA (photo. G. Koukas) • 365. Photo. Archive Excavation at Aghios Andreas, Siphnos (photo. Ch. Televantou) • 366. Photo. Archive XXI EPCA (photo. G. Koukas) • 367. Photo. Archive XXI EPCA (photo. Z. Papadopoulou) • 368. Photo. Archive XXI EPCA (photo. G. Koukas) • 369, 370. Photo. Archive XXI EPCA (photo. P. Pantou) • 371, 372 Photo. Archive XXI EPCA (photo. Z. Papadopoulou) • 373. Photo. Archive XXI EPCA (photo. P. Pantou) •375, 376. Photo. Archive Archaeological Receipts Fund • 377. Photo. Archive Ph. Zapheiropoulou (photo. E. Eliadis) • 378. Photo. Archive MELISSA publishing house • 379-381. Photo. Archive Ph. Zapheiropoulou (photo. E. Eliadis) • 382. Photo. Archive Ph. Zapheiropoulou (photo. Ph. Zapheiropoulou) • 383. Photo. Archive Ph. Zapheiropoulou (photo. E. Eliadis) • 384. Photo. Archive XXI EPCA (photo. Y. Kourayos) • 385-387. Photo. Archive MELISSA publishing house (photo. E. Eliadis) • 388. Photo. Archive Ph. Zapheiropoulou (photo. E. Eliadis) • 389. Photo. Archive XXI EPCA • 390. Photo. Archive NAM • 391. Photo. Archive XXI EPCA (photo. Y. Kourayos) • 395. Photo. Archive V. Lambrinoudakis • 396. Photo. Archive Naxos Museum (photo. Ch. Papanikolopoulos) • 397. Photo. Archive O. Philaniotou (photo. O. Philaniotou) • 398. Photo. Archive MELISSA publishing house • 399, 400. Photo. Archive Naxos Museum (photo. Ch. Papanikolopoulos) • 401, 402. Photo. Archive XXI EPCA (photo. O. Philaniotou) • 403, 404. Photo. Archive Naxos Museum (photo. Ch. Papanikolopoulos) • 405. Photo. Archive XXI EPCA (photo. O. Philaniotou) • 406, 407. Photo. Archive Naxos Museum (photo. Ch. Papanikolopoulos) • 408-414. Photo. Archive V. Lambrinoudakis • 415. Photo. Archive TOUBIS publishing house • 416. Photo. Archive MELISSA publishing house • 417. Photo. Archive V. Lambrinoudakis • 418-420. Photo. Archive Naxos Museum (photo. Ch. Papanikolopoulos) • 421. Photo. Archive Ph. Zapheiropoulou (photo. Ph. Zapheiropoulou) • 422. Photo. Archive O. Philaniotou (photo. O. Philaniotou) • 423. Photo. Archive XXI EPCA (photo. O. Philaniotou) • 424. Photo. Archive Naxos Museum (photo. Ch. Papanikolopoulos) • 425. Photo. Archive MELISSA publishing house • 426. Photo. Archive O. Philaniotou (photo. O. Philaniotou) • 427 Photo. Archive XXI EPCA (photo. Kanakis) • 428. Photo. Archive XXI EPCA (photo. O. Philaniotou) • 429, 430. Photo. Archive MELISSA publishing house • 431, 432. Photo. Archive Amorgos Researches (photo. L. Marangou) • 433. Photo. Archive German Archaeological Institute • 434. Photo. Archive of Aigiali • 435. Photo. Archive German Archaeological Institute • 436. Photo. Archive PAT (photo. L. Marangou) • 437, 438. Photo. Archive of Arkesine (photo. L. Marangou) • 439. Photo. Archive PAT (photo. G. Makris) • 440. Photo. Archive of Minoa (photo. I. Despotidis) • 441, 442. Photo. Archive of Minoa (photo. L. Marangou) • 443. Photo. Archive of Minoa (photo. Y. Patrikianos) • 444. Photo. Archive of Minoa (photo. I. Despotidis) • 445. Photo. Archive of Minoa (photo. L. Marangou) • 446-449. Photo. Archive XXI EPCA (photo. I. Patrikianos) • 450. Photo. Archive XXI EPCA (photo. M. Marthari) • 451. Photo. Archive XXI EPCA • 452, 453. Photo. Archive XXI EPCA (photo. I. Patrikianos) • 454. Photo. Archive XXI EPCA • 455. Photo. Archive Ministry of the Aegean (photo. S. Tsoulellis) • 456, 457. Photo. Archive V. Vasilopoulou • 458. Photo. Archive MELISSA publishing house • 459. Photo. Archive XXI EPCA • 460. Photo. Archive MELISSA publishing house • 461, 462. Photo. Archive XXI EPCA • 463. Photo. Archive Ministry of the Aegean • 464. Photo. Archive NAM (photo. C. Xenikakis) • 465. Photo. Archive Association of Melians in Athens • 466. Photo. Archive MELISSA publishing house • 467. Photo. Archive NAM • 468. Photo. Archive MELISSA publishing house • 469, 470. Photo. Archive NAM (photo. R. Parisis) • 471. Photo. N. Vitsonits • 472, 473. Photo. Archive I. Trianti (photo. E. Eliadis) • 474. Le Louvre © RMN (photo. H. Lewandowski) • 475, 476. Photo. Archive Excavation at Akrotiri Thera (photo. D. Sakatzis) • 477. Photo. Archive Ch. Doumas (photo. Ch. Doumas) • 478. Photo. Archive Excavation at Akrotiri Thera (photo. Ch. Papanikolopoulos) • 479, 480. Photo. Archive Excavation at Akrotiri Thera (photo. S. Marinatos) • 481. Photo. Archive Excavation at Akrotiri Thera • 482. Photo. Archive Excavation at Akrotiri Thera (photo. A. Voliotis) • 483-487. Photo. Archive Excavation at Akrotiri Thera (photo. Ch. Papanikolopoulos) • 488-490. Photo. Archive Excavation at Akrotiri Thera (photo. A. Voliotis) • 491. Photo. Archive MELISSA publishing house (photo. D. Sakatzis) • 492. Book *Sea Routes,* ed. N. Stampolidis, Museum of Cycladic Art 2003, 391, fig. 602 • 493. Photo. Archive XXI EPCA (photo. D. Sakatzis) • 494, 495. Photo. Archive MELISSA publishing house (photo. D. Sakatzis) • 496. Photo. Archive XXI EPCA (photo. Ch. Sigalas) • 497. Photo. Archive XXI EPCA (photo. D. Sakatzis) •498. Photo. Archive MELISSA publishing house • 499-503. Photo. Archive XXI EPCA (photo. C. Antziletou) • 504. Photo. Archive D. Philippidis • 505. Photo. Archive XXI EPCA (photo. Ch. Televantou) • 506. Photo. Archive XXI EPCA (photo. G. Staikopoulos) • 507. Photo. Archive XXI EPCA (photo. Ch. Televantou) • 508. Photo. Archive Ministry of the Aegean (photo. S. Tsoulellis) • 509, 510. Photo. Archive XXII EPCA (photo. M. Michalaki-Kollia) • 511-514. Photo. Archive XXII EPCA (photo. A. Dreliosi-Irakleidou) • 515, 516. Photo. Archive XXII EPCA (photo. K. v. Eickstedt) • 517. Photo. Archive XXII EPCA (photo. A. Dreliosi-Irakleidou) • 518. Photo. Archive XXII EPCA (photo. T. Marketou) • 519. Photo. Archive XXII EPCA (photo. G. Kasiotis) • 520. Photo. Archive XXII EPCA • 521. Photo. Archive XXII EPCA (photo. C. Xenikakis) • 522. Photo. Archive XXII EPCA (photo. G. Kasiotis) • 523. Photo. Archive XXII EPCA (photo. M. Michalaki-Kollia) • 525. Photo. Archive XXII EPCA • 526. Photo. Archive Archaeological Receipts Fund • 527. Photo. Archive XXII EPCA • 528-531. Photo. Archive MELISSA publishing house (photo. N. Kaseris) • 532-535. Photo. Archive XXII EPCA (photo. D. Bosnakis) • 536. Photo. Archive XXII EPCA • 537, 538. Photo. Archive MELISSA publishing house (photo. N. Kaseris) • 539. Photo. Archive XXII EPCA (photo. D. Bosnakis) • 540. Photo. Archive ADAM publishing house • 541, 542. Photo. Archive of Kardamaina, Kos (photo. G. Kokkorou-Alevra) • 544-546. Photo. Archive XXII EPCA (photo. M. Michalaki-Kollia) • 547. Photo. Archive XXII EPCA (photo. G. Kasiotis) • 548. Photo. Archive XXII EPCA (photo. M. Filimonos-Tsopotou) • 549. Photo. Archive Ministry of the Aegean (photo. S. Tsoulellis) • 551. Photo. Archive XXII EPCA (photo. M. Filimonos-Tsopotou) • 552, 553. Photo. Archive XXII EPCA (photo. E. Pharmakidou) • 554, 555. Photo. Archive XXII EPCA (photo. T. Marketou) • 556. Photo. Archive XXII EPCA • 557. Photo. Archive XXII EPCA (photo. T. Marketou) • 558. Photo. Archive XXII EPCA (photo. E. Pharmakidou) • 559. Photo. Archive (photo. T. Marketou) • 560. Photo. Archive Archaeological Receipts Fund • 561. Le Louvre © RMN (photo. H. Lewandowski) • 562, 563. Photo. Archive XXII EPCA • 564, 565. Photo. Archive XXII EPCA (photo. B. Kaseris) • 576, 577. Photo. Archive XXII EPCA (photo. B. Kaseris) • 578. Photo. Archive NAM • 579, 580. • 581. Photo. Archive TOUBIS publishing house • 582, 583. Photo. Archive XXII EPCA (photo. Ph. Zervaki) • 584, 585. Photo. Archive XXII EPCA • 586. Photo. Archive MELISSA publishing house • 589. Photo. Archive ADAM publishing house • 590. Photo. Archive Zakros excavation • 591. Photo. Archive Zakros excavation (photo. S. Tsavdaroglou) • 592. Photo. Archive XXV EPCA (photo. S. Alexandrou) • 593. Photo. Archive W. & E. Myers • 594. Photo. Archive ADAM publishing house • 595. Photo. Archive W. & E. Myers • 597. Photo. Archive XXV EPCA (photo. S. Alexandrou) • 598. Photo. Archive W. & E. Myers • Photo. Archive MELISSA publishing house • 600. Photo. Archive ADAM publishing house • 602. Photo. Archive Monastiraki Excavation (photo. A. Kanta) • Photo. Archive EfA (photo. J.-Cl. Poursat) • 670. Photo. Archive W. & E. Myers • 608, 609. Photo. Archive ADAM publishing house • 610, 611. Photo. Archive G. Rethemiotakis • 612. Photo. Archive A. Vlachopoulos (photo. A. Vlachopoulos) • 613. Photo. Archive ADAM publishing house • 614. Photo. Archive MELISSA publishing house • 615. Photo. Archive W.-D. Niemeier • 616, 617. Photo. Archive MELISSA publishing house • 618, 619. Photo. Archive British School at Athens (photo. G. Papadakis) • 620. Photo. Archive XXV EPCA (photo. E. Eliadis) • 621. Photo. Archive XXV EPCA (photo. M. Andreadaki-Vlazaki) • 622. Photo. Archive Herakleion Museum (photo. G. Papadakis) • 623. Photo. Archive Zakros Excavation (photo. S. Tsavdaroglou) • 624. Photo. Archive Herakleion Museum (photo. G. Papadakis) • 626. Photo. Archive XXV EPCA • 627. A. Vlachopoulos (photo. A. Vlachopoulos) • 628, 629. Photo. Archive XXV EPCA (photo. E. Eliadis) • 630. Photo. Archive XXV EPCA (photo. S. Alexandrou) • 631. Photo. Archive MELISSA publishing house • 632. Photo. Archive Kavousi Excavation • 633. Photo. Archive T. Brogan (photo. T. Brogan) • 634. Book *Eastern Mediterranean*, eds N. Stampolidis, A. Karetsou, Herakleion Crete 1998, 84 • 635. Book *Eastern Mediterranean*, eds N. Stampolidis, A. Karetsou, Herakleion Crete 1998, 219 • 636. Photo. Archive T. Brogan (photo. T. Brogan) • 637. Photo. Archive I. Levendi (photo. I. Levendi) • 638. Photo. Archive American School of Classical Studies (photo. A. Frantz) • 640. Photo. Archive ADAM publishing house • 641. Book *Sea Routes,* ed. N. Stampolidis, Museum of Cycladic Art 2003, 65, fig. 19 • 642. Book *Sea Routes,,* ed. N. Stampolidis, Museum of Cycladic Art 2003, 569, fig. 1147 • 643. Book *Eleutherna*, ed. N. Stampolidis, 2004, 282, fig. 360• 644. Photo. Archive ADAM publishing house • 645. Book *Eleutherna*, ed. N. Stampolidis, 2004, 132, fig. 23. • 646. Photo. Archive British School at Athens • 647, 648. Photo. Archive Excavation at Azorya Kavousi • 649. Photo. Archive British School at Athens • 651-653. Photo. Archive A. Vlachopoulos (photo. A. Vlachopoulos) • 654. Photo. Archive N. Vogeikoff • 656, 657. Photo. Archive XXV EPCA (photo. V. Niniou-Kindeli) • 658, 659. Photo. Archive Mochlos Excavation • 660. Photo. Archive XXV EPCA (photo. E. Eliadis) • 661. Photo. Archive ADAM publishing house • 662. Photo. Archive W. & E. Myers • 663. Photo. Archive ADAM publishing house • 664. Photo. Archive XXV EPCA • 665. . Book *Eleutherna*, ed. N. Stampolidis, 2004, 186, fig. 86 • 666. Photo. Archive IENAE (photo. C. Petrinos) • 667. Photo. Archive IENAE (photo. K. Jackney) • 668, 669. Photo. Archive IENAE (photo. C. Xenikakis) • 672-678. Photo. Archive Ephorate of Underwater Antiquities (photo. P. Vezyrtzis) •679, 680 Photo. Archive NAM • 681 Photo. Archive Excavation at Palaiopoli, Andros (photo. L. Palaiokrassa-Kopitsa) • 682, 683. Photo. Archive EfA (photo. J.-Y. Empereur) • 684, 685. Photo. Archive Ephorate of Underwater Antiquities (photo. P. Vezyrtzis) • 686, 687. Photo. Archive NAM